MICHELIN
GUIDE

NEW YORK CITY

MICHELIN

Michelin Travel Partner

Société par actions simplifiées au capital de 11 288 880 EUR
27 Cours de l'Ile Seguin - 92100 Boulogne Billancourt (France)
R.C.S. Nanterre 433 677 721

© **Michelin, Propriétaires-Éditeurs**

Dépôt légal septembre 2016

Printed in Canada - septembre 2016
Printed on paper from sustainably managed forests
Impression et Finition : Transcontinental (Canada)

Dear Reader

I t's been an exciting year for the entire team at the MICHELIN guides in North America, and it is with great pride that we present you with our 2017 edition to New York City. Over the past year our inspectors have extended their reach to include a variety of establishments and multiplied their anonymous visits to restaurants in our selection in order to accurately reflect the rich culinary diversity this great city has to offer.

As part of the Guide's highly confidential and meticulous evaluation process, our inspectors have methodically eaten their way through all the five boroughs with a mission to marshal the finest in each category for your enjoyment. While they are expertly trained professionals in the food industry, the Guides remain consumer-driven and provide comprehensive choices to accommodate your every comfort, taste, and budget. By dining and drinking as "everyday" customers, they are able to experience and evaluate the same level of service and cuisine as any other guest. This past year has seen some unique advancements in New York City's dining scene. Some of these can be found in each neighborhood introduction, complete with photography depicting our favored choices.

Our company's founders, Édouard and André Michelin, published the first MICHELIN guide in 1900, to provide motorists with useful information about where they could service and repair their cars as well as find a good quality meal. In 1926, the star-rating system was introduced, whereby outstanding establishments are awarded for excellence in cuisine. Over the decades we have made many new enhancements to the Guide, and the local team here in New York City eagerly carries on these traditions.

As we take consumer feedback seriously, please feel free to contact us at: michelin.guides@michelin.com. You may also follow our Inspectors on Twitter (@MichelinGuideNY) and Instagram (@michelininspectors) as they chow their way around town. We thank you for your patronage and truly hope that the MICHELIN guide will remain your preferred reference to New York City's restaurants.

Contents

Dear Reader   3
The MICHELIN Guide   6
How to Use This Guide   8

Where to **Eat**   10

Manhattan   12

▶ Chelsea   14
▷ Chinatown & Little Italy   34
▶ East Village   48
▷ Financial District   94
▶ Gramercy, Flatiron & Union Square   104
▷ Greenwich & West Village   140
▶ Harlem, Morningside
  & Washington Heights   194
▷ Lower East Side   216
▶ Midtown East   236
▷ Midtown West   272
▶ SoHo & Nolita   322
▷ TriBeCa   348
▶ Upper East Side   364
▷ Upper West Side   394

The Bronx   412

Brooklyn   434

▶ Downtown   436
▶ Fort Greene & Bushwick   454
▶ Park Slope   474
▶ Sunset Park & Brighton Beach   488
▶ Williamsburg   504

Queens   534

Staten Island   584

Indexes   607

Alphabetical List of Restaurants   608
Restaurants by Cuisine   620
Cuisines by Neighborhood   632
Starred Restaurants   648
Bib Gourmand   651
Under $25   653

Subway Map   656

The MICHELIN Guide

"This volume was created at the turn of the century and will last at least as long."

This foreword to the very first edition of the MICHELIN guide, written in 1900, has become famous over the years and the Guide has lived up to the prediction. It is read across the world and the key to its popularity is the consistency in its commitment to its readers, which is based on the following assurances.

→ Anonymous Inspections

Our inspectors make anonymous visits to restaurants to gauge the quality of cuisine offered to the everyday customer. They pay their own bill and make no indication of their presence. These visits are supplemented by comprehensive monitoring of information—our readers' comments are one valuable source, and are always taken into consideration.

→ Independence

Our choice of establishments is a completely independent one, made for the benefit of our readers alone. Decisions are discussed by the inspectors and editor, with the most important considered at the global level. Inclusion in the Guide is always free of charge.

→ The Selection

The Guide offers a selection of the best restaurants in each category of comfort and price. A recommendation in the Guides is an honor in itself, and defines the establishment among the "best of the best."

→ Annual Updates

All practical information, the classifications, and awards, are revised and updated every year to ensure the most reliable information possible.

→ Consistency & Classifications

The standards and criteria for the classifications are the same in all countries covered by the Michelin Guides. Our system is used worldwide and easy to apply when selecting a restaurant.

→ The Classifications

We classify our restaurants using XxXxX-X to indicate the level of comfort. A symbol in red suggests a particularly charming spot with unique décor or ambience. The ✿✿✿-✿ specifically designates an award for cuisine. They do not relate to a chef or establishment and are unique from the classification.

→ Our Aim

As part of Michelin's ongoing commitment to improving travel and mobility, we do everything possible to make vacations and eating out a pleasure.

How to Use This Guide

Areas or neighborhoods
Each area is color coded...

Average Prices

👞	Under $25
$$	$25 to $50
$$$	$50 to $75
$$$$	Over $75

Symbols

💷	Cash only
🕭	Wheelchair accessible
🌣	Outdoor dining
🍳	Breakfast
🥂	Brunch
🦐	Dim sum
🍷	Notable wine list
🍶	Notable sake list
🍸	Notable cocktail list
🍺	Notable beer list
🚗	Valet parking
✧	Private dining room

The Bronx

Manhattan ▶ Chelsea

Tiger Cat Cafe 😊

America

B2 715 Zhe Court Dr. (bet. Little Ave. & Fan Dr.)

Phone: 224-224-2424
Web: www.tigercatfancafe.com
Price: $$

🕭

🌣

Named for the owner's beloved tabby cat, th
exudes warmth form the welcoming waitstaff to
curtains, the pet portraits in the dining room. A l
from the neighborhood's hustle and bustle, the s
contemporary dining room stocked with shelve
ingredients.
Sample dishes like quinoa salde tossed se
salmon and soy sauce dressing, or juicy, tende
beef. round out the offerings. And old school s
fish dishes and even venison. The most uniqu
mango infused coconut sorbet served a soy b
bowl.
Hearty portions and tuna treats available t
your feline buddies bring smiles to the regul

Uptown Jeanine

A2 1957 Hart Blvd. (bet. 45th & 46th Ave

Phone: 646-212-2929
Web: www.eatatuptownjeanine.com
Price: 👞

🥂

✧

Uptown Jeanine's interior is classier th
granite tables equipped with grill tops
and a glass-enclosed exhibition kitche
Bein with the usual but exquisite bane
fermented bean paste soup, and sepo
funky, garlicky, and a total pleasure.
Since 2005, the sunny spot has ser
an entire Cornish game hen stu
jujubes, ginger, annise and garlic
bowl of delicately flavored ginse
bobbing with tofu arrives piping
nutty, telltale flavor of fermentec
have it

72

16

Restaurant Classifications by Comfort

	More pleasant if in red
X	Comfortable
XX	Quite comfortable
XxX	Very comfortable
XxxX	Top class comfortable
XxXxX	Luxury in the traditional style
▤	Small plates

Map Coordinates

Manhattan ▲ Chelsea

San Francisco ▲ Nob Hill

Sonya's Palace ❀

Italian   XXxX

A4   100 Reuther Pl. (at 30th St.)

Dinner Mon – Sat

Subway: 23rd St (Eighth Ave.)
Phone: 917-222-1155
Web: www.sonyasfabulouspalace.com
Price: $$$$

Home cooked Italian never tasted so good than in this pretentious palace. The decor claims no big name designers, and while the Murano glass light fixtures are chic and the velveteen-covered chairs are comfortable, this isn't a restaurant where millions of dollars were spent on the interior.

Instead, food is the focus here. THe restaurant's name may not be Italian, but it nonetheless serves some of the best pasta in the city, made fresh in-house. Dishes follow the seasons, thus ravioli maybe stuffed with fresh ricotta and herbs in summer, and pumpkin in fall. Most everyting is liberally dusted with Parmigiano Reggiano, a favorite ingredient of the chef. Start meals with an immaculately fresh caprese salad, then sample a crisp pie from the Neapolitan wood-burning pizza oven. One bite of her lasagna, rich with creamy ricotta and hearty Bolognese, will have you cheering "Mamma mia," while oversized portions have some crying "basta!"

For Dessert, you'll have to deliberate between the likes of creamy tiramisu, ricotta cheesecake, and the homemade geltao. One thing's for sure: you'll never miss your nonna's cooking when eat at Sonya's..

17

107

Manhattan _____12
The Bronx _____412
Brooklyn _____434
Queens _____534
Staten Island _____584

Where to Eat

Manhattan

Chelsea

DIVERSITY IN DINING

Chelsea is a charming residential neighborhood combining modern high-rises and sleek lofts with classic townhouses and retail stores aplenty. To that end, this nabe is a shopper's paradise, offering everything from computer marts and high fashion boutiques, to **Chelsea Market**—the city's culinary epicenter. And let's not forget the art: this neighborhood's once-dilapidated warehouses and abandoned lofts are currently home to over 200 prominent galleries as well as the artists who contribute to them. Naturally, find a burgeoning cultural scene. To feed its well-educated, art-enthusiast residents, and out-of-towners on pilgrimage here, Chelsea teems with casual cafeterias. Those old-world Puerto Rican luncheonettes that used to dot Ninth Avenue have now given way to mega-hip temples of fusion cooking—where diners are accommodated in stylish digs and the cocktail menu packs a potent punch. Carousers party until last call at such high-energy hangouts as **1 OAK**, launched by greenmarket-obsessed chef, Alex Guarnaschelli's Butter Group. Patrons of this hot spot may then jump ship to the likes of **Marquee**, but remain loyal to such late-night stalwarts as **Robert's Steakhouse at Scores New York**. Nestled inside the Penthouse Executive Club,

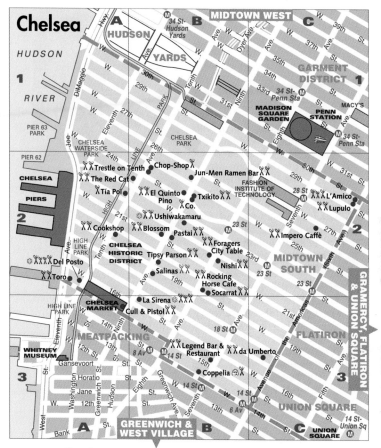

Chelsea

MIDTOWN WEST

HUDSON

RIVER

PIER 63 PARK

PIER 62

CHELSEA PIERS

HUDSON YARDS

34 St-Hudson Yards

CHELSEA WATERSIDE PARK

HIGH LINE PARK

CHELSEA HISTORIC DISTRICT

CHELSEA MARKET

HIGH LINE PARK

WHITNEY MUSEUM

MEATPACKING

GARMENT DISTRICT

MADISON SQUARE GARDEN

PENN STATION

MACY'S

34 St-Penn Sta

FASHION INSTITUTE OF TECHNOLOGY

MIDTOWN SOUTH

FLATIRON

UNION SQUARE

14 St-Union Sq

GRAMERCY, FLATIRON & UNION SQUARE

GREENWICH & WEST VILLAGE

Trestle on Tenth • Chop-Shop
The Red Cat •
Tía Pol
El Quinto Pino
Txikito
Co.
Ushiwakamaru
Cookshop • Blossom
Pastai
Del Posto
Toro
Tipsy Parson
Salinas
Nishi
Rocking Horse Cafe
Socarrat
La Sirena
Cull & Pistol

Jun-Men Ramen Bar
L'Amico
Lupulo
Impero Caffè
Foragers City Table

Legend Bar & Restaurant
da Umberto
Coppelia

Gansevoort
Horatio
Jane
Bank

---

it's really all about the "meat" at this fortress of flesh, where gentlemen seem far more interested in the likes of char-rich steaks on their plates than those ladies perched on their laps.

Located above Manhattan's mean streets and atop an elevated freight railroad, **The High Line** is a lengthy public space with a large presence in Chelsea. Populated by yuppies and young families, and punctuated by acres of

indigenous greenery as well as surprisingly stunning views of the Hudson, this city-center oasis also offers unique respites for refreshment. For instance, **Bubby's High Line** is perpetually packed for its impressive repertoire of food and drink. Envision young locals ordering off a kid's menu; or late-night revelers devouring a "midnight brunch" and you will begin to understand what this neighborhood is all about. Too rushed to dwell over dessert?

Their retail store sells pastries and ice cream sandwiches to-go, after which a shot of single-origin drip espresso at **Blue Bottle Coffee Café** is not just fitting, but first-class. As history would have it, the last functional freight train that passed through The High Line had cars filled with meat. It therefore seems only natural that **The Taco Truck** churns out Mexican street eats to ease the summer heat. Nearby, **Terroir at The Porch** is an open-air, full-service café with small plates, wine, and beer to boot. Seal such stellar sips with a cooling kiss from **L'Arte del Gelato**. Sound like bliss? It is.

In 1997, the 1898 Nabisco factory reopened as **Chelsea Market**, a fabled culinary bazaar whose brick-lined walkways are cramped with stores selling everything—from lemons to lingerie. Carb-addicts begin their circuitous excursion here at **Amy's Bread**, where artisan-crafted loaves are as precious as crown jewels. Then they might linger at **Bar Suzette** for scores of fluffy crêpes. Meanwhile, the calorie-counters collect at **Beyond Sushi** for healthy renditions of this Japanese staple, wrapped here in black rice and topped with tofu.

From Asian signatures to everyday Italian, **Buon Italia** will not only help stock your pantry for a night in with *nonna*, but sates those inevitable hunger pangs while you're at it—a stand upfront sells cooked foods and sandwiches to crowds on the run. Other welcome members to this epicurean community include **Dickson's Farmstand Meats** for house-made pâté; **Sarabeth's** or **Fat Witch Bakery** for holiday goodies; **Creamline** for comfort food classics; and **Ronnybrook** for dairy products. Keep trekking northward before sealing the deal at **The Grill at La Piscine** (on the rooftop of Hôtel Americano) with a bite of any kind, but sure sip of *vino*!

Blossom

Vegan

B2

187 Ninth Ave. (bet. 21st & 22nd Sts.)

Subway: 23 St (Eighth Ave.)
Phone: 212-627-1144
Web: www.blossomnyc.com
Price: $$

Lunch & dinner daily

Unpretentious and welcoming, this is a vegan favorite with spot-on spicing and delicious surprises. The cream-colored interior is dim with dark velvet curtains and votive candlelight reflected in round mirrors. The vibe may seem moody come evening, but the staff is always warm and affable.

Huge portions and the bold flavors of smoked tempeh, spinach, pine nuts, and cremini mushrooms prove the power of vegetables to dedicated carnivores. Follow this with meaty and woodsy grilled seitan, glazed with violet-mustard and served over a mélange of roasted salsify and sautéed kale surrounded by horseradish cream. Come dessert, try the hand-churned cashew ice cream or a lemony cheesecake with a mixed berry reduction and coconut-cookie crust.

Chop-Shop

Asian ✗

B2

254 Tenth Ave. (bet. 24th & 25th Sts.)

Subway: 23 St (Eighth Ave.)
Phone: 212-820-0333
Web: www.chop-shop.co
Price: $$

Lunch Mon – Sat
Dinner nightly

Though the name might bring to mind an auto repair garage, the concrete floors at this industrial-chic establishment are accented not by grease and grime, but by reclaimed pine, vintage lights, and sunlight streaming in through its soaring windows.

The eclectic menu roams across Asia with a bevy of stir-fried, sizzled, and steamed dishes, each of them as deliciously flavorful and balanced as the last. Subtlety reigns in the crispy bits of fried beef dressed with a nicely calibrated sweet and spicy orange sauce; while fried rice is revved up with potent Thai green curry paste and pocked with shrimp, egg, and basil. Sweet tooths will appreciate that desserts here are mouthwateringly complex, too, as in the rich and silky coconut crème caramel.

Co.

B2

P i z z a

230 Ninth Ave. (at 24th St.)

Subway: 23 St (Eighth Ave.)
Phone: 212-243-1105
Web: www.co-pane.com
Price: $$

Lunch Tue – Sun
Dinner nightly

Head to Co. for something other than those Naples-aping pizzerias that have come to monopolize the whole of New York. A serious destination for its dedicated take on pies, this carb haven pays equal attention to the dough and toppings, with outstanding results. These are the ways of celebrated baker and chef, Jim Lahey, who perfected his yeasty, smoky flavors at Sullivan Street Bakery (a few doors away) and is NYC's resident expert on bread-making.

Amid wood-paneled walls, wine racks, and modern-looking mirrors, crowds savor innovative combinations, such as spicy merguez with smoked pepper sauce, pecorino, and mint on a puffy crust. Nightly specials include a creamy leek and celeriac soup, finished with olive oil and freshly ground black pepper.

Cookshop

A2

A m e r i c a n

156 Tenth Ave. (at 20th St.)

Subway: 23 St (Eighth Ave.)
Phone: 212-924-4440
Web: www.cookshopny.com
Price: $$

Lunch & dinner daily

It's a delight just to enter this beautiful neighborhood mainstay, with its airy, impeccably clean, and sunlight-flooded dining room. The plant-filled space is furnished with ethically-sourced American oak tables as well as a wall of banquettes; and the bar is perfect for solo dining. And all this charm awaits you even before you sink your teeth into Cookshop's ultra-delicious food.

Chef de Cuisine Andrew Corrigan's contemporary, product-driven, and Mediterranean-inspired menu focuses on local sourcing, and includes dishes like ricotta *gnudi* with brown butter-apple sauce; grain salad with sesame, pomegranate and poached egg; or grilled bigeye tuna with dried fig *anchoiade*. Breakfast is served during the week, while weekends offer a full brunch menu.

Coppelia

Latin American 🍴

B3

207 W. 14th St. (bet. Seventh & Eighth Aves.)

Subway: 14 St (Seventh Ave.)   Lunch & dinner daily
Phone: 212-858-5001
Web: www.coppelianyc.com
Price: $$

Think of ultra-casual Coppelia as a favorite anytime Latin-American diner, ready to please with its enormous menu served 24 hours a day, seven days a week. The space is long and narrow, including a counter for solo guests, checkerboard floors, and cheery yellow walls. Come midnight, the booths are hopping.

The Havana salad has nothing to do with its namesake city but is an unbeatable combination of curly kale, queso fresco, toasted pepitas, crunchy mustard seeds, and tomatoes tossed in lemony vinaigrette. Crisp and flaky empanadas have both classic and quirky fillings, ranging from shredded chicken and chorizo to sweet corn. Save room for a towering slice of carrot cake featuring the unique twist of Manchego cheese and zesty lime frosting.

Cull & Pistol

Seafood 🍴🍴

A3

75 Ninth Ave. (in Chelsea Market)

Subway: 14 St - 8 Av   Lunch & dinner daily
Phone: 646-568-1223
Web: www.cullandpistol.com
Price: $$

Cull & Pistol is a sensational seafood spot. This breath of fresh salt-laden air is replete with reclaimed teak tables, brushed steel chairs, and a zinc-topped raw bar groaning with crimson-red crab claws, chilled lobster, shrimp cocktail, and clams from all shores.

It's an impressive start tailed by a vast oyster menu and deeply comforting classics that may be slurped up at two-tops inside the cozy space. Then, a whole fish salt-baked in a hefty cask is cracked open, teasing diners with plumes of thyme- and lemon-scented steam. At lunch, the clambake is a briny, heavenly mash-up of lobster, mussels, Dickson's sausage, corn on the cob and fingerling potatoes, served family-style in a rich shellfish broth. Dessert is pure and sweet bliss.

da Umberto

Italian

C3

107 W. 17th St. (bet. Sixth & Seventh Aves.)

Subway: 18 St	Lunch Mon – Fri
Phone: 212-989-0303	Dinner Mon – Sat
Web: www.daumbertonyc.com	
Price: $$$$	

There is a finely tuned harmony to dining at such classic New York restaurants as this one. The Italian menu is familiar and unpretentious, the kitchen is adept, and ingredients are superb. But, what truly sets it apart is an ability to serve exactly what you crave without seeming trite or predictable. Even the look is a perfectly conjured mix of warm neutrals with a sleek yet informal Northern Italian style and impeccably timed servers.

Start with the traditional antipasto and then proceed to one of the daily specials like veal Milanese or a lavish dish of *garganelli* with mushrooms and black truffles. When the dessert cart rolls around, expect an array of excellent house-made sweets like pristine berries under whisked-to-order *zabaglione*.

El Quinto Pino

Spanish

B2

401 W. 24th St. (bet. Ninth & Tenth Aves.)

Subway: 23 St (Eighth Ave.)	Lunch Sat – Sun
Phone: 212-206-6900	Dinner nightly
Web: www.elquintopinonyc.com	
Price: $$	

This convivial tapas spot, compliments of Chef/co-owners Alex Raij and Eder Montero, is small but oh-so-warm and friendly. A bustling bar greets you upon entry; behind that lies a sweet little dining space with large windows, mismatched chairs, and a huge woven mural. Service is engaging and attentive. The food may hit the table swiftly, but nonetheless, the multiple courses are very well paced.

This kitchen has a talent for frying to perfection, but the highlight of the menu is arguably their lineup of warm, crusty *bocadillos* (sandwiches). The menu offers a full range of Spanish tapas that include regional touches from areas like Andalusia, Asturias or Menorca—and clever combinations like the garlic shrimp with ginger and jalapeño or delicious shrimp po' boy.

Del Posto

Italian 🍴🍴🍴🍴

A2

85 Tenth Ave. (at 16th St.)

Subway: 14 St - 8 Av
Phone: 212-497-8090
Web: www.delposto.com
Price: $$$$

Lunch Mon – Fri
Dinner nightly

Neighbors like the High Line, Whitney Museum and Chelsea Market immediately position Del Posto at the height of fashion. And with the names Batali, Bastianich, and Ladner behind it, its cuisine and setting are opulent beyond words. A sense of European luxury is clear in the beautifully dressed tables, polished marble, and windows draped in fine silks and billowing fabric.

Balconies sit over the large and striking bar with live piano music pouring through the room. By the time a rich Italian red touches your lips, and that crusty baguette with an irresistible globe of cultured cream speckled with black pepper and emerald-green olive oil hits the table, you are basking in the splendor of it all. Follow that with canapés that are as dramatic as the room.

Every dish from Co-owner/Executive Chef Mark Ladner's team is gorgeously crafted, but next-level pasta is what makes this kitchen truly soar. Indulge in a slim block of 100-layer lasagna, browned à la minute and set on a streak of bright pomodoro sauce. Equally sumptuous is *caserecci all'Amatriciana* tossed in a very Del Posto mélange of onions, porcini *trifolati*, and tuna belly creatively standing in for the traditional *guanciale*.

Foragers City Table

Contemporary ✕✕

B2

300 W. 22nd St. (at Eighth Ave.)

Subway: 23 St (Eighth Ave.)
Phone: 212-243-8888
Web: www.foragersmarket.com
Price: $$

Lunch Sat – Sun
Dinner nightly

This restaurant-cum-market is an offshoot of an independent grocer in DUMBO, though its kitchen philosophy seems to have arrived via California. The dining room radiates functionality through large and unencumbered windows as well as basic hardwood tables. It's staffed and patronized by the sort of local-loving sycophants who consider it an honor to dine here—and it actually is.

Chef Nickolas Martinez and his team will impress you with their skilled cooking featuring local produce from the market's own farm in Columbia County. Heirloom tomatoes are whirled into a lush gazpacho; artisanal dried pasta produced in Brooklyn from organic grain is deliciously dressed; and roasted chicken with Hudson Valley corn polenta is comfort food extraordinaire.

Impero Caffè

Italian ✕✕

C2

132 W. 27th St. (bet. 6th & 7th Aves.)

Subway: 28 St (Seventh Ave.)
Phone: 917-409-5171
Web: www.imperorestaurants.com
Price: $$$

Lunch & dinner daily

One of New York's favorite chefs, Scott Conant, has returned to serve his signature take on hearty Italian dining. The setting combines ivory walls, light wood floors, soft lighting, and feels somewhat cache, tucked beneath the newly constructed Euro-chic Innside hotel.

The menu is based in an array of pasta, such as twists of *gemelli* slicked with chicken liver *sugo* and topped with a dollop of deliciously savory Calabrian *neonata*, made from anchovies, sweet red peppers, and chilies. More straightforward creations include pockets of ricotta-stuffed *raviolini* in a chunky ragù of stewed red and gold cherry tomatoes. Commence your meal here with a classic *fritto misto* of calamari, rock shrimp, and more. Then finish with a buttery pineapple upside down cake and vanilla gelato.

Jun-Men Ramen Bar

Japanese 🍴🍴

B2

249 Ninth Ave. (bet 25th & 26th Sts.)

Subway: 23 St (Eighth Ave.)
Phone: 646-852-6787
Web: www.junmenramen.com
Price: 💰

Lunch & dinner Mon – Sat

This cool West Chelsea ramen shop is a hot ticket—and with less than two dozen seats, a short wait can be expected at lunchtime. Slick and bright, the grey and white space is accentuated by the stainless steel implements of the open kitchen, where two hot tub-sized stock pots of pork broth bubble away.

That marrow-rich broth is the foundation for a succulent bowlful of toothsome straight noodles topped with simmered bamboo shoots, delightfully fatty *chasu*, *shoyu tamago* with a liquid gold yolk, and a splash of fermented garlic oil for good measure. Spicy miso and kimchi are delicious variations on the theme, while small plates offer tastes like pork buns, fried sweet potatoes, and yellowtail crudo dressed with pickled mango and kimchi.

L'Amico

Italian 🍴🍴🍴

C2

849 Sixth Ave. (at 30th St.)

Subway: 28 St (Broadway)
Phone: 212-201-4065
Web: www.lamico.nyc
Price: $$

Lunch & dinner daily

French-born Chef Laurent Tourondel knows New Yorkers can never get enough pizza—especially not when it's this divine. The restaurant's stunning rustic-contemporary interior was conceived by Brooklyn-based design studio, Crème, and the look is a breath of fresh air—soft, warm lighting washes across an open layout room dotted with vibrant green plants, reclaimed slats, ceiling beams, and Windsor-style walnut chairs.

The kitchen's ingredient-driven menu was built around its beautiful, copper-clad wood-fired ovens, so naturally, excellent pizzas and pastas abound. But, appetizers like veal-and-pork meatballs "al forno", and entrées like a wood oven-roasted chicken are tempting additions. Tack on one of their lovely cocktails for a full-on *festa*.

La Sirena

Italian

B3

88 Ninth Ave. (bet. 16th & 17th Sts.)

Subway: 14 St - 8 Av
Phone: 212-977-6096
Web: www.lasirena-nyc.com
Price: $$$

Lunch & dinner daily

Here come empire-builders Chef Mario Batali and partner Joe Bastianich to rev up the Chelsea scene even further with this revamp of the Maritime Hotel's dining room.

La Sirena is anchored by a pretty lounge (with its limited menu) where the custom mosaic-tiled floor endures a nightly stampede of stilettos, as a wall of glass overlooking an expansive patio allows the sunset to glint off the gleaming bar. For proper dining, seek out the cached dining rooms where sleek leather furnishings and very fine service offer hushed comfort.

Having honed his skills at Del Posto and Babbo, Chef Josh Laurano has been ordained to execute this New York-style take on Italian dining. Pastas such as creamy *lasagne al pesto e patate* or zesty *tonnarelli neri* with seafood are sure to be a highlight and best enjoyed as the *bis* portion, split between you and your guest. *Panelle*, mint, and pomegranate molasses combine for a Sicilian-inspired backdrop to succulent lamb chops. When asked if you would like bread, your answer should be enthusiastically affirmative—the freshly baked semolina loaf is fabulous.

Campari-soaked *babà* is an untraditional but nonetheless delightful pastry nicely paired with basil gelato.

Legend Bar & Restaurant

B3

Chinese ✗✗

88 Seventh Ave. (bet. 15th & 16th Sts.)

Subway: 14 St (Seventh Ave.)
Phone: 212-929-1778
Web: www.legendrestaurant88.com
Price: ⊘⊘

Lunch & dinner daily

While Legend may offer a nice variety of Asian fare, just stick to the Sichuan specialties and be thoroughly rewarded. Find one of the many highlights in supremely flavorful and tender Chong Qing spicy chicken, loaded with viciously good dried chilies. The house duck is a traditional presentation of roasted and crisped meat with wraps as well as a host of accoutrements, including crushed peanuts, fragrant herbs, scallions, and very tasty plum sauce. Bok choy with black mushrooms is a crunchy, simply delicious departure from the intensity of other dishes you may face here.

The dining room has a certain hip and chic feel that fosters a lively happy hour scene. Colorful fabrics, striped walls, and statues of deities make for an attractive space.

Lupulo

C2

Portuguese ✗✗

835 Sixth Ave. (at 29th St.)

Subway: 28 St (Seventh Ave.)
Phone: 212-290-7600
Web: www.lupulonyc.com
Price: $$

Lunch & dinner daily

Located at the base of Eventi, a Kimpton Hotel, Chef George Mendes' elegant restaurant is a beautiful, industrial-chic ode to the casual home cooking of Portugal. Food voyeurs should vie for a seat at the bar, where they can eye fresh seafood lined up in plump, shimmering rows or enjoy the action behind the glass wall of the semi-open kitchen. Otherwise, a seat in the bustling dining room, decked out in gorgeous Portuguese tiles and hip lobster-trap lights, ought to do the trick.

Try the *espargos assados*, a dish of tender, spit-grilled spring asparagus topped with shaved dried sea urchin, sorrel, olive oil and a dust of sea salt; or the wickedly good *frango piri-piri*, grilled to perfection and served with its mouthwatering namesake pepper sauce.

Nishi

Contemporary   XX

B2

232 Eighth Ave. (bet. 21st & 22nd Sts.)

Subway: 23 St (Eighth Ave.)
Phone: 646-518-1919
Web: www.momofuku.com
Price: $$$

Lunch & dinner daily

With Nishi, David Chang and his crackerjack team venture west into Chelsea, quickly garnering the kind of devoted following that their other restaurants produced before it. The slender space features a cool, minimal décor, with communal seating at long honey-colored wood slabs; pale walls; and a nice selection of artwork.

Of course, as with his other joints, you're not here to look. The menu is downright delicious, incorporating products from Chang's fermentation-focused Brooklyn lab, Momofuku Foods. Custard-smooth tofu with plump orange beads of smoked trout roe, finely diced Tokyo turnip, and nori is splashed with fermented rye *bonji*; while perfectly chewy *chitarra* is laced in a vivid red chili sauce, tender squid, and Thai basil.

Pastai

Italian   XX

B2

186 Ninth Ave. (bet. 21st & 22nd Sts.)

Subway: 23 St (Eighth Ave.)
Phone: 646-688-3463
Web: www.pastainyc.com
Price: $$

Lunch & dinner daily

To call it simply an "artisanal pasta bar" would be selling Pastai short. It also happens to be attractive and thoroughly likable, repurposing milk bottles as water pitchers and displaying bright flowers, pennytiles, and wainscoting beneath its vintage ceiling. Wooden communal tables enhance the very pleasant atmosphere.

The white-tiled kitchen and pasta station are front and center, keeping the menu's focus on everyone's mind. Tart and aromatic fresh-lemon pasta arrives twirled in a sort of broccoli rabe "pesto" with roasted tomatoes and creamy burrata. Handcrafted ravioli are so delicate and translucent that snips of asparagus and ricotta stuffing appear milky-green. Desserts like the lemon-olive oil cake are deliciously simple.

The Red Cat

Chelsea

American ✗✗

B2

227 Tenth Ave. (bet. 23rd & 24th Sts.)

Subway: 23 St (Eighth Ave.)
Phone: 212-242-1122
Web: www.theredcat.com
Price: $$

Lunch & dinner daily

If crowds indicate quality (and downtown they often do) then this clear favorite is still going strong after more than 15 years. Loyal customers as diverse as the city itself flood the long bar and richly colored room for lunch, dinner, or just for a finely mixed cocktail and snack. Flowers give the space a touch of luxury; Moorish lanterns add warmth.

The pleasures here are straightforward, beginning with a smoky bowl of charred eggplant dip, with a healthy splash of sherry vinegar, garlic, and herbs, served with fresh bread. Don't miss schmaltz-fried eggs on top of crispy potato rosti, piled with buttery sautéed spinach and tender brisket. Crunchy cinnamon churros with a spiced chocolate ganache and guava-caramel sauce are a decadent finish.

Rocking Horse Cafe

Mexican ✗✗

B2

182 Eighth Ave. (bet. 19th & 20th Sts.)

Subway: 14 St - 8 Av
Phone: 212-463-9511
Web: www.rockinghorsecafe.com
Price: $$

Lunch & dinner daily

A Chelsea classic since 1988, this Mexican café has a split personality. The front room—with vibrant orange walls, glowing lanterns, bare tabletops, and a long bar—is a bright, casual place to sample tequila cocktails or crunch into handmade tortilla chips and smoky salsa. Beyond a blue mosaic wall, the back room is a down-to-earth dining spot with a relaxed feel.

The distinctive menu includes the likes of *cordero enchipotlado*, chipotle braised lamb shank with caramelized onions, roasted tomatoes, and epazote over a creamy bed of *cotija*-spiked polenta; or blue corn *crepas de pato* stuffed with duck confit. The wise diner who ventures beyond commonplace dishes here is rewarded with complex, from-scratch cooking with soul.

Salinas

Spanish XX

B2

136 Ninth Ave. (bet. 18th & 19th Sts.)

Subway: 18 St   Dinner nightly
Phone: 212-776-1990
Web: www.salinasnyc.com
Price: $$$

What's not to love here? Even if the lip-smacking tapas menu didn't draw customers in droves, a sexy décor dressed in oodles of fresh roses and the warm glow of candlelight would do the trick. A slender hallway opens up into a narrow dining hall featuring dark walls; tufted velvet banquettes; and a backyard dining area topped by a retractable roof.

The Spanish cuisine, skillfully rendered by chef and San Sebastian native, Luis Bollo, arrives as intricate tapas or hearty large plates, depending on your appetite. Tuck into *arroz brut a la plancha,* a tender, griddled cake of short grain brown rice, studded with savory merguez, peas, and raisins; or baked *fideuà* sauced with squid ink and topped with shaved *sepia,* garlicky aïoli and watercress sprouts.

Socarrat

Spanish XX

B2

259 W. 19th St. (bet. Seventh & Eighth Aves.)

Subway: 18 St   Lunch & dinner daily
Phone: 212-462-1000
Web: www.socarratnyc.com
Price: $$

True, Soccarat is named for that ridiculously tasty burnished rice crust at the bottom of the paella pan. And yes, this place serves one of the city's best. The *paella de la huerta* with chicken combines spicy house-made chorizo, chickpeas, artichokes, tomatoes, and more in one traditional hot flat-bottom pan built for two (or more). However, there is much more on the menu to explore, especially during their highly regarded brunch-time feast of steak *a la plancha* with eggs, or an *ensalada mixta* tossing greens, asparagus, boiled egg, tuna, and olives.

Glossy walls reflect the convivial room's gentle light, while mirrors and portraits lend depth and color. Communal tables are packed with your newest old friends and tapas-loving locals.

Tía Pol

A2

205 Tenth Ave. (bet. 22nd & 23rd Sts.)

Subway: 23 St (Eighth Ave.)
Phone: 212-675-8805
Web: www.tiapol.com
Price: ⊝⊜

Lunch Tue – Sun
Dinner nightly

You'll think you've died and gone to Barcelona. This cozy little tapas den kicks up to boisterous levels in its bustling and festive front area, where servers uncork bottles and the wine flows as guests cue up for tables in the front or back dining room. The wait is all part of the fun, of course, and service is as cheery, efficient and casual as you'd hope it to be.

Originally opened in 2004, owners Heather Belz & Mani Dawes offer a scrumptious array of small plates like creamy black rice plated with shaved cuttlefish and pale green parsley purée; or a thick wedge of potato-studded tortilla Española, laced with delicious garlicky aïoli. Don't miss the skirt steak, a must-try when it hits the specials menu.

Tipsy Parson

✗✗

B2

156 Ninth Ave. (bet. 19th & 20th Sts.)

Subway: 18 St (Eighth Ave.)
Phone: 212-620-4545
Web: www.tipsyparson.com
Price: $$

Lunch & dinner daily

The masculine bar shelved with books and premium spirits, dining room bric-a-brac, and French doors overlooking a garden clearly convey familiar, homey comfort. Dining here is like visting at an old friend's house, starting with drinks in the living room and ending on the back porch. But with much better food.

The chive buttermilk biscuit is a distinctive, flaky force to be reckoned with. Clear Southern flavors are further explored with sour pickles and thick slices of green tomatoes both dredged in cornmeal and deep-fried to piping hot perfection, served with buttermilk dressing, avocado salad, tomato jam, and hatch chile salsa. Small plates like "big damn shrimp" do not disappoint, but save room for the superb cornflake-topped crumble for two.

Toro

Spanish ✗✗

A2

85 Tenth Ave. (entrance at 15th St. & Eleventh Ave.)

Subway: 14 St - 8 Av
Phone: 212-691-2360
Web: www.toro-nyc.com
Price: $$

Dinner nightly

Trendy location? Check. Sleek, warehouse-sized space? Check. Floor-to-ceiling windows filled with romantic sunsets? Check. In brief, Toro is a head-turner graced with intent service and extraordinary food. Begin with inventive (and strong) crowd-pleasing sips at the impressive bar before settling in to a comfy communal table.

The music gets louder at sundown, but find yourself fixated on such deeply flavorful *pinchos* as *sardina y mantequilla de cabra* (crusty bread spread with goat butter and preserved sardines) or aged duck ham kissed with olive oil, lemon zest, and sweet, delicious fat. Links of smoky, tender chorizo set over chickpea stew is a comforting creation, while inky-dark *sepia risotto en su tinta* made with orzo is rich, buttery, and perfect.

Trestle on Tenth

Contemporary ✗✗

B2

242 Tenth Ave. (at 24th St.)

Subway: 23 St (Eighth Ave.)
Phone: 212-645-5659
Web: www.trestleontenth.com
Price: $$

Lunch & dinner daily

West Chelsea's non-stop canteen is favored by a steady stream of gallerists, fashionistas, and tourists out for a jaunt along the High Line. Despite the glitz of this ascendant neighborhood, the look here is cozy, sociable, and downright humble. Pastas may veer from the Austrian theme but are nonetheless delicious. Try the tagliatelle tossed in a buttery broth of clams, parsley, and garlic. Calf's liver here is outrageously funky and just as delicious, tender and supremely fresh beneath carmelized onions and a sweet wine reduction. The *Nusstorte* is a symphony of cruncy walnuts, sticky caramel, and Madagascan vanilla ice cream. Wash it all down with a Swiss wine or craft beer.

Rocket Pig is the restaurant's highly popular offshoot next door.

Ushiwakamaru ✿

J a p a n e s e ✗✗

B2

362 W. 23rd St. (bet. Eighth & Ninth Aves.)

Subway: 23rd St (Eighth Ave.)
Phone: 917-639-3940
Web: N/A
Price: $$$$

Dinner Mon – Sat

Now firmly settled into its Chelsea home in a former tavern, Ushiwakamaru may no longer have that underground feel of a *sushi-ya* that only the most dedicated aficionados know about. However, it remains home to luxe sushi and excellent fish.

The brief menu lists wallet-friendly à la carte specials, small plates, and cooked items like sautéed lobster and asparagus, but you may choose to ignore all that. Chef Hideo Kuribara's true focus is on the very impressive omakase, served as a choice of 14 or 20 superb courses. A bowl of pickled cucumber stimulates the appetite as a series of cold dishes arrive, with highlights like chopped horse mackerel with green onion and shiso leaf. Then move on to sashimi that proves just how incredibly fresh the fish here is.

Delve into perfectly cut octopus simply dressed with salt, pepper, and a squeeze of lemon; or needlefish served with a bowl of grated ginger, green onion slivers, and soy for dipping. Each morsel of nigiri is crafted at the dining counter and presented on a ceramic slab, ready to be plucked with your fingers. Expect large, cool mouthfuls of Japanese sea urchin, lightly torched fatty tuna with truffle salt, and rich shad brushed with soy.

Txikito

Spanish

B2

240 Ninth Ave. (bet. 24th & 25th Sts.)

Subway: 23 St (Eighth Ave.)   Dinner nightly
Phone: 212-242-4730
Web: www.txikitonyc.com
Price: $$

Start off with a "gin tonic" and taste what the fuss is all about. Always packed, delicious, and passionate, this Basque spot conveys a world of regional cuisine, thanks to Chefs Alex Raij and Eder Montero. Colorful touches and a chalkboard of daily specials lend an informal Spanish feel. Closely spaced tables remind you that you're in New York.

The Basque menu offers both small and large plates that often seem simple but are rich, tasty, and downright special—don't miss the anchovies! Their worthy signature octopus carpaccio (*pulpo*) is cut into remarkably thin slices, dressed in lemon, marjoram, and *piment d'Espelette*. If the umami-rich *laminas de setas*—citrus-marinated king oyster mushrooms offset with salty Marcona almonds—is available, get it.

Feast for under $25 at all
restaurants with ⊜.

Chinatown & Little Italy

As different as chow mein and chicken cacciatore, these two neighborhoods are nonetheless neighbors and remain as thick as thieves. In recent years, their borders have become increasingly blurred, with Chinatown gulping up most of Little Italy. It is said that New York cradles the maximum number of Chinese immigrants in the country, and settlers from Hong Kong and mainland China each brought with them their own distinct regional cuisines.

EAT THE STREETS

Chowing in Chinatown can be delectable and delightfully affordable. Elbow your way through these cramped streets to find a flurry of markets, bubble tea cafés, bakeries, and more. Freshly steamed pouches of chicken, seafood, and pork are all the rage at **Vanessa's Dumpling House**, a neighborhood fixture with a long counter and longer queue of hungry visitors. There is lots more deliciousness to be had in this 'hood—from feasting on freshly pulled noodles; ducking into a parlor for a scoop of black sesame ice cream; or breezing past a market window with crocodile meat on display—claws included! **New Kam Man** is a bustling bazaar offering everything from woks to wontons; and Vietnamese mecca, **Tan Tin-Hung**, is a mini but "super" market proffering the best selection of Vietnamese ingredients in town—red perilla, *rau ram*, and *culantro* are ready for your home kitchen. For more instant gratification, be sure to binge on salty eats from **New Beef King**. Imagine a spicy blend of jerky and barbecue—this neat and mod spot has it all. Over on Mulberry Street, **Asia Market Corp.** is a sight for sore eyes as shelves spill over with Malaysian, Indonesian, and Thai specialties. The space is tight, but the range of imported goods is nothing less than right.

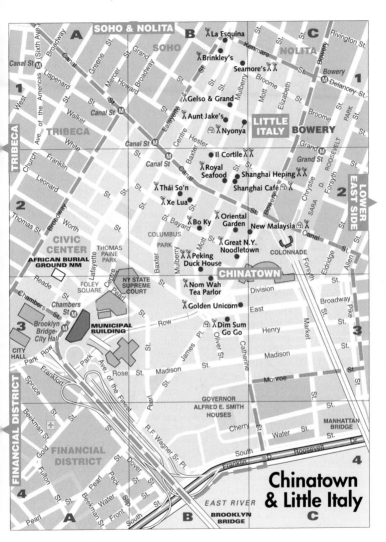

Chinatown
& Little Italy

Find celebrity chefs at these Asian storefronts, haggling over flipping fish and quality produce, before sneaking under the Manhattan Bridge for a crusty *bánh mì*. Moving on to chilies and curry pastes, **Bangkok Center Grocery** boasts every ingredient necessary for a Thai-themed feast—not to mention their publications and friendly owner! Fans of Cantonese cuisine join the line outside **Big Wong King**, where comfort food classics (congee and roast duck) are as outstanding as the setting is ordinary. **Amazing 66** is a brightly lit, bi-level darling with two dining rooms. Here dishes arrive almost as swiftly

as the crowds go in and out, making it a spot where taste and efficiency are of superlative quality. Then dim sum is obligatory and weekend brunch is a longtime tradition at **Jing Fong**. Take the escalator up a floor to arrive at this mainstay, where the service is gruff but the Hong Kong-style treats are very tasty. For a more snug vibe, head to **Tai Pan Bakery** for pastries. The exquisitely light sponge cake at **Kam Hing Coffee Shop** has made it a worthy competitor in the "Best bakeries around town" contest; just as artisan bakeshop, **Fay Da**, has been serving its Chinese treats with a modern twist to the community for near-infinity. Klezmer meets Cantonese at the **Egg Rolls and Egg Creams Festival**, an annual summer street celebration honoring the neighboring Chinese and Jewish communities of Chinatown and the Lower East Side. Every year during Chinese New Year, partygoers pack these streets, with dragons dancing down the avenues accompanied by costumed revelers and firecrackers.

LITTLE ITALY

The Little Italy of Scorsese's gritty *Mean Streets* is slowly vanishing into what may now be more aptly called Micro Italy. The onetime stronghold of a large Italian-American population has dwindled today to a mere corridor—Mulberry Street between Canal and Broome. But, the spirit of its origins still pulses in century-old markets, cramped delis, gelato shops, and mom-and-pop trattorias. Seasoned palates love **Piemonte Ravioli** for homemade sauces, as well as dried and fresh pastas—available in all shapes with a variety of fillings. **Alleva Dairy** (known for its ricotta) is the oldest Italian cheese store in the country; while **Di Palo Fine Foods** boasts imported *salumi*, and cheeses. Primo for pastries and espresso, fans never forget to frequent **Ferrara's Bakery and Café** on Grand Street. Of course, during warmer months, Mulberry Street becomes a pedestrian zone with one big alfresco party—the **Feast of San Gennaro** is particularly raucous. While these days you can get better Italian food elsewhere in the city, tourists and old-timers still gather to treasure and bathe in the nostalgia of this nabe.

Aunt Jake's

Italian

 B1

151 Mulberry St. (bet. Grand & Hester Sts.)

Subway: Canal St (Lafayette St.)
Phone: 646-858-0470
Web: www.auntjakesnyc.com
Price: $$

Lunch & dinner daily

This pleasant, light-filled atrium is a Little Italy newcomer that has quickly set itself apart from the gimmicky red-sauce joints surrounding it. Instead, Aunt Jake's is a lovely retreat for settling into well-priced, home-style cooking that centers around fresh, hand-made pasta.

Start with sautéed mushrooms in a garlicky red-pepper marinade set over fresh arugula. While the menu does offer some pre-determined combinations, this is a place to pick your favorite pasta and pair it with any one of their tasty sauces. Try their house-made *cavatelli*, cooked to a perfect al dente, and tossed with creamy rabbit ragù.

The front counter is not just an attraction for its pasta making station, but it is also where all those to-go orders are doled out.

Bo Ky

Chinese

B2

80 Bayard St. (bet. Mott & Mulberry Sts.)

Subway: Canal St (Lafayette St.)
Phone: 212-406-2292
Web: N/A
Price:

Lunch & dinner daily

If you're drawn to those bare bones sort of places where food quality, beyond-warm service, and value speak for itself, this is your Chinatown slam dunk. Bo Ky's steamed-up windows (from the succulent meats roasting inside) are an invitation to come in and get cracking on a perfect bowl of wonton and noodle soup.

Succulent braised duck is a house specialty here. Served with its sweetened dark soy braising liquid and pickled, crunchy daikon, this is a Teochew specialty but with a definite Vietnamese touch. Its textural interplay is as first-rate as the kitchen's other favorite item, namely a crispy fried shrimp-and-scallion roll wrapped in bean curd skin. Spice fiends can turn up the heat at home—their addictive secret-recipe sauces are for sale by the jar!

Brinkley's

Gastropub ✗

B1

406 Broome St. (at Cleveland Pl.)

Subway: Spring St
Phone: 212-680-5600
Web: www.brinkleyspubs.com
Price: $$

Lunch & dinner daily

This gorgeous restaurant draws a stylish young crowd, who wander in for post-work cocktails or a delicious kickstart to their Saturday night. Brinkley's interior is part British pub, part glam downtown restaurant—with sleek, sparkling black and white checkered floors; a long zinc bar; wooden banquettes; and a pressed-tin ceiling.

Provenance and sustainability highlight this menu of decadent American bar favorites, with a strong focus on local ingredients and quality produce. Think fried pickle chips in Genesee beer batter, served with spicy jalapeño-mayo sauce; or wildly fresh lobster club packed with peppery arugula, crispy pancetta, and a swipe of bright green avocado. Save room for the delicious cheesecake featuring a dark Oreo-cookie crust.

Dim Sum Go Go 😊

Chinese ✗

B3

5 East Broadway (at Chatham Sq.)

Subway: Canal St (Lafayette St.)
Phone: 212-732-0797
Web: N/A
Price: $$

Lunch & dinner daily

This wildly popular dim sum joint is still packed to the gills most days, and for good reason: the Cantonese fare and dim sum served up at this bright, contemporary spot is as good as the food you'll find trekking out to those super-authentic places in far-flung Queens. Even better, they take reservations—and dim sum orders are taken by the staff as opposed to rolled around on the traditional cart, helping ensure the food stays super fresh.

If the price seems a bit higher than its competitors, you'll find it's worth it for dishes like sweet shrimp, rolled in rice paper and laced with dark soy sauce; plump snow pea leaf dumplings spiked with vibrant ginger and garlic; rich, tender duck dumplings; or an irresistibly flaky baked roast pork pie.

Gelso & Grand

B1

186 Grand St. (at Mulberry St.)

Subway: Spring St
Phone: 212-226-1600
Web: www.gelsoandgrand.com
Price: $$

Lunch & dinner daily

It may be located smack in the middle of tourist-trappy Little Italy, but Gelso & Grand is a special place for creative and contemporary Italian food. The space is attractively industrial, with small tables and large windows that fling open for prime people-watching in warm weather. It may also be a bit pricy for the neighborhood, but that difference goes straight into the quality local ingredients and skillful cooking.

Begin with a pretty fan of tuna carpaccio garnished with tomato jam, candied ginger chips, and buttery green olives. Wood-oven fired pizzas are popular, but don't skip out on house pasta such as the roasted lasagna, layered in breaded eggplant fried golden brown, melted mozzarella, chunky Bolognese, and creamy tomato sauce.

Golden Unicorn

Chinese ✗

B3

18 East Broadway (at Catherine St.)

Subway: Canal St (Lafayette St.)
Phone: 212-941-0911
Web: www.goldenunicornrestaurant.com
Price: $$

Lunch & dinner daily

This age-old dim sum parlor, spread over many floors in an office building, is one of the few Cantonese spots that actually has the space and volume to necessitate its parade of steaming carts brimming with treats. While Golden Unicorn's system is very efficient and part of the spectacle, arrive early to nab a seat by the kitchen for better variety and hotter items.

A helpful brigade of suited men and women roam the space to offer the likes of exquisitely soft roast pork buns, or congee with preserved egg and shredded pork. Buzzing with locals and visitors, it is also a favorite among families who appreciate the kid-friendly scene as much as the delectable, steamed pea shoot and shrimp dumplings, pork *siu mai*, and rice rolls stuffed with shrimp.

Great N.Y. Noodletown

 Chinese

 B2

28 Bowery (at Bayard St.)

Subway: Canal St (Lafayette St.)
Phone: 212-349-0923
Web: N/A
Price: 😊😊

Lunch & dinner daily

When heading to Great N.Y. Noodletown, invite plenty of dining companions to share those heaping plates of roasted meats and rice and noodle soups served at this bargain favorite. Locals stream in until the 4:00 A.M. closing bell for their great Cantonese fare—food is clearly the focus here, over the brusque service and unfussy atmosphere. Guests' gazes quickly pass over the imitation wooden chairs to rest on the crispy skin of suckling pig and ducks hanging in the window.

These dishes are huge, so forgo the rice and opt instead for deliciously chewy noodles and barbecue meats. Incredible shrimp wontons, so delicate and thin, and the complex, homemade *e-fu* noodles demonstrate technique and quality to a standout level that is rarely rivaled.

Il Cortile

 Italian

B2

125 Mulberry St. (bet. Canal & Hester Sts.)

Subway: Canal St (Lafayette St.)
Phone: 212-226-6060
Web: www.ilcortile.com
Price: $$

Lunch & dinner daily

Beyond this quaint and charming façade lies one of Little Italy's famed mainstays, ever-popular with dreamy eyed dates seeking the stuff of Billy Joel lyrics. The expansive space does indeed suggest a nostalgic romance, with its series of Mediterranean-themed rooms, though the most celebrated is the pleasant garden atrium (*il cortile* is Italian for courtyard), with a glass-paneled ceiling and abundant greenery.

A skilled line of chefs present a wide array of familiar starters and entrées, from eggplant *rollatini* to chicken Francese; as well as a range of pastas, such as *spaghettini puttanesca* or *risotto con funghi*. Several decades of sharing family recipes and bringing men to one bent knee continues to earn Il Cortile a longtime following.

La Esquina

B1

114 Kenmare St. (bet. Cleveland Pl. & Lafayette St.)

Subway: Spring St (Lafayette St.)   Lunch & dinner daily
Phone: 646-613-7100
Web: www.esquinanyc.com
Price: $$

When La Esquina opened it was a breath of bright air, offering enjoyably fresh cuisine that stood tall among the paltry selection of Manhattan Mexican. Thankfully, the city's south-of-the-border dining scene has evolved since then. However, this idol remains a fun and worthy option. More playground than restaurant, the multi-faceted setting takes up an iconic downtown corner and draws a hip crowd to the grab and go taqueria, 30-seat café, and lively subterranean dining room-cum-bar. The spirit here is not just alive but kicking with classic renditions of tortilla soup; *mole negro enchiladas* filled with excellently seasoned chicken; as well as the likes of *carne asada* starring black Angus sirloin with *mojo de ajo*.

A baby sib in Brooklyn continues to thrive thanks to its retro vibe.

New Malaysia 😊

C2

46-48 Bowery (bet. Bayard & Canal Sts.)

Subway: Canal St (Lafayette St.)   Lunch & dinner daily
Phone: 212-964-0284
Web: N/A
Price:

Mad for Malaysian? Head to this lively dive, sequestered in a Chinatown arcade. Proffering some of the best Malaysian treats in town, including all the classics, New Malaysia sees a deluge of regulars who pour in for a massive offering of exceptional dishes. Round tables cram a room furnished with little more than a service counter. Still, the aromas wafting from flaky *roti canai* and Melaka crispy coconut shrimp keep you focused on the food.

Capturing the essence of this region are brusque servers who speedily deliver abundant and authentic bowls of spicy-sour *asam laksa* fragrant with lemongrass; *kang-kung belacan*, greens with dried shrimp and chili; and *nasi lemak*, the national treasure starring coconut rice, chicken curry, and dried anchovies.

Nom Wah Tea Parlor

B3

13 Doyers St. (bet. Bowery & Pell St.)

Subway: Canal St (Lafayette St.) Lunch & dinner daily
Phone: 212-962-6047
Web: www.nomwah.com
Price: ⊜⊜

First things first: You don't go to Nom Wah Tea Parlor for the décor or the service. The latter is polite and ultra-speedy, but otherwise forgettable. And the décor offers little more than pleather booths and a diner-style counter. None of this matters, for once the kitchen starts dropping its lip-smacking Chinese-American fare down with aplomb, you'll be in dim sum heaven.

Begin with soft and tender shrimp-and-snow pea leaf dumplings, before moving on to unique bean curd skin rolls tucked with savory Chinese pork. Downright terrific pan-fried dumplings are filled with pink shrimp and fragrant chives. Don't leave without sampling the restaurant's "Original Egg Roll," which is basically a massive umami bomb, easily split between four people.

Nyonya

B1

199 Grand St. (bet. Mott & Mulberry Sts.)

Subway: Canal St (Lafayette St.) Lunch & dinner daily
Phone: 212-334-3669
Web: www.ilovenyonya.com
Price: ⊜⊜

S

Nyonya flaunts a comfy setting composed of brick walls and basic wood tables, but really, everyone's here for their popular Malaysian food. Speedy servers steer lively diners through the varied menu—and perhaps even away from such delicacies as *prawn mee*, an exceptionally spiced and sour shrimp broth with silky noodles, pork, vegetables and bean sprouts floating in its goodness.

Asians and other locals know to stick to such faithful and deeply satisfying dishes as *nasi lemak*, which is a delightful combo of coconut rice, pickled veggies, crispy anchovies, curried chicken and hard-boiled egg. *Mee siam* spotlights noodles stir-fried with tofu and shrimp in a chili sauce that puts all others to shame, while coconut batter-fried jumbo prawns are nothing short of—omg—wow!

Oriental Garden

Chinese

B2

14 Elizabeth St. (bet. Bayard & Canal Sts.)

Subway: Canal St (Lafayette St.)
Phone: 212-619-0085
Web: www.orientalgardenny.com
Price: $$$

Lunch & dinner daily

A daily destination for dim sum, Oriental Garden is a treasure among tourists, foodies, and wealthy Chinese residents. The place is known to get packed as crowds pour in for top-notch dumplings, whose prices seem to escalate with its popularity. So, be sure to reserve ahead for a seat in this group-friendly den, decked with kitschy fish tanks and food photo-covered menus boasting delicious dim sum.

Set menus are widely appealing and have been known to unveil such tasty crowd-pleasers as steamed watercress and pork dumplings; crispy fried shrimp wontons; and crab claws. Equally worthy (read: safe) options include a duo of lettuce wraps with minced duck and pork served with hoisin; or one massive oyster cooked in its shell with classic black bean sauce.

Peking Duck House

Chinese

B2

28 Mott St. (bet. Chatham Sq. & Pell St.)

Subway: Canal St (Lafayette St.)
Phone: 212-227-1810
Web: www.pekingduckhousenyc.com
Price: $$

Lunch & dinner daily

It's worth your while to wend through Chinatown's teeming sidewalks to delight in the eponymous house specialty here. Once inside, however crowded, the neutral-toned interior adds a calming effect to the many tables gearing up for their bird's arrival, and the mode of transport is a linen-draped cart. The duck is deftly carved and dramatically served by the chef himself, so push in your chair and prepare for a festive DIY feast of warm, soft pancakes, cool cucumbers, scallions, and sweet hoisin. Although the duck is what makes this a destination, there are several other entrées like sizzling sliced beef with scallops; and live lobster with ginger and scallions. To begin, the clear golden broth of the duck wonton soup is an appropriate prelude to the main event.

Royal Seafood

 Chinese

B2

103 Mott St. (bet. Canal & Hester Sts.)

Subway: Canal St (Lafayette St.) Lunch & dinner daily
Phone: 212-219-2338
Web: N/A
Price:

 Bright, chaotic, and jam-packed with a multi-generational Chinese crowd, this well-priced favorite has dim sum lovers lined up and waiting in droves. Dinnertime brings a quieter vibe, along with an extensive Cantonese menu. The sizable room is decked with round tables draped in pink linens and kitschy Chinese touches. This communal scene has friends and strangers alike dining side by side.

Join the masses and feast on the likes of steamed dumplings, nicely crafted and filled with mushrooms, vegetables, ground pork, and peanut; or seafood and greens. The shrimp wrapped in yellow bean curd skin are crisply fried, not at all greasy, and completely delicious. Pan-fried wontons are thin and delicate yet exploding with flavor from garlic and chives.

Seamore's

Seafood

B1

390 Broome St. (at Mulberry St.)

Subway: Spring St Lunch & dinner daily
Phone: 212-730-6005
Web: www.seamores.com
Price: $$

 You'll feel like you stepped into a seafood shack in Montauk for an hour or two when you visit Seamore's—a breezy, whitewashed seafood restaurant courtesy of Michael Chernow, co-founder of the beloved Meatball Shop. The design of this space is complementary to the menu—fresh, clean, and stylish, with high ceilings, distressed wood planks, and bare wooden tables framed by metal-lined wooden chairs.

On the menu, you'll find a short list of sharable plates like guacamole, ceviche, and tuna poke; followed by a lineup of healthy salads, fish sandwiches, tacos and even a burger if you're so inclined. The "Reel Deal" of the day offers fresh-off-the-boat fish prepared to delicate perfection, and paired with three inventive seasonal sides.

Shanghai Café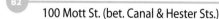

Chinese ✗

B2

100 Mott St. (bet. Canal & Hester Sts.)

Subway: Canal St (Lafayette St.)
Phone: 212-966-3988
Web: N/A
Price: ⊜

Lunch & dinner daily

This quirky café is a Chinatown stalwart. Busy booths line one wall, while big round tables are popular for gathering families. Note the dumpling station upfront, where agile chefs assemble these mouthwatering parcels.

Regulars know to arrive early for lunch to make the most of their vast menu, appetizing to vegetarians and omnivores alike. Servers are remarkably capable, balancing trays of addictive steamed juicy buns and cold dried bean curd, or soft rice cakes stir-fried with chicken and shrimp. The "queen" mushroom is sized for a king; its thick slices cooked until tender and bathed in an umami-rich brown sauce. The salty pork slices and fresh, crunchy bamboo shoots arrive in a broth so nourishing that you will slurp to the last drop.

Shanghai Heping

Chinese ✗✗

B2

104 Mott St. (bet. Canal & Hester Sts.)

Subway: Canal St (Lafayette St.)
Phone: 212-925-1118
Web: N/A
Price: $$

Lunch & dinner daily

When faced with the long, no-frills menu, there should read a caution sign to not miss out on the crab and pork soup dumplings. The plump, juicy filling and flavorful broth held in each delicate wrapper with soy-ginger seasoning explain the afternoon crowd lunching out of takeout boxes on the entrance in.

Large bamboo steamer baskets line most tables, and the seared pan-fried pork dumplings are not to miss either. Cold appetizers shine like dark soy- and sugar-cooked bamboo shoots with wheat gluten; and thinly-sliced, earthy stir-fried eel with chives. There are larger, steaming hot plates to choose from like Shanghai rice cakes with beef. The sweet "Eight Jewel Rice" dessert matches a mound of sticky rice with red bean paste, red dates, and golden raisin "jewels."

Thái Son

 **Vietnamese**

B2

89 Baxter St. (bet. Bayard & Canal Sts.)

Subway: Canal St (Lafayette St.)   Lunch & dinner daily
Phone: 212-732-2822
Web: N/A
Price: 🍴

Thái So'n is by far the best of the bunch in this Vietnamese quarter of Chinatown. It's neither massive nor fancy, but it's bright, clean, and perpetually in business. One peek at the specials on the walls (maybe golden-fried squid strewn with sea salt) will have you begging for a seat in the crammed room.

Speedy servers scoot between groups of City Hall suits and Asian locals as they order the likes of *cha gio*, pork spring rolls with *nuoc cham*; or *goi cuon*, fantastic summer rolls filled with poached shrimp and vermicelli. Naturally, *pho* choices are abundant, but the real star of the show is *pho tai*—where raw beef shavings are cooked to tender perfection when combined with a scalding hot, savory broth replete with herbs, sprouts, and chewy noodles.

Xe Lua

Vietnamese ✗

B2

86 Mulberry St. (bet. Bayard & Canal Sts.)

Subway: Canal St (Lafayette St.)   Lunch & dinner daily
Phone: 212-577-8887
Web: N/A
Price: 🍴

Fantastic food is the sole focus of this Vietnamese dive. The décor—albeit stark—highlights a semi-tropical theme and the crowd might be touristy, but don't let that deter you as the food is wonderfully authentic and very reasonable.

Condiments atop each table serve to enhance even the most humble *goi cuon* stuffed with grilled pork and vermicelli. *Muc chien don* is a plate of chewy, crisped squid tossed in salt, pepper, and tailed by cucumbers and red onion for ample tang; while the house special *pho xe lua* reveals a rich, savory broth full of noodles, brisket, and beef tendon. Combine this with sprouts, chilies, and herbs for a surefire delight.

Enjoy dessert with a Vietnamese iced coffee that will give even your great-aunt Grace the shakes.

East Village

L ong regarded as the capital of cool, the East Village was once a shadier incarnation of Tompkin's Square Park and second home to squatters and rioters. However, the neighborhood today is safer, cleaner, and far more habitable. And while cheap walk-ups filled with struggling artists or aspiring models may be a thing of the past, the area's marked gentrification hasn't led to any sort of dip in self-expression or creativity. In fact, reflecting the independent and outspoken spirit for which this neighborhood is known, the East Village flaunts a distinct personality and vibrant dining landscape.

CHEAP EATS

B udget-friendly bites abound in these parts. Family-run **Veselka**, located in the heart of this 'hood has been serving traditional Ukrainian specialties for over 60-years, and is a fitting homage to the area's former eastern European population. After a night of bar-hopping or other mischief, grab a restorative bite of salt and fat at **Crif Dogs**, where deep-fried hot dogs are doled out until 4:00 A.M. Along these streets, find a number of food-related endeavors that are the product of laser-focused culinary inspiration. **Banh mi Zon** for instance is a smash for crackling-skinned Vietnamese pork sandwiches. **Superiority Burger** is a hot spot loved for its lip-smacking vegan take on

the classic burger; while **Luke's Lobster** has expanded into a city-wide network presenting rolls stuffed with crustaceans straight from Maine. For ramen, Japanese-import **Ippudo** churns out steaming bowlfuls to its boisterous patrons. Meanwhile, **Brodo** (the brainchild of Hearth

Chef/owner Marco Canora) is a trendsetting storefront (window?) dispensing comforting bowls of broths that are available in three sizes and types—the Hearth broth, Organic Chicken, and Gingered Grass-fed beef. Others may join the constant queue of students looking for a crusty slice of white from **Artichoke Basille's Pizza** on 14th Street. And while on the topic of cravings of all stripes, the sensory assault around St. Mark's Place offers an immersion in Asian savors that is delightfully kitschy and incredibly worthwhile. Discover a taste of Korea by way of **Korilla**, a food truck sensation brought stateside by Chef Edward Song. Located on the first floor of a brick structure just off Cooper Square, this mostly take-out barbecue spot is beloved for pearly-white tofu coated with crimson-red, fire-hot *gochujang* and crowned by leafy bok choy. If that doesn't have you salivating, duck into **Boka** for spicy Korean fried chicken. Or, follow the scent of *takoyaki* frying and sizzling *okonomiyaki* at **Otafuku**. Hungry hordes know to look for the red paper lanterns that hang outside haunts like **Yakitori Taisho**; while taste buds are always tingling at divey *izakayas* such as **Village Yokocho**. And yet, among this area's sultry sake dens, none rival the outrageous offering at subterranean **Decibel**—rife with eats and beats.

A SWEET SIDE

Badass attitude and savory dishes aside, the East Village also has a very sweet side. **Moishe's Bake Shop** is a Kosher delight where challah, rugelach, and marble sponge cake have been on the menu since 1978. In operation since 1894, **Veniero's Pasticceria & Caffé** brings yet another taste of the Old World to these newly minted locals. This Italian idol draws long lines, especially around holiday time, for baked goods. And, don't forget to make these sweets just a bit more beautiful with a shipment of flowers from **Fleurs Bella**. There can never be a dearth of caffeine in the city, and

chic-geeks love **Hi-Collar**—a nifty, Japanese-esque coffee house bedecked with a brass counter and back wall accented by rice paper screens. Stay late and you may even be served some sake. Chef-cum-celebrity, David Chang's dessert darling on the move, but is now a top-seller for signatures like the Bea Arthur—a swirl of vanilla, *dulche de leche*, and crushed Nilla wafers. The craft cocktail movement has taken firm root in this "village" of trend, where many subtly (and even undisclosed) locations offer an epicurean approach to mixology. **Death & Co.** is a dimly lit, hot-as-hell spot that is packed to the gills, but when in need of a more intimate scene, check out the secret passageway inside **Crif Dogs** to access **PDT**—Please Don't Tell—where Benton's Old-Fashioned crafted from bacon-smoked Bourbon may just be every cocktail critic's dream come true. Cached behind a wall in a Japanese restaurant, **Angel's Share's** snazzy bartenders shake and stir for a civilized crowd,

Momofuku Milk Bar also rents space here and serves clever variations on dessert. Pastrami pockets, "Compost" cookies, and soft-serve have sweet teeth swooning (and returning). **Big Gay Ice Cream** may have started life as a modest truck while **Mayahuel's** creations lead to south-of-the-border-style fun. Finally, polished **Pouring Ribbons**, devoted to vintage Chartreuse, continues to be praised in the nabe as a sanctuary of sorts among those in-the-know.

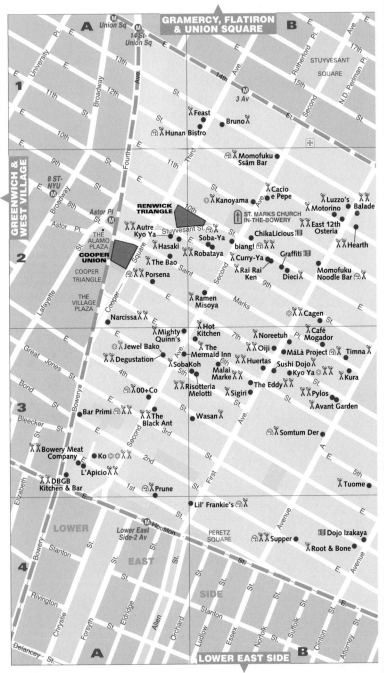

STUYVESANT SQUARE

M 3 Av

X Feast
Bruno X

🍴 X Hunan Bistro

8 ST-NYU
M

🍴 X Momofuku Ssäm Bar

X Cacio e Pepe

❄ Kanoyama
X Luzzo's
X Motorino
X Balade

RENWICK TRIANGLE
🕆 ST. MARKS CHURCH IN-THE-BOWERY

X X Autre
Kyo Ya
Soba-Ya
ChikaLicious 🍴
X East 12th Osteria

Astor Pl
M
X Hasaki
biang! X X
X X Hearth

THE ALAMO PLAZA
X Robataya
Curry-Ya
Graffiti 🍴

COOPER UNION
X The Bao
X Rai Rai Ken
Dieci X
Momofuku Noodle Bar 🍴

COOPER TRIANGLE
X X Porsena

THE VILLAGE PLAZA
X Ramen Misoya
❄ X X Cagen

Narcissa X X
X Mighty Quinn's
X Hot Kitchen
X Noreetuh
Café Mogador

❄ Jewel Bako
X Oiji
MáLà Project 🍴 X Timna

X X Degustation
X The Mermaid Inn
X X Huertas
Sushi Dojo X

X SobaKoh
Malai Marke X X
Kyo Ya ❄ X X Kura

X 00+Co
Risotteria Melotti
X Sigiri
The Eddy X X
X X Pylos

X X The Black Ant
X Wasan
X Avant Garden

Bar Primi X X

🍴 X Somtum Der

X X Bowery Meat Company
Ko ❄ X X

X X DBGB Kitchen & Bar
L'Apicio X X

🍴 X Prune
X Tuome

Lil' Frankie's 🍴 X

LOWER
M Lower East Side-2 Av
PERETZ SQUARE
🍴 X X Supper
🍱 Dojo Izakaya

EAST
X Root & Bone

SIDE

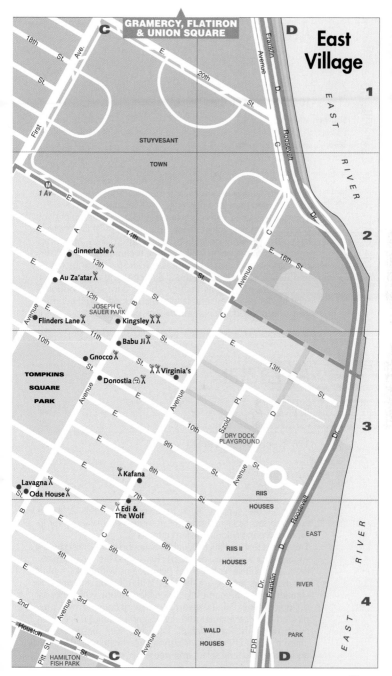

Autre Kyo Ya

10 Stuyvesant St. (bet. Third Ave. & 9th St.)

Subosway: Astor Pl
Phone: 212-598-0454
Web: www.autrekyoya.com
Price: $$

Lunch Sat – Sun
Dinner Tue – Sun

If you love the popular Japanese kaiseki house Kyo Ya, then you'll *really* love its hip new sibling, Autre Kyo Ya. The inside of the restaurant is warm and homey, and while it's less sophisticated than its older sister, it's a lot more fun.

The space is lined with cozy banquettes, a bar, and plenty of nooks for intimate conversation. But the real highlight here is the food, a unique collection of Japanese dishes amped up with French influences and cooking techniques—think *pâté de Campagne*; a crispy cauliflower with spicy peanut sauce; and Berkshire pork belly Kamadaki rice pot in a garlic-ginger sauce. Other highlights include chilled corn soup, bobbing with tender edamame and laced with leek oil; and the terrific goma tofu "cocktail" in a bonito-seaweed broth.

Au Za'atar

188 Avenue A (at 12th St.)

Subway: 1 Av
Phone: 212-254-5660
Web: www.auzaatar.com
Price: $$

Lunch & dinner daily

Don't let the simple décor fool you—what this Arabian-French bistro lacks in ambience, it more than makes up for in mouthwatering Middle Eastern cuisine.

The menu features such delights as lamb shank braised with Armagnac and prunes, delicious char-grilled meats, and many meze. Of course, every meal here begins with fresh, piping hot pita. Hot, tender, and brushed with olive oil, the bread is sprinkled with the namesake spice blend along with a hearty dollop of labne. Pair it with an appetizer of *batinjan makdous*, pickled baby eggplants stuffed with garlic-walnut paste, then move on to the *kafta* kebab. Juicy and well-seasoned, this charred ground beef skewer arrives plated with grilled tomato and onion, crunchy salad, and rice pilaf.

Avant Garden

B3

130 E. 7th St. (bet. Avenue A & First Ave.)

Subway: 1 Av   Dinner nightly
Phone: 646-922-7948
Web: www.avantgardennyc.com
Price: $$$

This tight but artsy little jewel box of a restaurant, courtesy of Ravi DeRossi, aims to give vegan food some well-deserved polish. Avant Garden's dynamic menu couldn't have arrived at a better time, as New York diners are hungry for more upscale meatless options. This is excellent food that just happens to be vegan.

Try the cold, salt-baked sweet potato with puréed watercress, crispy jicama and Meyer lemon; or avocado, paired with white asparagus, crunchy radishes, strawberries, and garlicky grilled ramps. Sheets of pasta are tossed with pesto, tomatoes, French string beans and Kalamata olives. Their thick slices of toast topped with cremini mushrooms, sweet onion marmalade, toasted walnuts and *herbs de Provence* are destined to become a signature item.

Babu Ji

C3

175 Avenue B (at 11th St.)

Subway: 1 Av   Dinner Mon – Sat
Phone: 212-951-1082
Web: www.babujinyc.com
Price: $$

For excellent Indian food by way of Melbourne, there is no better place than this "mister." Rest assured that nothing is lost in translation here: fabulous spicing leads to dishes that are fragrant, light, and flavorful. The best way to dine may be to let the kitchen take charge through the tasting menu, presented in a series of metal vessels. Begin with a signature scallop coconut curry or try tender butter chicken, marinated in ginger, garlic and yogurt, then simmered in a rich tomato sauce. *Batata vada* features crushed potatoes coated in chickpea flour and fried to crisp perfection.

The energy is high in this sleek room, though nothing is as high as the decibel level. And if you think restaurants have become noisy, well, nothing will prepare you for Babu Ji.

Balade

B2

Lebanese ✕✕

208 First Ave. (bet. 12th & 13th Sts.)

Subway: 1 Av   Lunch & dinner daily
Phone: 212-529-6868
Web: www.baladerestaurants.com
Price: $$

Honing in on the cuisine of Lebanon, Balade is a welcoming and tasty Middle Eastern experience fronted by a cheerful red awning. The spotless room is accented with tile, brick, and wood; and each table bears a bottle of private label herb-infused olive oil.

The menu begins with a glossary of traditional Lebanese ingredients and the explanation that *Balade* means "fresh, local." The meze; grilled meat-stuffed sandwiches; and Lebanese-style pizzas called *manakeesh* topped with the likes of lean ground beef, chopped onion, and spices are all fresh-tasting indeed. House specialties are also of note, like the *mujaddara crush*—a platter of lentils and rice topped with crispy fried onions as well as a salad of cool, chopped cucumber and tomato.

The Bao

A2

Chinese ✕

13 St. Marks Pl. (bet. Second & Third Aves.)

Subway: Astor Pl   Lunch & dinner daily
Phone: 212-388-9239
Web: N/A
Price: $$

Trade the hustle and bustle of Chinatown for the equally boisterous St. Marks Place as a destination for excellent soup dumplings. This being the East Village, the dining room is chic but low-key with a pale earthy color scheme framing a communal table and metal chairs.

As for the menu, the restaurant's name says it all: the *bao* are absolute perfection. Presented in a bamboo steamer with soy and vinegar dipping sauce, each parcel is artfully dimpled, delightfully toothsome, and plumped with tasty broth and seasoned meat. Save room for sampling some of their other delicious specialties, including julienned celery stalks stir-fried with dried tofu; diced chives tossed with ground pork and fermented black beans; or XO sauce-fried rice.

Bar Primi 😊

A3

Italian ✖️✖️

325 Bowery (at 2nd St.)

Subway: Bleecker St
Phone: 212-220-9100
Web: www.barprimi.com
Price: $$

Lunch & dinner daily

Chef Sal Lamboglia and Chef/owner Andrew Carmellini clearly know what they wanted to do in this kitchen: make excellent Italian (and Italian-American) food with a delicious twist here and surprise ingredient there. The result is a restaurant we would all want to have just around the corner. Great wine, a friendly service team, and two floors of comfortable seating make it easy for guests to pile in, night after night.

Start with meatballs, a far cry from the generic kind, stuffed with nutty Fontina and braised until tender in a chunky tomato *sugo*. Pasta here rivals Italy, especially the spaghetti with small, briny clams and spicy *'njuda* crumbles topped with breadcrumbs and parsley. Daily specials are also a delight as is the simply delicious hazelnut gelato.

biáng! 😊

B2

Chinese ✖️✖️

175 Second Ave. (bet. 10th & 11th Sts.)

Subway: Astor Pl
Phone: N/A-N/A
Web: www.biang-nyc.com
Price: $$

Lunch & dinner daily

Jason Wang, the chef wunderkind behind lauded fast-food mini chain, Xi'an Famous Foods, steps up his Northern Chinese game to sit-down material with the popular biang! Tucked into a deep space, the dining room is clean, capacious, and furnished with a commanding black-topped bar, white brick walls and reclaimed wood beams.

His cooking, which hails from the Shaanxi province located toward the center of China, may begin with the likes of tender spicy and sour lamb dumplings; or a bright fiddlehead fern salad laced with Sichuan pepper oil and Chinese black vinegar. Then savor a plate of stewed oxtail *biang-biang* "ripped" noodles, or fragrant pao mo lamb soup topped with cilantro and served with pickled garlic cloves and red chili sauce.

The Black Ant

✗✗

A3

60 Second Ave. (bet. 3rd & 4th Sts.)

Subway: Astor Pl
Phone: 212-598-0300
Web: www.blackantnyc.com
Price: $$

Lunch Sat – Sun
Dinner nightly

Bringing a dose of Mexico City chic to the East Village, this restaurant takes its name from the ancient Mesoamerican fable of an ant and incorporates that imagery throughout the setting. Black and white checkerboard flooring, blackboard wall tiles bearing white ants, and a very cool giant ant mural reinforce the theme.

The menu is an unrestricted look at Mexican cuisine. It is only fitting that specialties here include the Climbing Ant cocktail combining tequila, Aperol, and *mole* bitters; freshly-mashed guacamole seasoned with crushed ant salt; and grasshopper-crusted shrimp tacos. Insect-free creations are just as appealing, as in tacos stuffing tender masa tortillas with large chunks of battered and fried cod cheek, aïoli, and cabbage-mango slaw.

Bowery Meat Company

✗✗

A3

9 E. 1st St. (bet. Bowery & Second Ave.)

Subway: 2 Av
Phone: 212-460-5255
Web: www.bowerymeatcompany.com
Price: $$$$

Dinner nightly

It's official: Bowery Meat Company with its cozy velvet booths, dusky blue floor-to-ceiling drapery, and dark wood details honors the swagger of the steakhouse archetype. However, crowds of millennials lend a fresh and energetic face to this buzzy downtown address.

A list of specially selected oysters from the raw bar—like Kumamotos from Washington State dressed with spicy wasabi leaf and citrusy lemon—or zucchini carpaccio with feta and toasted pistachios may prelude this Meat Company's red-blooded roster. Speaking of which, one may relish a bone-in filet mignon au poivre, dry-aged New York strip, as well as grilled pork ribeye with spicy Korean barbecue sauce. And, don't overlook those side dishes—the sour cream and onion hash brown is a must.

Bruno

Contemporary ✗

B1

204 E. 13th St. (bet. Second & Third Aves.)

Subway: 3 Av
Phone: 212-598-3080
Web: www.brunopizzanyc.com
Price: $$$

Lunch Sat – Sun
Dinner nightly

With an edgy design and ambitious menu that goes well beyond pizza, Bruno is an extraordinary surprise to its East Village surrounds. Inside this narrow room lined with small tables and a dining counter, the service team offers more than skater style—they consistently put each guest's comfort and enjoyment first. And the casual downtown crowd is gobbling it all up, late into the night. They take few reservations, so arrive early or be prepared to wait.

You might want to skip the (very good) pizza altogether. Those in the know start with an elegant duck liver mousse that is more than worthy of the some of the best uptown kitchens. Their superb skill and creativity is clear in the seared local squid, dusted with dried chilies and sumac, then set over charred onion leaves in green chili sauce with sorrel.

Cacio e Pepe

Italian ✗

B2

182 Second Ave. (bet. 11th & 12th Sts.)

Subway: 3 Av
Phone: 212-505-5931
Web: www.cacioepepe.com
Price: $$

Dinner nightly

This charming Italian *gioiello* has welcomed diners for more than a decade now. But in relaying its pleasures, one must partake in the eponymous house specialty. This fresh *tonnarelli* tossed with pasta water, olive oil, cracked black pepper, and a showering of pecorino is pure delight. Those willing to branch out will find other pasta dishes here as equally pleasing, like the *maltagliati* dressed with a savory monkfish ragù revved up with olives, capers, and an unexpected hit of ginger. Mussels in black pepper "soup" is a savory bowl of mollusks and broth with garlicky croutons for soaking up the enticingly salty liquid.

Exposed brick and wood furnishings complement the *zucca*-orange walls lined with wine bottles offered on the all-Italian list.

Café Mogador

Moroccan

B3

101 St. Marks Pl. (bet. First Ave. & Avenue A)

Subway:	1 Av	Lunch & dinner daily
Phone:	212-677-2226	
Web:	www.cafemogador.com	
Price:		

The key to this beloved café's long-term success is its popular array of tasty, crowd-pleasing Moroccan favorites. A veritable landmark in the East Village, the decades-old hangout is as inviting as ever—and despite the constant crush of its brainy-hip set, it remains inexplicably fresh-faced.

Open from morning to night, breakfast offers the likes of eggs any style sided by hummus and tabouli, whereas afternoon fare may include tasty specials like *bastila* or *harira*—a hearty and fragrant soup. Chicken tagine is excellent: try it with fluffy couscous and *charmoula*, a spicy green herb sauce, or order it Casablanca-style with chickpeas, raisins, and onions.

If the East Village isn't hip enough, do ferry across the river to their bright outpost in Williamsburg.

ChikaLicious

Contemporary

B2

203 E. 10th St. (bet. First & Second Aves.)

Subway:	Astor Pl	Dinner Thu – Sun
Phone:	212-475-0929	
Web:	www.chikalicious.com	
Price:		

Named for Pastry Chef/owner Chika Tillman, this sweet spot presents an all-encompassing dessert experience that somehow manages to impress without overkill. The chic white space offers counter seating overlooking a lab-clean kitchen, where the team prepares elegant jewels that start as butter, sugar, and chocolate. À la carte is offered, but the best way to appreciate this dessert bar is to select the prix-fixe. Feasts here may begin with an amuse-bouche of Darjeeling tea gelée with milk sorbet; followed by a mascarpone semifreddo topped with espresso granita. Then finish with pillowy cubes of coconut-marshmallow *petits fours*.

Dessert Club across the street tempts with delish cookies, cupcakes, and shaved ice for a grab-and-go fix.

Cagen ✿

B2

414 E. 9th St. (bet. Avenue A & First Ave.)

Dinner Tue – Sun

Subway: Astor Pl
Phone: 212-358-8800
Web: www.cagenrestaurant.com
Price: $$$$

Boasting soothing textured walls the color of sand, sturdy but comfortable furnishings, and cool slate flooring, this serene and serious space is just what one would expect of a high-end Japanese dining room. But, beyond this quotidian look is a kitchen that turns out very exciting—and quite unexpected—food. Tables are an available option, but a seat facing Chef Toshio Tomita at the pristine elm counter is the place to be.

While the menu offers both à la carte dining and a sushi-only omakase, the Chef's Counter omakase is by far the best experience to be had here. This meal begins with a playful platter of bites (envision smoked ham *katsu*) to break the ice and stimulate the palate for the kitchen's sparkling sashimi. Slices of Hokkaido octopus, marinated bonito, and snapper are a treat, dressed not only with freshly ground wasabi root and top-notch soy sauce, but also the chef's signature *chimichurri*—a touch of fusion that signals his decade-plus years of working at Nobu. Another highlight is the chilled handmade soba served with spicy buckwheat sprouts and a divine dipping sauce.

Cooked dishes, like fried soft-shell crab with watermelon salad, and impressive nigiri round out Cagen's *kappo*-style meal.

Curry-Ya

Japanese

214 E. 10th St. (bet. First & Second Aves.)

Subway: Astor Pl   Lunch & dinner daily
Phone: 866-602-8779
Web: www.nycurry-ya.com
Price:

Complex, warming, and perfumed with fruity sweetness, slow-cooked *wafuu* (or Japanese-style) curry is a highly popular national treat. Tantalizingly draped over a mound of steamed short grain rice, each bowl calls for one of the kitchen's tasty embellishments such as panko-crusted fried shrimp, pan-fried hamburger steak, Berkshire pork, or chicken *katsu*. The menu, albeit brief, also offers inspiring starters like flavor-packed tofu skin as well as green bean salad tossed with nutty parmesan and a crushed-olive dressing.

Brought to you by Bon Yagi this local jewel has only 14-seats set along a white marble counter that is lined with bowls of pickles and dried onion flakes. Yes, the space may seem simple, but it's a spectacular destination to dig in and enjoy.

DBGB Kitchen & Bar

French

299 Bowery (bet. First & Houston Sts.)

Subway: 2 Av   Lunch Fri – Sun
Phone: 212-933-5300   Dinner nightly
Web: www.dbgb.com
Price: $$

Nestled into a sleek, warm space with low lighting and copper pots lining the shelves, legendary Chef Daniel Boulud's DBGB Kitchen & Bar radiates a hip, easy charm. The staff is equally cool, shuffling trays of juicy burgers and coq au vin from table to table with easy grace. The divided space offers myriad seating options, from a lively bar to a fun brasserie and more. Boulud is a master at charcuterie, so a country-style pâté campagnard with cornichons and sourdough toast points is a great way to start your evening. From there, you might opt for the juicy Beaujolaise pork link with mushroom, onion, and bacon, served with braised *lentilles du Puy*. If you can drum up twelve or more friends, the "Whole Beast Feast" offers an unforgettable family-style dinner.

Degustation

A3

239 E. 5th St. (bet. Second & Third Aves.)

Subway: Astor Pl   Dinner nightly
Phone: 212-979-1012
Web: www.degustation-nyc.com
Price: $$$

This cozy tapas bar packs a big punch thanks to the winning combination of Chef Nicholas Licata and proprietor Jack Lamb. At the center of the action is an open kitchen with surround counter seating—from here you can watch the fast-moving, amicable chefs work up their delicious magic.

Chef Licata's fare is stylish and inventive, with one eye on Spain and the other meandering around the Mediterranean. Crispy chicken croquetas are paired with smoky aïoli; while a bowl of milky burrata is bathed in bright green herbs and served atop cubes of toasty bread. Paella arrives bursting with blue prawns, chorizo, and irresistible socarrat; and a classic dessert of *torrija* (basically a fancier version of French toast) is crowned with creamy *cajeta* and sea salt.

Dieci

B2

228 E. 10th St. (bet. First & Second Aves.)

Subway: Astor Pl   Dinner nightly
Phone: 212-387-9545
Web: www.dieciny.com
Price: $$

This terrific Japanese-Italian(ish) spot pulls off more complicated flavor combos than its Lilliputian kitchen would lead you to believe. The marriage of the two disparate culinary styles find happy union in pan-roasted lamb chops with nutty sesame sauce and a soy reduction; or *linguine alle vongole*, finished with a thatch of radish sprouts. A wickedly good bed of crab and cod roe cream sauce is paired with pillowy gnocchi, then rounded out with shiso and a smattering of *shichimi togarashi*.

The postage stamp-sized space is romantic and understated, featuring large mirrors, flickering votives and steel-encased windows popped by bright floral arrangements. The dessert offering is small, but lovely—it's the perfect way to finish a lingering dinner for two.

dinnertable

C2

Contemporary

206 Avenue A (bet. 12th & 13th Sts.)

Subway: 1 Av
Phone: N/A
Web: www.dinnertable.nyc
Price: $$

Dinner Tue – Sat

This 20-seat gem is tucked behind The Garret East, a polished East Village bar with round, silver banquettes and shimmering mosaic surfaces. Make your way through the packed room and you'll find the speakeasy-like dinnertable—a small space furnished with a smattering of seats and the ubiquitous counter.

The talented kitchen behind this concept has created a menu of surprisingly elegant comfort food. Black sea bass is seared to pearly perfection and paired with tomatillo *puttanesca*; just as a supremely light *lasagna Bolo* for two is formed into rosettes filled with robiola, herbs, and a perfect tomato sauce. For a small fee, they will even add caviar to anything on the menu.

Dojo Izakaya

B4

Japanese

38 Avenue B (bet. 3rd & 4th Sts.)

Subway: 2 Av
Phone: 212-253-5311
Web: www.dojoizakaya.com
Price:

Lunch & dinner daily

If dinner in Tokyo isn't in the cards, make your way to this Alphabet City nook for the next best thing. Inside the *izakaya*, just large enough to accommodate you and a small entourage, black walls produce a vibe that's cozy, not claustrophobic, and gentle prices give way to bold flavors.

The luscious array of pleasingly authentic cooked items on offer are best washed down by a cold beer or glass of sake. Highlights include *kani korokke*, temptingly gooey and creamy crabmeat-flecked croquettes; pork neck *kushiyaki*, slices of sweet, toothsome, fatty meat charred on a bamboo skewer and brushed with a savory glaze; as well as *mentaiko onigiri*, a grilled rice ball stuffed with spicy cod roe, dusted with sesame seeds, and wrapped in sheet of toasted nori.

Donostia

C3

155 Avenue B (at 10th St.)

Subway: 1 Av
Phone: 646-256-9773
Web: www.donostianyc.com
Price: 🍴🍴

Lunch Sat – Sun
Dinner nightly

A little bite of Barcelona can be found just across from Tompkins Square Park at this bar *de conservas*. A mural depicting the Basque countryside frames the slender quarters. Most diners choose the marble counter seating, but there are also a handful of tables.

An array of small bites makes up Donostia's menu. Find Spanish cheeses and *charcutería* of Iberico pork, but the true star here are the *conservas*. To refer to these as canned seafood would be technically correct but improper—digging into a few is obligatory. Among the temptations, expect a delicate miniature *tartalata* filled with smooth sea urchin and toothsome octopus. Also try meaty chunks of oil-cured bonito with spicy salsa *roja*, potato chips, and mini loaf-shaped crackers called *picos*.

East 12th Osteria

B2

197 First Ave. (at 12th St.)

Subway: 1 Av
Phone: 212-432-1112
Web: www.east12osteria.com
Price: $$

Lunch Sat – Sun
Dinner nightly

On the one hand, this is a straightforward little corner osteria. On the other, Chef Roberto Deiaco's exciting cooking is a delicious presentation of Italian tastes and technique. The front of house is run by the chef's wife, Giselle, who lends a personal and intimate air that's hard to fake and increasingly rare. The room glows with good vibes that radiate across the hardwood floor, marble bar, and tin ceiling.

Contemporary highlights accent the coastal Italian-focused menu of *fritto di mare* neatly piling hot and delicately crisp calamari, red mullet, jumbo shrimp and a zucchini blossom. *Tagliolini all'uovo* is twirled with basil pesto, *ricotta salata*, and black truffle; and slowly braised veal cheeks are coddled with *pinot bianco gremolata* sauce and polenta.

The Eddy

Contemporary

B3

342 E. 6th St. (bet First & Second Aves.)

Subway: 2 Av
Phone: 646-895-9884
Web: www.theeddynyc.com
Price: $$

Dinner nightly

Seasonal American cuisine and a serious carte of libations (wines included) are the forte at this innovative gem on Curry Row. Headlined by Chef Brendan McHale, this wee bistro is appealingy rustic with whitewashed walls and handsome wood beams.

The Eddy's menu defies easy categorization and offers cleverly constructed cooking. Fried beef tendons are a puffed and crunchy snack dabbed with charred onion cream and sweet trout roe. Delicate ricotta gnocchi with toasted hazelnuts showcases spring's sweet peas and pickled ramps, while golden spotted tilefish is seared and plated with squid ink Hollandaise, saffron broth, rice beans, and braised artichokes. Cardamom panna cotta with rhubarb granita and olive oil relays the menu's spirit to the finish line.

Edi & The Wolf

Austrian

C4

102 Avenue C (bet. 6th & 7th Sts.)

Subway: 1 Av
Phone: 212-598-1040
Web: www.ediandthewolf.com
Price: $$

Lunch Sat – Sun
Dinner nightly

This is as much an Austrian *heuriger* (wine tavern) that one can find in New York. While the menu has some modern and creative elements, the décor is comprised of wood planks and thick coils of rope for an attractively barn-like feel. That cozy and disheveled character makes you forget where you are—same goes for the superb list of German and Austrian wines. On warm days, head to the equally pleasing and tiny back patio.

Most everyone knows to go for the schnitzel, served with potato salad, cucumbers, and lingonberries. Still, you won't go wrong with a host of rustic small plates like crisped Brussels sprouts tossed in pork ragout with scallions and pickled mustard seeds, or perhaps roasted beets with pickled walnuts, walnut milk, and dill.

Feast

 Contemporary

B1

102 Third Ave. (bet. 12th & 13th Sts.)

Subway:	3 Av	Lunch Sat – Sun
Phone:	212-529-8880	Dinner nightly
Web:	www.eatfeastnyc.com	
Price:	$$	

This arrival with the straightforward but promising moniker is a rustic and textbook amalgam of wood, brick, and tiles.

The kitchen consistently offers several prix-fixe menus, served family-style. These might be based on specials from the farmer's market or even inclulde a nose-to-tail meal of lamb, including merguez stew; as well as a lasagna layering shank, broccoli rabe, and goat cheese. If you're not up for a whole feast, dine à la carte on meaty, ocean-fresh oysters capped by cocktail sauce aspic; or a *nouveau* take on incredibly tender chicken and "dumplings" of liver-stuffed pan-fried gnocchi and wisps of crisped skin. End with the awesome Valrhona chocolate pudding—leaving a single dark chocolate cookie crumb behind is impossible.

Flinders Lane

 International

C2

162 Avenue A (bet. 10th & 11th Sts.)

Subway:	1 Av	Lunch & dinner daily
Phone:	212-228-6900	
Web:	www.flinderslane-nyc.com	
Price:	$$	

This is a perfect spot to meet friends for a drink and stay for a meal that is not only tasty but intriguing, as it strives to reflect the myriad cultures and flavors of Australian cuisine. The room feels like a cool cabin, with Edison bulbs, high ceilings, and a wall tagged in graffiti as a nod to the restaurant's namesake street in Melbourne.

Asian influences underscore many dishes here, such as fragrant and pleasantly funky (if not spicy) coconut curry laksa with grilled shrimp, fried bean curd, and clear rice noodles. The roasted Australian lamb is downright outstanding, cooked to perfection and crusted with wattleseed for sweet and nutty crunch, served alongside a cucumber salad and minted yogurt on a bed of harissa.

Gnocco

C3

Italian ✗

337 E. 10th St. (bet. Avenues A & B)

Subway: 1 Av
Phone: 212-677-1913
Web: www.gnocco.com
Price: $$

Lunch & dinner daily

A casual *tavolata* with a lovely back garden, Gnocco is a neighborhood staple with a homey touch. The restaurant charms with creaky wood floors and exposed brick walls accented by abstract paintings. The wood-burning oven at the entrance sets a warm tone, and greets guests with the heady aroma of freshly baked bread.

The signature *gnocco* (sweet, salty pillows of fried bread) can be ordered as an appetizer, side, or even as a dessert with Nutella. Pizzas shine on this carb-centric menu, thanks to that blistered thin crust hanging over the plate's edge. The *Amatriciana* layers tart tomato sauce with sweet red onion, shreds of pancetta, and a heavy-handed sprinkle of red pepper flakes. The *torta al cioccolato* with chocolate mousse makes a fine dessert.

Graffiti

B2

Contemporary

224 E. 10th St. (bet. First & Second Aves.)

Subway: 1 Av
Phone: 212-464-7743
Web: www.graffitinyc.com
Price: $$

Dinner Tue – Sun

An instant hit since its inception in 2007, this cool cub brought to you by Chef/owner Jehangir Mehta is still going strong and baby boy is quite the dreamboat. Dressed with tightly-packed square communal tables and beaded ceiling lights, petite Graffiti may be dimly lit, but an exposed brick wall glossed with a metallic finish and hugging framed mirrors is all brightness.

Feeding a pack of 20 on newspaper-wrapped tables are Indian-inspired sweet and savory small plates. Highlights may include squares of watermelon and feta cubes cooled by a vibrant mint sorbet; and soft, pillowy eggplant buns spiked with toasty cumin. Adventurous palates however are bound to find much to admire in such inventive items as the green mango *paneer* or zucchini-hummus pizza.

Hasaki

Japanese

A2

210 E. 9th St. (bet. Second & Third Aves.)

Subway: Astor Pl
Phone: 212-473-3327
Web: www.hasakinyc.com
Price: $$

Lunch Wed – Sun
Dinner nightly

Since the mid-eighties, this local darling has been doing a solid business thanks to its high quality ingredients, skilled kitchen, and excellent value. For under $20, the soba lunch set will warm the heart of any frugal fan of Japanese cuisine. This generous feast features a bowl of green tea noodles in hot, crystal-clear dashi stocked with wilted water spinach and fish cake, accompanied by lean tuna *chirashi*, yellowtail, and *kanpyo*. The *ten-don*, a jumbo shrimp tempura served over rice, is just as enticing. The à la carte offerings draw crowds seeking delish sushi as well as a host of tasty cooked preparations; a Twilight menu is nice for early birds.

The dining room has a clean and spare look, with seating available at a number of wood tables or sizable counter.

Hearth

Italian

B2

403 E. 12th St. (at First Ave.)

Subway: 1 Av
Phone: 646-602-1300
Web: www.restauranthearth.com
Price: $$$

Lunch Sat – Sun
Dinner nightly

Duck your head into beloved Hearth, its loyal patrons buzzing about as happy as ever, and you might not even notice that the kitchen has moved on to some new and exciting things. It's still delicious Italian, yes, but now the ingredients are more carefully sourced, on the healthy side, and with a deep commitment to GMO-free grains, less butter, and no processed oils.

The renewed focus on vegetables, grains and brodi is a winning combination. The kitchen lights up in the vegetable arena, braising Sorana beans to perfection with sage, garlic, and mackerel "bottarga"; or topping carrot and beet tartare with cured egg yolk, chervil and breadcrumbs. Meat lovers, take heart—Hearth's beloved braised rabbit, ribollita and variety burger are still available.

Hot Kitchen

Chinese ✗

104 Second Ave. (bet. 6th & 7th Sts.)

Subwayː Astor Pl
Phone: 212-228-3090
Web: www.hotkitchenny.com
Price: $$

Lunch & dinner daily

True to its name, Hot Kitchen adds a dash of fiery Sichuan cooking to a neighborhood already rife with international delights. Whitewashed brick walls, chili-red beams, an orange accent wall, and ebony furnishings detail the tidy space.

Steer clear of the Chinese-American portion of the menu; instead, partake in the memorable house specialties featuring dried chilies, Sichuan peppercorns, and pickled peppers that singe with abandon. However, a handful of straightforward items do bring relief from the spicy onslaught, as in minced pork with pickled cabbage in a light, sour broth; chunks of dark and salty-sweet braised beef and potatoes; and myriad hotpots (a recent menu addition).

A second location can be found in Midtown East on 53rd Street.

Huertas

Spanish ✗✗

107 First Ave. (bet. 6th & 7th Sts.)

Subway: Astor Pl
Phone: 212-228-4490
Web: www.huertasnyc.com
Price: $$$

Lunch Sat – Sun
Dinner nightly

Huertas is lovely—even lovelier than you might expect for its gritty location. The casual space is deep, with a long bar pouring cider or sherry, dedicated counter where a host of cured meats including *jamón* is sliced, and larger tables in the back.

The Basque-leaning menu showcases *pintxos* like stuffed and batter-fried squash blossoms, duck *croquetas*, and skewers of white anchovies with olives and pickled peppers. The selection of *conservas* promises the type of fare that only the Spanish can do, as in *zamburiñas* in a complex tomato sauce with lemon, herbs, and bread topped with a heavy drizzle of mayo. A handful of larger *platos* round out the menu with dishes like deep-fried porgy with toasted garlic, pickled chilies, and manzanilla olives.

Hunan Bistro

Chinese ✗

B1

96 Third Ave. (bet. 12th & 13th Sts.)

Lunch & dinner daily

Subway: 3 Av
Phone: 212-388-9855
Web: N/A
Price: $$

Delicious, lip-scorching Hunan fare makes its way to the East Village and everyone's just a little bit happier for it. Tucked into a narrow space with dark wood paneling, industrial lighting and large planters, Hunan Bistro offers swift, but warm and helpful, service—and an all-together welcoming dining space for exploring this intriguing cuisine.

Dinner might kick off with razor-thin slices of pig ear, tossed with a confetti of green onions and glistening with smoky chili oil; or crunchy, sour pickled cabbage topped with red chilies and cilantro. Next up? Toothsome *dan dan* noodles beneath a thatch of ground pork with loads of chili oil, black vinegar and Sichuan pepper; or perfectly cooked, shell-on crawfish laced in a wildly good chili sauce.

Kafana

Eastern European ✗

C3

116 Avenue C (bet. 7th & 8th Sts.)

Lunch Sat – Sun
Dinner nightly

Subway: 1 Av
Phone: 212-353-8000
Web: www.kafananyc.com
Price: $$

If the Eastern European intelligentsia needed somewhere to plan a revolution or maybe just talk politics, they would meet here. Walls papered with Cyrillic newspapers set a deliciously covert scene, yet overall, the effect is inviting.

The menu highlights Serbian fare that is hard to find in Manhattan. That said, some specialties will seem familiar, like *zeljanica*, a buttery wedge of classic phyllo pie folded with chopped spinach, garlic, herbs, and feta. Unique dishes feature dried prunes stuffed with crumbly cheese, rolled in chicken liver and bacon. Also try gently dredged and fried spearing fish, piled on butcher paper with urbenes dip. *Ćevapi* are the catchall for sausages from the same area and here they highlight finely ground pork with herbs.

Jewel Bako ✿

Japanese 🍴

239 E. 5th St. (bet. Second & Third Aves.)

Subway: Astor Pl
Phone: 212-979-1012
Web: www.jewelbakosushi.com
Price: $$$

Dinner Mon – Sat

Only a discretely marked door and tiny glass windows mark the entrance to this beloved sushi *bijou*. Once inside, you'll find a deeply elegant scene highlighting sloped bamboo slats that frame a row of beautifully plated, close-knit tables. There's a gorgeous blonde wood sushi bar in the back, while gentle jazz music plays in the background. The overall effect is very appealing and particularly serene.

Service is excellent and begins at the door, with the reserved host carefully attending to your belongings. The waiters have an eagle eye for detail, managing to be so polite and unobtrusive that you're able to enjoy intimate conversation.

You can choose a fixed price omakase and leave it all up to the talented Chef Shimao Ishikawa. Either way, you're in for a culinary treat. The quality and seriousness of the kitchen remains excellent with each passing year, turning out exquisite dishes like seasonal lobster sashimi (so fresh it may still be squirming on the plate) laced with ponzu— its head and innards later presented in a savory miso soup. The sashimi that follows is equally astounding, from the impeccable slicing technique to the fish quality, much of it seasonal and flown in directly from Japan.

Kanoyama ❀

Japanese ✗

B2

175 Second Ave. (at 11th St.)

Subway:	3 Av	Dinner nightly
Phone:	212-777-5266	
Web:	www.kanoyama.com	
Price:	**$$$**	

The spotlight shines here on the seriously talented Chef Noboyuki Shikanai and commands the rear room's attention as he performs his magic before the few coveted seats along his omakase counter. Beyond this, the space has a row of tables where you might observe a group indulging in a tuna rib that appears large enough to have come from a cow: first sliced raw, then cooked to enjoy this incredibly fresh fish both ways.

Ancillary rooms almost feel like a sushi-ya within a sushi-ya. The service team is swift and friendly even as they work in the shadow of their master.

Kanoyama's omakase is a profoundly personal experience, as Chef Shikanai slices, cuts, and brushes, dabs, and perfects each morsel before presenting it to you with cupped hands, to be taken with your fingers. Pieces are precisely crafted yet delicate and beautiful in that traditional Edo-mae style. Overall, the meal is a progression from light, firm fish to vivid, buttery salmon and toro with exciting stops along the way, like cherry trout *hakozushi* (box-pressed) or jackfish with grains of Icelandic sea salt and a drizzle of lemon. Finish with an extraordinary block of cake-like *tamago* topped with a silken yolk.

Kingsley

Contemporary

C2

190 Avenue B (bet. 11th & 12th Sts.)

Subway: 1 Av
Phone: 212-674-4500
Web: www.kingsleynyc.com
Price: $$$

Lunch Sat – Sun
Dinner Tue – Sun

The crowds are clamoring for a table at this East Village charmer, and for good reason: Kingsley's splurge-worthy cuisine is sophisticated, surprising, and delicious. And the cozy space makes for a rare oasis amid the neighborhood's raucous dining scene.

Featuring an interesting juxtaposition of flavors and textures while being reminiscent of classic fare, dinner here might begin with a summer bean salad starring cranberries, rattlesnake and ridiculously fresh Romano beans paired with bacon marmalade, crème fraîche and sautéed spicy greens. Soft, chewy wild rice noodles is topped with stir-fried mushrooms and Asian greens, just as a heavenly Wagyu Basses-Côtes steak arrives with velvety Fairy Tale eggplant, grilled potato, and a streak of *chimichurri*.

Kura

Japanese

B3

130 St. Mark's Pl. (bet. Avenue A & First Ave.)

Subway: Astor Pl
Phone: 212-228-1010
Web: N/A
Price: $$$$

Dinner Mon – Sat

From first glance, Kura is everything that a personal, well-run, and very authentic Japanese restaurant should be. Inside, the master dons a traditional *samue* and greets each guest who approaches the L-shaped counter, as he begins to prepare the next course. Also find a few tables in the front of the room where groups manage to squeeze in.

The menu offers four different levels of omakase, beginning with the likes of braised fava beans; a whole stuffed squid brushed with a sweet-salty reduction; as well as rice topped with nori and *ikura*. Settle into the ten-piece nigiri, presented as an array of hyper-seasonal fish dabbed with soy, gently torched, or wrapped in cured cherry leaf. Finish with a familiar and delicious cube of chilled *tamago* and miso soup.

Ko ✿ ✿

8 Extra Pl. (at 1st St.)

Subway: 2 Av
Phone: 212-500-0831
Web: www.momofuku.com
Price: $$$$

Lunch Thu – Sat
Dinner Tue – Sat

Let the awards, accolades and press keep coming—for there is still nothing quite like David Chang's beloved Ko. Head down a quiet alley in the otherwise hopping East Village, and you'll come upon a door sporting only Chang's proverbial peach. Behind it lies a gorgeous, street-hip space with 40 seats, 22 of them forming a U-shaped counter around the bustling and open kitchen.

There is no à la carte at Ko, only the multi-course menu for the evening, which you're given in print. Dishes are delivered by the chefs, who briefly describe each ingredient while servers slip seamlessly between guests filling drinks. It's a unique style that brings you right into the action.

Dave Chang is a veritable rock star chef by any standard (and longtime lieutenant Sean Gray is something like his Keith Richards)—so you're in expert hands from the start. The strength of his food lies as much in its texture as in its taste: fresh black bass is paired with jalapeño, shiso and consommé jelly; while charcoaled potato in lobster emulsion is topped with herbs for a simple, but otherworldly, dish. A buttery slice of duck farce pie, studded with black truffle and paired with sunchokes and turnip, is a culinary revelation.

Kyo Ya ✿

Japanese ✕✕

94 E. 7th St. (bet. First Ave. & Avenue A)

Subway: Astor Pl	Dinner Tue – Sat
Phone: 212-982-4140	
Web: N/A	
Price: **$$$**	

Tucked away down a discreet flight of steps in an unremarkable East Village building, it's easy to cruise right past Kyo Ya. But what a shame it would be to miss this brilliant kaiseki jewel. If the mostly Japanese crowd doesn't tell you you're onto something special, the relentless charm and hospitality of the staff will win you over completely.

This is a cozy and intimate room with lots of polished wood and displays of lovely Japanese ceramics. A row of counter seats cuts down the middle of the space, along with a smattering of small tables and a six-seat counter at the back is reserved for those having the kaiseki menu.

Kyo Ya's dishes are delicate, exquisite, and perfectly balanced. And as if that weren't enough, most of them use authentic, imported ingredients, which are not commonly found in domestic kitchens. A ten-course kaiseki, for example, might unveil a soft ball of fresh edamame tofu in a delicate, clear fish broth flavored with junsai as well as sweet and earthy spaghetti squash. Then chewy *kuruma-fu* is served in a winter melon soup bobbing with spicy pink peppercorns, mizuna and *kinira ohitashi*. A finish of crispy shishito pepper tempura and cherry tomato make it downright excellent.

L'Apicio

 Italian XX

A3

13 E. 1st St. (bet. Bowery & Second Ave.)

Subway: 2 Av
Phone: 212-533-7400
Web: www.lapicio.com
Price: $$

Dinner nightly

Despite being named for an 18th century Italian cookbook, this buzzy trattoria is a contemporary hit.

A downtown vibe courses throughout the swanky den that is slightly rustic and industrial—this setting is worth dressing up for. Half of the room is devoted to the bar, and the private dining room is best suited to exhibitionists who enjoy dining within glass walls in the center of the room.

Bright flavors and skilled creativity combine in their tailored selection of Italian plates designed for grazing. Start with dishes like fried green tomatoes capped with sweet basil pesto and milky mozzarella, or fresh agnolotti stuffed with sweetbreads. Finish with a wedge of moist olive oil cake sweetened with crème fraîche and *Vin Santo*-soaked raisins.

Lavagna

Italian X

C3

545 E. 5th St. (bet. Avenues A & B)

Subway: 2 Av
Phone: 212-979-1005
Web: www.lavagnanyc.com
Price: $$

Lunch Sat – Sun
Dinner nightly

The little menu at this neighborhood fixture proves that quality trumps size. Lavagna's kitchen is snug but still manages to make ample use of a wood-burning oven to bake everything from delicate *pizzette* to whole roasted fish. Pastas are always a treat, while other tasty options can include pan-fried smoked *scamorza* paired with a roasted red pepper topped crostini, juicy rack of lamb, or a slice of spot-on *crostata* filled with seasonal fruit and dressed with caramel sauce.

Framed mirrors, a pressed-tin ceiling, and candlelight produce a mood that is almost as warm as the genuinely gracious service, which ensures that regulars receive the royal treatment. That said, everyone who steps through these doors feels welcome and well taken care of.

Lil' Frankie's

Italian

B4

19 First Ave. (bet. 1st & 2nd Sts.)

Subway: 2 Av
Phone: 212-420-4900
Web: www.lilfrankies.com
Price: ⊝⊝

Lunch Sat – Sun
Dinner nightly

Frank Prisinzano's pizzeria combines a series of intimate rooms for a laid-back vibe that's perfectly in step with the neighborhood. An open kitchen is in one room, a pizza oven in another, and a third boasts a wall of window panels that open for alfresco dining. Framed photos and colorful vinyl tablecloths add character.

The Neapolitan-style pizza is always a hit, perhaps topped with bright tomato sauce, fresh mozzarella, and slices of spicy salami. Also savor the likes of fava bean purée with dandelion greens for a thick and homey soup. Garlic bread, baked pasta of the day, and whole eggplant with *peperoncino* oil are all flame-kissed creations from the wood-burning oven. Stop by during weekend brunch for "killer pancakes" made with buckwheat flour.

Luzzo's

Pizza

B2

211-13 First Ave. (bet. 12th & 13th Sts.)

Subway: 1 Av
Phone: 212-473-7447
Web: www.luzzospizza.com
Price: $$

Lunch & dinner daily

A treasured century-old coal oven is the heart of this quirky Neapolitan-style pizza parlor, lined with exposed brick, mismatched chairs, and kitschy knickknacks. Italian music plays softly beneath the buzz of this ever-busy restaurant, as loyal crowds wait patiently outside for the piping hot pies topped with melting mozzarella.

A deep understanding of the art of bread baking is evident in every pie pulled from the coal-burning oven. The *diavola* features a tender, black-blistered crust topped with thin slices of spicy-salty salami, light and chunky tomato sauce beneath dollops of mozzarella. Round, square, and even puffy fried pies are all crafted with care at this convivial spot. For dessert, the *zeppole di Nutella* are an unabashed crowd-pleaser.

Malai Marke

 Indian XX

318 E. 6th St. (bet. First & Second Aves.)

Subway: Astor Pl
Phone: 212-777-7729
Web: www.malaimarke.com
Price: $$

Lunch & dinner daily

The name of this Curry Row resto translates to "extra cream" in Hindi tea stall slang, and rich and flavorful is indeed the order of the day. The clean, narrow space is bright and contemporary, with black tile wainscotting and copper pots hanging from exposed brick.

From the kitchen, *tangra*-style Calcutta-Chinese specialties are a new offering, however it is best to focus your attention on the preparations originating from the Southwest coast. Seafood and coconut factor heavily in Lata Shetty's shrimp *ajadina*, a dry-gravy stir-fry rich with red chillies and myriad spices. Chicken *chutney wala* is simmered in a bright yellow cream sauce seasoned with tart-sweet green mango chutney; and pumpkin *sabji* is another fantastic offering that also happens to be vegetarian. Win win!

MáLà Project

Chinese X

122 First Ave. (bet. 6th & 7th Sts.)

Subway: 1 Av
Phone: 212-353-8880
Web: www.malaproject.nyc
Price: $$

Lunch & dinner daily

Add this delicious newcomer to the growing list of Chinese restaurants that are finally giving Manhattanites a chance to feast on spice levels once reserved for the outer boroughs. Inside MáLà Project's two rooms, find seating that includes a long group-friendly communal table tucked into a nook, exposed brick walls, beautiful floors, and big green leafy plants.

Dinner could go in any number of delicious directions, but a MáLà dry pot might be the most fun. Diners are given a choice of ingredients—meat, poultry, seafood, vegetables, rice—and then asked their desired degree of spiciness. A pot of lamb, bok choi, wood ear mushrooms, shrimp balls, and chicken gizzards make their way into a wok with a fragrant "secret sauce" and a complex spice oil.

The Mermaid Inn

Seafood ✗

96 Second Ave. (bet. 5th & 6th Sts.)

Subway: Astor Pl
Phone: 212-674-5870
Web: www.themermaidnyc.com
Price: $$

Dinner nightly

This laid-back and inviting seafood spot has been a neighborhood favorite for over a decade now, spawning locations in Greenwich Village and the Upper West Side. A steady stream of guests lines the bar early in the week for Monday's five to seven happy hour with freshly shucked oysters, snack-sized fish tacos, and other specially priced bites. For a hearty plate after your nosh, try blackened catfish dotted with crawfish butter alongside hushpuppies, or the lobster roll with Old Bay fries. On Sunday nights, look out for lobsterpalooza—a whole lobster accompanied by grilled corn on the cob and steamed potatoes.

At the end of your meal there's no need to deliberate over dessert. A demitasse of perfect chocolate pudding is presented compliments of the house.

Mighty Quinn's

Barbecue ✗

103 Second Ave. (at 6th St.

Subway: Astor Pl
Phone: 212-677-3733
Web: www.mightyquinnsbbq.com
Price:

Lunch & dinner daily

From its humble beginnings as a Smorgasburg favorite, Mighty Quinn's continues to impress with its "low and slow smoked barbecue." And, boasting seven permanent outposts spanning from the Upper East side, to Williamsburg. This rustic and casual wood-lined space feels young and energetic with crowds of hungry diners lined up to the door.

Cafeteria-like service features cleaver-wielding cooks proffering pulled pork, ribs, and more. Selections are sliced, weighed, and piled high before you even make it to the sides and vats of house pickles. Go for the baked beans, made with black-eyed peas and meaty burnt ends for plenty of umami. The best reason to come here may be the wonderfully wobbly-tender brisket, pink-tinged with smoke and thinly crusted in spice.

Momofuku Noodle Bar

Asian ✗

B2

171 First Ave. (bet. 10th & 11th Sts.)

Subway: 1 Av
Phone: 212-777-7773
Web: www.momofuku.com
Price: $$

Lunch & dinner daily

This elder member of David Chang's culinary empire is hipper and hotter than ever. A honey-toned temple of updated comfort food, decked with blonde wood counters and a sparkling open kitchen, the service here may be brisk. But rest assured, as the menu is gutsy and molded with Asian street food in mind.

Those steamed buns have amassed a gargantuan following thanks to decadent fillings like moist pork loin kissed with Hollandaise and chives. Additionally, that bowl of springy noodles doused in a spicy ginger-scallion sauce is just one instance of the crew's signature work. Korean fried chicken with seasonal greens is fit for a king; while more modest items, including desserts like candy apple truffle, are beautifully crafted and rightfully elevated to global fame.

Momofuku Ssäm Bar

Contemporary ✗

B2

207 Second Ave. (at 13th St.)

Subway: 3 Av
Phone: 212-254-3500
Web: www.momofuku.com
Price: $$

Lunch & dinner daily

A sure sign of impending middle age, this East Village elder (favorite) has undergone some bodywork, and in typical Manhattan style maintains its perpetual youth. Gone are those uncomfortable backless chairs—an obvious sign of the maturing hip crowd's desire for comfort. The vibe remains convivial, but the indisputable star of the show is Dave Chang's cooking style, which features Korean and Japanese ingredients flirting with European and Californian influences. There's smartly sourced charcuterie and an enticing raw bar to kick things off, but one mustn't leave without trying the pork buns—pillow-soft and laced with hoisin, they are an absolute indulgence. And that flat iron steak? It's grilled to perfection, paired with *chicharrón* chips and asparagus tips for a heavy-on-flavor crowd-pleaser.

Motorino

349 E. 12th St. (bet. First & Second Aves.)

Subway: 1 Av

Phone: 212-777-2644

Web: www.motorinopizza.com

Price: 🍜

Lunch & dinner daily

What started out as a Neapolitan-style pizzeria in Brooklyn has grown into a global chain with locations in Hong Kong and Manila. Cloaked in the scent of wood-fired pies, Motorino is praised as an all-day spot that's easy on the wallet. True, it may be smaller than the newer, slightly grander Williamsburg outpost, but these pizzas leave nothing to be desired.

Blackboard specials convey the product-focused sensibilities that begin with a lunchtime prix-fixe pairing a green salad of mint, beet greens, and red onion in balsamic vinaigrette with a perfectly charred and chewy pie. The foundation of each pizza is its outstanding crust spread with crushed tomatoes, gobs of melting fresh mozzarella, and perhaps a generous layering of spicy sausage slices.

Narcissa

25 Cooper Sq. (at 5th St.)

Subway: Astor Pl

Phone: 212-228-3344

Web: www.narcissarestaurant.com

Price: $$

Lunch & dinner daily

André Balazs' Standard East Village hotel is where you will find one of downtown's snazziest dining rooms. Richly stained wood furnishings in contrasting hues pair beautifully with tanned leather banquettes, sienna table linens, and perfectly calibrated lighting. The overall effect is warmer than a Malibu sunset.

Chef John Fraser (of Dovetail) has assembled a formidable team to realize his vision of polished farm-to-table dining, starring seasonal produce from The Farm at Locusts on Hudson. Beets take a turn in the rotisserie oven and arrive for your pleasure as a warm salad with hearty bulgur, pickled cucumber, and a pool of horseradish cream. Poussin is roasted whole and set atop steel cut oats slicked with jus, spicy sausage, and oven-wilted radicchio.

Noreetuh

 Fusion

B3

128 First Ave. (bet. 7th St. & St. Marks Pl.)

Subway: Astor Pl
Phone: 646-892-3050
Web: www.noreetuh.com
Price: $$

Dinner Tue – Sun

For a taste of something different, make a beeline to this unique Hawaiian-flavored spot. Headed by a trio of Per Se veterans, Noreetuh features an intimate setting of two slender dining rooms adorned with hexagonal mirrors and shelving units used to store bottles from the impressive wine list.

Bigeye tuna poke strewn with seaweed, diced macadamia nuts, and pickled jalapeños is just one of the delicious highlights on offer, while plump shrimp seasoned with crushed garlic and arranged over a bed of sticky rice and baby romaine is another fine choice. For dessert, the signature take on bread pudding boasts caramelized slices of custard-soaked King's Hawaiian bread with rum raisins and a knockout scoop of pineapple ice cream.

Oda House

 Central Asian

C3

76 Avenue B (at 5th St.)

Subway: 2 Av
Phone: 212-353-3838
Web: www.odahouse.com
Price: $$

Lunch Fri – Sun
Dinner nightly

For a taste of something different, the inviting Oda House serves up intriguing specialties from Georgia. The vibe is simple and rustic with pumpkin-stained walls, exposed brick, and wood furnishings. Of course, this nation's proximity to Azerbaijan, Turkey, and Armenia results in a vibrant and diverse cuisine.

A liberal use of spices, kebabs, *khinkali* (oversized meat-and-cheese dumplings), and *khachapuri*, typify the kitchen's preparations. But, more classic dishes may reveal *satsivi* or boiled chicken served cool in a warmly spiced and seasoned walnut sauce, accompanied by *gomi* (hominy grits in a mini cauldron studded with rich and stretchy cheese).

Balance out this hearty feast with a bright garden salad perfectly dressed with green *ajika* sauce.

Oiji

Korean

119 First Ave. (bet. E. 7th St & St. Marks Pl.)

Subway: Astor Pl
Phone: 646-767-9050
Web: www.oijinyc.com
Price: $$

Dinner Tue – Sun

Oiji's modern take on Korean dining is a reminder that this food is so much more than barbecue. Devoid of smoky tabletops, the dining room is small and attractive, with an open kitchen to sneak peeks at the very talented chefs as they prepare a cuisine rooted in culinary tradition, but with creative and refined touches.

Signature dishes do not disappoint, so try the wonderfully original pine-smoked mackerel, balancing the rich fish with citrus-soy sauce. Cold buckwheat noodles are a cool and contemporary nest of dark and chewy noodles topped with half of a slow-cooked egg, sesame seeds, and loads of scallions. And finally, *gochujang* chicken showcases nicely braised drumsticks with a variety of wintery vegetables in a spicy, tart and garlicky sauce.

Porsena

Italian XX

21 E. 7th St. (bet. Second & Third Aves.)

Subway: Astor Pl
Phone: 212-228-4923
Web: www.porsena.com
Price: $$

Dinner nightly

Sophisticates of all ages flock to this neighborhood favorite to be enveloped by a warm, welcoming, and upbeat vibe. Euro-chic Porsena also boasts adept servers who can be seen strutting about with appetizing platters of aromatic food.

As always, Chef Sara Jenkins proves herself to be a talent and a pro through presentations that are unfussy yet remain uniquely flavorful and always special. The menu rotates with the seasons, but standbys cannot be missed, like wild escarole salad with crisp leaves wilting in hot anchovy dressing; or huge rounds of *anelloni* tossed with spicy lamb sausage, peppery mustard greens, and breadcrumbs. If offered, get the lasagna expertly layering pasta sheets with a creamy béchamel and hearty veal-prosciutto ragù.

Prune ⊙

Contemporary ✗

A3

54 E. 1st St. (bet. First & Second Aves.)

Subway: 2 Av
Phone: 212-677-6221
Web: www.prunerestaurant.com
Price: $$

Lunch Sat – Sun
Dinner nightly

This beloved neighborhood bistro won locals' hearts many moons ago, but Chef/owner/writer Gabrielle Hamilton's evolving talents keep them loyal. The tiny space packs a big punch—both for its sweet décor, which is surprisingly comfy to linger in, and for the kitchen's adventurous food. From greeting to check, Prune delivers the whole package—and consistently at that. Chef Hamilton's dishes are soulful and unpretentious. Savor tender stewed tripe Lyonnaise in a luxurious broth with carrots, celery and bay leaf; or perfectly poached chicken in a fatty, delicious, restorative stock with ham and oxtail. Guests can also watch the excitement unfold in the mini, open kitchen while nursing a drink.

Nightly specials, listed on the chalkboard, are always worth perusing.

Pylos

Greek ✗✗

B3

128 E. 7th St. (bet. First Ave. & Avenue A)

Subway: Astor Pl
Phone: 212-473-0220
Web: www.pylosrestaurant.com
Price: $$

Lunch Wed – Sun
Dinner nightly

Restaurateur Christos Valtzoglou has found the winning formula with this longstanding hideaway in the vibrant East Village. Pylos continues to sparkle as brightly as the Aegean Sea on a summer day. And, taking its name from the Greek translation of "made from clay," this contemporary taverna also features a ceiling canopy of suspended terra-cotta pots, dressing up a room with rustic whitewashed walls and lapis-blue insets.

Pale-green stemware and stark white crockery are used to serve Greek wines and a menu of rustic home-style cooking. *Gigantes* are baked in honey-scented tomato-dill sauce; grilled marinated octopus is drizzled with balsamic reduction; and *aginares* moussaka is a creamy vegetarian take on the classic made with artichokes.

Rai Rai Ken

Japanese

B2

218 E. 10th St. (bet. First & Second Aves.)

Subway: Astor Pl
Phone: 212-477-7030
Web: N/A
Price:

Lunch & dinner daily

By virute of its expansive space and comfortable ambience, Rai Rai Ken is a popular neighborhood haunt. Make your way inside to arrive in a room that boasts a pristine, neat and tidy look with blonde wood seating and signature red vinyl stools. An array of pots remain bubbling and steaming behind the counter.

Rest assured the menu's star attraction—those thin and toothsome ramen noodles—are just as delicious, served with four near-addictive, fantastically complex broth variations: *shio*, *shoyu*, miso, and curry. Each bowlful is chock-full of garnishes, like slices of roasted pork, boiled egg, nori, fishcake, and a nest of springy noodles. Grab a business card before leaving as loyal diners are rewarded with a complimentary bowl after ten visits.

Ramen Misoya

Japanese

B2

129 Second Ave. (bet. St. Marks Pl. & Seventh St.)

Subway: Astor Pl
Phone: 212-677-4825
Web: www.misoyanyc.com
Price:

Lunch & dinner daily

With 30 locations worldwide, Ramen Misoya brings its trademark ambrosial bowlfuls to New York City. The earthy dining area dons a bamboo-lined ceiling as well as a TV monitor that is internally looped to broadcast the kitchen's every move.

The ramen offering here differentiates itself by centering on a trio of miso-enriched broths: *shiro* is a white miso fermented with rice *koji* (starter); *kome-miso* is richer tasting; and *mame-miso* is a strictly soybean product. The mouth-coating soup is delicious alchemy. Each slurp is a multifaceted distillation of pork and chicken bones with savory-salty-sweet notes, stocked with excellent noodles, vegetables, and the likes of panko-crusted shrimp tempura, fried ginger chicken, or slices of house-made *cha-su*.

Risotteria Melotti

Italian ✗✗

B3

309 E. 5th St. (bet. First & Second Aves.)

Subway: Astor Pl
Phone: 646-755-8939
Web: www.risotteriamelottinyc.com
Price: $$

Lunch & dinner dail

By specializing in risotto, this unique family-owned spot rises above the city's endless proliferation of Italian dining options. The Melotti family produces rice in Veneto and this stateside location is sister to Isola della Scala in Verona.

Scenes from the film *Riso Amaro* on a mounted television add atmosphere to the rustic surrounds, where the air is filled with the sounds of stirring as each order is prepared. A bread basket stuffed with rice cakes precedes plates of risotto *al limone e gamberi* made with lemon juice and studded with morsels of pan-seared shrimp. More complex *risotti* may be presented in a crispy Monte Veronese cheese cup and showcase Amarone wine. Here, each creamy and toothsome grain displays impressive technique.

Robataya

Japanese ✗✗

B2

231 E. 9th St. (bet. Second & Third Aves.)

Subway: Astor Pl
Phone: 212-979-9674
Web: www.robataya-ny.com
Price: $$

Lunch & dinner daily

Irasshaimase! This is the kind of intensely authentic place where welcomes are shouted to guests upon entering. At peak times, wait among Japanese expats and young couples lining the sidewalk. Aim straight for the counter to appreciate the theatrics of it all, where orders are acknowledged with more shouts flying from Japanese servers to chefs. The energy is high, but so are the standards for their expertly grilled meats and vegetables.

Kneeling cooks use long wooden paddles to deliver dishes hot off the robata, like *gyu tataki*, seared beef filet topped with tobiko and scallions on a bed of red onions with ponzu. Technical mastery is clear in a salt-packed sea bream's subtle smoky flavors emphasizing the delicacy of such white, flaky fish.

Root & Bone

B4

200 E. 3rd St. (bet. Avenues A & B)

Subway: 2 Av
Phone: 646-682-7080
Web: www.rootnbone.com
Price: $$

Lunch & dinner daily

Down-home cooking, fried chicken, and a cocktail are just the thing at this cramped but cozy café. The packed room is difficult to take in during the dinner rush, but pretty touches include whitewashed brick walls, a pressed-tin ceiling, and glass-paned cabinets stocked with crockery.

You might even adopt a drawl while reading through Root & Bone's pleasing menu. Grandma Daisy's warm angel biscuits are incredibly light and fluffy—especially alongside that salty-sweet, dark chicken-maple jus for dipping. The signature sweet tea-brined fried chicken is prepared in a designated corner of the room, filling the space with tempting aromas. Shrimp and grits with Virginia country ham has a Yankee touch thanks to the addition of Brooklyn lager to the sauce.

Sigiri

B3

91 First Ave. (bet. 5th & 6th Sts.)

Subway: 1 Av
Phone: 212-614-9333
Web: www.sigirinyc.com
Price: ☙

Lunch & dinner daily

Located above street level in a neighborhood better known for Indian cuisine, this is a welcoming Sri Lankan retreat. The décor is basic and tidy, with bright walls, colorful tablecloths, and a large window for people-watching along First Avenue. Service is well-paced, but each dish is made to order and may take some time to arrive.

No matter what, do not miss the sharp and savory dry-fish curry. Balanced with peppery notes, fluid veins of sour tamarind, and countless other wonderful spices, this dish is an absolute must. Other highlights include the chicken biryani made with meaty cashews, sweet raisins, and abundant saffron to permeate each grain of rice. Finish with a coconut rice pudding redolent of cloves, cinnamon, and nutmeg.

Sobakoh

B3

309 E. 5th St. (bet. First & Second Aves.)

Subway: 2 Av
Phone: 212-254-2244
Web: www.sobakoh-nyc.com
Price: ⊖⊖

Lunch & dinner daily

SobaKoh presents a purist approach to soba—and our bellies are all the happier for it. The restaurant takes its name from the Japanese term for buckwheat flour, and here the product is organic, grown upstate and in Canada. The result is delightfully soft, light and chewy noodles that mercifully make its way into 20 or more dishes on Chef/owner Hiromitsu Takahashi's outstanding menu. Those hankering for sashimi can sate their craving with dishes like the cold octopus; or cool and creamy uni.

Featuring a small, spare and immaculate arena, with exposed brick and bare tables, the space is very cozy and homey. A square-windowed spot, which can be seen from the street and the dining room, offers a chance to see Takahashi in action.

Soba-Ya 🐸

B2

229 E. 9th St. (bet. Second & Third Aves.)

Subway: Astor Pl
Phone: 212-533-6966
Web: www.sobaya-nyc.com
Price: ⊖⊖

Lunch & dinner daily

There's a ton of Japanese restaurants that line this stretch of the East Village, so why Soba-Ya? Why *not* Soba-Ya, its ultra-dedicated patrons would argue—for the buckwheat soba as well as the hearty udon on tap here are consistently off-the-charts good. Co-owner and mini-mogul, Bon Yagi, favors authenticity over flash in his establishments. And here he employs that traditional aesthetic to sweet perfection; along with a graceful, but simply appointed dining space; and quiet, well-timed service.

A meal might begin with sea urchin and grated mountain yam, kissed with wasabi and crispy, toasted nori; then transition to a seasonal noodle dish like warm soba mingled with plump, pickled oysters, mountain yam, cilantro and tempura root vegetables.

Somtum Der

B3

85 Avenue A (bet. 5th & 6th Sts.)

Subway: 2 Av
Phone: 212-260-8570
Web: www.somtumder.com
Price: $$

Lunch & dinner daily

Tucked along the fringes of Alphabet City, a little taste of authentic Isaan Thai awaits. Originally based out of Bangkok, the New York outpost of Somtum Der offers a cozy little enclave for the East Village set, stylishly accented with bright pops of red, and a welcome glimpse of the kitchen's *somtum* station. There, you'll spy large glass jars of peanuts, dried red chilies, and spices—the contents of which are ground by mortar and pestle to produce what some claim is the city's best green papaya salad.

Order big here, for the portions aren't massive and the food is so terrific you'll inevitably want more. The kitchen is happy to kick things up a notch, spice-wise, but you'll need to request the hotter end of the spectrum for greater authenticity.

Supper

B4

156 E. 2nd St. (bet. Avenues A & B)

Subway: 1 Av
Phone: 212-477-7600
Web: www.supperrestaurant.com
Price: $$

Lunch Sat – Sun
Dinner nightly

This is the kind of fuss-free Italian cooking that true New Yorkers keep in regular rotation. The dark, quirky interior spreads across multiple rooms for a relaxed setting.

There is no better salvo to this style of dining than their complementary beans soaked in olive oil with chilies, garlic, and parsley. Follow with thick, shareable portions of bruschetta, slathered with chicken liver and bits of sea salt. Their "extraordinary platter of vegetables" is just that, and serves as a reminder that few cuisines can work such wonders with roasted fennel, sautéed escarole, grilled asparagus, and more. Veal Milanese is just as delicious as those fancy midtown joints, but half the price.

The adjacent wine bar is a worthy stop to sip from an incredible list.

Sushi Dojo

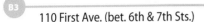

Japanese ✗

B3

110 First Ave. (bet. 6th & 7th Sts.)

Subway: Astor Pl
Phone: 646-692-9398
Web: www.sushidojonyc.com
Price: $$$

Dinner Tue – Sat

Even after the departure of its talented and rebellious chef, Sushi Dojo's 14-seat counter and smattering of tables stay decidedly packed with sushi hunters-in-the-know. In fact, this den still feels a bit cult-like, with diners waiting patiently outside for a chance just to sample the goods.

The chef's choice menu is highly recommended, offering great value for this level of skill and quality. With much of it ariving straight from Japan, the fish is pristine and ultra-seasonal. Counter customers are locked into the omakase (and won't regret it), but diners can also opt for à la carte. Either way, expect the likes of red snapper, fried shrimp head, yellowtail from Australia, blue fin from Greece, buttery Hokkaido scallop, and even a dollop of creamy uni.

Timna

Middle Eastern ✗

B3

109 St. Marks Pl. (bet. First Ave. & Avenue A)

Subway: Astor Pl
Phone: 646-964-5181
Web: www.timna.nyc
Price: $$

Lunch Sat – Sun
Dinner Tue – Sun

Diners may end up arguing about which of Timna's divine, complex Middle Eastern dishes is the most memorable, but almost everything whipped up by Chef Nir Mesika (formerly of Zizi Limona in Williamsburg) will have you buzzing. Tucked below street level, the deep, narrow space features plenty of exposed brick and a welcoming bar up front.

Start with the addictive *kubaneh*, a Yemenite brioche-and-challah hybrid served with crushed tomato sauce, butter-thick yogurt, and jalapeño salsa. For a refreshing treat, tuck into the Chinatown salad—glass noodles tossed with a pesto of fragrant herbs, palm sugar, and fish sauce, then topped with tempura green beans. Finish the evening with a yuzu tart featuring piña colada-panna cotta and sweet strawberry coulis.

Tuome

B3

Fusion

536 E. 5th St. (bet. Avenues A & B)

Subway: 2 Av
Phone: 646-833-7811
Web: www.tuomenyc.com
Price: $$

Dinner Mon – Sat

Chef Thomas Chen's intimate venue flaunts petite East Village bones, a warm glow cast over the hip crowd, and a too-loud playlist that may cause indigestion for anyone older than a Millenial.

Asian accents filtered through the mind of this chef reveal a playful lineup including Treviso chicory spears, which are brushed with creamy Caesar dressing and plated with warm, buttery croutons, clementine segments, and toasted sunflower seeds. Black bass is expertly seared and sauced with New England-style clam chowder pocked with Chinese sausage and perfectly complemented by a side of banana leaf-wrapped sticky rice enriched with duck fat. If you still have room for dessert, order the hot, crisp, and mildly sweet Chinese beignets that can satisfy any sweet tooth.

Virginia's

C3

Contemporary ✗✗

647 E. 11 St. (bet. Avenues B & C)

Subway: 1 Av
Phone: 212-658-0182
Web: www.virginiasnyc.com
Price: $$

Dinner Tue – Sat

Perfectly East Village in scale, this intimate yet ambitious bistro is composed of two slender rooms unified by butterscotch-colored banquettes and whitewashed brick walls hung with framed vintage menus. Fine stemware and items presented on wooden boards lend an upscale manner to the experience.

Chef Christian Ramos takes risks while building upon a steady foundation from time spent as a sous chef at Per Se. A crostino of fava bean tapenade and shredded squash is a bright summertime treat—best paired with an icy glass of rosé. Pan-seared striped bass with wedges of new potato, is sauced with saffron-infused cockle broth; and the black-and-white sablé arranged with a taste of cocoa nib mousse and candied pistachios offers a sweet finish.

Wasan

Japanese ✕

108 E. 4th St. (bet. First & Second Aves.)

Subway: 2 Av
Phone: 212-777-1978
Web: www.wasan-ny.com
Price: $$

Dinner nightly

Welcome to a new style of Japanese cooking, where dishes may seem familiar, but the ingredients are often surprising. Foie gras, anyone? Start with elegant seasonal rolls, like the *ehou*, which is wrapped in nori and pickled ginger with a dense mouthful of uni, shrimp, *tobiko*, shiitake and more. The chef's philosophy is clear in the intriguing red, green, and white "cheese tofu" in a pool of dashi with tomatoes and asparagus. Bento boxes may feature almond-crusted chicken, assorted sashimi, and a wintry crème brulée.

The recommended tasting menu is a nice complement to the 18 sake flight—surely delicious, but perhaps more memorable if you don't finish them all.

The dining room is neutral, vaguely modern, and run by a very hospitable service team.

00+Co

Vegan ✕

65 Second Ave. (bet 3rd & 4th Sts.)

Subway: Bleecker St
Phone: 212-777-1608
Web: www.matthewkenneycuisine.com
Price: $$

Lunch & dinner daily

There are wine bars and then there is this amazing concept from plant-based food guru, Matthew Kenney. But lets just dwell on this space for a moment. Fitted out with tall, communal tables, backlit wine shelves, and beautiful artwork, the scene inside is both sexy and urbane.

With his unique vision behind 00 & Co, the chef contends he is "crafting the future of food." There is no dairy or meat here; and by the taste of things, no one's missing it either. A long, tantalizing lineup of low-gluten pizza and "not pizza" dominate the menu, along with occasional specials like a wickedly good sweet potato *cavatelli*. A vegan cheese plate might feature creamy truffled cashew or almond ricotta. All washed down with exquisite organic wine? Food nirvana, indeed.

New York City's Financial District is home to some of the world's largest companies. Previously cramped with suits of all stripes, this buzzing business center is becoming increasingly residential thanks to office buildings being converted into condos and a sprouting culinary scene. Every day like clockwork, Wall Street warriors head to such lunch-only stalwarts as **Delmonico's** for signature Angus boneless ribeye. If that's too heavy on the heart (or expense account), change course to **Industry Kitchen**, the lunch spot with a waterfront view and authentic wood-fired pizzas.

NOSTALGIC NIGHTS

At sundown, bring a picnic basket and catch the Shearwater for a memorable sail around Manhattan. Alternatively, step aboard **Honorable William Wall**, the floating clubhouse of the Manhattan Sailing Club, anchored in the New York harbor from May through October every year. Not only does this stunning platform let you get up, close, and personal with Lady Liberty herself, but it also proffers a perfect view of the evening sailboat races—don't forget to have a drink while you're at it! During the summer, weekend trips to Governor's Island—a lush parkland featuring playing fields and hills—are not just popular but make for a wonderful escape among families and friends alike. In fact, all of the city's carnivores make sure to convene here every October for the hugely famous

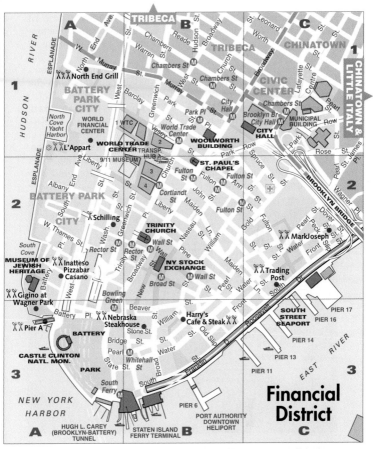

Financial District

and always delicious festival **Meatopia**. Recently recuperated public markets also point to the residential boom in this quarter. Case in point: the burgeoning **Staten Island Ferry Whitehall Terminal Greenmarket** (open on Tuesdays and Fridays) is housed within the large and well-designed Staten Island Ferry Terminal, and deserves plenty of praise for sourcing local and farm-fresh produce to the community from a host of independent vendors.

BARS & BEVVIES GALORE

Despite the destruction wreaked by Superstorm Sandy, restaurants downtown seem to have bounced back into buzzing mode with finance whizzes drowning their worries in martinis, and reviewing portfolios over burgers and beer. One of the neighborhood's largest tourist draws, **South Street Seaport**, is flanked by a collage of fantastic eateries and convivial, family-friendly bars. The legendary **Fraunces Tavern** is a fine specimen on Pearl Street that includes a restaurant and museum paying homage to early American history. While they proffer an impressive selection of brews and cocktails, crowds also gather here for comprehensive brunch- lunch- and dinner-specials. Every self-respecting New Yorker loves happy hour, which is almost always buzzing here with over 130 craft beers a moment to relish some of their homemade punch before perusing the cocktail menu—a work of art in and of itself. Then wash down this kitchen's Irish-influenced eats with the same nation's drink of choice at South Street's **Watermark Bar**. Speaking of bars, revelers may also lounge in style at **Livingroom Bar & Terrace**, accommodated in the sleek **W Hotel,** and accoutered with towering windows set above

and ciders to boot. Thanks to such flourishing destinations, buttoned-up suits have learned to loosen their ties and chill out with locals over the creative libations at **The Dead Rabbit**. This delightful, multi-award-winning watering hole has been drawing city slickers to Water Street as much for specialty cocktails as for their well-conceived décor and small plates. If the ground floor's sawdust proves too rustic for your taste, head up to **The Taproom** for a whiff of elegance. While here, take

specially designed seats that afford unobstructed views of the glimmering skyline. By cooking up classic plates in conjunction with a litany of enticing martinis, this spot remains a coveted summer venue for concerts, corporate events, and other celebrations.

BITES ON-THE-GO

Jamaican food sensation **Veronica's Kitchen** carries on the food-cart craze in the FiDi with its spectrum of flavorful Caribbean classics.

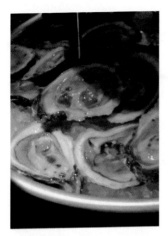

Locals never seem to tire of the food from here, and return on the regular for smoky and deliciously tender jerk chicken. Similarly, carb lovers rejoice at **Adrienne's Pizzbar**'s brick oven pies and other Italian delights, after which **Financier Patisserie** is a dream for tantalizing sweets. Top these off with a steaming cuppa' joe at one of the numerous vendors nearby and heave a satisfied sigh. Even food-focused events like the **Stone Street Oyster Festival** play to this district's strengths—what better way to lift your spirits and celebrate the local Blue Point harvest in September than by slurping up oysters, outdoors on narrow, sinuous, and very charming Stone Street? Located in the shadows of the monumental and glitzy World Trade Center is **Hudson Eats**—a substantial food court complete with an impressive lineup of nibbles and sips. If visions of a grilled cheese sammie scattered with chunks of fresh lobster come to mind, you have arrived in the right place. Finally, custom pastries and cakes from **The Café District** (in Brookefield Place) deliver much decadence to the local palate by way of unique fillings, frostings, and toppings. Even chocolate lovers are welcome here to gorge on truffles, nougats, toffee, and biscuits.

Gigino at Wagner Park

A3   Italian ✕✕

20 Battery Pl. (in Wagner Park))

Subway: Bowling Green
Phone: 212-528-2228
Web: www.gigino-wagnerpark.com
Price: $$

Lunch & dinner daily

To find food this tasty in a rather touristy neck of the woods is a welcome surprise. A setting that boasts views of the Statue of Liberty, Ellis Island, and Hudson River is unique enough that they could probably get away with less than this very good Italian-ish food.

In warmer months, the best seats are on the patio amid blinking harbor lights and a gorgeous vista. A tastefully subdued dining room and unpretentious service make it a pleasant place to while away an evening.

This is a kitchen that cuts no corners, especially in the superb potato gnocchi coated in a silky tomato ragù with braised meatballs. And, *melanzane alla Sorrentina* features layers mozzarella, basil, and chunky tomato sauce with thick slices of fried eggplant.

Harry's Cafe & Steak

B3   American ✕✕

1 Hanover Sq. (bet. Pearl & Stone Sts.))

Subway: Wall St (William St.)
Phone: 212-785-9200
Web: www.harrysnyc.com
Price: $$

Lunch & dinner Mon – Sat

The historic Hanover Bank Building is the home to two different restaurants (albeit one kitchen). Enter through Stone Street and find the "Café." Or enter through Pearl Street and make your way into the casual, cavern-like steakhouse—a bustling space donning a convivial atmosphere with snug rooms, roomy booths, and an elegant vibe. Both are equally charming and polished—and ripe for a business meal.

Start with mushroom bisque, extra rich with a splash of Sherry and dollop of crème fraîche, or Harry's salad chockablock with grilled hearts of palm, peppers, tomatoes, and mushrooms. Other successful entrées include the succulent beef Wellington whose tender baby carrots in a savory wine jus are rendered to melt-in-your-mouth precision.

Inatteso Pizzabar Casano

Italian

A2

28 West St. (at 2nd Pl.))

Subway: South Ferry
Phone: 212-267-8000
Web: www.inattesopizzabar.com
Price: $$

Lunch & dinner daily

This well-designed contemporary "pizzabar" serves tasty cooking that won't break the bank. The dining room is attractive and wood paneled, while the modern bar also offers views of the two pizza ovens, churning out their most popular menu option. However, other offerings merit exploration. Don't miss the wonderful pasta, like oversized ravioli stuffed with spinach, ricotta, and pecorino, in a choice of smooth tomato or sage-butter sauces. Other interesting and flavorful dishes include the *agnolotti di barbabietole*, with braised beet greens, Swiss chard, and cheese stuffed into fresh beet pasta and served in a buttery *"brodo"* finished with poppy seeds.

Also try their café just steps away, serving fresh morning croissants and afternoon tea.

MarkJoseph

Steakhouse

C2

261 Water St. (bet. Peck Slip & Dover St.)

Subway: Fulton St
Phone: 212-277-0020
Web: www.markjosephsteakhouse.com
Price: $$$

Lunch Mon – Fri
Dinner nightly

Well positioned on a historic and touristy stretch to attract diners from near and far, MarkJoseph is more approachable than the clubby competition, but rest assured that these steaks are treated with the utmost care. The dining room looks rather masculine, flaunting chairs with plush fabric and dark brown pinstripes.

This is the kind of place where the namesake salad does away with lettuce, leaving a refreshing combo of poached shrimp, porky bits of *lardons*, string beans and beefsteak tomatoes. Meticulously chosen, aged, and cooked steak, often served sizzling on platters for two or more, is what distinguishes this dedicated and skilled kitchen. Most meals here may be bookended by seafood platters and unapologetically decadent desserts.

L'Appart

French ✕✕

225 Liberty St. (at West St.)

Subway: World Trade Center
Phone: 212-981-8577
Web: www.lappartnyc.com
Price: $$$$

Dinner Tue – Sat

Tucked within the sprawling French markets of Le District, L'Appart is not so much a dining room as the crown jewel comprised of everything those surrounding boulangeries, cheese markets, and butchers can offer.

Through two nondescript doors and a small brass plate etched with its Liberty Street address, find an impeccably decorated interior that resembles an elegant Parisian apartment (hence the abbreviated name). Stunning New York Harbor views wake you from that reverie.

Chef Nicolas Abello starts meals on a high note with canapés simply called "Nico's snacks" that range from a cool, fragrant Charentais melon soup with a hint of mulling spices, to a spoonful of smoky eggplant topped with the perfect counterpoint of sweet, dense prawn. This may be the prelude to a picturesque ensemble of foie gras with mango purée, pickled Finger grapes, green gooseberries, pecan slices, and more. Herb-crusted Colorado lamb filet is downright flawless, accompanied by a copper pot of *confit byaldi*, layering thin slices of baked vegetables and served with a wonderfully salty goat cheese "samosa." The choice of prix-fixe menus ranges in the number of dishes offered, but the cheese supplement is always a steal.

Nebraska Steakhouse

 Steakhouse

B3

15 Stone St. (bet. Broad & Whitehall Sts.))

Subway: Bowling Green
Phone: 212-952-0620
Web: www.nebraskasteakhousenyc.com
Price: $$$

Lunch & dinner Mon – Fri

Marked by a relatively modest and discreet façade, Nebraska Steakhouse remains a well-tread fixture in the FiDi. This classic watering hole with equally brazen diners hovering around a tiny, narrow, and well-soaked bar evokes that old-timey city tavern scene. Inside, the vibe is lively, drinks are strong, and their appetizing offerings are expertly handled.

Finding the door isn't a cakewalk and manipulating the crowd takes some negotiating, but rest assured that the end result is worth it. Yes, those steaks are on-point, but smoked trout salad followed by 22-ounces of tender and juicy grilled lamb Porterhouse chops never fails to sate.

In contrast with the gruff service, a pecan pie studded with chocolate chips and heavy cream is so sweet.

North End Grill

American

A1

104 North End Ave. (at Murray St.))

Subway: Chambers St (West Broadway)
Phone: 646-747-1600
Web: www.northendgrillnyc.com
Price: $$$

Lunch & dinner daily

Its contemporary look features that same stunning combination of white umbrella-like fixtures, black-stained walls, and midnight blue banquettes. However, the reigning chef in the open kitchen reveals a menu shift towards grilled foods, updated comfort favorites, and charcuterie.

Start with an artfully arranged terrine layering strips of pig's ear topped with green beans and mustard vinaigrette. The flavors of wood infuse every element of a thick, blistered pizza decked with potatoes, pancetta, sweet onions, and gently poached eggs. French sensibilities shine in the simply grilled Colorado lamb chops with ribbons of zucchini, baby leeks, and carrots. For dessert, the creamsicle pie bursts with the taste of candied orange, whipped cream, and childhood.

Pier A

A3

American XX

22 Battery Pl. ((inside Battery Park))

Subway: Rector St
Phone: 212-785-0153
Web: www.piera.com
Price: $$$

Lunch & dinner daily

Situated on a pier off the Hudson River, this three-story Victorian—a rambunctious New York landmark replete with a prominent clock tower and enormous promenade—is hardly your average watering hole. After all, where else can you slurp bivalves and sip craft beers among pressure gauges from 19th century steamships while taking in a view of the Statue of Liberty? The menu's tempting seafood options include a dozen types of fresh, plump oysters; lobster mac and cheese studded with greens and bacon and served in a cast iron skillet; as well as mini lobster rolls with a citrusy remoulade.

While the fare here begs for brews, grown-ups craving quiet conversation, a proper martini, and an ultra-hearty Tomahawk steak should head upstairs to Pier A Harborhouse.

Schilling

A2

Austrian X

109 Washington St. (bet. Carlisle & Rector Sts.)

Subway: Rector St
Phone: 212-406-1200
Web: www.schillingnyc.com
Price: $$$

Dinner Mon – Sat

If anyone's willing to set up shop in unlikely places, it's the talented Eduard Frauneder, who has quietly tucked his newest creation into the Financial District. The 70-seat restaurant, designed by Florian Altenburg, features a striking glass-panel garage door and sleek interior with exposed barn wood and steel columns that make use of the building's original features. In back, a U-shaped bar pours some terrific Viennese-inspired cocktails.

At Schilling, Frauneder's contemporary take on Austrian fare gets a Mediterranean touch, as in wild mushroom ravioli with sorrel sauce, baby shiitake, and courgette fondant. Don't miss tender, perfectly braised lamb shoulder set over pistachio crumble, couscous, harissa, and zippy mustard greens to cut the richness.

Trading Post

C2

170 John St. (at South St.))

Subway: Fulton St
Phone: 646-370-3337
Web: www.tradingpostnyc.com
Price: $$

Lunch & dinner Mon – Sat

A reprieve from the neighborhood's many pubs and quick-serve joints, this popular restaurant occupies three floors of a historic building across from the Rockwell-designed Imagination Playground. Stylish and eclectic with a maritime theme, the massive space boasts a rollicking bar and whiskey cellar plus an upscale second floor with water views and an elegant library.

The menu is just as wonderful and wide-ranging, with everything from flatbreads to skirt steak to lobster fried rice. Highlights include a healthy and delicious quinoa salad, studded with butternut squash, morsels of creamy feta, dried cranberries, and a drizzle of reduced balsamic vinegar. Jumbo shrimp plated with wilted kale, plump butter beans, and braised tomato is an impressive entrée.

Sunday brunch plans?
Look for the 🍴 !

Gramercy, Flatiron & Union Square

Anchored around the members-only Gramercy Park, this neighborhood of the same name is steeped in history, classic beauty, and tranquility. Even among thoroughbred New Yorkers, most of whom haven't set foot on its private paths, the park's extreme exclusivity is the stuff of legends—because outside of the residents whose homes face the square, Gramercy Park Hotel guests are among the few permitted entrance.

Bounded by tourist-y Union Square and the fashionably edgy Flatiron District, Gramercy is a quiet enclave that also boasts of beautiful brownstones, effortlessly chic cafés, artisanal restaurants, and haute hotels. Channel your inner Dowager Countess of Grantham as you nibble on dainty finger sandwiches at the refreshed **Lady Mendl's Tea Salon**, a Victorian-style parlor tucked inside the Inn at Irving Place. Stroll a few blocks only to discover assorted pleasures at **Maury Rubin's City Bakery**, a popular haunt for fresh-baked pastries and—in true New York City style—pretzel croissants. Old-timers love the warm chocolate *babka* from **Breads Bakery** and Mediterranean delights from **Lamazou Cheese**. For those who like a little spice, trek a few blocks north to **Curry Hill**, where restaurants focused on the greasy takeout formula reside alongside such choice ingredient paradises as **Foods of India**.After combing these aromatic shelves, head on over to nearby, **Kalustyan's**, an equally celebrated spice emporium showcasing exceptional products like orange blossom water and some thirty-plus varieties of dried whole chilies. Similarly, **Desi Galli** is a quick-serve spot for street food faves—think delicious stuffed bread. Here, pick either a white or wheat *paratha* or *roomali roti* (griddled flatbread) to be filled with the likes of lamb *keema*, spicy *channa* and potato masala, or chicken *tikka*. The vibrant-green mint chutney served on the side is quite sublime.

FLATIRON DISTRICT

Named after one of the city's most notable buildings, the Flatiron District is a commercial center-turned-residential mecca. Engulfed with trendy clothing stores and chic restaurants, the area today is a colorful explosion of culture and shopping. A few blocks to the west is the welcoming Madison Square Park with its own unique history and vibe. Ergo, it is only fitting that visitors are greeted by the original outpost of burger flagship, **Shake Shack**, serving its signature fast food from an ivy-covered kiosk. While burgers and Chicago-style dogs are all the rage, it is their house-made custard that has patrons fixated and checking the online "custard calendar" weekly for favored flavors.

Tourists looking to trend it up should hang with the cool kids at the Ace Hotel, who take their sip from **Stumptown Coffee Roasters** to savor in the hipster-reigning lobby. The equally nifty **NoMad Hotel** is home to Gotham's first **Sweetgreen** and socialites watching their waistline along with "Silicon Alley" staffers can't get enough of their cold-pressed juices and frozen yogurt. A long way from clean tastes, barbecue addicts remain committed to the **Big Apple Barbecue Block Party** held every June. This weekend-long fiesta features celebrity pit masters showing off their "smoke" skills to hungry aficionados. Another frequented spectacle is **Eataly NY**, founded by Oscar Farinetti but brought stateside by Mario Batali and Joe Bastianich. This *molto* glam marketplace incorporates everything Italiano under one roof, including a dining hall with delicious eats, regional specialties, and aromatic food stalls.

UNION SQUARE

Nearby Union Square is a formidable historic landmark characterized by a park with tiered plazas that host political protests and rallies. Today it may be best known for its **Greenmarket**—held on Mondays, Wednesdays, Fridays, and Saturdays—heaving with seasonal produce. Beyond the market, find some fine wine to complement your farm-to-table meal from **Union Square Wines and Spirits**, or **Italian Wine Merchants**. Further evidence of this *piazza*'s reputation as a culinary center is the flourishing presence of **Whole Foods** and the city's very first **Trader Joe's** —both set within just blocks of each other.

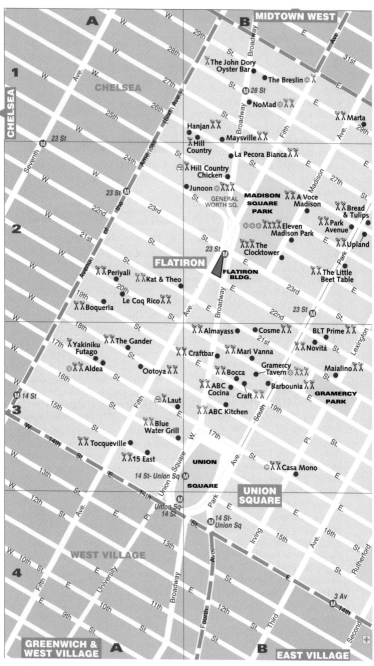

A

B

W. 29th St.

Broadway

Ave.

W. 28th St.

31st

1

CHELSEA

W. 27th St.

M 28 St

The John Dory
Oyster Bar

The Breslin ❀

W. 26th St.

NoMad ❀❀

Broadway

E.

W. 25th St.

Marta

Hanjan

E.

23 St

Maysville

Ave.

29th

Seventh

W. 24th St.

Hill
Country

Fifth

La Pecora Bianca

W.

Hill Country
Chicken

23 St M

Madison

27th

22nd

23rd St.

Junoon ❀

MADISON
SQUARE
PARK

A Voce
Madison

Bread
& Tulips

2

Avenue of the Americas (Sixth Avenue)

W. 21st St.

GENERAL
WORTH SQ.

❀❀ Eleven
Madison Park

Park
Avenue

W.

23 St

The
Clocktower

Upland

W. 20th St.

FLATIRON

M

FLATIRON
BLDG.

Park

The Little
Beet Table

Periyali

Kat & Theo

23rd

W. 19th St.

Le Coq Rico

Broadway

Ave.

E.

22nd

23 St M

Lexington

Boqueria

W. 18th St.

Almayass

Cosme

BLT Prime

Yakiniku
Futago

The Gander

21st

Novitá

3

W. 17th St.

Craftbar

Mari Vanna

Seventh

Aldea

Ootoya

Bocca

Gramercy
Tavern ❀❀

Maialino

W. 16th St.

Fifth

ABC
Cocina

Craft

Barbounia

GRAMERCY
PARK

14 St

M

Laut

South

ABC Kitchen

E. 19th

W. 15th St.

Blue
Water Grill

W.

E. 17th

Pl.

St.

Tocqueville

14th St.

St.

W. 13th St.

15 East

University

UNION
SQUARE

Ave.

St.

Casa Mono

14 St- Union Sq M

W. 12th St.

Broadway

Union Sq.

UNION
SQUARE

Park

Fourth

14 St

14 St-
Union Sq

Irving

15th

16th

WEST VILLAGE

University

13th St.

Ave.

St.

Rutherford

4

W. 10th St.

Fifth

E.

W.

11th

Broadway

Fourth

12th St.

Third

3 Av

M 14th

9th St.

Second

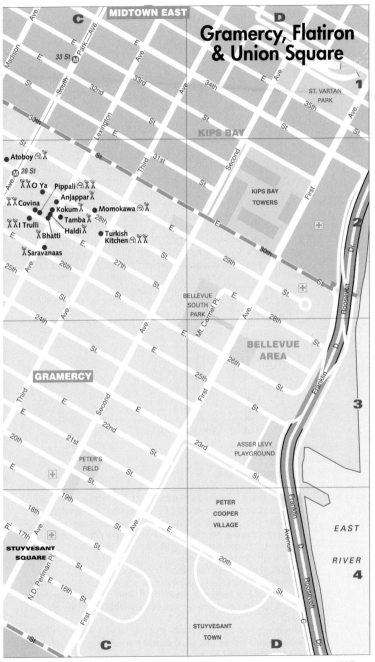

Gramercy, Flatiron & Union Square

MIDTOWN EAST

KIPS BAY

ST. VARTAN PARK

KIPS BAY TOWERS

● Atoboy

Ya

Pippali
Anjappar
Covina
Kokum ● Momokawa
Tamba
I Trulli
Haldi
Bhatti
Turkish Kitchen
Saravanaas

BELLEVUE SOUTH PARK

BELLEVUE AREA

GRAMERCY

PETER'S FIELD

ASSER LEVY PLAYGROUND

PETER COOPER VILLAGE

STUYVESANT SQUARE

EAST

RIVER

STUYVESANT TOWN

ABC Cocina

B3

38 E. 19th St. (bet. Broadway & Park Ave. South)

Subway: 23 St (Park Ave. South)　　　　　　　　　Lunch & dinner daily
Phone: 212-677-2233
Web: www.abccocinanyc.com
Price: $$

Let your eyes wander from the Carnevale Studio bungee chairs to the Fog Linen aprons worn by the staff, and take in all the beauty and brands. It might come in handy later, as just about everything you see—from crockery to utensils—is available for sale in the surrounding floors of ABC Carpet & Home. And of course, everything is gorgeous; for many, the setting alone is worth a trip.

The eclectic menu can seem hard to pin down but it is infused with South American flavors (and drinks). Start with a bright red celebration of the season in the tomato and peach gazpacho with chili and basil. Finish with a wedge of wonderfully moist almond sponge cake frosted with almond-kissed buttercream, and maybe a salted caramel cookie filled with "impossible" dulce de leche.

ABC Kitchen

Contemporary ✕✕

B3

35 E. 18th St. (bet. Broadway & Park Ave. South)

Subway: 23 St (Park Ave. South)　　　　　　　　　Lunch & dinner daily
Phone: 212-475-5829
Web: www.abckitchennyc.com
Price: $$

Jean-Georges Vongerichten's farm-to-table restaurant lets you indulge your cravings whilst playing up your eco credentials, because this is a place that takes its social responsibilities seriously and whose ethos is writ large upon the menu, with suppliers acknowledged and policies explained. They describe their extensive menu as "locally sourced and globally artistic." Fortunately their food is more convincing than their semantics—the glossy tuna sashimi is served at just the right temperature; a burger is pepped up with pickled jalapeños; and a toothsome panna cotta comes with delicious glazed figs.

This accent on freshness finds its reflection in the pure white wholesomeness of the place and the youthful enthusiasm of the service team.

Aldea ❀

Mediterranean ✖✖

31 W. 17th St. (bet. Fifth & Sixth Aves.)

Subway: 14 St - 6 Av Dinner Tue – Sat
Phone: 212-675-7223
Web: www.aldearestaurant.com
Price: $$$

A perfect climate and great scenery—it's easy to see the appeal of life on the Mediterranean. George Mendes' cheerful restaurant may not transport you there, but you will leave feeling as though your serotonin levels have received a timely boost.

Those who like to eat while deciding what to eat will delight in an appealing *petisco* or snack—the crisp and refreshing gin and tonic macaron for example—served to kick off the four-course meal. The menu reflects the seasons and is full of dishes to match that Southern European climate: they are bright, sunny, and you feel they are doing you good. Nothing says the Med more than *bacalhau*—here served grilled and set over earthy-sweet sunchoke purée, finished tableside with enriched soy sauce. The kitchen is equally adept at more warming, comforting dishes—try the grilled quail with butternut squash and pumpkin seeds. Aim for items that remain truer to their Portuguese heritage rather than Japanese embellishments.

The restaurant comes decorated with birch wood and shades of blue and is spread over two narrow rooms. Thanks to the open kitchen, the first floor has more buzz, but ask for the more intimate mezzanine level if on a date.

Almayass

Lebanese
Lebanese

 B3

24 E. 21st St. (bet. Broadway & Park Ave. South)

Subway: 23 St (Park Ave. South)   Lunch & dinner daily
Phone: 212-473-3100
Web: www.almayassnyc.com
Price: $$

Armenian influences steer the Lebanese cuisine here to a unique and rather elegant place. While this family-run operation has numerous Middle Eastern locations, this is their sole U.S. outpost. Polished service befits the upscale room, installed with vivid artwork and tables generously sized for feasting.

Beginning with a selection of fresh and flavorful meze is absolutely necessary. Cold options include *kabis*, an assortment of spicy pickled vegetables; and *moutabbal Almayass*, a magenta-colored spread of mashed beets seasoned with sesame paste, lemon, and garlic. Or opt for hot, succulent, and Armenian *mantee*—little pockets stuffed with beef, earthenware-baked, and doused with tart yogurt. A selection of Lebanese producers headlines the wine list.

Anjappar

Indian

 C2

116 Lexington Ave. (at 28th St.)

Subway: 28 St (Park Ave. South)   Lunch & dinner daily
Phone: 212-265-3663
Web: www.anjapparusa.com
Price: $$

Step inside this Curry Hill standout to unearth a dining room that is festive without being kitschy. Carved woodwork and a palette of red and ivory embolden the tasteful setting.

Specializing in the cuisine of the Chettinad region, this South Indian kitchen showcases freshly ground spice blends and a particular fondness for eggs. This is clear in items like *nattukozi* (country chicken) *biryani* featuring a fluffy mound of fragrant basmati studded with a hard-boiled egg and pieces of bone-in chicken, sided by onion gravy, chopped fresh onion, and tomato-studded *raita*. Also sample the *meen kolambu;* chunks of kingfish in a brick-red curry redolent with mustard seeds, coarse ground black peppercorns, red chilies, and bits of fresh and aromatic curry leaf.

Atoboy 🙂

Korean ✗

C2

43 E. 28th St. (bet. Madison & Park Aves.)

Subway: 28 St (Park Ave. South)
Phone: 646-476-7217
Web: www.atoboynyc.com
Price: $$

Dinner Mon – Sat

Together with his wife, Ellia, Chef Junghyun Park wows diners from start to finish at this Gramercy hot spot with their unapologetic love for Korean food. The fact that they eschew any kind of city pretense in favor of a deeply welcoming atmosphere simply adds to the allure.

With its polished cement floors, posters designed by the owners, and row of communal tables, the interior is clean and industrial, and the enticing menu woos diners with its adventurous—yet approachable—take on Korean food. Here you may find creamy braised eggplant with sweet snow crab, tomato, and lemon; or tender squid stuffed with minced pork, shrimp and paired with a Korean-leaning *chimichurri*. Close out with firm, oily mackerel swimming in a flavorful soy-green chili bath and set atop cubes of braised daikon.

A Voce Madison

Italian ✗✗

B2

41 Madison Ave. (entrance on 26th St.)

Subway: 28 St (Park Ave. South)
Phone: 212-545-8555
Web: www.avocerestaurant.com
Price: $$$

Lunch Mon – Fri
Dinner Mon – Sat

This modern beacon of Italian cooking remains a steadfast draw for the stylish Flatiron business set. With its handsome walnut floors, plush leather chairs and abstract art, the interior is casually elegant—and the same can be said about the cooking.

Don't pass up on the focaccia, which hits the spot when dipped into fruity olive oil. But hungry hordes should also save room for the burrata, accompanied by an Italian-style salsa composed of peppers, basil, and more of that golden olive oil. Then look forward to homemade orecchiette, served in a sumptuous veal ragù with grated parmesan and chickpeas, while the deliciously dense chocolate bread pudding—complete with smoked Caribbean chocolate ganache and pine nut gelato—makes for an enticing dessert.

Barbounia

B3

250 Park Ave. South (at 20th St.)

Subway: 23 St (Park Ave. South)
Phone: 212-995-0242
Web: www.barbounia.com
Price: $$

Lunch & dinner daily

Barbounia brings the pleasures of the Mediterranean to a primo locale. The welcome is warm, the ceilings are notably high, and the floor-to-ceiling bar is considerably stocked (note the wine list and its surprisingly large selection from Greece). The dining room is crowded with tables, so go for the cozy corner banquettes overlooking the action.

The rustic, satiating fare is ideal for sharing. Thick pieces of octopus are grilled to a buttery softness and served over marinated chickpeas with olives, oregano, and a slick of *labneh*. Order the *shakshuka* and a cast iron skillet arrives bursting with flavor and bubbling at the table, with a piquant paprika-spiked tomato sauce topped with baked eggs and studded with roasted peppers and merguez.

Bhatti

C2

100 Lexington Ave. (at 27th St.)

Subway: 28 St (Park Ave. South)
Phone: 212-683-4228
Web: www.bhattinyc.com
Price: ⊜⊜

Lunch & dinner daily

This Northern Indian eatery is praised for its array of tasty grilled meats and kebabs that emerge from the *bhatti* (open-fire grill). Quality ingredients and a skilled kitchen combine with delicious results as in *hariyali chooza*, nuggets of white meat chicken marinated in an herbaceous blend of mint, cilantro, green fenugreek, chilies, and hung curd; or the unique house specialty *galouti kebab*, made from fragrantly spiced lamb ground so fine and incredibly tender that it's almost pâté-smooth. Hearty dishes such as *khatte baingan*, silky chunks of eggplant stewed in a tangy onion-tomato masala and garnished with pickled ginger root, wrap up temptations.

The room is kitsch-free and tastefully done with dark wood furnishings set against red-and-gold wallpaper.

BLT Prime

Steakhouse XX

B3

111 E. 22nd St. (bet. Lexington Ave. & Park Ave. South)

Subway: 23 St (Park Ave. South)   Dinner nightly
Phone: 212-995-8500
Web: www.bltprime.com
Price: $$$

Oh, to spend a night amongst the lush temptations of BLT Prime, where sizzling cuts of Prime Angus beef dabbed with butter waft by, and glossy, high-end reds swirl in glasses. It's the kind of place your friend might argue: if we're going to do it, let's do it right. It's dark, it's loud, it's sexy—hip, but masculine. There's a lot to love here.

Steak might be the most popular option from this kitchen, but these chefs' talents run deep. An excellent starter of cheese popovers arrive light as a feather, their golden crust giving way to a savory, custardy filling. A bright lobster salad, rendered in the style of a Cobb, hits its mark with nearly a pound of meaty lobster, ripe avocado, crispy pancetta, buttermilk ranch dressing, and a soft-boiled egg.

Blue Water Grill

Seafood XX

A3

31 Union Sq. West (at 16th St.)

Subway: 14 St - Union Sq   Lunch & dinner daily
Phone: 212-675-9500
Web: www.bluewatergrillnyc.com
Price: $$

This New York institution has become an iconic part of the Union Square landscape. The stately building is a former bank, with century-old architectural details and marble aplenty.

As the name would suggest, the menu leans heavily on seafaring classics with an ample raw bar and sushi counter. But more than anything, this kitchen aims to please, with starters like pork belly sliders topped with tangy fennel-lettuce slaw on a brioche bun. Octopus tentacles are crisp yet perfectly tender inside, served resting atop chickpeas with a deep-red tomato and roasted pepper ragout infused with smoked paprika. Fish is always perfectly handled and often rises well above its accompaniments on the plate.

Live jazz is a nightly draw to the downstairs lounge.

Bocca

Italian   XX

39 E. 19th St. (bet. Broadway & Park Ave. South)

Subway: 23 St (Park Ave. South)
Phone: 212-387-1200
Web: www.boccanyc.com
Price: $$

Lunch Mon – Fri
Dinner nightly

This trattoria hits all the right notes—and throws in a few novel riffs—to make it as a neighborhood favorite. The Roman cuisine has few faults, and the comfortable setting feels genuine with its parchment-lacquered walls, displayed wine storage, and framed posters of Federico Fellini's classics.

Bocca is owned by the team behind Cacio e Pepe in the East Village, so you can expect delicious and dramatically presented *tonnarelli cacio e pepe*. However, the talented kitchen offers temptations aplenty, such as a bowl of fresh, rich-tasting *spaghetti alla chitarra* brilliantly dressed with cherry tomato sauce and 'nduja. Twice-cooked pork belly with braised cabbage and celery mostarda is another fine example of their hearty, regional flavors.

Boqueria

Spanish   XX

53 W. 19th St. (bet. Fifth & Sixth Aves.)

Subway: 18 St (Seventh Ave.)
Phone: 212-255-4160
Web: www.boquerianyc.com
Price: $$

Lunch & dinner daily

Named after Barcelona's famed market, Boqueria does that vibrant emporium proud with an array of ingredient-driven tapas. Their tortilla Española is a true classic, served as a towering wedge of organic eggs, tender potatoes, and sweet onions. Kale reaches new heights as a sweet and earthy salad tossed with a rainbow of cumin-roasted carrots, toasted sunflower seeds, pomegranate arils, and a lush swipe of tangy *labne*. *Bombas de la Barceloneta* are crunchy, beef-stuffed potato *croquetas* plated with salsa verde and silken, garlicky aïoli.

Envision high banquettes amid creamy hues, a white marble bar area filled with wooden boards of Spanish cheeses, olives in terra-cotta bowls, and crowds cooing over classic tapas like *pan con tomate. Delicioso.*

Bread & Tulips

 Italian

 B2

365 Park Ave. South (at 26th St.)

Subway: 28 St (Park Ave. South)
Phone: 212-532-9100
Web: www.breadandtulipsnyc.com
Price: $$

Lunch Mon – Fri
Dinner Mon – Sat

One of the best things about the New York City food scene is that you don't have to empty your pockets to eat well. Case in point: Bread & Tulips. It's cute, it's economical and it's very well-located. The menu is casual, rustic Italian, featuring a healthy roster of pizzas, pasta and simple, well-prepared entrées. Uniquely, each of the pastas can be substituted with gluten-free variations.

Housed in the lower level of the swanky Hotel Giraffe, this warm and rustic dining room is dressed in wood, metal and exposed brick—with bright artwork lining the walls and decorative baskets doubling as lampshades. When the weather's right, you can sneak up to the rooftop for a cocktail, a limited food menu and a bird's eye view of the city.

The Clocktower

Contemporary

 B2

5 Madison Ave. (bet. 23rd & 24th Sts.)

Subway: 23 St (Park Ave. South)
Phone: 212-413-4300
Web: www.theclocktowernyc.com
Price: $$$

Lunch & dinner daily

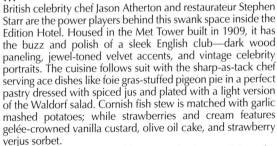

British celebrity chef Jason Atherton and restaurateur Stephen Starr are the power players behind this swank space inside the Edition Hotel. Housed in the Met Tower built in 1909, it has the buzz and polish of a sleek English club—dark wood paneling, jewel-toned velvet accents, and vintage celebrity portraits. The cuisine follows suit with the sharp-as-tack chef serving ace dishes like foie gras-stuffed pigeon pie in a perfect pastry dressed with spiced jus and plated with a light version of the Waldorf salad. Cornish fish stew is matched with garlic mashed potatoes; while strawberries and cream features gelée-crowned vanilla custard, olive oil cake, and strawberry verjus sorbet.

Given its particularly notable spirit selection, a visit to the Gold Bar is crucial.

The Breslin

B1

16 W. 29th St. (bet. Broadway & Fifth Ave.)

Subway: 28 St (Broadway)
Phone: 212-679-1939
Web: www.thebreslin.com
Price: $$$

Lunch & dinner daily

This lively, low-lit gastropub only keeps getting better with time. Dining here has never been more civilized (especially at off hours) now that The Breslin takes reservations.

Service is hip but great, thanks to that certain careful informality that only a skilled team could manage.

The cooking reflects everything that makes April Bloomfield totally unique and original. Chicken liver sounds like a simple starter, but here it arrives faultless with a rosy color and elegant texture beneath a pretty pink layer of gelée, alongside crusty slices of grilled country toast drizzled with olive oil. Seafood sausage is a signature dish that demonstrates superlative charcuterie skills, from the snap of each link to the tender seafood interior, decadently bathed in beurre blanc. Incomparable vegetables prove the breadth of this kitchen's talent, so save room for sides like crisp cauliflower florets with harissa and coriander, or broccoli rabe with abundant anchovies and Calabrian chilies.

Desserts are far more elevated than rustic, such as the chocolate caramel "candy bar" layered with crumbly almond-graham cracker crust, cocoa nib ice cream, and a sprinkle of sea salt to bring the flavors together.

Casa Mono ✿

Spanish ✖✖

B3

52 Irving Pl. (at 17th St.)

Subway: 14 St - Union Sq
Phone: 212-253-2773
Web: www.casamononyc.com
Price: $$$

Lunch & dinner daily

Casa Mono is tiny, jammed, and totally New York. Furnished with a few closely packed tables that moan under the excess of mouthwatering plates as well as that mighty counter framed by a handful of seats, this grotto-like wine bar is loud, communal—and an absolute thrill.

Then consider the service, which moves like clockwork and confirms that this is no slipshod show. The staff may be brisk in their presentation of the kitchen's ambitious renditions of tapas, but with flavors so delicious and concepts inventive, so be it. A faithful mix of locals and hungry out-of-towners convene for fantastic bite-sized eats like buttery bone marrow with smoked caper chermoulah—a house signature that is rich, flavorful, and entirely unmissable. Even the humble *bacalao* fritter attains new heights here as a deep-fried, fluffy delight coupled with sweet-citrusy *alioli*. Lastly, fallback plates like razor clams *a la plancha* in garlic-parsley sauce remain outstanding, consistent, and full of Spanish soul. This kitchen isn't frightened to explore, so skill and innovation are at the forefront of every morsel, including the thick, creamy, and luscious *crema Catalana con buñuelos*. One word comes to mind: bliss.

Oenophiles may head next door to the drinking-focused sidekick, Bar Jamón.

Cosme

B3

35 E. 21st St. (bet. Broadway & Park Ave. South)

Subway: 23 St (Park Ave. South)   Lunch & dinner daily
Phone: 212-913-9659
Web: www.cosmenyc.com
Price: $$$$

The uni tostada is reason enough to visit this sleek, ersatz-industrial space courtesy of Mexico's most celebrated chef, Enrique Olvera. Add in flattering lighting, a great bar and a seductive atmosphere and you have a restaurant in high demand—so don't be surprised if that visit of yours isn't necessarily at the hour of your choosing.

One glance at the menu of sharing plates will also tell you this is no ordinary Mexican restaurant. Tender beef tongue with coffee oil, crispy octopus with hazelnut *mole*—the cooking is clever, innovative and, at times, surprisingly delicate. And yet, not everything works. The milk chocolate dessert with tomatoes may be a little too challenging for some tastes, but there's no doubting the kitchen's ambition and imagination.

Covina

XX

C2

127 E. 27th St. (bet. Lexington Ave. & Park Ave. South)

Subway: 28 St (Park Ave. South)   Dinner nightly
Phone: 212-204-0225
Web: www.covinanyc.com
Price: $$$

Covina swings into town complements of husband-wife duo, Tim and Nancy Cushman—names synonymous with restaurant royalty in Boston. Inside, the colorful dining room features a u-shaped bar and bustling open kitchen; while the café up front offers sandwiches and pastries to-go.

The thoughtful menu aims for a Cal-Med sensibility, and achieves it with balance and polish. Dinner might begin with curried cauliflower accompanied by peas, cilantro-mint chutney, and charred garlic yogurt. Then move on to plump wood-grilled Gulf shrimp with creamy polenta and smoked Oaxacan *pasilla chile* sauce; or even homemade fennel pork sausage with salsa verde. Don't miss the signature *farfalle* of farro, milled in-house, and tossed with braised greens, pine nuts and parmesan.

Craft

American

B3

43 E. 19th St. (bet. Broadway & Park Ave. South)

Subway: 14 St - Union Sq
Phone: 212-780-0880
Web: www.craftrestaurantsinc.com
Price: $$$$

Lunch Mon – Fri
Dinner nightly

It's been years since Tom Colicchio first opened Craft to great acclaim, but the easy charms of the celebrity chef-cum-TV personality's downtown institution haven't waned a bit. The room still bustles most nights of the week with stylish types who appreciate the triple threat of cozy décor, elegant fare and a crackerjack service team.

As the name suggests, guests «craft» together a meal from seasonal, perfectly executed dishes featuring pristine ingredients. Dinner might kick off with a cured slice of crudo, served with shaved fennel, radish and micro greens in a Meyer lemon dressing. Don't leave without trying one of Chef Colicchio's legendary pastas, like a gorgeous tangle of *capellini* with lemon zest, grated cheese, ramps and Calabrian chilies.

Craftbar

Contemporary

B3

900 Broadway (bet. 19th & 20th Sts.)

Subway: 14 St - Union Sq
Phone: 212-461-4300
Web: www.craftrestaurantsinc.com
Price: $$

Lunch & dinner daily

Its ersatz industrial aesthetic and the rumble of the subway below combine to create a sense of energy and toil—although the service team can sometimes fail to embrace these concepts with any great vigor. But never mind because, as the name suggests, there's a big bar here, and a menu that has something for everyone.

There is quite a pronounced Asian flavor in many of the dishes, such as the big bowl of PEI mussels with Makrut lime, chili paste, and Sichuan pepper. Those, however, who prefer their culinary influences a little more homegrown, will find much comfort in the "double stack" burger. Anyone mindful of the heart—its health, not its emotional state—will be reassured by the presence of ingredients like kale on the menu.

Eleven Madison Park ✿ ✿ ✿

Contemporary 𝐗𝐗𝐗𝐗

B2

11 Madison Ave. (at 24th St.)

Subway: 23 St (Park Ave. South)
Phone: 212-889-0905
Web: www.elevenmadisonpark.com
Price: $$$$

Lunch Fri – Sun
Dinner nightly

Chef Daniel Humm's cooking is clever, innovative and even a little whimsical; it is as often robust as it is delicate. This variety and depth is what sets him apart from other chefs, and puts Eleven Madison Park on the vanguard of America's dining evolution. As before, no menu is presented here, but a conceptual shift means that diners are now empowered to choose their preferences for a number of courses.

The myriad plates that subsequently appear are dramatic, like the gueridon presentation of asparagus in rosemary broth cooked sous-vide in a pig's bladder, but also display extraordinary understanding of technique, as in the dry-aged duck.

The restaurant is housed within the sort of grandeur that could only ever have belonged to a financial institution. It's a hard space to fill; conversations don't so much hang in the air as float up to the vast ceiling and never return. But somehow the room's sheer scale and the well-spaced tables allow you to feel cocooned in your own world. Considerable help comes courtesy of the engaging staff as they explain each dish in loving terms but without ever sounding too virtuous. They also know when to talk and when to leave you to enjoying your meal.

15 East

Japanese ✗✗

A3

15 E. 15th St. (bet. Fifth Ave. & Union Sq. West)

Lunch & dinner Mon – Sat

Subway: 14 St - Union Sq
Phone: 212-647-0015
Web: www.15eastrestaurant.com
Price: $$$

A Japanese restaurant divided in two: you can perch at the counter and watch the sushi chefs in action or you can go next door and sit at a table in a slickly run, narrow room decked out in earthy tones. Either way, you'll be well looked after by an attentive team.

The menu is also divided—between sushi and sashimi from the bar, and hot dishes from the kitchen. There is an impressive selection of the former, with the sashimi being particularly worthy. The hot dishes range from the traditional to the more innovative and adapted. Avoid the over-generously battered tempura and go instead for the soba noodles, made in house and served with a choice of topping such as uni or *ikura*, or the rich squid ink risotto with spear squid.

The Gander

Contemporary ✗✗

A3

15 W. 18th St. (bet. Fifth & Sixth Aves.)

Lunch & dinner daily

Subway: 14 St - Union Sq
Phone: 212-229-9500
Web: www.thegandernyc.com
Price: $$

At this elegant outpost Chef Jesse Schenker imbues each dish with distinct originality. The space flows from an inviting front lounge to a cozy back dining room, dressed with burlap ceiling pendants and ivory terrazzo flooring.

Go for the three or four-course prix-fixe dinner to experience this clever and delightful cuisine. Creamy anchovy dressing and meaty bacon join in the chef's take on this classic reinterpretation of a wedge salad. Risotto-style beluga lentils balance intense mushroom stock with a subtle hit of jalapeños. Many dishes highlight delicious restraint, like the pan-roasted branzino with foamy and mild foie-gras veloute. Finish with the slender bar of chocolate torte with white chocolate-miso ganache and fennel ice cream.

Gramercy Tavern

Contemporary

B3

42 E. 20th St. (bet. Broadway & Park Ave. South)

Subway: 23 St (Park Ave. South)
Phone: 212-477-0777
Web: www.gramercytavern.com
Price: $$$$

Lunch & dinner daily

In a roll-call of New York's most beloved restaurants of the last couple of decades, Gramercy Tavern would be high on many people's list. It is one of those places that manage the rare trick of being so confident in its abilities that it can be all things to all people. You'll probably leave happy whether you've come on a date or are here to impress the in-laws; whether you're closing a deal or simply lubricating the thought processes behind a deal.

The "Tavern" side is the better one for lunch, especially if there are only two of you and you can sit at the bar—it doesn't take bookings so get here early and join in the grown-up "I'm not really queuing, I'm just standing here" queue outside. The "Dining Room" is for those who like a little more pomp with their pappardelle, and really comes into its own in the evening.

The cooking is the perfect match for the warm and woody surroundings: this is American food sure of its footing and unthreatening in its vocabulary. The main component, be it sea bass or pork loin, is allowed to shine and there is a refreshing lack of over-elaboration on the plate that demonstrates the confidence of the kitchen.

Haldi

Indian

C2

102 Lexington Ave. (bet. 27th & 28th Sts.)

Subway: 28 St (Park Ave. South)
Phone: 212-213-9615
Web: www.haldinyc.com
Price: $$

Lunch & dinner daily

It takes serious effort for an Indian restaurant to stand out from the crowd in jam-packed Curry Hill, but by highlighting the cuisine of Calcutta and its faction of Jewish immigrants, this *desi* diner does just that. Haldi translates to turmeric in Hindi, and the space is fittingly decorated with splashes of yellow throughout.

Executive Chef Hemant Mathur heads up this operation, where a cadre of skilled cooks routinely turn out the likes of such unique plates as *mangshor* chop, a crunchy ground lamb-and-potato patty served with cilantro chutney; or fish-fry Calcutta-style served with mustard-and-onion relish. Chicken *makmura*, featuring minced chicken meatballs cooked in a rich, creamy curry made from almonds and cashews, makes for a fine finale.

Hanjan

Korean

B1

36 W. 26th St. (bet. Broadway & Sixth Ave.)

Subway: 28 St (Broadway)
Phone: 212-206-7226
Web: www.hanjan26.com
Price: $$

Lunch Mon – Fri
Dinner Mon – Sat

This contemporary take on Korean cuisine continues to thrive and is cherished among locals and visitors alike. A convivial crowd gathers along a cluster of tables in the petite space where ivory ceramic pieces are set against grey walls.

Small plates arranged as "traditional" and "modern" highlight quality ingredients and stimulating presentations. The signature house-made tofu is unmissable: these chilled scoops of quivering soybean curd are a toasty shade of brown, sprinkled with slivered green onion and sesame seeds, and accompanied by soy sauce and perilla vinaigrette. Lunch is limited to a handful of starters, *bi bim bap*, and popular noodle dishes, perhaps mixing pork belly and vegetables doused in black bean sauce. Dinner is a better bet.

Hill Country

B a r b e c u e ✗

B1

30 W. 26th St. (bet. Broadway & Sixth Ave.)

Subway: 28 St (Broadway)
Phone: 212-255-4544
Web: www.hillcountryny.com
Price: $$

Lunch & dinner daily

Manhattan's Hill Country offers as succulent a barbecue experience as one can hope for without actually stepping onto the rolling hills of central Texas. This rollicking roadhouse proudly displays its Lone Star heritage throughout; the lower level doubles as a live country music venue and the ground floor is arranged with counters dispensing the mouthwatering victuals.

Consider your meat options, but don't fret 'cause it's all good, whether you choose lean (or moist) brisket, pork ribs, or smoked chicken to name just a few of the treats. Have your meal ticket stamped, then pick from a plethora of sides and sweets to complete your feast.

Downtown Brooklyn recently welcomed its own Hill Country Barbecue, adjacent to the Hill Country Chicken offshoot.

Hill Country Chicken

A m e r i c a n ✗

B2

1123 Broadway (at 25th St.)

Subway: 23 St (Broadway)
Phone: 212-257-6446
Web: www.hillcountrychicken.com
Price: ⊜⊜

Lunch & dinner daily

Gussied up in a happy palette of sunny yellow and sky blue, this 100-seat homage to deep-fried down-home country cooking serves exemplary fried chicken offered in two varieties. The "classic" sports a seasoned, golden-brown skin; "Mama El's" is skinless and cracker-crusted. Both are available by the piece or as part of whimsically named meals, like the "white meat solo coop."

Step up to the counter and feast your eyes on cast-iron skillets of chicken, as well as sides like creamy mashed potatoes, pimento macaroni and cheese, or grilled corn salad with red peppers and green onion. And then there's pie. More than 12 assortments, baked in-house and available by the slice, whole, or blended into a milkshake for a drinkable take on "à la mode."

I Trulli

C2

122 E. 27th St. (bet. Lexington Ave. & Park Ave. South)

Subway: 28 St (Park Ave. South)   Lunch & dinner daily
Phone: 212-481-7372
Web: www.itrulli.com
Price: $$$

Warm, ambient, and widely appealing, this precious restaurant is known for crafting Italian food with a light touch. Neither young nor hip, it's a neighborhood stalwart that still lures locals with its sublime covered garden, fantastic (and affordable) wine list, and charming dining room of white walls and flickering candles. Their enoteca next door is perfect for a glass of *vino* with friends.

Then there's the menu, which is unabashedly pleasing, beginning with the *panelle*, chickpea fritters with goat cheese and a Sicilian-style caponata. House "musts" include *panzerotti*, mini-Apulian crispy calzones with tomato and mozzarella. Stuffed pastas are a huge draw—think of *ravioli per Olivia* oozing with ricotta and tossed in a light pistachio sauce.

The John Dory Oyster Bar

B1

1196 Broadway (at 29th St.)

Subway: 28 St (Broadway)   Lunch & dinner daily
Phone: 212-792-9000
Web: www.thejohndory.com
Price: $$

Straddling a stylish corner and just at the "hip" of the Ace Hotel, the local mishmash of industrial lofts, artsy company headquarters, and modeling agencies is a proper fit for this beloved gem. Inside, you'll find fish posters adorning the walls, a copper-topped bar lined with Crayola-bright bar stools, and candles as well as twinkling sconces that offer an intimate vibe, despite the lofty ceilings.

Chef Bloomfield is a master of deceptively simple, rustic dishes executed with top-notch ingredients and impeccable care. A warm weather oyster pan roast arrives with plump, luscious oysters and crostini slathered with uni butter. Then look forward to heavenly, house-smoked char pâté sliders, which get a kick from crème fraîche, chili powder and chives.

Manhattan ▶ Gramercy, Flatiron & Union Square

Junoon ✿

B2 Indian XXX

27 W. 24th St. (bet. Fifth & Sixth Aves.)

Subway: 23 St (Sixth Ave.) Lunch & dinner daily
Phone: 212-490-2100
Web: www.junoonnyc.com
Price: **$$$**

Creative cuisine, attention to detail and stunning décor set Junoon apart from its upscale Indian associates. Step through the restaurant's ebony wood doors, and you'll find a dramatic, welcoming space adorned with treasures from the subcontinent. The large bar up front, replete with two antique *jhoolas* (swings) crafted from Burmese teak, delivers sophistication and fun—and by day, lunch is served in the light and airy (Patiala) room.

Dinner guests are treated to the more theatrical room, walking along the length of the space through an ancient wooden arch and carved panels, seemingly afloat in a reflecting pool. This leads to an amber-tinted dining area where tables are luxuriously spaced. The overall effect is exotic, luxe and transporting—not easily forgotten.

The talented kitchen team is particularly adept at bringing out contrasting flavors and textures in vegetarian dishes. A plate of *kofta paneer,* highlighting soft cottage cheese-like dumplings with a crisp exterior, puddled in a mustard-greens curry studded with English peas and abundant chilies, reaches epic heights when paired with a cheese-filled naan. But for a truly regal affair, opt for the chicken biryani—aromatic, moist and perfectly spiced.

Kat & Theo

 Mediterranean **XX**

 A2

5 W. 21st St. (bet. Fifth & Sixth Aves.)

Subway: 23 St (Broadway)
Phone: 212-380-1950
Web: www.katandtheo.com
Price: $$$

Lunch & dinner Mon – Sat

Chef Paras Shah (of Per Se, El Bulli, and Momofuku Noodle Bar) joins Pastry Chef extraordinaire, Serena Chow, to head up the kitchen at this gorgeous Gramercy charmer. The space is dramatic and cozy, with velvet booths (facing the kitchen, be still our hearts) and an exposed brick dining room with rustic wood beams and a working fireplace.

The dinner menu offers up seasonal, intricately composed small plates, as well as contemporary entrées that show a touch of Asian technique laced with Mediterranean inspiration. Pristine monkfish with Bordelaise sauce is coupled with mashed turnip and roasted sunchoke; while a dessert called Maple & Milk offers a unique play on *tres leches* cake, sporting crunchy meringue, fennel powder and brown-butter ice cream.

Kokum

 Indian **X**

 C2

106 Lexington Ave. (bet. 27th & 28th Sts.)

Subway: 28 St (Park Ave. South)
Phone: 212-684-6842
Web: www.kokumny.com
Price: $$

Lunch & dinner daily

The specialties of India's southern coastline are the focus at this gratifying Shiva Natarajan venue. Named after the tart tropical fruit, Kokum is prettied by a mural of fishing boats on a sandy stretch and exposed filament bulbs reflecting warmly off bronzed mirror panels.

Delights from Kerala, Chennai, and Mangalore anchor the menu. Roasted in a banana leaf with diced tomato and spices, the fish *pollichathu* is infused with sweetness and accompanied by fried tapioca root. *Kori gassi* is chicken in a rich curry containing plenty of dried red chilies but tempered by coconut milk and flecked with curry leaf. Carb fans can't resist the fragrant mound of vegetable biryani, drizzled with saffron butter, topped with fried onions and crushed *papadum*.

La Pecora Bianca

Manhattan ▶ Gramercy, Flatiron & Union Square

Italian XX

B2

1133 Broadway (at 26th St.)

Subway: 28 St (Broadway)
Phone: 212-498-9696
Web: www.lapecorabianca.com
Price: $$$

Lunch & dinner daily

Owner Mark Barak is behind this vibrant and rustic Italian charmer, which arrives like a breath of fresh air along this burgeoning stretch of Broadway. Inside the glass-walled dining space, you'll find a nearly open kitchen in the back, and a handsome white marble counter that doubles as a café and panini bar by day.

Utilizing sustainable artisan grains and other Italian-leaning ingredients that are produced domestically whenever possible, Chef Simone Bonelli manages to push out gorgeous and easy-breezy dishes. A small plate of roasted cauliflower is paired with mascarpone, pickled raisins, and almonds; while tender, curly house-made *einkorn gramigna* is cooked to chewy perfection and tossed with soft broccolini, sweet pork sausage, garlic and chili.

Laut

Asian X

A3

15 E. 17th St. (bet. Broadway & Fifth Ave.)

Subway: 14 St - Union Sq
Phone: 212-206-8989
Web: www.lautnyc.com
Price: $$

Lunch & dinner daily

Laut is a unique Malaysian restaurant that is at once cheerful and authentic yet never challenging or inaccessible. It is likewise true to its downtown spirit, in a room that features dim lighting and exposed brick adorned with chalk drawings of orchids and water lilies.

The personable staff and menu of Southeast Asian delights are as steady as the constant crowd. Popular choices include *roti telur*, a thin and slightly crisped yet pliable pancake stuffed with scrambled eggs, onions, and peppers, paired with fragrant coconut chicken curry. The *nasi lemak* is a dome of coconut rice surrounded with sweet chili shrimp, hard-boiled egg, roasted peanuts, and dried anchovies for mixing into an outrageously good mélange of Malaysian flavors.

Le Coq Rico

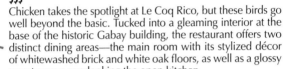

French ✕✕

A2

32 E. 20th St. (bet. Broadway & Fifth Ave.)

Subway: 23 St (Park Ave South) Lunch & dinner daily
Phone: 212-267-7426
Web: www.lecoqriconyc.com
Price: $$$

Chicken takes the spotlight at Le Coq Rico, but these birds go well beyond the basic. Tucked into a gleaming interior at the base of the historic Gabay building, the restaurant offers two distinct dining areas—the main room with its stylized décor of whitewashed brick and white oak floors, as well as a glossy counter area overlooking the open kitchen.

There is a list of chicken breeds to choose from including Plymouth Rock, New Hampshire and Rohan Farm Duck. The menu offers plenty to mull over—imagine eggs, soups, and salads of sautéed guinea fowl and artichokes à la Barigoule. Finally, mains like chicken fricassee sided by rice pilaf or Maine lobster served with shellfish jus are just as delightful as a dessert of vanilla raspberry *Vacherin* with ice cream.

The Little Beet Table

American ✕✕

B2

333 Park Ave. South (bet. 24th & 25th Sts.)

Subway: 23 St (Park Ave South) Lunch & dinner daily
Phone: 212-466-3330
Web: www.thelittlebeettable.com
Price: $$

The product-focused, gluten-free food popularized by the fast-casual Little Beet now has a more elegant home in this Gramercy dining room outfitted with potted greenery and bold artwork.

It should come as no surprise that these beets are divine, whether in a salad of tender grilled wedges plated with strained yogurt, savory pumpkin seed granola, and young arugula; or used to brightly tint a creamy risotto topped with carrot purée and whipped ricotta. But while lovingly prepared vegetables make a strong showing on the menu, it's not all rabbit food here. Other recommendations include tuna tataki dressed with a charred jalapeño vinaigrette; and salmon, cooked so gently it's positively silken, plated with a creative interpretation of caponata.

Manhattan ▶ Gramercy, Flatiron & Union Square

Maialino

Italian XX

 B3

2 Lexington Ave. (at 21st St.)

Subway: 23 St (Park Ave South)   Lunch & dinner daily
Phone: 212-777-2410
Web: www.maialinonyc.com
Price: $$

Housed inside the legendary Gramercy Park Hotel, Danny Meyer's Maialino is one of the sexiest *hosterias* in town—buzzing day to night with New Yorkers in all their trendy glory. Reservations are always a good idea here, though you can always try for a seat at the charming bar, with its tasty little *salumi* and bread stations.

The menu is deliciously simple and hearty: well-sourced food rendered to sweet satisfaction. A starter of tender fried artichokes is paired with lemon aïoli, and al dente *bucatini all'Amatriciana* arrives with well-rendered pork bits, *guanciale*, tomato sauce and pecorino. Of course, the Berkshire pork chop, served with tender, braised turnips and a sweet-and-sour plum *mostarda*, remains a perpetual highlight.

Mari Vanna

Russian XX

 B3

41 E. 20th St. (bet. Broadway & Park Ave. South)

Subway: 23 St (Park Ave South)   Lunch & dinner daily
Phone: 212-777-1955
Web: www.marivanna.ru/ny
Price: $$

The beautiful setting matches the beautiful people at Mari Vanna, a Russian restaurant lined with Louis XV chairs, dripping crystal chandeliers and wallpapered walls filled with sepia-hued photos. A serious array of infused vodkas line one wall, and Monday "Key" nights after 9:00 P.M. are devoted to V.I.Ps only with special keys.

There's a lot of fun to be had at a place like this, that's for sure, but the food remains as delicious as ever: witness a golden caviar platter paired with crème fraîche, finely sieved eggs, and buttery crêpes. Chicken *tabaka* arrives crispy-skinned and fragrant with garlic, served with tender green beans, whipped yogurt and herbs; while silky beef Stroganoff is coupled with fluffy *kasha* and blended with sour cream and dill.

Marta

Italian ✗✗

B1

29 E. 29th St. (bet. Madison Ave. & Park Ave. South)

Subway: 28 St (Park Ave. South)   Lunch & dinner daily
Phone: 212-651-3800
Web: www.martamanhattan.com
Price: $$

Channeling the success of boutique hotel-style Italian dining, Danny Meyer and his team apply a similar mindset to this latest venture located at the Martha Washington hotel. A former woman's lodging, the space was recently given a dramatic makeover to accommodate the lobby level restaurant—a sharp-looking open layout complete with a dining counter overlooking wood-fired pizza ovens.

Like Maialino, Marta is helmed by Chef Nick Anderer and boasts a Roman accent. But, that's where the similarities end. Crispy, thin-crust pizza is the main attraction on this pasta-free menu: the Margherita, for instance, is a crackling delight from the *pizze rosse* listing, while the *anatra* combining duck confit, fennel, and golden raisins is a novel *pizze bianche*.

Maysville

American ✗✗

B1

17 W. 26th St. (bet. Broadway & Sixth Ave.)

Subway: 23 St (Sixth Ave.)   Lunch & dinner daily
Phone: 646-490-8240
Web: www.maysvillenyc.com
Price: $$

All hail the brown stuff: named for a Kentucky port town that produced one of the first Bourbons shipped out of state, Maysville is a gorgeous shrine to all things whiskey. Bottles of the stuff line shelves that face the marble-topped bar, set alongside other decorative features like gilt-framed mirrors and charcoal sketches. It's a lovely and handsome setting, with pops of bright color delivered by flower arrangements placed atop the bar.

This is a great spot for a quick lunch or leisurely dinner, but those who cherish the quiet should opt for off-peak hours. No matter when you arrive, the food is divine—running the gamut from green tomato carpaccio with buttermilk, mint and shallots, to whole-smoked trout with charred red onion and pickled mushrooms.

131

Momokawa

C2

157 E. 28th St. (bet. Lexington & Third Aves.)

Subway: 28 St (Park Ave. South)
Phone: 212-684-7830
Web: www.momokawanyc.com
Price: $$

Lunch & dinner daily

Momokawa is *the* place for reasonably priced shabu-shabu in a rather high-priced part of town. The steep spiral staircase isn't much more comfortable than the postage stamp-sized dining room and tables. They all but disappear once you've ordered, and the rapid-fire kitchen begins delivering dense *goma* tofu with enticingly smoky dashi and sea urchin, or deep-fried bits of soy-marinated chicken and thickly battered shrimp.

With your tabletop burner set a safe distance back from the wall (heed the scorch marks) begin the main event, dipping platters of raw meat, vegetables, and herbs to cook in pots of boiling broth. Options include dark duck broth, bobbing with brightly spiced meatballs, cabbage, watercress and springy noodles to finish down to the last slurp.

Novitá

B3

102 E. 22nd St. (bet. Lexington Ave. & Park Ave. South)

Subway: 23 St (Park Ave South)
Phone: 212-677-2222
Web: www.novitanyc.com
Price: $$$

Lunch Mon – Fri
Dinner nightly

Enjoyable and quietly elegant, Novitá boasts a genuine Italian sensibility both in setting and service. The small size and low ceilings foster a surprisingly serene ambience that is all but disappearing in the city. Prices are not cheap, but the quality is high. The cooking does not necessarily break new ground, but is nonetheless good. Rather than explore the costlier dishes that perhaps feature Kobe beef or black truffles, it's best to stick to the tried-and-true favorites.

Start with a superb combination of pan-fried shiitake caps filled with shrimp and scallions. Then, move on to tiny orechiette mingled with just the right amount of slow-cooked and fiery lamb ragù, broccoli rabe, and grated cheese. The espresso-soaked tiramisù is a perfect pick-me-up.

NoMad ❀

1170 Broadway (at 28th St.)

Subway: 28 St (Broadway)
Phone: 212-796-1500
Web: www.thenomadhotel.com
Price: $$$$

Lunch & dinner daily

The reputation of the seductively louche NoMad hotel, housed within a strikingly bohemian Beaux-Arts building, owes much to the considerable talents of Will Guidara and Chef Daniel Humm of Eleven Madison Park, as they look after all things relating to food and drink.

The glass-roofed Atrium is the chief pleasure dome but a meal in NoMad's land is a moveable feast and some prefer eating in the more languid surroundings of the Parlour, where there's a little less head swiveling and competitive dressing. Wherever you sit, you'll find the service confident and engaging and the menu hugely appealing.

Don't come expecting the culinary pyrotechnics of Eleven Madison Park: here it's about familiar flavors in more approachable, less intricate dishes, but with the same care and understanding of ingredients. Chicken—which, if we're honest, would be the final meal of choice of many of us— is the undoubted star; they roast a whole bird, pimp it up with foie gras and black truffle and serve it for two. Bone marrow adds depth to beef, while asparagus with bread sauce shows the kitchen is equally adept when subtlety is required. For dessert, look no further than the aptly named "Milk & Honey."

Manhattan ▶ Gramercy, Flatiron & Union Square

Ootoya

A3

8 W. 18th St. (bet. Fifth & Sixth Aves.)

Subway: 14 St - 6 Av
Phone: 212-255-0018
Web: www.ootoya.us
Price: $$

Lunch & dinner daily

This Japanese chain boasts more than 300 locations throughout Asia, and now claims three more here in the Big Apple. Thankfully the chic interior does nothing to convey chain dining. Instead, the look is understated with wood slats, ikebana, and muted tones. Ootoya's budget-friendly pricing ensures a full house.

Hearty, home-style fare is the hallmark of their expansive menu of (mostly) cooked specialties. House-made tofu, rice bowls, fried free-range chicken with sweet-and-sour sauce, and pork *katsu* are but just a few of the product-focused items on offer. The lunch sets are an excellent value, built around fine quality fish such as *saikyo* miso-marinated grilled salmon with *chawan mushi*, steamed brown rice, and grains, accompanied by a heartwarming miso soup.

O Ya

C2

120 E. 28th St. (bet. Lexington Ave. & Park Ave. South)

Subway: 28 St (Park Ave. South)
Phone: 212-204-0200
Web: www.o-ya.restaurant
Price: $$$$

Dinner Tue – Sat

Hidden along a workaday street in Gramercy, just adjacent to the Park South Hotel, this lively sushi den keeps things sleek and stylish. A small line of banquette tables hug a wall, offering a cozy seating option, but arguably the best place to be is at the lovely wooden counter, where guests can watch the talented *itamaes* (up to five at a time) up close and personal.

O Ya offers nigiri, sushi, cooked vegetables and meats— and many of the à la carte items make appearances in their wonderful omakase. The endless array of service pieces are stunning, almost to the point of distraction, but in the end the food is the star. On the surface, this is Japanese cooking, but the kitchen uses its high-end ingredients to creatively push the boundaries.

Park Avenue

Contemporary 🍴

B2

360 Park Ave. South (at 26th St.)

Subway: 28 St (Park Ave. South)	Lunch & dinner daily
Phone: 212-951-7111	
Web: www.parkavenyc.com	
Price: $$$	

This Flatiron corner with an identity crisis is now the latest incarnation of the uptown stalwart known for changing inspiration with each season. Larger than its previous digs, Park Avenue is a sprawling canvas on which design firm AvroKO works its magic.

The restaurant remains a family affair, with father and son Alan and Michael Stillman steadily steering the concept alongside Chef/partner Craig Koketsu. Just like the décor, the menu fully celebrates the seasons. Hearty wintertime flavors have featured mustard seed vinaigrette, Manchego, and chestnut honey-drizzled kale-and-chorizo salad. The whimsical "everything" crusted branzino is set on a smear of smoked cream cheese; and sticky toffee pudding is graced with brûléed bananas.

Periyali

Greek 🍴

A2

35 W. 20th St. (bet. Fifth & Sixth Aves.)

Subway: 23 St (Sixth Ave.)	Lunch Mon – Fri
Phone: 212-463-7890	Dinner nightly
Web: www.periyali.com	
Price: $$$	

Relaxing and stylish for grown-ups, Periyali serves the kind of straightforward Greek cooking that remains blissfully unconcerned with trends. Think grilled octopus is boring? Think again, when presented with charcoal-grilled morsels, marinated for two days in red wine and finished with olive oil and parsley sauce. Salmon may not be native to Greece, but it gets its due respect here, wrapped with herbs and baked in phyllo, served alongside stewed okra. A puréed dish of fava *kremidaki* showcases a terrific blend of textures, colors, and flavors that is the heart and soul of this rustic kitchen.

The dining room echoes the culinary theme with a suspended wall of shimmering decorative fish, abundant flower arrangements, and a back room flooded with natural light.

Pippali

Indian **XX**

C2

129 E. 27th St. (bet. Lexington Ave. & Park Ave. South)

Subway: 28 St (Park Ave. South) Lunch & dinner daily
Phone: 212-689-1999
Web: www.pippalinyc.com
Price: $$

Pippali offers a pleasing study on the myriad regional cuisines of India with an array of sensational curries, seafood dishes, and so much more. On-point service makes it a dream destination for date night or dinner with friends, and a muted color scheme in the sleek dining room provides an ideal backdrop for the kitchen's rout of boldly seasoned dishes.

Standards are done right, but focus on their specialties for a unique perspective: *melagu chemeen* is a must—black pepper-rubbed Chilean sea bass simmered in a coconut-rich red chili curry; while Bombay *dabeli* unveils soft buns slathered with spicy mashed potatoes and crispy *sev*. Presentations are careful and unfussy, as found in *baingan ka salan* replete with peanut, sesame, and of course, more spice.

Saravanaas

Indian **X**

C2

81 Lexington Ave. (at 26th St.)

Subway: 28 St (Park Ave. South) Lunch & dinner daily
Phone: 212-679-0204
Web: www.saravanabhavan.com
Price: ≋

This Curry Hill branch of the international chain Saravana Bhavan is one of the neighborhood's most popular dining spots. The monochromatic white interior has taken a beating over the years, but that's easy to look past when the eats are as cheap and tasty as these. The completely vegetarian menu is an authentic array of curries, breads, and weekend-only biryani, but the real head-turners are those table-long *dosas*. They arrive as crisp, tactile favorites on a metal tray ready to be picked apart and dunked into luscious *sambar* and refreshing chutneys.

The *milagai podi* onion *dosa*, a crispy rice-and lentil-flour crêpe spread with dried spices and a deliciously offensive amount of chopped red onion, is just one of many worthwhile treats.

Tamba

C2

103 Lexington Ave. (bet. 27th & 28th Sts.)

Subway: 28 St (Park Ave. South)   Lunch & dinner daily
Phone: 212-481-9100
Web: www.tambagrillandbar.com
Price: $$

Tamba's food may be very good, but the genuine hospitality delivered by owner Mr. Malik and his team of servers is memorable. These are the touches that set it well above its Curry Hill brethren.

Billed as an Indian grill, many dishes are char-kissed and arrive fresh from the tandoor like succulent *jalpari* (jumbo shrimp); mint *paneer tikka*; or *haryali* kebab, skewered chunks of white meat chicken marinated in an herbaceous coriander-mint purée served over a bed of salad greens and browned onions. Other favorites include *channa saag*, toothsome chickpeas and finely chopped spinach simmered in onion, tomato, ginger, and fragrant spices. Tamba's special naan is studded with bits of *tandoori* chicken and is a delicious complement to everything on the menu.

Tocqueville

A3

1 E. 15th St. (bet. Fifth Ave. & Union Sq. West)

Subway: 14 St - Union Sq   Lunch Mon – Sat
Phone: 212-647-1515   Dinner nightly
Web: www.tocquevillerestaurant.com
Price: $$$

In a city that's getting more casual by the second, it's a treat to step into Tocqueville's decadent foyer. Stunning fresh flower arrangements decorate the host stand and there's wood-paneled storage for your coat. A jacketed server might guide you into the spacious, double-height dining room, passing a fabulous bar along the way. You feel tended to at this dining retreat—in the best way possible.

The food, of course, holds it own refinement. Marco Moreira and his wife Joann Makovitzky more than utilize their proximity to Union Square Greenmarket, depositing the neighborhood bounty into their seasonally driven menu with generous abandon. Delights may reveal Cato Farm Bloomsday cheddar salad, followed by chesnut Napoleon or Black Mission fig cheesecake.

137

Turkish Kitchen 🍴

Turkish ✗✗

C2

386 Third Ave. (bet. 27th & 28th Sts.)

Subway: 28 St (Park Ave. South)
Phone: 212-679-6633
Web: www.turkishkitchen.com
Price: $$

Lunch Sun – Fri
Dinner nightly

Turkish Kitchen showcases all the classics but excels in the preparation of grilled meats. Indulge in *yogurtlu karisik*, a dish of moist and smoky char-grilled lamb, chicken, and spicy kebabs on a cooling bed of garlic-scented yogurt sauce and pita bread. Pillowy beef dumplings also wade in a pool of that signature garlicky yogurt sauce topped with paprika-infused oil and a dusting of sumac, oregano, and mint. A wide selection of Turkish wines makes a fine accompaniment to a hearty meal.

Dangling globe light fixtures give the entrance to this cavernous, multi-level restaurant with floor-to-ceiling windows a modern glow. Tables are topped with pristine white cloths and set between black and white striped chairs; cherry-red walls lend a pop of color.

Upland

Mediterranean ✗✗

B2

345 Park Ave. South (at 26th St.)

Subway: 28 St (Park Ave. South)
Phone: 212-686-1006
Web: www.uplandnyc.com
Price: $$$

Lunch & dinner daily

The stars must have aligned to bring Chef Justin Smillie, restaurateur Stephen Starr, and design firm Roman Williams together to form this bright spot along Park Avenue South. Everything seems to click at Upland—the restaurant's interior design is urbane but cozy, with vintage flooring and glowing jars of preserved lemons and backlit wine bottles lining the walls. Earthy and bountiful, it's the perfect backdrop for Smillie's gorgeous Mediterranean-influenced dishes.

A meal in this kitchen's capable hands might reveal a small plate of crispy duck wings, glossy with yuzu sauce; or a plate of *estrella*, star-shaped tubular pasta with crushed chicken livers, herbs, and pecorino. Finish the feast with a wonderful yuzu soufflé, laced with calamansi curd.

Yakiniku Futago

Japanese

37 W. 17th St. (bet. Fifth & Sixth Aves.)

Subway: 18 St (Seventh Ave.)
Phone: 212-620-0225
Web: N/A
Price: $$$

Lunch Mon – Sat
Dinner nightly

Oh, but you're in for a treat at Yakiniku Futago, where the Korean barbecue on offer is actually Japanese at heart. There are only a handful of *yakiniku* spots in the city, and this one is particularly cool. Inside the sleek Gramercy space, the details are grand, with reclaimed wood plank floors, walls alternately covered in exposed brick and Japanese scribes, as well as a dramatically lit bar lined with premium spirits.

During the popular lunch, only a small but divine selection of ramen is available, accompanied by a rich *tonkotsu* broth. The thing that sets a meal apart at this Japanese jewel is the stunning beef quality—cuts like black Wagyu or Hamideru *kalbi* are fantastically creamy, bold in meaty flavors and rich with fatty notes.

Look for **red** couverts, indicating a particularly pleasant ambience.

Manhattan ▶ Gramercy, Flatiron & Union Square

139

Once occupied by struggling artists, poets, and edgy bohemia, Greenwich Village today continues to thrive as one of New York City's most artsy hubs. With Washington Square Park and NYU at its core, this area's typically named (not numbered) streets wear an intellectual spirit as seen in its many cafés, indie theaters, and music venues.

ASSORTED PLEASURES

Mamoun's has been feeding students for decades with some of the best falafel in town. Area residents however have been known to experience similar gratification at **Taïm**, which features updated renditions of this fried delight. Chase down these savory treats with one of their smoothies or opt for a cup of fair trade coffee at **Kopi Kopi,** known for its Indonesian flair. Whether in the mood to linger or pick up a jar to-go, find yourself rubbing shoulders with natives craving authentic Spanish flavors at nearby **100 Montaditos**. Also captivating the culinary elite are those delicate, very satisfying rice- and lentil-flour crêpes served with character and flair at food truck sensation, **N.Y. Dosas**. For crêpes in their original, faithful form along with other excellent French goodies, stop by **Patisserie Claude**, or unearth a slice of Italy by way of old-time bakeries and butchers also settled here. **Faicco's Pork Store** as well as **Ottomanelli & Sons Meat Market** have been tendering their treats for over 100 years now. Take home a round of parsley and cheese sausage or tray of arancini—even though the staff insist that one must be eaten warm, before

leaving the store. Setting aside the dusty floors and minimal décor, **Florence Prime Meat Market** in operation for over 70 years, is every gourmand's go-to spot for Christmas goose, Newport steak, and so much more. And really, what goes best with meat? Cheese, of course, with **Murray's Cheese Shop** initiating hungry neophytes into the art and understanding of their countless varieties. Completing Italy's culinary terrain in Greenwich Village is **Raffetto's**, whose fresh, handmade pastas never cease to please. From here, hop countries to arrive in London via **A Salt & Battery**, whose fish and chips are crafted from the finest ingredients and served with a range of first-rate sides. Think—curry sauce, Heinz baked beans, and mushy peas. Of course, no Village jaunt is complete without pizza, with some of the finest to be found coal-

fired and crisp, only by the pie, at **John's of Bleecker Street**. **Joe's** is another local gem dishing up thin-crust selections that promise to leave you with a lifetime addiction. Close this feast with a uniquely textured scoop from **Cones**, available in surprisingly tasty flavor combinations...even watermelon!

WEST VILLAGE

Located along the Hudson River and extending all the way down to Hudson Square, the West Village is predominately residential, marked by angular streets, quaint shops, and charming eateries. Once known as "Little Bohemia," numerous old-fashioned but resilient food favorites continue to thrive here and offer a taste of old New York. For a nearly royal treat, stop by **Tea & Sympathy** for high tea, followed by a full Sunday supper of roast beef and Yorkshire pudding. **Dominique Ansel Kitchen** serves up more delectable pastries topped with an abundance of French flair. Over on Commerce Street, fans are swooning over **Milk & Cookies**' unapologetically sinful goodies. These are reputedly as sensational as the breakfast and burgers always on offer at **Elephant & Castle**. The influential **James Beard Foundation** is also situated steps away, in a historic 12th Street townhouse that was once home to the illustrious food writer. But, if Tex-Mex is more your speed, then join the raucous twenty-something's at **Tortilla Flats**. Known as much for Bingo Tuesdays as for their potent house margaritas,

it's a guaranteed good time. Manhattan's love for brunch is a time-tested affair that continues to thrive in this far west stretch. Find evidence of this at **La Bonbonniere**, a pleasant little diner whose brazen and beautiful creations are excelled only by their absurdly cheap prices. Pack a basket of egg specialties and enjoy a picnic among the urban vista of roller skaters and runners at Hudson River Park.

While strolling back across bustling Bleecker, let the overpowering aromas of butter and sugar lead you to the original **Magnolia Bakery**. Proffering over 128 handmade treats, this official sweet spot is a darling among tourists and date-night duos. **Li-Lac** is one of the city's oldest chocolate houses dispensing the best hand-crafted treats and chocolate-covered pretzels in town—take your pick between dark and milk! Beyond bakeries, the bar scene in the West Village is always abuzz. Night owls pound through an assortment of pints at the **Rusty Knot**, while relishing cheap eats

NEW YORK CITY

and fantastic live music. Equally expert mixologists can be found pouring "long drinks and fancy cocktails" at **Employees Only**; just as bartenders reach inventive heights at **Little Branch**—where an encyclopedic understanding of the craft ensures dizzying results. At the foot of Christopher Street and atop the Hudson River waterfront, **Pier 45** is a particularly lovely destination for icy cold drinks, hot dogs, and sunbathing.

MEPA

Everyone from fashionistas, curious locals, and stiletto-clad socialites make the pilgrimage further north to the notoriously chic Meatpacking District. Once home to slaughterhouses, prostitution services, and drug dens, today MePa is packed with moneyed locals and savvy tourists looking to get their snack, sip, and groove on. Thanks to the huge success of the High Line—an abandoned 1934 elevated railway that is now a 19-block-long park—

these once-desolate streets now cradle some of the city's coolest restaurants and hottest nightclubs. As if in defiance of these cautious times, luxury hotels, "starchitect" high-rises, and festive bistros have risen—and these modish minions cannot imagine being elsewhere. But, in the midst of all this glitz find **Upholstery Store**, a precious gem when it comes to cocktails served in a repurposed furniture store. **The Standard hotel** is the social hub with beer and bratwursts running the show every summer at **The Biergarten**. Come fall, hipsters soak up the scene at **Kaffeeklatsch**, a pop-up shop preparing hot beverages for freezing skaters doing the rounds at Standard Plaza; while foodies flock to **Valbella** for Northern Italian cooking. Finally, obfuscated by this haute hotel, **Hector's Café** is a modest holdout that continues to feed the few remaining meatpackers here—usually all day, everyday.

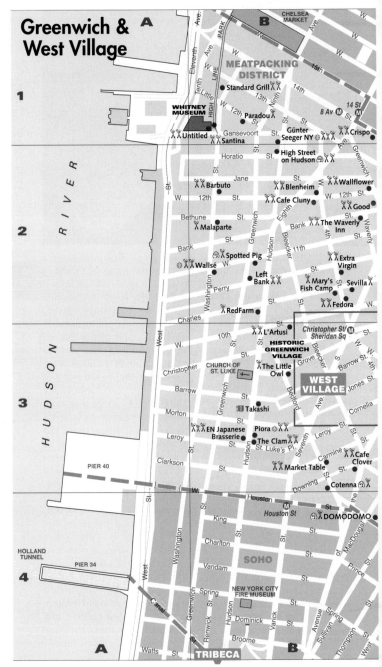

Greenwich & West Village

A **B**

CHELSEA MARKET

MEATPACKING DISTRICT

1

Standard Grill

Paradou

WHITNEY MUSEUM

Untitled Santina

Gansevoort St.

Günter Seeger NY

Crispo

14 St
8 Av

Horatio St.

High Street on Hudson

Jane St.

Barbuto

Blenheim

Wallflower

W. 12th St.

Cafe Cluny

Good

2

RIVER

Bethune St.

Malaparte

The Waverly Inn

Bank St.

Spotted Pig

Extra Virgin

Wallsé

Left Bank

11th St.

Perry St.

Mary's Fish Camp

Sevilla

RedFarm

Fedora

Charles St.

L'Artusi

Christopher St/
Sheridan Sq

HISTORIC GREENWICH VILLAGE

10th St.

CHURCH OF ST. LUKE

The Little Owl

Grove St.

Barrow St.

3

HUDSON

Christopher St.

Barrow St.

Takashi

WEST VILLAGE

Jones St.

Morton St.

EN Japanese Brasserie

Piora

Cornelia St.

Leroy St.

The Clam

Cafe Clover

PIER 40

Clarkson St.

Market Table

Cotenna

Houston St.

Houston St

DOMODOMO

HOLLAND TUNNEL

PIER 34

King St.

Charlton St.

SOHO

4

Vandam St.

NEW YORK CITY FIRE MUSEUM

Spring St.

Dominick St.

Prince St.

Broome St.

Watts St.

TRIBECA

A **B**

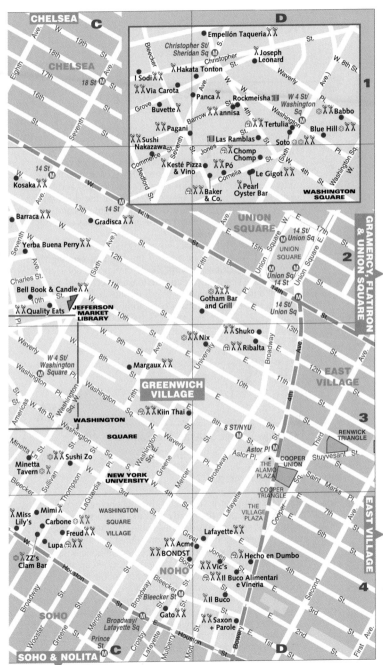

CHELSEA C   D

Empellón Taqueria ✕ ✕

CHELSEA

Christopher St/
Sheridan Sq Ⓜ

✕ Joseph
Leonard

Ⓜ 18 St

✕ Hakata Tonton

I Sodi ✕ ✕
✕ ✕ Via Carota
Panca ✕
Rockmeisha ▥   W 4 St/
Washington
Sq

Grove   Buvette ✕
✕ ✕ annisa
✕ ✕ Babbo

✕ ✕ Pagani

Ⓐ ✕ ✕ Tertulia

Blue Hill ✕ ✕

✕ ✕ Sushi
Nakazawa

▥ Las Ramblas

Soto Ⓐ✕✕   1

✕ Chomp
Chomp

✕ Kesté Pizza
& Vino

✕ ✕ Pó

Le Gigot ✕ ✕

Kosaka ✕ ✕

Ⓐ ✕ ✕ Baker
& Co.

✕ Pearl
Oyster Bar

WASHINGTON
SQUARE

GRAMERCY, FLATIRON & UNION SQUARE

Barraca ✕ ✕

Gradisca ✕ ✕

UNION
SQUARE

14 St/
Union Sq Ⓜ

Yerba Buena Perry ✕ ✕

UNION
SQUARE

Ⓜ Union Sq/
14 St

Gotham Bar
and Grill Ⓐ✕✕✕

Ⓜ 14 St/
Union Sq

Bell Book & Candle ✕ ✕

✕ ✕ Quality Eats

JEFFERSON
MARKET
LIBRARY

Ⓐ✕ Nix

✕ ✕ Shuko

Ⓐ✕✕ Ribalta

Margaux ✕ ✕

EAST
VILLAGE

GREENWICH
VILLAGE

WASHINGTON

Ⓐ ✕ ✕ Kiin Thai

SQUARE

8 ST/NYU Ⓜ

RENWICK
TRIANGLE

Minetta
Tavern Ⓐ✕

Ⓐ ✕ ✕ Sushi Zo

Astor Pl Ⓜ
Astor Pl.

COOPER
UNION

NEW YORK
UNIVERSITY

THE
ALAMO
PLAZA

COOPER
TRIANGLE

✕ Miss
Lily's

Mimi ✕

WASHINGTON

Carbone Ⓐ✕✕

Freud ✕ ✕

SQUARE

THE
VILLAGE
PLAZA

EAST VILLAGE

Lupa Ⓐ✕✕

VILLAGE

Lafayette ✕ ✕

Ⓐ ZZ's
Clam Bar

✕ ✕ Acme
✕ ✕ BONDST

Ⓐ ✕ Hecho en Dumbo

NOHO

✕ Vic's

Ⓐ ✕ ✕ Il Buco Alimentari
e Vineria

Bleecker St Ⓜ

✕ Il Buco

SOHO

Broadway/
Lafayette Sq Ⓜ

Gato ✕ ✕

✕ ✕ Saxon
+ Parole

Prince
St Ⓜ

C   D

SOHO & NOLITA

145

Acme

Contemporary ✗✗

9 Great Jones St. (bet. Broadway & Lafayette St.)

Subway: Broadway - Lafayette St
Phone: 212-203-2121
Web: www.acmenyc.com
Price: $$

Dinner nightly

Be prepared to wait a bit at this long-standing NoHo favorite, where the lines are long but the rewards well worth your time. Inside, weathered floor planks, leather banquettes, and brass details lend Acme a sexy brasserie style that the downtown set loves to hunker down in. Descend a flight of stairs, and you'll find a cozy after-dinner reprieve with serious cocktails, moody environs and music.

Talented Chef Brian Loiacono (of Daniel and db Bistro Moderne) has recently taken over the kitchen, sending the menu in a less fussy, Italian-French direction. Get started with silky chicken liver spread over toasted ficelle and dusted with salt and herbs; or sweet shards of blue crab paired with ripe watermelon, in a tomato consommé with cool, creamy cucumber.

annisa

Fusion ✗✗

13 Barrow St. (bet. Seventh Ave. South & W. 4th St.)

Subway: Christopher St - Sheridan Sq
Phone: 212-741-6699
Web: www.annisarestaurant.com
Price: $$$

Dinner nightly

Anita Lo's menu is informed by her heritage and her peregrinations, and she clearly puts much effort into seeking out the best seasonal produce available. The Asian element of the fusion equation is quite pronounced yet there is also plenty of choice for those who prefer their influences to come from more Westerly cuisines. As a result, one can start with black sea bass sashimi with trout roe and follow it up, by way of contrast, with a "tasting of lamb" with cauliflower. Dishes are quite delicate creations and come with some flavor combinations that will certainly perk up your taste buds.

The dining room exudes warmth; the service is self-assured and, given that annisa means "women" in Arabic, it is fitting that the wine list makes a point of featuring many female wine growers.

Babbo

110 Waverly Pl. (bet. MacDougal St. & Sixth Ave.)

Subway: W 4 St - Wash Sq
Phone: 212-777-0303
Web: www.babbonyc.com
Price: $$$

Lunch Tue – Sat
Dinner nightly

While a restaurant can rarely be all things to all people, it should certainly adapt to the various needs and moods of its customers. Come for lunch at Babbo, for example, and there'll be Stan Getz playing gently in the background to accompany the quiet clinking of cutlery and the soft murmur of conversation. Turn up for dinner with friends and Led Zeppelin or Tom Petty will be the soundtrack to the far more excitable vibe.

Mario Batali's Village stalwart is a thoroughbred now heading inexorably towards its 20th birthday. The reason for its longevity is pretty apparent as soon as you walk in: the place just feels right, everything they do they have practiced, and every need you have and every request you make will be accommodated. It's also a decidedly handsome space, with the first floor room adorned with fresh flowers and a staircase leading to a bright, raised second level.

The menu offers a comprehensive selection of Italian dishes whose rustic appearance belies their skilled creation. The homemade pasta dishes are an obvious strength and the kitchen can show a remarkably light touch when required, especially with certain classic desserts like panna cotta.

Baker & Co.

Italian ✕✕

D2

259 Bleecker St. (bet. Cornelia & Jones Sts.)

Subway: W 4 St - Wash Sq
Phone: 212-255-1234
Web: www.bakernco.com
Price: $$

Lunch & dinner daily

With only a few years on the downtown circuit, this chic charmer is already a bonafide Village sweetheart. Brought to you by the team behind the wildly popular Emporio and Aurora, Baker & Co. is housed in the beloved and much-missed Zito & Sons Bakery—and the interior features a long, welcoming bar, cozy, wood-lined banquettes, as well as a vibrant red-and-white mosaic floor.

The kitchen smartly relies on the same formula that put their other outposts on the map: honest, unfussy Italian rendered with a deft hand and deep attention to ingredients. Consider the luscious burrata, paired with pencil-thin roasted asparagus, cured fish roe and a drizzle of salsa verde; or the tender branzino with asparagus, toasted hazelnuts, arugula and chili flakes.

Barbuto

Italian ✕✕

B2

775 Washington St. (at 12th St.)

Subway: 14 St - 8 Av
Phone: 212-924-9700
Web: www.barbutonyc.com
Price: $$

Lunch & dinner daily

When New Yorkers dream of living in the West Village, Barbuto has a place in that dream, too. Springtime lunches with garage doors open to the sidewalk, and a feast of refined, simple dishes have earned Jonathan Waxman a devoted following in a neighborhood already full of charming restaurants. Casually professional service and the dimly lit dining room's dose of California cool enhance the experience. Barbuto's roast chicken deserves its legendary status, but other dishes tempt too. A *cavolo nero* salad of thinly sliced black kale and crunchy breadcrumbs tossed in a creamy dressing of anchovies and pecorino puts the average kale salad to shame. Linguini is coated with black pepper, egg, pancetta, and cheese in one indelible plate of carbonara.

Barraca

Spanish

C2

81 Greenwich Ave. (at Bank St.)

Subway: 14 St - 8 Av
Phone: 212-462-0080
Web: www.barracanyc.com
Price: $$

Lunch Fri – Sun
Dinner nightly

Spanish for "shack," rustic Barraca charms with timber ceilings and vats of sangria behind the bar. Blue chairs pop against all the wood and brick, bringing a Mediterranean feel to the intimate space. Banquettes line one side of the restaurant, suggesting cozy evenings of sharing *coca de atùn* (flatbread) or *pan tomate.*

Empanadas are flaky and crusty, filled with thyme-laced beef, spring onion, allspice, and cheese. Classic *croquetas* are crackling outside and creamy within, resting on a dab of aïoli. But such snacks are just a prelude to the excellent paella; choose one version studded with shellfish and sweet peppers, or mix and match two or three different "flavors."

Crusty churros finish off an evening of pure Spanish pleasure.

Bell Book & Candle

American

C2

141 W. 10th St. (bet. Greenwich Ave. & Waverly Pl.)

Subway: 14 St (Seventh Ave.)
Phone: 212-414-2355
Web: www.bbandcnyc.com
Price: $$$

Lunch Sun
Dinner nightly

Funky, relaxed, and locally minded, the idea behind this farm-to-table style of dining might seem overdone if the cooking here wasn't so very good. Enter carefully down a steep set of stairs to find low ceilings, large canvas artwork, and comfortable seating that lets you settle in and ponder just how very local the lettuce can be (answer: the rooftop).

In fact, much of the produce here was harvested from their aeroponic rooftop gardens, while the rest is sourced from local purveyors. From start to finish, the American fare is consistently pleasing. Highlights include crispy fried P.E.I. oysters with jalapeño-buttermilk dressing, thick and juicy grilled sausage with house pickles and flatbread, and gooey chocolate brownies with pistachio ice cream.

Blenheim

B2

American

283 W. 12th St. (at W. 4th St.)

Subway: 14 St (Seventh Ave.)
Phone: 212-243-7073
Web: www.blenheimhill.com
Price: $$$$

Lunch & dinner daily

Blenheim's been buzzing around the food world for good reason. Clearly, it takes its farm-to-table ethos seriously as the restaurant draws vegetables and livestock of guinea hens, black angus beef and heritage pig from its very own farm upstate. There may be no more genuine expression of this kitchen than the farm eggs—their yolk bright, orange and fresh. Other technically impressive dishes may highlight chestnut pappardelle with pork ragout, or braised beef short rib paired with roasted sunchoke and maitake mushrooms.

Combined with a sultry and chic interior, featuring plush upholstery, pearly white bar stools, and smoky globes that drop down over tables, the effect is sublime. Date-night material, indeed.

The sun is out – let's eat alfresco! Look for 🛋.

Blue Hill ☘

American 𝗫𝗫

D1

75 Washington Pl. (bet. Sixth Ave. & Washington Sq. Park)

Subway: W 4 St - Wash Sq

Dinner nightly

Phone: 212-539-1776
Web: www.bluehillfarm.com
Price: $$

Chef Dan Barber's iconic venue remains the paragon of farm-to-table dining in Manhattan by virtue of its seasonal lineup of pampered product. Everything on the menu is sourced from the Stone Barns Center (home to Blue Hill's Westchester farm) as well as a number of local producers.

Blue Hill's intimate space has been hosting a devoted foodie following for an impressive 15-some years, and service in this former speakeasy—where fresh flowers and candlelight cast a romantic spell—is nothing less than excellent.

The adept kitchen turns out contemporary cuisine, which in turn showcases the astounding quality stocked in the larder and allows vegetables to shine at all times. Asparagus spears are gently roasted to preserve their natural earthiness and coupled with vibrant beet yogurt, as well as stinging nettles cream for a perfect balance in flavor. Then, moist striped bass draped atop fennel purée is decked with soft, sweet currants and toasted salty pine nuts to form a succulent and satisfying entrée. Familiar desserts highlight still more of the kitchen's best, as is the case with light and custard-y brioche bread pudding coupled with a quenelle of pleasantly bitter cocoa nib cream.

BONDST

C4

6 Bond St. (bet. Broadway & Lafayette St.)

Subway: Bleecker St   Dinner nightly
Phone: 212-777-2500
Web: www.bondstrestaurant.com
Price: $$$

There's no denying that BONDST is still trendy after all these years; it even manages to stay sexy with sheer fabric panels, wispy tree branches, dark leathers, and private spaces. The three-story interior fills nightly with a very European crowd. (Romantics head downstairs; Bacchanalians go up.)

High quality fusion dishes may seem more crowd-pleasing than inventive, but are nonetheless delicious. Behind the wood sushi bar, the buzzing kitchen rolls mountains of maki, like paper-thin slices of pristine scallops balanced with a thick soy-jalapeño sauce and *yuzu kosho*. The *soba nomi* "risotto" is a wickedly rich and unmissable dish of glistening buckwheat soba folded with trout butter, king crab, and shrimp beneath a thatch of bonito flakes and gold paper.

Buvette

C1

42 Grove St. (bet. Bedford & Bleecker Sts.)

Subway: Christopher St - Sheridan Sq   Lunch & dinner daily
Phone: 212-255-3590
Web: www.buvette.com
Price: $$

Charming and proudly French, Buvette serves delicious Gallic plates to a notably svelte set. While carb addicts can barely fit into these wee seats, it's worth the squeeze for Chef Jody Williams' famously rustic cooking. Inside, everything comes alive with jazz and chatter. Instagrammable dishes take their cue from French classics and may feature crusty olive oil-drizzled country bread slathered with fluffy scrambled eggs, salty prosciutto, and nutty parmesan. Then await croissants—fresh, buttery, and flaky—served with sweet fruit preserves for a typically French and very decadent treat.

If not up the block at her other spot or across the pond in Paris, you may even find the chef herself holding meetings over a potent, frothy, and flawless cappuccino.

Cafe Clover

Contemporary XX

B3

10 Downing St. (at Sixth Ave.)

Subway: Houston St
Phone: 212-675-4350
Web: www.cafeclovernyc.com
Price: $$$

Lunch & dinner daily

This fab arrival to secluded Downing Street takes clean eating to sophisticated heights with expertly rendered vegetable, seafood and meat dishes. Inside, the triangular space is impossibly chic and embodies a particularly unique spirit, featuring mercury-glass mirrors, blue leather banquettes, and beautiful lighting.

In the kitchen, Chef David Standridge whips up fantastic fare, like a summer succotash with sweet corn fava, cherry tomatoes, chanterelle mushrooms and baby kale; or a delicious pairing of quinoa tagliatelle and chickpea spaghetti. Bright, cold watermelon cubes arrive juicy and sweet come summer, tossed with nut powder and loads of micro herbs; while soft chickpea flour hushpuppies are set over lentils and paired with a jalapeño aïoli dip.

Cafe Cluny

Contemporary XX

B2

284 W. 12th St. (at W. 4th St.)

Subway: 14 St - 8 Av
Phone: 212-255-6900
Web: www.cafecluny.com
Price: $$

Lunch & dinner daily

This warm and cozy café flaunts its feminine persona with more than a touch of Village cool (and some occasional aloofness). There are ample windows for people-watching, or let your eyes wander to the botany drawings along the walls and bird sculptures decorating nooks.

The Cluny burger accompanied by golden fries is a sure-fire hit; it arrives topless to showcase the perfectly charred and glistening meat. Once fully dressed with your choice of Bibb lettuce, tomato, and red onion slices, it literally drips with goodness—maybe right onto those beautifully crisped fries. Come dessert, go for a simple and outrageously good plate of biscotti, served in a "jenga" arrangement of bittersweet chocolate and walnut or pistachio and anise flavors.

Carbone

Italian

C4

181 Thompson St. (bet. Bleecker & Houston Sts.)

Subway: Houston St
Phone: 212-254-3000
Web: www.carbonenewyork.com
Price: $$$$

Lunch Mon – Fri
Dinner nightly

With nostalgia at the forefront, Carbone is plain gorgeous. While this big, bold, and beautiful ode to Italian-Americana comes alive at night under the low lights, lunch is equally admired among brash bankers with big appetites and Valentino-donning divas. That same sense of history pervades the entire space, which highlights plush banquettes, impressive ceramics, and glittering chandeliers. Was the striking tiled-floor inspired from a certain restaurant scene in *The Godfather*? Probably.

Mid-century classics are what this menu is all about, but exalted ingredients, skill, and presentations will excite even the most cynical savant. Stylish servers—who work the floor with a little flirt and lot of flair—remain in character while presenting top antipasti like crusty garlic bread, *soppressata*, and fresh, particularly divine olive oil-dunked mozzarella. A Caesar salad tossed tableside with carb-worthy croutons and gently pickled white anchovies hits the ball out of the park, while pale-yellow, ricotta-filled tortellini over an intensely rich and meaty ragù is a laudable delight.

Desserts like a proper cheesecake set atop a cookie-crumb base and laced with lemon curd is New York in all its old-school glory.

Chomp Chomp 🐶

Singaporean ✗

D2

7 Cornelia St. (bet. Bleecker & W. 4th Sts.)

Subway: W 4 St - Wash Sq
Phone: 212-929-2888
Web: N/A
Price: $$

Dinner nightly

Named for the legendary Chomp Chomp Food Centre in Singapore, this eatery takes its cues from the same nation's delicious street foods. Owned by Simpson Wong, Chomp Chomp's interior features cool, concrete floors and industrialist fixtures, reclaimed school chairs and mirrors, as well as flickering votive candles. Tables are closely packed or communal—the latter making it the ideal place to bring a big group and order one of everything.

Popular items may include succulent, head-on cereal prawns, Hainanese chicken, or savory carrot cake, a dish which bears little resemblance to the sweet American dessert. This version is fried in sweet soy sauce and packed with radish, fish, Chinese sausage and a flutter of chives. Sound odd? It's anything but.

The Clam

Seafood ✗✗

B3

420 Hudson St. (at Leroy St.)

Subway: Houston St
Phone: 212-242-7420
Web: www.theclamnyc.com
Price: $$

Lunch & dinner daily

Hugging a corner of the West Village, this shellfish charmer is courtesy of Mike Price and Joey Campanaro. The restaurant's huge windows flood the space with daylight, showing off exposed white brick walls and dark wood accents; by night, pretty sconces cast a soft cozy glow. You should be prepared to wait (and yes, it's worth it), but the bustling bar is a fun spot to gather with friends.

The focus at The Clam is, of course, its namesake ingredient, but the menu also features seafood, meat and vegetarian options. Try a delicious tangle of spaghetti and clams in a bright red sauce with glistening greens, chili pepper and scallions; or crispy sweet pea risotto balls served over charred onion-chili crema. The gingerbread ice cream sandwich is unbeatable.

Cotenna

Italian

B3

21 Bedford St. (bet. Downing & Houston Sts.)

Subway: Houston St   Lunch & dinner daily
Phone: 646-861-0175
Web: n/a
Price: $$

Cotenna arrives on the New York restaurant scene courtesy of seasoned chef, Roberto Passon, a veteran on the city's food landscape. Tucked inside a tiny spot in a charming nook of the Village, Cotenna makes up for its diminutive size with a big personality, homey décor (wine and prosciutto line the walls) and warm service.

Everything here—from the pastas to the *cicchetti*, *contorni* and *carpaccio e zuppe*—is executed with great care, employs excellent ingredients, and is reasonably priced. *Vongole originate*, that classic Italo-American dish, finds new life with a delicate breadcrumb stuffing and loads of lemon and oregano. And save room for the *polpette pomodoro* or any of the flat-out delicious pastas—especially the soft, pillowy *gnocchi sorrentina*.

Crispo

Italian

B1

240 W. 14th St. (bet. Seventh & Eighth Aves.)

Subway: 14 St (Seventh Ave.)   Dinner nightly
Phone: 212-229-1818
Web: www.crisporestaurant.com
Price: $$

Tucked just below street level, this low-lit Italian-American restaurant boasts a Mediterranean vibe, not to mention a warm bonhomie not usually found along bustling 14th Street. Inside, you'll find low ceilings crossed by dark wood beams and brick walls adorned with artwork. Wood-framed windows open up to a little jewel box terrazzo and deep in the rear, a small semi-open kitchen completes the rustic look.

The menu at Crispo offers a solid range of traditional entrées, along with a nice antipasto selection and handful of daily specials. Pastas are always a good bet—plump ravioli are stuffed with creamy spinach and savory braised short rib, then laced in a nutty and buttery red wine sauce studded with mushroom as well as shaved parmesan.

DOMODOMO

B4

138 W. Houston St. (bet. MacDougal & Sullivan Sts.)

Subway: Houston St   Dinner nightly
Phone: 646-707-0301
Web: www.domodomonyc.com
Price: $$

Situated just below street level, DOMODOMO is sleek and lovely, with carefully constructed wood furnishings and a long, smooth blonde wood counter. The buzz at the bar is magnetizing, and service is stellar with each sitting, as diners are presented with a small bowl of water and cleansing hand towel.

Sushi is plentiful in New York, of course, but this kitchen ups the ante of their hand rolls with top-notch nori, rice, and fish. The cutting techniques are just as flawless, and while some combinations are familiar and others quirky and inspired, each roll is filled with an array of pristine ingredients. Highlights include spicy salmon with grilled tomato; finely chopped tuna with wasabi; and light, perfectly crisp shrimp tempura with mango salsa.

Empellón Taqueria

D1

230 W. 4th St. (at 10th St.)

Subway: Christopher St - Sheridan Sq   Lunch Thu– Sun
Phone: 212-367-0999   Dinner nightly
Web: www.empellon.com
Price: $$

If you build it, they will come: straddling a prime corner of the West Village, Empellón Taqueria packs them in most nights of the week—catering to a spirited group of young diners who arrive both solo and in groups. The draw is Chef/owner Alex Stupak's outstanding tacos, but the hip spot itself, which is awash in vibrant artwork, whitewashed walls and long communal tables, is also a big part of the fun.

Here the menu presents a wide and varied selection of tacos, which run the gamut from authentic to progressive—though anyone wishing to explore the kitchen's formidable talent should do a little wandering. And finally, foodies won't want to miss the nutty, verdant guacamole or the crackerjack salsas so savory and transcendent, they are worth trying as is.

EN Japanese Brasserie

Japanese   🍴🍴🍴

B3

435 Hudson St. (at Leroy St.)

Subway: Houston St
Phone: 212-647-9196
Web: www.enjb.com
Price: $$$

Lunch & dinner daily

EN doesn't pander to the spicy tuna-loving set, but effectively pays homage to highly seasonal Japanese cooking. In such simple and delicate food, flawless execution is a must so don't be hesitant to ask for a recommendation. The knowledgeable and genuine servers are happy to offer their opinion on items, be it the ground Kurobuta pork mixed with *natto*; or gently fried *agedashi* tofu floating in a thick, glossy dashi with mushrooms. Silken *chawanmushi* in a glazed stone cup is paired with kernels of charred corn for a delightful bit of bite, while Aburi sea trout is fanned sashimi-style across a striking onyx plate.

Lofty ceilings, large windows, and a glass wall lined with shelves of sake attract a young, professional, and fashionable clientele.

Extra Virgin

Mediterranean   🍴🍴

B2

259 W. 4th St. (at Perry St.)

Subway: Christopher St - Sheridan Sq
Phone: 212-691-9359
Web: www.extravirginrestaurant.com
Price: $$

Lunch & dinner daily

Thanks to its idyllic West Village setting, this is where the beautiful people go to eat beautifully. Everything is effortless, pleasant, and as smooth as the Jack Daniels caramel sauce drizzled on a warm buttery apple tart at meal's end. Regulars may seem to pop in and out of the friendly bar area, but visiting mortals need weekend reservations.

Start with a salad of roasted beets, crisp endive, and grassy watercress in apple-vinaigrette capped with a coin of pistachio-crusted goat cheese. Classic daily specials are always a hit, like Monday's baked lasagna, Tuesday's Bourbon-glazed meatloaf, or Wednesday's lemon sole almondine served with cauliflower gratin and tender haricots verts. On Sundays, swing by for a nice big bowl of spaghetti and meatballs.

Fedora

Contemporary XX

B2

239 W. 4th St. (bet. Charles & 10th Sts.)

Subway: Christopher St - Sheridan Sq
Phone: 646-449-9336
Web: www.fedoranyc.com
Price: $$$

Dinner nightly

An ode to the New York old guard, Fedora still attracts the creative, the moneyed and the young. It's a sort of dreamlike supper club where well-crafted cocktails flow into endless conversations, the words absorbed into the crevices of the original carved wooden bar as they have for generations. No longer a renowned literati haunt, Fedora remains an attractive homage to the Village of yore.

Tuck your bag and coat into the cubby above the banquette and set off on an adventure in contemporary cuisine, one that mixes barbecue cream with smoked salmon and highlights the distinctive wines of Jura. This builds to the excellent and gargantuan crispy duck with perfectly lacquered skin accented by a date-barbecue sauce that's pure hedonistic inspiration.

Freud

Austrian XX

C4

506 La Guardia Pl. (bet. Bleecker & Houston Sts.)

Subway: Bleecker St
Phone: 212-777-0327
Web: www.freudnyc.com
Price: $$

Lunch & dinner daily

The hospitality is warm and food irresistible at this welcoming spot on LaGuardia Place, flanking NYU's sprawling footprint. Inside, you'll find a décor that's part-rustic part-bistro and the sum is something elegant and familiar. The bar boasts sensational flower arrangements; and the wines by the glass are particularly unique. At Freud, you're meant to linger.

The Austrian-German menu is small but gorgeously executed by Eduard Frauneder. Following suit, the kitchen consistently delivers ingredients and dishes that go beyond nostalgia. And though the desserts ring familiar, Frauneder's versions are an absolute must. This especially after such comforting mains as dark rye späetzle and silky Hemlock hen, served over buckwheat porridge studded with greens.

Manhattan ▶ Greenwich & West Village

159

Gato

Mediterranean ✕✕

C4

324 Lafayette St. (bet. Bleecker & Houston Sts.)

Subway: Bleecker St.
Phone: 212-334-6400
Web: www.gatonyc.com
Price: $$

Dinner nightly

Bobby Flay's gorgeous Gato is a great place to kick off a Saturday night in the Big Apple, though you certainly won't be the only one with that idea. Models, city-slickers, and bearded locals alike pile into this Rockwell Group-designed space, though the enormous and industrial-chic interior—with its big, bustling bar and humming open kitchen—can certainly handle the volume.

Don't skip the Bites Menu, a must-do starter where you get to choose three openers from a long list of creative combinations like an eleven-layer potato cube, tucked with luscious cream, butter and loads of garlic. Then linger over a chorizo crépinette featuring bright apricot *mostarda*; or a white bean spread, folded with feta, garlic and walnut-piquillo relish.

Good

American ✕✕

B2

89 Greenwich Ave. (bet. Bank & 12th Sts.)

Subway: 14 St - 8 Av
Phone: 212-691-8080
Web: www.goodrestaurantnyc.com
Price: $$

Lunch Tue – Sun
Dinner nightly

Creamy walls and lime green wainscoting frame this cozy and comfortable little slice of Americana that has been pleasing Greenwich Village residents since 2000. Good also happens to be great for date night—the intimate bar pours top-shelf spirits and the muted dining room is dressed with crisp white linens. Everything has a certain serenity, even when it's bubbling at happy hour.

Chef/owner Steven J. Picker's menu puts his own signature on tempting seasonal cooking. Beautifully seared squid and Japanese eggplant grilled until silky are adorned with summer beans, cherry tomatoes, and mint. Turkey scallopini is crisp and light, set atop a bed of frisée, shaved celery, and *ricotta salata*. Long live the tortilla-crusted, jalapeño-kicked mac and cheese!

Gotham Bar and Grill

American XXX

D2

12 E. 12th St. (bet. Fifth Ave. & University Pl.)

Subway: 14 St - Union Sq
Phone: 212-620-4020
Web: www.gothambarandgrill.com
Price: $$$

Lunch Mon – Fri
Dinner nightly

Warm, personable, and genuine, this elegant idol has everything a New York restaurant needs to stand the test of time. Inside, find towering floral arrangements and lofty ceilings hung with fabric-draped fixtures, which soften the room's appearance. The interior is vast, but the sunken dining area, elevated bar, and smartly divided room feel more classic than overdone. The service team exemplifies on-the-ball excellence.

This kitchen's distinctive seasonal American cooking is a reminder that good food never goes out of style. Begin with the clean and bright flavors of a simple-sounding seafood salad combining succulent shrimp, tender lobster meat, and grilled Spanish octopus in citrus vinaigrette garnished with salad greens. Move on to explore pasta like Taleggio-filled tortellini in a creamy sauce dotted with butternut squash and tender chopped chicken. Desserts alone are worth a visit, especially to indulge in the elegant and picture-perfect apple tarte Tatin for two, filled with fruit so tender their centers are as lush as custard. Caramelized juices oozing from the apples lend complex flavor to the flaky golden pastry crust.

The greenmarket lunch prix-fixe offers superb value and quality.

Günter Seeger NY ✿

Contemporary ✗✗✗

B1

641 Hudson St. (bet. Gansevoort & Horatio Sts.)

Subway: 14 St - 8 Av   Dinner Mon – Sat
Phone: 646-657-0045
Web: www.gunterseegerny.com
Price: $$$$

&

Downtown New York will always be a place for contemporary fine dining, but Chef Seeger boldly goes against the tide of others offering serious cooking in casual settings. Here, find a dining room that feels like a part of his own home, decorated with his own artwork, wine collection, floral arrangements, and tiered drum chandeliers covered in rosy fabric. Much of the staff wear a formal mien and the orchestrated service reflects that—as do their uniforms, which are as serious as American Gothic, but still modern.

Local farmers and producers influence the nightly tasting menu with exquisite ingredients that shine in the kitchen's very capable hands. This is the eponymous chef's first foray into NY's dining scene (he is still a household name in his previous home city of Atlanta). And here he crafts a seasonal cuisine that is refined and elegant, yet also restrained and muted. Highlights include a cool and intensely fresh snap pea gazpacho with wild mint and shallots, followed by a supremely tender beef tenderloin in a pinot noir-jus reduction.

Desserts like the *rote grütze* (red groats) with vanilla cream and green juniper berries make it immediately clear why this is a kitchen of serious standing.

Gradisca

Italian

 C2

126 W. 13th St. (bet. Sixth & Seventh Aves.)

Subway: 14 St (Seventh Ave.) Dinner nightly
Phone: 212-691-4886
Web: www.gradiscanyc.com
Price: $$

 If one could choose an Italian mother, it would be *"mamma,"* the pasta maker at Gradisca. Walking into this quaint brownstone is like taking a step into a trattoria in Emila Romagna, complete with Fellini posters, napkin-covered bread baskets, and a smiling bartender pouring a glass of violet-scented Sangiovese. Pasta plays front and center here and is luckily always handmade. Gorgeous, rose-shaped tortellini are stuffed with mounds of *prosciutto* and spinach, before being finished with a perfect plum tomato sauce. *Secondi* are also a must and may include the sublime *cotoletta alla Bolognese*, a perfectly breaded and pan-fried free-range chicken cutlet topped with a creamy truffle-béchamel and served with a warm spinach *budino*.

Hakata Tonton

Japanese

D1

61 Grove St. (bet. Bleecker St. & Seventh Ave. South)

Subway: Christopher St - Sheridan Sq Dinner nightly
Phone: 212-242-3699
Web: N/A
Price: $$

A serious devotion to pork and Japanese spirit is what makes this Kyushu soul food different from anything else around.

The restaurant may have expanded, but the hopping front room still feels tight with close tables, a small counter and service that is, well, pretty bad. Then again, you are all here for the pork, which is impeccable. Hot pots are a must, but they may need to simmer on your tabletop burner for 20 minutes before eating, so go ahead and munch on a grilled pig's foot served in a bowl with yuzu rind and vinegar sauce. Then, dive into that wonderfully savory pork broth bobbing with vegetables, scallions, tofu, dumplings, pork belly, and much more.

The reasonably priced tasting menu is the best way to explore their range of interesting items.

Hecho en Dumbo

Mexican ✗

D4

354 Bowery (bet. 4th & Great Jones Sts.)

Subway: Bleecker St
Phone: 212-937-4245
Web: www.hechoendumbo.com
Price: $$

Lunch Sat – Sun
Dinner nightly

Even after happy hour ends and the margaritas are a few dollars more, the crowds continue to flock here for reliably excellent Mexican fare. Weekend waits can be long and that happy hour is one of the area's best, so expect a lively atmosphere. While it may be theoretically possible to fend off the need to order guacamole the moment you enter, give into it. Cool, creamy, and delicious, dotted with white onion, slivers of fiery jalapeño and cilantro, it is the best way to enjoy their fantastic tortilla chips. Then mouthwatering tacos arrive fully loaded with the likes of tender ribeye, cilantro, onions, and a squeeze of lime alongside an array of salsas.

The highlight however may be the open kitchen in the back, serving the "chef's table" its own prix-fixe.

High Street on Hudson

American ✗✗

B2

637 Hudson St. (at Horatio St.)

Subway: 14 St - 8 Av
Phone: 917-388-3944
Web: www.highstreetonhudson.com
Price: $$

Lunch daily
Dinner Wed – Sun

Fresh off the success of their wildly popular Philadelphia restaurant, High Street on Market, Chef Eli Kulp has opened up this lovely little spot, just steps south of MePa to well-deserved acclaim. Breakfast, lunch and dinner are available, with a focus on grains, sandwiches and wickedly good homemade breads.

This airy and entertaining corner space is bright and welcoming, with a fully open kitchen and small side counter to view the action within. Grilled cheese finds delicious refinement in thick slices of homemade roasted potato bread, aged cheddar and delicious cultured butter. Roasted, perfectly singed broccoli is tossed with herbed mayo and paired with juicy blistered grapes, shaved cucumber, radicchio and spicy, toasted Marcona almonds.

Il Buco

Italian

D4

47 Bond St. (bet. Bowery & Lafayette St.)

Subway: Bleecker St
Phone: 212-533-1932
Web: www.ilbuco.com
Price: $$

Lunch Mon – Sat
Dinner nightly

Il Buco is a *molto* charming amalgam of antique knickknacks, porcelain dishes, and polished copper pots. The hardest seats to nab are found downstairs, but the rustic dining room remains as inviting as ever, with tables full of vittles and *vino*. The kitchen showcases meticulously sourced ingredients that sing the praises of regional Italian know-how, like a mound of arugula, petite mustards, and chrysanthemum greens that top a rather tiny veal Milanese cooked to moist perfection. Thick ribbons of toothsome homemade tagliatelle tossed with myriad mushrooms, melted leeks, and pecorino emit a lovely aroma, befitting this unique and pretty pearl. Meanwhile, the porchetta—served once a year as a sort of sidewalk celebration—is still one of the best in town.

Il Buco Alimentari e Vineria

Italian

D4

53 Great Jones St. (bet. Bowery & Lafayette St.)

Subway: Bleecker St
Phone: 212-837-2622
Web: www.ilbucovineria.com
Price: $$

Lunch & dinner daily

This is the kind of cooking and scene that makes us all wish we were Italian. Start with a stroll through the *alimentari* (located up front) to grab some pickled beans and serious cheeses. Then, head towards the rustic dining area in the back, which oozes warmth and comfort. Note the meticulously conceived copper roof, open kitchen, and other decorative accents that set a picturesque backdrop for a delicious meal. The food here is authoritative and tasty, with a nice representation of Italian cooking from breakfast through dinner. The porchetta *panino* is timeless, amazing and vies to be the finest around. Skillfully crafted pasta includes textbook-perfect *bucatini cacio e pepe*. Finish with an *affogato*, topping a scoop of vanilla gelato with hot espresso.

I Sodi

C1

Italian ✗✗

105 Christopher St. (bet. Bleecker & Hudson Sts.)

Subway: Christopher St - Sheridan Sq   Dinner nightly
Phone: 212-414-5774
Web: www.isodinyc.com
Price: $$

Manhattan has classic Italian and new Italian, but not many *thoughtful* Italian restaurants. Tuscany native Rita Sodi is out to change that with this trattoria. She consciously selected every aspect of the design, from the linen napkins to the thick, striated glass windows that hide the modern space from the marauding groups of young people on Christopher Street.

Inside this oasis, Negronis prep palates for al dente rigatoni and hearty, meat-focused dishes like the *coniglio in porchetta*. This exceptional rabbit preparation combines bacon-wrapped loin with a sweet wine- rosemary- and garlic-sauce. The herbal quality of such savoriness brings out the almost austere nature of the lean rabbit, showing how truly intuitive and innovative Italian cooking can be.

Joseph Leonard

D1

Contemporary ✗

170 Waverly Pl. (at Grove St.)

Subway: Christopher St - Sheridan Sq   Lunch & dinner daily
Phone: 646-429-8383
Web: www.josephleonard.com
Price: $$

Seven years into the game, this tiny West Village charmer tucked into a sweet corner location on a historic block, is still packing them in every night. Sure, the happy hour is a good enough deal to warrant a weekly visit and yes, the staff is ultra kind and professional. But, the real deal with Joseph Leonard is that it's hard to go wrong with their clear, focused and delightful menu—whether you're inclined toward fish, meat or the smaller vegetable plates.

After a dabble with the ever-changing vegetable appetizers, try your hand at a tender poblano pepper stuffed with quinoa, black bean purée and cojita cheese, then laced in a smoky tomato sauce. Round it all out with a decadent three-layer slab of carrot cake with ample cream cheese frosting.

Kesté Pizza & Vino

Pizza 🍴

D2

271 Bleecker St. (bet. Cornelia & Jones Sts.)

Subway: W 4 St - Wash Sq Lunch & dinner daily
Phone: 212-243-1500
Web: www.kestepizzeria.com
Price: 🍴🍴

Mamma mia! New York's love affair with Kesté shows no sign of stopping. This kitchen begins with a puffy, blistered crust that's perfectly salty and tangy, then tops it with ingredients like roasted butternut squash purée, smoked mozzarella and basil. And while its ingredients seem to have taken a small hit in recent years, that crust is still on point.

Co-owner Roberto Caporuscio presides over the American chapter of Associazione Pizzaiuoli Napoletani, and his daughter, Giorgia, oversees the in-house pizza making operations. Diners can choose from more than 22 pizzas (including a few gluten-free options), a roster of *calzoni*, and nightly pie specials.

The restaurant is teeny-tiny, but diners are encouraged to linger, in true Italian hospitality.

Kiin Thai 😊

Thai 🍴🍴

C3

36 E. 8th St. (bet. Greene St. & University Pl.)

Subway: 8 St - NYU Lunch & dinner daily
Phone: 212-529-2363
Web: www.kiinthaieatery.com
Price: $$

Smack in the middle of NYU turf and on a street choking with fast-casual eateries, Kiin Thai cuts an impressive figure design-wise, with its lofty ceilings and light-filled interior. While value-driven lunch specials might on occasion affect quality, the kitchen continues to push out precise renditions of Central and Northern Thai dishes.

Khao soi is a gorgeous orange-hued curry with chewy noodles, tender braised chicken, hard-boiled egg, and the requisite condiments needed to amp the dish up to an incendiary level. Other faves include fish *hor mok*—a custardy curry with striped sea bass, coconut milk, and duck eggs—topped with herbs and Makrut lime; or the excellent *hor nueng gai* with chicken, Thai eggplant, and rice, delicately steamed in banana leaf.

Kosaka

C2

220 W. 13th St. (bet. Greenwich & Seventh Aves.)

Subway: 14 St (Seventh Ave.)
Phone: 212-727-1709
Web: www.kosakanyc.com
Price: $$$$

Dinner Tue – Sat

Lauded chef Yoshihiko Kousaka, formerly of Jewel Bako, takes the wheel at this wonderful sushi house, partnering with Key Kim and Mihyun Han to offer two shimmering and new omakase menus. The room is sleek and modern, with a handsome Japanese sensibility and a counter for 12, along with three small tables. A relaxed, but deeply attentive service staff rounds out this wonderful little gem.

Much of the fish laid out over the course of the night is imported from Tokyo's Tsukiji Fish Market, though some of it is procured from local purveyors. But each bright, immaculate slice—be it King salmon with smoked soy sauce, scallop with sea grapes and yuzu, or kelp-cured and pressed striped jack—is wildly fresh, cut-to-order, and seasoned with the lightest hand possible.

Lafayette

D4

380 Lafayette St. (at Great Jones St.)

Subway: Bleecker St
Phone: 212-533-3000
Web: www.lafayetteny.com
Price: $$

Lunch & dinner daily

Chef Andrew Carmellini's homage to French cuisine lures patrons inside with its attractive baked-goods counter up front lined with organic breads and tempting pastries. From here, the room unfolds into a series of seductive spaces where one finds a rotisserie oven spinning bronzed birds, a backlit bar with an amber glow, and columns clad in warm honey and blue tile.

The cooking is nothing short of stellar, right from that Niçoise salad with thick slices of rare tuna, briny black olives, barely poached green beans, soft potatoes, and hard-boiled egg, to a local fillet of trout finished with mustard sauce and well-dressed frisée salad. Desserts are borderline irresistible, especially the mille-feuille Lafayette with chocolate crémeux and caramel-poached pear.

L'Artusi

Italian

228 W. 10th St. (bet. Bleecker & Hudson Sts.)

Subway: Christopher St - Sheridan Sq
Phone: 212-255-5757
Web: www.lartusi.com
Price: $$

Lunch Sun
Dinner nightly

This polished, airy West Village charmer is a magnet for beautiful people—or maybe it's just that everyone looks gorgeous in L'Artusi's romantically lit room, divvied up into three dining options and a quiet mezzanine, alongside its more traditional dining area. A semi-open kitchen, polished and gleaming with stainless steel, pushes out wickedly good Italian dishes like tender potato gnocchi in a rabbit cacciatore, laced with garlic, sweet tomato, rosemary and sage; or perfectly charred octopus paired with creamy potatoes spiked with chilies, olives and savory pancetta.

Polish that off with a drink from their generous list of *aperitivi* or fantastic selection of wines by the glass, and you'll be feeling quite beautiful yourself by dinner's end.

Las Ramblas

Spanish

170 W. 4th St. (bet. Cornelia & Jones Sts.)

Subway: Christopher St - Sheridan Sq
Phone: 646-415-7924
Web: www.lasramblasnyc.com
Price:

Lunch Sat – Sun
Dinner nightly

Sandwiched among a throng of attention-seeking storefronts, mighty little Las Ramblas is easy to spot, just look for the crowd of happy, munching faces. The scene spills out onto the sidewalk when the weather allows.

Named for Barcelona's historic commercial thoroughfare, Las Ramblas is a tapas treat. A copper-plated bar and collection of tiny tables provide a perch for snacking on an array of earnestly prepared items. Check out the wall-mounted blackboard for *especiales*. Bring friends (it's that kind of place) to fully explore the menu, which serves up delights such as succulent head-on prawns roasted in a terra-cotta dish and sauced with cava vinegar, ginger, and basil; or béchamel creamed spinach topped by a molten cap of Mahón cheese.

Left Bank

B2

Contemporary 🗶🗶

117 Perry St. (at Greenwich St.)

Subway: Christopher St - Sheridan Sq

Phone: 212-727-1170

Web: www.leftbanknewyork.com

Price: $$

Dinner nightly

This idyllic neighborhood spot is still in high demand and packed with "locals." Its near-bucolic Village setting and faux-farmhouse décor are a perfect match for the pleasure-driven cooking. A rotating selection of art makes the whitewashed walls stand out.

Be sure to begin with the "nosh" section—a changing array of *bruschette* can be a meal unto itself while lightly poached shrimp and heirloom tomatoes served on a thick slab of sourdough bread with basil and a sprinkle of parmesan feels so right. The "bar steak" is practically a standard order, cooked to a perfect medium rare and served with herb butter and *chimichurri* over crisp French fries. Desserts are simple and well-made, like the creamy ricotta cheesecake with poached pear and fruit preserve.

Le Gigot

D2

French 🗶🗶

18 Cornelia St. (bet. Bleecker & W. 4th Sts.)

Subway: W 4 St - Wash Sq

Phone: 212-627-3737

Web: www.legigotrestaurant.com

Price: $$$

Lunch & dinner Tue – Sun

At first glance, Le Gigot transports guests to an inviting little family-owned bistro—the kind you'd only find in *La Ville-Lumière*. The service exceeds expectations with uncharacteristic warmth that brings a welcoming vibe to the nostalgic dining room.

Tasty renditions of classic bistro fare dominate the menu, so expect the cooking to be familiar and pleasing. The *petit bouillabaisse* begins as a saffron fish broth with a red-peppery North African accent to elevate the traditional fish and seafood dish. Their cassoulet is a beloved Toulousaine version with duck confit, bacon, cannellini beans, herbs, and luscious pork. Finally, brioche pudding conjures all that is simple and good in a dessert, with crème anglaise, berries, and whipped cream.

The Little Owl

American ✗

B3

90 Bedford St. (at Grove St.)

Subway: Christopher St - Sheridan Sq
Phone: 212-741-4695
Web: www.thelittleowlnyc.com
Price: $$

Lunch & dinner daily

Straddling a picturesque corner of the West Village, with a name that could charm the pants off the grizzliest city diner, The Little Owl has a lot going for it up front. Light pours from the windows as people stand outside, catching up and chatting with friends. Inside, bright flowers dot the quaint room; and a thoughtful service staff ushers you through your meal.

And then there's Chef Joey Campanaro, who hits his seasonal menu out of the park, weaving top-notch ingredients into comforting fare that's as rustic as it is disciplined. An Italian wedding soup is sourced from local urban gardens and loaded with tender little *polpettine*; while a beautifully seared halibut arrives with fluffy chive-mashed potatoes and a drizzle of lemon crème fraîche.

Lupa 😋

Italian ✗✗

C4

170 Thompson St. (bet. Bleecker & Houston Sts.)

Subway: W 4 St - Wash Sq
Phone: 212-982-5089
Web: www.luparestaurant.com
Price: $$

Lunch & dinner daily

Is there anything more lovely than a lazy weekend lunch at Batali and Bastianich's Lupa? You'd be hard-pressed to convince the regulars who flock here in droves day and night for the amicable service, interesting wines, and otherworldly pasta.

Everything on the menu is so lovingly sourced: witness a warm spinach and pancetta salad tossing a perfect mix of vibrant greens with warm, smoky bacon; or starter of plump, marinated sardines laced with oil and coarse salt and served over a bed of miniscule cubes of cucumber and celery. But the star of the show remains the pasta, which may reveal decadent bavette *cacio e pepe,* a classic dish from Lazio. It's nothing short of sweet satisfaction, dotted with sharp pecorino and freshly ground black pepper.

Malaparte

B2

Italian

753 Washington St. (at Bethune St.)

Subway: 14 St - 8 Av
Phone: 212-255-2122
Web: www.malapartenyc.com
Price: **$$**

Lunch Sat – Sun
Dinner nightly

Tucked into one of those idyllic, tree-lined West Village corners that looks straight off a movie set, Malaparte is the kind of cozy, romantic spot you need in your date night rolodex. Bare wood tables; large, framed windows for people-watching; low lighting; and exposed brick walls all lend a hand in creating that perfect *osteria* vibe.

As if that weren't enough to sustain a loyal following, Malaparte takes its home-style Italian cooking to the next level. Try one of the excellent pizza specials; the *dadi di tonno scottato*, a dish of wildly fresh seared tuna tossed in avocado-sesame dressing; the bang-on lasagna Bolognese, a silky version of this classic dish boasting an exquisitely good veal and pork ragù; or the melt-in-your-mouth chocolate mousse.

Margaux

C3

Mediterranean

5 W. 8th St. (bet. Fifth & Sixth Aves.)

Subway: W 4 St - Wash Sq
Phone: 212-321-0111
Web: www.margauxnyc.com
Price: **$$**

Lunch & dinner daily

Tucked away on the bottom floor of the Martlon Hotel, with a clientele that looks like it just stepped off the cover of Hamptons Magazine, Margaux is like walking into a bit of Paris in the best possible way. Curved banquettes line the wall, porcelain potted plants abound, and the bar—furnished with red leather stools and clever art posters—is worth a visit alone.

Begin with a gorgeous chilled gazpacho, drizzled with excellent Sicilian olive oil and finished with torn basil. Then move on to delicate spaghetti pocked with plump Manila clams, tender spigarello, garlic and a flutter of chili pepper, before relishing a seared slice of Arctic char served over blistered cherry tomatoes, summer squash, grilled asparagus and blanched pea leaves.

Market Table

American ✗✗

B3

54 Carmine St. (at Bedford St.)

Subway: W 4 St - Wash Sq
Phone: 212-255-2100
Web: www.markettablenyc.com
Price: $$

Lunch & dinner daily

Think of this bright little corner as the template for a perfect neighborhood restaurant—one that everyone dreams of having nearby. The vibe is unpretentious yet cool, with a young, attentive service staff. The windowed room feels barnyard-chic, with a chalkboard wall listing wine and cheese offerings beneath reclaimed ceiling beams.

The menu is stocked with the kind of dishes that never disappoint—think bucatini tossed with fried eggplant and creamy burrata in a chunky tomato sauce. The kitchen's knack for making simple food vivid is clear in the impeccably cooked strip loin, served with carrots, haricots verts, and shishitos brought together with smoked chili "pesto." "Take it easy" and choose to end your meal with either a liquid or solid dessert.

Mary's Fish Camp

Seafood ✗

B2

64 Charles St. (at W. 4th St.)

Subway: Christopher St - Sheridan Sq
Phone: 646-486-2185
Web: www.marysfishcamp.com
Price: $$

Lunch & dinner Mon – Sat

This West Village seafood shack is much more than just a destination for lobster rolls. Located on an irresistibly cute corner with large windows, Mary's Fish Camp tempts with creative daily specials scrawled on a chalkboard, sweet and briny raw offerings, and nostalgic desserts like hot fudge sundaes. Crowds pack into the curving stainless steel counter while white, lazy fans spin overhead.

The summery space offers lots of choice, but the lobster roll should not be overlooked. A toasted bun is overflowing with hunks of tender, sweet meat dressed in the perfect proportion of mayonnaise and lemon juice, with a mountain of shoestring fries on the side. Begin the meal with spicy Key West conch chowder and then end with a slice of Americana—banana cream pie.

173

Mimi

C4

185 Sullivan St. (bet. Bleecker & Houston Sts.)

Subway: Spring St (Sixth Ave.)
Phone: 212-418-1260
Web: www.miminyc.com
Price: $$$

Lunch Sun
Dinner nightly

Lucky are the diners who get to call this cozy bistro their neighborhood spot, for manning the kitchen is the passionate 25-year-old chef, Liz Johnson. It's a postage stamp-sized bistro—the tables are tight and a small bar welcomes walk-ins—but the look and feel of Mimi's is warm and classic. Find fresh flowers lining the room and a service staff that's as unobtrusive as it is efficient.

Johnson's seasonal menu changes frequently, but dinner might begin with a thick slice of *pâté en croute*, the peppercorn-studded pâté surrounded by silky liver mousse; or firm, pickled Kohada (a fish in the Herring family) draped over puffs of *pommes dauphine*. Finally, *gnocchi Parisienne* is laced in brandade cream with watercress, stewed peppers and tender sweet corn.

Miss Lily's

C4

132 W. Houston St. (at Sullivan St.)

Subway: Houston St
Phone: 646-588-5375
Web: www.misslilysnyc.com
Price: $$

Lunch & dinner daily

Authentic Jamaican flavors and thumping reggae go hand-in-hand amid Miss Lily's bright orange booths, retro artifacts, and Formica-topped tables. Wide-open windows overlooking buzzy Houston Street merely add to the allure. A well-stocked bar and bins filled with produce set the mood for enjoyable classics brought to you at the hands of glam servers.

Start with jerk chicken that is insanely moist yet nearly black with intense spices, served with a Scotch bonnet sauce that will have your mouth tingling for hours. Then cool down with Melvin's "body good" salad tossing kale, radish, celery, and apples in a citrus-ginger vinaigrette. From the Jamaican Sampler—think curry goat, oxtail stew, and callaloo—to a boozy rum cake, this Caribbean queen reigns supreme.

Minetta Tavern

Gastropub 🍴

113 MacDougal St. (at Minetta Ln.)

Subway: W 4 St - Wash Sq
Phone: 212-475-3850
Web: www.minettatavernny.com
Price: **$$$**

Lunch Wed – Sun
Dinner nightly

While this circa 1937 setting has been restored and refreshed, nothing here changes and that is its beauty. This quintessential New York tavern is still surrounded by dark wood, checkerboard tiled floors, and those framed caricatures. The astute service team handles the crowds and energy as well as ever—they even don the same white-aproned livery seen in *Mad Men*. It's that kind of place.

The menu's dedication to bistro classics (like oxtail and foie gras terrine) and New York steakhouse fare ensure its longevity. Trust them to prepare a steak tartare that is beyond textbook perfect, comprised here of pristine beef tenderloin, anchovy, capers and more, crowned with a tiny quail's egg. This kitchen has a way with meat that goes far beyond the burger on everyone's lips, thanks to beef that promises the deep, telltale flavors of dry-aging. Their massive pork chops draped in *sauce charcutière* have an intense crust that is blackened but never burnt, concealing a juicy interior that is no small feat for such a large piece of meat.

The bittersweet chocolate soufflé is, was, and probably always will be crowd-pleasing and delicious, especially when served with a melting scoop of Bourbon-pecan ice cream.

Nix ⣿

Vegetarian ✗✗

72 University Pl. (bet. 10th & 11th Sts.)

Subway: 14 St - Union Sq   Dinner nightly
Phone: 212-498-9393
Web: www.nixny.com
Price: $$$

Named for the 19th century Supreme Court case that ultimately decided tomatoes are indeed a vegetable, Nix is a bright young starlet backed by some heavy hitters. Chefs John Fraser (of Dovetail's beloved meatless Mondays) and Nicolas Farias are crafting a vegetarian cuisine that makes you wonder if meat might be holding back vegetables—here they shine without it.

The service team is as on-point and well-versed as a letter from the editor (Condé Nast's former Editorial Director is a partner and frequently oversees the dining room). No surprise that it fills with a unique crowd of fashionista foodies that are as visually appealing as those light fixtures sculpted from juniper roots. Green plants and skylights keep everything looking healthy and bright—it's a welcoming scene.

The two à la carte menus offer intriguing vegetarian options or a more concise vegan one, which has many of the same compositions minus the dairy. Playful highlights include crisply charred avocado *a la plancha* served in a pool of tomato water, salted and spiked with jalapeño, finished with bits of fresh mozzarella. Fuji apple sorbet begins as a fragrant dessert, then pops with the inventive flavors of candied olive and lime.

Pagani

 Italian

 289 Bleecker St. (at Seventh Ave. South)

Subway: Christopher St - Sheridan Sq   Lunch & dinner daily
Phone: 212-488-5800
Web: www.paganinyc.com
Price: $$

This charmer from a scion of the Lusardi family brings a much-needed jolt of romance to bustling Bleecker Street. With several other established restaurants under their watch, this family's experience shines in the details at Pagani. Here the ambience is hip and rustic (think reclaimed wood, distressed walls and white marble). There's a fully stocked bar churning out clever cocktails and killer Italian wines; and you can even catch live music several nights a week.

Start with the grilled artichokes featuring toasted walnuts, mint and lemon zest. And, then take time to enjoy the house-made *ricciatelle* folded in a light mushroom sauce with pignoli nuts, garlic and arugula; or juicy pork tenderloin paired with zucchini-studded risotto and sweet dried plums.

Panca

 Peruvian

 92 Seventh Ave. South (bet. Bleecker & Grove Sts.)

Subway: Christopher St - Sheridan Sq   Lunch & dinner daily
Phone: 212-488-3900
Web: www.pancany.com
Price: $$

First thing's first: go to the impressive wood bar lined with bottles of pisco and grab a handful of the wickedly good roasted Peruvian corn. Then settle into the rather lively and colorful dining room, or just ogle at the many *ceviche* options on the menu, another hallmark of the cuisine. If you choose to sit outside, be prepared to give up the interior's cantina-like vibe.

Explore the *tiradito* (think of it like *ceviche's* cousin), which highlights sashimi-like cuts of seafood like fluke, shrimp, and octopus served on a duo of peppery *aji amarillo* or *rocoto* sauces. Panca gives equal honor to those other pillars of its national cuisine, serving a cilantro-stewed chicken accompanied by pitch-perfect garlic rice and potatoes topped with salsa *criolla*.

Manhattan ▶ Greenwich & West Village

177

Paradou

B1

8 Little W. 12th St. (bet. Greenwich & Washington Sts.)

Subyway: 14 St - 8 Av
Phone: 212-463-8345
Web: www.paradounyc.com
Price: $$

Lunch Sat – Sun
Dinner Thu – Sun

For a restaurant that refuses to take itself too seriously, the crowd-pleasing bistro cuisine here is no joke. At home along a cobblestoned street in the clubby Meatpacking District, Paradou offers a handful of tables and a stocked bar. Move past the vintage French liquor ads and down a brick-lined hallway to find a year-round back garden outfitted with chandeliers, a high glass roof, and tables crafted from vintage wine crates.

The menu's foundation is Provençal cooking, but its lighthearted spirit feels free to stray. Begin with Amish bacon "crack"—chili-spiked bacon jerky made from Pennsylvania Amish pigs. The duck breast is expertly seared, with crisp skin and a pink center. Don't skip the springy crêpes, filled with Nutella and ripe bananas.

Pearl Oyster Bar

D2

18 Cornelia St. (bet. Bleecker & W. 4th Sts.)

Subway: W 4 St - Wash Sq
Phone: 212-691-8211
Web: www.pearloysterbar.com
Price: $$

Lunch Mon – Fri
Dinner Mon – Sat

It's not hard to find a lobster roll in this city, and for that we can thank Rebecca Charles. This seafood institution—inspired by Charles' childhood summers spent in Maine—has been stuffing sweet lobster meat into split-top rolls since 1997. The two-room setting offers a choice: counter seating or table service. Wood furnishings and white walls are low-key; beachy memorabilia perks up the space.

Start the meal by slurping your way through a classic chilled shellfish platter before tucking into that signature lobster roll, served alongside a tower of shoestring fries. The kitchen shines in daily specials, too, such as the grilled lobster served with corn pudding or pan-roasted wild bass. A hot fudge sundae is an appropriately nostalgic finish.

Piora

B3

430 Hudson St. (bet. Morton St. & St. Luke's Pl.)

Subway: Christopher St - Sheridan Sq
Phone: 212-960-3801
Web: www.pioranyc.com
Price: $$$

Dinner Tue – Sun

It's hard to tell from the name, but this delightful retreat has a distinctly polished, upscale and intimate sensibility. A simple glow from the window in the evening hints at the treats to come. Then make your way inside, and you'll find a gorgeous interior with a few communal tables, a marble-topped bar, as well as cozy two-tops. Designed by architect Stephanie Goto, the interior is a sophisticated blend of white, woods, and gorgeous branch-like light fixtures with exposed bulbs.

So yes, you'll be talking about the splendid décor, but rest assured as it won't be long before the first-rate food and graceful service catches your attention. Chris Cipollone is an accomplished chef, and his food is a marriage of equals between Italian and Asian. The result is sublime, refined and innovative fare.

Dinner must begin with hot, pillowy monkey bread served in a cast iron pot, dusted with sea salt and served with rosemary-scented *lardo* as well as roasted seaweed butter. From there, imagine black garlic- and squid ink-*bucatini* studded with meaty Dungeness crab, maitake mushrooms and Fresno chilies; or savory suckling pig with mustard seeds, grilled sweet onions, orange and oven-roasted cabbage.

Pó

 Italian **XX**

D2

31 Cornelia St. (bet. Bleecker & W. 4th Sts.)

Subway: W 4 St - Wash Sq   Lunch Wed – Sun
Phone: 212-645-2189   Dinner nightly
Web: www.porestaurant.com
Price: $$

Sometimes the best design begins with a simple and humble concept. Case in point: Po', a lovely spot with a cozy ambience; good wine list; charming staff; and excellent Italian food. By day, the narrow space feels open and airy—especially in summer, when they prop the windows open and ceiling fans swirl lazily overhead. Come nightfall, it's a date night dream, with low lighting and an old-fashioned romantic vibe.

Get your night started with *polpette di carne*, a trio of silky meatballs braised in tomato sauce with *caciocavallo* and a thatch of fresh herbs. And then move on to a tangle of spinach tagliatelle with a rich *ragù alla Bolognese*; or a succulent grilled pork chop, served over tender braised cabbage, with a pear-and-cranberry mostarda.

Quality Eats

American **XX**

C2

19 Greenwich Ave. (bet. Christopher & 10th Sts.)

Subway: Christopher St - Sheridan Sq   Lunch Wed – Sun
Phone: 212-337-9988   Dinner nightly
Web: www.qualityeats.com
Price: $$

This neighborhood tavern has the kind of food you could nosh on every day—and excellent versions of it, at that. Duck inside and you'll find a deep, narrow space with an elevated back dining room. Up front, a hip and hopping bar set amid a series of two-tops beckons lone diners and cozy lovebirds.

Steak plays a big role in this kitchen's menu—and rightfully so, for it's fantastic. But almost everything here, from the seasonal greens to the delicious sides and fresh-from-the-skillet monkey bread, aims to please. A bright, crisp spring pea salad gets a salty hit of pecorino and drizzle of vinaigrette; while a dish named Don Ameche (beautifully-seared filet mignon fanned over sourdough toast spread with creamy chicken liver mousse) is downright brilliant.

RedFarm

Asian ✕

B2

529 Hudson St. (bet. Charles & 10th Sts.)

Subway: Christopher St - Sheridan Sq	Lunch Sat – Sun
Phone: 212-792-9700	Dinner nightly
Web: www.redfarmnyc.com	
Price: $$	

The hot spot for upscale (and of the moment) Chinese food, RedFarm packs in the flavor, the noise, as well as the people. On any given night, the line will snake out the door, and a wait is inevitable to score a seat at their communal table in this industrial space. It's worth any hassle, though, when you sit down to experience the farm-to-table, Asian-fusion concept from big names in the business like Joe Ng & Ed Schoenfeld.

The freewheeling kitchen relishes experimenting with local ingredients. Try the bright green pea leaf and shrimp dumplings, which stand out beautifully in their near-translucent casing; or wok-fried Dungeness crab and crawfish in a thick and spicy basil-ginger sauce.

For some Peking duck fun, head downstairs to Decoy.

Ribalta 😋

Italian ✕✕

D3

48 E. 12th St. (bet. Broadway & University Pl.)

Subway: 14 St - Union Sq	Lunch & dinner daily
Phone: 212-777-7781	
Web: www.ribaltapizzarestaurant.com	
Price: $$	

It all starts with the dough. That said, Ribalta's mother version apparently started nearly a century ago and has been kept alive to feed the masses since. Today, it rises for 72 hours before being baked into a crust that is so light and digestible that you might be tempted to go for a second, very authentic Margherita, topped with that perfect balance of tomato sauce, mozzarella, olive oil, and basil. Pasta dishes are just as strong, so sample a duo of wonderfully tender gnocchi, thickly dressed in pesto or an excellent *penne rigate con ragù Napolitano* loaded with ground pork and beef.

The food may be substantial, but the space feels like *La Grande Mela* thanks to red leather banquettes, creatively tiled white walls, and planks suspended from the lofty ceiling.

Rockmeisha

Japanese

 D1

11 Barrow St. (bet. Seventh Ave. South & W. 4th St.)

Subway: Christopher St - Sheridan Sq Dinner Tue – Sun
Phone: 212-675-7775
Web: N/A
Price:

Tightly-packed bar height tables fill this tiny *izakaya*-style restaurant, a quirky canteen with a menu designed for fun. The young crowd sips Sapporo or sake against a soundtrack of old school rock; and the décor, not far behind, ranges from vinyl records to a framed beer ad featuring Japanese women in bathing suits. The space is cramped yet fun, the atmosphere lively and loose.

An appropriately moist leek omelet shows the kitchen's deft execution of simple dishes. Meaty, deep-fried chicken wings coated in a nose-tingling vinegar-based buffalo sauce are an optimal drinking accompaniment, as is a bowl of *chashu* ramen with milky pork bone broth, delicate noodles, pork belly, pickled ginger, sliced scallions, and a generous sprinkling of sesame seeds.

Santina

Seafood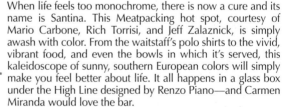

 B1

820 Washington St. (at Gansevoort St.)

Subway: 14 St - 8 Av Lunch & dinner daily
Phone: 212-254-3000
Web: www.santinanyc.com
Price: $$$$

When life feels too monochrome, there is now a cure and its name is Santina. This Meatpacking hot spot, courtesy of Mario Carbone, Rich Torrisi, and Jeff Zalaznick, is simply awash with color. From the waitstaff's polo shirts to the vivid, vibrant food, and even the bowls in which it's served, this kaleidoscope of sunny, southern European colors will simply make you feel better about life. It all happens in a glass box under the High Line designed by Renzo Piano—and Carmen Miranda would love the bar.

Notionally described as "Italian coastal cuisine," the food's about fish, vegetables, and sharing; and comes with an obvious health dividend. Be sure to start with *cecina* made with chickpea flour and try the surprisingly light rice and pasta dishes.

Saxon + Parole

Contemporary

D4

316 Bowery (at Bleecker St.)

Subway: Bleecker St
Phone: 212-254-0350
Web: www.saxonandparole.com
Price: $$$

Lunch Sat – Sun
Dinner nightly

Named after two 19th century racehorses, this spirited hipster-magnet is the creation of Executive Chef Brad Farmerie and the AvroKO Hospitality Group. Rich wood tones and warm lighting achieve a clubby atmosphere, from the buzzing long bar and communal table to the intimate, serene dining room's banquettes dressed with pristine linens.

Begin with a palate-pleasing surprise in cocktails like the celery gimlet. Then, sample rotating house-made "pots" filled with mousses like eggplant topped with a sweet-sour relish and taro chips, or chicken liver with port and pepper jelly served with grilled sourdough bread. Seared branzino over cranberry bean and kale stew with tomato-caper broth and shaved fennel highlights wonderfully complementary flavors.

Sevilla

Spanish

B2

62 Charles St. (at W. 4th St.)

Subway: Christopher St - Sheridan Sq
Phone: 212-929-3189
Web: www.sevillarestaurantandbar.com
Price: $$

Lunch & dinner daily

Yellowed menus that haven't changed in decades make this old-school Spanish stalwart seem like a relic. Still, no one comes here to be surprised. Rather, they are plowing through their favorite renditions of paella, ranging from vegetable to seafood with chicken and chorizo. The paella Valenciana also adds clams, mussels, and lobster claws. Prices are low, portions are large, and lively crowds are always happy.

Dishes are made to order, so if that *arroz con pollo* takes 30 minutes to get to your table, know that it will be worthy of the wait. It arrives as a massive amount of saffron-tinged rice and tender bone-in chicken dotted with green onions, pepper strips, lots of garlic, chorizo, and peas. Come dessert, you cannot go wrong with the flan.

Shuko

Japanese XX

D3

47 E. 12th St. (bet. Broadway & University Pl.)

Subway: 14 St - Union Sq
Phone: 212-228-6088
Web: www.shukonyc.com
Price: $$$$

Dinner Mon – Sat

Jimmy Lau and Nick Kin, both Masa alumni, have created a cool, high-end sushi bar for a young and eager crowd. They've certainly nailed the ultra-discreet façade—anyone who's eaten out in Tokyo will know the feeling of walking past a place a couple of times before finding its door. The centerpiece of the windowless room is the three-sided counter fashioned out of white ash—it's a thing of beauty which you'll find yourself unable to resist stroking every now and again.

Drinks aside you have just one choice to make—to have the omakase or the marginally more expensive kaiseki. Even for Edomae-style sushi, the size is quite diminutive, with the best pieces being those that push a little at the boundaries. The rice could be better but there's no doubting the quality of the fish.

Spotted Pig

Gastropub X

B2

314 W. 11th St. (at Greenwich St.)

Subway: Christopher St - Sheridan Sq
Phone: 212-620-0393
Web: www.thespottedpig.com
Price: $$$

Lunch & dinner daily

It's impossible to tell if the famously talented April Bloomfield ever imagined the massive draw her restaurant would have, but years ago, when Spotted Pig sashayed its way into the West Village, NY'ers were more than ready to fall in love with the gastropub.

However, it is the cooking that has been the main draw here—even if you are teetering on a wooden stool or knocking elbows with pencil-thin hipsters in this cozy, bi-level space. Outstanding staples like burgers, pan-seared mackerel, or gnudi—ricotta "gnocchi" laced with brown butter, sage and parmesan—have a cultish following; while creamy burrata spread on sourdough with fava and mint, as well as a perfectly roasted *poussin* served with Sherry vinegar and grilled ramps are favorites for good reason.

Soto ❀ ❀

Japanese ✗✗

D1

357 Sixth Ave. (bet. Washington Pl. & W. 4th St.)

Subway: W 4 St - Wash Sq
Phone: 212-414-3088
Web: N/A
Price: $$$

Dinner Mon – Sat

Simply put, Soto is a special place. The smallish room is bright, spotless, and modern with few adornments other than a wall of decorative wood. The sushi counter fills with very serious diners served by a staff that never seems to miss a beat.

The à la carte menu showcases Chef Sotohiro Kosugi's consummate perfectionism through signature starters, such as *goma* tofu and *zuke* carpaccio with sesame and watercress salad. Other contemporary originals feature an inventive combination of the finest sea urchin wrapped in thin slices of squid and shiso in a Tosa soy reduction, using white kelp in place of nori. Don't be surprised to find some other items layered in mounds of caviar, truffles or other premium ingredients. Still, the nigiri are every meal's highlight, served as an array of impeccably chosen seafood and precisely prepared rice that is nothing short of a master class in Japanese cuisine. While some of the supremely fresh fish are brushed with sauces, the true, clean flavor of each morsel is never masked. Expect deliciously marinated mackerel from Japan, Long Island fluke, Russian sea urchin, and much more.

The omakase here is memorable, marvelous, and absolutely worth it.

Standard Grill

Contemporary ✗✗

848 Washington St. (bet. Little W. 12th & 13th Sts.)

Subway: 14 St - 8 Av   Lunch & dinner daily
Phone: 212-645-4100
Web: www.thestandardgrill.com
Price: $$

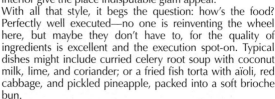

This clubby, popular restaurant makes it's home in the even more popular Standard Hotel, which is nestled under the most popular High Line. Takeaway? It's a *trés* trendy crowd you'll run with at the Standard Grill, where vintage plaid-uniformed servers, penny-tiled floors and a chic downtown interior give the place indisputable glam appeal.

With all that style, it begs the question: how's the food? Perfectly well executed—no one is reinventing the wheel here, but maybe they don't have to, for the quality of ingredients is excellent and the execution spot-on. Typical dishes might include curried celery root soup with coconut milk, lime, and coriander; or a fried fish torta with aïoli, red cabbage, and pickled pineapple, packed into a soft brioche bun.

Sushi Nakazawa

Japanese ✗✗

23 Commerce St. (bet. Bedford St. & Seventh Ave. South)

Subway: Christopher St - Sheridan Sq   Dinner Mon – Sat
Phone: 212-924-2212
Web: www.sushinakazawa.com
Price: $$$$

Sushi lovers can breathe a sigh of relief—after an oh-so-brief closing, beloved Sushi Nakazawa has emerged sexier, more spacious and more delicious than ever. Even better? It's much easier to score a seat now. Updates include an elegant new lounge where a limited selection of sushi is served à la carte, accompanied by some inventive spins on their extensive wine, beer and sake list.

Whether you land in the main dining room or the lounge, the gorgeous fish on offer is of outstanding quality. Indulge in a truly luxurious flight of creamy uni hailing from Maine, Santa Barbara, and Hokkaido; scallop spiked with bold, bright citrusy notes and wrapped in excellent nori; or a perfectly restrained slice of Atlantic bluefin, barely kissed with soy sauce.

Sushi Zo ✿

Japanese ✕✕

C3

88 W. 3rd St. (bet. Sullivan & Thompson Sts.)

Subway: W 4 St - Wash Sq   Dinner Tue – Sat
Phone: 646-405-4826
Web: www.sushizo.us
Price: $$$$

This LA import has sushi that rivals the best in New York but is served with a laid-back vibe that is a welcomed change of pace. Sushi Zo is nonetheless ambitious, serving superlative fish and seafood that is pristine, delicious, and well beyond reproach.

The petite space is serene and showcases a particularly lovely mix of blonde wood and exposed brick, decorated with little more than birch branches. Their nightly omakase menu has only two turns at the counter as well as the handful of tables, so plan well in advance if you want to approach this multi-course feast.

Begin with a plump Kumamoto oyster served with a slightly sweet ponzu sauce and lime zest in the company of spectacular sashimi. Their exquisite nigiri—with bright flavors and skilled torch work—is sure to be the highlight of your meal thanks to halibut with lemon and sea salt, belt fish with wasabi, and *shima aji* with yuzu juice and lime zest. Each long slice of perfectly fresh fish drapes off the delicate *shari*; those generous proportions belie Sushi Zo's origins as a California-based *sushi-ya* that is unafraid to flout tradition. Finish with a delicate and palate-cleansing fish-bone consommé and sphere of house mochi.

Takashi

B3

Japanese

456 Hudson St. (bet. Barrow & Morton Sts.)

Subway: Christopher St - Sheridan Sq   Dinner nightly
Phone: 212-414-2929
Web: www.takashinyc.com
Price: $$

Takashi Inoue honors his Korean ancestry and Osaka upbringing with a delicious array of *yakiniku* favorites at this cozy space. Tremendous care, planning, and sourcing of specialty cuts went into the design of the menu before the restaurant opened its doors to acclaim. Inside, you'll find high tech grills gracing the tables and cutesy cartoons depicting beefy cuts, offal and innards on the walls.

The carte is exotic to say the least (*testicargot*, anyone?), filled with meats, surprises like tripe, or even *namagimo*—fresh raw liver with sesame oil and roasted rock salt. The kitchen's *yakiniku* (table-grilling) specialties are presented to you to cook at your own pace and may include items like *shio-tan* (tongue) marinated in soy, apples, and orange marmalade.

Tertulia 😊

D1

Spanish ✗✗

359 Sixth Ave. (bet. Washington Pl. & W. 4th St.)

Subway: W 4 St - Wash Sq   Lunch & dinner daily
Phone: 646-559-9909
Web: www.tertulianyc.com
Price: $$

With a Spanish soul and tastefully raw space, Chef Seamus Mullen's Tertulia is big-hearted and boasts a surprisingly healthy side to its menu. The narrow room decked with a long wood bar and colorful tiles evokes those casual eateries in Spain, rife with a buzzing open kitchen and chalkboards scribbled with cheeses. The bites here are healthy but equally bright with flavor. *Tosta matrimonio* is a flax and quinoa crisp topped with black and white anchovies, slow-roasted tomato, and sharp sheep's milk cheese. Also, try *bocata de delicata*, a satisfying sandwich of slices of charred delicata squash, roasted red peppers, Swiss chard, and cheddar cheese.

For a sweet fix try the *pastel de almendras*, a chocolate-covered almond cake with Pedro Ximénez syrup and a side of peanut butter icecream.

Untitled

 American ✗✗

B1

99 Gansevoort St. (at Washington St.)

Subway: 14 St - 8 Av   Lunch & dinner daily
Phone: 212-570-3670
Web: www.untitledatthewhitney.com
Price: $$

Who can outshine a world-renowned museum like the Whitney? Danny Meyer can—especially when his trendy restaurant, Untitled, is housed on site. Located by the entry to the popular High Line, the stunning, modern restaurant is a work of art itself, with floor-to-ceiling windows, sleek red chairs, and a beautiful semi-open kitchen.

Talented Chef Michael Anthony oversees the operations here, and the results are anything but ordinary. Witness this vegetable-focused carte reveal the likes of marinated mussels with fava, yellow eye beans and edible flowers; or *stradette* tossed with broccoli rabe pesto, French beans, and mushrooms. Then throw caution to the wind and close out with a triple-layer peanut butter and blueberry crunch cake.

Via Carota

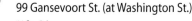 Italian ✗✗

C1

51 Grove St. (bet. Bleecker St. & Seventh Ave. South)

Subway: Christopher St - Sheridan Sq   Dinner nightly
Phone: 212-255-1962
Web: www.viacarota.com
Price: $$

Occasionally, predictability can be a beautiful thing, especially when it comes to rave-worthy Italian cooking. Via Carota is not so much robotically perfect as it is pleasing—in fact it's the kind of place where dishes can (and should) be piled on. Italian style and artistry combine in this homey space that features bare wood farm tables, sideboards, and whitewashed brick. A no-reservations policy means long waits that are actually worth it, so join those lines.

Diners may start nibbling on deep-fried olives that are plump, piping hot, and stuffed with pork sausage. Then, a luscious (and unmissable) risotto *cacio e pepe* arrives loaded with ecorino and fresh pepper. For dessert, the simple-sounding flourless chocolate cake is downright excellent.

Vic's

Italian XX

D4

31 Great Jones St. (bet. Bowery & Lafayette St.)

Subway: Bleecker St   Lunch & dinner daily
Phone: 212-253-5700
Web: www.vicsnewyork.com
Price: $$

The eatery formerly known as Five Points has been reinvented as an Italian-leaning restaurant complete with exposed brick walls and the requisite red pizza oven. Though the dining room is bright and airy, a notable bar program—especially in Italian inflections such as homemade limoncello—prove there's more to this joint than meets the eye.

The best bites are unfussy updates of familiar dishes, such as rye rigatoni with rich braised lamb, fragrant torn oregano, and a sprinkling of sharp cheese. A silky, satisfying nest of *cacio e pepe* is heavy on the black pepper and nutty pecorino, and that red pizza oven produces thin, crisp pies topped with tomato, basil, and sharp pecorino. For dessert, a *bomboloni* of ricotta and chocolate is worth the splurge.

Wallflower

French XX

B2

235 W. 12th St. (bet. Greenwich Ave. & W. 4th St.)

Subway: 14 St (Seventh Ave.)   Dinner nightly
Phone: 646-682-9842
Web: www.wallflowernyc.com
Price: $$

When a Daniel restaurant veteran opens a casual little cocktail lounge and dining room, the locals will come and never leave. Xavier Herit spent seven years as head bartender at the renowned spot, and his expertise clearly shows in the impressive wine list and complex cocktails—he even crafts a house-made pinot noir syrup for the Scotch-based Père Pinard.

The prix-fixe is a true deal in this neighborhood, especially with choices from the raw bar and charcuterie. For heartier fare, try the country pâté or rabbit terrine, both classically prepared and perfectly seasoned. Silky beef short ribs are deeply comforting, garnished with bacon, mushroom, cipollini, and just the right amount of brawny sauce. The coffee-chocolate *pot de crème* is deliciously intense.

Wallsé

 Austrian ✗✗

B2

344 W. 11th St. (at Washington St.)

Subway: Christopher St - Sheridan Sq   Dinner nightly
Phone: 212-352-2300
Web: www.kg-ny.com
Price: $$$

Austrian cuisine is known for being hearty and immeasurably satisfying, but the great strength of Wallsé is that you don't have to have spent the day skiing in Innsbruck to appreciate its cooking because the adept kitchen has a lightness of touch and is not rigidly tied to tradition. There are some foods that just feel right at certain times of the year. When the nights draw in and there's a little chill in the air, there are certain words whose very presence on a menu summon feelings of comfort and warmth—and those words surely include spaetzle, schnitzel, and strudel.

Whether you've chosen the gamey and fork-tender venison cheek goulash or have gone for the *tafelspitz*, you'll find that the dishes here are harmonious, nicely balanced, easy to eat, and even easier to return to enjoy again and again.

The restaurant is divided into two rooms, both dominated by striking paintings that may even portray the chef himself. The clientele is a largely sophisticated bunch with an inherent understanding of how restaurants work which, in turn, creates an easy, relaxing atmosphere.

The wine list also merits examination, if only to discover there's more to Austrian wine than Grüner Veltliner.

ZZ's Clam Bar ✿

Seafood ✗

169 Thompson St. (bet. Bleecker & Houston Sts.)

Subway: Spring St (Sixth Ave.)   Dinner Tue – Sat
Phone: 212-254-3000
Web: www.zzsclambar.com
Price: $$$$

If you forget about your bank statement, don't arrive faint with hunger, and leave your cynicism at the door—you'll love ZZ's Clam Bar. With just four marble tables and a small counter, this is as intimate as it gets. But you first have to navigate the bouncer at the door who'll only allow admittance with a reservation. This at least ensures that, when you're inside this *bijou* spot, the door doesn't swing open every minute.

Once in, you're handed a cocktail list—these are, without doubt, some of the best in town and fully justify the lofty prices. The short seafood menu comes with a couple of choices under headings like "crudo," "seared" and "ceviche." Before you do anything else, order the trout roe on toast—it's a beautiful thing and will linger long in the memory.

This is not the place for everyone. Some won't see past some of the more pretentious elements and affectations and the prices can be eye-watering—the Chianina beef carpaccio comes in at over $100. However, judicious ordering before you plunge into the cocktails, like having clams instead of caviar, can at least keep your final bill from escalating too wildly. It also helps that the place is run with considerable charm, patience and care.

Harlem, Morningside & Washington Heights

This upper Manhattan pocket is best known for its 1920s jazz clubs that put musicians like Charlie Parker and Miles Davis on the map. Home to Columbia University, this capital of African-American, Hispanic, and Caribbean culture lives up to its world-renowned reputation as an incubator of artistic and academic greats. Having officially cast off the age-old stigma of urban blight, these streets are now scattered with terrific soul food joints and authentic African markets that make Harlem a vibrant and enormously desired destination.

buildings. When they're not darting to and from classes, resident scholars and ivy-leaguers from Columbia University can be found lounging at the **Hungarian Pastry Shop** with a sweet treat and cup of tea. Special occasions may call for an evening gathering at **Lee Lee's Baked Goods**. Rather than be misled by its plain-Jane façade, prepare yourself for gratification here by way of the most delicious and decadent rugelach in town. When spring approaches, stroll out onto the terrace and enjoy an apricot-filled treat in the breeze.

MORNINGSIDE HEIGHTS

Considered an extension of the Upper West Side, park-lined Morningside Heights is frequented for its big and bold breakfasts. Inexpensive eateries are set between quaint brownstones and commercial

WEST HARLEM

Further north lies Harlem, a sanctuary for the soul and stomach. Fifth Avenue divides this region into two very unique sections: West Harlem, a hub for African-American culture; and East Harlem, a pulsating Spanish district also referred

to as "El Barrio." Beloved for its sass and edge, West Harlem is constantly making way for booming gentrification and socio-cultural evolution. One of its most visible borders is **Fairway**, a Tri-State area staple that draws shoppers of all stripes. Pick up one of their goodies to-go or simply savor the same while sifting through the extensive literary collection over at the historic Schomburg Center for Research in Black Culture. When the sun sets over the Hudson River, find locals and savvy tourists slipping into **Patisserie des Ambassades**, where a modern, chic décor does much to lure—for breakfast, lunch, and dinner. Not only do the aromas from fresh-baked croissants, *éclairs au chocolat*, and cream-filled beignets waft down the block, but they also ensure long lines at all times. Every August, **Harlem Week** brings the community together for art, music, and food. Join the fun and take in some of the most soulful tunes in town. Both east and west of Central Harlem, food has always factored heavily into everyday routine, and

the choices are as varied as the neighborhood itself. From Mexican and Caribbean, to West African cuisine, there are rich culinary delights to be had. **Lolo's Seafood Shack** cooks up Caribbean-infused steampots and serves them out of a counter; while **Manna's** on Frederick Douglass Boulevard attracts diners to its soul food steam table, where church groups rub shoulders and share stories with backpacking visitors. Fried food junkies fantasize over Chef Charles Gabriel's acclaimed buffet and amazing fried chicken at **Charles Country Pan Fried Chicken**, but for an evening at home, comb the shelves at **Harlem Shambles**, a true-blue butcher shop specializing in quality cuts of meat and poultry that promise to enhance every meal.

EAST HARLEM

Over in East Harlem, Spanish food enthusiasts and culture pundits never miss a trip to **Amor Cubano** for home-style faves. If smoked and piggy *lechón* served with a side of sultry, live Cuban beats isn't your idea of a good time, there's always that counter of divine Caribbean eats at **Sisters**; or juicy jerk chicken at **Winston & Tee Express Jerk Chicken**. Not pressed for time? Choose to scope the tempting taco truck and taqueria scene along "Little Mexico" on East 116th Street—otherwise known as the nucleus of New York City's Mexican communities.

Almost like a vestige of the Italian population that was once dominant in this district, **Rao's** remains a culinary landmark. Operated from a poky basement and patronized by bigwigs like Donald Trump or Nicole Kidman, it is one of the city's most difficult tables to secure. The original benefactors have exclusive rights to a seat here and hand off reservations like rent-controlled apartments. But, rest assured as there is other enticing Italian to be enjoyed at **Patsy's Pizzeria**, another stronghold in East Harlem, famous for its hot coal oven (and occasionally its pizza). Of course **Hot Bread Kitchen**, a tenant of **La Marqueta marketplace**, continues to flourish for its global selection at both breakfast and lunch, and is reputed to be quite the holy haven among carb addicts.

WASHINGTON HEIGHTS

Set along the northern reaches of Uptown, Washington Heights offers ample food choices along its steep streets. From Venezuelan food truck sensation **Patacon Pisao**, to restaurants like **Malecon** preparing authentic *morir soñando*, *mangu*, and *mofongo*, this colorful and lively neighborhood keeps dishing it out. In fact, the Tony award-winning musical *In The Heights* is a tribute to the ebullient district, where Dominican and Puerto Rican communities have taken root. Late-nighters never tire of the Latin beats blasting through the air here, after which a visit to Puerto Rican *piragua* carts selling shaved ice in a rainbow of tropical flavors seems not only nourishing, but also necessary. Locals queue up in lines around the block outside **Elsa La Reina del Chicharrón** for crunchy, deep-fried *chicharrónes*, after which palates may be quenched with *jugos naturales* or natural juices made from cane sugar and fresh fruit for a healthy treat. Need some sweet after this abundant savory feast? **Carrot Top Pastries** continues to entice passersby with assorted cookies, colorful cakes, and deliciously moist sweet potato pies. First-rate fish markets and butcher shops also dot these hilly blocks, and less than ten bucks will get you a plate of traditional pernil with rice and beans at any number of diners nearby. Hungry hordes can be found ducking into **La Rosa Fine Foods** for fish, meat and vegetables; while nearby in Inwood, **Piper's Kilt** is a standing relic among German and Irish settlers for its accurate renditions of their country's cuisines. Settle into a booth and order a pint to go with "Irish nachos" or "Kilt burgers." It's just like continental Europe here, only minus the jet lag!

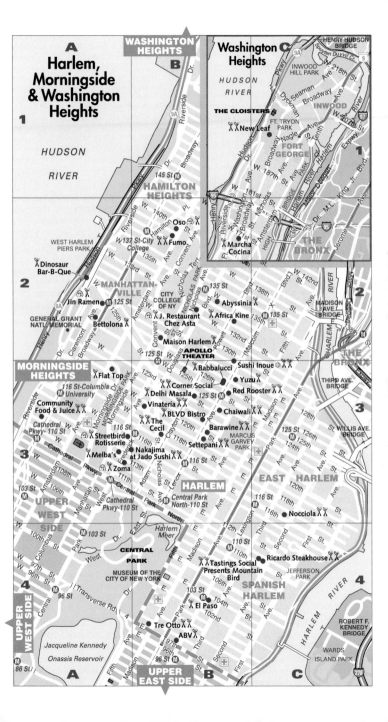

ABV

Gastropub

B4

1504 Lexington Ave. (at 97th St.)

Subway: 96 St (Lexington Ave.)
Phone: 212-722-8959
Web: www.abvny.com
Price: $$

Lunch Sat – Sun
Dinner nightly

This Americana gastropub's sophisticated cooking and no-nonsense mien are a perfect fit for its location straddling Carnegie Hill and East Harlem. Residents flock to the welcoming surrounds outfitted with tufted honey-tan leather banquettes and an open kitchen.

Craft beers and small-producer wines comprise the beverage selection at ABV (alcohol by volume) and the menu is an impressively prepared lineup of seasonally skewed creations. Expect autumnal butternut squash cannelloni boasting local ricotta and pumpkin seed-marjoram pesto, or lip-smacking buttermilk-brined fried chicken with kimchi-cabbage slaw and crumbly cornbread topped with a melting pat of butter. A summertime offering of Frog Hollow peach sorbet headlines the short but sweet dessert choices.

Abyssinia

Ethiopian

B2

268 W. 135th St. (bet. Adam Clayton Powell Jr & Frederick Douglass Blvds.)

Subway: 135 St (St. Nicholas Ave.)
Phone: 212-281-2673
Web: www.harlemethiopianfood.com
Price:

Lunch & dinner daily

Abyssinia's expansion couldn't be better timed, for the local Ethiopian population surrounding its Harlem location has grown by leaps and bounds in recent years. Expanded digs means no one leaves hungry, including the gluten-intolerant diners lining up for the *injera*—a sour-dough risen flatbread with a uniquely spongy texture that performs the task of cutlery, and is also ideal for sopping up all the amazing flavors from this authentic kitchen.

The dining room is spacious and flooded with natural light; the staff gracious; and the décor simple, clean and functional. This is essentially light, healthy, and spicy cooking, and the best way to experience it is to come with a group and order a slew of entrées to sample. Whatever you do, save room for the delicious slow-cooked beef *awaze tibs*.

Africa Kine

B2

2267 7th Ave. (bet. 133rd & 134th Sts.)

Subway: 135 St (Lenox Ave.)　　　　　　　　　Lunch & dinner daily
Phone: 212-666-9400
Web: www.africakine.com
Price:

Following the closure of the original location a few years ago, fans of Senegalese cuisine are happy to see the return of this West Harlem café run by a pair of Dakar-natives. A giant fork and spoon hung on the wall are whimsical decorative accents in a room of pale yellow hues and faux marble-topped tables, where placemats double as menus displaying Africa Kine's myriad offerings.

Keep it simple with grilled fish or meat sided by salad, or opt for more succulent items such as peanut butter-enriched lamb *mafe* or *suppa kandja* (lamb and fish simmered in an okra and golden palm oil sauce). Note that some dishes are only available on certain nights, and although lunch is a more limited affair, Senegal's national treasure, *thiebou djeun*, is always on offer.

Babbalucci

Italian

B3

331 Lenox Ave. (bet. 126th & 127th Sts.)

Subway: 125 St (Lenox Ave.)　　　　　　　　　Dinner nightly
Phone: 646-918-6572
Web: www.babbalucci.com
Price: $$

 A wood-fired pizzeria named after a snail? Yes—and there's actually a snail pizza on the menu. But, regardless of your preferred choice of topping, say *salame piccante* or Sicilian tuna, Babbalucci's 12- or 16-inch pies are light, thin, and pleasantly crisp. Other delicious offerings include small plates such as wood-fired radicchio paired with blistered cherry tomatoes and luscious burrata, all given a drizzling of *vin cotto*, as well as exceptional pastas like penne slicked with a ricotta-enriched tomato sauce hit with *pepperoncini* and fresh mint.

And, thanks to an inviting location set back from the fray of 125th Street and a beautiful brick pizza oven within, the setting at this rustic Harlem newcomer is every bit as divine as its food.

Barawine

B3

200 Lenox Ave. (at 120th St.)

Subway: 116 St (Lenox Ave.)
Phone: 646-756-4154
Web: www.barawine.com
Price: $$

Lunch Sat – Sun
Dinner nightly

Amid the leafy, brownstone-lined Mount Morris Park Historic District, Barawine is an inviting dining room overseen by Fabrice Warin (formerly the sommelier at Orsay). This eye-catching space entices Lenox Avenue passersby to step in, sip and sup, either perched at the bar area's communal table or seated in the quieter, more intimate back dining room. Whitewashed walls attractively double as wine storage throughout.

The crowd-pleasing menu defies classification and embraces myriad influences. Quinoa salad with tofu and seaweed will please the disciplined, while mac and cheese loaded with béchamel, Gruyère, and diced ham calls out to more indulgent palates. Pan-seared branzino with aromatic herbs and a drizzle of balsamic is a treat for all.

Bettolona

A2

3143 Broadway (bet. LaSalle St. & Tiemann Pl.)

Subway: 125 St (Broadway)
Phone: 212-749-1125
Web: N/A
Price: $$

Lunch & dinner daily

This Morningside Heights darling gets incredibly high marks from Columbia University students for their pasta and pizza. The little room is crowded with locals fueling up on delightful *lasagna verdi*, meaty linguine Bolognese, or those puffy, crusty delights that constantly emerge from the wood-burning oven.

The succulent array of items includes pizza *affumicata* spread with crushed tomato, fresh cherry tomatoes, smoked fresh mozzarella, and crumbles of sausage. The chicken breast Marsala is stuffed with spinach, gooey fontina, mushrooms, and is a tasty example of their heartier cooking.

Lodged under the elevated (and rumbling) 1 train, Bettolona is inviting nonetheless, featuring closely arranged wood tables, brick walls, and a rustic vibe.

BLVD Bistro

Southern ✕

239 Lenox Ave. (at 122nd St.)

Subway: 125 St (Lenox Ave.)
Phone: 212-678-6200
Web: www.boulevardbistrony.com
Price: $$

Lunch Sat – Sun
Dinner Tue – Sat

Tucked into the base of a corner brownstone, this southern restaurant delivers the best of old Harlem: warm hospitality, a feel-good, soulful soundtrack, and flaky biscuits slathered with apple butter.

Filled with dark leather booths and high wood tables, the intimate dining room boasts a convivial atmosphere that's only enhanced by the chef's presence as he greets his devoted customers.

After those buttery biscuits, a decadent meal might continue with rich seven cheese macaroni, topped with crumbled bacon. Cornmeal-crusted grouper receives careful execution, resulting in flaky flesh and a crunchy crust. The sides shine, too, including red beans and rice with a hint of thyme and a smoky stew of black eyed peas with Andouille sausage.

The Cecil

International ✕✕

210 W. 118th St. (bet. Adam Clayton Bld. & St. Nicholas Ave.)

Subway: 116 St (Frederick Douglass Blvd.)
Phone: 212-866-1262
Web: www.thececilharlem.com
Price: $$

Lunch Sat – Sun
Dinner nightly

With The Cecil, Harlem proves it's a destination for serious eats once and for all. Neon signage marks this entrance—inside, the lounge's provocative artwork sets a fun and sexy tone for the evening. This place is hopping. Always.

A meal here is a trip around the globe, with a carte that dips down into Africa, Asia, South America and the US South. Executive Chef Joseph "JJ" Johnson heads the kitchen and his range is both wide and skilled in dishes like crudo with hibiscus tea and cinnamon; duck leg confit; or chili lobster with udon. The wine list features varietals from South Africa, labels from Richard Parson's Tuscany vineyard, Il Palazzone, and African-American sommelier André Hueston Mack's Mouton Noir winery. For weekend revelry, head to sister act Minton's for dinner and live jazz.

Chaiwali

274 Lenox Ave. (bet. 123rd & 124th Sts.)

Subway: 125 St (Lenox Ave.) Lunch & dinner Tue – Sun
Phone: 646-688-5414
Web: www.chaiwali.com
Price: $$

A tea house in theory, Chaiwali's two-floor setting respects the cozy confines of a 19th century brownstone that has been prettily renovated into an utterly unique locale by owner Anita Trehan. Metal lanterns complement exposed brick walls, a vivid mural swathes the second floor seating area, and the back garden is charmingly discreet. All in all, it's a striking space that adds some zest to Harlem's melting pot.

Indian flavors are reinterpreted here with an eye on contemporary tastes—read kale is prominently featured. Dinner brings more substantial food in items like smoky mashed eggplant paired with warm, buttery *paratha*; or spice-dusted crunchy fish with okra "fries" and a streak of tomato-harissa sauce. A cup of the lushly fragrant chai is a must.

Community Food & Juice

American

2893 Broadway (bet. 112th & 113th Sts.)

Subway: Cathedral Pkwy/110 St (Broadway) Lunch & dinner daily
Phone: 212-665-2800
Web: www.communityrestaurant.com
Price: $$

As part of Columbia University's sprawl, this address is a godsend for students, faculty, and locals from morning to night. Although it's spacious with plenty of outdoor options, the popular spot doesn't accept reservations—and has the lines to prove it. Executive Chef/partner Neil Kleinberg (also of downtown fave Clinton St. Baking Company) turns out joyful fare, and the weekly blueberry pancake special is just one reason why this place gets so much love.

For lunch, a kale salad with artichoke hearts, pickled carrots, and crispy chickpeas is anything but rote. Come dinnertime, the fish or steak of the day has revealed pan-seared mahi-mahi with roasted cauliflower and black truffle beurre blanc, or grilled strip steak brushed with glistening teriyaki.

Manhattan ▶ Harlem, Morningside & Washington Heights

Corner Social

American

B3

321 Lenox Ave. (at 126th St.)

Subway: 125 St (Lenox Ave.)   Lunch & dinner daily
Phone: 212-510-8552
Web: www.cornersocialnyc.com
Price: $$

Boasting a bar where everybody knows your name and a kitchen that churns out locally sourced, sustainably farmed, and flat-out delicious food, it's no surprise that locals are proud to call this welcoming gathering place their own. With its lively playlist and warm, cozy demeanor (think exposed brick and dim amber lighting), Corner Social is made for sharing a meal with good friends.

Start with the guacamole, which comes with thick, crispy tortillas from Hot Bread Kitchen, a nearby incubator whose mission is to train and employ immigrant women. Entrée options abound, from a buttermilk-fried chicken sandwich, to hanger steak drizzled with warm, house-made steak sauce and propped up by crispy potato wedges dusted with parmesan and white truffle salt.

Delhi Masala

Indian

B3

2077 Adam Clayton Powell Jr. Blvd (bet. 123rd & 124th Sts.)

Subway: 125 St (Lenox Ave.)   Lunch & dinner daily
Phone: 212-666-8600
Web: www.delhimasalanyc.com
Price: $$

Harlem has been long overdue for authentic Indian food, and Delhi Masala has come to the rescue. Inside, find an attractive and comfortable dining room with gray tile flooring, faux-brick walls, colorful fabrics, and wood tables.

The menu offers an expertly prepared lineup of Indian favorites such as vindaloo and tikka masala curries, vegetarian dishes, and griddled breads. Fresh tandoori shrimp arrives with excellent charred, tangy flavor; and tender chunks of chicken Xacuti, a specialty from Goa, are simmered in a roasted coconut-based sauce tinted earthy red with spices and browned onions. Even that old standby, *saag paneer*, finds new depth here when nicely seasoned and prepared with finely chopped spinach that is not bogged down by cream or ghee.

Dinosaur Bar-B-Que

Barbecue

A2

700 W. 125th St. (at Twelfth Ave.)

Subway: 125 St (Broadway)   Lunch & dinner daily
Phone: 212-694-1777
Web: www.dinosaurbarbque.com
Price: $$

&

Huge, loud, and perpetually packed, this way west Harlem barbecue hall draws crowds from near and far. The bar area is rollicking, and for that reason kept separate from the dining quarters. There, wood beams and slats, swirling ceiling fans, and oxblood leather booths fashion a comfortable—and quieter—setting.

The scent of wood smoke wafting through the red brick structure (which coincidentally once served as a meatpacking warehouse) only heightens the diners' carnivorous cravings. Minimize decision-making and order the Extreme Sampler: a heaping feast of apple cider-brined smoked chicken, dry-rubbed slow-smoked pork ribs, and lean Creekstone Farms brisket. Add on a creative side or two—perhaps the barbecue fried rice studded with bits of pulled pork?

El Paso

Mexican

B4

1643 Lexington Ave. (at 104th St.)

Subway: 103 St (Lexington Ave.)   Lunch & dinner daily
Phone: 212-831-9831
Web: www.elpasony.com
Price: $$

El Paso is an East Harlem cantina that serves some of the most gratifying south-of-the-border fare in town. True-blue residents as well as those new to this evolving neighborhood crowd its affable rooms, where margaritas, ice-cold cerveza, and smiles flow freely. Stucco walls and decorative metal work grace the interior, while the covered back patio has a breezy mien.

Tacos, quesadillas, and ceviche kick off cooking that hits all the right notes. Zesty guacamole is freshly mashed and served up in a *molcajete* with warm tortilla chips. Bold citrus- and tequila-braised *carnitas Michoacanás* are kissed by green chilies and expertly paired with a bowl of hearty black beans and tender tortillas for wrapping. The silken flan offers a sweet finish.

Flat Top

Contemporary 🍴

A3

1241 Amsterdam Ave. (at 121st St.)

Subway: 116 St (Broadway)
Phone: 646-820-7735
Web: www.flattopnyc.com
Price: $$

Lunch & dinner daily

Morningside Heights' scholarly set, already familiar with Jin Ramen, has been quick to adopt this bistro from the same team of partners. A mural of the Harlem Viaduct gives the low-key setting a sense of place, while friendly service accentuates the neighborly vibe.

Global accents mark Flat Top's cuisine in starters like a caprese salad with burrata, or shrimp ceviche. Meanwhile entrées have included black pepper-flecked roasted chicken breast. The latter is presented sliced over steamed Yukon gold potatoes and a mouthwatering herb sauce made from puréed cilantro, roasted jalapeños, and hint of cream. For dessert, a dressed-up chocolate cake is layered with whipped ganache, crispy bits of *feuilletine*, and presented with a side of Guinness ice cream.

Fumo

Italian 🍴🍴

B2

1600 Amsterdam Ave. (at 139th St.)

Subway: 137 St-City College
Phone: 646-692-6675
Web: www.fumorestaurant.com
Price: $$

Lunch & dinner daily

The setting at Fumo is undeniably chic, with bright white walls, light wood tables, and dark leather furnishings. A wood-fired pizza oven is in back, while the front offers sidewalk seating under a protective awning. Attractive shelving lined with canned tomatoes frames the bar area and dining room.

The menu offers Italian favorites, executed with a deft hand and solid ingredients. Pizzas are 12-inches and come *rosso* or *bianco*, topped with the likes of vodka sauce, wild mushrooms, or charred vegetables. Excellent pastas, like the penne Caprese, are tossed with tomato sauce, fresh basil, and creamy mozzarella. A neatly deboned branzino arrives subtly flavored with fresh herbs and beautifully seasoned, alongside wilted spinach and a wedge of lemon.

Jin Ramen

A2

Japanese ✗

3183 Broadway (bet. 125th St. & Tiemann Pl.)

Subway: 125 St (Broadway)   Lunch & dinner daily
Phone: 646-559-2862
Web: www.jinramen.com
Price: ⊖⊖

All you really need to know is that this is the hands-down best ramen above 59th Street. Sure, decorative elements are simple, and it hardly matters that this gem is hidden behind the 125th Street station's brick escalator. What comes from the kitchen however deserves kudos. The menu is concise but full of classics like pan-fried *gyoza* served with an addictive sesame-seed flecked dipping sauce. *Shio*, *shoyu*, and miso ramen are all delightful, but the *tonkatsu* ramen is a special treat. This piping hot, almost creamy, mouthcoating distillation of pork bones is deliciously rich and stocked with fragrant *chasu*, pickled bamboo shoots, slivered green onion, and a soft-boiled egg.

For added fun, visit Kissaten Jin—an offshoot serving homestyle bites and soba made by a master.

J. Restaurant Chez Asta

B2

Senegalese ✗

2479 Frederick Douglass Blvd. (bet. 132nd & 133rd Sts.)

Subway: 135 St (Frederick Douglass Blvd.)   Lunch & dinner daily
Phone: 212-862-3663
Web: N/A
Price: ⊖⊖

Impressive in its authenticity, this Senegalese café is a rare bird in a neighborhood of vibrant dining choices. Meals here are exquisitely prepared and brim with unique flavors and scents, resulting in a truly transporting experience.

Spotless and comfy, the dining room offers a clutch of wood tables sturdy enough to support the heaping portions of chicken *yassa* or lemon-marinated chicken cooked with onions; as well as *souloukhou*, fish and vegetables in a peanut sauce. For a true taste of the country's flavors, go with the *thiebou djeun*, a one pot wonder of broken rice infused with tomato and Scotch bonnet pepper. It's cooked with fish, cabbage, okra, and cassava, and speckled with *xóoñ* (those crusty, toothsome bits scraped from the bottom of the pan).

Maison Harlem

B2

341 St. Nicholas Ave. (at 127th St.)

Subway: 125 St (St. Nicholas Ave.)
Phone: 212-222-9224
Web: www.maisonharlem.com
Price: $$

Lunch & dinner daily

A steady stream of locals, phone-toting tourists and City College academics filling these well-worn wooden tables proves that this bistro has little trouble attracting a crowd. Floor-to-ceiling windows, dark red banquettes, and quirky touches like vintage Gallic posters or football jerseys tacked to the walls lend a whiff of whimsy.

Maison Harlem's menu plays around with culinary traditions, with results that may include a classic rendition of coq au vin with smoky lardons, browned button mushrooms, and fresh noodles to garnish the wine-braised chicken pieces. Sticking to tradition, ratatouille is a sunny bowlful of diced and stewed summer vegetables. The tarte Tatin layers thick but spoon-tender caramelized apple wedges over outrageously buttery pastry.

Marcha Cocina

B2

4055 Broadway (at 171st St.)

Subway: 168 St
Phone: 212-928-8272
Web: N/A
Price: $$

Lunch Fri – Sun
Dinner nightly

Colors evoke the Caribbean at Marcha, a narrow restaurant known for authentic Spanish tapas. A long bar dominates the sea-blue and sunny-yellow room filled with high tables and a convivial crowd. The music is a touch loud, the service is refreshingly down-to-earth, and the food impresses beyond what its neighborhood bar-vibe might suggest.

The menu is broad and affordable, which makes a perfect excuse to sample widely. Staples from tender *tortilla Espanola* to *gambas al ajillo* are delicious executions of classic tapas. Ribbons of luscious Spanish ham are on handsome display in the *hongos e higos coca*, a chewy flatbread also topped with mushrooms, figs, and buttery almonds. It would be blasphemy to skip the dates wrapped in bacon or the thick-cut yucca fries.

Melba's

Southern

A3

300 W. 114th St. (at Frederick Douglass Blvd.)

Subway: 116 St (Frederick Douglass Blvd.)
Phone: 212-864-7777
Web: www.melbasrestaurant.com
Price: $$

Lunch Sat – Sun
Dinner nightly

With its colorful spirit and lineup of Southern classics, this comfortable spot—as charming and lovely as its namesake owner, born-and-bred Harlemite Melba Wilson—is a perfect reflection of the neighborhood's flavor, culture, and past. It's a place to gather and relax over good food and drinks, from Auntie B's mini-burgers slathered in a smoky sweet sauce to a golden-brown and berry-licious fruit cobbler that's nothing short of heaven on a plate.

Equally enticing is the Southern fried chicken—darkly bronzed, and salty sweet when paired with Melba's iconic eggnog waffles.

Expect other surprises like spring rolls stuffed with black-eyed peas, collards, and cheddar cheese, as well as a healthy minded grilled vegetable Napoleon with buffalo mozzarella.

Nakajima at Jado Sushi

Japanese

B3

2118 Frederick Douglass Blvd. (bet. 114th & 115th Sts.)

Subway: Cathedral Pkwy/110 St (Broadway)
Phone: 212-866-2118
Web: www.jadosushi.com
Price: $$$

Dinner Tue – Sun

Although you could easily satisfy your appetite with a crispy shrimp maki at this Harlem *sushi-ya*, you'd be missing the point of what makes Nakajima at Jado so special—its strictly-at-the-counter omakase.

While the dark, stylish room boasts such details as pretty light fixtures and a sleek wall of mirrors, Chef Kunihide Nakajima's impressive handiwork shines even brighter than the décor. The meal may start off with a refreshing bite leading to succulent sashimi, which has featured profoundly creamy Kumamoto oysters, flash-boiled live lobster, and slivers of luminous Montauk fluke. The fluke is featured again come sushi time, now aged for three days and brushed with *nikiri*. Other bites may reveal golden eye snapper and Santa Barbara sweet shrimp.

New Leaf

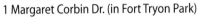 American ✗✗

C1

1 Margaret Corbin Dr. (in Fort Tryon Park)

Subway: 190 St
Phone: 212-568-5323
Web: www.newleafrestaurant.com
Price: $$

Lunch daily
Dinner Tue – Sun

Talk about wowing your dinner date. Located in a 1930's slate and fieldstone cottage tucked away in Upper Manhattan's Fort Tryon Park, New Leaf Café was opened as part of the New York Restoration Project. With its stone walls and arched windows, the interior is just lovely. And lunch out on the flagstone terrace is downright stunning—offering unparalleled views of the dramatic Palisades and (if you squint a bit) the George Washington Bridge.

Delicious and modern American food is the name of the game at this kitchen, with a menu that touches on some usual crowd favorites (think juicy burgers and soft beignets) along with trendy, veggie-based items like avocado smeared on toasted crostini; a bowl of greens and grains; and falafel burger.

Nocciola

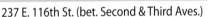 Italian ✗✗

C3

237 E. 116th St. (bet. Second & Third Aves.)

Subway: 116 St (Lexington Ave.)
Phone: 646-559-5304
Web: www.nocciolanyc.com
Price: $$

Lunch & dinner daily

The transformation of this East Harlem address into a pleasing trattoria is a breath of fresh air for the neighborhood. Run by the team behind El Paso, the slender space has been minimally re-touched but nevertheless feels cozy and inviting with its dark-stained wood furnishings and warm brown-shaded walls.

The menu boasts house-made pastas like silken fettuccine treated to a soaking of *Domenico* sugo—a hearty amalgam of sweet fennel sausage, pan-fried spicy meatballs, and pork ragù in a bright tomato sauce. A roasted whole fish is beautifully done, expertly de-boned and dressed with a touch of *salmoriglio*, charred lemon and young arugula. Top off this confident cooking with a block of classic tiramisu that boasts an ample dusting of cocoa powder.

Oso

B2

Mexican 🍴

1618 Amsterdam Ave. (bet. 139th & 140th Sts.)

Subway: 137 St-City College
Phone: 646-858-3139
Web: www.osoharlem.com
Price: $$

Lunch Sat – Sun
Dinner nightly

This chic little Mexican restaurant, whose name means "bear" in Spanish, sits opposite the City College of New York. The charming space is dressed in wood tables, warm lighting, and a Dia de los Muertes mural gracing a corner. One black-tiled dining counter is lined with vintage white metal stools, while another small bar faces the tidy open kitchen where the cooks hand-make tortillas at a steady clip.

The cuisine of Mexico City inspires Oso's menu with a concise, impressive offering of dishes like braised octopus tostada with mandarin salsa, guava-chipotle glazed ribs, and authentic tacos and *antojitos*. Come summer, don't miss the wonderful radish salad, served warm with fresh cilantro, serrano peppers, anchovies, and tomato vinaigrette.

Red Rooster

B3

American 🍴🍴

310 Lenox Ave. (bet. 125 & 126th Sts.)

Subway: 125 St (Lenox Ave.)
Phone: 212-792-9001
Web: www.redroosterharlem.com
Price: $$$

Lunch & dinner daily

So many things make Red Rooster special, not the least of which is Chef Marcus Samuelsson whose head-spinning achievements include inventive world-renowned cooking, penning cookbooks, and bringing the New Harlem Renaissance to Lenox Avenue. Downstairs, find live music at Ginny's Supper Club. Up front, The Nook serves sweets and sandwiches to-go. And in the center, the Red Rooster celebrates Harlem, the African-American diaspora, and great food.

Start with a brilliantly simple wedge of crumbly, buttery corn bread. Then, move on to the likes of highly spiced and "dirty" basmati rice with sweet shrimp and swirls of lemon aïoli; or try their interpretation of South African "bunny chow" served as lamb stew on a sesame bun with fried egg and fresh ricotta.

Ricardo Steakhouse

Steakhouse

C4

2145 Second Ave. (bet. 110th & 111th Sts.)

Subway: 110 St (Lexington Ave.)
Phone: 212-289-5895
Web: www.ricardosteakhouse.com
Price: $$

Lunch Fri – Sun
Dinner nightly

Walk up to the entrance of Ricardo Steakhouse on a Saturday night and don't be surprised to see imposing doormen focused on crowd control. Beloved by longtime locals, this place remains very popular for its genuine, ungentrified East Harlem vibe. Beyond its polished façade and wood-framed doors find small tables, eye-catching artwork, and on occasion, a formidable DJ. The menu combines whimsical wording and Latin influences with starters that range from empanadas or fried calamari to raw bar offerings. Heaping entrées (listed under "Da Meats") include the Ricardo Special, a grilled platter pairing tender skirt steak and a juicy pork chop with black beans, rice, and fried plantains.
A few blocks north, Ricardo Ocean Grill is also satisfying crowds.

Settepani

Italian

B3

196 Lenox Ave. (at 120th St.)

Subway: 125 St (Lenox Ave.)
Phone: 917-492-4806
Web: www.settepani.com
Price: $$

Lunch & dinner daily

This stylish little corner spot dares to (re)discover the true strength of regional Italian flavors through a handful of Sicilian specialties. Inside, floor-to-ceiling windows and a bar area popular with locals make this a nice spot to pop in for a glass of Nero d'Avola. Flickering votive candles, whitewashed brick walls, and bare tables lend an upscale feel, while the hands-on owners canvass the room to help guests order or answer any questions.

Start with *insalata polipo alla Siciliana*, combining the bold tastes of capers, olives, and red onion with grilled octopus, chickpeas, and warm potatoes drizzled in excellent olive oil. Their rendition of *pasta con sarde* is wow-inducing featuring *perciatelli* in a thick sardine- tomato and fennel bulb frond-sauce.

Streetbird Rotisserie

A3

Fusion ✕

2149 Frederick Douglass Blvd. (at 116th St.)

Subway: 116 St (Frederick Douglass Blvd.)
Phone: 212-206-2557
Web: www.streetbirdnyc.com
Price: $$

Lunch & dinner daily

Chef Marcus Samuelsson's latest Harlem hot spot is a funky corner devoted to slow-roasted chicken and old-school street-style. Wade through the boisterous, rum punch-fueled crowd and enter this party to find splashes of custom graffiti, eye-popping murals, and lighting fixtures made from cassette tapes, drum sets, and bicycle tires.

Despite all this sensory overload, it is impossible not to notice the plump, auburn birds spinning in the glass-fronted oven. Tender, juicy, and exceptionally flavorful, they steal the show and are supported by the chef's signature mash-up of global flavors: green papaya salad, jasmine fried rice, and cornbread. Not feeling the poultry? Opt for the spicy *piri-piri* catfish with crispy shallots and avocado.

Tastings Social Presents Mountain Bird

C4

Contemporary ✕✕

251 E. 110th St. (bet. Second & Third Aves.)

Subway: 110 St (Lexington Ave.)
Phone: 212-744-4422
Web: www.tastingsnyc.com
Price: $$

Lunch Sun
Dinner Tue – Sat

The inspiration for Chef Kenichi Tajima and wife Keiko's popular venture no doubt sprung from the popularity of their initial and well-loved incarnation of Mountain Bird. It's clear they were missed as this hot spot, in collaboration with the events organization Tastings Social, stays hopping most nights.

This area has wanted for serious food for a while, and Mountain Bird brings it with style—the dining space, tucked into the ground floor of a red row house, is intimate with a small bar and a smattering of wood tables. As the name implies, the menu bears a whimsical devotion to poultry, featuring dishes like hand-cut ostrich tartare; black truffle chicken wings and duck leg-and-turkey sausage cassoulet; along with a nightly seafood and vegetarian option.

Sushi Inoue ✿

B3

381 Lenox Ave. (at 129th St.)

Subway: 125 St (Lenox Ave.)   Dinner Tue – Sun
Phone: 646-766-0555
Web: www.sushiinoue.com
Price: $$$$

For truly amazing sushi, head to the heart of Harlem, where Chef Shinichi Inoue—formerly of Sushi Azabu—now presides over this discreet and unexpected addition to the neighborhood.

Inside the small establishment, bamboo blinds obscuring the scene outside combined with hushed and genuine hospitality produce a sense of calm and refinement. The Nagasaki-born chef works behind a display of sparkling fillets and a dark counter arranged with 14 *washi* placemats and sets of lacquer chopsticks. It is here that a concise list of omakase options is prepared increasing in price with the additions of tempura, sashimi and an uni tasting.

Chef Inoue personally looks after every detail of the meal—from the blended soy sauce to the house miso recipe. Pickled ginger placed on your tray ushers in the expertly crafted nigiri, and while the grated wasabi root that sparks most pieces can be a bit aggressive at times, the procession is rather delightful. Highlights include a buttery bite of *shima aji* from Kyushu island; *shiro ika* dressed with salt and *sudachi*; soy-marinated tuna with mustard and toasted sesame seeds; and fatty tuna from Boston—one of the rare pieces not found in Japanese waters.

Tre Otto

Italian XX

B4

1410 Madison Ave. (bet. 97th & 98th Sts.)

Subway: 96 St (Lexington Ave.)
Phone: 212-860-8880
Web: www.treotto.com
Price: $$

Lunch & dinner daily

East Harlem's favorite neighborhood trattoria has triumphantly returned following a move next door. Thanks to proprietors Louis and Lauren Cangiano, the popular surrounds—complete with cheery red walls, exposed brick, and penny-tile floors—are as cozy and welcoming as ever.

Tre Otto's mouthwatering menu boasts home-style dishes made from recipes gathered over time. Antipasti include a luscious salad of shaved fennel and orange segments crowned by tender grilled octopus drizzled with zesty *salmoriglio* sauce. Freshly made trenette pasta is twirled with pesto *Trapanese*, a divinely rich combination of tomatoes, almonds, garlic, and basil; while the flavors of pizza, topped with red onions, capers, and tuna, call Sicily's sparkling coastline to mind.

Vinatería

Italian XX

B3

2211 Frederick Douglass Blvd. (at 119th St.)

Subway: 116 St (Frederick Douglass Blvd.)
Phone: 212-662-8462
Web: www.vinaterianyc.com
Price: $$

Lunch Sat – Sun
Dinner nightly

Adding to Harlem and its hidden charms is Vinatería, an Italian darling brimming with wines to accompany each sublime bite. Not only is it cozy, but the attractive slate-toned room etched in chalk with scenes of decanters and menu specials will augment your appetite.

The semi-open kitchen in the back unveils such treasures as house-cured sardines with fiery piquillo peppers and crunchy croutons; or a salad of earthy golden and red beets mingled with yogurt, oranges, arugula, crunchy pistachios and tossed with a lemon vinaigrette. Herbs plucked from their copper planters may be featured in an impeccably grilled rosemary-marinated pork blade served with rich mashed potatoes; or desserts like citrus-glazed rosemary panna cotta bathed in chamomile grappa.

Yuzu

B3

Japanese ✗

350 Lenox Ave. (bet. 127th & 128th Sts.)

Subway: 125 St (Lenox Ave.)
Phone: 646-861-3883
Web: www.yuzunewyork.com
Price: $$

Lunch & dinner Tue – Sun

Add sushi to Harlem's burgeoning lineup of eateries that are delighting residents and luring curious foodies uptown. The space is spare but fits in well within the *sushi-ya* archetype. An L-shaped counter and numerous tables compose the seating options in the room, which is painted pale yellow to reference the namesake citrus fruit. Yuzu's personable staff lends an amiable tone to the vibe.

Chef Tomoyuki Hayashi is highly skilled, so expect to be pleased from start to finish. Sushi platters are a good show of skill, and may be composed of lean tuna, torched salmon, and unagi nigiri, plus well-constructed maki. Cooked options include cold and hot small plates such as yuzu- and miso-marinated seafood or grilled bluefin tuna belly.

Zoma 😊

A3

Ethiopian ✗

2084 Frederick Douglass Blvd. (at 113th St.)

Subway: 116th (Frederick Douglass Blvd.)
Phone: 212-662-0620
Web: www.zomanyc.com
Price: ⊜⊜

Lunch Sat – Sun
Dinner nightly

Smart, cool, modern, and always welcoming, Zoma may well be this city's most serious Ethiopian restaurant. The crowded bar emits a golden light from below to showcase its premium spirits, and the ambient dining room is filled with locals from this thriving community.

Attention to detail is clear from the steaming hot towel for cleaning your hands to the carefully folded *injera* used for scooping up their chopped salads, chunky stews, and saucy vegetables. Unusual starters might include green lentils with a cold and crunchy mix of onions, jalapeños, ginger, white pepper, and mustard seeds. The *doro watt*—a chicken dish of the Amhara people—is a very traditional stew with a berbere sauce of sun-dried hot peppers and ground spices.

The Lower East Side is one of New York City's most energetic, stylish, and fast-evolving neighborhoods. Bragging a plethora of shopping, eating, and nightlife, this high-energy hub proudly retains the personality of its first wave of hard-working immigrants. But, thanks to a steady stream of artists and entrepreneurs over the last few decades as well as a real estate uprising, the area faces constant transformation with an influx of high-rises breaking through trendy boutiques and galleries. And yet, some nooks remain straight up dodgy as if in defiance of such rapid development; while others feel downright Village-like in stature and spirit.

AROUND THE WORLD

Visit the Lower East Side Tenement Museum for a glimpse of the past before trekking its enticing, ethnically diverse streets. Then for a taste of yore, traipse into **Russ & Daughters** for appetizing tidbits including smoked, cured fish and hearty bagels. This nosher's delight was instituted in 1914 but continues to be mobbed even today, especially during the holidays when that "ultimate

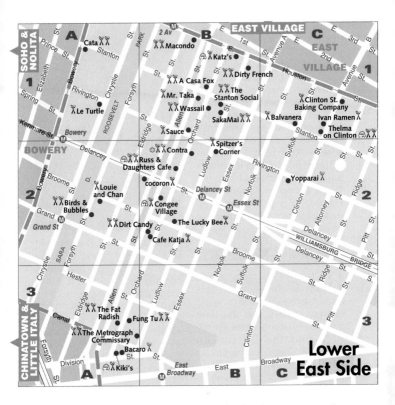

Cata

Macondo

Katz's

Dirty French

A Casa Fox

Mr. Taka

The Stanton Social

Clinton St. Baking Company

Le Turtle

Wassail

SakaMai

Balvanera

Ivan Ramen

Thelma on Clinton

Sauce

Contra

Spitzer's Corner

Russ & Daughters Cafe

Yopparai

Louie and Chan

cocoron

Birds & Bubbles

Congee Village

Dirt Candy

The Lucky Bee

Cafe Katja

The Fat Radish

Fung Tu

The Metrograph Commissary

Bacaro

Kiki's

WILLIAMSBURG BRIDGE

Lower East Side

salmon and caviar" package is nothing short of...you guessed it...ultimate! Also inhabiting these streets are German, Italian, and Chinese residents, whose opposite cultures have triggered a host of diverse and tasty eats 'n treats. Find signs of this at **Nonna's LES Pizza** where the red, white, and green squares are known to tug at all the right nostalgic strings. **Palà**, which boasts a vast list of gluten-free and vegan selections, is not far behind with homesick hordes craving a host of heartwarming pies. Meanwhile, an afternoon spent at **Gaia Italian Cafè** breezing through magazines and biting into delicious *dolci* or perfect biscotti will take you back to Rome on a dime. This toasty spot may be mini in size, but cooks up flavors that are big and bright. **Tiny's Giant Sandwich Shop** is yet another unpretentious but wholly irresistible gem where sandwiches rule the roost and are slung at all times. Ground zero for partygoers, punk rockers, and scholars, this Rivington Street paragon is a rare treat highlighting fresh ingredients and creative presentations. While on the topic of a spirited scene, **New Beer Distributors** is a warehouse-y beer shop in operation since 1968. Housing numerous bottles and cans from the globe over, craft beer aficionados will adore perusing its metal racks for rare (read exotic) varietals. Then, if sweet is what you need, **Economy Candy** is a flourishing emporium of old-time confections. Moving from one timeless pleasure to another are two very different takes on one nostalgic treat. **Morgenstern's Finest Ice Cream** bills itself as a New American ice cream parlor, while **Ice & Vice** boasts highly experimental flavors. Try a scoop of fernet black walnut, or a pint of smoked dark chocolate as respective proof.

ETHNIC FUN

By the 1950s, the ethnic mosaic that defined this district intensified with a surge of new settlers, but this time they were mainly from Puerto Rico and the Dominican Republic. These communities continue to dot the culinary landscape today, so come to savor such favorites as *mofongo* or *pernil*. Dominican *especiales* and creamy *café con leche* at **El Castillo de Jagua** keep the party pumping from dawn till dusk, while sugar junkies find their fix at **Tache Artisan Chocolate**—launched by pastry chef, Aditi Malhotra. Try the tequila-infused dark chocolate ganache, which lasts for a moment in your mouth but leaves an impression that will remain for a lifetime. Rivington Street is a perfect hybrid of the Old World and New Order. During the day, the mood here is chill with locals looking to linger at cozy coffee houses. Come sunset, these streets start to fill with raucous carousers looking to land upon a scene-y restaurant

or popular party spot. Further south, Grand Street is home to well-manicured residential complexes scattered amid shops and catering to a cadre of deep-rooted residents. While here, carb-addicts should be afraid, very afraid, of **Kossar's Bialys** flooded with bagels, *bialy*, and *bulkas*. Then there's **Doughnut Plant** proffering inventive offerings crafted from age-old recipes. To replicate that classic deli experience at home, pick up pickles to-go from **The Pickle Guys**—settled on Essex and stocked with barrel-upon-barrel of these briny treats.

Fire escape-fronted Orchard Street is venerated as the original hub of the 'hood. Once dominated by the garment trade with stores selling fabrics and notions, it tells a different tale today with sleek eateries set amid trendy boutiques selling handmade jewelry and designer skateboards. Even tailors remain a cult favorite here, offering cheap, while-you-wait service. At lunchtime, find them at sandwich-slinging hot spots like **Black Tree**.

Concurrently, **Cup & Saucer** is a teatime treasure serving everything under the sun, while **Dimes** (the café that exudes Cali-cool on Canal Street) is a reliable resource for three square meals a day. It's packed to the rafters during peak hours, so shoppers looking to cool their heels may drop by **Il Laboratorio del Gelato**, located on Ludlow.

ESSEX STREET MARKET

Every self-respecting foodie makes the pilgrimage to **Essex Street Market**, a treasure trove of gourmet food. Frequented for its top produce merchants, butchers, bakers, and fishmongers all housed under one roof, this public bazaar expounds on their expertise by way of cooking demonstrations and wine tastings that keep crowds coming back. Burned-out browsers however may rest their feet and calm a craving at **Essex** or even **Shopsin's General Store** known for an encyclopedic carte (and cranky owner). Finally, everything from chocolate (at **Roni-Sue's**); rice balls (at **Arancini Bros**); or cheese (at **Saxelby Cheesemongers**) make this pleasure palace an enticing destination for gastronomes and curious palates alike.

A Casa Fox

XX

B1

173 Orchard St. (bet. Houston & Stanton Sts.)

Subway: 2 Av
Phone: 212-253-1900
Web: www.acasafox.com
Price: $$

Lunch Fri – Sat
Dinner Tue – Sat

A Casa Fox is a bold and bright darling that serves superlative Latin fare with fantastic authenticity and a whole lotta love. This is largely thanks to Chef/owner Melissa Fox, who can be seen in the open kitchen or checking on guests in the snug space, filled with Mexican tiles, wide plank floors, and a warming fireplace.

Be sure to begin any meal with a selection of empanadas, as in pulled pork with caramelized onion, chorizo and aged manchego, or the outstanding *carne enchorizada* (seasoned ground beef with onions, tomatoes, yucca, chayote, and potatoes). Other dishes might include *camarones a las brazes*, grilled shrimp in a sour-orange marinade wrapped in smoky bacon; or chicken *tostones*, its pulled meat on a well-grilled round of masa with *crema* and mango salsa.

Bacaro

X

A3

136 Division St. (bet. Ludlow & Orchard Sts.)

Subway: East Broadway
Phone: 212-941-5060
Web: www.bacaronyc.com
Price: $$

Dinner Tue – Sun

Heavy iron candelabras, crumbling stone walls, and communal wooden tables lend a sultry vibe to this underground labyrinth, named for a Venetian *bacaro* (or counter for casual grazing of snacks and wine). The first floor's marble-topped bar beckons for small bites and a glass of wine, while nooks beneath those low stone ceilings in the downstairs dining room call for a romantic evening over candlelight.

Crafted by Frank DeCarlo, the same chef/owner of Peasant in NoLita, Bacaro's menu highlights the best of Venetian cuisine. *Bigoli con sugo d'anatra* brings together whole-wheat pasta with tender, pulled duck, a tomato-cream sauce, and shavings of salty parmesan. For dessert, the velvety flourless chocolate cake topped with dried apricots, is as decadent as the setting.

Balvanera

Argentinian 🍴

C1

152 Stanton St. (at Suffolk St.)

Subway: Delancey St
Phone: 212-533-3348
Web: www.balvaneranyc.com
Price: $$

Dinner nightly

A balanced taste of Argentina is the centerpiece of this lively bistro, which is a destination for beautifully marbled, expertly grilled meats and super-fresh veggies. Service is attentive and free of attitude in a neighborhood where this is all too common, and whitewashed brick walls alongside tightly packed wooden tables highlight the low key, welcoming scene.

Balvanera's versatile menu is designed for sharing, from the authentically flaky empanadas with a zippy *chimichurri* to succulent house-made chorizo, served simply with a slice of smoky roasted red pepper. Meats are a must, including the dry-aged, grilled bone-in rib eye, garnished with crisp watercress. To balance all that meat, dig into sweet roasted carrots with frisée, orange, and pepitas.

Birds & Bubbles

American 🍴🍴

A2

100B Forsyth St. (bet. Broome & Grand Sts.)

Subway: Grand St
Phone: 646-368-9240
Web: www.birdsandbubbles.com
Price: $$

Lunch Sat – Sun
Dinner nightly

This chic and cozy restaurant celebrates the unique and utterly delightful pairing of fried chicken and crisp, sparkling wine. Whodathunkit? Sarah Simmons—a savvy chef who pioneered one of the city's most popular pop-up restaurant concepts, City Grit. In 2014, she transitioned into this brick and mortar space, replete with a sexy, low-lit dining room and a fairytale-esque back garden strung with twinkling lights.

The menu is all part of the fun, with dishes listed under cheeky titles like the "Winner Winner Chicken Dinner" or "Fowl Play." This is elevated Southern comfort food at it's best: think buttermilk-brined chicken, deviled eggs and black eyed peas; interesting salads (Southern fattoush, anyone?); and a rotating selection of market sides.

Cafe Katja

Austrian

B2

79 Orchard St. (bet. Broome & Grand Sts.)

Subway: Delancey St
Phone: 212-219-9545
Web: www.cafekatja.com
Price: $$

Lunch Tue – Sun
Dinner nightly

Beer mugs are clinking and schnapps is flowing at the rustic Cafe Katja. After slowly expanding to neighboring storefronts over the past few years, the owners have now realized its much-deserved grandeur without losing its charm. Expats plus locals are de rigueur here, and routinely stop in for incredibly delicious and unbelievably hearty eats.

Co-chef and owner Erwin Schrottner (who hails from outside Graz) keeps everything authentic, from house-made bratwurst platters to the mustard sour cream. The pretzels arrive straight from Europe as divine carbo-bombs served with *liptauer* cheese and butter. The idea of warm chocolate cake may seem passé, but this rendition with terrifically bittersweet orange marmalade is a treat for all the senses.

Cata

A1

Spanish

245 Bowery (at Stanton St.)

Subway: 2 Av
Phone: 212-505-2282
Web: www.catarestaurant.com
Price: $$

Dinner nightly

Blue plaid and jean-clad waiters set the casual tone for Cata, a downtown-cool restaurant with a long bar and glass case displaying the day's fresh seafood. Distressed mirrors, vaulted ceilings, and iron accents fill the dark, cavernous space with a certain broody, old-world vibe. Long communal tables are ideal for groups lingering over small plates and an extensive list of gin-based cocktails.

Nibbling should be the strategy here, starting with whole deviled eggs stuffed with tangy-sweet *gribiche* beneath a single crunchy fried oyster. Crispy bite-sized bombas filled with creamy potato, Manchego, and Serrano ham sit in a very nice, mildly spicy tomato sauce. Paella is ever-pleasing with head-on shrimp, chorizo, and a satisfying *socarrat* at the bottom of the pan.

Clinton St. Baking Company

A m e r i c a n ✗

C1

4 Clinton St. (at Houston St.)

Subway: 2 Av
Phone: 646-602-6263
Web: www.clintonstreetbaking.com
Price: ⌖

Lunch daily
Dinner Mon – Sat

Having finally expanded to include the space next door, the comfort level and service of this brunch-focused *bijou* has greatly improved. And, what started as a bakery is now a legend—one that draws a perpetual crowd waiting for ample rewards. A little bit country and a little bit food lab, this kitchen has achieved such success in NY that the owners now have outposts in Japan and Dubai.

Breakfast for dinner is always a treat, especially when golden-brown Belgian waffles are served with warm maple butter and topped with buttermilk-brined fried chicken for a flawless marriage of sweet and savory. Lighter but still lovely, chicken tortilla soup sees a pile of crunchy fried tortilla strips over hearty broth bobbing with carrots, celery, and shredded chicken.

cocoron

J a p a n e s e ✗

B2

61 Delancey St. (bet. Allen & Eldridge Sts.)

Subway: Delancey St
Phone: 212-925-5220
Web: www.cocoronandgoemon.com
Price: ⌖

Lunch & dinner Tue – Sun

Don't mind the manga posters or the menu's colorful cartoons—this is a serious destination for all things soba. The room is cramped and the furniture flimsy, yet a seat at the counter facing the open kitchen promises excellent cold, warm, and dip soba noodles. Service underwhelms and the scene is quirky, but the focus here is solely on the noodles and noodles alone.

Curry dip soba arrives as a shallow bamboo basket of firm, chilled noodles just as a heavily spiced sauce with pork, ginger, and green onion bubbles away in a clay pot set atop a small flame. Dunk these strands of cold soba into the hot broth and let the slurping begin. Then rest assured that when you're done, the curry is fortified with hot soba water to form a delicious and drinkable soup.

Congee Village

Chinese ✗

B2

100 Allen St. (bet. Broome & Delancey Sts.)

Subway: Delancey St   Lunch & dinner daily
Phone: 212-941-1818
Web: www.congeevillagerestaurants.com
Price: ⬥⬥

From the edge of Chinatown comes Congee Village, with its neon-etched sign that shines bright at night. Coveted for its fantastic cooking (check the front window for a slew of accolades), the menu also has a Cantonese focus. Service is basic and the décor kitschy at best, but it's clean, tidy, and tons of fun.

This soothing namesake porridge comes in myriad forms— ladled into a clay pot with bits of crispy roasted duck skin, or mingled with pork liver and white fish to form an intense and rich flavor combination. Pair it with dunkable sticks of puffy deep-fried Chinese crullers for a satisfying contrast in texture. Less adventurous palates may deviate into such solid standards as sautéed short ribs and sweet onions tossed in a smoky black pepper sauce.

Dirt Candy

Vegetarian ✗✗

B2

86 Allen St. (bet. Broome & Grand Sts.)

Subway: Grand St   Dinner Tue – Sat
Phone: 212-228-7732
Web: www.dirtcandynyc.com
Price: $$

East Village foodies and health nuts can't seem to get enough of this culinarily nourishing vegetarian temple. Chef Amanda Cohen and team have now comfortably settled into their bigger and bolder digs, where industrial elements meld with white walls and the chic bar proffers both cocktails and consolation seating. Sound too good to be true? It isn't.

Dirt Candy's menu is best described as a bounty of creativity, with options like "Fennel," a hearty salad of raw and pickled shavings with black bean cake and caramelized yogurt spread *carta di musica*; as well as "Carrots," the orange veggies roasted with jerk spices and served over a carrot waffle with peanut *mole* sauce. Desserts are every bit as inspired, like a chocolate tart peppered with caramelized onions.

Contra ❀

Contemporary ✗✗

B2

138 Orchard St. (bet. Delancey & Rivington Sts.)

Subway: 2 Av   Dinner Tue – Sat
Phone: 212-466-4633
Web: www.contranyc.com
Price: $$$

Minimal, industrial, and in harmony with the cool neighborhood, this is the kind of classic downtown spot that draws trendy millennials from afar. Seating is either intimate or cramped, and the music is lively or loud, all depending on your mood. Enthusiastic servers add to the room's energy.

Offering six courses for under $70, their prix-fixe is renowned not just for its ambition and creativity but also as one of the best values in town. While the menu format may be fixed, dishes change frequently to reflect the young chefs' wide-ranging talents and contemporary flair. The hallmarks of this kitchen are clean flavors and unfussy technique, as in raw shrimp shimmering with brown butter, served with *tardivo di Treviso*, matcha powder, pink grapefruit, and reddish strips of pickled radish. Then, thin slices of trumpet mushrooms served over a brunoise of Asian pear are balanced with cilantro and dill in a citrusy lemongrass broth, for perfect balance of flavor and texture. Impressive skill is behind the visual appeal in the fluke fillet, beautifully cooked and set in a creamy pool of almond broth with golden tomato segments.

A few doors down, sibling Wildair serves natural wines with signature snacks.

Dirty French

French ✕✕

180 Ludlow St. (bet. Houston & Stanton Sts.)

Subway: 2 Av   Lunch & dinner daily
Phone: 212-254-3000
Web: www.dirtyfrench.com
Price: $$$

Dirty French is Major Food Group's stab at a hotel restaurant—and what a theatrical, charismatic stab it is. Settled in the Ludlow Hotel, this space shares the neighborhood's irreverent attitude, from the pink neon signs at the door to the casual kicks on the hipster waiters. Tables are tightly packed and lively conversations drown out funky music.

This truly unique restaurant designs French-inspired bistro fare with colonial meanderings. Start off with fluffy flatbread slathered with *fromage blanc*. Then, sample the exquisitely executed mille-feuille of trumpet mushrooms in a verdant pool of green curry with pickled hot peppers. Duck *à l'orange* has crackling-crisp skin and tender meat alongside rice pilaf topped with crunchy shallots.

The Fat Radish

Contemporary ✕✕

17 Orchard St. (bet. Canal & Hester Sts.)

Subway: East Broadway   Lunch Tue – Sun
Phone: 212-300-4053   Dinner nightly
Web: www.thefatradishnyc.com
Price: $$

British-leaning yet focused on local and seasonal cooking, this kitchen showcases two ways to indulge—choose between creative vegetarian dishes or old-world classics that are always worth the splurge. The farmhouse-style interior is a nice contrast to the Lower East Side setting, with exposed brick walls, charmingly mismatched wooden seats, and a distressed mirror listing daily specials.

Guests may be torn between the hearty Scotch egg or macrobiotic plate. Yet the casual-cool servers will be quick to point out that just as much detail goes into the burger as the roasted cauliflower over braised lentils with sheep's milk yogurt. Finish the meal in British style with a slice of banoffee pie, with layers of banana, caramel toffee, and fluffy whipped cream.

Fung Tu

Asian ✗✗

A3

22 Orchard St. (bet. Canal & Hester Sts.)

Subway: East Broadway
Phone: 212-219-8785
Web: www.fungtu.com
Price: $$

Dinner Tue – Sun

A drinks list that includes a selection of Fino sherries, a seven-course tasting menu and snacks before the starters—it's fairly apparent that Jonathan Wu's modern Chinese restaurant ploughs its own furrow. It's an intimate, narrow room with a discernible sense of time and place. The dishes are designed for sharing although that's more than you can say for the tables—their size means you'll need to do some juggling or fairly rapid distributing to make room.

Highlights are the entrées such as the very moreish fried rice with crab, which goes very nicely with the whole steamed fish with fennel and tangerine peel. The less convincing dishes are those whose influences are a little more nebulous, like the scallion pancake with smoked chicken.

Ivan Ramen

Japanese ✗

C1

25 Clinton St. (bet. Houston & Stanton Sts.)

Subway: Delancey St
Phone: 646-678-3859
Web: www.ivanramen.com
Price: $$

Lunch & dinner daily

This delicious little *ramen-ya* couldn't have landed on a more fitting spot. It may appear rough around the edges, but the ultra-hip 'hood and its affinity for indie rock beats fit Ivan's scene to a tee. Then consider their sweet staff gliding within the snug space filled with packed seats, and realize how serious a treat this is.

Solo diners head to the counter for a view of the action-packed kitchen, while others look for a seat from which to admire that mural of manga cutouts. Find them launching into pickled daikon with XO sauce and sesame seeds for a 'lil crunch and whole 'lotta flavor. Displaying a flare for non-traditional ingredients, *paitan* ramen with tender chicken confit in a chicken-and-kombu broth makes for a singular, savory, and tasty highlight.

Katz's

Deli ✖

205 E. Houston St. (at Ludlow St.)

Subway: 2 Av
Phone: 212-254-2246
Web: www.katzsdelicatessen.com
Price: 😊

Lunch & dinner daily

 One of the last-standing, old-time Eastern European spots on the Lower East Side, Katz's is a true NY institution. It's crowded, crazy, and packed with a panoply of characters weirder than a jury duty pool. Tourists, hipsters, blue hairs, and everybody in between flock here, so come on off-hours. Because it's really *that* good.

Walk inside, get a ticket, and don't lose it (those guys at the front aren't hosts—upset their system and you'll get a verbal beating). Then pick up your food at the counter and bring it to a first-come first-get table; or opt for a slightly less dizzying experience at a waitress-served table.

Nothing's changed in the looks or taste. Matzo ball soup, pastrami sandwiches, potato latkes—everything is what you'd expect, only better.

Kiki's

Greek

130 Division St. (at Orchard St.)

Subway: East Broadway
Phone: 646-882-7052
Web: N/A
Price: $$

Lunch & dinner daily

This is where to find excellent home-style Greek cooking at unbeatable prices. Everything tastes fundamentally right and good, from the perfectly tender braised and grilled octopus to those moist and smoky lamb chops—the aromas alone guarantee that you will dine well here. Start with a superb spanakopita that balances flaky filo with just the right amount of chopped spinach dotted with onion and feta. Saganaki entices with salty and springy Greek cheese wrapped in filo that manages to stay crisp beneath a rich drenching of honey and sesame seeds.

The tavern-like space feels attractively dark, cozy, fills up quickly, and doesn't take reservations so expect a wait. The servers and staff are a stylish and laid-back mirror image of the neighborhood.

Le Turtle

Contemporary

A1

177 Chrystie St. (at Rivington St.)

Subway: Bowery
Phone: 646-918-7189
Web: www.leturtle.fr
Price: $$

Dinner nightly

Experience and style converge at this beautiful destination and instant favorite of the cool kids in town.

The cuisine is not only as attractive as the setting, but sophisticated flavors ensure its success. Kohlrabi bisque is deliciously creamy, with ambitious garnishes like smoked cabbage, pickled mustard seeds, and bits of intensely rich lamb belly to make it savory and very memorable. Straightforward skill is clear in the scored curls of squid served with a refreshing salsa verde, embellished with *oroblanco*. Every flavor is perfectly complementary in the dense and buttery hazelnut financier, from the chewy caramelized edges to the quenelles of lemon yogurt sorbet and pear purée.

A moderately priced list showcases unique and interesting French wines.

Louie and Chan

Italian

A2

303 Broome St. (bet. Eldridge & Forsyth Sts.)

Subway: Grand St
Phone: 212-837-2816
Web: www.louieandchan.com
Price: $$

Lunch Sat – Sun
Dinner nightly

With a name that nods to the convergence of Chinese and Italian immigrants in this part of lower Manhattan, Louie and Chan is a dimly lit, tightly packed restaurant with inspired cooking. The main space feels more bar than dining room, with intentionally scruffy walls decorated with distressed mirrors. Service is friendly and a young crowd keeps things lively.

Cocktails are Asian-inspired while the menu uses Italy as its muse. Delicate gnudi arrive in a rustic bowl of tender lamb ragù topped with a dollop of smoked ricotta. A wood-burning oven is responsible for the blistered crust pizzas, including the *bacio del diavolo*, decked with tart tomato sauce, chunks of 'nduja, house-made mozzarella, and spicy whole Calabrese peppers.

The Lucky Bee

Asian ✗

B2

252 Broome St. (bet. Ludlow & Orchard Sts.)

Subway: Delancey St
Phone: 844-364-4286
Web: www.luckybeenyc.com
Price: $$

Dinner nightly

This inviting Southeast Asian-inspired restaurant is housed in a quirky retro space accented by bold prints and neon lights. It's a small restaurant, but it practically pulsates with energy. Cocktails are made with local honey to support the NYC Bee Keepers Association, as fun 70s music plays loudly overhead. Tuck into tender pork and sesame dumplings drizzled with a sharp black vinegar reduction, fermented black beans, and sesame seeds; or try a bowl of glistening duck *larb* tossed with mint, basil and raw onions for a crunchy surprise.

Don't miss Thai specialties like *khao soi*, a Northern Thai noodle curry with chicken, pickled mustard greens and a nest of fried noodles in rich coconut broth; or coconut-braised short rib with an excellent green curry.

Macondo

Latin American ✗✗

B1

157 E. Houston St. (bet. Allen & Eldridge Sts.)

Subway: 2 Av
Phone: 212-473-9900
Web: www.macondonyc.com
Price: $$

Lunch Sat – Sun
Dinner nightly

Readers of Gabriel Garcia Marquez will be familiar with this Latin American restaurant's name—Macondo is the fictional setting of *100 Years of Solitude*. Here on the Lower East Side (and at the West Village outpost), it is an intimate small plates restaurant with a long bar of counter seating, semi-open kitchen, and exposed brick walls with stocked shelves of Latin pantry ingredients.

Sharing is the strategy here, from the crispy chicken croquettes to the raw kale and manchego salad with crunchy roasted pumpkin seeds and a sweet kick from sticky dried dates, topped with a lemon-chipotle dressing. Be prepared to battle over the last bite of *arroz con pollo*, a piping-hot cast iron pan of plump bomba rice, piquant chorizo, tender chicken, and cherry tomatoes.

The Metrograph Commissary

American ✗✗

A3

7 Ludlow St. (bet. Canal & Hester Sts.)

Subway: East Broadway   Dinner nightly
Phone: 347-348-0617
Web: www.metrograph.com
Price: $$

Located on the second floor of The Metrograph theater—a small, independent two-screen movie house in the Lower East Side—The Commisary channels an old Hollywood vibe. Picture retro furniture, potted palms, and plenty of cozy nooks to relax in. The food is simple but sophisticated for the neighborhood, offering a lovely American slant on bistro fare. Even the concessions downstairs are worth perusing for their unusual selection.

The menu is brief but tempting, with small plates of steak tartare, fluke crudo and burrata getting play next to classic salads (think Waldorf and kale Caesars), as well as pleasing entrées like roasted chicken, steak frites and brown butter trout. Comforting sides like mac-and-cheese and steamed broccoli make it a truly American affair.

Mr. Taka

Japanese ✗

B1

170 Allen St. (bet. Stanton & Rivington Sts.)

Subway: 2 Av   Lunch & dinner daily
Phone: 212-254-1508
Web: www.mrtakaramen.com
Price: $$

When the chef of a successful Tokyo *ramen-ya* opens a spot in NY, success is virtually guaranteed. Mr. Taka may seem small and simple, but the food is fun and distinctive.

The cooking here is a delicious break from tradition, thanks to ramen that ranges in toppings from avocado to the richest slice of pork belly on this side of the Pacific. Of course, all of these garnishes depend on the broth—the spicy miso ramen is made with chicken and bonito, wafting with aromas that are at once spicy, savory, and sweet. These thick ribbons of noodles have a springy, bouncy texture that is never lost within the mounds of bean sprouts, scallions, soft-boiled egg, and much more. Other highlights include a crunchy *hijiki* salad and piping-hot batons of deep purple sweet potato tempura.

Russ & Daughters Cafe

Deli

127 Orchard St. (bet. Delancey & Rivington Sts.)

Subway: Delancey St
Phone: 212-475-4881
Web: www.russanddaughterscafe.com
Price: $$

Lunch & dinner daily

From white-jacketed servers to that pristine counter, this updated yet model LES café channels the very spirit and charm of its mothership, set only blocks away. The adept kitchen follows suit, taking the original, appetizing classics and turning them on their heads to form an array of proper and profoundly flavorful dishes.

Regulars perch at the bar to watch the 'tender whip up a cocktail or classic egg cream, while serious diners find a seat and get noshing on hot- and cold-smoked Scottish salmon teamed with potato crisps. The result? A thrilling contrast in flavor and texture. Caramelized chocolate babka French toast is crowned with strawberries for a sweet-savory treat; and "eggs Benny" with salmon, spinach, and challah never fails to peg a bruncher.

SakaMai

Japanese

157 Ludlow St. (bet. Rivington & Stanton Sts.)

Subway: Delancey St
Phone: 646-590-0684
Web: www.sakamai.com
Price: $$$

Dinner nightly

Nestled smack in the middle of the Lower East Side's nightlife hub, this stylish Japanese gastro lounge is a must-do for the adventurous eater. SakaMai's wheelhouse is transforming highbrow ingredients (maybe foie gras, Wagyu beef, luscious uni and caviar) into delicious small plates that pair exceptionally with their formidable Japanese liquor and sake list.

The menu is arranged into a collection of interesting, *izakaya*-style, shared plates, but there is a $65 tasting menu available as well for those with serious appetites. Dishes often blend Japanese technique with non-traditional ingredients like radicchio or parmesan. Don't miss the *yakisaba*—box-pressed nigiri topped with smoky, grilled mackerel, crispy *lardo Ibérico*, and scallions.

Sauce

Italian X

B1

78-84 Rivington St. (at Allen St.)

Subway: 2 Av
Phone: 212-420-7700
Web: www.saucerestaurant.com
Price: $$

Lunch Sat – Sun
Dinner nightly

What would you expect from a spot called Sauce? Some serious and very delicious red sauce—naturally! Serving Italian-American comfort food with a nostalgic décor to match, Sauce stays modern with its local, hipster-friendly playlist, and quirky ambience—the attractive crowd doesn't hurt either. It's a fun meal to say the least.

Pasta is made in-house daily, with specials that feature potato-kale gnocchi or the signature ricotta *cavatelli* showered with pecorino. The menu highlights regional specialties from Little Italys across the country, including SF's cioppino and classic *Nuyorkese* tomato gravy like *nonna* used to make. Try the robust Sergio Leone steak smothered in tomato sauce and topped with a fried heritage egg for tons of fun and flavor.

Spitzer's Corner

 Gastropub

B2

101 Rivington St. (at Ludlow St.)

Subway: Delancey St
Phone: 212-228-0027
Web: www.spitzerscorner.com
Price: $$

Lunch & dinner daily

Spitzer's is a spirited corner eatery dedicated to craft brews and gastropub fare in a buzzing locale. Large glass windows overlook the heart of the neighborhood, providing an entertaining vantage point for people-watching over pints of nutty Bronx Pale Ale. There are large communal tables made of reclaimed wood and chalkboards listing comfort food classics.

This is a cozy drinking den, and its kitchen focuses on food that pairs well with suds. Tables are laden with quality renditions of burgers and mac 'n cheese. Spinach and artichoke dip is equally comforting, topped with broiled cheese and served with char-grilled pita. A fried chicken sandwich sees generous chunks of crunchy thigh meat stuffed into potato rolls with butter lettuce and a pickle.

The Stanton Social

B1

99 Stanton St. (bet. Ludlow & Orchard Sts.)

Subway: 2 Av
Phone: 212-995-0099
Web: www.thestantonsocial.com
Price: $$

Lunch Sat – Sun
Dinner nightly

This stylish downtown looker has been going strong for over a decade now. Unlike the hip spots that burn brightly then fade, The Stanton Social still has the stuff—best evidenced, perhaps, by the throngs of beautiful young things that fill its seats every weekend. That said, it's not so cool that you won't find a family with kids squeaking through the door for an early dinner.

Inside the generous space, you'll find sultry purple velvet booths and dark wooden tables. The thumping music and dim lights give it a clubby vibe, as does the bar and lounge upstairs. The food is equally eclectic and playful, with a delicious shareable menu that includes the popular French onion soup dumplings, a "Big Sexy Burger," and Mexican street corn ravioli.

Thelma on Clinton

C1

29A Clinton St. (bet. Houston & Stanton Sts.)

Subway: Essex St
Phone: 212-979-8471
Web: www.thelmaonclinton.com
Price: $$

Lunch Sat – Sun
Dinner Mon – Sat

With its cozy bistro décor and sincere, down-to-earth service, Thelma on Clinton is the kind of unpretentious restaurant everyone wants around the corner from home.

Owner Melissa O'Donnell is a longtime fixture on New York's restaurant scene, and Thelma is her latest contribution—this time, in her old Salt Bar space. Does she kill it? She kills it. And she might just get double credit for producing such delicious fare in a kitchen smaller than some local apartment kitchens. Kick things off with the scrumptious bacon-wrapped dates, laced in a irresistible, sticky maple sauce. Then move on to tender spring pea and asparagus risotto showered with Grana Padano cheese; or olive oil-poached codfish in a lovely citrus sauce.

Wassail

Vegetarian

162 Orchard St. (bet. Rivington & Stanton Sts.)

Subway: 2 Av
Phone: 646-918-6835
Web: www.wassailnyc.com
Price: $$

Dinner nightly

Everyone's buzzing about Wassail's awesome list of 90+ ciders from around the world, but there are a few more delectable reasons to check out this modern and much loved tavern. The vegetable- and grain-focused menu is contemporary in style, and the technique, seasonality, and personality the kitchen brings to each dish will sway even the most adamant carnivore.

Though the menu is small, you can't really miss here. Soft, chewy sweet potato dumplings are perfectly caramelized, topped with pea shoots and baby bok choy, then laced in a luscious sweet-and-sour coconut broth with smashed coriander seeds. But leave room as it would be a sin to skip such brilliantly executed desserts as a rich, fudgy devil's food cake with milk jam and sage ice cream.

Yopparai

Japanese

C2

151 Rivington St. (bet. Clinton & Suffolk Sts.)

Subway: Delancey St
Phone: 212-777-7253
Web: www.yopparainyc.com
Price: $$$

Dinner Mon – Sat

Guests ring a buzzer to gain access to this clandestine *izakaya*. Inside, you'll find a stylish, serene cubby hole—reservations are a must on popular nights—where every point of your experience has been thoughtfully considered, from the two-person bar stools to the kimono-clad servers with answers at the ready. Two chefs perform their magic in view: one works the grill station while the other tackles sashimi and steamed dishes. A small kitchen in the back pushes out occasional items as well. The menu offers barbecue dishes, *robata* specials, as well as other seasonal delights. But you'll have the most fun ordering a little of everything—each new presentation is truly an artful revelation.

Housed just down the block, Azasu is the modern and much loved sibling.

Midtown East

An interesting mix of office buildings, hotels, high-rises, and townhouses, Midtown East is one of the city's most industrious areas. Home to the iconic Chrysler Building and United Nations Headquarters, the vibe here is buzzing with suits, students, and old-timers wandering its streets. Whether it's that reliable diner on the corner, a gourmet supermarket, or fine dining gem, this neighborhood flaunts it all. Close on the heels of its global theme, **Adana Grill** is a highly enjoyable Turkish takeout spot, where items are grilled to order. The wait is long and entirely worth it. Residents of neighboring Beekman and Sutton Place are proud of their very own cheese shop (**Ideal Cheese**); butcher (**L. Simchick Meats**); bagel and lox shop (**Tal Bagels**); and to complete any dinner party—renowned florist (**Zeze**). While **Dag Hammarskjöld Plaza Greenmarket** is for the most part dwarfed by Union Square, come Wednesdays it presents just the right amount of produce to feed hungry locals. Then sample a bit of chic at Paris-based café **Rose Bakery**, set inside the very haute and hip Dover Street Market. It may be tucked behind a soaring cement column sheathed in colorful macramé, but turn a corner to find display cases filled with fresh salads and tempting sweets.

GRAND CENTRAL TERMINAL

Built by the Vanderbilt family in the 19th century, **Grand Central Terminal** is a 21st century food sanctuary. An ideal day at this titanic and particularly

gorgeous train station may begin with a coffee from **Joe's**. Later, stop by one of Manhattan's historic sites, the **Grand Central Oyster Bar & Restaurant**, nestled into the cavernous lower level. This gorgeous seafood respite presents everything from shellfish stews and pristine fish, to an incredible raw bar and more. Then take a turn—of taste—and head to **Neuhaus**, venerable chocolatiers who craft their delicacies from exceptional ingredients. Others may stop by family-owned and renowned **Li-Lac Chocolates** for such nostalgic confections as dark chocolate-covered pretzels or beautifully packaged holiday gift boxes. Of course, no trip to this Terminal is complete without a visit to the "whispering gallery" where low, ceramic-tiled arches allow whispers to sound more like shouts. Just beyond, the loud dining concourse hums with lunch stalls ranging from **Café Spice** for Indian or **Eata Pita** for Middle Eastern. **Mendy's** is midtown's go-to for everything kosher—think pastrami and brisket mingled in with some Mid-Eastern eats. Then, finish with the sweetest treats— maybe red velvet cupcakes at the Terminal's very own **Magnolia Bakery** outpost. Moving on to the market, Eli Zabar has expanded

his empire, and continues to proffer the freshest fruits and vegetables at **Eli Zabar's Farm to Table**. But, for an impressive assortment of pastries and cakes, **Eli Zabar's Bread & Pastry** is your best bet. In addition to its myriad fishmongers, butchers, and bakers, home cooks and top chefs are likely to find the best selection of spices here—at one of the market's better-kept secrets, **Spices and Tease**, specializing exotic blends and...you guessed it...unique teas. But, if you're among hungry hordes with time to spare, make sure to visit one

237

of the several prized restaurants situated beneath Grand Central's celestial ceiling mural for a stellar night. And finally, if the scene in the Terminal is too corporate for your liking, then head on over to **Urbanspace Vanderbilt**. This lively food hall may exist in the heart of commercial Manhattan, but it showcases over 20 cutting-edge culinary concepts, and is a recent destination.

JAPANTOWN

Trek a few blocks east of Lexington to find a very sophisticated Japantown, where scores of *izakaya* and restaurants are scattered among hostess clubs. Salarymen frequent old-world hangouts like **Riki**, **Ariyoshi**, and **Tsukushi**, or even rookies like **Lucky Cat**. Favored **BentOn Cafe** is a retail outpost of a bento delivery service, but tenders daily changing bentos at terrific value. Expats with ladies in tow linger over the psuedo-Italian spread at **Aya**, just as the yuppy crews may opt for a light bite from **Cafe Zaiya** or **Dainobu** (both bustling deli-cum-markets). **Nishida Shoten** is cherished for comforting noodles soups; **Hinata Ramen** is an all-time gem for steaming bowls of ramen. Red meat fiends join the lines outside **Katsu-Hama** or **Yakiniku Gen** for delicious grilled meats. Looking

to impress your out-of-town guests? Plan a Japanese-themed evening by stocking up on gleaming ceramics, cookware, and authentic produce from specialty emporium, **MTC Kitchen**. A few blocks south, younger and quieter Murray Hill has its own distinct vibe. Here, fast-casual finds thrive thanks to thirty-somethings sating late-night cravings. Meanwhile, **The Kitano**, one among a handful of Gotham's Japanese-owned boutique hotels, continues to lure thanks to its sleek vibe, live tunes at **JAZZ at Kitano**, and traditional kaiseki cuisine served at their very own subterranean hot spot, **Hakubai**.

SWEETS AND SPIRITS

Slightly north, owner and pastry chef, Stephane Pourrez, brings French flair and baked treats to **Éclair** on 53rd Street. Presenting a lineup of pastries, cakes, macarons, and of course, those eponymous eclairs, this sweet midtown spot also houses some of *the* flakiest croissants in town. Steps away indulge in wine and Mediterranean-inspired small plates at petite **Pierre Loti**.

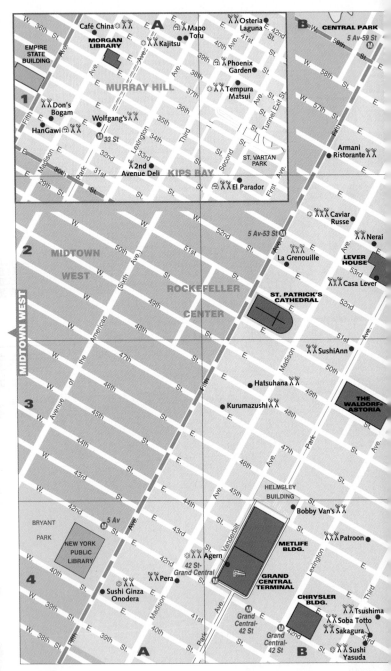

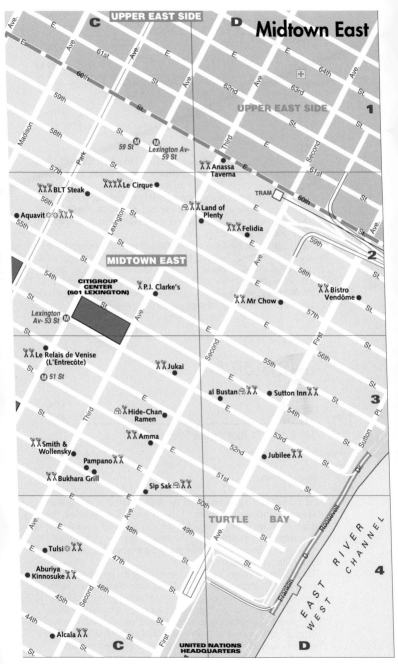

Aburiya Kinnosuke

C4

213 E. 45th St. (bet. Second & Third Aves.)

Subway: Grand Central - 42 St
Phone: 212-867-5454
Web: www.aburiyakinnosuke.com
Price: $$$

Lunch Mon – Fri
Dinner nightly

Call it a trip to Tokyo without the tariff. This dark, sophisticated Japanese *izakaya* is tucked down a side street in bustling midtown. Grab an intimate table for two or join the crowd at the open kitchen counter surrounding the smoky *robata* grill. The waiters talk up the omakase, but it's worth trusting your own instincts to guide you on a personalized tour through their authentic offerings.

The *sukiyaki* is a must-try seasonal offering of tender marbled beef served in a hot pot bobbing with a beaten egg, tofu, vegetables, and noodles. Other favorites include smoky bamboo shoots fresh off the *robata* with shaved bonito; and their legendary *tsukune*, a tender ground chicken meatball brushed with teriyaki and dipped in raw egg.

al Bustan

D3

319 E. 53rd St. (bet. First & Second Aves.)

Subway: Lexington Av - 53 St
Phone: 212-759-5933
Web: www.albustanny.com/
Price: $$

Lunch & dinner daily

Lebanese specialties are fired up with aplomb at Al Bustan, where a moneyed Middle Eastern crowd dominates the space, along with a steady stream of locals (including diplomats from neighboring UN). Inside, glittering chandeliers hang from a beam-lined ceiling and neat white leather chairs impart an air of elegance.

The expansive menu boasts a slew of meze, house specials, and a knockout dinner prix-fixe. Kick things off with a crunchy fattoush salad; or *sambousek jibneh*, a baked pastry bubbling with salty feta. You can't go wrong adding a *mashawi* (mixed grill platter for sharing) to your order; or for that matter, *kouzi*, a giant, round of flaky homemade phyllo stuffed with heavenly spiced rice, peas, carrots and tender gamey lamb.

Agern

S c a n d i n a v i a n

B4

89 E. 42nd St. (at Vanderbilt Ave.)

Subway: Grand Central - 42 St
Phone: 646-568-4018
Web: www.agernrestaurant.com
Price: **$$$$**

Lunch Mon – Fri
Dinner nightly

When Claus Meyer opens a New York restaurant, there is an undeniable "Noma factor" that has locals running to the door (hidden as it is on the corner of Vanderbilt and 42nd). The design is gorgeous, drinks are outstanding, and the location is ideal for midtown business lunches—of a certain type. Dining here is pleasing as well as cerebral and unapologetically expressive of the New Nordic food scene, without a flight to Copenhagen. They may be using local ingredients, but that distinctive Scandinavian style dominates every dish.

Bitter, sour, and fermented flavors reappear throughout each meal, perhaps beginning with a snack that combines icy oysters with pine needles. The salt and ash-baked beet is an instant signature that summarizes the kitchen's talents: it is cracked tableside for a dramatic presentation of earthy, sweet beets balanced with an aggressively acidic vinegar sauce, crème fraîche, leaves and shoots, all accompanied by their fantastic bread. This may seem like a lot of fuss, but it is unpretentious and thoroughly delicious. Desserts might virtually explode with rhubarb, sorrel, and the flavors of a summer garden.

Also try the adjacent takeout spot for simpler lunches and pastries.

Alcala

C4

246 E. 44th St. (bet. Second & Third Aves.)

Subway: Grand Central - 42 St
Phone: 212-370-1866
Web: www.alcalarestaurant.com
Price: $$$

Lunch Mon – Fri
Dinner nightly

This cozy Spanish eatery is a stone's throw from the United Nations, drawing a lively evening mix of sophisticated international clientele and neighborhood regulars. With its buttery yellow walls and homey little bar stocked with delicious Spanish wines, Alcala might remind you of an old Spanish *finca*, but at heart it's also one of those old school New York haunts, where the waiters and cooks have been in place forever and you wouldn't dream of kicking your meal off without a drink.

The dishes are delicious, well-prepared, and ample. Try the *sardinas a la parrilla*, laced with hot pimiento oil; fresh, grilled branzino in a bright tomato coulis; or the *tarta de aresse*, a rich custard pie with mouthwatering crème anglaise and strawberry coulis.

Amma

C3

246 E. 51st St. (bet. Second & Third Aves.)

Subway: 51 St
Phone: 212-644-8330
Web: www.ammanyc.com
Price: $$

Lunch & dinner daily

Vibrant family-style South Asian cooking is appropriately set within this former townhouse, as *amma* is the word for mother in several South Indian languages. And manners are a must, as this "home" is adjacent to the UN, and service is attentively buttoned-up.

Find generously-portioned options from both the north and south subcontinent. Street snack Bombay *bhel puri* is colorfully seasoned with tamarind water and mango powder-laced *chaat masala*. Hard-to-find menu items such as *bagharey baingan* or eggplants simmered in a thick, rich peanut curry, make you feel like you've been let in on a little secret and invited to the neighbor's party. Pistachio *kulfi* is a satisfyingly sweet, cardamom-spiced finale which makes another neighborly visit inevitable.

Anassa Taverna

D1

Greek ✗✗

200 E. 60th St. (at Third Ave.)

Subway: 59 St
Phone: 212-371-5200
Web: www.anassataverna.com
Price: $$

Lunch & dinner daily

Two floors of whitewashed brick walls and large windows dressed with sheer drapery provide a respite for weary shoppers and a sociable clientele at this contemporary taverna. The upstairs dining room is sedate, but remains your best bet when crowds pack the ground-level bar area.

Anassa's menu is an honest presentation of Greek specialties, including a platter of spreads, sushi-quality charcoal-broiled octopus, and a selection of Mediterranean and North Atlantic fish to be grilled and dressed with extra virgin olive oil, fresh lemon, and capers. Nightly specials add further variety to the extensive menu. Don't miss Wednesday's luscious slow-roasted pork shoulder served fork-tender in a parchment bundle with fresh herbs and wedges of lemon potatoes.

Armani Ristorante

B1

Italian ✗✗

717 5th Ave. (at 56th St.)

Subway: 5 Av - 53 St
Phone: 212-207-1902
Web: www.armanirestaurants.com
Price: $$$

Lunch daily
Dinner Mon – Sat

At Giorgio Armani's Fifth Avenue restaurant what you're wearing is as important as what you're eating. Overlooking the famous street, models serve as (distracted) staff members and bartenders are pure showstoppers—to no one's surprise. Would you expect anything less of the man whose luxurious Armani Casa furniture lines the space?

His streamlined and modern aesthetic prevails, right down to the glistening, ruby-red tuna tartare. Each cube cut by hand, the sea-fresh fish rolls in truffle oil and chives with briny sea beans and trout roe for a fantastic play on texture. Equally precise, the pan-seared spring flounder is infused with a coriander reduction, fresh porcini, and fennel with an airy foam that looks so good it may as well be Photoshopped.

Aquavit

Scandinavian XxX

65 E. 55th St. (bet. Madison & Park Aves.)

Subway: 5 Av - 53 St
Phone: 212-307-7311
Web: www.aquavit.org
Price: $$$$

Lunch Mon – Fri
Dinner Mon – Sat

No detail goes unnoticed at this sleek Scandinavian beauty, where black-suited servers line the room waiting to assist guests and fur-covered benches are presented for your handbags. The overall design of Aquavit is clean, elegant and contemporary—with dark floors, wood tabletops, and sleek, high-backed leather chairs. Courses arrive in equally beautiful, but minimalist, dishware like wood boxes, slate platters, and glazed earthenware.

Aquavit does many things well, but what makes it one of the more unique restaurants in the city is the kitchen's ability to take bold Scandinavian flavors like dill, lingonberry, smoke or brine, and soften them into impeccably balanced, whimsical and elegant dishes. Take for example, a silky cut of Arctic char, which is delicately poached in brown butter and set atop velvety new potato purée, then paired with dill béarnaise, salt-cured cucumber, chive blossoms, new potatoes and briny beads of Kalix Löjrom.

Finally, don't miss the namesake aquavit, offered in house-made flavors like anise-caraway-fennel, fig-cardamom, or elderflower-Meyer lemon; or the imported variety in flavors like white cranberry (from Sweden) or caraway-anise (from Norway).

Bistro Vendôme

D2

French ✗✗

405 E. 58th St. (bet. First Ave. & Sutton Pl.)

Subway: 59 St
Phone: 212-935-9100
Web: www.bistrovendomenyc.com
Price: $$

Lunch & dinner daily

The nearby residents of Sutton Place fit Bistro Vendôme, a classic sort of spot where three cozy dining rooms, top-notch service, and excellent food come together seamlessly. Often glimpsed gliding across the restaurant, the husband-and-wife owners warmly cater to locals during pleasant but humming dinner hours. The space makes everyone feel lucky—such solid dining options don't typically exist this far east.

Familiar and well-done classics may include an enjoyably but never overwhelmingly flavorful fish soup, served with Gruyère, *rouille*, and croûtes. Well-executed striped bass arrives with a bed of zucchini cooked in a fragrant tomato-saffron broth; while an *ile flottante* with caramel sauce is like an ode to the Parisian bistro.

BLT Steak

C2

Steakhouse ✗✗✗

106 E. 57th St. (bet. Lexington & Park Aves.)

Subway: 59 St
Phone: 212-752-7470
Web: www.bltsteak.com
Price: $$$$

Lunch Mon – Fri
Dinner nightly

There is no mistaking the fact that this is a corporate chain. However, the experience of dining here is just as much about fun as it is food. In fact, those massive and airy popovers set quite the lively tone for a meal capped off with miniature brownies.

No need to spend much time perusing the starters or salads. Feasts here should focus on a martini and a nicely cooked steak, like a Porterhouse served sliced alongside outstanding béarnaise and blue cheese sauces (skip the herbed butter). Do not, under any circumstances, hold back when choosing sides. Sirens are surely singing from that tower of crisp and thickly battered onion rings, mini cast-iron pots of creamed spinach, or those mod-ish potato skins covered in cheddar, sour cream, and scallions.

Bobby Van's

✕✕

B4

230 Park Ave. (in East Walkway & 46th St.)

Subway: Grand Central - 42 St
Phone: 212-867-5490
Web: www.bobbyvans.com
Price: $$$$

Lunch Mon – Fri
Dinner Mon – Sat

♿

🍽

Nestled at the base of The Helmsley building near Grand Central lies Bobby Van's, a perennial favorite of the expense-account set. Its classic steakhouse atmosphere—gruff but prompt service, noisy post-work bar scene, and gargantuan portions—is met with commendable dishes that reach beyond the normal chop shop fare.

While the beef speaks for itself, the kitchen's execution takes common combos to the next level: mozzarella and tomatoes are drizzled in flavorful balsamic and olive oil with a chiffonade of basil and shallots; while soft-shell crabs arrive perfectly battered and tempura fried. This massive special, with crisp asparagus and bed of sautéed spinach, showcases great culinary technique and seasonality not expected from a midtown lunch hangout.

Bukhara Grill

✕✕

C3

217 E. 49th St. (bet. Second & Third Aves.)

Subway: 51 St
Phone: 212-888-2839
Web: www.bukharany.com
Price: $$$

Lunch & dinner daily

🍽

In NYC's ever-expanding realm of Indian dining, Bukhara Grill has stood the test of time with excellence. Glimpse their expert chefs who seem contentedly trapped behind a glass kitchen wall. Featuring a noisy and yuppie set, this tri-level space is decorated (albeit oddly) with clunky wooden booths, closely set tables, and private rooms.

Peek into the kitchen for a whiff of *tandoori* treats and Mughlai specialties. *Dahi aloo papri* or spicy potatoes and chickpeas tossed in yogurt and tamarind is a predictably perfect starter. The signature, wickedly creamy *dal* Bukhara will have you coming back for more (tomorrow). Even if the service may range from sweet to clumsy, hand-crafted breads meant to sop up the likes of *sarson ka saag* remain a crowning glory.

Café China ❀

Chinese ✗✗

13 E. 37th St. (bet. Fifth & Madison Aves.)

Subway: 34 St - Herald Sq
Phone: 212-213-2810
Web: www.cafechinanyc.com
Price: $$

Lunch & dinner daily

Blink and you'll miss its inconspicuous façade, but what a shame, for Café China is a little journey into the magnificent pleasures of Sichuan cuisine by way of midtown. Inside find a long, narrow space fitted with seductive portraits of 1930's Shanghai starlets, bright red chairs, bamboo planters and a dominating marble-and-wood bar.

After struggling with their on-again-off-again popularity, this kitchen is back to their A-game, producing Sichuan (and Sichuan-influenced) dishes with aplomb. Their particular strength lies in the elegant and effortless contrast of complex flavors, even when the prep is decidedly simple—as in the delicious steamed eggplant and ginger sautéed duck.

Pickled vegetables achieve harmonious balance between sour and fiery notes; while thinly sliced conch pairs perfectly with tingly chili oil. Sichuan pork dumplings arrive in a delicate wrapper and atop a delicious bath of soy and chili oil. But save space to savor the Chungking chicken, alternately tender and crispy, with abundant dried chilies, scallions and sesame seeds. Spicy cumin lamb, fried to gamey perfection and tossed with sesame seeds, chili peppers and cilantro, is yet another smoky treat.

Casa Lever

Italian

B2

390 Park Ave. (entrance on 53rd St.)

Subway: Lexington Av - 53 St
Phone: 212-888-2700
Web: www.casalever.com
Price: $$$$

Lunch Mon – Fri
Dinner Mon – Sat

It must be mildly dispiriting to be the chef at Casa Lever because your food has much to compete with. Firstly, the restaurant boasts a hugely impressive and ever expanding collection of Andy Warhol portraits, ranging from the Shah of Iran to Rudolf Nureyev. Secondly, most of the customers are here for the business of business and their chief concern is closing a deal, not hearing about the provenance of ingredients.

For those who are interested, the food shows considerable care and flair. The focus is on northern parts of Italy but dishes like the excellent lobster gnocchetti or the sea urchin linguine are more than a match for classics like veal Milanese. Those unhindered by financial imperatives could try coming during truffle season.

Don's Bogam

Korean

A1

17 E. 32nd St. (bet. Fifth & Madison Aves.)

Subway: 33 St
Phone: 212-683-2200
Web: www.donsbogam.com
Price: $$

Lunch & dinner daily

At Don's Bogam, the food is fantastic and service indulgent. So, reserve ahead as every seat is filled—from the festive bar up front right down to those fun two-tops sporting blazing grills. Make no mistake—this is no average K-town joint. Inside, a top-notch venting system lets diners enjoy a smoke-free evening of exceptional grilled meats. Start wtih deep-fried pork *mandu*, which are crisp, on-point, and extra divine. Wonderfully flaky *buchu gochu pajeon* is studded with chives for perfect flavor; while pork belly marinated in red wine is smoky and supremely tender.

For the ultimate payoff, opt for the memorable beef platter featuring thinly sliced *macun* and *yangneuym galbi* set beside king trumpet mushrooms—meaty and mouthwatering in their own right.

Caviar Russe ✿

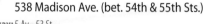

Contemporary 𝗫𝗫𝗫

B2

538 Madison Ave. (bet. 54th & 55th Sts.)

Subway: 5 Av - 53 St
Phone: 212-980-5908
Web: www.caviarrusse.com
Price: $$$$

Lunch daily
Dinner Mon – Sat

No playful pun, no name-check for grandma, no oblique reference to a geographical landmark—whoever christened this restaurant clearly wanted to attract a certain type of customer.

This is not the place where you should order by pointing vaguely at the menu—that way lies trouble because you may find yourself having to re-mortgage your apartment to pay for the 250 grams of Osetra caviar you've just inadvertently requested. Best leave that section of the carte to the oligarchs and retired dictators and concentrate on the main menu. Here you will find contemporary dishes of surprising delicacy and precision, with a pleasing bias towards wonderful seafood and shellfish, such as scallops with ricotta gnudi, or delicious bluefin tuna with uni and asparagus.

You get buzzed in at street level, which adds a bit of mystery to proceedings. Up the stairs and you'll find yourself in a lavish little jewel box, with colorful murals on the wall, Murano chandeliers hanging from an ornate ceiling, and semi-circular booths. The only thing missing is James Bond's nemesis drumming his fingers on the table in the corner.

El Parador 🐶

B2

325 E. 34th St. (bet. First & Second Aves.)

Subway: 33 St
Phone: 212-679-6812
Web: www.elparadorcafe.com
Price: $$

Lunch & dinner Mon – Sat

This neighborhood mainstay boasts over fifty years of success. With their fantastic menu, killer margaritas, and dedication to hospitality, El Parador is worthy of its status as a beloved destination. The intimate space is decked with ornate wood chairs, red banquettes, and wood plank ceilings, while white brick walls are hung with artwork and artifacts.

The bountiful menu offers favorites like taco trays and nachos in three varieties, as well as a rotating menu of daily specials (be sure to try the fish of the day). Fill up on *aguachile de camaron*, deliciously classic shrimp ceviche in lime juice and jalapeño; or tender, falling-off-the-bone baby-back ribs served with tequila-chili *guajillo* salsa, cabbage slaw, and braised *camote*.

Margaritas are a must, but of course.

Felidia

D2

243 E. 58th St. (bet. Second & Third Aves.)

Subway: Lexington Av - 59 St
Phone: 212-758-1479
Web: www.felidia-nyc.com
Price: $$$$

Lunch Mon – Fri
Dinner nightly

Cookbook author, television series host, and restaurateur Lidia Bastianich has been behind this flagship restaurant and greeting customers since 1981. Service could use a little finesse and some of Bastianich's charm, but the elegant décor inspires dressing up for dinner and the exceptional wine list offers a vast collection of Italian choices.

Signature *paste* sparkle here, such as *cacio e pere* ravioli stuffed with delicate pear and bathed in black pepper and pecorino. Massive portions of scallops, squid, a split langoustine, and lobster star in the *grigliata* drizzled with lemon vinaigrette. Rely on Lidia to deliver a cannoli that lives up to its true potential—envision narrow tubes filled with lemony ricotta cream spilling into the center of the plate.

HanGawi

Korean

A1

12 E. 32nd St. (bet. Fifth & Madison Aves.)

Subway: 33 St
Phone: 212-213-0077
Web: www.hangawirestaurant.com
Price: $$

Lunch Mon – Sat
Dinner nightly

Beyond an ordinary façade lies this serene, shoes-off retreat with traditional low tables, Korean artifacts, and meditative music. Said footwear is stored in cubbies, seating is the color of bamboo, and clay teapots adorn the back wall. The setting is soothing, but the atmosphere is surprisingly convivial, with groups gabbing over stuffed shiitake mushrooms and green tea.

The *ssam bap* offers a fun DIY experience with a long platter of fillings. Dark leafy lettuce and thin, herbaceous sesame leaves are topped with creamy slices of avocado, crunchy bean sprouts, pickled daikon, carrot, cucumber, radish, and three rice options—white, brown, and a nutty, purple-tinged multigrain. Topped with miso *ssam* sauce, each bite is a fresh burst of uplifting textures.

Hatsuhana

Japanese

B3

17 E. 48th St. (bet. Fifth & Madison Aves.)

Subway: 47-50 Sts - Rockefeller Ctr
Phone: 212-355-3345
Web: www.hatsuhana.com
Price: $$$

Lunch Mon – Fri
Dinner Mon – Sat

It's been around since the beginning of time (in NYC Japanese restaurant years) but this is no lesser a destination for excellent sushi. With a retro décor that spans two floors and a business that's run like a machine, Hatsuhana is a go-to for corporate dining.

Though the rave reviews came decades ago, their traditional *Edomae* sushi still holds its own. Fish is top quality, the army of chefs have solid knife skills, and rice is properly prepared. This reliability draws a host of regulars who develop relationships with the *itamae*. Stick to the counter and go omakase: the sushi will be surprisingly impressive with accommodations for the spicy tuna-set. At lunch, the "Box of Dreams" is an aptly named must-order.

Hide-Chan Ramen

C3

248 E. 52nd St. (bet. Second & Third Aves.)

Subway: Lexington Av - 53 St
Phone: 212-813-1800
Web: www.hidechanramen.nyc
Price:

Lunch Mon – Sat
Dinner nightly

Real, genuine *tonkotsu*-style ramen is happening right here in NY, thanks to Hideto Kawahara, whose *ramen-ya* roots run deep in Japan. These noodles are cooked exactly as customer-specified and arrive perfect every time—even for the savviest and most discerning salarymen who tend to pour in late Friday nights for the post-work, post-bar scene. But on cold days, arrive early for lunch or risk a line that is sure to snake down the stairs. In addition to their springy ramen floating in rich, fortifying broth, include other treats like crispy *gyoza*, traditional *takoyaki*, and steamed buns. For those who want to shy away from noodles, the *dons* are surprisingly good.

The setting is appropriately informal, while service can be spacey at times.

Jubilee

D3

948 First Ave. (bet. 52nd & 53rd Sts.)

Subway: Lexington Av - 53 St
Phone: 212-888-3569
Web: www.jubileeny.net
Price: $$

Lunch & dinner daily

Settled into sleek Sutton Place, Jubilee is New York City's very own version of *Cheers*. Affluent families are in full force here, while friends gather on weeknights to mingle over wine and fine French-Belgian cuisine. The European-inflected nautical décor screams quaint coastal elegance with perpetually packed tables and a bar where everybody knows your name. A silky, saffron-scented fish soup, accompanied by grated Gruyère, a few croûtes, and pot of *rouille* is deliciously classic and incredibly sumptuous. But before filling up, be sure to sample the sole *meuniere*—a delicate fish seared perfectly and served with sautéed spinach leaves. If that doesn't sound like the best way to end a long day, their popular crème brûlée offers the ultimate fix.

Jukai

C3

Japanese ✗✗

237 E. 53rd St. (bet. Second & Third Aves.)

Subway: Lexington Av - 53 St   Dinner Mon – Sat
Phone: 212-588-9788
Web: www.jukainyc.com
Price: $$$

If you can't make it to Tokyo by dinnertime, this subterranean den is the next best thing. Smartly styled in wood and bamboo, it's packed with expats lingering over elaborate meals attended to by an amicable staff.

The menu is traditional, though the chef's unique influences are well expressed in a massive oyster "sashimi" that's sliced in half on the shell and served with a mirin-soy dip and grated radish. To allow for a wide sampling of their top quality sashimi—from fluke and scallop to uni—opt for the tasting menu, and be sure to request the premium shabu-shabu. Thinly sliced Washu is swished in a bubbling dashi and coupled with noodles, bok choy, tofu, mushrooms, and two drinkable dipping sauces—ponzu as well as a signature sesame shabu-shabu sauce.

Kurumazushi

B3

Japanese ✗✗

7 E. 47th St., 2nd fl. (bet. Fifth & Madison Aves.)

Subway: 47-50 Sts - Rockefeller Ctr   Lunch & dinner Mon – Sat
Phone: 212-317-2802
Web: www.kurumazushi.com
Price: $$$$

Mimicking Tokyo's tucked-away restaurant style, this sushi destination is located up a dark staircase in a midtown building and through a sliding door. The focal point of the room is the sushi bar, where Chef/owner Toshihiro Uezu meticulously prepares each morsel in a minimal space.

For the full theatrical experience, brace your wallet and settle into the omakase. The undeniable quality of each ingredient is center stage, displayed simply on stone glazed pottery.

Take a cue from the Japanese and limit conversation: the succession of sashimi and sushi is quick, and all senses should work together without distraction to savor the smooth, buttery fatty tuna, Spanish mackerel (with its lightly blistered skin), pearly white sea bream, and rich *unagi*.

Kajitsu

A1

125 E. 39th St. (bet. Lexington & Park Aves.)

Subway: Grand Central - 42 St   Dinner Tue – Sun
Phone: 212-228-4873
Web: www.kajitsunyc.com
Price: $$$

It's the way of the modern world that we think of the changing of the seasons more in terms of our wardrobe rather than our food—but a meal at Kajitsu could change that. This Japanese vegan restaurant serves shojin cuisine based on the precepts of Buddhism—if you're in search of an antidote to the plethora of steakhouses in the city, this is it. The traditionally decorated space on the second floor is a sanctuary of peace and tranquility and offers table or counter seating and service that is as charming as it is earnest.

Such is the skill of the kitchen you'll forget in no time about the absence of fish or meat. It's all about balance, harmony and simplicity—and allowing the ingredients' natural flavors to shine, whether it's the delicate onion soup with mizuna and potato, or the visually arresting *hassun* which could include everything from mountain yam to burdock root.

Your period of contemplation and newfound respect for your fellow man may come to a juddering halt when you find yourself back on Lexington but, for a few moments at least, you'll feel you connected with nature.

La Grenouille

French ✗✗✗

B2

3 E. 52nd St. (bet. Fifth & Madison Aves.)

Subway: 5 Av - 53 St   Lunch & dinner Tue – Sat
Phone: 212-752-1495
Web: www.la-grenouille.com
Price: $$$$

La Grenouille is a bastion of old-world glamor and manners with an exorbitant budget for floral arrangements. Although this storied enclave still attracts a devoted following, there's always room for local newbies and blinged-out tourists. Everyone looks good in this lavish space, where red velvet banquettes, polished wood veneer, and softly lit tables bathe the room in rose and apricot hues.

Classic and classy, this French cuisine deserves high praise. Delicate ravioli is stuffed with chopped lobster hinting of tarragon and dressed with creamy, tart beurre blanc; an exquisitely tender-seared beef filet arrives with *pommes Darphin* and a lick of perfect sauce *au poivre*; and for dessert, the *île flottante* is heaven under a cloud of spun caramel.

Land of Plenty 😊

Chinese ✗✗

D2

204 E. 58th St. (bet. Second & Third Aves.)

Subway: 59 St   Lunch Mon – Fri
Phone: 212-308-8788   Dinner nightly
Web: www.landofplenty58.com
Price: $$

Why do they call it Land of Plenty? Chewy Chongqing noodles puddled in a chili oil broth with ground pork, peanuts and sesame seeds; luscious bean curd bathed in…yes…more chili oil with toasted peanuts, Sichuan peppercorns, and scallions. Then imagine vibrant green snow pea sprouts dusted with salt and garlic, tender pork dumplings swimming in a Sichuan soy- peanut- and chili-bath that's spicy, sweet and salty all at once. And those are just a few of the plentiful reasons.

Though the focus here is definitely the food, this fiery haven feels more elegant than the other Sichuan spots in midtown. Tucked into a sleek, clean, subterranean space, the décor features marble floors and mosaic-tile walls. A professional service staff helps further set the tone.

Le Cirque

 C2

151 E. 58th St. (bet. Lexington & Third Aves.)

Subway:	59 St	Lunch Mon – Fri
Phone:	212-644-0202	Dinner Mon – Sat
Web:	www.lecirque.com	
Price:	**$$$$**	

This primavera-pasta legend brought stateside by Sirio Maccioni, continues to thrive in this tony locality. Its doors may have originally opened to a very different Manhattan, but the timeless cuisine still packs the house. The dramatic interior alone warrants a visit: a beautiful semi-circular dining room flaunting arching banquettes, soaring windows, and elaborate canopies overhead.

The kitchen team currently holding court blends time-honored recipes with delicious new additions. Don't miss the *salade de homard*, featuring lobster, fennel and pineapple, mingled with creamy avocado mousse and a lobster dressing. The *paupiette* of black bass, wrapped in thin sheets of potato, laced with a red wine sauce and served over melted leeks, is yet another delight.

Le Relais de Venise (L'Entrecôte)

C3

590 Lexington Ave. (at 52nd St.)

Subway:	51 St	Lunch & dinner daily
Phone:	212-758-3989	
Web:	www.relaisdevenise.com	
Price:	**$$**	

Sibling to the Paris original, this midtown outpost boasts a prime location and exceptional value. Inside, it's no amateur show and there's just one menu option—but what an impressive one it is. Start with green salad tossed in a light mustard vinaigrette before slicing into a juicy steak, dressed with the kitchen's mouthwatering (and top secret!) sauce. Of course, it is only upon the arrival of salty, crunchy frites when your meal will truly start to sing. Desserts aren't a highlight; so opt instead for another glass of *vin* from their moderately priced list.

The décor is classic and the staff, dressed in sassy outfits, are the very image of Paris-chic. So sit back, relax, and take it all in—and find that for a moment, you'd forgotten you were in Manhattan.

Mapo Tofu

✗

A1

338 Lexington Ave. (bet. 39th & 40th Sts.)

Subway: Grand Central - 42 St   Lunch & dinner daily
Phone: 212-867-8118
Web: N/A
Price:

"How many?" That's the greeting at this temple of "ma la," where enticing aromas are sure to lure you in. Find yourself among executives and locals slurping up a host of chili oil specialties (don't wear white!). This is the kind of place where dragons go to recharge their breath.

Some may peruse the menu—rife with typos—for daily specials, but most blaze their tongues with Sichuan pickles or chilled noodles tossed in an intense sesame vinaigrette. The place is named after a humble dish, but many items surprise with bold flavors like silky fish fillets swimming in a spicy broth with Napa cabbage, or camphor tea-smoked duck. Peppercorns in stir-fried chicken unite subtle sweetness with intense heat, while sponge squash offers a cooling, textural finale.

Mr Chow

Chinese ✗✗

D2

324 E. 57th St. (bet. First & Second Aves.)

Subway: 59 St   Dinner nightly
Phone: 212-751-9030
Web: www.mrchow.com
Price: **$$$$**

Oh Mr Chow, how you hook the hordes with your flavorful fusion and fancy prices! Perhaps it's your retro scene decked in black-and-white, lacquered Asian-accented chairs, and glinting mirrors. Or, maybe it's the noodle guy's theatrical display of hand-pulling? Whatever the hype, this guy still has it and Sutton suits with their wealthy wives party here like it's 1999.

Attentive service, stimulating drinks, and a combo of Chow originals as well as Cantonese classics executed with surprising skill keep these uptown crowds returning time and again. The signature chicken *satay* in all its neon-orange glory followed by squab with lettuce are signature choices, but the Beijing duck prix-fixe accompanied by their famous water dumplings is probably the way to go.

Nerai

Greek **XX**

B2

55 E. 54th St. (bet. Madison & Park Aves.)

Subway: 5 Av - 53 St
Phone: 212-759-5554
Web: www.nerainyc.com
Price: $$$

Lunch & dinner daily

Nerai endeavors to transport diners to Santorini, creating a stark contrast to its rather stiff midtown surrounds. A resort-chic vibe echoes through the whitewashed walls, sea-blue accents, and lots of cool marble. But the holiday ends there, as this crowd is all about business—especially at lunch.

The fresh, light cuisine begins with beautifully prepared starters like tender, enticingly charred octopus atop chickpeas, roasted pepper, and quick-pickled onions drizzled with lemon and olive oil. Grilled sea bass is a flawless shade of white, salty and crisp-skinned alongside seasonal vegetables like zucchini and buttery pea purée. Finish with the lovely *portokalopita* topped with a scoop of bittersweet chocolate sorbet boldly flavored with orange.

Osteria Laguna

Italian **XX**

B1

209 E. 42nd St. (bet. Second & Third Aves.)

Subway: Grand Central - 42 St
Phone: 212-557-0001
Web: www.osteria-laguna.com
Price: $$

Lunch & dinner daily

A little bit corporate (it is midtown, after all) and a little bit casual (daytrippers from nearby Grand Central), Osteria Laguna has nailed its audience and delivers a perfect blend to suit both worlds. Inside, it's delightfully rustic, complete with the requisite Italian ceramic plates and wooden chairs with rush seating.

Crowd-pleasers like pastas, pizzas from the wood-burning oven, *antipasti*, salads, and nicely done fish, starch, and vegetables comprise the menu at this better-than-average gem. The friendly service can be spotty, but the perfectly crisped wood-fired pizzas are always spot on. The portions are abundant, perhaps even too much given the tiny tables, but the prices aren't, so you can treat your out-of-town friend and keep the change.

Pampano

 Mexican

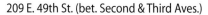

C3

209 E. 49th St. (bet. Second & Third Aves.)

Subway: 51 St
Phone: 212-751-4545
Web: www.richardsandoval.com
Price: $$$

Lunch Mon – Fri
Dinner nightly

Nothing screams you need a trip to Acapulco like a stressful day in midtown, and we've got your remedy. Pampano, a popular Mexican seafood restaurant, offers two types of oases for the weary worker: downstairs, you'll find a lively bar (especially come happy hour) with a few small tables to enjoy their *botanas* menu; upstairs, you'll find a transporting, beachy dining space with whitewashed ceilings, wicker chairs, lazy ceiling fans, and an outdoor patio.

Don't miss the fresh guacamole; excellent rotating list of ceviches, plump with off-the-boat fish and humming with bright lime; or grilled grouper, marinated in *achiote* and wrapped in banana leaf.

Next door, Pampano Taqueria keeps the hungry lunch crowds at bay with delicious tacos on the fly.

Patroon

American

B4

160 E. 46th St. (bet. Lexington & Third Aves.)

Subway: Grand Central - 42 St
Phone: 212-883-7373
Web: www.aretskyspatroon.com
Price: $$$$

Lunch & dinner Mon – Fri

For those in the know, this elegant canteen needs no introduction. Patroon exudes the air of a private club—one where suited professionals huddle over drinks at the sleek bar; and dining rooms fill with power lunchers who smoke cigars on the rooftop.

That this restaurant draws a devoted crowd of regulars should come as no surprise; the maître d' and his gracious servers are top-notch and the kitchen team is highly competent. Come dinnertime, the classic cooking is especially impressive: bracing ceviche may feature Long Island fluke; then Dover sole is plated tableside; and light yet satisfying leek gratin caters to diners who would rather invest the calories elsewhere—say a fine pour from the well-curated wine list or a perfect crème brulée for dessert.

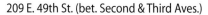

Manhattan ▶ Midtown East

261

Pera

Turkish ✕✕

A4

303 Madison Ave. (bet. 41st & 42nd Sts.)

Subway: Grand Central - 42 St   Lunch & dinner daily
Phone: 212-878-6301
Web: www.peranyc.com
Price: $$

For flavorful Turkish food infused with contemporary influence, Pera serves to please. Lunch does big business in this attractive dining room, layered in a chocolate-brown color scheme and packed with corporate types as well as visitors looking for a sleek place to sojourn mid-day. Acoustics can be loud, but with food so fine, you'll want to stay awhile. Dinner is more low-key but the menu always brims with simple, good quality, and slightly renovated plates like warm hummus with *pastirma*; lentil and bulgur tartare; or watermelon chunks tossed with salty feta, tomatoes, and olive oil. A forkful of their model and deliciously tender chicken *adana* with a side of addictively crispy fries has wide appeal and makes for a fitting feast—at all times.

Phoenix Garden ☺

Chinese ✕

B1

242 E. 40th St. (bet. Second & Third Aves.)

Subway: Grand Central - 42 St   Lunch & dinner daily
Phone: 212-983-6666
Web: www.phoenixgardennyc.com
Price: $$

This fuss-free and no-frills basement joint shows Chinatown that delicious Chinese food for a great value can exist outside of its borders. Forgo ho-hum lunch deals and pop in at dinnertime for a delectable selection of Cantonese cooking.

The vast menu can take some navigating, so chat up the servers for their expert advice in order to get the goods. Highlights include exquisite salt-and-pepper shrimp, shell-on, butterflied, flash-fried and tossed with sliced chilies and garlic; sautéed snow pea leaves in an egg-white sauce of sweet crabmeat, carrots, and snow peas; sizzling eggplant casserole studded with minced pork and ham; and crispy Peking duck sliced tableside, rolled up in pancakes, and layered with hoisin, cucumber, and scallions.

P.J. Clarke's

Gastropub ✗

915 Third Ave. (at 55th St.)

Subway: Lexington Av - 53 St
Phone: 212-317-1616
Web: www.pjclarkes.com
Price: $$

Lunch & dinner daily

Old time and on the ball, P.J. Clarke's drips with New York history—ad men and business execs have patronized this pour house for generations, and with good reason. Besides a dazzling medley of drinks, the kitchen sends out a crowd-pleasing menu showcasing solid technique. Following its repute, the distinct décor spotlights notable artifacts, worn floors, and smartly dressed tables.

Weekends draw a touristy set, but who's complaining with an amazing Bloody Mary so close at hand? Highlights include potato chips with an outrageously gooey blue cheese gratin; braised short rib spring rolls with horseradish-tinged sour cream; and tuna tartare tacos filled with scallion and sesame seeds. The cheeseburger is as classic and on-point as the staff itself.

Sakagura

Japanese ✗✗

211 E. 43rd St. (bet. Second & Third Aves.)

Subway: Grand Central - 42 St
Phone: 212-953-7253
Web: www.sakagura.com
Price: $$$

Lunch Mon – Fri
Dinner nightly

Got sake on the brain? You'll need to book in advance, but tucked away in the basement of a midtown office building, Sakagura is an amazing little hideaway with a phenomenal sake list (including seasonal selections) and a smattering of delicious small plates for pairing. All this fabulousness may have gone to their head a bit as the service seems a bit lacking these days, but it's worth it for that flash of authentic Tokyo by way of midtown.

A couple of gems off the massive menu include the *uzaku*, grilled eel with cucumbers and seaweed in vinaigrette; perfectly chewy soba noodles presented in a traditional basket with dipping sauce, scallion, and wasabi; and tender *tori karaage*, a delicious Japanese fried chicken marinated in sake, soy, and ginger.

2nd Avenue Deli

Deli

A1

162 E. 33rd St. (bet. Lexington & Third Aves.)

Subway: 33 St   Lunch & dinner daily
Phone: 212-689-9000
Web: www.2ndavedeli.com
Price: 😎

While the décor may be more deli-meets-deco and there's a tad less attitude, this food is every bit as good as it was on Second Avenue. Ignore the kvetching and know that this is a true Jewish deli filled with personality, and one of the best around by far.

The menu remains as it should: kosher, meat-loving, and non-dairy with phenomenal pastrami, pillowy rye, tangy mustard, perfect potato pancakes, and fluffy matzoh balls in comforting broth. Have the best of both worlds with the soup and half-sandwich combination.

Carve a nook during midday rush, when in pour the crowds. The deli also does takeout (popular with the midtown lunch bunch), and delivery (grandma's latkes at your door). Giant platters go equally well to a bris or brunch.

Sip Sak

Turkish

C3

928 Second Ave. (bet. 49th & 50th Sts.)

Subway: 51 St   Lunch & dinner daily
Phone: 212-583-1900
Web: www.sip-sak.com
Price: $$

Tucked inside a charming, bistro-like setting with pressed-tin ceilings and cool white marble-top tables, this neighborhood favorite just keeps getting better with age. Owner Orhan Yegen runs a tight ship, directing his staff and kitchen as they entice diners with a meze of citrusy olives, delicious hummus, garlicky *cacik*, and creamy *tarama*.

Kick things off with a starter of plump shrimp cooked in a downright addictive garlic and parsley sauce; or tuck into an equally earthy Greek salad with a Turkish twist featuring pickled cabbage, crumbled feta, and a poached artichoke heart filled with dilled fava beans. For dinner, skip the seafood and opt for fragrant and hearty lamb meatballs, served over rice pilaf with a grilled tomato and pile of mixed greens.

Smith & Wollensky

 Steakhouse

C3

797 Third Ave. (at 49th St.)

Subway: 51 St
Phone: 212-753-1530
Web: www.smithandwollensky.com
Price: $$$$

Lunch Mon – Fri
Dinner nightly

Sitting proudly on this corner for 40-some years, Smith & Wollensky is a bona fide institution. This is the kind of clubby steakhouse where stellar martinis are still poured tableside and the regulars get their names engraved on a plaque. It's where business deals go down and a number of old-time guys live it up. Begin with dangerously warm and buttery Parker House rolls before savoring a beefsteak tomato-onion salad finished with house dressing and blue cheese. Spoon-licking plates of creamed spinach, hashbrowns, or onion rings are a must alongside the all-time favorite Colorado rib steak—beautifully marbled, deliciously fatty, bone-on and big enough for three.

For those who prefer a bit of blare with their meat, Wollensky's Grill next door is ideal.

Soba Totto

Japanese

B4

211 E. 43rd St. (bet. Second & Third Aves.)

Subway: Grand Central - 42 St
Phone: 212-557-8200
Web: www.sobatotto.com
Price: $$

Lunch Mon – Fri
Dinner nightly

It's a jam-packed lunchtime operation here at Soba Totto, where business folks gather and quickly fill the popular space. As the name suggests, everyone arrives in droves for the tasty homemade soba. Dinnertime brings a mellower vibe, and a crowd of beer- and sake-sipping patrons ordering tasty plates of spicy fried chicken and *yakitori* galore.

Midday features several varieties of lunch sets. Tasty appetizers may unveil a salad of assorted pickles and simmered daikon in a sweet ginger dressing. Skip over the fried seafood in favor of the *soba totto gozen* set, which includes the wonderful soba in fragrant *dashi*; or try one of the many delicious *dons* topped with tasty tidbits like sea urchin and salmon roe or soy-marinated tuna, grated yam, and egg.

SushiAnn

Japanese

B3

38 E. 51st St. (bet. Madison & Park Aves.)

Subway: 51 St
Phone: 212-755-1780
Web: www.sushiann.net
Price: $$

Lunch Mon – Fri
Dinner Mon – Sat

Step through the serene, bamboo-filled entrance and into this dedicated sushi den. The mood is respectfully formal yet friendly, thanks to the focused kitchen staff who are happily interacting with guests. Just arrive with a sense of what (and how much) you'd like to eat and insist upon omakase.

Let the day's catch dictate your meal and take a seat at the counter, where only the glassed-in display of fish and mollusks separates you from this team of skilled, disciplined chefs. The omakase may be wildly varied depending on the day (and your chef), but high standards are always maintained and each crunchy morsel is treated with integrity. A ceramic dish of sashimi may reveal a glistening array of mild giant clam, firm *tai*, and tuna that melts in the mouth.

Sutton Inn

American

D3

347 E 54th St. (bet. First & Second Aves.)

Subway: Lexington Av - 53 St
Phone: 646-370-3045
Web: www.suttoninnrestaurant.com
Price: $$$

Dinner Tue – Sat

This charming American bistro flies a bit under the radar, but has all the things you'd want in a neighborhood restaurant. It's exceptionally quaint and cozy; the guests are friendly and often local; and the vibe is perfectly laid-back. And while the space is decidedly unflashy, the refined dishes showcase a delicious interplay between quality ingredients and the notable talents of the kitchen.

Kick things off with a mouthwatering bowl of chilled corn soup, served sweet and creamy and garnished with roasted poblano peppers, gouda, *pico de gallo*, and fresh cilantro. Then move on to a lovely fillet of bluefish, roasted to crispy-outside-and-tender-inside perfection, and served over nutty wild rice with snap pea slivers and a mild green curry emulsion.

Sushi Ginza Onodera

Japanese ✗✗

461 Fifth Ave. (bet. 40th & 41st Sts.)

Subway: 42 St - Bryant Pk
Phone: 212-390-0925
Web: https://onodera-group.com/en/
Price: $$$$

Lunch Mon — Fri
Dinner Mon — Sat

Purity of flavor and experience is what makes this *sushi-ya* so very unique and worth its price tag. Of course, the elegant room has a great deal more to offer thanks to an impressive Bizen-yaki tile wall, well-spaced seats along the blonde wood counter, and hand-painted crystal sake glasses. But that perfectly seasoned rice and fish (some of it wild-caught from Japan) are the foundations of this omakase, showcasing nigiri presented at a leisurely pace so guests can savor each bite.

When your *itamae* presents those beautifully scored and deliciously pungent Hokkaido sardines, the finely sliced chives, grated daikon, bead of wasabi, and brush of soy sauce that garnish it make every flavor delicate and memorable. Slices of poached monkfish liver are velvety, ultra-rich, and prove that these chefs are at the top of their game. Bonito is gently cold-smoked and infused with flavor yet maintains the texture of fish in its "raw" state, further enhanced by soy-sesame-chive sauce.

No element of tradition is forgotten here: when your chef and servers offer you a deep bow upon your departure, they will hold it until you are down the street and out of sight. Such adherence to cultural respect is not often found in this day and age.

Sushi Yasuda ✿

B4

Japanese ✗✗

204 E. 43rd St. (bet. Second & Third Aves.)

Subway: Grand Central - 42 St
Phone: 212-972-1001
Web: www.sushiyasuda.com
Price: $$$$

Lunch Mon – Fri
Dinner Mon – Sat

There is a Spartan appearance to this sushi temple, where honey-toned bamboo slats are by far the warmest feature. Reservations require confirmation and punctuality, but to sushi-loving diehards, this is just the cost of admission.

Avoid the tables packed with suits (this is midtown, after all) and request a seat at the sleek counter—it's where the magic happens. Your experience here depends entirely on the soft-spoken, attentive, and very focused *itamae* working before you, as his signature style will guide your meal. Their mission is to ensure that each diner receives a wide variety of fish that has just been cut, formed and dressed moments before it is eaten.

The kitchen lives up to its hype by ignoring new wave trends in favor of serving classically assembled and spectacularly fresh sushi. Every item is handled with the utmost care, especially the progression of sashimi highlighting the ample textures of mackerel, tuna, and salmon. Outstanding clams and scallops are seasoned with a touch of lemon and sea salt flakes to enhance their natural taste; while nigiri featuring Maine and Japanese uni tastings underscore the subtle differences in flavor.

Tempura Matsui

222 E. 39th St. (bet. Second & Third Aves.)

Subway: Grand Central - 42 St
Phone: 212-986-8885
Web: www.tempuramatsui.com
Price: $$$$

Dinner nightly

Tempura may be considered a more common pleasure in Japan, but it has been refined to an art form at this home to succulent morsels of fish and vegetables. There is no equal in the city and the kitchen's delicate hand and authenticity is particularly clear in the lightly seasoned batter that sparingly coats each bit of food before it is quickly fried and rendered crisp. The skill here is so great that they could probably get away with serving lesser quality fish, but still, these are often imported from Tsukiji market in Tokyo at their peak of freshness. Don't miss the sweet shrimp wrapped in shiso leaf and butterflied Japanese whiting served with purple sweet potato.

Meals are bookended with premium sashimi and cooked dishes that are just as enticing, like seared butterfish with a tiny radish, spring pea, and onion. Tilefish is prepared with flavors that seem to conjure spring thanks to cherry leaves, uni, and braised broccoli over sticky rice with sesame and goji berries.

The best place to appreciate the kitchen's artistry is from the counter where chefs can be found carefully dipping each little golden nugget of food in and out of boiling oil, then promptly placing it before you.

Though sadly Chef Matsui has passed away, his disciples carry on.

Tsushima

Japanese XX

B4

210 E. 44th St. (bet. Second & Third Aves.)

Subway: Grand Central - 42 St   Lunch & dinner daily
Phone: 212-207-1938
Web: usushimanyc.com
Price: $$

A shiny black awning marks the entrance to this slightly antiseptic yet considerably authentic sushi bar. A few rooms done in traditional Japanese style provide seating choices at this den, which hums with business groups on the run as well as neighborhood dwellers seeking fantastic value lunches and terrific quality sushi in the evening.

Choose to dine at their sushi counter or at a table in the well-lit dining room, attended to by speedy servers. Then, dive into generously sized lunch specials featuring perhaps a colorful *chirashi*, headlining yellowtail, salmon, *tamago*, and amberjack set deftly over well-seasoned sushi rice. Sticky-glazed eel, nicely grilled and plenty fatty, is an absolute must as is the impressive omakase for dinner.

Wolfgang's

Steakhouse XX

A1

4 Park Ave. (at 33rd St.)

Subway: 33 St   Lunch & dinner daily
Phone: 212-889-3369
Web: www.wolfgangssteakhouse.net
Price: $$$$

Wolfgang's is no stranger to the bustling New York steakhouse scene. From the lunch hour business crowd to the lively, post-work bar scene, Wolfgang's jams in locals and tourists alike—each coming for the classic fare and precise Manhattans. The service can be gruff at times, but they have a good track record of squeezing you into a table or perch at the bar without a reservation.

Once seated, the bone-in Porterhouse, cooked rare, is the only way to go. It arrives sizzling in its own fat, perfectly seasoned. Save space for a slice of bacon—a must-order appetizer—creamed spinach, and crispy German potatoes with yet more salt and fat (at this point, why not?). Just beware: while dishes are sized to share, they're priced like Maseratis.

Tulsi

C4

211 E. 46th St. (bet. Second & Third Aves.)

Subway: Grand Central - 42 St
Phone: 212-888-0820
Web: www.tulsinyc.com
Price: $$$

Lunch Mon – Sat
Dinner nightly

Those who like their Indian food served in style with nary a seizure-inducing colored light in sight should head along to Tulsi. This midtown gem, adorned with billowing muslin and neutral tones, provides its savvy diners with tranquil, sophisticated surroundings that go hand-in-hand with the sweet-natured staff.

The cuisine, best enjoyed at dinner, is also markedly different from the norm. For the appetizers, the kitchen takes the sort of snacks you can find streetside on Chowpatty and, by putting its own spin on them, raises them to new heights. Cauliflower Manchurian, highlighting deliciously fried florets tossed in zingy chili-tomato sauce, is nothing less than textbook-perfect. You may also travel north by way of *zafrani jhinga* or tandoor-roasted shrimp served with a delightful combo of crispy okra, *upma*, and spicy eggplant chutney. Then *kasuri seekh kabab* is sparked with gooseberry relish for all-out enjoyment, while the buttery black *dal* must be tailed by an outstandingly light and fluffy naan for a definitive finish.

As a nod to local tastes spicing can be assertive, but those familiar with India—and anyone who knows their silly mid-on from their backward point—will still find much to savor here.

More diverse than its counterpart (Midtown East) but still rather gritty in parts, Midtown West presents a unique mix of tree-lined streets and ethnic enclaves amid glitzy glass-walled towers. It is also home to numerous iconic sights, including now well-known **Restaurant Row**—the only street in all five boroughs to be proudly advertised as such. The fact that it resides in an area called Hell's Kitchen and highlights an impressive range of global cuisines, is sealing evidence of this nabe's devotion to good food.

EAT THE STREETS

Also referred to as "Clinton," Hell's Kitchen is a colorful mosaic of workaday immigrants, old-timey residents, and young families. Gone are the Prohibition-era dens, which are now replaced by swanky restaurants, boutique hotels, and hip bars. **Little Brazil**, set only steps from bustling Sixth Avenue, showcases samba and street food every summer on Brazilian Day. And, speaking of the same nation, tourist-centric **Churrascaria Plataforma** is an all-you-can-eat Brazilian steakhouse showing off their wares via waiters, armed with skewers of succulent roasted meat. Midtown may be choked by cabs and corporate types on the go, but in true Big Apple-style the residents demand (and

streets oblige with) outstanding eats in varying venues. Under the guidance of the Vendy Awards and the blog—Midtown Lunch—discover a changing lineup of speedy and satisfying street food faves as well as delis stocked with everything from Mexican specialties and dried chilies to farm-fresh produce. Those in a hurry hustle over to **Tehuitzingo** for over 17 types of tacos, but if seeking a more reliable scene, find a seat at **Tulcingo del Valle** where tortas are turned out alongside burritos and burgers. Carnivores also revel over those perfectly pink patties laced with crispy fries at Le Parker Meridien's **burger joint**, but if barbecue

PEOPLE
WHO LOVE
TO EAT
ARE ALWAYS
THE BEST PEOPLE
IF YOU'RE
AFRAID OF
BUTTER
USE CREAM
- JULIA C HILD

is what floats your boat, trek to the wilds of Eleventh Avenue and into **Daisy May's** for smoky, succulent 'cue. In need of a more rare treat? **K-town** is a dark horse-like quarter that has been known to sneak up and surprise. Its instant and unapologetically authentic vibe owes largely to the prominence of aromatic barbecue joints, karaoke bars, and of course, grocers hawking everything from fresh tofu to handmade dumplings.

Macy's is across the street and may sport a frenzied scene, but tucked into its quiet crypt is **De Gustibus**, a cooking school and stage for culinary legends. Trek further along these midtown streets and find that equal attention is tendered to cooking as to arranging storybook mannequins behind the velvet ropes of glossy department stores. Shop till you drop at Bergdorf; then cool your heels over caviar and croissants at the *très* French and fancy **Petrossian**. Others may opt to stir things up with a martini and tasty small plate served out of

the stately **Charlie Palmer at the Knick**, comfortably situated in the Knickerbocker Hotel in Times Square.

Switching gears from specialty spots to mega markets, **Gotham West Market** is one of Manhattan's most favored gourmet feats. Settled along Eleventh Avenue, this culinary complex cradles a number of chef-driven stalls and artisanal purveyors offering tapas, charcuterie, sammies, and everything in between. Of special note is the first stateside outpost of **Ivan Ramen**, where the rockstar chef's global fan base slurp down bowlfuls of these wispy rye noodles bobbing in a sumptuous broth. **City Kitchen** is yet another formidable bazaar featuring a rustic-industrial setting and outfitted with kiosks from **ilili Box, Gabriela's Restaurant & Taqueria Bar, Luke's Lobster, Dough** and more. Of course, cached beneath the graceful Plaza hotel is the tastefully decorated **Plaza Food Hall**. Here, a dizzying array of

comestibles is on full-display and makes for a fine attraction—or distraction? Curated by mega-watt personality, Todd English, this 32,000-square-foot space is a perfect meeting spot if you're looking to sip, savor, and shop. Beginning with caviar, lobster rolls, or sushi; and closing with coffee or cupcakes, this veritable tour de force perfectly typifies the city's culinary elite.

FOOD FIXES

A few steps west and Gotham City's eclectic identity reveals yet another facet,

where Ninth Avenue unearths a wealth of eats. A wonderful start to any day is practically certified at **Amy's Bread**, where fresh-baked baguettes lend countless restaurant kitchens that extra crumb of culture. But, it is their famously colorful cakes and cookies that tempt passersby off the streets and into the store. Across the way, **Poseidon Bakery** is a winner for Greek sweets. It is also the last place in town that still crafts their own phyllo dough by hand—a taste of the spanakopita will prove it. Then, even its moniker depicts another district, **Sullivan Street Bakery's** one and only retail outlet is also housed along this stretch—a location so perilously far west in the Manhattan mindset that its success is worth its weight in gold. Just as Jim Lahey's luxurious loaves claim a cult-like following, so do the fantastic components (a warm Portuguese-style roll?) at **City Sandwich**. Meanwhile, theater-lovers and Lincoln Tunnel-bound commuters know to drive by **The Counter** and place an order for hand-crafted burgers, proclaimed to be a "must try before you die." New Yorkers in the know never tire of the lure behind **La Boîte**'s spice blends, or the sumptuous cured meats and *formaggi* found at **Sergimmo Salumeria**. Find more such salty goodness at veteran butcher, **Esposito Meat Market**, proudly purveying every part of the pig alongside piles of offal. Thirsty travelers should keep heading further south of Port Authority Bus Terminal to unearth an enclave rich with restaurants and food marts. Here, foodies start their feasting at **Ninth Avenue International Foods** proffering such pleasures as olives, spices, and spreads. But, among their outstanding produce, find the renowned *taramosalata* (as if prepared by the gods atop Mount Olympus themselves). Then consider the fact that it also features on the menu of many fine-dining destinations nearby, and know that you're in for truly something special.

TIME WARNER CENTER

Finally, no visit to this district is complete without paying homage to the epicurean feat that is the **Time Warner Center**. Presiding and preening over Columbus Circle, high-flying chefs indulge both themselves and their pretty patrons here with ground-breaking success. Discover a range of savory and sweet delights indoors—from **Bouchon Bakery's** colorful French macarons, to the eye-popping style and sass of **Ascent Lounge**. Located on the fourth floor, **Center Bar** (brought to you by Michael Lomonaco) is a sophisticated perch for enjoying a champagne cocktail while taking in the views of lush Central Park. This is classic New York—only more glossy and glamorous than usual.

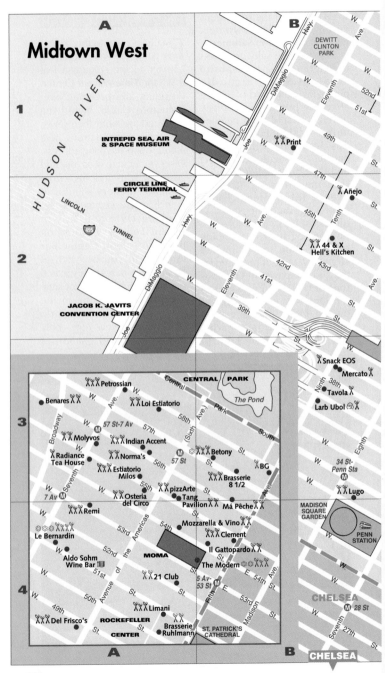

Midtown West

A

B

HUDSON RIVER

DEWITT CLINTON PARK

INTREPID SEA, AIR & SPACE MUSEUM

CIRCLE LINE FERRY TERMINAL

LINCOLN TUNNEL

495

JACOB K. JAVITS CONVENTION CENTER

Joe DiMaggio Hwy.

Eleventh Ave.
Tenth Ave.
Ninth Ave.
Eighth Ave.

W. 52nd St.
W. 51st St.
W. 49th St.
W. 47th St.
W. 45th St.
W. 43rd St.
W. 42nd St.
W. 41st St.
W. 39th St.

Print
Añejo
44 & X Hell's Kitchen

Snack EOS
Mercato
Tavola
Larb Ubol

CENTRAL PARK

The Pond

Central Park South

Petrossian
Benares
Loi Estiatorio

Broadway
Seventh Ave.
7 Av

W. 57th St.
57 St-7 Av
W. 58th St.
57 St
W. 56th St.
W. 55th St.
W. 54th St.
W. 53rd St.
W. 52nd St.
W. 51st St.
W. 50th St.
W. 49th St.

Molyvos
Indian Accent
Radiance Tea House
Norma's
Estiatorio Milos
pizzArte
Tang Pavilion
Osteria del Circo
Remi
Le Bernardin
Aldo Sohm Wine Bar
21 Club
Del Frisco's
Limani
Brasserie Ruhlmann

Betony
BG
Brasserie 8 1/2
Má Pêche
Mozzarella & Vino
Clement
Il Gattopardo
The Modern

5 Av-53 St
Fifth Ave.
Madison Ave.

MOMA

34 St-Penn Sta
Lugo

MADISON SQUARE GARDEN

PENN STATION

CHELSEA

28 St
Seventh Ave.
W. 27th St.

ROCKEFELLER CENTER

ST. PATRICK'S CATHEDRAL

A

B

CHELSEA

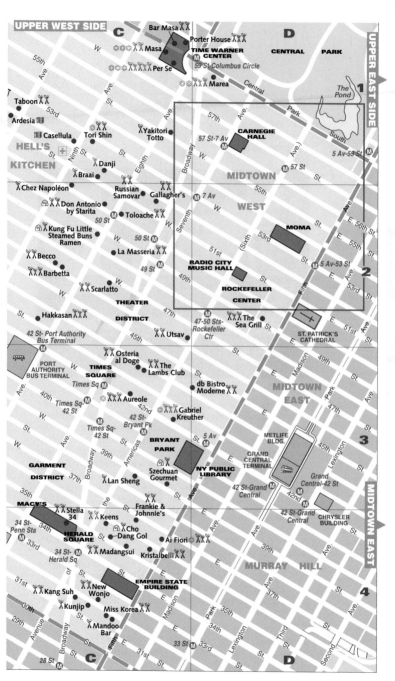

UPPER WEST SIDE

C

Bar Masa 🍴🍴

Porter House 🍴🍴🍴

D

CENTRAL   PARK

UPPER EAST SIDE

W. ❄❄❄ 🍴🍴 Masa

TIME WARNER
CENTER
Ⓜ
59 St-Columbus Circle

55th Ave.

❄❄❄ 🍴🍴🍴🍴🍴 Per Se

❄❄ 🍴🍴🍴🍴 Marea

Central

The
Pond

1

Taboon 🍴🍴

53rd St.

57th

57 St-7 Av

CARNEGIE
HALL

South

Park

Ⓜ 5 Av-59 St

Ardesia 🍶

🍴🍴 Tori Shin

57 St. (Av.)

5 Av-59 St

🍶 Casellula

Ninth St.

🍴 Yakitori
Totto

W.
57th

Ⓜ 57 St

HELL'S
KITCHEN

✚

🍴 Danji

Eighth St.

MIDTOWN

E. 56th St.

🍴 Braai ●

55th

WEST

Ave.

E. 55th St.

🍴 Chez Napoléon ●

Russian
Samovar ●

🍴🍴
Gallagher's

Ⓜ 7 Av

Broadway

MOMA

Sixth St.

E. 55th St.

🐦🍴🍴 Don Antonio
by Starita

50 St Ⓜ

Toloache 🍴🍴

Seventh (Sixth) St.

53rd

Ⓜ 5 Av-53 St

53rd St.

🐦🍴 Kung Fu Little
Steamed Buns
Ramen

W.
50 St Ⓜ

51st

🍴🍴 Becco

● La Masseria 🍴🍴

RADIO CITY
MUSIC HALL

2

🍴🍴🍴 Barbetta

49 St Ⓜ

49th

St.

ROCKEFELLER

53rd St.

🍴🍴 Scarlatto

W.

THEATER

CENTER

Fifth

● Hakkasan 🍴🍴🍴

DISTRICT

47th

47-50 Sts-
Rockefeller
Ctr

🍴🍴🍴 The
Sea Grill St.

ST. PATRICK'S
CATHEDRAL

51st Ave.

42 St- Port Authority
Bus Terminal

🚌
Ⓜ

45th

🍴🍴 Utsav ●

St.

49th

Madison

PORT
AUTHORITY
BUS TERMINAL

W.

🍴🍴 Osteria
al Doge

TIMES
SQUARE

Times Sq Ⓜ

🍴🍴 The
Lambs Club

St.

47th

MIDTOWN
EAST

Park

40th

Times Sq-
42 St Ⓜ

❄ 🍴🍴🍴 Aureole

42nd

● db Bistro
Moderne 🍴🍴

E.

W.

Ⓜ
42 St-
Bryant Pk

❄🍴🍴🍴 Gabriel
Kreuter

5 Av
Ⓜ

METLIFE
BLDG.

45th

Lexington

St.

St.

Times Sq-
42 St Ⓜ

BRYANT
PARK

St.

E.
42nd

47th

GARMENT
DISTRICT

Broadway

39th

Americas

the

● Szechuan
Gourmet

NY PUBLIC
LIBRARY

GRAND
CENTRAL
TERMINAL

Grand
Central-42 St

3

37th

🍴 Lan Sheng

St.

42 St-Grand
Central Ⓜ

42 St-Grand
Central Ⓜ

42nd Ⓜ

35th

MACY'S

🍴🍴 Stella
34

🍴🍴 Frankie &
Johnnie's

E.

CHRYSLER
BUILDING

34 St-
Penn Sta

34th

🍴🍴 Keens

39th

St.

Ave.

Third St.

33rd

🐦🍴 Cho
Dang Gol

● Ai Fiori ❄🍴🍴🍴

MURRAY   HILL

D

34 St- Ⓜ
Herald Sq

🍴🍴 Madangsui

Kristalbelli 🍴🍴

Ave.

37th

31st

🍴🍴 Kang Suh

🍴🍴 New
Wonjo

EMPIRE STATE
BUILDING

Park

35th

4

🍴 Kunjip

Miss Korea 🍴🍴

Madison

34th

30th

Avenue

🍴 Mandoo
Bar

33 St Ⓜ

33rd

29th

Broadway

St.

31st

Fifth St.

Lexington

Second

28th Ⓜ

C

St.

St.

D

HERALD
SQUARE

HELL'S
KITCHEN

MIDTOWN EAST

Ai Fiori

C4

400 Fifth Ave. (bet. 36th & 37th Sts.)

Subway: 34 St - Herald Sq
Phone: 212-613-8660
Web: www.aifiorinyc.com
Price: $$$$

Lunch Mon – Fri
Dinner nightly

Elegantly accessed either by a sweeping spiral staircase or the Langham Place hotel elevator, Ai Fiori stands proudly above its busy Fifth Avenue address. Walls of windows and espresso-dark polished wood dominate the space. The Carrara marble bar and lounge furnished with silvery tufted banquettes are ideal for solo diners; large florals, brown leather chairs, and square columns adorn the formal dining room. No matter where you sit, the servers are attentive, the linens are thick, chargers are monogrammed with a goldleaf "F" and every last detail is very, very lovely.

As one might expect of a Michael White restaurant, pastas here are masterful. Begin with perfectly al dente spaghetti evenly coated in subtly sweet tomato sauce with flakey crabmeat, gently spiced red chilies, and grated *bottarga*. Fish courses can be even more enticing. Dine on some of the brightest, freshest halibut known to this city, served on an excellent mix of smoky butter beans, chopped pancetta, artichokes, crispy golden croutons, and wonderfully minerally *cavolo nero*.

Finish your meal on a tasty note with a passion fruit curd and mango jelly tartlet along with a crunchy cookie to accompany your cup of strong, hot coffee.

Aldo Sohm Wine Bar

Contemporary

A4

151 W. 51st St. (bet. Sixth & Seventh Aves.)

Subway: 50 St (Broadway)
Phone: 212-554-1143
Web: www.aldosohmwinebar.com
Price: $$

Lunch Mon – Fri
Dinner Mon – Sat

Step through this buffed metal doorway to find an oenophile's fantasy where Zalto stemware is stacked high and each polished glass is ready to be filled by one of the 200 selections brilliantly curated by Le Bernardin's super-star sommelier, Aldo Sohm. Over 40 wines on the list are offered by the glass. A tailored crowd sits and sips—perhaps on an oversized U-shaped sofa, a comfy counter, or handful of tall tables.

The scene is luxe but also comfortable, featuring crystal fixtures, vivid artwork, and a stylish array of bric-a-brac stacked high to the soaring ceiling. Tapas-sized snacks are designed for sharing with wine consumption in mind and include a plate of cheeses, charcuterie, harissa-roasted carrots, or chicken drumstick prepared coq au vin-style.

Añejo

Mexican

B2

668 Tenth Ave. (at 47th St.)

Subway: 50 St (Eighth Ave.)
Phone: 212-920-4770
Web: www.anejonyc.com
Price: $$

Lunch & dinner daily

This modern Mexican gem produces truly unique small plates, conceptualized by talented Chef Angelo Sosa. The intimate, tavern-like space is rustic and sexy, with low ceilings that give it a sultry, date-night vibe. A long, wooden bar stretches down the length of the room, facing rows of exotic tequila and mescal—and the downtown TriBeCa location even houses a downstairs speakeasy. Don't miss the namesake margarita—a top-shelf refresher made with fresh lime juice and agave nectar.

The menu offers a wide variety of creative small plates like guacamole with charred pineapple, rabbit *mole*, as well as tacos stuffed with short rib or crispy shrimp. There are lots of dishes to choose from and the plates arrive as they are cooked—tapas-style, naturally.

Ardesia

Contemporary

C1

510 W. 52nd St. (bet. Tenth & Eleventh Aves.)

Subway: 50 St (Eighth Ave.)   Dinner nightly
Phone: 212-247-9191
Web: www.ardesia-ny.com
Price: $$

This is one of the area's best spots for grabbing an *aperitivo* and bite after work. Service is young, friendly, and knowledgeable, so make sure to ask for a recommendation as it can yield tasty rewards. Towering ceilings and a wall of windows seem to augment the rather petite space; and a chalkboard wall lists wines available by the glass, even if the most impressive selections are only offered by the bottle on the menu.

Contemporary small plates begin with notable cheese offerings like ricotta Ginepro, cold-smoked sheep's milk, and pale yellow Ossau Iraty accompanied by a walnut covered in date-coconut jam and thick, crusty bread from Amy's. Sample skewers lined with garlicky shrimp or spiced lamb. Then finish with a sweet and earnest take on homemade s'mores.

Bar Masa

Japanese

C1

10 Columbus Circle (in the Time Warner Center)

Subway: 59 St - Columbus Circle   Lunch & dinner Mon – Sat
Phone: 212-823-9800
Web: www.barmasanyc.com
Price: $$$

Make no mistake: Masa's adjacent lounge is by no means a bargain substitute for the stunner next door. Bar Masa remains as hopping as when it first opened, and on any given night every tightly packed seat is perpetually filled—thanks in part to a no-reservations policy. Despite the crowds, softly lit Japanese limestone walls give the room an air of serenity.

The long list of creative sips are excellent, so lay your lips on a cucumber mint gimlet while eagerly awaiting selections off the extensive menu. Serious effort is blatantly apparent: raw petals of *sakura* trout are tantalizingly dressed; pudding-soft tofu and perfectly ripe avocado are a heavenly pairing for an *uramaki*; and fluffy wild mushroom fried rice is sprinkled with wasabi salt.

Aureole ✿

Contemporary XxX

135 W. 42nd St. (bet. Broadway & Sixth Ave.)

Subway: 42 St - Bryant Pk
Phone: 212-319-1660
Web: www.charliepalmer.com
Price: $$$$

Lunch Mon – Fri
Dinner nightly

Nestled smack dab in the middle of the melee that constitutes modern-day Times Square, Aureole's message is clear from the moment you enter its serene glass façade: drop your bags (and perhaps your shoulders) and relax—it's time to be pampered by a truly exquisite seafood-centric meal in a luxurious setting.

Up front, you'll find the Liberty Room, home to a lively bar that's ideal for an after-work drink or pre-dinner cocktail; and a small collection of handsome, walnut-topped tables comprising a more casual dining area. Toward the back of the restaurant, the formal dining room cuts an impressive, elegant figure with sexy low lighting, crisp white tablecloths, and polished table settings.

Dinner might begin with a beautifully composed peekytoe crab salad, sporting vibrant green avocado panna cotta, juicy watermelon and sea beans; and then move on to a gorgeous slice of fresh Alaskan black cod in a sweet and savory marinade, paired with crisp snap peas, bok choy, and *choy sum*. End with a stunning finale like the elegantly prepared Saint Honoré, a flaky tuile topped with a flower-shaped pinwheel piped with silky Manjari chocolate mousse and dotted with light-as-air *choux* puffs.

Barbetta

Italian

C2

321 W. 46th St. (bet. Eighth & Ninth Aves.)

Subway: 50 St (Eighth Ave.) Lunch & dinner Tue – Sat
Phone: 212-246-9171
Web: www.barbettarestaurant.com
Price: $$$

It doesn't get more old-world New York than this iconic Restaurant Row institution. Opened in 1906, Barbetta is a testament to proper dining out: men are required to don dinner jackets, outerwear is mandatorily checked, and a brigade of starched servers flit about the hushed and gilded surrounds. Perhaps unsurprisingly, the impossibly romantic patio has been the backdrop for countless marriage proposals. The kitchen's Northern-influenced specialties are listed on thick cardstock, and each selection is highlighted by the year of its addition to the menu. Linguine with *pesto alla Genovese* is as scrumptious today as it was in 1914; while luscious rabbit *alla Piemontese*, dating back to the Clinton era and braised in white wine and lemon, is equally divine.

Becco

Italian

C2

355 W. 46th St. (bet. Eighth & Ninth Aves.)

Subway: 50 St (Eighth Ave.) Lunch & dinner daily
Phone: 212-397-7597
Web: www.becco-nyc.com
Price: $$

This Restaurant Row stalwart has no shortage of competition, but remains unrivaled when it comes to sating diners and theatergoers with reliably hearty Italian food. This is all thanks to culinary authority Lidia Bastianich, her impresario son Joe, and longtime Executive Chef William Gallagher.

Becco's pleasing vision of this country's cuisine includes a unique trio of tableside pasta offerings—perhaps rustic penne *arrabiata* if you're lucky—as well as delightfully savory Belgian ale-roasted pulled pork with salsa verde. Then, *sarma* honors the family's Istrian heritage with meat-stuffed cabbage in a lush tomato sauce. And, the wine list includes bottles priced at $29, with selections from their own highly regarded label.

Benares

 Indian XX

A3

240 W. 56th St. (bet. Broadway & Eighth Ave.)

Subway: 59 St - Columbus Circle
Phone: 212-397-0707
Web: www.benaresnyc.com
Price: $$

Lunch & dinner daily

Unassuming inside and out, Benares serves solid Northern Indian fare in a casual setting. The South Asian clientele is testament to its authenticity. The décor may seem a bit limited, but find thoughtful touches like a colorful glass chandelier and a framed painting of women washing clothes along the Ganges (in the restaurant's namesake city).

Fragrant spice mixtures abound as seen in succulent and crunchy shrimp marinated with *ajwain*, garlic, and ginger, then grilled in the tandoor. Curry offerings showcase boldly satisfying comfort food, such as bowls of fork-tender *rezala*, the goat served bone-in with fragrant saffron and creamy yogurt. Any meal here should be accompanied by pillow-soft naan, and thick cucumber raita dotted with a pungent masala.

BG

American X

B3

754 Fifth Ave. (at 58th St.)

Subway: 5 Av - 59 St
Phone: 212-872-8977
Web: www.bergdorfgoodman.com
Price: $$$

Lunch daily
Dinner Mon – Sat

On the 7th floor of Bergdorf Goodman, BG offers ladylike posh to the label-conscious clientele of this fashion emporium. The Kelly Wearstler-designed brasserie combines springtime hues with hand-printed Chinoiserie wallpaper, gilded fixtures, and lacquered accents.

Large windows frame killer Central Park vistas and highlight the well-coiffed crowd savoring a number of fine salads. However, the carte du jour offers more vibrant dining with decadent renditions of American comfort favorites, like lobster mac and cheese. The silken tomato basil soup is enriched with just the slightest hint of cream; and Israeli couscous is infused with smoked paprika and stocked with seared black bass and shellfish.

Afternoon tea is a suitably refined affair.

Betony ❀

Contemporary ✗✗✗

41 W. 57th St. (bet. Fifth & Sixth Aves.)

Subway: 57 St
Phone: 212-465-2400
Web: www.betony-NYC.com
Price: $$$$

Lunch Mon – Fri
Dinner Mon – Sat

Midtown and Betony go together like caviar and blinis. Serious funds have been invested to create this smart, grown-up restaurant and its gilded features, wood paneling, and well-spaced tables provide very comfortable surroundings in which to do business or impress friends. The experienced service team, though, do a good job in ensuring the atmosphere never veers into the terminal seriousness that blights many a formal restaurant.

When one surveys this luxurious backdrop and the impeccably manicured clientele, it is perhaps something of a surprise to find that the food is adventurous and creative. Chef Bryce Shuman and his kitchen team know all the latest cooking techniques and are not afraid to use them. Ravioli with smoked potato shows off their delicate touch but the grilled short rib demonstrates that they also know how to create layers of flavor.

The smattering of canapes that kick off the meal are best enjoyed with a drink. Speaking of drinks, make sure you start by ordering a milk punch—the kitchen isn't the only team here who has some clever ideas and the ability to see them through.

Braai

South African

 329 W. 51st St. (bet. Eighth & Ninth Aves).)

Subway: 50 St (Eighth Ave.)　　　　　　　　　Dinner nightly
Phone: 212-315-3315
Web: www.braainyc.com
Price: $$

 From its ground floor townhouse home, Braai tantalizes with its first-rate South African cuisine. Two tables sit up front in a snug patio, which dovetails into a slender dark wood space. Drawing inspiration from the surrounding region, wide planks make up the floors while an arched ceiling is thatched with straw. Yet, the African-inspired décor in the dining room is anything but cliché.

Compensating for its somewhat sloppy service is a menu resplendent with new and balanced flavors that are at once evident in frikkadel, a classic dish of baked meatballs in broth, or even calamari drenched in wine-lemon emulsion. Bunny chow, a street eat of lamb curry ladled into a bread bowl, is a winner here.

Brasserie 8 1/2

Contemporary

 9 W. 57th St. (bet. Fifth & Sixth Aves.)

Subway: 57 St　　　　　　　　　　　Lunch Sun – Fri
Phone: 212-829-0812　　　　　　　　　Dinner nightly
Web: www.patinagroup.com
Price: $$$

Dress-up, descend that sweeping staircase, and make a grand entrance upon stepping into this well-lit, spacious, grown-up canteen. The serene lounge, with just a handful of tables and walls boasting original works by Henri Matisse and Pablo Picasso, is a rarefied gift that feels worlds away from midtown's cacophony. The masculine, clubby aura of the dining room showcases ivory terrazzo floors, exotic wood veneer-lined walls, polished metal columns, and more artwork.

Talented Chef Franck Deletrain brings a traditional vision of brasserie cooking in items such as coq au vin; or *saucisson chaud*, braised pork sausage nestled in a bed of *lentils du Puy*. Finish with pear poached in spiced red wine, accompanied by mascarpone and pistachio financiers.

Brasserie Ruhlmann

French ✗✗

45 Rockefeller Plaza (bet. Fifth & Sixth Aves.)

Subway: 47-50 Sts - Rockefeller Ctr
Phone: 212-974-2020
Web: www.brasserieruhlmann.com
Price: $$$

Lunch & dinner daily

True, some New Yorkers may think of this place as kind of touristy, but this is quintessential brasserie cooking in an equally quintessential Manhattan setting at the base of Rockefeller Center, overlooking its plaza. There is little debate that this French *bijou* offers some of the best people-watching around. The décor pays homage to its art deco namesake, Émile-Jacques Ruhlmann, through edgy lines and geometric prints.

Some dishes may be on the menu more for pleasing the crowds than reflecting tradition (hence the sushi rolls). Still, the *croque monsieur* is everything you dream it to be—impossibly rich with paper-thin and salty *jambon de Paris*, creamy béchamel, and a dangerously good layering of melted Gruyère over thick slices of brioche.

Casellula

American ▤

401 W. 52nd St. (bet. Ninth & Tenth Aves.)

Subway: 50 St (Eighth Ave.)
Phone: 212-247-8137
Web: www.casellula.com
Price: $$

Dinner nightly

Casellula oozes with warmth in both look and feel. Dark wood tables, exposed brick, and flickering votives are a sight for sore eyes, while the delightful staff is so attentive and friendly, that you may never want to leave.

Small plates are big here, while medium ones feature tasty sandwiches (crunchy *muffulettas* stuffed with fontina and cured meats) and shrimp tacos splashed with *salsa verde*. Pity the lactose intolerant, as cheese (and lots of it) followed by dessert (maybe a pumpkin ice cream "sandwich" pecked with brown butter caramel?) are part and parcel of the special experience at this petite place. Feeling blue? They've got that and much more with over 50 different varieties, perfectly complemented by an excellent and vast wine list.

Chez Napoléon

 C2

French ✗

365 W. 50th St. (bet. Eighth & Ninth Aves.)

Subway: 50 St (Eighth Ave.)
Phone: 212-265-6980
Web: www.cheznapoleon.com
Price: $$

Lunch Mon – Fri
Dinner Mon – Sat

Oh-so-popular and family-run by the Brunos since 1982, this atmospheric bistro is not to be missed for its unapologetically creamy and butter-dreamy plates of traditional French cuisine. It's not polite to discuss age, but let's just say that Chef/ *grandmère*, Marguerite Bruno, has steadily commanded this kitchen for an impressive tenure.

The scene is *magnifique*. Take in the creaky wood floors and parchment-colored walls hung with French-themed jigsaw puzzles. Then indulge in chilled silky leeks dressed with the famous house vinaigrette; sautéed veal kidneys in mustard-cream sauce; and steak *au poivre* with black or green peppercorn sauce. Plan ahead when ordering so you have time (and space) for a classic dessert soufflé sided with crème anglaise.

Cho Dang Gol

C4

Korean ✗

55 W. 35th St. (bet. Fifth & Sixth Aves.)

Subway: 34 St - Herald Sq
Phone: 212-695-8222
Web: www.cdgnyc.com
Price: 🥢

Lunch & dinner daily

For a change of pace in bustling Koreatown, Cho Dang Gol offers the barbecue-weary an opportunity to explore some of this nation's more rustic cooking. Soft tofu is the specialty of the house and for fitting reason (it's downright delicious). But, bubbling casseroles and spicy stews are equally heartwarming. The menu also offers favorites like flaky *pajeon*, satisfying *bibimbap*, and marinated meats. A sautéed tofu trio with pork belly is stir fried with glassy sweet potato noodles and kimchi, in an excellent sweet and spicy red pepper sauce.

The interior has a simple, homey appeal—its cozy dining room simply decorated with close-knit wood tables. The occasional burst of sound drifting down from the upstairs karaoke bar promises a little post-dinner fun.

Clement

  XXX

B4

700 Fifth Ave. (at 55th St.)

Subway: 5 Av - 53 St
Phone: 212-956-2888
Web: www.peninsula.com/NewYork
Price: $$$

Lunch daily
Dinner Tue – Sat

Sometimes we need to be served by someone older than our socks, be addressed by our name rather than as "you guys," be able to converse without recourse to sign language, and to sit in a chair designed by someone familiar with the concept of upholstery. The handsomely attired Clement, at the Peninsula Hotel, provides all this and more, and is ideal for those times when we need to feed our inner grown-up.

The kitchen does its bit too by avoiding spurious reinvention and instead focusses on producing wholesome, satisfying and adroitly prepared contemporary dishes. Start with a perky tuna crudo, have the wonderfully succulent milk-fed veal chop which has been given time to rest before being served, and end with pumpkin pie with silky cinnamon ice cream.

Danji

  X

C1

346 W. 52nd St. (bet. Eighth & Ninth Aves.)

Subway: 50 St (Eighth Ave.)
Phone: 212-586-2880
Web: www.danjinyc.com
Price: $$

Lunch Mon – Fri
Dinner Mon – Sat

Thanks to tall communal tables that practically fill the dining room, Chef Hooni Kim's Hell's Kitchen hot spot is both festive and bustling. Attractive and smartly designed, its silk panels, pottery, and striking display of spoons are further enhanced by a flattering lighting scheme.

Equally impressive are the menu's myriad small plates, each of them a refreshing take on Korean specialties. Blocks of soft tofu are quickly deep-fried and boldly dressed with *gochujang* and a ginger-scallion vinaigrette. Poached daikon rings accompanied by bok choy, are glazed with a dark and spicy sauce and stacked high for dramatic presentation. Vegetarian highlights include spicy, crispy dumplings filled with tofu, vegetables, and cellophane noodles.

Culinary Agents

Find the best jobs. Find the best people.

CulinaryAgents.com

db Bistro Moderne

 Contemporary ✗✗

D3

55 W. 44th St. (bet. Fifth & Sixth Aves.)

Lunch & dinner daily

Subway: 5 Av
Phone: 212-391-2400
Web: www.dbbistro.com
Price: $$$

Chef Daniel Boulud's midtown canteen is fashioned by Jeffrey Beers and dons a contemporary demeanor. The front lounge is abuzz with post-work and pre-theater gaggles, while well-behaved crowds in the back are seated in a walnut-paneled space dressed with mirrors and black-and-white photography. Like its setting, the menu is inventive and unites classic bistro cooking with market-inspired creations. That lush *pâté en croute* is a buttery pastry encasing layers of creamy country pâté, guinea hen, and foie gras, dressed with huckleberry compote, toasted pine nuts, and pickled enoki mushrooms. Wild rice-crusted fluke presented with Hawaiian blue prawn and sauce *Américaine* further demonstrates the kitchen's contemporary leanings.

Del Frisco's

 Steakhouse

A4

1221 Sixth Ave. (at 49th St.)

Lunch Mon – Fri
Dinner nightly

Subway: 47-50 Sts - Rockefeller Ctr
Phone: 212-575-5129
Web: www.delfriscos.com
Price: $$$

Prime, aged, corn-fed beef is the main attraction at this sprawling, outrageously successful outpost of the Dallas-based steakhouse chain. Portions range from the petite filet to a 24-ounce Porterhouse that will make any Texan proud. The menu begins with a suitably rich feast of cheesesteak egg rolls or white clam flatbread, but then does an about face with a knife-and-fork Caesar salad. Lunch is an affordable way to sample their classics.

Complementing its McGraw-Hill Building home, Del Frisco's flaunts a masculine look with a large L-shaped bar, dramatic wrought-iron balcony, wood accents, and towering windows. The mezzanine dining area, accessible by a sweeping staircase, enjoys a quieter ambience. Del Frisco's Grille in Rockefeller Plaza is another option.

Don Antonio by Starita 😊

P i z z a ✖✖

309 W. 50th St. (bet. Eighth & Ninth Aves.)

Subway: 50 St (Eighth Ave.)
Phone: 646-719-1043
Web: www.donantoniopizza.com
Price: $$

Lunch & dinner daily

Don Antonio's knows its way around a pie. The namesake outpost, located in Naples, has been running strong since 1901. And if that isn't enough street cred to send you running to Antonio Starita and Roberto Caporuscio's beloved pizzeria, then perhaps the generous buzz surrounding Caporuscio's other New York venture, Kesté, will do the trick.

Don Antonio's signature pie is the Montanara Starita—a lightly fried pizza laced with fresh house-made tomato sauce, smoked mozzarella and basil, then finished in the wood-fired oven. Oh, but who could stop there with treasures like the *salsiccia e friarielli* pizza to sample. This beauty arrives with sweet, crumbled fennel sausage, smoked mozzarella, bitter rapini greens and a glossy swirl of EVOO.

Estiatorio Milos

G r e e k ✖✖✖

125 W. 55th St. (bet. Sixth & Seventh Aves.)

Subway: 57 St
Phone: 212-245-7400
Web: www.milos.ca
Price: $$$

Lunch & dinner daily

This Greek restaurant offers such deliciously singular focus on the sea that dinner here feels like a relaxing jaunt to the Mediterranean coast. Feast your eyes on the ever-present bounty of iced fish, flown in fresh and displayed in the back of the cavernous room where a well-dressed, business-minded crowd gathers.

Oregano plants atop each table are snipped into bowls of olive oil to accompany the fine bread that precedes the selection of raw bar specialties and grilled fish. The day's bounty may reveal charred *barbouni*, or red mullet, dressed with olive oil, capers, and a sprig of flat leaf parsley. Side dishes unveil *chtipiti*—a mouthwatering spread made from roasted red peppers and barrel-aged feta that you'll want to slather on everything.

44 & X Hell's Kitchen

American ✗✗

B2

622 Tenth Ave. (at 44th St.)

Subway: 42 St - Port Authority Bus Terminal
Phone: 212-977-1170
Web: www.44andx.com
Price: $$

Lunch & dinner daily

The moniker is a mouthful, but this modern bistro's endearing appeal has attracted eclectic crowds since opening on a block west of no-man's land. Today, this corner of Hell's Kitchen is a solid, mature venue offering a vast number of draws. Cute servers in black t-shirts are gracious and attentive, presenting updated renditions of spirited comfort food. Lobster tacos with charred tomato salsa, crunchy buttermilk fried chicken accompanied by a chive waffle and maple syrup jus, as well as pan-roasted mahi mahi with lobster and scallop risotto emerge from the skilled kitchen. House-baked apple pie is a lovely sweet special to ward off the chill of an autumn evening.

Sister spot 44 ½ offers more casual cooking in an equally delightful setting.

Frankie & Johnnie's

Steakhouse ✗✗

C4

32 W. 37th St. (bet. Fifth & Sixth Aves.)

Subway: 34 St - Herald Sq
Phone: 212-947-8940
Web: www.frankieandjohnnies.com
Price: $$$

Lunch Mon – Fri
Dinner Mon – Sat

No surprise that this is a former speakeasy. The first floor is dedicated to drinking at the bar and booths filled with people sipping martinis before splitting to Penn Station. Head upstairs, beyond an artistically assembled mound of wax over the vestibule, to enter this classic dining room. Spacious tables, crisp linens, and swift service ensure a steady business clientele.

All in all, Frankie & Johnnie's is the kind of place where you shouldn't have to look at the menu. Just go with a nicely marbled, medium rare Porterhouse steak sliced tableside and served with the bone for gnawing. Traditional sides like whipped potatoes or creamed spinach push the limits with butter and cream. For dessert, the cheesecake is prepared with solid New York know-how.

Gabriel Kreuther ❀

C3

Contemporary XX

41 W. 42nd St. (bet. Fifth & Sixth Aves.)

Subway: 42 St - Bryant Pk
Phone: 212-257-5826
Web: www.gknyc.com
Price: $$$$

Lunch Mon – Fri
Dinner Mon – Sat

Proving that the death of fine dining has been grossly exaggerated, Alsace-born Gabriel Kreuther's eponymous midtown restaurant offers artfully designed surroundings, creative and eye-catching food, and service that is formal and quite ceremonial.

It's certainly a striking room, with columns of reclaimed wood juxtaposed with creamy white leather seating and a glass wall offering glimpses of the impressively calm goings-on in the kitchen. The table settings are immaculate too, with delicate glassware, cups and bowls that you can't stop stroking, and surgically thin modern cutlery that you'll either love or hate.

The chef's classical culinary upbringing underpins his modern creations and his Alsatian heritage plays a role too. Alongside *kugelhopf*, you'll also find sauerkraut—it makes an appearance in one of his more theatrical dishes where it's mixed with sturgeon, garnished with caviar and presented at the table with the lifting of a glass cloche filled with applewood smoke. The desserts, if you can get past their somewhat pretentious monikers ("revisited" or "ethereal" anyone?) show that the pastry section is also given license to push boundaries.

Gallagher's

Steakhouse ✕✕

C2

228 W. 52nd St. (bet. Broadway & Eighth Ave.)

Lunch & dinner daily

Subway: 50 St (Broadway)
Phone: 212-586-5000
Web: www.gallaghersnysteakhouse.com
Price: $$$

A multi-million dollar renovation hasn't glossed over any of Gallagher's iconic character. Walls covered with photos of horses and jockeys harken back to the seasoned stallion's former proximity to the old Madison Square Garden. The menu's "other soup" is a sly reference held over from Prohibition days; and diners still walk past the window-fronted meat locker where slabs of USDA Prime beef are dry-aged.

Gallagher's fresh sparkle is exhibited by the display kitchen, set behind glass panes. The chefs here turn out contemporary-minded fare like hamachi crudo with a yuzu-jalapeño vinaigrette to go with choice cuts of meat grilled over hickory. The rib steak is a bone-in ribeye that arrives mouthwateringly tender with a side of warm and savory house sauce.

Hakkasan

Chinese ✕✕✕

C2

311 W. 43rd St. (bet. Eighth & Ninth Aves.)

Subway: 42 St - Port Authority Bus Terminal
Phone: 212-776-1818
Web: www.hakkasan.com
Price: $$$$

Lunch Sat – Sun
Dinner nightly

If this sensual and sophisticated lair doesn't come to mind when you crave quality Cantonese cooking, it's high time you added it to the list. Behind its front door lies a long, moodily-lit corridor that leads to a massive dining room, which, thanks to cobalt-blue glass, Carrara marble, and mirrors, feels intimate despite its size.

The equally elegant menu underscores mouthwatering dishes like jasmine tea-smoked chicken and stir-fried sugar pea pods with crabmeat and scallops; or bamboo steamers full of scallop *siu mai* topped with tobiko, King crab noodle rolls, as well as truffle and roasted duck *bao*. The prix-fixe dim sum, a wallet-friendly delight that synchs perfectly with Hakkasan's luxe tenor, is yet another decadent surprise.

Il Gattopardo

Italian ✗✗

B4

13-15 W. 54th St. (bet. Fifth & Sixth Aves.)

Subway: 5 Av - 53 St
Phone: 212-246-0412
Web: www.ilgattopardonyc.com
Price: $$$

Lunch & dinner daily

This *leopard's* take on Italian dining favors elegance over rusticity. Set within two Beaux Arts townhouses (once home to a Rockefeller family member), the restaurant is an understated sprawl of ivory walls contrasted with dark-stained floors and smoky mirrors.

The smartly attired staff attends to a buttoned-up crowd digging into pricey but pleasing fare like shaved artichoke salad with organic frisée, lemon, olive oil, and *bottarga di muggine*. Here, veal scaloppini is a pounded filet layered with grilled eggplant and smoked provolone, alongside braised escarole studded with black olives. Like everything else at Il Gattopardo, the *cassata Siciliana*—with its candied fruit and bright green almond paste—is a dressed-up take on the classic.

Indian Accent

Indian ✗✗✗

A3

123 W. 56th St. (bet. Sixth & Seventh Aves.)

Subway: 57 St
Phone: 212-842-8070
Web: www.indianaccent.com
Price: $$$

Lunch & dinner Mon – Sat

Nestled inside the posh Le Parker Méridien hotel, Indian Accent offers gorgeously plated food with a decidedly modern spin. An outpost of the highly acclaimed original in Delhi, the New York space is sleek and exotic, with purple banquettes, brass details and a shimmering gold-accent wall. The service is polished and professional, with the knowledgeable staff carefully walking you through a customized prix-fixe menu selected from various parts of the carte.

Celebrated chef Manish Mehrotra heads the talented kitchen, serving up impressive starters like freshly griddled *phulka* paired with jackfruit, green chili sauce, and micro sprouts. Perfectly tender sea bass is then coupled with herbed barley, trout roe, and puddled in creamy coconut sauce.

Kang Suh

 Korean ✗✗

C4

1250 Broadway (at 32nd St.)

Subway: 33 St
Phone: 212-564-6845
Web: www.kangsuhnyc.com
Price: $$

Lunch & dinner daily

A longtime favorite of Korean barbecue fans, this lively yet homey joint delivers an authentic and charming experience. Donning an old-school vibe, the room may seem trapped in time, but rest assured as there is delish food and free-flowing soju on deck here. Bypass the first floor and find a roost on the second level, where warm, almost maternal servers with a sense of humor present an array of fragrant grilled meats.

The *haemool pa jeon* is a flaky seafood pancake and excellent starter that may be trailed by delicate slices of *galbi* sizzling on the grill. Further indulge this meat feast with *jaeyook gui* or marinated pork grilled to pink perfection. Yet still be sure to save room for *boodae chongol*—a bubbling stew of kimchi, pork, vegetables, and noodles.

Keens

Steakhouse ✗✗

C4

72 W. 36th St. (bet. Fifth & Sixth Aves.)

Subway: 34 St - Herald Sq
Phone: 212-947-3636
Web: www.keens.com
Price: $$$

Lunch Mon – Fri
Dinner nightly

It's not just carnivores who'll appreciate this most classic of steakhouses; Anglophiles, social historians, Scotch lovers and pipe smokers will also find themselves revelling in the immeasurably appealing atmosphere of Keens and its palpable sense of times past. Established in 1885, it suggests a Dickensian Gentleman's club, with its dark wood panelling and low ceiling lined with thousands of clay pipes, although these days the customers are mostly deal-making business types rather than extravagantly whiskered thespians.

Follow their lead and drape your jacket over the back of your chair, roll up your sleeves and attempt to gain control over a Porterhouse steak, dry-aged in-house, or finish their legendary mutton chop in one sitting.

Kristalbelli

Korean ✗✗

8 W. 36th St. (bet. Fifth & Sixth Aves.)

Subway: 34 St - Herald Sq
Phone: 212-290-2211
Web: www.kristalbelli.com
Price: $$$

Lunch Mon – Fri
Dinner nightly

This sophisticated restaurant boasts a distinctly uptown vibe—the interior features sparkling crystal grills and the kitchen presents a menu filled with French inflections. Each marble table seats four and the premise of these signature grills is that they cook the meat faster—with no smoke. The upstairs bar, Juga, offers a dim and clubby venue for pre-dinner drinks or a private party.

Don't miss such chef-driven dishes as *galbi*, a plate of perfectly seared Wagyu short rib in soy-garlic marinade, served with roasted maitake mushrooms and polenta studded with chive brunoise, pickled radish and scallion salad. Or make like the locals and dive into a robust silken tofu stew brimming with fiery red chili pepper broth, tender zucchini, clams and squid.

Kung Fu Little Steamed Buns Ramen 😊

Chinese ✗

811 Eighth Ave. (bet. 48th & 49th Sts.)

Subway: 50 St (Eighth Ave.)
Phone: 917-388-2555
Web: www.kfdelicacy.com
Price: 😊😊

Lunch & dinner daily

With its lineup of traditionally prepared comfort food, this steamy joint kicks Hell's Kitchen's Chinese competitors to the curb. Set among the bright lights of the Theater District yet more indicative of the noodle houses found south of Canal Street or along Flushing Avenue, the perpetually packed gem offers a so-so ambience but very friendly service.

Hand-pulled and hand-cut noodles are stir-fried with a number of mouthwatering accompaniments; while the dumpling variety is so great it's almost impossible to focus. Herb-spiked pork and shrimp wonton soup is well worth the 20-minute wait, allowing diners plenty of time to devour pan-fried Peking duck bundles and scallion pancakes stuffed with sliced beef; or steamed buns full of mushroom and bok choy.

Kunjip

C4

Korean ✗

32 W. 32nd St. (bet. Broadway & Fifth Ave.)

Subway: 34 St - Herald Sq
Phone: 212-216-9487
Web: www.kunjip.com
Price: 🍴

Lunch & dinner daily

The first thing you need to know about this wildly popular restaurant is that it's open 24 hours. The second thing you need to know is that it's actually good. Even better news? An expansion has created additional seating in this two-level dining room, done up in spare, earthy hues and traditional wooden screens. It's classic, clean and simple—the message is clear. At Kunjip, the focus is most decidedly on the food.

Barbecue is always popular, and is done quite well at dinner. The menu, however, reaches much wider with a long list of hearty soups (a big hit with the lunch crowd), stews, and casseroles. Everything is excellent, but a steaming bowl of *galbitang*—bobbing with tender and fatty short rib, glass noodles and juicy daikon slivers—truly transcends.

Manhattan ▶ Midtown West

La Masseria

C2

Italian ✗✗

235 W. 48th St. (bet. Broadway & Eighth Ave.)

Subway: 50 St (Eighth Ave.)
Phone: 212-582-2111
Web: www.lamasserianyc.com
Price: $$

Lunch & dinner daily

Stone, stucco walls, and exposed wood beams warm this bright and popular Theater District standby. The convenient location ensures that every large white-clothed table in the dining room is routinely full, and spot-on service delivered by smartly attired team keeps the mood upbeat.

When it comes to the food, the menu chooses homey Italian comforts over theatrics. Homemade stuffed fresh mozzarella allows the character of each ingredient—peppery arugula, roasted eggplant—to shine. Don't miss a selection of pasta *fatta in casa*. Entrées include a tender, juicy, expertly pounded veal chop with wedges of crisply roasted potatoes and a zippy chopped tomato and black olive salad. Finish with a warm and buttery inverted apple tart topped with vanilla ice cream.

297

The Lambs Club

American ✕✕

C3

132 W. 44th St. (bet. Broadway & Sixth Ave.)

Subway: Times Sq – 42 St   Lunch & dinner daily
Phone: 212-997-5262
Web: www.thelambsclub.com
Price: $$$

Thanks to the culinary expertise of Chef Geoffrey Zakarian, the curiously un-apostrophized Lambs Club delivers a reliably good dining experience thanks to cooking that is far more capable than the somewhat generic menu would suggest. Moments of subtle innovation never come at the expense of flavor and there's an appealing clarity and freshness to dishes like homemade spaghetti with crab and chili, a well-judged tuna tartare, and a smooth panna cotta.

At lunch the large fireplace goes some way to compensating for the lack of windows. Dinner feels more intimate and less corporate—something that the society of thespians to which the name refers would surely have preferred. Just get to the table first so you can snare the banquette rather than the oddly low-set chairs.

Lan Sheng

Chinese ✕

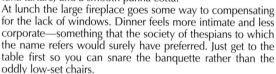

C3

60 W. 39th St. (bet. Fifth & Sixth Aves.)

Subway: 42 St – Bryant Pk   Lunch & dinner daily
Phone: 212-575-8899
Web: N/A
Price: $$

Midday hordes gathered outside its plain-Jane façade evidences the popularity of this midtown Sichuan stop. While its interior appears to be getting even more disheveled by the day, high-backed banquettes and colorful accent lights provide a respite of sorts once you make it through the doors. Recent experiences have indicated inconsistent cooking, but the fiery and smoky specialties here are still praiseworthy. Nibble on a crispy pile of camphor tea-smoked duck while waiting for the more standout items to arrive. These may include miso- and chili-simmered whole fish showered with green onion; strips of bitter melon dressed with black bean sauce; or shredded potatoes shined with oil, vinegar, and hit with dried red as well as thinly sliced green chilies.

Larb Ubol 😊

Thai ✕

B3
480 Ninth Ave. (bet. 36th & 37th Sts.)

Subway: 34 St - Penn Station
Phone: 212-564-1822
Web: www.larbubol.com
Price: 😊😊

Lunch & dinner daily

The *larb* here really is good enough to be the restaurant's namesake as these spicy, crunchy, salty and herb-y salads sing with flavor. Yet Larb Ubol does much more with equal skill: the sheer size of their massive chicken wings defy nature, yielding enough crisp-skinned and chili-coated meat to satisfy any appetite. *Yum moo krob* mixes impossibly tender pork with abundant green chilies in a fish sauce dressing for a brilliant counterpoint in flavor; while *kai jeow*, a Thai-style omelet, is an unexpectedly comforting dish that highlights excellent technique. There may be a choice of three fillings, but the pickled garlic can't be beat.

The space itself is no more than basic; the location is, well, meh. Service is friendly, though not necessarily speedy.

Limani

Greek

A4
45 Rockefeller Plaza (entrance on 50th St.)

Subway: 47-50 Sts - Rockefeller Ctr
Phone: 212-858-9200
Web: www.limani.com
Price: $$$

Lunch & dinner daily

This splashy Rockefeller Center canteen has positioned itself as a top contender for formal Greek dining. The ethereal space is all gleaming white surfaces and colorful mood lighting; whole fish are displayed on ice, and an onyx reflecting pool sits in the center of it all.

Limani's dressed-up crowd nibbles on contemporary Hellenic delights executed with aplomb. The raw bar offers icy treats—oysters, sashimi, and ceviche—and globally sourced catch is the foundation of cooked preparations, like grilled Canadian halibut dressed with olive oil and capers. *Gigantes* cooked in a tomato sauce redolent of dill and anise are a worthy side dish; while *karidopita*, spiced walnut cake soaked with honey, makes for a sweet Greek finish.

Le Bernardin

Seafood

A4

155 W. 51st St. (bet. Sixth & Seventh Aves.)

Subway: 50 St (Broadway)
Phone: 212-554-1515
Web: www.le-bernardin.com
Price: $$$$

Lunch Mon – Fri
Dinner Mon – Sat

Eric Ripert's paean to all things piscatorial is unquestionably one of the daddies of the New York dining scene. No one gets to occupy this amount of prime midtown real estate for this long without knowing exactly what they're doing—and doing it supremely well. Run with consummate ease by a well-organized team, its influence stretches beyond merely the entertaining of big-hitters and even bigger spenders.

But however celebrated, the sine qua non of any self-respecting seafood restaurant must be the ability to cook a piece of fish absolutely perfectly and, in this, Le Bernardin displays deftness and consistency. Just try the luxuriantly buttery wild striped bass and you'll get the idea.

"Almost Raw," "Barely Touched," and "Lightly Cooked" are the headings under which you'll find an impressive array of dishes. The influences are global but the cooking is underpinned by a mastery of technique; ingredients are of unimpeachable quality and the kitchen has the confidence to never overcrowd a plate so that the fish always remains the star of the show.

Loi Estiatorio

Greek **XX**

132 W. 58th St. (bet. Sixth & Seventh Aves.)

Subway: 57 St
Phone: 212-713-0015
Web: www.loiestiatorio.com
Price: $$

Lunch Mon – Fri
Dinner nightly

Chef, cookbook authority, and restaurateur Maria Loi has moved her refined take on traditional Greek cuisine to this midtown location. The room is tastefully decorated, with dark leather furnishings and panoramic photos of sun-bleached coastline that hang on the pale walls.

Lovers of Greek cuisine will revel in the cooking's familiar scents and flavors, while marveling at the kitchen's unique, inspired spin on the classics. It's possible to feast on starters alone like *ladolemono*-dressed grilled octopus with fava bean purée, or *papoutsakia* (stuffed eggplant topped with caramelized béchamel sauce). But, don't overlook the entrées—rooster, braised in red wine as well as spiced tomato sauce and served over Greek pasta, is especially decadent.

Lugo

Italian **XX**

1 Penn Plaza (entrance on 33rd St.)

Subway: 34 St - Penn Station
Phone: 212-760-2700
Web: www.ldvhospitality.com
Price: $$

Lunch & dinner Mon – Fri

In a blah locale that's overshadowed by tourists, this café shines bright as a recommendation for Italian food. The cavernous space boasts a clubby vibe and boisterous businessmen make this a lively choice. Light streaming in from lofty windows shows off a white-tiled bar area framed by black-and-white photographs, and a pastel-green Vespa adds an extra dose of charm. But, look past the somewhat staged design and focus on the food—you'll be pleasantly surprised. The menu is executed with unexpected elegance and care.

Tables may cradle snacks like warm hand-pulled mozzarella, Neapolitan-style pizza, and mains like Mediterranean branzino with *puttanesca*. Deftly prepared pasta like ridged tubes of *rigatoncini* with Bolognese is a worthy indulgence.

Madangsui

Midtown West
Manhattan ►

Korean

35 W. 35th St. (bet. Fifth & Sixth Aves.)

Subway: 34 St - Herald Sq   Lunch & dinner daily
Phone: 212-564-9333
Web: www.madangsui.com
Price: $$

With a menu that reads like a who's who list of Korean all-star dishes, Madangsui is one of those old-school joints that regulars and first-timers seem to enjoy equally well—most likely because when they do any one of their classic Korean dishes, they hit it out of the park.

The setting is clean and simple (think Korean barbecue hall) and the staff genuinely warm and friendly, but the lip-smacking roster of classics is the real draw here. Past the lineup of terrific *bi bim baps* is an excellent array of *mandu* that are fried to perfection and piped with tender ground pork and vegetables. Then indulge in *japchae*, a sweet potato noodle stir fry; or one of their popular lunch specials—perhaps a bowl of refreshing *naengmyeon* served in icy cold broth.

Mandoo Bar

Korean

2 W. 32nd St. (bet. Broadway & Fifth Ave.)

Subway: 34 St - Herald Sq   Lunch & dinner daily
Phone: 212-279-3075
Web: N/A
Price: ⊛

Tasty, cheap, quick, and clean, Mandoo Bar knows exactly who it is and what it does well. A neon pink "M" lights up the front window, through which passersby can glimpse a sort of grandmotherly chef folding dumplings with myriad fillings. Each wrapper color indicates what is tucked within, with green for vegetable, white for pork, and pink for seafood.

True to its name, these *mandoo* can be found on every table. Crisp fried pork *goon mandoo* are half-moon shaped and seared until brown and blistered, stuffed with minced pork seasoned with Chinese chives. Simple flavors are the hallmarks of their boiled vegetable dumplings—enticingly plump and chewy. The full kitchen also offers an array of larger dishes, like *jap chae* and *bi bim bap*.

Má Pêche

Fusion ✗✗

B4

15 W. 56th St. (bet. Fifth & Sixth Aves.)

Subway: 57 St
Phone: 212-757-5878
Web: www.momofuku.com
Price: $$

Lunch & dinner daily

Midtown's version of Momofuku is a soaring space furnished in sleek blonde wood and located on the lower level of the boutique Chambers hotel. Like all siblings, this "Lucky Peach" family member strives to make its own voice heard—and it does so successfully.

Dim sum Momofuku-style is the name of the game here, so be sure to keep an eye out for trays filled with their iconic pork buns. However, non dim sum items are also worth ordering to experience this chef's true abilities. A raw bar wagon is stocked with torched sea scallop crudo dressed with yuzu and olive oil, as well as hot treats like succulent jerk chicken wings. Dessert is yet another surefire hit, as goodies from Milk Bar star and may include birthday cake truffles, or blueberry-miso soft-serve.

Mercato

Italian ✗

B3

352 W. 39th St. (bet. Eighth & Ninth Aves.)

Subway: 42 St - Port Authority Bus Terminal
Phone: 212-643-2000
Web: www.mercatonyc.com
Price: $$

Lunch & dinner daily

Italian hospitality with a Pugliese accent is on display at Mercato, a rustic trattoria in the western midtown hinterlands. The space is country-chic, with distressed wood tables, soft, exposed bulbs, and vintage signs. The atmosphere is inviting and the menu is inspired by the classic dishes of Puglia, the birthplace of owner Fabio Camardi.

First get a drink in your hand, then start with *fave e cicoria*, a straightforward purée of fava beans and garlicky chicory greens. A well-rounded Italian meal must have pasta, so be sure to indulge in the likes of orecchiette with broccoli rabe and garlic, enhanced by anchovies and breadcrumbs. For something deeply satisfying, try the fennel-dusted porchetta with a hearty side of potato and green cabbage mash.

Manhattan ▶ Midtown West

Marea ✿ ✿

Seafood ✗✗✗

D1

240 Central Park South (bet. Broadway & Seventh Ave.)

Subway: 59 St - Columbus Circle
Phone: 212-582-5100
Web: www.marea-nyc.com
Price: $$$$

Lunch & dinner daily

There are some restaurants that have a discernible pulse that makes you immediately aware you've arrived somewhere a little special. At this elegant and refined Italian restaurant you aren't so much as welcomed in as taken in hand and enveloped in a sort of benevolent bubble of care. It's a grown up establishment with a suitably urbane clientele who all look at home in this part of town. Sit in the main dining room where all the action happens, rather than in the alcove off the bar—which is undoubtedly—Siberia.

As the name suggests, seafood and shellfish lie at the heart of the menu. And needless to say, the ingredients are not only of irreproachable quality but are also treated with respect and deftness by the kitchen, whether it's the brilliant white halibut or the salt-baked wild bass. Start with the crudo, and then head for a generous bowl of homemade pasta such as tagliolini with clams and calamari, followed by a whole fish or a classic entrée.

It's not of course compulsory to stick to fish—the lamb chops make a worthy alternative. The wine list is a deserving tome and along with the big names are some lesser known growers who merit investigation.

Masa ✿✿✿

Japanese 🍴🍴

10 Columbus Circle (in the Time Warner Center)

Subway: 59 St – Columbus Circle
Phone: 212-823-9807
Web: www.masanyc.com
Price: $$$$

Lunch Tue – Thu
Dinner Mon – Sat

To taste what may be the continent's best sushi, experience the quiet, contemplative, and very exclusive ceremony of Chef Masa Takayama's omakase. Everything here carries a certain weight, beginning with the heavy wooden door and carrying through to the bill. The room of course is as unchanging and calming as a river stone, set amid blonde hinoki wood and a gargantuan forsythia tree. Yes, you'll forget it's on the fourth floor of a mall.

Attention to detail is unsurpassed and at times it may seem like a bit much, but a reverential spirit is part of your meal here. Service displays the same smooth grace, with servers at-the-ready carrying their hot towels, fingerbowls, tea, and bits of insight.

Awaken the palate with a sweet chunk of hairy crab meat dressed in citrusy yuzu beneath creamy tomalley. This may be followed by the chef's signature glass coup of minced toro and a very fine—and very generous—pile of Osetra caviar. Maine uni is downright epic, served in its shell with caramelized custard and paper-thin, melting sheets of white truffle. The chef's selection of sushi is unrivaled; the rice is firm and temperate, garnishes are subtle, and quality of fish is supreme.

305

Miss Korea

C4

Korean 〨〨

10 W. 32nd St. (bet. Broadway & Fifth Ave.)

Subway: 34 St - Herald Sq

Phone: 212-594-4963

Web: www.misskoreabbq.com

Price: $$

Lunch & dinner daily

24-hour access to delicious Korean food? Yes please, Miss Korea. Located in the heart of K-Town, this popular restaurant is guaranteed to have a line out the door during peak dinner hours, but once inside you'll find a fairly serene décor, with each of its floors dedicated to a unique aspect of Korean culture.

The first floor offers the most robust menu; the second floor is more intimate, with Zen-like private dining rooms and a set menu featuring Imperial cuisine. Each floor is packed with blonde wooden tables fixed with grills. However, make sure to go for the outstanding clay pot *galbi* highlighting tender USDA Prime beef short ribs marinated on the bone for 24 hours, then cut tableside and grilled to heavenly perfection on the spot.

Molyvos

A3

Greek 〨〨

871 Seventh Ave. (bet. 55th & 56th Sts.)

Subway: 57 St - 7 Av

Phone: 212-582-7500

Web: www.molyvos.com

Price: $$

Lunch & dinner daily

Yes, it's true: the city has upped its Greek game in recent years. But Molyvos has more than earned its OG status—having served fresh, Mediterranean cuisine to a loyal uptown crowd for nearly twenty years. The secret to its longevity lies in the kitchen's beautifully simple and enjoyable food, smart, polished service, and casually elegant setting (tables covered in white cloth and a spare, rustic aesthetic).

Executive Chef Carlos Carreto and collaborating partner, Diane Kochilas (whose books are on sale in the restaurant), oversee this terrific menu. Among a host of delicious sounding (and tasting) options is the octopus carpaccio spotlighting a tender terrine topped with arugula, capers and sumac-and fennel pollen-dusted red onion slivers.

The Modern ⍟⍟

Contemporary 🍴🍴🍴

B4

9 W. 53rd St. (bet. Fifth & Sixth Aves.)

Subway: 5 Av - 53 St
Phone: 212-333-1220
Web: www.themodernnyc.com
Price: $$$$

Lunch Mon – Fri
Dinner Mon – Sat

It goes without saying that The Modern has one of the city's most prized locations, designed to capture the iconic feel of the MoMA in which it is seamlessly housed.

A brief closure for an ambitious kitchen renovation and nip-tuck of the dining rooms brings The Modern back better than ever. Art enthusiasts have always appreciated its timeless and glorious surrounds and are sure to notice the improved acoustics, which facilitate quiet conversation and match the calm of the view over the sculpture garden. The state-of-the-art kitchen should allow the team to grow into its full creative potential—both in the dining room and at the buzzy bar.

Chef Abram Bissell and crew are truly wowing these globe-trotting patrons with excellent food and warm, well-timed service. Appealing dishes showcase clean flavors and may include roasted cauliflower composed with creamy crab butter, almond-cauliflower purée, and crabmeat. Delicate balance and top ingredients are at the height of an exceedingly tender lobster "marinated with truffles" and served in a luscious sauce with radishes and bright herbs.

For dessert, rhubarb bread pudding is topped with vanilla-mascarpone mousse for a bit of flourish and whole lot of fun.

Mozzarella & Vino

A4

33 W. 54th St. (bet. Fifth & Sixth Aves.)

Subway: 57 St
Phone: 646-692-8849
Web: www.mozzarellaevino.com
Price: $$

Lunch & dinner daily

Spoiler alert: as the moniker of this midtown treasure implies, the star of the show here is *mozzarella di bufala*. Bring your appetite to the pretty, narrow space, which features whitewashed brick and taupe walls lined with mirrors and brown leather banquettes, and attempt to choose a version (there are many) of the milky cheese.

Can't decide? Our favorites saw it rolled with grilled sweet peppers hinting of anchovies and presented sliced over arugula, as well as diced and stuffed into a trio of golden-brown, crumb-coated *arancini* filled with sweet pea-studded creamy rice. A salad of avocado and shaved fennel with citrus segments and fresh mint is a refreshing starter, and the short list of entrées indulges with a hearty, oven-baked pasta of the day.

New Wonjo

C4

23 W. 32nd St. (bet. Broadway & Fifth Ave.)

Subway: 34 St - Herald Sq
Phone: 212-695-5815
Web: www.newwonjo.com
Price: $$

Lunch & dinner daily

New Wonjo offers a delightful respite in this jam-packed quarter of K-town. The modest space is spread over two floors and is mighty popular for barbecue-seeking groups. The fact that these grills still use charcoal only adds to the overall lure. And no matter the time, one can expect to find hordes of diners huddling around platters of marinated beef short ribs (*kalbi*) or thinly sliced pork belly (*samgyupsal*).

Non-barbecue delights include *mandoo*, *chap chae* and *cochu pa jeon*. But, keep room to savor soups like *ban gye tang*—a soothing *ginseng*-infused broth bobbing with a sticky rice- garlic- and jujubes-stuffed chicken. *Gopdol bi bim bap* with minced beef, a runny egg, and other spicy condiments is wonderfully flavorful but only incendiary upon request.

Norma's

American 🍴🍴

A3

119 W. 56th St. (bet. Sixth & Seventh Aves.)

Subway: 57 St
Phone: 212-708-7460
Web: www.parkermeridien.com
Price: $$

Lunch daily

Serving heaping platters of breakfast well into the afternoon, Norma's may have been inspired by the humble diner but rest assured that she is no greasy spoon. Tables at this Le Parker Meridien dining room are bound to be filled with business types already dealing over the first meal of the day. Upscale touches include tables wide enough to accommodate a laptop beside your plate, a polished staff, and gratis smoothie shots.

The menu adds personality with whimsically titled dishes like "bing popping waffles" or "Normalita's huevos rancheros." The crunchy French toast's outrageously good sweetness begins with a marshmallow-y layering of crisped rice, gilded with a sprinkling of powdered sugar, ramekin of caramel sauce, and individual bottle of maple syrup.

Osteria al Doge

Italian 🍴🍴

C3

142 W. 44th St. (bet. Broadway & Sixth Ave.)

Subway: Times Sq - 42 St
Phone: 212-944-3643
Web: www.osteria-doge.com
Price: $$

Lunch & dinner daily

Just a stone's throw from the Broadway hustle lies this little oasis of rustic hospitality. Follow its blue awning into a charming dining room and you'll find cozy banquettes, friendly black-and-white uniformed servers with nary a pretense among them, and a romantic second-level balcony offering magical date night possibilities.

Dinner kicks off with a basket of bread, olive oil, and a few delicious briny olives. The menu, despite its Venetian slant, presents those familiar yet well-conceived Italian-American staples (cue the dessert tray loaded with over-the-top cream-filled sweets). Of course, specials are usually crafted with the best of the season and are worth trying—maybe chewy *tagliolini alla chitarra* served in a veal ragù and laced with mushrooms as well as finely diced carrots.

309

Osteria del Circo

A3

Italian

120 W. 55th St. (bet. Sixth & Seventh Aves.)

Subway: 57 St
Phone: 212-265-3636
Web: www.circonyc.com
Price: $$$

Lunch Mon – Fri
Dinner nightly

Step right up to this humming destination for a tasteful take on the Big Top, courtesy of the Maccioni family. The setting is a riot of theme and color: a trapeze hangs figurines above the entrance, red-and-white fabrics billow from the tent-like ceiling, harlequin-upholstered seating surrounds tables set with cobalt goblets, and animal sculptures are stationed throughout.

The crackerjack menu highlights thin-crust pizzas and the classic Tuscan fish soup, *cacciucco alla Livornese*. *Scaloppine alla Sirio* topped with sautéed mushrooms and green peas is an appropriate signature, but that's not to discount such Italian-American classics as clams casino, eggplant *Parmigiana*, and chicken Marsala, which also punctuate the lineup.

Petrossian

A3

French XXX

182 W. 58th St. (at Seventh Ave.)

Subway: 57 St - 7 Av
Phone: 212-245-2214
Web: www.petrossian.com
Price: $$$

Lunch & dinner daily

With such exemplary attributes—location, historic setting, and a refined staff—this French bastion smacks of old-world indulgence. The exterior's detailed stonework features frolicking cherubs and griffins, while a wrought-iron door guards the entrance. Inside, the dining room harkens back to the '80s with its mirrored bar and pink-and-black granite. Lalique crystal fixtures add a touch of timeless bling.

The best way to begin a meal at Petrossian is to partake in some caviar, smoked salmon, or foie gras (all available for purchase next door in the boutique). Then dive into a bowl of borscht, served with tiny meat-filled pastries, before treating your palate to seared diver sea scallops with sweet English peas, plump morels, *bottarga*, and parmesan nage.

Per Se ❀ ❀ ❀

Contemporary XXXXX

C1

10 Columbus Circle (in the Time Warner Center)

Subway: 59 St - Columbus Circle
Phone: 212-823-9335
Web: www.perseny.com
Price: $$$$

Lunch Fri – Sun
Dinner nightly

There is no more dramatic departure from the soulless Time Warner Center than entering through the iconic blue doors to Per Se. An upscale sense of calm—the kind that only money can buy—soaks the atmosphere. Some might say that the ease with which one can now get a reservation here may herald the end of this certain style of fine dining, yet New York will always have a special place in its heart for Per Se, with all its bells and whistles and that incomparable park view. That said, the dining room seems more for tourists and celebrants than New Yorkers.

Chef Thomas Keller continues to raise the bar with meals that express artistry and seasonality right down to the moment. This is expressed with tremendous consistency throughout both tasting menus, with a superb vegetarian option. Meat courses attain new heights with the likes of Snake River Farms *calotte de boeuf*, served remarkably tender within a crisp exterior, paired with a deeply flavored and memorable Bordelaise sauce, *pommes Maxime* and glazed pearl onions.

Desserts are more contemporary than classic yet always put pleasure first, like the fluffy little orbs of strawberry and vanilla. But always save room for the chocolates. Always.

pizzArte

Manhattan ▶ Midtown West

Italian

A3

69 W. 55th St. (bet. Fifth & Sixth Aves.)

Subway: 57 St
Phone: 212-247-3936
Web: www.pizzarteny.com
Price: $$

Lunch & dinner daily

The serene, slender, bi-level dining room that is pizzArte stands in stark contrast to the workaday bustle outside its doors. A bar and a domed wood-burning pizza oven populate the first floor, while the upstairs is filled with closely set tables and gallery-white walls displaying original art.

Expect the room to be packed with a chic, Italian-accented clientele who flock here for blissfully authentic Neapolitan-style pizzas. These are baked to perfect pliability with a bit of char, topped with impeccable ingredients like creamy *mozzarella di bufala*, broccoli rabe, and sausage. Fine cooking skills are displayed in the *paccheri al baccala*, tossing pasta tubes with cherry tomatoes, plump Sicilian capers, intense Gaeta olives, and firm fillets of cod.

Porter House

Steakhouse

C1

10 Columbus Circle (in the Time Warner Center)

Subway: 59 St - Columbus Circle
Phone: 212-823-9500
Web: www.porterhousenewyork.com
Price: $$$$

Lunch & dinner daily

Michael Lomonaco's flagship steakhouse offers unparalleled views of Central Park from its Time Warner Center perch. Here, tables are well-spaced and allow for fine dining, but look for those few intimate booths located in the front bar area—they make for a great escape on busy nights. The views certainly distinguish this handsome retreat from the pack, as do its carefully selected aged meats, quality fish, and expert sides. The kitchen puts out a tasty helping of sweet and spicy onion rings, buttermilk-battered and deep-fried in portions designed for linebackers. The beautifully marbled ribeye is aged for more than 45 days and would be delicious simply seared, though a chili rub adds an aggressive spice. Cool down with a lightly dressed purslane salad.

Print

American ✖✖

B1

653 Eleventh Ave. (at 48th St.)

Subway: 50 St (Eighth Ave.)
Phone: 212-757-2224-
Web: www.printrestaurant.com
Price: $$

Lunch & dinner daily

Travel to these western hinterlands and breath a whiff of Californian sensibility. Print's home, off the lobby of the Ink48 hotel, has an easy-breezy layout that unites lounging and supping in a space that is pleasantly moody and particularly cozy.

The talented team behind this locavore kitchen takes its mission seriously: there is a full time forager on payroll, water is poured into recycled glasses, the kitchen composts, and the menu highlights the provenance of ingredients. Seasonality and simplicity are shown in creations like a wintertime salad of watercress, blood orange, Medjool dates, crushed Marcona almonds, and sherry vinaigrette.

During the summer, ride up to the 16th-floor Press lounge for drinks, small plates, and killer views.

Radiance Tea House

Asian ✖

A3

158 W. 55th St. (bet. Sixth & Seventh Aves.)

Subway: 57 St - 7 Av
Phone: 212-217-0442
Web: www.radiancetea.com
Price: $$

Lunch & dinner daily

Radiance Tea House is a delicious midtown curiosity. The ordinary locale obscures its presence, but one step inside reveals an unexpected world of green tea and tranquility. Walls are shelved with books about tea and wellness to peruse or purchase, as well as a selection of tea tins and ceramic ware.

Arrive during the lunchtime peak and the scent of rice wine vinegar wafts through the air from tables loaded with dumplings and dipping sauce. A vast selection of loose-leaf blends is offered to be enjoyed alongside chicken wontons with house-made chili oil, green tea soba noodles with sesame sauce, and shrimp-stuffed baby bok choy.

Tea lovers note that a traditional Chinese tea ceremony can be booked one day in advance for a minimum of two persons.

Remi

A4

Italian

145 W. 53rd St. (bet. Sixth & Seventh Aves.)

Subway: 7 Av
Phone: 212-581-4242
Web: www.remi-nyc.com
Price: $$

Lunch Mon – Fri
Dinner nightly

This well-orchestrated production delights every sense. Designed by Adam Tihany, Remi's slim interior captivates with inlaid wood floors, a striped banquette evoking a gondolier's shirt, Venetian mural, and trio of blown glass chandeliers. A glass wall overlooks a courtyard where seating is offered in warmer weather.

The lengthy menu of Northern Italian specialties is perfectly at home, starting with *carciofi alla Veneziana*—roasted baby artichoke hearts atop a vibrant herb purée, garnished with pitted black olives, roasted garlic cloves, and pecorino. Then, move on to beautifully served *tortelli di zucca* stuffed with roasted squash and *mostarda alla Mantovana*, dressed with drizzles of browned butter, grated cheese, and fried sage.

Russian Samovar

C2

Russian

256 W. 52nd St. (bet. Broadway & Eighth Ave.)

Subway: 50 St (Broadway)
Phone: 212-757-0168
Web: www.russiansamovar.com
Price: $$

Lunch & dinner daily

Which came first: the vodka or the celebs? It's hard to say when it comes to this hot spot, which caters to hockey players, Russian intelligentsia, and vodka aficionados alike. Our bets are on that beautiful vodka selection, available in all kinds of flavors, qualities, and sizes (shot, carafe, or bottle).

Nestled into the bustling Theater District, Russian Samovar is both quirky and elegant—with low lighting, glass panels, and musicians tickling the piano and violin. The staff is attentive, sweet, and can walk you through delicious fare like fresh salmon-caviar blini, prepared tableside; *pelmeni*, tender veal dumplings served with sour cream and honey mustard; or milk-cured Baltic herring, paired with pickled onions, potatoes, and carrots.

Scarlatto

Italian **XX**

C2

250 W. 47th St. (bet. Broadway & Eighth Ave.)

Subway: 50 St (Eighth Ave.)
Phone: 212-730-4535
Web: www.scarlattonyc.com
Price: $$

Lunch & dinner daily

Dip down below street level to find a lovely exposed brick interior displaying rows of wine bottles and glass beaded wall sconces to match the sparkly tiara crowning Audrey Hepburn in a framed still from *Roman Holiday*.

The menu doesn't offer many surprises but this is cooking that—just like a little black dress—never goes out of style. Among the array, search out *polpette al pomodoro*, house-made meatballs in a tomato ragù, or bean soup with fresh pasta. Their *pollo Parmigiana* is a "red sauce" classic, made with breaded and fried chicken breast draped in a bright tomato sugo beneath a bounty of grated and caramelized parmesan, served atop a mound of al dente spaghetti. Also of special note is a prix-fixe dinner that is offered throughout the evening.

The Sea Grill

Seafood **XxX**

D2

19 W. 49th St. (bet. Fifth & Sixth Aves.)

Subway: 47-50 Sts - Rockefeller Ctr
Phone: 212-332-7610
Web: www.patinagroup.com
Price: $$$

Lunch Mon – Fri
Dinner Mon – Sat

This seafood-centric grill looks onto the iconic Rockefeller Center ice-skating rink and is framed by a wall of windows. Inside, find a cool aqua-accented space that inspires dressing up. Yes, tourists flock here after a spin on the ice, but it is also popular among business crowds—especially at lunch when the bar is bustling with sharp suits munching on lobster tail with a martini on the side.

The food itself is light and fresh. In-season you may find soft-shelled crab, served alongside a seaweed salad with citrus-marinated hearts of palm. The Northeast supplies many local seafood choices, such as the Block Island golden snapper *a la plancha*, with tangy cherry-tomato vinaigrette. Dependable and familiar classics like jumbo lump crab cakes are also on offer.

315

Snack EOS

B3

522 Ninth Ave. (at 39th St.)

Subway: 42 St - Port Authority Bus Terminal
Phone: 646-964-4964
Web: www.snackeos.com
Price: $$

Lunch & dinner daily

This wood-paneled gem is nestled amongst the busy stretch of Ninth Avenue in the shadows of Port Authority. Think of it as a miniature oasis of Mediterranean hospitality, for at Snack EOS, the service is warm and genuine; the space simple but cozy; and the menu full of pristine seafood and simply prepared meats, bursting with fragrant herbs.

The kitchen churns out a variety of dips (cool and creamy tzatzikis and nutty *muhammara* made with piquant harissa) and small plates (like saganaki and roasted octopus) to start. It's the perfect prelude for heartier dinner fare like *halloumi* skewers or lamb loin. And there's even a reasonably priced three-course prix-fixe. Drinkers should take note of the beer and wine list, which offers unique Greek and Mediterranean options.

Stella 34

C4

Italian **XX**

151 W. 34th St. (entrance at 35th St. & Broadway)

Subway: 34 St - Herald Sq
Phone: 212-967-9251
Web: www.patinagroup.com
Price: $$

Lunch & dinner daily

Windows overlook the Empire State Building at the long and light-filled Stella 34, located on the sixth floor of Macy's. The space is contemporary—with mosaic-tile floors, bare tabletops, and coffee-colored banquettes. But the food is pure comfort, with three wood-burning ovens churning out Neapolitan-style pizzas.

A meal at the curvaceous bar would best begin with some *salumi* and *formaggi*, or *pappa al pomodoro* thick with bread, tomato, Tuscan kale, white beans, and Pecorino Romano. Pasta is as enticing as the crispy pizzas—*cresta di gallo* satisfies with escarole *maccheroni* (in the shape of a rooster's crest) tossed with tomatoes, red onion, chilies, *guanciale*, and pecorino. For dessert, the renowned Vivoli gelato arrives here straight from Florence.

Szechuan Gourmet

C3

Chinese ✗

21 W. 39th St. (bet. Fifth & Sixth Aves.)

Subway: 42 St - Bryant Pk
Phone: 212-921-0233
Web: N/A
Price: $$

Lunch Mon – Fri
Dinner nightly

Come lunchtime, midtown office workers with a jones for the tingly heat of Sichuan peppercorns or the burn of bright red chili oil know exactly where to go. A queue for tables is nearly obligatory, but the pace settles down in the evening and on weekends. Inside, red lanterns and pink linens accent the bustling room and servers attend to tables where specialties are piled high.

Though the menu is vast, you can't go wrong by tearing into the best scallion pancakes in town; or cool, hand-shredded chicken draped in a creamy sesame paste and chili oil. Smoked tofu shreds tossed with Asian celery and toasted sesame oil; or wok-tossed jumbo prawns with a crispy shell of peppercorns and spiced salt are the reason for those long lines.

Taboon

C1

Middle Eastern ✗✗

773 Tenth Ave. (at 52nd St.)

Subway: 50 St (Eighth Ave.)
Phone: 212-713-0271
Web: www.taboononline.com
Price: $$

Lunch Sun
Dinner nightly

Taboon's namesake brick-walled, wood-fired oven is burning a bit brighter these days since Chef Efi Nahon has returned to Hell's Kitchen's finest Middle Eastern dining room. That oven not only provides a heartwarming welcome and sets the whitewashed interior aglow, but it is also responsible for baking the incredible plank of bread that is alone worth a trip here.

Bring friends because this midtown marvel's recently revised menu is best enjoyed by grazing the list of zesty meze like house-made scallop and crab sausage *shakshooka* with poached quail egg, or wild mushroom bread pudding with creamy talleggio and romesco. Vegetables aren't spared the flames, as in a luscious and healthy pile of roasted broccolini splashed with orange oil.

317

Tang Pavilion

A3

65 W. 55th St. (bet. Fifth & Sixth Aves.)

Subway: 57 St
Phone: 212-956-6888
Web: www.tangpavilionchinese.com
Price: $$

Lunch & dinner daily

This longstanding, elegant Chinese favorite is a delightful contrast to its brassy midtown location. Set foot inside the hushed dining room featuring pale peach walls dressed with black lacquer trim. Jacketed servers dote on a dressy crowd savoring Shanghainese specialties.

The kitchen offers countless delectable house delicacies emphasizing the regional focus. Honey ham Shanghai-style is a sweet and salty treat dressed with dates and lotus seeds. The "eight jewels with hot paste" is a mouthwatering spiced stir-fry of mushrooms, bamboo shoots, wheat gluten, scallops, chicken, and shrimp. Green beans with tofu sheets is a gorgeously simple combo of soybeans and paper-thin ribbons of bean curd skin judiciously bathed in a light, broth-based sauce.

Tavola

B3

488 Ninth Ave. (bet. 37th & 38th Sts.)

Subway: 42 St - Port Authority Bus Terminal
Phone: 212-273-1181
Web: www.tavolahellskitchen.com
Price: $$

Lunch & dinner daily

This Hell's Kitchen pizzeria is housed in the former Manganaro's Grosseria Italiana, a family-run emporium dating back to 1893. Bright and clean but boasting the patina of its long existence, the dining room now greets guests with a wall of Italian products and a sky-lit double pizza oven.

The wood-burning dome crafted of volcanic clay from Mt. Vesuvius produces an array of blistered, chewy, quality-topped pies such as the *Baresa*, bearing sweet fennel sausage, broccoli rabe, and roasted breadcrumbs. Grilled local calamari with lemon-caper *salmoriglio* can be found among the starters. The pastas are also an excellent choice, especially *lasagna della casa*, stacking fresh sheets with bright and saucy veal ragù, ricotta, and *mozzarella di bufala*.

Toloache

Mexican   **XX**

251 W. 50th St. (bet. Broadway & Eighth Ave.)

Subway: 50 St (Broadway)   Lunch & dinner daily
Phone: 212-581-1818
Web: www.toloachenyc.com
Price: $$

This original location of midtown's Mexican hot spot continues to prosper and for ample reason. An extensive selection of tequilas flow freely from the spirited bar, chunky guacamole is endlessly mashed from ripe avocados, and a host of tasty tacos emerge from the kitchen in this two-story dining room—decked with Talavera tiles and copper lanterns. Toloache puts a contemporary spin on each of its zesty dishes as seen in *callos de hacha*, highlighting seared scallops over a bed of melting quinoa-studded cheese and accompanied by roasted porcinis. Then move on to those tacos with beer-braised beef brisket (*suadero*), tomatillo, and horseradish *crema*, but finish with a flavorful helping of *camarones* Toloache—fresh shrimp draped with a vibrant dried cascabel salsa.

21 Club

American   **XX**

21 W. 52nd St. (bet. Fifth & Sixth Aves.)

Subway: 5 Av - 53 St   Lunch Mon – Fri
Phone: 212-582-7200   Dinner Mon – Sat
Web: www.21club.com
Price: $$$

This fabled institution has been in business for over 85 years, and there's nothing slowing it down. Once a speakeasy, 21 Club has wined and dined everyone, from movie stars and music moguls to moneyed locals. Add to that its lantern-holding jockeys, townhouse exterior, leather- and wood-paneled dining room, and know this is a classic through and through. Gentlemen, don't forget to don your jackets here.

The menu is a perfect accompaniment to the setting featuring "Clayton's jumbo lump crab meat" dabbed with mustard and topped with cucumber; or a splendid oxtail ravioli in a rich bone marrow-brown butter sauce. The Dutch apple pie with cheddar crumble and sarsaparilla ice cream offers a delightful contrast in taste, texture, and will guarantee your favor.

319

Tori Shin ❀

Japanese ✗✗

362 W. 53rd St. (bet. Eighth & Ninth Aves.)

Subway: 50 St (Eighth Ave.)
Phone: 212-757-0108
Web: www.torishinny.com
Price: $$$

Dinner nightly

Now firmly settled into its midtown location, Tori Shin continues to honor the decidedly Japanese art of grilling—thanks to Chefs Shu Ikeda and Atsushi Kono.

A small bar pouring sake, shochu, and Japanese whiskey welcomes patrons into this multi-level dining room, featuring myriad table seating options that include a popular mezzanine with gold leaf walls. This may be a serious and sophisticated restaurant, but the warm service as well as the upbeat and energetic atmosphere keep it approachable.

The focus here is on organically raised chicken parts sizzling over the *binchotan*-fired grill, where embers are coaxed or cooled with extreme care. Unique and varied skewers are the high point of dining here, so be sure to try crisped wing, seared heart, and creamy liver—all of which need nothing more than a few grains of salt to express true flavor. Ordering à la carte is another fun way to explore the menu, which may also offer grilled vegetables and favorites like chicken *cha-shu*. But, the omakase is a worthy progression that may include *kara-age*, chicken and duck *tsukune*, blistered shishito peppers, and—you guessed it—bowls of springy ramen.

Utsav

Indian

C2

1185 Sixth Ave. (entrance on 46th St.)

Subway: 47-50 Sts - Rockefeller Ctr
Phone: 212-575-2525
Web: www.utsavny.com
Price: $$

Lunch & dinner daily

Meaning "festival" in Sanskrit, Utsav is an upscale hideaway perched on a suspended corridor between two office buildings. The ground floor features a bar and small plaza with outdoor seating, while the upstairs dining room is swathed in gold fabric and spacious with floor-to-ceiling windows. Orchid-topped tables look even prettier once the food arrives.

The wallet-friendly and over-flowing lunch buffet brings office workers in by droves, while the early evening prix-fixe is popular with the pre-theater crowd. Delights include tandoori chicken *kali mirch* liberally seasoned with crushed black pepper, as well as Hyderabadi shrimp curry with a bright red tamarind and chili sauce so tasty it begs to be sopped up by hot wedges of *aloo paratha*.

Yakitori Totto

Japanese

C1

251 W. 55th St. (bet. Broadway & Eighth Ave.)

Subway: 57 St-7 Av
Phone: 212-245-4555
Web: www.tottonyc.com
Price: $$

Lunch Mon – Fri
Dinner nightly

To say that this *yakitori-ya* nails authenticity is an epic understatement. Its discreet signage and second-floor location feels more Tokyo than Manhattan; J-pop dominates the playlist and the crowd is a reassuring mix of native-speakers and in-the-know foodies. Best of all is the aroma from sizzling skewers, deftly prepared over a charcoal fire. Kitchen classics are also popular, but the house specializes in grilled chicken parts like *soriresu* (chicken oyster) highlighting a layer of succulent skin. Equally tasty are charred shiitakes and *niku yaki*, dense rice wrapped in a thin shaving of pork belly and grilled until golden.

For dessert, *annin* tofu showcases silky apricot kernel "tofu" appealingly garnished with frozen raspberry and mint.

SoHo & Nolita

SoHo (or the area South of Houston) and Nolita (North of Little Italy) prove not only that New York City has a penchant for prime shopping and divine dining, but that the downtown scene lives on now more than ever.

SHOPPING CENTRAL

Halfway through the 20th century, SoHo's cast iron structures gave way to grand hotels, theaters, and commercial establishments. Thanks to such large-scale development, housing costs

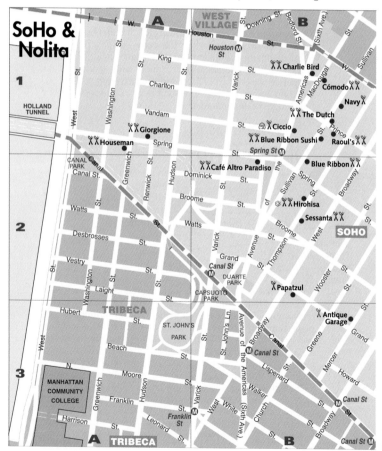

SoHo & Nolita

soared and artists absconded to adjoining Chelsea. And yet, these streets remain true to their promise of sun-drenched restaurants and sleek cafés filled with wine-sipping sophisticates, supermodels and tourists. Locals fortunate enough to live in SoHo's pricey condos, know to stock up on cheese and meats from **Despaña Tapas Café**— they may even prepare a traditional tortilla Española for you with advance notice. **Broome Street Bar** is beloved for burgers (served on pitas) and desserts, which must be followed by a fantastic selection of sips at **Despaña Vinos y Mas**—the wine boutique next door. Scattered with fancy boutiques, these residents are here to stay and entertaining guests is bound to be a breeze—after a visit to **Pino's Prime Meat Market** complete with quality options. The butchers here know the drill and are happy to engage rookies as they break down some of the best game

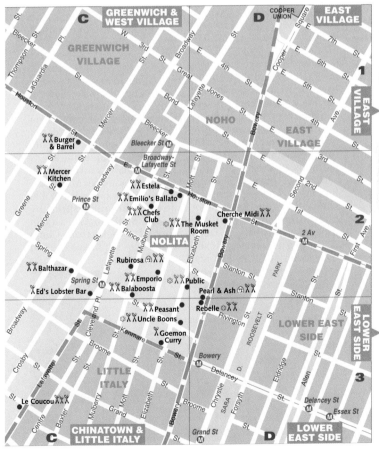

in town. On the flip side, vegetarians take great pride in **The Butcher's Daughter**, a meat-free emporium with the sole purpose of treating, cutting and carving regionally sourced and sustainable produce.

If yearning for regional Italian specialties, sample the brick oven-baked prosciutto rolls at old-time treasure, **Parisi Bakery**; or, the signature square pizza along with Sicilian arancini at **Prince St. Pizza**. Sugar junkies find their fix at **Vosges Haut Chocolat**, where sweets reach new heights of innovation. Try "The Goose's Golden Eggs" featuring real bacon caramel in half-shelled chocolate eggs for a truly exquisite and decadent experience, before heading over to **MarieBelle**, another renowned cocoa queen, combining exotic ingredients and precise methods to create precious "chocolate jewels." For the Big Apple's most cherished cheeses, coffees, and other condiments, the original Broadway location of **Dean & Deluca** is always packed with locals, food lovers, and

hungry office workers. And of course, for bagels in their best form, **Black Seed Bagels** on Elizabeth Street is a perpetual dream. Others may wait till the clock strikes happy hour, before sampling the sips at **Astor Wines & Spirits**, whose selection displays amazing variety and is every barkeep's creed. Weekly tastings and wine-related events here are exemplary and focused on unique varietals, so book ahead. **City Winery** over on Hudson Square (equipped with grapes, barrels, storage, and expertise) is a bona fide destination for oenophiles to make their own private-label wine. But, if sweet is your favorite way to seal a meal, then follow your nose to **Little Cupcake Bakeshop** on Prince or **Maman** (a café on Center Street) for comforting French baked goodies. Meanwhile, home shoppers frequent **Global Table** for its international accessories with simple lines and vivid finishes. Avoid hunger pangs inevitable after a shopping spree by visiting **Smile to Go**, a quiet spot set blocks from Canal that serves big breakfasts and light lunch bites.

NIGHTS OUT IN NOLITA

Nolita may have been an integral part of Little Italy back in the day, but today it is its own distinctive district and explodes with swanky boutiques, sleek restaurants, and hip bars. Located farther east than tourist-heavy SoHo, this neighborhood is also home to slightly cooler (read cosmopolitan) groups. Not unlike its name, Nolita's eclectic residents shun the typical nine-to-five drill and reject SoHo's scene-y hangouts in favor of more intimate spots that invariably begin with the word "café." At the top of this list is **Café Habana**, offering that ubiquitous diner vibe and four square meals a day—breakfasts may include sunny-side-up eggs topped with *salsa verde* and *salsa ranchera*. Amazing Mexico City-style corn on the cob is also available for takeout next door at **Café Habana To Go**; while **Cafe Gitane** is an exquisite hipster hangout, well-tread at all times for wonderful French-Moroccan food served with stellar cocktails. The ethos in Nolita is simple yet resolute—to do a single thing very well. This may have been inspired by **Lombardi's** on Spring Street, which claims to be America's very first pizzeria (founded in 1905). The fact that they still serve these coal oven-fired delicacies by the pie (not the slice) clearly hasn't been bad for business, and lines continue to snake out the door if not the block. Hopping cuisines from Italy to Israel, **Hoomoos Asli** draws a trail of twenty- and thirty-somethings for fluffy pitas packed with crispy falafel and outstanding hummus. The décor and service may be rudimentary at best, but serious effort goes into the food as well as that refreshing side of tart lemonade.

Top off this plethora of eats at the aromatic and ever so alluring **Dominique Ansel Bakery**. Formerly an executive pastry chef at Daniel, the chef here is now fulfilling his own dessert dreams with a spectrum of specialty cakes, tarts, cookies, and pastries. For a taste of dessert bliss, follow instructions and eat the made-to-order "Magic Soufflé" piping hot. Desserts are best matched with coffee, so head on over to **La Colombe**—a Philadelphia-based roaster located nearby on Lafayette Street. If date-night duos aren't closing the deal here over one of their eco-friendly blends, then find them sweetening things up at **Rice to Riches** bringing comfort food to this edgy nook in bowls of creamy rice pudding. The fact that these are

Cheesecake bears the moniker "special" for good reason. Embellished with fruit toppings and fun flavors like amaretto or coconut custard, Eileen's divine creations continue to control the downtown scene, chasing those Junior's fans back to Brooklyn. Of course, one of the greater challenges that this neighborhood poses is the decision of where to end the day or night. But, savvy locals know full well that tucked into these vibrant streets are scores of snug bars, each with its own sleek city feel. Originally a speakeasy during the Prohibition era, today **Fanelli Café** is one of the city's oldest establishments offering an array of simple pub grub, beers and cocktails. But, date-night duos looking to end the night with a bit of sweet should head to **Sweet & Vicious**, which pours concoctions that have been said to leave you starry-eyed. And between these countless dinners and drinks, Nolita also caters to New York City's culinary elite by virtue of its numerous wholesale kitchen supply stores, all settled and thriving along the Bowery.

appended with quirky names like "Sex Drugs and Rocky Road" or "Fluent in French Toast" only adds to this sugar den's supreme appeal. For more such rich and creamy goodness, **A.B. Biagi** brings the craft of traditional Italian gelato-making infused with a taste of Brazil to the core of Nolita. Their wide range of light yet very luscious gelatos and sorbets highlights exotic flavors including passion fruit as well as goat cheese with orange peel and anise. Cheesecake addicts take note that **Eileen's Special**

Antique Garage

B3

Turkish 🍴

41 Mercer St. (bet. Broome & Grand Sts.)

Subway: Canal St (Broadway)   Lunch & dinner daily
Phone: 212-219-1019
Web: www.antiquegaragesoho.com
Price: $$

Complete with high ceilings and the beat-up bones of a former garage, this sultry spot combines vintage furniture as well as a haphazardly cool collection of paintings and mirrors, gilded objects, and jewel-toned carpets to create a quintessential Bohemian-chic hangout. Adding to this unbeatable atmosphere, live jazz is a common occurrence.

Ottoman cuisine rules this kitchen with bowlfuls of well-made meze, like spicy olives perfect for sharing after a day of browsing the neighborhood's boutiques and galleries. The menu's bigger bites—grilled meats and pan-fried beef-stuffed *manti* drizzled with thick yogurt and tomato sauce—are equally delicious. And though gluten-free pasta makes an appearance on the menu, it's best left for the willowy fashionista-types.

Balaboosta

C2

Middle Eastern 🍴🍴

214 Mulberry St. (bet. Prince & Spring Sts.)

Subway: Spring St (Lafayette St.)   Lunch Tue – Sun
Phone: 212-966-7366   Dinner nightly
Web: www.balaboostanyc.com
Price: $$

It's hard to walk by and avoid falling in love with this thoroughly charming Mediterranean favorite and its keen (if wandering) eye on Sephardic cuisine.

A small bar serves cocktails and organic wines while the dining room is full of bare tables, exposed brick walls, and shelves lined with bottles and books. Like the main arena, this kitchen bears a bright, friendly vibe. Here, smoke and fire take center stage in the shrimp cazuela, a tagine of plump shrimp, chickpeas, preserved lemons, and fiery jalapeño. Tender striped bass with crispy skin is a thoroughly comforting dish, served on a bed of sautéed mushrooms, buttery spinach and chewy black gnocchi, drizzled with crab bisque. Linger over *kanafeh*, syrup-soaked shredded filo dough stuffed with cheese.

Balthazar

C2

French ✗✗

80 Spring St. (bet. Broadway & Crosby St.)

Subway: Spring St (Lafayette St.)   Lunch & dinner daily
Phone: 212-965-1414
Web: www.balthazarny.com
Price: $$$

As ageless as its beautiful patrons, the brassy and mirrored Balthazar should be called "quintessentially SoHo" because it invented the term. One of the benchmark brasseries from serial restaurateur Keith McNally, the attractive space is housed in a former tannery. Those whiffs of leather have been replaced by red awnings, scents of pastries, and an excellent oyster-filled raw bar completing its Parisian transformation.

It seems as though every other table is topped with their bestselling steak frites—hardly a value but expertly prepared and served with a heaping side of fries. On the delicate side, sautéed skate is served with sweet raisins and tart capers; while silky beef tartare with shallots, herbs, and Worcestershire spreads just like butta.

Blue Ribbon

B2

Contemporary ✗✗

97 Sullivan St. (bet. Prince & Spring Sts.)

Subway: Spring St (Sixth Ave.)   Dinner nightly
Phone: 212-274-0404
Web: www.blueribbonrestaurants.com
Price: $$$

Blue Ribbon stays open until the wee hours, serving somewhat simple but particularly memorable food to SoHo's stylish set. Moreover, this unaffectedly warm and *very* classic bistro boasts zero pretense and deserves all praise that comes its way. Its décor may have stayed the same through the years— think timeless—but those bar seats remain a hot ticket.

This "chef's canteen" as it is typically hailed is well-tread for masterpieces like fresh shucked oysters; smoked trout salad tossed with sour cream and zippy horseradish; or matzo ball soup—enjoyable, aromatic, and full of root vegetables. Fried chicken with mashed potatoes takes home the gold medal for comfort classics, while banana-walnut bread pudding with caramel sauce is the very essence of decadence.

Blue Ribbon Sushi

B1

Japanese ✕✕

119 Sullivan St. (bet. Prince & Spring Sts.)

Subway: Spring St (Sixth Ave.)   Lunch & dinner daily
Phone: 212-343-0404
Web: www.blueribbonrestaurants.com
Price: $$$

Set just below street level and down the block from its eldest sibling, Blue Ribbon Sushi is an inviting spot to watch the masters at work. A sushi bar dominates the space, with colorful sake bottles and premium spirits on display. The low, wood-covered ceilings and polished tables provide an intimate setting, while the counter is a prime perch for a solo diner.

The staff may point to Americanized options, but it's best to trust the expert chefs and go with an omakase. The menu divides itself into *Taiheiyo* ("Pacific") offerings, like the *kohada* spotted sardine, or a sweet and briny giant clam, and *Taiseiyo* ("Atlantic"), perhaps featuring fluke fin or a spicy lobster knuckle. Maki tempts with the *karai kaibashire*, with spicy minced scallop and smelt roe.

Burger & Barrel

C1

Gastropub ✕✕

25 W. Houston St. (at Greene St.)

Subway: Broadway - Lafayette St   Lunch & dinner daily
Phone: 212-334-7320
Web: www.burgerandbarrel.com
Price: $$

Comfort food becomes downright elegant at this urbane gastropub, where clubby leather booths, louvered blinds, and requisite chalked-up blackboards stay on the approachable side of cool. When the long bar and closely set tables are at capacity, conversations bouncing off the wood-paneled walls can reach a dull roar. Still, the atmosphere stays relaxed.

The modern pub menu covers all the bases with panache, though you won't go wrong sticking with a griddled Bash burger. Pan-roasted Scottish salmon is straightforward goodness, cooked just as ordered and set over a colorful seasonal succotash, drizzled with basil oil purée. Desserts can be novel and fun, as in miniature sugar cones filled with vanilla ice cream, completely covered in a dark chocolate shell.

Café Altro Paradiso

Italian ✖️✖️

234 Spring St. (bet. Sixth Ave. & Varick St.)

Subway: Spring St (Lafayette St.)
Phone: 646-952-0828
Web: www.altroparadiso.com
Price: $$

Lunch Wed – Sun
Dinner nightly

Sommelier Thomas Carter and Chef Ignacio Mattos, aka Team Estela, work their magic again—this time at a chic Italian café that's warm, welcoming and completely packed. What's their secret? At Café Altro Paradiso, a buzzing bar and inviting dining room help set the scene; but the real draw is Mattos' honest, straightforward and delicious Italian cooking. Kick things off with a wildly fresh crudo dressed with olive oil, caper berry slivers, parsley and a squeeze of lemon; or a bright fennel salad with Castelvetrano olives and diced provolone. Homemade *lasagnette* is delicious, tucked with silky trumpet mushrooms, leeks and parmesan. Chicken Milanese is rustic and ample, accompanied by lemon, Dijon, and a salad of radicchio, farro and pine nuts.

Charlie Bird

Italian ✖️✖️

5 King St. (entrance on Sixth Ave.)

Subway: Houston St
Phone: 212-235-7133
Web: www.charliebirdnyc.com
Price: $$$

Lunch & dinner daily

Of all the out-of-the-way restaurants that dot this stretch of SoHo, none are hipper than Charlie Bird. You'll be greeted by a blast of music upon entry, where a long bar leads to a brick-lined dining space with leather seats. From there, things just take off: along with a clever menu, upbeat service, and a thoughtful wine list brimming with Puglian reds and organic Catalonians, the kitchen delights long before Chef/co-owner Ryan Hardy's renowned pastas hit your plate. Think rigatoni with fennel-roasted suckling pig; or *spaghetti alla carbonara* formed into a ball and topped with buttery spring onions, smoked bacon, and a bright yellow duck egg.

Baby sib Pasquale Jones offers similar modern-Italian cuisine with an emphasis on Neapolitan wood-fired pizzas.

Manhattan ▲ SoHo & Nolita

331

Chefs Club

C2

275 Mulberry St. (bet. Houston & Jersey Sts.)

Subway: Broadway - Lafayette St
Phone: 212-941-1100
Web: www.chefsclub.com
Price: $$$$

Dinner nightly

Like a never-ending All-Star game featuring the country's best dishes, the innovative concept behind Chefs Club (by *Food & Wine*) is a rotating lineup of the magazine's "Best New Chefs" honorees over the years. If that isn't exciting enough, the space itself is visually stunning, featuring a state-of-the-art open kitchen with a striking blue-tile backdrop; a sensational modern bar; and lots of loud music to set the mood.

Dinner might include a cool, creamy spring pea soup dotted with pickled pearl onions and fresh herbs; or expertly smoked and seared Hudson Valley foie gras paired with sunchoke purée, apple chips, and buttermilk-thyme jam. Squab *à la plancha* is then glazed with sage-honey and served over grilled confit leeks with a giblet ragout.

Cherche Midi

D2

282 Bowery (at Houston St.)

Subway: 2 Av
Phone: 212-226-3055
Web: www.cherchemidiny.com
Price: $$$

Lunch & dinner daily

Restaurateur Keith McNally went back to his bistro roots with Cherche Midi, his restaurant on a bustling SoHo epicenter of sorts. Romantic, French, and timeless, this inviting space is filled with spectacular flower arrangements, burgundy leather booths, antique mirrors, and a semi-circular bar with wood stools.

A *pot de fromage* sets the tone for the meal. This luscious parmesan custard, served with toast points slathered in anchovy butter, is simple, satisfying with just the right amount of richness. At lunch, a steak sandwich with aged Gruyère and bacon marmalade on a Balthazar-baked brioche bun is a hit. For dinner, indulge in elevated classics like the bone-in skate wing meunière with onion-fennel soubise. Don't forget some pencil-thin pommes frites on the side.

Ciccio

B1

190 Sixth Ave. (bet. Prince & Vandam Sts.)

Subway: Spring St (Sixth Ave.)
Phone: 646-476-9498
Web: www.ciccionyc.com
Price: $$

Lunch Mon – Fri
Dinner nightly

Chef/owner Giacomo Romano defines this brilliant little restaurant as an *alimentaria*—a place where patrons can find ever-changing temptations day or night. This may mean hearty *ribollita* for lunch or satisfying pasta for dinner. The sunny space is a former antique store that fashions a raw look through whitewashed brick walls and blonde wood tables.

Simple, unpretentious food is the signature here, in dishes like *insalata di carota*, mixing sweet roasted carrots, peppery arugula, and pumpkin seeds—grab wedges of bread to soak up its citrusy vinaigrette. Fresh pasta is a must, especially the *strisce alla Chiantigiana* tossed with a reduction of wine, *guanciale*, and red onions. End with a perfect espresso or rich and oozing molten chocolate cake.

Cómodo

B1

58 MacDougal St. (at King St.)

Subway: Houston St
Phone: 646-370-4477
Web: www.comodonyc.com
Price: $$

Lunch Sat – Sun
Dinner Mon – Sat

This charming, candlelit restaurant flaunts a Latin tilt while maintaining its very American, homey feel. Away from artsy SoHo, this quiet slice of the neighborhood draws locals looking for an unfussy meal with bright flavors. The small space has exposed brick, two long communal tables, a semi-open kitchen, and carefully chosen music.

Detail sets Cómodo apart, beginning with a thick, deep evergreen cilantro soup poured tableside, over a mound of fresh crab, smoky roasted poblano peppers, and tart goat cheese. The interesting and very approachable dishes go on to include lamb sliders on *pão de queijo* (Brazilian bread made with cheese and cassava) finished with a pop of chipotle cream. Coffee-rubbed slow-roasted pork shoulder shouldn't be missed.

The Dutch

A m e r i c a n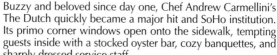

B1

131 Sullivan St. (at Prince St.)

Subwail: Spring St (Lafayette St.)
Phone: 212-677-6200
Web: www.thedutchnyc.com
Price: $$$

Lunch & dinner daily

Buzzy and beloved since day one, Chef Andrew Carmellini's The Dutch quickly became a major hit and SoHo institution. Its primo corner windows open onto the sidewalk, tempting guests inside with a stocked oyster bar, cozy banquettes, and sharply dressed service staff.

The menu is just as seductive as the space, familiar but with fresh updates. Highlights include a roundabout take on the plump fried oyster po' boy, made here with mustard-pickled okra remoulade. Tasty pastas refresh the menu consistently; you might find black *rigatini* tossed with tender squid and spicy pork sausage, finished with fiery breadcrumbs. Desserts are divine, with fresh pies made daily, such as salted lime with passion fruit, *nata de coco*, and coconut sorbet.

Ed's Lobster Bar

S e a f o o d

C2

222 Lafayette St. (bet. Kenmare & Spring Sts.)

Subway: Spring St (Lafayette St.)
Phone: 212-343-3236
Web: www.lobsterbarnyc.com
Price: $$

Lunch & dinner daily

Thanks to Ed's, there's no need to leave the city for an outstanding lobster roll. This seafood-driven favorite is a pitch-perfect encapsulation of the Northeast coast with a lively NY vibe. Inside the white-brick room, the gleaming marble bar is definitely the place to sit.

With a mean Bloody Mary, pristine raw bar, and daily chalkboard specials, Ed's has amassed a loyal following; aim for off-peak times to avoid the wait. Shareable appetizers of sweet and briny Ipswich clams are lightly fried for amazing salty-crisp contrast. And entrées, like linguini bathed in olive oil with lemony-garlic clams and toasted breadcrumbs, are pleasant but never the real draw—that mayo- and butter-rich lobster roll keeps crowds a coming and is worth every calorie.

Emilio's Ballato

Italian 🍴🍴

C2

55 E. Houston St. (bet. Mott & Mulberry Sts.)

Subway: Broadway - Lafayette St
Phone: 212-274-8881
Web: N/A
Price: $$

Lunch & dinner daily

This unassuming Houston St. standard is an unsung hero, even if many walk past Emilio's gold- and red-etched window and write it off as some run-of-the-mill red sauce joint. Step inside the narrow, weathered space, where owner Emilio Vitolo offers each guest a personal welcome and a genuine Italian-American experience.

The menu is filled with pasta classics like Roman *cacio e pepe*, tossed with sharp pecorino cheese and freshly ground black pepper. Signature specialties include *pollo Emilio*, a delicately breaded chicken cutlet draped in lemon-caper sauce; and plump clams *oreganata* speckled with garlicky breadcrumbs. Crisp cannoli shells filled with vanilla- and cinnamon-tinged ricotta cream rival any other version found from Palermo to Siracusa.

Emporio

Italian 🍴🍴

C2

231 Mott St. (bet. Prince & Spring Sts.)

Subway: Spring St (Lafayette St.)
Phone: 212-966-1234
Web: www.emporiony.com
Price: $$

Lunch & dinner daily

Everything at Emporio has been strategically placed, from canned tomatoes by the open kitchen to the pressed-tin ceiling and reclaimed wood accents. It's this Italian-inspired café's attention to detail that has made it a local mainstay, filled with gorgeous crowds and friendly servers. Here, everyone shares conversation over sips set to go with complimentary spreads or "aperitivo" like crispy pancetta with rosemary.

Although the space is small, flavors are huge, and the same attention that went into décor goes into the food—from grass-feed beef to excellent handmade *orecchiette* with cauliflower and shrimp. For a real treat, try a Nutella calzone—its wonderfully thin dough oozing with hazelnut-chocolate and topped with fresh cream and hazelnut crumbs.

Estela

C2

47 E. Houston St. (at Mulberry St.)

Subway: Broadway - Lafayette St

Phone: 212-219-7693

Web: www.estelanyc.com

Price: $$$

Lunch Sat – Sun

Dinner nightly

This boisterous little hot spot is the perfect place to meet friends for a night of sharing small plates over a good bottle of wine. The talented duo of Chef Ignacio Mattos and Co-owner Thomas Carter have mastered exactly how to keep the vibe cozy yet festive and packed with chic crowds. Dimly lit globe lights overhead and small marble tables prevent things from feeling claustrophobic.

The bold and creative cooking features dishes like beef and sunchoke tartare, with each morsel of meat and root vegetable cut to the exact same size and faintly glistening with egg yolk and olive oil alongside country bread. An appetizing range of textures underscore the rice in squid ink sauce folded with bits of fried rice and tender squid set over romesco.

Giorgione

A1

307 Spring St. (bet. Greenwich & Hudson Sts.)

Subway: Spring St (Sixth Ave.)

Phone: 212-352-2269

Web: www.giorgionenyc.com

Price: $$

Lunch Mon – Fri

Dinner nightly

In far west SoHo, beyond Chanel and Balenciaga, find this long-time resident cherished for its quiet location where Spring Street locals enjoy a slower pace—much like Italy itself. Founded by Dean & Deluca's Giorgio Deluca, the stylish and distinctly Italian L-shaped room focuses on straightforward pizza, outstanding pastas, and serious desserts.

You can't go wrong with the handful of pastas on the menu, such as the lovingly crafted pouches of spinach and ricotta ravioli in a light tomato sauce. Delicately grilled lamb chops with *peperonata* and rosemary-roasted new potatoes are simple yet beguiling. Try one (or two) noteworthy desserts, including the flaky *crostata* filled with rich chocolate ganache and bright green *pistacchio di Bronte*.

Goemon Curry

Japanese

C3

29 Kenmare St. (bet. Elizabeth & Mott Sts.)

Lunch & Dinner Tue – Sun

Subway: Bowery
Phone: 212-226-1262
Web: N/A
Price:

Directly next door to Yoshihito Kira's "cocoron" lies this unique venture devoted to Japanese-style curry. Dressed sparingly in wood and concrete, this sliver of a space displays a shelf lined with large glass jars full of the spices used to compose its made-from-scratch blend.

Diners choose the desired heat level for their curry, a rich and spicy treat that can be embellished with everything from deep-fried shrimp to *tandoori* chicken. For something a bit different yet no less delicious, dig into the *yakuzen* soup curry, a warming chicken- and bonito-infused broth stocked with root vegetables, boiled egg, and delicately thin ground chicken-stuffed dumplings. Of course, don't forget about the *koshihikari* rice with pickles that arrive on the side.

Houseman

American

A1

508 Greenwich St. (bet. Canal & Spring Sts.)

Lunch Mon– Fri
Dinner nightly

Subway: Spring St (Sixth Ave.)
Phone: 212-641-0654
Web: www.housemanrestaurant.com
Price: $$

Just around the corner from the legendary Ear Inn, you'll find this amazing offering courtesy of Chef/owner Ned Baldwin. Sporting a small, but sharply designed interior by Louis Yoh, replete with schoolhouse chairs and reclaimed bowling alley wood tables, Houseman's seasonal menu isn't extensive, but each dish is extremely well-sourced—not to mention well-executed, with the help of co-chef, Adam Baumgart.

Kick things off with a grilled tomato salad, bursting with fresh herbs, salty feta and smoky shishito peppers. Then linger over a superbly fresh, slashed, and fried whole black sea bass, laced in a tarragon-forward herby sauce; or excellent, beer-braised sausage links, served with sweet caramelized onions and roasted banana peppers.

337

Hirohisa

Japanese 🍴🍴

 B2

73 Thompson St. (bet. Broome & Spring Sts.)

Subway: Spring (Sixth Ave.)
Phone: 212-925-1613
Web: www.hirohisa-nyc.com
Price: $$$

Lunch Mon – Fri
Dinner Mon – Sat

There's nothing like a discreet entrance to raise expectations—and Hirohisa is nicely concealed on Thompson Street. When you do find it, you enter into a stylish, beautifully understated and meticulously laid out room that looks like a page from *Wallpaper* magazine. It's run with considerable charm by an unobtrusive and very courteous Japanese team.

The two-page menu is easy to decipher with clear headings. However, you might just be better off giving in and letting the chefs decide by going for the balanced and seasonal dishes from the seven- or nine-course omakase. Two things will quickly become clear: the ingredients are exceptional and the technical skills of the chefs considerable. This is food that is as rewarding to eat as it is restorative. Standouts include the lingering, complex flavors of Kumamoto oysters wrapped in Wagyu beef carpaccio topped with Maine sea urchin, perfectly grilled Japanese *kinki*, and anything with their homemade tofu.

There are tables available, but it's so much more satisfying to sit at the counter and engage with the smiling chefs—this way, you may even find that there are a few more dishes in their repertoire than they advertise.

Le Coucou

French

 C3

138 Lafayette St. (at Howard St.)

Dinner nightly

Subway: Canal St (Lafayette St.)
Phone: 212-271-4252
Web: www.lecoucou.com
Price: $$$

In 2006, Chef Daniel Rose made a name for himself when he opened his popular bistro in Paris called Spring. And now France's favorite American ex-pat, who hails from Chicago, has come home to debut this elegant restaurant with Philadelphia-based restauranteur Stephen Starr. Here at stylish Le Coucou, you'll find whitewashed walls, velvet chairs and custom glass chandeliers, as well as a lineup that does more than justice to classic French cuisine.

Arranged under three headings (*hors d'oeuvres*, *gourmandises*, and *poissons et viands*), this menu offers such ace dishes as oysters with seaweed butter, and veal terrine with pickled milkweed. Fried quail with herb butter and lemon confiture, or duck with foie gras and black olives leaves a lasting impression.

Mercer Kitchen

Contemporary

 C2

99 Prince St. (at Mercer St.)

Lunch & dinner daily

Subway: Prince St
Phone: 212-966-5454
Web: www.themercerkitchen.com
Price: $$$

Whether you're here to pick at a salad or up your intake of carbs, Jean-Georges' slick restaurant within the Mercer Hotel has something for you. It has been an inexorable part of the SoHo scene for almost two decades, and ergo, knows what its customers want and how to keep them coming back. Those customers are quite an international bunch and the restaurant provides them with stylish surroundings and a healthy dose of glamour. The occasional sighting of someone from the sunny side of Celebrity Street helps too.

The extensive menu is an appealing document, with everything from hot dogs to pizza, seafood platters to roast chicken. Servings are reassuringly generous yet the kitchen has a commendably light touch—try the wonderful Peekytoe crab fritters.

The Musket Room

Contemporary XX

D2

265 Elizabeth St. (bet. Houston & Prince Sts.)

Subway: Broadway - Lafayette St   Dinner nightly
Phone: 212-219-0764
Web: www.themusketroom.com
Price: $$$

New Zealander Matt Lambert appears to be on a mission to debunk some stereotypes and defy a few expectations about his homeland. For a chef raised in a country famous for its wild, rugged terrain and obsession with rugby, his contemporary cuisine is surprisingly subtle, thoughtful and at times even quite delicate—and if you come here expecting to find lamb on the menu, you'll probably be disappointed.

It is obvious that this is a kitchen with a mastery of all the modern culinary techniques. Don't go thinking this is all about presentation though, because the dishes really do deliver on flavor and are ridiculously easy to eat. Nothing demonstrates the ability here more than the succulent New Zealand venison accompanied by "flavors of gin" which are dots of juniper meringue, fennel, and a licorice-infused sauce. Even that antipodean classic, the pavlova, is given a new lease of life by not so much being deconstructed as being reinvented, as a subtle and delicious delicacy made with passion fruit.

The warm and inviting room fits seamlessly into the neighborhood and comes with a 20-foot walnut timbered bar and lime-washed exposed brick walls.

Navy

Seafood ✗

B1

137 Sullivan St. (bet. Houston & Prince Sts.)

Subway: Spring St (Sixth Ave.)
Phone: 212-533-1137
Web: www.navynyc.com
Price: $$

Lunch & dinner daily

Only Navy could pull off a nautical-themed restaurant with repurposed WWII military duffle bags, panels of distressed copper, and antique sconces on the walls. Everything is beyond chic here, from the former bowling alley bench banquette, to that massive espresso machine used to serve coffee and pastries to early-to-rise SoHo-ites.

But seafood rules when the raw bar spouts oysters, clams, sea urchin, as well as bright Mediterranean white wine. The menu presents culinary hedonism at its finest, like mussel toast: plump mollusks, paprika, and caper aïoli spread over crunchy sourdough bread. Similarly, soft-shell crabs arrive atop a squash blossom pancake with hints of anchovy, and are accented with a dreamy blend of maple syrup.

Papatzul

Mexican ✗

B2

55 Grand St. (bet. West Broadway & Wooster St.)

Subway: Canal St (Sixth Ave.)
Phone: 212-274-8225
Web: www.papatzul.com
Price: $$

Lunch & dinner daily

Sangria and salsas are a heavenly match at SoHo's favorite cantina, where a boisterous crowd devours delightful Mexican cuisine. Decorated with masks and classic movie posters, Papatzul is abuzz with drinking buddies getting friendly with the bar's offerings and tables of friends scooping up every last drop from the signature salsa assortment—five varieties, each inspired by a different region of the country.

The talented kitchen churns out tacos and enchiladas at a steady clip. You can't go wrong with an order of enchiladas San Miguel, a creative rendition that stuffs *salsa roja*-soaked tortillas with sautéed kale, roasted sweet cherry tomatoes, and creamy goat cheese. If you still have room, go for the chocolate flan with cinnamon ice cream.

Pearl & Ash

Contemporary ✗✗

D2

220 Bowery (bet. Prince & Spring Sts.)

Subway: Bowery
Phone: 212-837-2370
Web: www.pearlandash.com
Price: $$

Dinner nightly

For small plates that spark contemplation, this deep, dark, and narrow restaurant delivers. Long wood tables line the room under a striking wall of boxes puzzle-pieced together to showcase collectibles like antique cameras. Shimmering subway tiles, an atmospheric soundtrack, and dim lighting lend a sultry feel.

House-smoked whole wheat bread arrives with freshly churned "chicken butter" (that's butter with chicken fat) and maple syrup. A lamb belly and *guajillo* pepper roulade rests in goat-milk yogurt, topped with crushed almonds, pea tendrils, and paper-thin slices of radish. Confit fingerling potatoes are buried under an avalanche of porcini purée with smoky chorizo over the top. The negroni ice cream sandwich has quickly risen to signature status.

Peasant

Italian ✗✗

C3

194 Elizabeth St. (bet. Prince & Spring Sts.)

Subway: Spring St (Lafayette St.)
Phone: 212-965-9511
Web: www.peasantnyc.com
Price: $$

Dinner Tue – Sun

Year after year, Peasant hits it out of the park—from the mouthwatering Italian food to the spot-on service to the utterly charming osteria spirit, Frank DeCarlo's ode to the Italian gathering spot is the essence of easy excellence. The décor is charmingly rustic—picture whitewashed walls, bare wood tables, and a bustling wine bar downstairs.

Kick things off with ricotta and otherworldly bread, fresh from the visible centerpiece hearth—which is the main method of cooking and sets this spot apart. But save room for house-made lasagna with braised rabbit ragù, creamy béchamel, and sweet root vegetables; tender razor clams in a fragrant white wine broth; succulent porchetta studded with garlic and rosemary; or stewed and perfectly chewy *trippa alla Romana*.

Public ❀

F u s i o n ✗✗

C2

210 Elizabeth St. (bet. Prince & Spring Sts.)

Subway: Spring St (Lafayette St.)
Phone: 212-343-7011
Web: www.public-nyc.com
Price: $$$

Lunch Sat – Sun
Dinner Tue – Sun

While other restaurants may copy one another right down to the linens, Public continues to chart its own course. The industrial décor may seem like a familiar trend in SoHo where nothing is cooler than a converted loading dock, but know that this was the original factory-cum-dining room design, complete with exposed brick and gunmetal gray stools. Yet there is undeniable warmth here, and not just from the attentive and friendly servers. Note the unique bronze mailboxes, where box-holders are delivered artisanal wines hand-selected by the chef, and private rooms contoured with billowing fabrics.

Asian and Mediterranean flavors weave together in an à la carte menu that is best described as inspired globetrotting. Start with a smooth Thai pumpkin soup that reflects the region in nothing more than name, yet is a deeply satisfying bowl redolent of coconut milk and curry paste. The accompanying "larb" of jicama, pickled chili, and crisped garlic finishes the dish with a clever deconstruction of flavors. Braised Australian lamb intensifies its accent with wondrously dark and savory Vegemite sauce.

A first-come, first-serve "Sunday Supper" is offered every Sunday with limited seating, and often sells out.

Rebelle

French ✕✕

D3

218 Bowery (bet. Prince & Spring Sts.)

Subway: Bowery
Phone: 917-639-3880
Web: www.rebellenyc.com
Price: $$$

Lunch Sat – Sun
Dinner nightly

Heat-seeking foodies on the hunt for the next big thing have found it at this chic bistro from the owners of Pearl & Ash. The dining room is as dim as a cave—its palette of concrete and ebony brightened only by a white marble bar and gracious team of servers who know when they're needed and seem to disappear when they're not. Rebelle has an edgy vibe—the space was once a burlesque bar, after all. But, beneath that veneer is impressive talent delivered with a sexy French accent.

While Chef Daniel Eddy's streamlined presentations and foam flourishes have contemporary flair, rest assured that classic technique is at the root of every dish. Lamb tartare is perfectly balanced, boasting *piment d'Espelette*-kissed cubes of meat tossed with green chickpeas, strained yogurt, and a slice of excellent toasted bread. Then, exceptionally tender pork loin is served over a mustard-tinged sauce with wilted greens, grilled spring onions, and a delicious bite of deep-fried headcheese.

For dessert, gâteau Saint-Honoré is seasonally reimagined as crisp layers of *pâte feuilletée*, mascarpone pastry cream, and fragrant wild strawberries adorned with tiny strawberry-caramel-lacquered profiteroles.

Raoul's

French 🍴🍴

B1

180 Prince St. (bet. Sullivan & Thompson Sts.)

Subway: Spring St (Sixth Ave.)
Phone: 212-966-3518
Web: www.raouls.com
Price: $$$

Lunch Sat – Sun
Dinner nightly

It's the nature of all great cities to constantly change but that doesn't mean severing ties to the past. Raoul's has been around since the '70s—which alone qualifies it as an "institution"—but this is no museum piece living on past glories. Wander in on any given night and you'll see a crowd of all ages united in their fondness for French food and their ability to enjoy themselves.

The menu wouldn't necessarily entice the passer-by on content alone but the kitchen has a surprisingly delicate touch that raises dishes above the ordinary, whether that's tender octopus with chickpea purée or succulent rack of lamb with oyster mushrooms. In the stampede to find all that is new, shiny and hot we shouldn't ignore those whose sin is mere longevity.

Rubirosa

Italian 🍴🍴

C2

235 Mulberry St. (bet. Prince & Spring Sts.)

Subway: Spring St (Lafayette St.)
Phone: 212-965-0500
Web: www.rubirosanyc.com
Price: $$

Lunch & dinner daily

Push through the dark red velvet curtain into Rubirosa's narrow, dimly lit dining room to discover how very cool nonna can be. Although it may be loud and cramped with the requisite 80's tunes blaring overhead, this adept Italian-American kitchen is bright with classic dishes and an heirloom Staten Island pizza recipe that's 55-years-old and counting.

The classic pie balances a crispy, cracker-thin crust with tart tomato sauce and oven-browned spots of salty, melting mozzarella. And the handmade pastas are highly recommended—you can't go wrong with a bowl of chewy *chittara* and its three hefty and hearty meatballs. Half portions allow diners to enjoy more of the favorable cooking here, and gluten-free pasta and pizza ensures everyone can enjoy it.

Uncle Boons

 Thai

7 Spring St. (bet. Bowery & Elizabeth St.)

Subway: Bowery   Dinner nightly
Phone: 646-370-6650
Web: www.uncleboons.com
Price: $$

Can't afford a trip to Thailand? No problem. This transporting little gem—compliments of talented husband-wife duo Matt Danzer and Ann Redding—brings the Northern Thai experience stateside with creative cuisine and whimsical drinks—Singha beer slushies anyone?

Tucked along the eastern edge of Spring Street, the dining room is den-like. A vibrant crowd keeps the place popping through the night, as does the gentle stream of Thai pop music in the background. Though tables are mini, the kitchen feels immense in its creative vision—a window into where the magic happens offers views of a slow-rotating rotisserie and crackling embers.

Danzer and Redding's dishes are certainly rooted in this nation's cuisine, but they give each dish a unique spin thereby infusing vibrant flavor into small plates, large plates, "charcoal-grilled goodies," desserts and drinking snacks. *Laab neuh gae* features delicious ground lamb tossed with pickled onion, lime, and fish sauce, while a banana blossom salad with rotisserie chicken and buttery cashew nuts arrives in an appetizing coconut dressing. For an epic end, go for grilled pork jowl, topped with watermelon radish, salted duck yolk, and a shake of sawtooth herb.

Sessanta

 Italian ✗✗

B2

60 Thompson St. (bet. Broome & Spring Sts.)

Subway: Spring St (Sixth Ave.)   Lunch & dinner daily
Phone: 212-219-8119
Web: www.sessantanyc.com
Price: $$$

Restaurateur John McDonald's latest venture finds him mining the unique flavors of Sicily, with the oh-so-talented Chef Jordan Frosolone helming the kitchen. Located in the SIXTY SoHo, Sessanta's mid-century Italian décor boasts vintage chandeliers, wood paneling, and a warm, earthy palette. The overall effect is retro, urban, and gorgeous.

So does the food hold up to the setting? Terrifically, for Chef Frosolone has a knack for sourcing ingredients and a memory for Sicilian flavors. Must-try dishes include near-perfect caponata with pignoli, *vincotto*, basil, and silky potato; sashimi-grade *crudo di tonno* with tart lime, zucchini ribbons, and caperberries; or *busiate* tossed with ruby-red shrimp, green zucchini, and *pomodori di Pachino*.

Remember, stars
(❀❀❀ ... ❀) are awarded
for cuisine only! Elements
such as service and décor
are not a factor.

DRINK AND DINE

TriBeCa is an established commercial center sprinkled with haute design stores, warehouses-turned-lavish lofts, and trendy drink-cum-dining destinations. Quite simply, this triangle below Canal is a cool place to eat, and its affluent residents can be seen splurging in restaurants whose reputations precede them. Of course that isn't to say that this area's famously wide, umbrella-shaded sidewalks aren't cramped with more modest hangouts. In fact, **Puffy's Tavern** is a favored neighborhood haunt with small bites, hearty sandwiches, and five flat-screens for the happy-hour crowds. Over on West Broadway, **Square Diner** is a local institution that takes you back in time via red vinyl booths and that diner counter cooking up the staples. Like every other Manhattan neighborhood, TriBeCa claims its own culinary treasures: **Bubby's** is a gem for comfort food; while **Zucker's Bagels & Smoked Fish** flaunts an updated décor and floors patrons with a taste of *bubbe*'s best. **Dirty Bird To Go** delivers fresh, all-natural chicken in

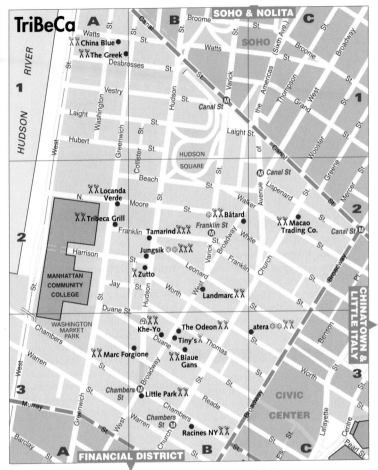

TriBeCa

A

B

C

HUDSON RIVER

Watts St.

X X China Blue ●

X X The Greek ●

Desbrosses St.

Vestry St.

Laight St.

Hubert St.

Washington St.

Greenwich St.

Collister St.

Hudson St.

Canal St.

Broome St.

Watts St.

SOHO

the Americas (Sixth Ave.)

Broome St.

Thompson St.

West St.

Grand St.

Broadway

St.

1

Canal St M

Laight St.

of

HUDSON SQUARE

Beach St.

Canal St M

Lispenard St.

Wooster St.

Greene St.

Mercer St.

X X Locanda Verde ●

N. Moore St.

X X Tribeca Grill ●

Franklin St.

Tamarind X X X

Jungsik ❄ ❄ X X X

X Zutto ●

Harrison St.

MANHATTAN COMMUNITY COLLEGE

Jay St.

Hudson St.

Worth St.

Leonard St.

Franklin St.

White St.

Walker St.

Avenue

❄ X X Bâtard ●

Franklin St M

Broadway

Varick St.

Church St.

X X Macao Trading Co. ●

Canal St M

2

Duane St.

Landmarc X X ●

WASHINGTON MARKET PARK

Chambers St.

Warren St.

Murray St.

Barclay St.

West St.

Greenwich St.

Duane St.

Broadway

Reade St.

Chambers St.

X X Marc Forgione ●

Khe-Yo X X ●

Tiny's ●

X X Blaue Gans ●

Chambers St M

Little Park X X ●

Racines NY X X ●

The Odeon X X ●

Thomas St.

Church St.

atera ❄ ❄ X X ●

Benson Pl.

Worth St.

Broadway

CIVIC CENTER

Lafayette St.

Centre St.

Pearl St.

Elk St.

3

CHINATOWN & LITTLE ITALY

its many glorious forms—try the buttermilk-fried or slow-roasted rotisserie and join its endless line of fans. And over on North Moore Street, **Smith & Mills** continues to make waves as a cocoon for fantastic eats plus spectacular drinks.

In keeping with its cutting-edge spirit, TriBeCa also offers a gourmet experience for any palate and price tag. **Grand Banks** bobs along the Hudson and is a summer special for seasonal oysters or a lobster roll, while winter calls for brunch at **Almond**, featuring delicious eggs, all things sweet, and...wait for it... homemade baby food! Here, tots can have their cake and eat it to, after which the adults can head over to **Chambers Street Wines** to keep the party going. Those looking for something to enjoy with their wine will rejoice over

the events sponsored by **New York Vintners**. These include free wine and cheese tastings and cooking demonstrations on how to decorate cupcakes with the kids—sip on a few sparkling varietals while you're at it!

BATHS & BAKERS

Work off a hangover at AIRE Ancient Baths, a luxury spa inspired by ancient civilizations and water-induced relaxation. They even offer rituals where you can soak in olive oil, cava, or red wine. The only downside? You can't drink it! Then, take your appetite to one of TriBeCa's numerous (and well-lauded) bakeries. **Sarabeth's** is an award-winning jam maker who turned this once humble retail store into the monstrous hit it is today. With its impressive array of cookies, cakes, preserves, and other sweets, this specialty spot knows how to play the culinary game with such solid competitors as **Duane Park Patisserie**,

known for pastries and seasonal specialties; or even **Tribeca Treats** for a plethora of decadent chocolates. Meanwhile, **Birdbath**, an integral part of the City Bakery clan, is admired for its eco-friendly philosophy as well as its unique selection of bites and bevvies. **Takahachi Bakery** on Murray Street is a modestly decorated but must-visit treasure for Japanese refreshers. While here, slurp up a *matcha* latte, but save room to snack on at least one macaron *sakura*.

AROUND THE WORLD

Korin is a culinary haven that flaunts an extensive and exquisite knife collection, plus tableware and gorgeous kitchen supplies. Not only do these products shine in many fine dining establishments, but they also bring to life the essence of food art. Chefs come here to get their blades worked on or to order a specific knife, while others may opt for the gorgeous gift sets that are sure to excite a friend or impress a colleague. Before this area became associated with top films from varying genres, director Bob Giraldi shot his mob- and food-themed movie *Dinner Rush* at famed eatery, **Gigino Trattoria**. However, thanks to the annual Tribeca Film Festival, a springtime extravaganza created by Robert DeNiro to revitalize the area after 9/11, TriBeCa is now the official home of twelve days of great films and community camaraderie. Scores of locals, tourists, and film buffs collect here every year to see the movies and share their views and reviews at hot spots like **Nish Nush**, a sidewalk show-stopper incorporating authentic Israeli hummus and crispy falafel into sandwiches, hearty platters, and healthy salads. From nourishing eats to heavenly treats, **Baked** is yet another tenant in TriBeCa. While the mothership continues to flourish in Red Hook, this considerably larger venture is beloved for breakfast, coffee and other sweet treats. Carb junkies craving more bread (maybe flatbread pizza?) but in a historic setting, should head to **Arcade Bakery** on Church Street. But, for those craving crêpes, sweet and savory selections abound at **By Suzette**—a mini counter on Chambers Street that is quickly gaining a major following. Speaking of laudable ventures, Chef David Bouley and team have created **Bouley Botanical**, a resourceful event space, designed to entice the senses and committed to celebrating every occasion in style. Outfitted with state-of-the-art sound and lighting equipment as well as an impressive exhibition kitchen, this greenhouse-inspired venue pledges to fit your every mood with the likes of yoga, pilates, and other wholesome practices.

atera

Contemporary 🍴🍴

77 Worth St. (bet. Broadway & Church St.)

Subway: Chambers St (Church St.)
Phone: 212-226-1444
Web: www.ateranyc.com
Price: $$$$

Dinner Tue – Sat

Such a high number of staff per guest might make one wonder if some are just there to dance along to the meal—and they kind of are. The mood is fun yet remains professional, and in fact quite a thrill if you're really into Bon Jovi. Yet the open kitchen's performance is far more engaging, as the numerous cooks coax each dish to perfection. The whole team is actually working as one to ensure the high quality and thorough enjoyment of your meal.

Start with an extraordinary salvo, such as a thin, warm waffle filled with cheddar cream cheese and generous slices of summer truffles from Provence. Follow that with foie gras custard and corn foam in a dense, aromatic lemon verbena broth. Those excellent broths and juices appear throughout the meal, whether green tomato-based to accompany scallops with horseradish powder and green apple, or as aromatic yuzu, green almonds, and celeriac paired with delicately poached lobster and brown butter.

Desserts can be a beautiful and awesome finish, especially the rhubarb sorbet with chocolate ganache and hazelnut cream over a bed of crumbled shortbread. Mignardises, like the lemon tart with mulberries, are so light and refreshing that there is always room for more.

Bâtard ❀

B2

Contemporary ✗✗

239 West Broadway (bet. Walker & White Sts.)

Subway: Franklin St
Phone: 212-219-2777
Web: www.batardtribeca.com
Price: $$$

Dinner Mon – Sat

239 West Broadway will be a familiar address to those who know their restaurants as it has hosted a number of seminal establishments over the years—namely Montrachet and Corton. Drew Nieporent's Bâtard restaurant is now firmly in situ and once again we have a talented chef making waves in TriBeCa.

Chef Markus Glocker's cooking is very precise and his dishes look quite delicate on the plate. But like a good featherweight they pack more of a punch than you're expecting. You'll even notice his Austrian roots in evidence in some of the dishes, such as short rib and *tafelspitz* terrine, or the Granny Smith and sweetbread strudel.

The room is comfortable and neat and the atmosphere grown-up yet animated. When it comes to service though, it appears that the restaurant has mistaken informality for indifference as it lacks coordination or direction. So you may need to remind yourself that you're here primarily for the food. But that food is very good indeed.

Blaue Gans

B3

 Austrian

139 Duane St. (bet. Church St. & West Broadway)

Subway: Chambers St (West Broadway)   Lunch & dinner daily
Phone: 212-571-8880
Web: www.kg-ny.com
Price: $$

This sleek, unbridled Viennese-style café feels almost smoky and well-worn, but never out of touch. Its walls are papered with vintage movie posters, while banquettes and tables dominate the dining space.

Blaue Gans' strong, loyal following (an increasingly rare feat in the city) is comprised of locals engaging in familiar banter at the bar or communal table. Everyone is here for the impressive Austrian cooking, which may unveil a beautiful bibb, pumpkin seed, and shaved radish salad with a light, creamy pumpkin oil dressing. Other classic treasures include pork Jäger schnitzel with mushrooms, bacon, and herbed spätzle; or classic *kavalierspitz* accompanied by salty creamed spinach and sweet-tart apple horseradish. Delish desserts will have you at hello.

China Blue

A1

Chinese

135 Watts St. (bet. Greenwich & Washington Aves.)

Subway: Canal St (Sixth Ave.)   Lunch & dinner daily
Phone: 212-431-0111
Web: www.chinabluenewyork.com
Price: $$

TriBeCa has been getting an elegant taste of Shanghai via this glossy restaurant, courtesy of Yiming Wang and Xian Zhang. Tucked into a landmarked neo-Flemish building, this is an upscale, uniquely charming dining room reimagined in dark wood and sea-foam walls. A handsome and full bar completes the scene.

Building on the success of their popular one-starred restaurant, Café China, the cadre of cooks are focused here on Shanghai (and a bit of Huaiyang) cuisine. The menu is filled with delicate soups; tender shredded eel sautéed with chives; and a good assortment of dim sum. Maybe delicate bean curd sheets wrapped around shitake mushrooms; cold, smoked carp, Suzhou-style; or slow-braised pork with bamboo shoots, baby bok choy and bowtie shaped yuba?

The Greek

A1

458 Greenwich St. (bet. Desbrosses & Watts Sts.)

Subway: Franklin St
Phone: 646-476-3941
Web: www.thegreektribeca.com
Price: $$

Lunch & dinner daily

This upscale *ouzerie* and taverna is a cozy den of Greek hospitality. Beyond the slender mahogany bar and mounted wine barrels, the rustic-chic dining room is meticulously decorated with vine-wrapped columns to echo the wine-centric theme, as well as plush sofas for sinking into the very relaxed vibe. The long bar is a lovely perch for the solo diner craving chicken souvlaki or just an afternoon frappé.

Begin with *keftedes*, tender beef meatballs slowly simmered in aromatic tomato sauce and topped with crumbled aged feta. Then move on to a thick yellow split pea purée folded with olive oil, capers, and bright lemon juice. The *mousaka* is bubbling perfection layered with potato, grilled eggplant, zucchini, and beef topped with eggy-buttery béchamel.

Khe-Yo

B3

157 Duane St. (bet. Hudson St. & West Broadway)

Subway: Chambers St (West Broadway)
Phone: 212-587-1089
Web: www.kheyo.com
Price: $$

Lunch & dinner daily

This Laotian hot spot serves up vibrant family-style plates brimming with tart and spicy notes that pack a punch—make that a Bang Bang, actually, as in the house sauce of mixed chilies, cilantro, fish sauce, and garlic served to diners as a welcome along with a basket of sticky rice.

The food is worth braving the wait and decibel levels, so sip a craft brew or cocktail before digging in. Start with a plate of wide rice noodles and bits of slow-cooked pork in a coconut-rich yellow curry garnished with herbs, bean sprouts, and slivered banana blossom. Banana leaf-steamed red snapper is another beautifully prepared item, served with crisped artichoke hearts, Chinese broccoli, and more of that sauce. Bright and bitter grapefruit sorbet is a fitting finish.

Jungsik

Korean

2 Harrison St. (at Hudson St.)

Subway: Franklin St
Phone: 212-219-0900
Web: www.jungsik.kr
Price: $$$$

Dinner Mon – Sat

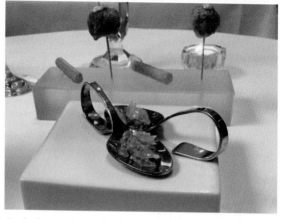

Cool, chic, and completely urbane, Jungsik is the epitome of contemporary elegance. Inside the large, neatly partitioned space, find rich browns and ivory furnishings with flattering lighting that is just bright enough to see your food clearly. The chairs are deep and tables are well spaced, but request a plush corner banquette for maximum comfort. Even the place settings show sculptural beauty through dark pottery and white porcelain. The ambience is fairly quiet and somewhat reflective.

The modern cuisine is confident, complex, and happens to be leaning much more toward Europe than Korea of late. No matter—the cooking remains profoundly enjoyable. At the same time, the most inspired dishes are the ones that retain their heritage, as in the dome of seaweed-seasoned rice with cubes of smoked and torched yellowtail, finished with slivered lettuce. Before the crispy red snapper arrives at the table, hot oil is poured overtop to cook the fish but also to yield incredibly crisped skin, served with a brunoise of hearty greens and potatoes and rich perilla vinaigrette.

Artful desserts include black raspberry and coconut sorbet with crumbles of spinach cake, yuzu meringue, and perfect berry slices.

Landmarc

Mediterranean XX

B2

179 West Broadway (bet. Leonard & Worth Sts.)

Subway: Franklin St
Phone: 212-343-3883
Web: www.landmarc-restaurant.com
Price: $$

Lunch & dinner daily

Chef/owner Marc Murphy's Landmarc is *the* TriBeCa destination for meeting friends over casual drinks and food that happens to be rib-sticking delicious. Downstairs, the bi-level space showcases thick steel cables suspending industrial art and a horseshoe bar flanking a large cooking fire that warms the soul and sizzles those lamb chops. The upstairs is more serene.

Meals may start with lighter plates of smoky and blistered shishito peppers flecked with crunchy sea salt. Then, move on to deeply satisfying (and reasonably priced) nightly pasta specials, like thick and buttery spaghetti *alla Bolognese.* "Landmarc classic" cheese plates are a reliable highlight. Miniature desserts mean that there is always room for a lemon-custard tart (or four).

Little Park

American XX

B3

85 West Broadway (at Chambers St.)

Subway: Chambers St (West Broadway)
Phone: 212-220-4110
Web: www.littlepark.com
Price: $$

Lunch & dinner daily

Little Park flaunts that upscale-downtown feel that TriBeCa seems to have trademarked. Yet Chef Min Kong delivers a personal and unique cuisine that distinguishes it from other Andrew Carmellini restaurants. Here, vegetables are often put front and center on the plate, with meat and seafood serving as accents. This means that the harmonious flavors of beet tartare with rye crumbs, dill, and smoked trout roe is just as impressive as the crisp-skinned tilefish with bok choy and black radish in toasted rice dashi. Masterful desserts include the frozen Meyer lemon "fluff" with meringue, orange sorbet, and candied ginger.

Diners take note—while the Smyth Hotel lobby bar operates at capacity early in the evening, this dining room starts buzzing at a later hour.

Locanda Verde

 A2

377 Greenwich St. (at N. Moore St.)

Subway: Franklin St

Phone: 212-925-3797

Web: www.locandaverdenyc.com

Price: $$$

Lunch & dinner daily

This ever-trendy yet refined Italian *ristorante* is as much coveted for its gorgeous setting as its lineup of rustic, tasty fare. The ambience is always abuzz and everyone looks beautiful amid low lights, a long bar, and walls adorned with wine bottles.

Breakfast verges on divine—think lemon pancakes and apple-cider donuts. Bare tables are packed throughout the day with a stylish crowd waxing poetic about crostini topped with blue crab and jalapeño. Also try terrific house-made pasta such as pappardelle with lamb Bolognese finished with a dollop of sheep's milk ricotta, or *paccheri* dressed in "Sunday night ragù." No one should leave without sampling superb sweets, like the apple and concord grape crostata with rosemary hazelnut brittle and brown butter gelato.

Macao Trading Co.

C2

311 Church St. (bet. Lispenard & Walker Sts.)

Subway: Canal St (Sixth Ave.)

Phone: 212-431-8750

Web: www.macaonyc.com

Price: $$$

Dinner nightly

Droves of curious downtowners continue their love affair with this cushy mainstay for Macanese cuisine. With nothing but a red light over a dark door to mark its entrance, make your way into this bi-level beauty, accoutered with heavy velvet drapes, double-height ceilings, and a dimly lit yet sexy bar. The mien is playful, buzz palpable, and first-rate drinks are flowing.

Start with the Tuscan kale-and-romaine salad, enticingly smoky with texturally perfect potato "croutons" and paprika vinaigrette. Then, move on to a Taipa steamboat (cross between a Chinese hotpot and Portuguese paella) teeming with briny shellfish, fried chicken wings, and linguiça. Sample a slice of their chocolate *diablo* cake for an indulgent and notably decadent finish.

Marc Forgione

Contemporary

B3

134 Reade St. (bet. Greenwich & Hudson Sts.)

Subway: Chambers St (West Broadway)
Phone: 212-941-9401
Web: www.marcforgione.com
Price: $$$

Lunch Sun
Dinner nightly

This eponymous restaurant is dark, sexy, and attracts an endless stream of downtown denizens. Abundant candles produce more atmosphere than light for the rustic room clad in exposed brick and salvaged wood. Aloof servers dressed in black seem to disappear into the background.

The innovative American food excites with bold flavors, as in barbecued oysters sprinkled with pancetta powder. Montauk fluke *en croute*, set over roasted cauliflower, hazelnuts, and capers topped with a buttery panel of toast, is dressed in *sauce proposal*—so named because the rich brown butter and golden raisin emulsion is said to have earned the chef a few romantic offers. It is delicious, but Chef Forgione deserves equal affection for those amazing butter-glazed potato rolls.

The Odeon

American

B3

145 West Broadway (at Thomas St.)

Subway: Chambers St (West Broadway)
Phone: 212-233-0507
Web: www.theodeonrestaurant.com
Price: $$$

Lunch & dinner daily

It's easy to see why The Odeon has been a part of the fabric of TriBeCa life for so long. Like watching a re-run of *Seinfeld*, it is reassuringly familiar, classically New York and, even when you know what's coming next, still eminently satisfying. The menu is a roll-call of everyone's favorites, from chicken paillard to beet salad, burgers to cheesecake. Cocktails are well made and beers carefully poured. Dishes are executed with sufficient care and portions are of manageable proportions.

The room comes with an appealing art deco feel and the terrace at the front pulls in the occasional passer-by. Service is personable and willing too, although after all this time the place could probably run itself.

Racines NY

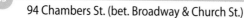

French **✗✗**

B3

94 Chambers St. (bet. Broadway & Church St.)

Subway: Chambers St (West Broadway)
Phone: 212-227-3400
Web: www.racinesny.com
Price: $$$$

Dinner Mon – Sat

The American outpost of this popular Parisian original cuts an elegant figure, with its wide marble bar and pristine flower arrangements. Throw in romantic low lighting, brick-lined walls and a tony TriBeCa address—and you have quite the operation.

The service can be a bit off-putting, which is a shame because Racines NY has an ace, even affordable, wine list that bears discussion and recommendations. As for the food, you'll pay for all that sexy ambience a little more than the cuisine currently merits—but certain dishes, like a rich chicken liver mousse served with grilled breads, make for an elegant bar snack. Paired with one of those excellent wines by the glass and a seat at that handsome bar, this is a recipe for a glam night on the town.

Tamarind

Indian **✗✗✗**

B2

99 Hudson St. (at Franklin St.)

Subway: Franklin St
Phone: 212-775-9000
Web: www.tamarindrestaurantsnyc.com
Price: $$$

Lunch & dinner daily

Building Tamarind cost a cool five million, and it shows—every inch of this soaring space oozes with grandeur. With its classic TriBeCa edifice and gorgeous marble bar (an ideal perch for post-work indulgence), the glass-fronted behemoth draws a posh crowd of Wall Streeters and well-heeled locals. Most impressive of all is the sleek display kitchen, outfitted with a gleaming tandoor that turns out exceptional Mughlai food like *nawab shami kabab* (lamb patties seasoned with ginger) and *hara bhara kabab* (pearl-white paneer mingled with bright emerald-green spinach). While service is mediocre at best and the kitchen may fall behind at peak times, mains like *kolambi pola* (prawns in a coconut-and-chili curry) make up for any gaffes and guarantee a return visit.

Tiny's

American ✗

B3

135 West Broadway (bet. Duane & Thomas Sts.)

Subway:	Chambers St (West Broadway)
Phone:	212-374-1135
Web:	www.tinysnyc.com
Price:	$$

Lunch & dinner daily

The name says it all—Tiny's is indeed tiny, but in that old New York, wood-burning fire, and pressed-tin ceiling kind of way. Enter this narrow Federal-style home (c. 1810) and sidle up to the beautiful people along the pew seats that overlook a poster of the Marlboro Man. Alternatively, head on up to the suitably named Bar Upstairs.

The setting is so rich with character that one could simply be satisfied by Tiny's fine burger, featuring dry-aged rib-eye and a side of cheddar tater tots. However, this is a surprisingly ambitious kitchen turning out some very clever dishes. The wild Coho salmon for example, is grilled to specification and plated with *vadouvan*-spiced beurre blanc; while the vanilla flan slicked with cold caramel syrup makes a wonderful finale.

Tribeca Grill

Contemporary ✗✗

A2

375 Greenwich St. (at Franklin St.)

Subway:	Franklin St
Phone:	212-941-3900
Web:	www.myriadrestaurantgroup.com
Price:	$$$

Lunch Sun – Fri
Dinner nightly

Beckoning business titans day and night, this corner restaurant is a destination for its big, bright dining room with well-spaced tables. Wall-to-wall windows overlook two quintessential TriBeCa streets, while exposed brick, moody artwork, and a spectacular bar smack in the center of the room complete the refined vibe.

Gigantone, large tubular pasta loaded with a braised short rib Bolognese beneath a dollop of fresh sheep's milk ricotta, makes a rich start to a meal. The decadence continues with seared scallops over creamy carrot risotto, topped with a truffled-Madeira vinaigrette, and brought over the top with a few fragrant shavings of black truffle. Desserts are as classic as the space; try the banana tart with malted chocolate and pecan ice cream.

Zutto

B2

77 Hudson St. (bet. Harrison & Jay Sts.)

Subway: Franklin St
Phone: 212-233-3287
Web: www.zuttonyc.com
Price: **$$**

Lunch & dinner daily

Exposed filament bulbs and a red brick wall give this cozy Japanese pub an inviting, industrial feel. There is a communal wood table for groups, small sushi bar, and long wall of banquettes and tables topped with linen napkins cleverly folded, origami-style. Service is eager, efficient, and less concerned with the flow of a leisurely meal.

Unlike many Japanese restaurants with one specialty, this *izakaya's* diverse menu includes bar snacks, sushi, steamed buns, and ramen. Tangy, spicy buffalo cauliflower is a playful take on wings, replacing chicken with bright orange chunks of deep-fried cauliflower tempered by a cool, creamy ranch sauce. The Zutto fried rice is another ideal drinking accompaniment, peppered with kimchi and pastrami beneath a runny egg.

Look for our symbol 🍺,
spotlighting restaurants
with a notable beer list.

Upper East Side

Famously expensive and particularly charming, the Upper East Side is flanked by lush Central Park on one side and the East River on the other. If watching barges and boats bob along the water from a dense metropolis doesn't sound like a perfect paradox, know that this prime area is predominantly residential and home to iconic addresses like Gracie Mansion. Closest to the park are posh diners catering to expats with expense accounts. But, walk a few steps east and discover young families filling the latest *sushi-ya*, artisanal pizzeria, or hot sidewalk spot. Carnegie Hill's **Lucy's Whey** is cheesy, but in a good way, stocked with a wide variety of cheeses and accouterments. They also have a

sit-down café where you can dig into salads, soup, and other types of gooey goodness—imagine panini-pressed ciabatta rolls stuffed with Iowa cheddar and locally sourced pickles...from Brooklyn, of course. Along First

and Second avenue, classic Irish pubs are packed with raucous post-grads who keep the party alive well through happy hour and into the wee hours.

SHOPPING CENTRAL

The most upper and eastern reaches of this neighborhood were originally developed by famous families of German descent. While here, make sure to join the queue of carnivores at **Schaller & Weber** as they hover over Austro-German specialties, including wursts for winter steaming or summer grilling as well as a plethora of pungent mustards to accompany them. This area also boasts a greater concentration of gourmet markets than any other part of town. Each of these emporiums are more packed than the next and make processing long lines an art of inspired efficiency. The presence of **Fairway**, a gourmet sanctuary showcasing everything from fresh produce and glistening meats, to seafood and deli delights, has made shopping for homemade meals a complete breeze. And, with such easy access to **Agata & Valentina**, a family-owned and operated food store whose famously cramped aisles are supplied with everything Italian, residents of the Upper East can't imagine residing elsewhere in the city. Outfitted with delicious gift ideas, baskets, and recipes, this epicurean haven brings an

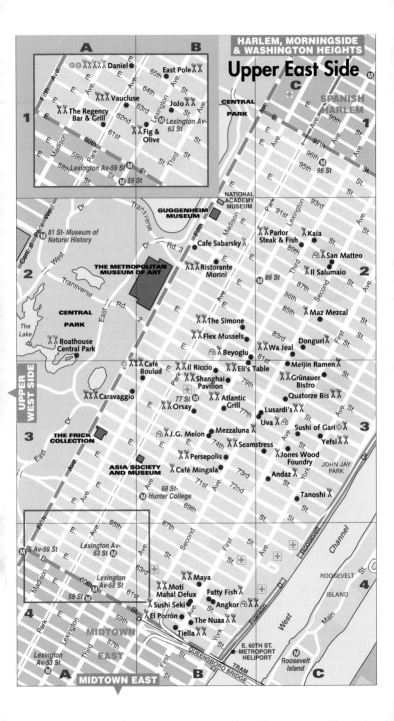

authentic European experience to the mean streets of Manhattan. A few steps west, **Citarella** pumps out its mouthwatering aroma of rotisserie chickens to entice passersby. Prime meats and rare produce are also on offer here, and contend with the abundant goodness available at **Grace's Marketplace**. In their expanded location, this beloved bazaar boasts more space, but no lesser quality, variety, or guests at the prepared foods counter. Such a savory spectacle is bound to

leave you starving, so grab a seat at their adjoining trattoria and devour some pasta or even a whole pizza. At the head of the gourmet game and celebrated as the reigning champion of everything uptown is Eli Zabar and his ever-expanding empire. **E.A.T.** is a Madison Avenue treasure selling all things edible in its casual café. Thanks to its vast offerings and appeal, other outposts (like **Vinegar Factory** and mega-mart **Eli's**) have sprouted and continue to prosper in this quarter. Meanwhile, **Corner Café & Bakery** is a gem among nannies and mommies with uniformed young'uns in tow for tasty salads, sammies, and fro-yo. Finally, every self-respecting foodie knows that **Kitchen Arts & Letters** flaunts the largest stock of food and wine publications in the country, and founder Nach Waxman is as good a source of industry insight as any book or blog around.

SUPPER, SWEETS AND SIPS

In spite of such large-scale shopping, still there are smaller purveyors to patronize here. **Lobel's** and **Ottomanelli** are among the best butchers in town; while **William Greenberg** continues to bake *babka* and Gotham's favorite black-and-white cookie. Just as **Ladurée**'s pastel-hued macarons bring a slice of the City of Lights to this enclave, **Glaser's Bake Shop** is reminiscent of everything Old World while **Lady M's** cakes fit right into its plush setting off Madison Avenue. Likewise, thirsty revelers will appreciate **Bemelmans Bar** or **The Jeffrey**, a railcar-like space serving stellar sips and pub grub. But, if in the mood for supper and a show, it doesn't get more classic than the storied hotel's, **Café Carlyle**. Finally, **Bar Pleiades** is another, more contemporary retreat, but just as elegantly uptown as one would expect with its quilted walls and lacquer finishes.

Andaz

C3

1378 First Ave. (bet. 73rd & 74th Sts.)

Subway: 77 St	Lunch & dinner daily
Phone: 212-288-0288	
Web: www.andazny.com	
Price: $$	

Simply stated, Andaz is one of *the* best Indian dining gems in the city's upper quarter. This demure space feels tidy and neutral beneath colorful ceiling pendants and wine shelves. A polite staff attends to the familiar coterie of neighborhood patrons.

The menu specializes in regional dishes that are spiced to your desired level. Sample rich bowls of *keema matar,* a thick and meaty stew of minced lamb and sweet peas in a spicy curry paste of dried red chilies, ginger, coriander, and cloves. Hearty vegetarian options include *paneer makhani,* brimming with cubes of diced house-made cheese in a decadent cream and butter-enriched tomato sauce; or lusciously seasoned and distinctly tart vegetable *vindaloo* stocked with cauliflower, potatoes, and sweet carrots.

Angkor ☻

B4

408 E. 64th St. (bet. First & York Aves.)

Subway: Lexington Av - 63 St	Dinner nightly
Phone: 212-758-2111	
Web: www.angkornyc.com	
Price: $$	

Connoisseurs of Southeast Asian cuisine, take note: in a city that prides itself on ethnic eats, this fresh bistro offers one of the few true places for Cambodian food in Manhattan.

Inside, the stone-accented Angkor is lined in richly-stained wood and filled with woven rattan furnishings and Buddha figurines. Owned by Minh and Mandy Truong, the husband--wife team who ran Chelsea's Royal Siam for 20 years, this menu certainly shares DNA with other Southeast Asian restaurants, offering classic items like grilled, marinated meat skewers, sour soups, spicy salads, and curries. But there are also more unique items to be explored, like delicious stir-fried specialties from Siem Reap; or *nyoam,* a traditional Khmer noodle dish sauced with thick red fish curry.

Atlantic Grill

Seafood ✕✕

B3

1341 Third Ave. (bet. 76th & 77th Sts.)

Subway: 77 St   Lunch & dinner daily
Phone: 212-988-9200
Web: www.atlanticgrill.com
Price: $$$

This gorgeous Grill's sprawling patio is a seafood oasis in the midst of urban chaos. It seems deceivingly vast until you round the bend to a second, beachy dining room decked with a marble sushi counter and rattan chairs—a taste of tropicana on Third Avenue. Despite its name, Atlantic Grill pulls influence from the Pacific (think delicious yet unapologetically unauthentic sushi).

Hints of *sriracha* and ginger keep things bright in bigeye tuna tartare, served in a glass jar glistening with sesame oil and avocado. Soft tacos filled with spicy shrimp and pineapple *pico de gallo* or red-miso Atlantic cod are filling and light at once. Brunch is a hit with twists on traditional fare.

Some whine about the prices, but considering the neighborhood, hush up!

Beyoglu

Turkish ✕

B2

1431 Third Ave. (at 81st St.)

Subway: 77 St   Lunch & dinner daily
Phone: 212-650-0850
Web: N/A
Price: $$

Upper East Siders can't get enough of the meze at cheerful Beyoglu and its enticing Turkish, Greek, and Lebanese cooking. Vibrant flavors enhanced by garlic and herbs start with chilled platters loaded with hummus, mashed eggplant spread (*patlican salatasi*), and salads like *kisir*, tabbouleh made with cracked wheat. The only other thing you'll need to fully enjoy the Beyoglu experience is a bowl of strained, house-made yogurt. That flatbread is pulled straight from the hot oven only to arrive on your table seconds later, gratis and absolutely gratifying.

Tile-topped tables and pistachio-green walls displaying painted flowers accent the interior. French doors separate the dining room from the sidewalk, but during warm weather both areas fill quickly.

Boathouse Central Park

American XX

A2

The Lake at Central Park (E. 72nd St. & Park Dr. North)

Subway: 68 St - Hunter College   Lunch & dinner daily
Phone: 212-517-2233
Web: www.thecentralparkboathouse.com
Price: $$$

The word "touristy" is mostly used pejoratively but there's no denying that sometimes visitors to the city know a good thing when they see one. Loeb Boathouse was built in 1954 and includes an outdoor bar and a restaurant whose glass wall folds away in the summer to give every table a great view of the lake. If you want to swap the chaos of the city and its cacophony of car horns for a couple of tranquil hours, then here's where to come.

The menu is a mix of American and European classics alongside less successful dishes of a more innovative persuasion. Try the robustly seasoned linguine with Little Neck clams or Scottish salmon with chickpea purée.

While brunch and lunch are year-long affairs, dinner is only served during warmer months.

Café Mingala

Burmese X

B3

1393B Second Ave. (bet. 72nd & 73rd Sts.)

Subway: 68 St - Hunter College   Lunch & dinner daily
Phone: 212-744-8008
Web: N/A
Price:

Café Mingala is a special destination—not simply because this is the only Burmese restaurant in all five boroughs. The cuisine itself is downright addictive and undeniably unique. This cross-cultural cuisine distills the flavors of Myanmar's neighbors—China, India, Thailand, and Malaysia—into its own luscious specialties.

The pickled green tea leaf salad combines chopped lettuce, bean sprouts, peanuts, sesame seeds, and bits of tea leaf all dressed with spiced oil and fresh lime. Follow this with *mo-goke* pork, from the "land of rubies" made with tender chunks of meat braised in a salty and sweet dark sauce. Café Mingala's signature dish is a flaky "thousand-layer" pancake, or *keema*, topped with ground beef and potatoes in a turmeric-rich curry.

Café Boulud ✿

French 𝕏𝕏𝕏

B3

20 E. 76th St. (bet. Fifth & Madison Aves.)

Subway: 77 St
Phone: 212-772-2600
Web: www.cafeboulud.com
Price: $$$$

Lunch & dinner daily

Taking its cue from classic French cuisine, Daniel Boulud's refined vision of food and beverage at the Surrey hotel is comprised of two spaces: the jewel box known as Bar Pleiades and this elegant, appealingly understated restaurant.

Inside, ritzy residents and in-the-know globetrotters dine in a well-groomed, secluded room furnished with plush carpeting, rich wood accents, and mirrored surfaces. Sparkling elements atop beautifully laid tables set off the spot's conviviality, and gallant, smartly-dressed servers display unwavering competence in their presentation of uniquely constructed and superb tasting compositions. Under the watch of Chef Aaron Bludorn, the kitchen makes culinary decisions that never disappoint. Classically done *poulet rôti* showcases evenly moist, crispy skinned chicken finished with a fragrant tarragon jus, while the Crescent Farms Pekin duck, cooked to a perfect pink and sprinkled with coarse salt, is served with currant-studded kasha for wonderful depth in flavor and texture.

For dessert, intricately layered crêpe cakes are garnished with rhubarb gelée and kissed with ricotta sorbet. And warm and springy madeleines—a house signature—send satisfied diners on their way.

Cafe Sabarsky

Austrian ✗

1048 Fifth Ave. (at 86th St.)

Subway:	86 St (Lexington Ave.)	Lunch Wed – Mon
Phone:	212-288-0665	Dinner Thu – Sun
Web:	www.kg-ny.com	
Price:	**$$**	

This Museum Mile *kaffeehaus* is so authentic it may as well be set along Vienna's *Ringstrasse*. Instead, find it in the Beaux Arts mansion—which is also home to Serge Sabarsky and Ronald Lauder's Neue Galerie, replete with 20th century Austrian-cum-German art and design. Located across from Central Park, this gorgeous ground-floor den is clad in dark-stained wood with diners seated along a banquette covered in Otto Wagner fabric.

Stunning cakes and pastries are displayed on a marble-topped sideboard. But first, order one of Chef Kurt Gutenbrunner's traditional specialties, including the city's best wiener schnitzel or hearty Hungarian beef goulash with creamy, herbed spätzle. When it's time for dessert, try a wedge of the chocolate, almond, and rum *Sabarskytorte*.

Caravaggio

Italian ✗✗✗

23 E. 74th St. (bet. Fifth & Madison Aves.)

Subway:	77 St	Lunch & dinner daily
Phone:	212-288-1004	
Web:	www.caravaggioristorante.com	
Price:	**$$$**	

Nestled among Madison Avenue boutiques and commanding a rather formal air, this highbrow Italian dining room is a good reason to dress up and splurge. The slender setting is adorned with silk-lined walls, sleek leather seating, and evocative artwork. The well-dressed staff is serious, but their hospitality is genuine.

The team of highly experienced co-chefs is equally intense in turning out their skilled cooking. Antipasti might include an elegant, warm octopus salad with baby artichoke and crispy potatoes, while heartier options may feature house-made *cavatelli* with jumbo crabmeat and sea urchin. Lunch offers a more pared-down experience, but a bowlful of velvety *pasta e fagioli* stocked with plump *borlotti* beans is a perfect post-shopping tonic.

Daniel ⁂ ⁂

French XXXXX

60 E. 65th St. (bet. Madison & Park Aves.)

Subway: 68 St - Hunter College   Dinner Mon – Sat
Phone: 212-288-0033
Web: www.danielnyc.com
Price: $$$$

The elegant façade, revolving door, sound of clinking glasses—even before you reach the dining room you feel a part of something special. This bastion of contemporary French cooking epitomizes the "special occasion," but even those with money to burn treat it with respect.

Translucent Limoges-tiled chandeliers hanging from the soaring ceiling dominate the dining room. If you're at one of the raised tables, you get to look down—literally rather than patronizingly—onto your fellow diners through neo-classical arches. Yet thanks to the personable service, such grandeur never stifles the animated atmosphere.

The kitchen is as sophisticated as the surroundings and reflects an obvious classical education, yet remains free from the tyranny of tradition. Behold the striking sea scallop ceviche with red and green sea lettuce, Lilliputian matchsticks of radish and cucumber, a burst of finger lime, and white sturgeon caviar. Young beets are baked in a seaweed-salt crust studded with cardamom and finished tableside with pistachios, chive aïoli and crème fraîche for a presentation that is as theatrical as delicious. Ruby peach mousse in a peach-colored white chocolate shell practically upstages summer's best fruit.

Donguri

309 E. 83rd St. (bet. First & Second Aves.)

Subway: 86 St (Lexington Ave.)
Phone: 212-737-5656
Web: www.donguriny.com
Price: $$

Dinner Tue – Sun

This cozy Yorkville hideaway has endured years of non-stop construction along Second Avenue and a more recent change in ownership and chef. Yet Donguri still perseveres as a highly recommendable venue. Service has lightened up of late, reflected in the genuine smiles of the small and gracious crew, but the cuisine's ethos remains very much unaltered.

Don't expect to dine on sushi here—there's more to Japanese cuisine after all as evidenced by their home-style cooked dishes. Nightly specials posted on the wall direct your attention to options like fried soft-shell crabs so pleasingly crispy and plump they don't need anything else. Okay, a squeeze of lemon if you must. Rice bowls topped with the likes of yellowtail and scallion are yet another specialty.

East Pole

133 E. 65th St. (bet. Lexington & Park Aves.)

Subway: 68 St - Hunter College
Phone: 212-249-2222
Web: www.theeastpolenyc.com
Price: $$$

Lunch & dinner daily

Just off Park Avenue's pre-war grandeur is this hip addition to the neighborhood, courtesy of the Fat Radish team. The cozy space is on the ground floor of a brownstone, so the setting is understandably narrow. East Pole's front bar is hopping, while black leather booths in the back allow parties to sit and enjoy an eclectic menu in relative peace.

The stimulating cooking here begins with a salad of roasted heirloom carrots with *hijiki*, diced avocado, and an Asian-inspired soy-and-sesame oil vinaigrette. Then move on to explore Kiev-style chicken, stuffed with garlic butter-enriched broccoli purée, or creamy fish pie stocked with cod, lobster, and fennel. The adult ice cream sundae is a boozy combo of Scotch-chocolate ice cream and Pimm's-soaked cherries.

Eli's Table

American American

B3

1413 Third Ave. (at 80th St.)

Subway: 77 St
Phone: 212-717-9798
Web: www.elistablenyc.com
Price: $$

Lunch Sat – Sun
Dinner nightly

Formerly known as Taste, Eli Zabar has redone the formal café located adjacent to his eponymous gourmet emporium. The facelift has revealed a more casual vibe—no tablecloths—but the scene is just about as casual as Upper East Siders can stomach. Inlaid geometric patterned flooring and an earthy palette remain, while a mural of the Côte d' Or is an attractive new touch signaling a more serious approach to wine.

Rooftop greens as well as bread and gelato made in-house at the market factor into the revised menu that boasts a sunny disposition in its affection for the Mediterranean. Expect to enjoy pig's ear salad with a mustard vinaigrette, plump sardines over olive oil-smashed potatoes, or fresh pappardelle twirled with wild mushrooms and a bit of cream.

El Porrón

Spanish

B4

1123 First Ave. (bet. 61st & 62nd Sts.)

Subway: Lexington Av - 59 St
Phone: 212-207-8349
Web: www.elporronnyc.com
Price: $$

Lunch & dinner daily

Black-and-white portraits of people pouring streams of wine into their mouths directly from *porróns*—blown glass wine vessels with long, tapered spouts—give you the idea of what this spot is all about. Dark colors give a cloistered feel to the intimate space, which is a pleasant contrast to its traffic-clogged location.

The kitchen churns out a graceful, all-encompassing array of tapas, large plates, and even paellas worth their 40-minute wait. Sample bites like canned *esparragos blancos Navarro*—their thick, tender stalks are served cool and dressed with Chardonnay vinaigrette—or *bacalao a la Vizcaina*, Basque-style salt cod with a sauce melding the flavors of roasted peppers, garlic, olives, and potatoes served in a bubbling hot *cazuela*.

Fatty Fish

B4

406 E. 64th St. (bet. First & York Aves.)

Subway: Lexington Av - 63 St

Lunch & dinner daily

Phone: 212-813-9338
Web: www.fattyfishnyc.com
Price: $$

Drifting through Manhattan's Yorkville neighborhood? Easygoing charm and creative Asian cooking make recommending Fatty Fish a cinch. Just past its distinctive orange awning, you'll find a homey interior with intimate rooms, creaky wood floors, and a staff that treats everyone like regulars. The cuisine pulls inspiration from myriad places, but it's all equally tempting.

At the sushi counter, you'll find skillfully knifed sashimi, *chirashi*, and maki. Cooked items might mean a well-crafted salmon burger, tucked between a soft brioche bun laced with wasabi aïoli, or crispy fish and chips, paired with ponzu aïoli. Other popular dishes include the honey-ginger glazed salmon; and jumbo shrimp in green curry, paired with jasmine rice.

Fig & Olive

B1

808 Lexington Ave. (bet. 62nd & 63rd Sts.)

Subway: Lexington Av - 63 St

Lunch & dinner daily

Phone: 212-207-4555
Web: www.figandolive.com
Price: $$$

This reliable, Mediterranean-inspired retreat is a popular post-museum (or post-shopping) pick. The sleek long bar glows beneath dangling light fixtures, while the shelf-lined walls are stocked with olive oils in verdant hues of green. Candles flicker over stone tables near plates of glistening olives.

An olive oil tasting showcases the stark nuances of different regions and makes an ideal start to a meal, served with fluffy rosemary *fougasse*. Then, move on to buttery, round tartlets of Gorgonzola dolce, caramelized figs, and chopped walnuts with a pile of arugula lending peppery spark. Nutty, truffle-infused risotto with meaty mushrooms is a high note. A shot glass of luscious chocolate mousse compensates for its paltry size with absolute decadence.

Flex Mussels

B2

Seafood ✗✗

174 E. 82nd St. (bet. Lexington & Third Aves.)

Subway: 86 St (Lexington Ave.)   Dinner nightly
Phone: 212-717-7772
Web: www.flexmusselsny.com
Price: $$

Featuring a focused menu of cleverly made, high-quality seafood, it's no surprise that this mussels haven was an immediate success. Still going strong, this setting is routinely packed to the gills, both up front where there is a bar and dining counter, as well as the proper dining room in the back, adorned with an abundance of maritime-themed artwork.

Expect to taste plenty of the namesake bivalve, hailing from Prince Edward Island. Priced by the pound and steamed in no fewer than twenty globally inspired broths, they are best with some killer hand-cut skinny fries. Mussels No. 23 refers to the nightly special, perhaps featuring a succulent bath of hot and sour soup bobbing with soft tofu, bits of pork, wood ear mushrooms, and dried red chili flakes.

Grünauer Bistro

C3

Austrian ✗✗

1578 First Ave. (at 82nd St.)

Subway: 86 St   Dinner nightly
Phone: 212-988-1077
Web: www.grunauernyc.com
Price: $$

Peter Grünauer's colorful Austrian bistro straddles a corner of the Upper East Side—its bright yellow-and-green painted façade giving way to a cozy room lined with dark wood, glazed ceramic urns and mirrored panels. Service is engaging and personable and the positive energy is palpable—after their meal, diners may be offered gratis shots of Hans Reisetbauer eau-de-vie.

Chef Thomas Slivovsky, formerly of Blaue Gans, puts together an enticing menu full of delicious Austrian elements—perhaps veal tongue and pickled vegetables with pumpkin seed pesto; chicken schnitzel with potato and cucumber salad; or beef goulash with spaetzle. Don't miss the meltingly tender chicken *paprikash*, slow-cooked in a bright paprika-seasoned sauce with creamy spaetzle.

Il Riccio

Italian XX

152 E. 79th St. (bet. Lexington & Third Aves.)

Subway: 77 St
Phone: 212-639-9111
Web: N/A
Price: $$

Lunch & dinner daily

Long-standing and low-key, this is just the right spot to recharge after an afternoon of perusing fabulous neighborhood boutiques or meandering through the nearby museums. Il Riccio has a cozy feel with warm ochre walls, simple furnishings, and an assemblage of photographs. Regulars know to head back to the enclosed garden to enjoy their meal.

The cooking here is fuss-free, pasta-focused, and lovingly dedicated to the Amalfi Coast. Favored dishes include roasted red peppers topped with salty, marinated white anchovies; or *fedelini primavera*, a rustic presentation of thin pasta strands tossed with an assortment of fresh vegetables and well-seasoned tomato sauce. Grilled fish dressed simply with olive oil and lemon rounds out the menu.

Il Salumaio

Italian X

1731 Second Ave. (bet. 89th & 90th Sts.)

Subway: 86 St (Lexington Ave.)
Phone: 646-852-6876
Web: www.ilsalumaiony.com
Price: ⊜

Lunch Fri – Sun
Dinner nightly

Yorkville residents have been doubly blessed by Fabio and Ciro Casella. First, their pizzeria San Matteo arrived on the scene with its wood-fired specialties. Now, the brothers bring more delightfully rustic fare by way of primo panini and pastas, to this underserved neighborhood.

The slender space seats only a handful, but sidewalk tables increase the accommodations. Cured meats and imported cheeses temptingly stocked in a refrigerator display case are skillfully manifested atop luscious plates like the Arthur Avenue—basically a *panino* bursting with ham, *salume*, mortadellla, and provolone. The *paccheri all'Amatriciana* or fat tubes of perfectly cooked pasta in a thick tomato ragù seasoned with onion, pancetta and *pecorino Romano*, is a delight unto itself.

J.G. Melon

 American ✗

B3

1291 Third Ave. (at 74th St.)

Subway: 77 St
Phone: 212-744-0585
Web: N/A
Price:

Lunch & dinner daily

Posterity will remember J.G. Melon as a classic and coveted New York institution. Make your way into this cave set upon a cozy Upper East corner, where the timeless vibe and cheery staff make up most of its allure. Drinks are steadily churned out at a dark wood bar, so arrive early to avoid the hordes.

The focus at this multi-generational saloon is the burger—perhaps paired with a lip-smacking Bloody Mary at brunch? The warm toasted bun topped with meat cooked on a griddle to rosy pink is coupled with onions, pickles, and crispy crinkle-cut fries. Be forewarned: you will go through the entire stack of napkins before finishing. Other simple pleasures include standards like salads, steaks, and eggs. Seal the meal with a chocolate chip-studded layer cake.

JoJo

 Contemporary ✗✗

B1

160 E. 64th St. (bet. Lexington & Third Aves.)

Subway: Lexington Av - 63 St
Phone: 212-223-5656
Web: www.jojorestaurantnyc.com
Price: $$$

Lunch & dinner daily

The key to longevity is to be part of the fabric of local life—and few places embody the very essence of their neighborhood more convincingly than this Jean-Georges Vongerichten bistro. It's reassuring to know that, on any given day, a few tables will be occupied by regulars who've been eating out since before most of us were on solids. The service is capable, confident and understandably patient and, while the menu leans towards the contemporary, there's nothing here to scare the horses. Invariably the best dishes are the simplest—the tuna tartare, baked salmon with mashed potato, and the chocolate cake with its cargo of rich, silky chocolate.

It's spread over two floors—ask for a table upstairs as the first floor can feel a little like a corridor.

Jones Wood Foundry

 C3

401 E. 76th St. (bet. First & York Aves.)

Subway: 77 St   Lunch & dinner daily
Phone: 212-249-2771
Web: www.joneswoodfoundry.com
Price: $$

 Jones Wood Foundry is a stateside take on a classic public house—the kind that Chef/partner Jason Hicks frequented during his childhood in England—that serves the same style of spot-on pub grub. The front bar is a choice spot to sip and savor from the selection of drafts. The space then opens up to a seating area of marble-topped tables, handsome button-tufted brown leather banquettes, and plush red velvet chairs. Beer-battered haddock and chips with tartar sauce, hearty meat pie of the day, and coronation chicken sandwich—the classic mid-century chicken salad dressed with intensely yellow, curry-tinged mayonnaise on toasted baguette—are a few of the true-blue hits. The vibe is charming, but dinner offers much more ambience than midday service.

Kaia

South African

C2

1614 Third Ave. (bet. 90th & 91st Sts.)

Subway: 86 St (Lexington Ave.)   Dinner nightly
Phone: 212-722-0490
Web: N/A
Price: $$

This South African wine bar takes its name from the word for shelter. It is owned by a native South African who chased her dreams of stardom to New York City, while building an impressive resume of work in some in the city's finer dining rooms. The space has a comfortable appeal, spotlighting a lively dining counter as well as high and low wood tables.

Discover a plethora of wines not just from South Africa, but also South America and New York. To accompany your glass, select from the interesting small plates like "spear and shield" of bacon-wrapped asparagus with cheddar-stuffed mushroom caps; or *vark ribbetjies en vark pensie*, a pork duo of ribs glazed with honey and *rooibos* tea plus belly braised in Indian pale ale dressed with candied kumquats.

Lusardi's

Italian

1494 Second Ave. (bet. 77th & 78th Sts.)

Subway: 77 St
Phone: 212-249-2020
Web: www.lusardis.com
Price: $$$

Lunch Mon – Fri
Dinner nightly

With its pumpkin-colored walls, dark woodwork, and vintage posters, this beloved old-school mainstay offers a menu that relishes in decadant Northern Italian cooking. Picture an array of fresh pasta and veal, richly embellished with cream, authentic cheeses, or truffle-infused olive oil.

The *insalata bianca* is a monotone-white yet delightfully refreshing composition of shaved fennel, sliced artichoke hearts, chopped endive, and slivered hearts of palm dressed with lemony vinaigrette and *Parmigiano Reggiano*, all singing with black pepper freshly ground tableside. *Paccheri* in *salsa affumicata* presents large pasta tubes draped with plum tomato sauce that has been enriched with creamy smoked mozzarella and strewn with bits of roasted eggplant.

Maya

Mexican

1191 First Ave. (bet. 64th & 65th Sts.)

Subway: 68 St - Hunter College
Phone: 212-585-1818
Web: www.richardsandoval.com
Price: $$

Lunch & dinner daily

Upscale Mexican dining thrives at Chef Richard Sandoval's *muy* popular Maya. Slick with polished dark wood furnishings, vibrant tiled flooring, and accent walls the color of a ripe mango, this is always a fun scene. Adding to the revelry is the Tequileria, Maya's bar with a serious focus on agave spirits.

Antojitos, such as squash blossom quesadillas and their trio of salsas, headline as starters. Tasty tacos are stuffed with smoked brisket and creamy chili slaw. Heartier dishes feature *huitlacoche* and wild mushroom enchiladas swathed in a creamy, fire-roasted poblano chile sauce. *Especialidades* like achiote-marinated carne asada with cactus-green bean salad and bacon-wrapped jalapeños display the kitchen's contemporary flair.

Maz Mezcal

C2

316 E. 86th St. (bet. First & Second Aves.)

Subway: 86 St (Lexington Ave.)
Phone: 212-472-1599
Web: www.mazmezcal.com
Price: $$

Lunch Sat – Sun
Dinner nightly

This family-run, longtime haunt still draws its legion of neighborhood regulars for satisfying and traditional Mexican food. The front room is brightened by turquoise walls and quirkily decorated with watermelon-themed artwork; while the back room is warmer with its terra-cotta-colored backdrop. Welcomes are personalized, and the dining rooms are filled with guests chatting and quizzing the staff about their latest news.

Chips and salsas are a crunchy and colorful precursor to Maz Mescal's commendable specialties. Family-friendly combination platters are a popular option, but a glimpse and whiff of the sizzling fajita platter might be all the enticement necessary to sway your decision. For dessert, brandy and Kahlua spike their take on the classic flan.

Meijin Ramen

C3

1574 Second Ave. (bet. 81st & 82nd Sts.)

Subway: 77 St
Phone: 212-327-2800
Web: www.meijinramen.com
Price: ⊜⊜

Lunch & dinner daily

One of the most ramen-deprived zones in the city is now home to this slurp-worthy spot. Sandwiched mid-block in a bustling locale, the wood plank façade confidently conveys an intriguing Japanese aesthetic, and the simple, earthy dining room delivers just that. But while the atmosphere is everything you'd expect from a noodle house, the cooking is a bit of a departure from the norm—further adding to MeiJin's rare-bird status.

Beef bones, instead of pork, are the foundation for the excellent broth, which is slow-simmered to extract a rich but refined essence and then seasoned with soy sauce, chili, oil, or miso and stocked with noodles. *Narutomaki* (fish cake), *menma* (braised bamboo shoots), and fried garlic chips are some samples of their tasty trimmings.

Mezzaluna

Italian ✗

1295 Third Ave. (bet. 74th & 75th Sts.)

Subway: 77 St   Lunch & dinner daily
Phone: 212-535-9600
Web: www.mezzalunanyc.com
Price: $$

Time and time again, this Italian idol hits the spot. Just take a look at the jubilant crowd huddled together at pink granite tables throughout the Euro-chic yet cozy room. One wall is yellow while another is completely lined with 77 depictions of the restaurant's name, beneath a sky-blue ceiling painted with clouds.

Neighborhood residents and savvy tourists know Mezzaluna's unfussy Italian cooking is guaranteed to be *delizioso*. Take for example the veal Milanese—pounded thin and delicately crunchy, simply topped with peppery wild arugula and sliced cherry tomatoes. Other hits include pizzas that emerge from a wood-burning oven unceremoniously stationed in a corner, or beef carpaccio with a choice of toppings like artichokes and *Parmigiano Reggiano*.

Moti Mahal Delux

Indian ✗✗

1149 First Ave. (at 63rd St.)

Subway: Lexington Av - 63 St   Lunch & dinner daily
Phone: 212-371-3535
Web: www.motimahaldelux.us
Price: $$

This corner spot marks the first American location of a fine dining chain that began in Delhi and now boasts outposts throughout India. Here in NYC, Moti Mahal Delux offers two distinct seating areas: an earth-toned dining room and windowed sidewalk atrium.

Their Northern-leaning cuisine traces back to the kitchens of the Mughal Empire, which brought Muslim influences to the Indo subcontinent. Lunch is limited, while dinner is more rewarding, featuring *tandoori* preparations like *anardana tikka*—grilled chicken infused with a pomegranate and black pepper marinade. Delightful flavors abound through the brick-red mutton curry flavored with spiced tomato, onion, and ginger; *paratha* dusted with dried mint; and mustard seed- and curry leaf-infused lemon rice.

The Nuaa

Thai **✗✗**

B4

1122 First Ave. (bet. 61st & 62nd St.)

Subway: 59 St　　　　　　　　　　　　Lunch & dinner daily
Phone: 212-888-2899
Web: www.thenuaa.com
Price: $$

The Nuaa offers a certain sultry vibe to this rather blah, trafficky stretch—it's dim and moody even in the middle of the day. Shimmering gold accents pop against the room's brown leather seating, carved woodwork, and dark palette.

Fans of Thai cuisine will enjoy the pleasantly pungent notes throughout the selection of salads and noodle dishes. Crunchy curried rice salad features deep-fried nuggets strewn with Thai sausage and lemongrass served with plenty of shallots, long beans, and lettuce, and a drizzle of Kaffir lime-mint vinaigrette. The *kanom jeen* features thin rice noodles soaked in a mildly spiced coconut-rich yellow curry that is generously stocked with huge lumps of crab meat, chopped pickled mustard greens, and caper berries.

Orsay

French **✗✗**

B3

1057 Lexington Ave. (at 75th St.)

Subway: 77 St　　　　　　　　　　　　Lunch & dinner daily
Phone: 212-517-6400
Web: www.orsayrestaurant.com
Price: $$$

With its mahogany paneling, hand-laid mosaic tiles, windows dressed with lacy café curtains, and pewter bar, this luxe brasserie is a painstakingly realized vision of art nouveau. Orsay proves its dedication to French tradition from the sidewalk seating to marble stairs leading up to a private room. The famous cheese soufflé sustains much of the well-dressed crowd here, but the classic menu brings much more. *Soupe de poisson* is a richly satisfying fusion of fish, tomatoes, fennel, and herbs; brook trout is presented *à la Grenobloise* with browned butter, capers, and finely diced croutons; and roasted pork tenderloin arrives with savoy cabbage, apples, and hard cider sauce. The soaked *baba au rhum* is as fine a rendition as any *à Paris*.

Parlor Steak & Fish

Contemporary ✗✗

 C2

1600 Third Ave. (at 90th St.)

Subway: 86 St (Lexington Ave.)   Lunch & dinner daily
Phone: 212-423-5888
Web: www.parlorsteakandfish.com
Price: $$$

Upper East Siders adore Parlor Steak & Fish, and no wonder—inside the big, clubby space, there's an ample front bar area (boasting a robust selection of top-shelf Belgian and American beers); handsome, dark-stained wood flooring; and French doors leading to the street. Downstairs, you'll find a private cellar dining room with a working fireplace.

Though this steakhouse recently changed their name to reflect the diversity of their menu, perfect cuts of dry-aged strips, filet mignon, and Berkshire pork chops continue to dominate the menu. But seafood lovers rejoice, for the new line-up of fish dishes—maybe tender lobster rolls, perfectly grilled swordfish, or slow-roasted salmon—and tempting raw bar items are market fresh and equally delicious.

Persepolis

Persian ✗✗

 B3

1407 Second Ave. (bet. 73rd & 74th Sts.)

Subway: 77 St   Lunch & dinner daily
Phone: 212-535-1100
Web: www.persepolisnewyork.com
Price: $$

Silky-smooth spreads, homemade yogurt, grilled meats, and fragrantly spiced stews have solidified Persepolis' reputation as one of the city's finest Persian restaurants. Linen-draped tables, spacious banquettes, and big windows facing Second Avenue fashion a look that inspires dressing up (or not). Service is always gracious, if at times earnest.

The kitchen shines with its eggplant *halim*, a creamy, steaming roasted eggplant and onion dip with tender lentils and a dollop of yogurt on top. A kebab duo of saffron-tinged chicken and grilled beef are both succulent successes, served with basmati rice flecked with bits of sour cherry. For dessert, try the tart-sweet Persian lemon ice studded with bits of rice noodles and doused in deep red cherry syrup.

Manhattan ▶ Upper East Side

Quatorze Bis

French XX

C3

323 E. 79th St. (bet. First & Second Aves.)

Subway: 77 St
Phone: 212-535-1414
Web: N/A
Price: $$

Lunch Tue – Sun
Dinner nightly

Savoring a meal at this ever-lovely bistro is like taking a break from the constant evolution that is life in New York City, where tastes change faster than you can tweet. The red-lacquer façade, claret-velvet banquettes, and sophisticated clientele are all much the same as when Quatorze Bis opened almost 25 years ago.

Though the ambience's timeless appeal is noteworthy, the traditional French cooking is their key to success. Frilly chicory, drizzled with hot bacon fat and red wine vinegar, and pocked with lardons, croutons, and shallots makes for a very hearty, *très* French salad. Seafood sausage is plump and studded with sweet red pepper and pine nuts. Daily specials keep the menu new, with dishes like striped bass served beside a creamy sorrel sauce.

The Regency Bar & Grill

Contemporary XX

A1

540 Park Ave. (at 61st St.)

Subway: Lexington Av - 59 St
Phone: 212-339-4050
Web: www.regencybarandgrill.com
Price: $$$

Lunch & dinner daily

The Regency Bar & Grill is beloved by sophisticated diners for its lovely art deco vibe, dark, matte-wood paneling and sparkling chrome fixtures. If that's not enough, grey velvet banquettes popped by red pillows, cream leather seating, as well as windows overlooking scenic Park Avenue is sure to lure. This is elevated hotel dining, to say the least.

Chef Brian Kevorkian takes the helm in the kitchen, dishing up contemporary, elegantly plated dishes. These may feature a cool three-bean salad tossed with roasted corn, red onion, watermelon radish, celery leaves, and grapefruit. Then fresh *piri piri* black cod may arrive drizzled with brick-red Portuguese chili and citrus sauce, accompanied by diced roasted eggplant, shaved fennel, and cherry tomatoes.

Ristorante Morini

Italian ✗✗✗

1167 Madison Ave. (bet. 85th & 86th Sts.)

Subway: 86 St (Lexington Ave.)
Phone: 212-249-0444
Web: www.ristorantemorini.com
Price: $$$

Lunch Mon – Fri
Dinner nightly

Altamarea Group's prime Madison Avenue corner boasts a lively street-level lounge and second story window-lined dining room where even children in tow are properly attired for lunch. Despite the high-rent address, Ristorante Morini offers an economical lunch prix-fixe, a late-night pasta special early in the week, and family-style Sunday supper.

Slick Italian dining is the draw here, as demonstrated by the likes of bigeye tuna crudo plated with pickled onions, nettle pesto, and fried salt-cured capers with a crouton-like crunch; or veal Milanese draped with prosciutto and melted fontina. Desserts continue to be a highlight, as in a cooling *coppa* of vanilla bean gelato and strawberry sorbet, whipped cream, basil, and crunchy meringue.

San Matteo

Pizza ✗

1739 Second Ave. (at 90th St.)

Subway: 86 St (Lexington Ave.)
Phone: 212-426-6943
Web: www.sanmatteopanuozzo.com
Price: 🍴🍴

Lunch Fri – Sun
Dinner nightly

This tiny pizzeria has made a big splash with its *panuozzo*, a regional specialty hailing from Campania that's a cross between a calzone and *panino*. The puffy plank of tender, salted dough emerges from San Matteo's hand-built, wood-fired oven crusty and smoke-infused before being sliced and stuffed with first-rate ingredients (highlights include the *ortolano's* fresh, house-made mozzarella, grilled eggplant, roasted sweet peppers, and baby arugula).

The room is graciously attended to and perpetually crowded with neighborhood folks stuffing their faces. In addition to the appetizing house signature, other favorites feature fresh salads such as escarole with Gaeta olives, capers, and gorgonzola; Neapolitan-style pizza; or the day's special baked pasta.

Sushi of Gari ✿

C3

Manhattan ▶ Upper East Side

Japanese 🍴

402 E. 78th St. (bet. First & York Aves.)

Subway: 77 St
Phone: 212-517-5340
Web: www.sushiofgari.com
Price: $$$$

Dinner Tue – Sun

Great things come in unassuming packages—such is the case at Sushi of Gari, where the handsome, but decidedly unflashy décor belies a transporting omakase experience.

Sold? A few insider tips from the regulars and you're on your way: make your reservation weeks in advance, as the dining room stays quite booked; score a seat only at the sushi counter, not just to enjoy those freshly scored slices of sushi straight from the chef's hand, but also because the congenial vibe at the bar surpasses the somewhat rushed experience at the tables; and do keep an eye on those prices, which can add up quicker than a trip to Target.

Sushi of Gari is Chef Masatoshi "Gari" Sugio's flagship restaurant, and the legendary chef's trademark creativity and skill shine in spades here. A night indulging in his omakase might include delicately seared kanpachi topped with a lightly poached quail egg; wildly fresh Japanese red snapper paired with pine nuts, bright greens, and fried lotus root; tender, seared toro with garlic and ginger sauce; or perfectly poached yellowtail, laced with sesame sauce and a sprinkle of chives.

Sound too good to wait for a reservation? Sushi of Gari also offers a booming takeout service.

Tanoshi

C3

Japanese

1372 York Ave. (bet. 73rd & 74th Sts.)

Subway: 77 St
Phone: 917-265-8254
Web: www.tanoshisushinyc.com
Price: $$$

Lunch & dinner Mon – Sat

Tanoshi isn't exactly the "sushi and sake bar" that the awning lists. It is BYO, so no sake, and a clipboard posted outside the door lists reservations for their two distinct dining rooms. (The right side is nicer.)

Settle into Chef Toshio Oguma's true expression of Edo-mae sushi, as you forgive the lacking service and ambience. Dinner here is omakase-only, with the exception of a few handwritten specials tacked to the wall. But all that is second to the sushi, which is handcrafted of loosely formed mounds of warm, *akazu*-seasoned rice, topped with perfectly fresh fish. Highlights include New Zealand king salmon that melts in the mouth, dense and tender amberjack topped with marinated cherry leaf, as well as bigeye tuna topped with wisps of kelp.

Tiella

B4

Italian

1109 First Ave. (bet. 60th & 61st Sts.)

Subway: Lexington Av - 59 St
Phone: 212-588-0100
Web: www.tiellanyc.com
Price: $$

Lunch Tue – Sat
Dinner nightly

Neapolitan specialties and gracious hospitality make Tiella absolutely worth seeking out. This railcar-sized space is set along a traffic-clogged stretch, but once inside, the ambience is sweet with espresso-tinted wood furnishings set against cream walls and exposed brick.

Petite pizzas baked in the wood-fired oven arrive bearing fresh mozzarella, spicy *'nduja*, and fava beans, among other tasty combinations. Starters include *gallette*, chickpea flour fritters stacked with *stracciatella* and shaved prosciutto, drizzled with fig syrup, and stuck with a sprig of rosemary. Enjoyable *primi* include risotto studded with diced artichokes, pancetta, and showered with shaved black truffle. Desserts like the lemon-soaked *delizia al limone* are homespun delights.

Uva

Italian ✗

1486 Second Ave. (bet. 77th & 78th Sts.)

Subway: 77 St
Phone: 212-472-4552
Web: www.uvanyc.com
Price: $$

Lunch Sat – Sun
Dinner nightly

Perpetually packed and always pleasing, this cousin of elegant Lusardi's is a rocking, rustic good time. Votive-filled nooks and fringed sconces cast a flattering light on the inviting room furnished with straw-seat chairs and wooden tables laden with wine bar-themed small plates.

Cheeses, meats, and salads are fine ways to start. The *insalata di manzo* is a tasty hybrid of all three—shaved lean beef topped by peppery young arugula, shaved parmesan, and pickled mushrooms. Join the crowds at the start of the week for Meatball Mondays offering three courses revolving around… you guessed it. Sample the hearty beef meatball ravioli garnished with sliced artichoke hearts, silky smooth tomato sauce, and a drizzle of extra virgin olive oil.

Vaucluse

French

100 E. 63rd St. (at Park Ave.)

Subway: 59 St
Phone: 646-869-2300
Web: www.vauclusenyc.com
Price: $$$

Lunch Sun – Fri
Dinner nightly

There is no shortage of good looks in this part of town and Chef Michael White's bold restaurant fits in nicely. It's certainly an impressive space, dressed in neutral tones. It's also a big space, with a bar that divides two dining rooms—the one on the upper level is less formal, while the lower level room has a more animated air.

The name refers to a *department* in France's southwest, but the cooking looks more to a typical brasserie for its influences. There is certainly a lot of choice on offer—bouillabaisse, *grillades* for those who like their food familiar, *fruits de mer*, salads and a notable selection of meat and fish.

The kitchen reveals its confidence by ensuring that plates are never overcrowded. Desserts, like Paris-Brest or crème brûlée, are a highlight.

Wa Jeal

Chinese ✗✗

C2

1588 Second Ave. (bet. 82nd & 83rd Sts.)

Subway: 86 St (Lexington Ave.)   Lunch & dinner daily
Phone: 212-396-3339
Web: www.wajealrestaurant.com
Price: $$

This Sichuan chili house is not merely weathering the local torrent of Second Avenue subway construction; their spotless room and tasty food will make you forget that the outside world exists. The ambience is upscale and appealing, combining pale walls, prescient images of wicked-red chilies, an engaging staff, and a substantial wine list.

The chef's specialties reveal the most noteworthy cooking, as in diced fish and crispy tofu stir-fried in a reddish-brown chili sauce speckled with chili seeds and sliced green onions. Sautéed chicken with spiced miso is another pleasure, mixing crisped, boneless pieces, wok-fried with roasted red chilies and charred jalapeños. Tender baby bok choy with garlic is a refreshing contrast to such potent flavors.

Yefsi

Greek ✗✗

C3

1481 York Ave. (bet. 78th & 79th Sts.)

Subway: 77 St   Dinner nightly
Phone: 212-535-0293
Web: www.yefsiestiatorio.com
Price: $$

Chef Christos Christou brings a wealth of experience to the kitchen of this Yorkville standout. Having manned the stoves at some of the city's Greek stalwarts, the Cyprus-native knows his way around his Aegean and Mediterranean coastal specialties.

Begin with salads showcasing superb feta or explore the array of luscious meze including zucchini and eggplant chips with tzatziki, octopus braised in *mavrodafni* or wine-spiked tomato sauce, and grilled sausages over black-eyed peas. Entrées entice with freshness and flavor, such as the wow-inducing nightly special of grilled tiger shrimp. Served head-on and lobster-like in size and texture, they are accompanied by a mound of creamy spinach rice and squeeze of fresh lemon— the perfect embellishment.

The Upper West Side is the epitome of classic New York. Proudly situated between Central Park and the Hudson River, this family-friendly neighborhood is one of the Big Apple's most distinct and upscale localities that has a near-religious belief in its own way of doing things. Whether it's because these charming streets cradle some of the best cafés in town, or that life here means constantly tripping over culture vultures destined for world-renowned Lincoln Center, area residents cannot imagine living elsewhere. On the heels of this famed institution is **Dizzy's Club Coca-Cola**—one of the better places to spend a night on the town. From its alluring vibe and exceptional jazz talent, to a stellar lineup of Southern food, audiences seem entranced by this imposing home to America's creative art form. The Upper West Side is also considered an intellectual hub— cue the distinguished presence of Columbia University to the north—and coveted real estate mecca with residential high-rises freckled amid quaint townhouses. In fact, legendary co-ops like *The Dakota* speak to the area's history, while agreeable eateries like **Épicerie Boulud** nourish its affluent tenants, hungry locals, and Ivy Leaguers on the run.

ALL IN THE FAMILY

Acknowledged for strolling, these sidewalks are stacked with charming diners and pre-war brownstones featuring polished parquet floors, intricate moldings, and bookish locals— arguing with equal gusto over the future of opera or if Barney Greengrass still serves the best sturgeon in town. One is also likely to find these deep-rooted residents browsing the shelves at **Murray's** for killer cheese; while more discerning palates may seek gratification at **Cleopatra's Needle**—an old-time jazz club-cum-Middle Eastern eatery named for the monument in Central Park. However, if stirring live performances and open mic (on Sunday afternoons) served with a side of Mediterranean cuisine doesn't fit the bill, then keep it easy indoors by stocking up on a selection of simple yet tasty sandwiches from **Indie Food and Wine**. Nestled inside the Elinor Bunin Munroe Film Center, this interesting café aims to entice the palates of visitors to Lincoln Center by way of Italian sandwiches and salads, finished with American flair. Sitting within

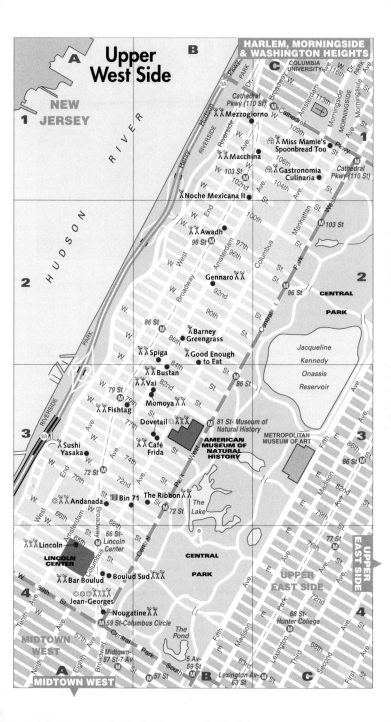

shouting distance, **The Tangled Vine** places fine wine and elegant eats under a warm and accessible spotlight. Presenting an extraordinary list of organic varietals, this boutique spot is also *the* perfect roost for a sip and small plate before heading south for a show...on Broadway, of course. But, if in the mood for familiar, old-time kitsch, find at seat at **The Cottage**, a Chinese-American standby serving nostalgic fare late into the night for area families and caffeinated scholars.

Migrating from the Far East and back to the Med, prepare for an evening in with *nonna* by stocking up on sips and other specialties from **Salumeria Rosi Parmacotto**. Regardless of your choice to dine-in or take-out, this Italian stallion is a guaranteed good time. Wallet-watching residents may rest easy as the price is always right at **Celeste**—known for churning out a perfect pizza as well as a regal Sunday afternoon repast. And in keeping with the value-meal theme, "Recession Specials"

are all the rage at legendary **Gray's Papaya**—the politically outspoken (check the window slogans) and quintessential hot dog chain.

BRUNCH AND BAKE

This dominantly residential region also jumped on the bakery-brunch bandwagon long before its counterparts; and its paths are rarely short on calorie-rich treats. From chocolates at **Mondel** or a trove of treasures at **Urbani Truffles**, to madeleines at **La Toulousaine**, the Upper West flaunts it all. In-the-know tenants get their sweet fix at **Levain**, where the addiction to chocolate chip cookies is only surpassed by their size. Meanwhile, not unlike **Magnolia's** cupcake following, **Grandaisy Bakery** is an Italian-inspired confectionary known to string along a coterie of sugar fiends. True to its posh surrounds, **Sugar & Plumm** is yet another master of the macaron. While cookies are also on offer here and a hit among kids, adults remain in awe of their brunch hits and sips.

A MEDLEY OF MARKETS

Such a "spirited" sense extends to all aspects of life in the Upper West Side—particularly food. For foodies and home cooks, the **Tucker Square Greenmarket** (anchored on West 66th and open on Thursdays and Saturdays) is popular for leafy greens and Mexican provisions—*papalo* anyone? Equally storied is the original **Fairway**, a culinary shrine to well-priced gourmet items. Intrepid shoppers should brave its famously cramped elevator to visit the exclusively organic second floor. Finally, no trip here is complete without a visit to **Zabar's**—home of all things kosher. Ogle their olives; grab some knishes to nosh on; then take the time to admire their line of exquisite kitchen supplies. But also remain assured that smaller purveyors still reside (and reign supreme) here. In fact, **Zingone Brothers**, once a fruit and vegetable stall, is now a famous, family owned-and-operated grocer that teems with conventional goodies...and treats you like a long-lost friend.

Andanada ⚬

A3

Spanish ✗✗

141 W. 69th St. bet. Broadway & Columbus Ave.

Subway: 72 St (Broadway)
Phone: 646-692-8762
Web: www.andanada141.com
Price: $$$

Lunch Sat – Sun
Dinner nightly

Wildly creative small plates, courtesy of Chef Manuel Berganza, take this vibrant Spanish favorite to the next level. A number of inventive items have graced the menu of late—a nod, perhaps, to Berganza's invigorated spirit. For instance, waffle-shaped *patatas bravas* arrive almost latke-like, light and tender with a golden exterior, and laced with aïoli as well as a tomato-based *brava* sauce. Another must from the menu includes the stuffed squid, plated on a black bean purée and filled with creamy black pudding, then garnished with herbed breadcrumbs, a brunoise of carrots, and smashed green peas.

Set off the busy stretch of Broadway, Andanada offers a lovely reprieve just below street level. Dim lights cast a soft glow over a dramatic mural of a bullfighter, giving the room a warm and sexy demeanor. Service is polished and nicely paced, even on weekend evenings when the place tends to be packed to the gills.

The crowd here is lively but sophisticated, and the space never feels too cramped to dine either at their date-friendly bar, in the pleasant glass atrium, or in the brick dining nook. Come Tuesday nights and at Sunday brunch, a guitarist and flamenco dancer may be found regaling the crowds.

Awadh

Indian

 B2

2588 Broadway (bet. 97th & 98th Sts.)

Subway: 96 St (Broadway)   Lunch & dinner daily
Phone: 646-861-3604
Web: www.awadhnyc.com
Price: $$

Awadh isn't an ordinary Indian spot, but one that advertises faithful flavors from Uttar Pradesh. This Northern Indian region excels in low- and slow-cooked *dum pukht* dishes, and the menu reads like a study in authenticity (there's no *tandoori* chicken in sight). Even the small room, polished and modern, is ideal for the city's well-traveled locals.

Top service and table settings further elevate the dining experience here, which begins with *aloo chutney pulao* or basmati rice scattered with silky potatoes and spiced peas. Couple this with *nali ki nihari* (perfectly pink lamb in a creamy cardamom-infused curry) or *khaas* chicken korma rich with nuts for a profound and regal repast. Then cool down over minty *pudina* raita, and just like that, you've become a regular.

Bar Boulud

French

A4

1900 Broadway (bet. 63rd & 64th Sts.)

Subway: 66 St - Lincoln Center   Lunch & dinner daily
Phone: 212-595-0303
Web: www.barboulud.com
Price: $$$

Somehow, Bar Boulud manages to be a destination for theatregoers while retaining the feel of a neighborhood spot. Both the ambience and cooking are unfussy, not overly structured, and anything but stuffy. The focus on wine is clear in everything from the abstract photographs of wine spills to the Jeroboam and Balthazar-sized bottles decorating the room. Take the time to explore this wine list and the daily specials.

The menu lists French classics, including wonderful charcuterie, cheese, pâtés, *tartes*, and *moules à poulettes*. Try the hearty onion soup, topped with a sourdough crouton and a melting layer of playfully stringy aged Swiss cheese. The croque madame is just as rich as expected, served with a fried egg and radish-frisée salad.

399

Barney Greengrass

Deli ✗

B2

541 Amsterdam Ave. (bet. 86th & 87th Sts.)

Subway: 86 St (Broadway) Lunch Tue – Sun
Phone: 212-724-4707
Web: www.barneygreengrass.com
Price: ☜

Bagels and bialys reign supreme in this culinary institution, set amid a culturally rich stretch dotted with lavish synagogues and purveyors of authentic deli delights. Not all are created equal, though, and little details make all the difference inside this sturgeon king, lauded for its weathered décor featuring muraled walls, a storied past, and service that is as authentically NY as can be. It's the sort of spot families flock to for brunch—imagine a triple-decker (tongue, turkey, and Swiss cheese) on rye paired with a pickle, of course.

Whether you take-out or eat-in, items like chopped liver with caramelized onions and boiled egg are sure to sate. Finish with a perfect black-and-white cookie, rugelach, or rice pudding, which are all favorites and fittingly so.

Bin 71

Italian

A3

237 Columbus Ave. (bet. 70th & 71st Sts.)

Subway: 72 St (Central Park West) Lunch & dinner Tue – Sun
Phone: 212-362-5446
Web: www.bin71.com
Price: $$

This little *enoteca* has been a smash-hit since day one and spawned its own cluster of knockoffs, though none have quite the same talent for pairing tasty little bites with excellent wines by the glass. The smartly designed space offers a marble U-shaped bar that makes use of every square inch but stays comfortable, especially for solo diners.

The Italian-leaning menu's small portions encourage diners to try a number of different plates. Start with gazpacho made from late-summer corn, avocado, and Jonah crab meat, or smoky-tender whole grilled squid. Meatballs are a delicious surprise, seasoned with cumin and fennel, then simmered in a deep golden sauce of white wine, bay leaf, and tangy lemon with nary a tomato in sight but plenty of bread for sopping.

Boulud Sud

Mediterranean XXX

20 W. 64th St. (bet. Broadway & Central Park West)

Subway: 66 St - Lincoln Center   Lunch & dinner daily
Phone: 212-595-1313
Web: www.bouludsud.com
Price: $$$

Far from a chichi French affair, Chef Daniel Boulud uses this ode to Mediterranean cuisine to explore all sides of the sea—from Morocco to Italy to Turkey and back again. Packed and lively, the dining room is airy with vaulted ceilings, natural lighting, and long striped banquettes. A semi-open kitchen allows a glimpse into the creation of deftly prepared delicacies.

The menu here is light yet dense with bright flavor, from the *crudo du jour* (perhaps cubes of hamachi with gently braised cauliflower, pignoli, white raisins, and herbs) to a tender octopus salad with Marcona almonds, arugula, and Jerez vinegar. Huge morsels of chicken with cous cous, wilted greens, and preserved lemons make a hearty dish, attractively served in a classic tagine vessel.

Bustan

Middle Eastern XX

487 Amsterdam Ave. (bet. 83rd & 84th Sts.)

Subway: 86 St (Broadway)   Lunch & dinner daily
Phone: 212-595-5050
Web: www.bustannyc.com
Price: $$

This colorful Upper Manhattan charmer bills itself as pan-Mediterranean, pulling inspiration from Italy, France, Spain, Morocco, Greece, Turkey and Israel. The result is darn good Middle Eastern food—and the inventive menu, together with the colorful space, done up in a blaze of color, shapes and textures, comes together to form something truly unique and special.

Dinner might begin with a plate of charred octopus sporting warm white bean *masabaha*, crushed green harissa, *bolargo* and *zhough*; or tender baby eggplant and grilled roasted eggplant stuffed with fragrant ground beef, *ras el hanout* and bulgur wheat. Then move on to stuffed lamb roulade, served with a fire-roasted eggplant and pepper purée, which is blended with yogurt-mint sauce for a bit of zest.

Café Frida

Mexican

B3

368 Columbus Ave. (bet. 77th & 78th Sts.)

Subway: 81 St - Museum of Natural History   Lunch & dinner daily
Phone: 212-712-2929
Web: www.cafefrida.com
Price: $$

Festive and friendly with happy hour margaritas that flow like the Rio Grande, Café Frida is almost better than it needs to be, considering its high-traffic location across from the Museum of Natural History. Overall, it feels like a rustic and welcoming hacienda. The extensive tequila list complements the relatively economical fare, showcasing traditional *moles*.

Peruse the menu while delving into the guacamole served in a *comal* with crisp chips and fiery habanero sauce on the side. Don't miss the clear and warming *sopa Azteca*, a restorative consommé bobbing with chicken, cactus leaf, and abundant vegetables as well as an array of accompaniments. Finally, *tlacoyos* spread with a creamy fava purée and slow-cooked pork carnitas, are *muy buenas*.

Fishtag

Seafood

A3

222 W. 79th St. (bet. Amsterdam Ave. & Broadway)

Subway: 79 St   Lunch Sat – Sun
Phone: 212-362-7470   Dinner nightly
Web: www.michaelpsilakis.com
Price: $$$

Slightly below street level in a classic townhouse, this charming restaurant from Chef Michael Psilakis offers the pleasures of the sea plus Mediterranean-inspired cuisine. Grab a seat at the marble-topped bar among exposed brick walls and wood panels for dishes that may be simple (grilled fish with greens, tomatoes, and olives) or inventive (headcheese-stuffed trout).

A modern Greek salad—tomato, cucumber, feta, olives, and grilled kale in a simple red wine vinaigrette—is a lovely start. Excellent bruschetta-like treats may bring an assortment of ingredients over sourdough bread, such as grilled prawns, tangy feta, and red chili peppers. Save room for sheep's milk dumplings with tomato fonduta, baby spinach, braised lamb, and white anchovies.

Dovetail ✿

 American 🗡🗡🗡

B3

103 W. 77th St. (at Columbus Ave.)

Subway: 81 St - Museum of Natural History
Phone: 212-362-3800
Web: www.dovetailnyc.com
Price: $$$

Lunch Sun
Dinner nightly

The name is apposite because this is one of those restaurants where all the elements fit together and complement each other perfectly, from the look of the room to the style of food and the tone of the service.

This large space has a chic and sophisticated feel, with pillars breaking it up into more manageable sections to ensure greater intimacy. The service is also just right: professional and structured yet undertaken with considerable warmth—you really feel as though you're being well looked after.

What sets this restaurant apart is that vegetables are given their own moment in the limelight rather than merely playing second fiddle to meat or fish. The ingredients are from the top drawer and the dishes are quite elaborate in design but pleasingly easy to eat. Fluke crudo comes at the perfect temperature so that maximum flavor is revealed; cauliflower velouté has a remarkable depth of flavor; and the sirloin and short rib reveals a kitchen strong on technique as well as an understanding of textures and the balance of flavors. It would seem churlish to end with anything other than their excellent chocolate soufflé.

Gastronomia Culinaria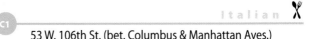

C1

Italian 🍴

53 W. 106th St. (bet. Columbus & Manhattan Aves.)

Subway: 103 St (Central Park West)   Lunch & dinner daily
Phone: 212-663-1040
Web: www.gastronomiaculinaria.com
Price: $$

Chef/owner Vincenzo Pezzilli opened this tiny gem a few years ago to a flood of attention—and the applause rightly continues. Pezzilli is so passionate and hands on at Gastronomia Culinaria that he can be found in-house most evenings, a very lucky thing for guests who get to enjoy all that delicious food he's carefully attending to.

This chef has deep roots in Rome, and as a result his pasta is, as you might expect, some of the best the city has to offer. Witness a nest of perfectly cooked pappardelle treated with cauliflower florets, buffalo mozzarella, pine nuts and raisins. Come solo, on a date, or with friends: the *hosteria* offers a row of private tables, a communal table, as well as a buzzing bar area with comfortable seats for single diners.

Gennaro

B2

Italian 🍴🍴

665 Amsterdam Ave. (bet. 92nd & 93rd Sts.)

Subway: 96 St (Broadway)   Dinner nightly
Phone: 212-665-5348
Web: www.gennaronyc.com
Price: $$

Despite its age, Gennaro hasn't lost its good looks or popularity—it still packs in hungry locals nightly, who aren't deterred by its borderline gritty surrounds or no-reservations policy. Come early or risk waiting, which isn't so bad considering their bar, whose by-the-glass offerings are vast and very appealing with both familiar and unusual Italian choices.

The menu can be overwhelming considering its long list of pastas and daily specials, so trust your gut and you can't go wrong. Start with the polenta, served almost *quattro stagione*-style, with gorgonzola, prosciutto, and sliced portobellos; before twirling your taste buds around chewy *bucatini* showered with pecorino and pepper. The tiramisu is a light, creamy, and fluffy slam dunk.

Good Enough to Eat

American ✗

B2

520 Columbus Ave. (at 85th St.)

Subway: 86 St (Broadway)
Phone: 212-496-0163
Web: www.goodenoughtoeat.com
Price: $$

Lunch & dinner daily

This is the place with the cows. You can't miss them—they are everywhere. And yet, Good Enough to Eat defies its own kitsch with undeniable charm, good food, and desserts that surpass expectation. Imagine the best coconut sponge cake you've ever had. This one is better. Stools swivel as if inviting guests to turn and face the display cases of cakes, cookies, and bread pudding throughout their meal.

As a prelude to your pie, choose from an enjoyable array of lunchtime salads and sandwiches. Dinner brings classic American fare like roasted chicken or meatloaf with gravy and mashed potatoes. Turn their downright gorgeous biscuits into pre-dessert with a thick layer of strawberry butter. Scoring a seat at brunch is a competitive sport, but well-worth the effort.

Lincoln

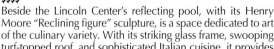

Italian ✗✗✗

A4

142 W. 65th St. (bet. Amsterdam Ave. & Broadway)

Subway: 66 St - Lincoln Center
Phone: 212-359-6500
Web: www.lincolnristorante.com
Price: $$$$

Lunch Wed – Sun
Dinner nightly

Beside the Lincoln Center's reflecting pool, with its Henry Moore "Reclining figure" sculpture, is a space dedicated to art of the culinary variety. With its striking glass frame, swooping turf-topped roof, and sophisticated Italian cuisine, it provides the ideal spot for pre- and post-show sustenance.

The chefs put on a different kind of show in their display kitchen behind a glass screen, presenting a seasonally inspired assortment of modern Italian fare. *Soppressata di polpo* blends aesthetics and flavor with a cross section of tender octopus rounds framed in beef tendon aspic garnished by sliced caper berries and pickled Tropea onions. The cooking is robust and generously proportioned, although the care and craftsmanship of previous years is no longer evident.

Jean-Georges ✿ ✿ ✿

Contemporary 〤〤〤〤

A4

1 Central Park West (bet. 60th & 61st Sts.)

Subway: 59 St - Columbus Circle   Lunch & dinner daily
Phone: 212-299-3900
Web: www.jean-georgesrestaurant.com
Price: **$$$$**

The crown-jewel restaurant of a crown-jewel Trump hotel, Jean-Georges reigns supreme over the Central Park dining scene. The restaurant's separate entrance can be something of a whirlwind as guests must pass through buzzing Nougatine to arrive at this refined silver-gray dining room. Still, those immense windows, columns, and twinkling views make it a very special place.

On weekdays, the feel is formal and business-driven, while weekends hum with tourists, socialites, and an easier vibe. The highly professional staff is one well-oiled and smooth machine. To dine here for the first time is to be blown away by brilliance; to come again and again is to realize that certain elements of the cooking flaunt more of a patina than a shine. Yet even certain menu classics continue to earn new accolades, especially the ever-memorable foie gras brûlée with dried sour cherries, pistachios, white Port gelée, and a spiced fig jam that leaves you weak in the knees. Desserts venture to rise above the savory dishes in theme and harmony. Grand finales include an homage to chocolate with hazelnut chocolate mille-feuille, chocolate pudding tart, and chocolate sable.

Lunch is a superb option for those who don't want to break the bank.

Macchina

Italian XX

2758 Broadway (at 106th St.)

Subway: 103 St (Broadway)
Phone: 212-203-9954
Web: www.macchina.nyc
Price: $$

Dinner nightly

As the name implies, Macchina combines an industrial design's raw edge and lots of iron with wood-fired Italian-American food just a stone's throw from Columbia University. A wall papered with newsprint, seasonal flower arrangements, and doors that swing open in warmer weather soften the look and feel.

Pizzas showcase quality ingredients, like *fior di latte*, pecorino, and cherry tomatoes over an impressively thin crust. Also try the finely tuned pastas, like carrot agnolotti "serpente" topped with amaretti and mint-hazelnut crumble in brown butter. "Al forno" items are an absolute highlight. Don't miss the cauliflower "steak," beautifully cooked in the wood-burning oven, served with the bold flavors of Castelvetrano olives, salsa verde, and sorrel.

Mezzogiorno

Italian XX

2791 Broadway (bet. 107th & 108th Sts.)

Subway: Cathedral Pkwy/110 St (Broadway)
Phone: 646-895-9624
Web: www.mezzogiorno.com
Price: $$

Lunch & dinner daily

This beautiful Italian gift arrives courtesy of Lorenzo and Nicola Ansuini, the talented Italian-born brothers behind the trailblazing SoHo outpost by the same name. Here on the Upper West Side, they bring their authentic Italian fare to a spacious, rustic dining room with a generous bar and an enclosed front patio that might just hold some of the best seats in the house.

Kick things off with the feather-light house-made gnocchi, topped with a feisty sausage ragout; or homemade *fazzoletti al rosmarino*—chewy, rosemary-laced "kerchiefs" served with earthy white beans, tomato and crushed pepper. Heartier items are equally delicious, so try *peposo dell'Impruneta*, a Florentine classic stew of beef shank braised in red wine with black pepper and fragrant sage.

Miss Mamie's Spoonbread Too

Southern ✗

C1

366 W. 110th St./Cathedral Pkwy. (bet. Columbus & Manhattan Aves.)

Subway: Cathedral Pkwy/110 St (Central Park West)   Lunch & dinner daily
Phone: 212-865-6744
Web: www.spoonbreadinc.com
Price: 🍋

Come to Miss Mamie's and plan to indulge, Southern style. This tiny institution recently got a makeover in the bright, clean dining room—think comfier wicker chairs, roomier tables, and lots of flower arrangements. Despite its more sophisticated appearance, the kitchen still embraces such tried-and-true classics as fried chicken thighs with black-eyed peas and collard greens, Louisiana catfish, and a creamy red velvet cake for dessert. Grab a fresh-squeezed lemonade and dive into the sampler, stocked with deep-fried shrimp, fall-off-the-bone beef short ribs, more fried chicken, and probably too many sides of cornbread stuffing and hop 'n John.

And if on offer dive in mouth first into a wedge of classically Southern banana pudding.

Momoya

Asian ✗✗

B3

427 Amsterdam Ave. (bet. 80th & 81st Sts.)

Subway: 79 St   Lunch & dinner daily
Phone: 212-580-0007
Web: www.momoyanyc.com
Price: $$

This longtime fixture is something of a local beacon, standing well above its competition, thanks to reliably good food and a consistently polished atmosphere. Everything here exudes subdued masculinity and sophistication, from the clean white marble bar and slate floors to the curving wood wall.

Begin with a highlight in the mushroom salad—these warm enoki are beautifully caramelized and dressed in yuzu-soy vinaigrette with shallots and freshly cracked pepper. *Yakitori* offerings are just as pleasing, like the tender cubes of grilled beef with pearl onions and scallions. Signature sushi rolls are American-style crowd-pleasers, such as the Greenwich made with spicy yellowtail, jalapeño and asparagus wrapped in yuba and topped with spicy eel sauce.

Noche Mexicana II

Mexican

B1

842 Amsterdam Ave. (at 101st St.)

Subway: 103 St (Broadway)   Lunch & dinner daily
Phone: 212-662-6900
Web: N/A
Price:

If you had a Mexican *tía*, you'd want her to be one of the lovely chefs pounding masa and wrapping tamales at Noche Mexicana II. This tasty corner is dominated by two veranda doors that open onto the sidewalk—a perfect setting for the specialties this talented kitchen sends out routinely. Imagine *huaraches con bistec* topped with tender beef and teeming with refried beans, bright tomatoes, and sour cream. Those who venture uptown will not be met with disappointment: *tomate verde mole* is accented with toasted pumpkin seeds and piquant chilies that cover the tender chicken; while brick-red *chilate* boasts plump shrimp swimming in a spicy *guajillo* broth with a sprinkling of cilantro and *queso fresco*. A fresh flan, the only dessert on the menu, is simply excellent.

Nougatine

Contemporary

A4

1 Central Park West (at 60th St.)

Subway: 59 St - Columbus Circle   Lunch & dinner daily
Phone: 212-299-3900
Web: www.jean-georgesrestaurant.com
Price: $$

Nougatine is a bright, stylish, and contemporary space on the ground floor of the Trump International Hotel—bookended by an open kitchen at one end and a huge picture window the other. What really sets it apart, however, is the service: the restaurant is run with lots of flair and no little professionalism by a vast army of servers—this is not one of the places where you need to use semaphore to get noticed by your waiter. The food is light and current and the lunch menu, with dishes taken from the main à la carte, is a positive steal—although the immaculately coiffured clientele do not seem the sort to be overly concerned by the concept of a bargain. Dishes like veal Milanese are confidently executed and it's worth leaving room for desserts, like apple tart.

The Ribbon

American ✗✗

B3

20 W. 72nd St. (bet. Central Park West & Columbus Ave.)

Subway: 72 St (Central Park West)
Phone: 646-416-9080
Web: www.theribbonnyc.com
Price: $$$

Lunch & dinner nightly

Eric and Bruce Bromberg, the talented brothers behind the city's Blue Ribbon empire, strike again. This time in an enormous, industrial-chic space featuring a bustling bar and long communal tables up front; and a handsome, light-filled dining room with a visible kitchen.

The Ribbon's well-sourced menu is an ode to classic American dishes, with a fantastic rotating butcher's board; a tempting raw bar; and a roster of burger variations, including oxtail and mushroom. Don't miss the house-made cavatelli tossed with shredded chicken, creamy artichoke hearts, blistered cherry tomatoes, and tender wilted spinach. The juicy, spit-roasted Amish chicken marinated in sage and Riesling, and served with spicy mustard and crispy sage leaves, is yet another highlight.

Spiga

Italian ✗✗

B2

200 W. 84th St. (bet. Amsterdam Ave. & Broadway)

Subway: 86 St (Broadway)
Phone: 212-362-5506
Web: www.spiganyc.com
Price: $$$

Dinner nightly

Located among classic brownstones, Spiga presents a setting and cuisine that is unrivaled in this neighborhood. Its style sets the scene for a romantic, relaxed meal and suits the area through exposed brick walls and wine bottles lining wood shelves. Servers charm with their thick, Italian accents and candles flicker on tightly packed, dark-wood tables.

A rotating list of Italian cheeses and cured meats makes a fine appetizer and prelude to a pasta course that shifts with the seasons. Soft, light potato and spinach gnocchi are executed precisely, with mascarpone, asparagus, and cherry tomatoes. Save room for the entrées, such as a pan-seared halibut fillet with clams and mussels in a tomato broth, set over a crispy polenta cake.

Sushi Yasaka

Japanese ✗

251 W. 72nd St. (bet. Broadway & West End Ave.)

Subway: 72 St (Broadway)
Phone: 212-496-8466
Web: www.sushiyasaka.com
Price: $$

Lunch & dinner daily

There are no decorative distractions at this efficient if spare *sushi-ya* located a few steps below street level. The simple space offers three rows of tables, unadorned white walls, and a well-lit counter in the rear, and is warmed up by enthusiastic servers. Devoted customers know the draw here is not atmosphere, but the quality and excellent value omakase.

Fish can be surprisingly luscious, especially the salmon, which has a remarkably clean finish and great salty note. The medium fatty tuna needs nothing more than a kiss of soy sauce. A 12-course omakase might also include giant clam, uni, sea eel, fluke, smelt roe, and for dessert, tamago. The *kanto* soba is excellent too, with a rich soy-bonito broth brimming with scallions, seaweed, and a fish cake.

Vai

Mediterranean ✗✗

429 Amsterdam Ave. (bet. 80th & 81st Sts.)

Subway: 79 St
Phone: 212-362-4500
Web: www.vairestaurant.com
Price: $$

Lunch Fri – Sun
Dinner nightly

Careful attention was paid to give this attractive space a special allure. The interior uses votive candles, dark wood, and exposed brick to great affect. The curving marble bar is an excellent spot for solo dining and proffers a nice happy hour. It also offers narrow views into the bustling kitchen, where Chef/owner Vincent Chirico is running a very energetic show.

The menu may feature under-represented pasta like perfectly chewy *spaccatelli* served as a sort of a carbonara with pancetta, creamy parmesan and a wonderfully runny egg. The crisp-skinned roasted chicken is delicious, warm, and elegant, set over braised kale and caramelized fingerling potatoes. Italian-American desserts like the white-chocolate cheesecake are predictably pleasing.

The Bronx

The Bronx

The only borough attached to the island of Manhattan, the Bronx boasts such awe-inspiring sights as the Bronx Zoo, Hall of Fame for Great Americans, as well as Yankee Stadium. However, it is also revered as a hotbed of culinary treasures. For instance, The New York Botanical Garden is devoted to education and hosts many garden- and food-related classes. In fact, the Botanical Garden's **Bronx Green-Up** is an acclaimed program aimed at improving inner-city areas by offering them agricultural advice and practical training. Located along the west side, Belmont is a residential quarter marked by various ethnic and religious groups. Once an Italian hub, its population is now comprised of Hispanics (primarily Puerto Ricans), African-Americans, West Indians, and Albanians. Much of the Bronx today consists of parkland, like Pelham Bay Park with its sandy Orchard Beach. And since a day at the beach is never complete without salty eats, you'll want to step into pizza paradise—**Louie & Ernie's**—for a seriously cheesy slice. Just as home cooks and haute chefs alike stock up on spices, herbs, and seeds from the myriad speciality stores around the way, thirsty travelers pop into **Gun Hill Brewing Co.** for an impressive bevy and more. Beyond, City Island is a gem of a coastal community teeming with seafood spots. **The Black Whale** is a local fixture frequented for its classic-meets-contemporary cuisine and quenching cocktails. Savor their offerings, either inside the quirky dining room or out in the garden. When the sun beats down, pop into **Lickety Split** for a cooling scoop of sorbet or ice cream, or both! Belmont's most renowned street, Arthur Avenue, is home to Italian food paradise—

The Arthur Avenue Retail Market. This enclosed oasis is a culinary emporium overrun with self-proclaimed foodies as well as famed epicureans, who can be seen prowling for quality pasta, homemade sausages, extra virgin olive oil, notorious heroes, heirloom seeds, and so much more. Some begin by diving into a ball of rich, gooey mozzarella at **Joe's Deli** (open on Sundays!). Others may grab them to go, along with pistachio-studded mortadella from **Teitel Brothers** or *salumi* from **Calabria Pork Store**.

Beyond this venerable marketplace, find early-risers ravenously tearing into freshly baked breads from either **Terranova** or **Addeo**— the choices are plenty. Come lunchtime, find a myriad of Eastern European eats. At **Tony & Tina's Pizzeria** skip the signatures and opt for Albanian or Kosovar *burek* (flaky rolls with sweet pumpkin purée). Just as **Xochimilco Restaurant** is a playground for families with tots, South Bronxite singles revel in Ecuadorian delights like *bollon de verde* at **Ricuras Panderia**. Then strolling southeast find **Gustiamo's** warehouse, which continues to flourish as a city-

wide favorite for regional Italian specialties including olive oils, pastas, and San Marzano tomatoes. Similarly, the butchers at **Honeywell Meat Market** can be seen teaching newbies a thing or two about breaking down a side of beef, which always reigns as king. But, over on Willis Avenue, Mott Haven's main drag, bright awnings designate a plethora of Puerto Rican diners and Mexican bodegas.

YANKEE STADIUM

Home to the "sultans of swat" (AKA the "Bronx Bombers"), **Yankee Stadium** is *the* spot for world-champion baseball. And what goes best with baseball? Big and bold bites of course, all of which may be found at the stadium's own food court. **Lobel's**, the ultimate butcher, is one such tenant and crafts perfectly marbled steak sandwiches to order. Even the Carbone-Torrisi boys have set up shop here at **Parm**, hooking fans with hearty sammies and heavenly sweets. The bromance continues at **Brother Jimmy's**, one of New York's

best-selling barbecue chains, cooking up the staples —think pulled pork, fried pickles, baked beans, and more. Refined palates will relish the farm-fresh produce from **Melissa's Farmers Market**, just as the cool kids are sure to swoon over the sips at **Tommy Bahama Bar**.

COMFORT FOODS

Eastchester, Wakefield, and Williamsbridge are home to diverse cultures, and ergo, each of their unique eats. Still, there are everyday vendors to be frequented here. Just as **Astor Prime Meats** proudly presents premium grade meats for every type of holiday feast, **G & R Deli** pays homage to the neighborhood's deep Italian roots by delivering authentic flavors in sausages and meat sauce sold by the quart. Then there's **Sal & Dom's** who stick with this line of duty by serving deliciously flaky *sfogliatelle*. Over on Grand Concourse, **Bate** and **Papaye** cook up a buffet of fresh, pungent Ghanian goodies for the surrounding West African

community. Indulge in this savory, smoky spread before closing over a treat at **Kingston Tropical Bakery**. **Valencia Bakery** is yet another sweet marvel among the borough's mighty Puerto Rican masses.

It is important to note that Asian food has officially arrived in the Bronx, with **Phnom Penh-Nha Trang Market** bagging a variety of important Vietnamese ingredients necessary for a Southeast Asian-themed dinner party. **Sabrosura** offers an excellent blend of Spanish and Chinese inspiration, and even purists can't help but crave their crispy yuca chips paired with sweet crabmeat. But, bringing it back to the basics, the hamburger craze rages on uptown at **Bronx Alehouse**, pouring a litany of beers. Bronx beer you say? You bet. And, there is an equally thrilling selection to be relished at **Jonas Bronck's Beer Co.** or **Bronx Brewery** over on East 136th Street. Hosts keep the house party hoppin' and stoves turning by stocking up on pantry staples for

late-night snacking from **Palm Tree Marketplace**. Also, find everything you may need here for a Jamaican-themed night. **Hunts Point Food Distribution Center** is another epicurean wonder, vital to NYC's food services industry. This expansive 329-acre complex of wholesalers, distributors, and food-processing vendors is also home to the **Hunts Point Meat Market** that sells every imaginable cut under the sun. Also housed within these grounds is the **Hunts Point Terminal Produce Market** supplying patrons with fantastic variety, as well as the famous **Fulton Fish Market**. This formidable network of stores caters to the city's most celebrated chefs, restaurateurs,

and wholesale suppliers. And such mouthwatering cruising is bound to result in a series of voracious cravings, all of which may be gratified at **Sam's Soulfood** located on the Grand Concourse, a classic joint oozing with potent doses of Bronx flavor.

RIVERDALE

Riverdale is not known for its culinary distinction. However, its winning location as the northernmost tip of the city affords it incredible views, and as a result, lavish mansions. Moneyed residents mingle with curious visitors over the aromatic offerings at **S&S Cheesecake**, or freshly baked babkas at the always-primped **Garden Gourmet** on Broadway. From here, those in need of more stirring sips may head to **Skyview Wines** boasting exceptional kosher varietals. Then, finish with style and flair at **Lloyd's Carrot Cake**, which has been doling out divine slices of red velvet or German chocolate cake to the community for over a quarter-century.

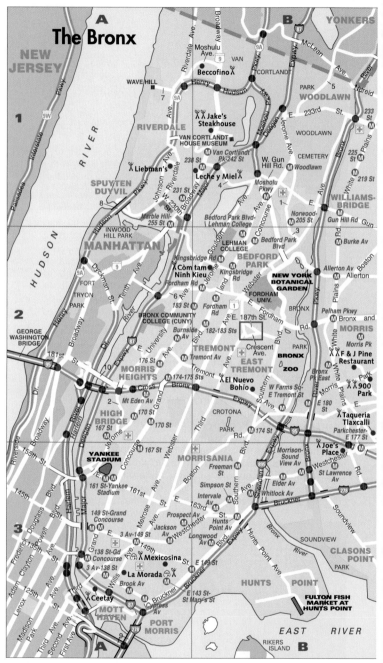

The Bronx

NEW JERSEY

NEW YORK

YONKERS

MANHATTAN

HUDSON RIVER

EAST RIVER

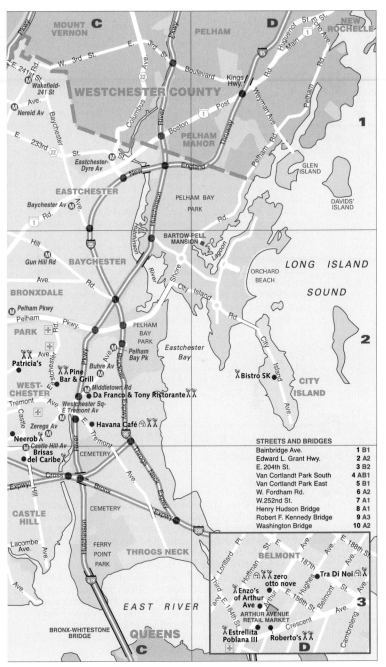

STREETS AND BRIDGES

Street/Bridge	Grid
Bainbridge Ave.	**1** B1
Edward L. Grant Hwy.	**2** A2
E. 204th St.	**3** B2
Van Cortlandt Park South	**4** AB1
Van Cortlandt Park East	**5** B1
W. Fordham Rd.	**6** A2
W.252nd St.	**7** A1
Henry Hudson Bridge	**8** A1
Robert F. Kennedy Bridge	**9** A3
Washington Bridge	**10** A2

Beccofino

Italian

B1

5704 Mosholu Ave. (at Fieldston Rd.)

Subway: Van Cortlandt Park-242 St   Dinner nightly
Phone: 718-432-2604
Web: www.beccofinorestaurant.com
Price: $$

Beccofino is an earnest neighborhood darling that is never taken for granted. Inside, string lights, exposed brick, and colorful, life-sized posters fashion a rustic bistro setting for indulging in their Italian-American favorites (with plenty of bread for sopping up sauces). Expect meals to be well-paced and the dedicated staff to ensure that everything is made to your liking.

Some dishes stray from being genuinely Italian but are nonetheless popular and surprisingly good, like seafood-stuffed manicotti topped with a generous amount of shrimp bisque and mild mozzarella. A crowd-pleasing chicken Milanese arrives as an insanely savory cutlet, pounded thin and sautéed, topped with broccoli rabe, chili flakes, spicy tomato sauce, and more melting mozzarella.

Bistro SK

French

D2

273 City Island Ave. (bet. Carroll & Hawkins Sts.)

Subway: Pelham Bay Park (& bus Bx29)   Lunch Sun
Phone: 718-885-1670   Dinner Tue – Sun
Web: www.bistrosk.com
Price: $$

In a neighborhood better known for seafood, this charming bistro breaks the mold with hearty plates of French fare. The husband-wife team lures locals into a snug, dimly lit space with marvelous mahogany-hued French onion soup finished with brandy and a sultry mound of Gruyère. Particular attention to the art of service shines through the dining room. A craving for classic Gallic dishes will surely be satisfied by cooking that is more solid than revelatory. Signatures include a tender roulade of chicken breast stuffed with spinach and mushrooms, served alongside French beans and fluffy, buttery mashed potatoes tucked with black olive for a bit of "wow!" For a finale, try the pineapple upside-down cake with a grilled ring of fruit and drizzle of caramel.

Brisas del Caribe

C3

1207 Castle Hill Ave. (bet. Ellis & Gleason Aves.)

Subway: Castle Hill Av
Phone: 718-794-9710
Web: www.brisasdelcaribe.net
Price: 😊😊

Lunch & dinner daily

Make your way inside this local charmer to find a room adorned with frescoes of Caribbean beach scenes and benches to ease the wait for tables. But really, everyone's eyes are drawn to the piles of food, *sopas*, and counters laden with freshly made cakes sold by the slice. While pernil rules in this borough—and Brisas indeed offers a great version—this kitchen's forte is Dominican food. In fact, find large families and groups of locals enjoying copious amounts of hot, tasty, and ridiculously affordable specialties.

Start with a hearty treat like *sancocho*, or go for *relleno de papa*, deep-fried mashed potatoes stuffed with cheese and ground meat. Then dive into a helping of the *patitas de cerdo*, a stew of pig's feet with cassava, potatoes, herbs, and strips of tripe.

Ceetay

A3

129 Alexander Ave. (at Bruckner Blvd.)

Subway: 3 Av - 138 St
Phone: 718-618-7020
Web: www.ceetay.com
Price: $$

Lunch Mon – Fri
Dinner nightly

Its location near Hunts Point and the burgeoning South Bronx art community may have put it on the foodie trail, but Ceetay has become known for inventive Asian cooking at its best. The open kitchen offers diners a view of the race among cooks cutting, washing, and packing up an endless number of takeout orders. The tiny dining room features Mason jar fixtures, a handcrafted bar, and a wall papered with yellowing Asian newspapers.

Creative specials include a seared square of sesame-studded rice "bruschetta" topped with avocado purée, tuna tartare, and frizzled onions. Don't miss such high-flying maki as the Kawasaki roll with a mishmash of crab, scallion, sweet glaze, and more. Traditional sushi here stands equally strong, with very nice *maguro*, *ebi*, and uni.

Còm tam Ninh-Kieu

Vietnamese

Vietnamese

B2

2641 Jerome Ave. (bet. 192nd & 193rd Sts.)

Subway: Kingsbridge Rd (Jerome Ave.) Lunch & dinner daily
Phone: 718-365-2680
Web: N/A
Price: 🍸

It's a bare bones operation at this Vietnamese joint, tucked beneath an elevated subway train and located on Jerome Avenue – but none of it will matter once you give yourself over to the amazing food. The large Vietnamese population that inhabits this pocket of the Bronx is undoubtedly in *pho* heaven—there are 16 varieties of the good stuff, packed with aromatic spices like star anise and coriander, and then served with a riot of Asian basil, crispy bean sprouts, chili slices and lime.

Those in the mood for a sandwich may opt for the delicious *bánh mì*, loaded with cilantro, jalapeño, pickled carrots, daikon radish and a dash of slow-burning chili paste. Or simply dive into the equally good *bánh mì dac biet*, layered with head cheese, *thit nguoi* and pâté.

Da Franco & Tony Ristorante

Italian 🍴🍴

C2

2815 Middletown Rd. (bet. Hutchinson River Pkwy. East & Mulford Ave.)

Subway: Middletown Rd Lunch & dinner daily
Phone: 718-684-2815
Web: www.dafrancoandtony.com
Price: $$

There is so much to love here, where sharply dressed servers dish up equal parts warmth, hospitality, and steaming bowls of scrumptious pasta. The menu leans heavily towards that nostalgic sort of red-sauce, Italian-American cooking that is again finding more and more respect, thanks to mouthwatering dishes like *merluzzo marechiaro* and veal scaloppini.

The interior is lovely, which is particularly important since you're in for a bit of a wait (everything is made fresh to order). But who could complain when tender knobs of potato gnocchi arrive tossed in basil pesto with plush gorgonzola cheese and walnuts. Their chicken *scarpariello* is perfectly caramelized, deeply flavored, and bathed in a sinfully thick wine broth, fragrant with rosemary.

El Nuevo Bohío

Puerto Rican

B2

791 E. Tremont Ave. (at Mapes Ave.)

Subway: West Farms Sq - E Tremont Av   Lunch & dinner daily
Phone: 718-294-3905
Web: www.elnuevobohiorestaurant.com
Price: 😊

On a prominent corner, windows filled with *lechòn* lure passersby with mouthwatering visions of shiny-skinned roast pork. Beloved by the local Puerto Rican community, the front room is minimally adorned and often filled with lines of those waiting for to-go orders. Snag a seat in the back—where bright walls are flooded with photos—for friendly table service.

Begin with *morcilla*, a thick blood sausage bright with chili peppers, cilantro, and garlic before moving on to the succulent *pernil*, pork shoulder roasted to a luxuriously crisp exterior and served with stinging garlic sauce, rice and beans, and plantains. Don't miss an array of complex *sopas*—from rich cow's feet soup with yucca and sweet potato to *asopado de carmarones*, a hearty combo of rice and shrimp.

Enzo's of Arthur Ave

Italian

D3

2339 Arthur Ave. (bet. Crescent Ave. & 186th St.)

Subway: Fordham Rd (Grand Concourse)   Lunch & dinner daily
Phone: 718-733-4455
Web: N/A
Price: $$

You'd be hard-pressed to find a soul with a bad word on this long-standing red-sauce restaurant nestled into the Bronx's thriving Arthur Avenue. Make your way past the front doors to enter into either their thumping dining room or expanded and jammed bar, come weekends. Servers whiz by, delivering plates of glistening clams *oreganata* and tender fish Livornese. Enzo's affable manager is usually a step behind, checking on your table like you're one of the family.

Begin with soft knobs of gnocchi in tegamino, with tomato, parmesan and a kiss of sage. Then dive into juicy pork chops floating in white wine sauce and topped with spicy pickled cherry peppers. Tender chicken breast arrives stuffed with prosciutto, mozzarella, and mushroom-cognac sauce.

Estrellita Poblana III

Mexican

D3

2328 Arthur Ave. (bet. Crescent Ave. & 186th St.)

Subway: Fordham Rd (Grand Concourse)   Lunch & dinner daily
Phone: 718-220-7641
Web: www.estrellitapoblanaiii.com
Price:

The Arthur Avenue area may be known as the artery of the Little Italy of the Bronx, but a Mexican restaurant shines here with its fluffy tamales loaded with tender, fragrant corn, and much more. The small interior is brightened with gold walls, a fuchsia ceiling, and three stars set in the fuchsia coffered ceiling. Exposed brick and a semi-open kitchen complete the comfortable scene.

Conversation is common between the pleasant servers and other diners, as searing hot *sopa* with shredded chicken and a nest of *fideos*, is placed on an immaculate table. The *bistec Estrellita* is served with a fiery habanero sauce, topped with *pico de gallo*, and flanked by a side of rice and beans. Flan is a lovely finish—though that generous steak may fulfill even the heartiest appetite.

F & J Pine Restaurant

Italian

B2

1913 Bronxdale Ave. (bet. Matthews & Muliner Aves.)

Subway: Bronx Park East   Lunch & dinner daily
Phone: 718-792-5956
Web: www.fjpine.com
Price: $$

This Bronx institution began as a simple storefront eatery in 1969. These days, Frankie & Johnnie's Tavern covers an entire city block, with a catering hall to boot. Locals, celebrities, Yankees and their fans alike love to roll in and pull up their sleeves in this large dining room, with its welcoming bar, visible pizza oven, backyard garden, and brass tags listing luminaries like "Rocco the Jeweler."

The Bastone family has been critical to the Bronx food scene for over 50 years now, and it shows through cooking that is as solid as it gets. No one is reinventing the wheel, but gargantuan portions of beloved Italian-American classics like stuffed pork chops, delicious pizzette, tender stuffed artichokes, and fresh seafood pastas more than hit the spot.

Havana Café

 Latin American ✗✗

C2

3151 E. Tremont Ave. (at LaSalle Ave.)

Subway: N/A   Lunch & dinner daily
Phone: 718-518-1800
Web: www.bronxhavanacafe.com
Price: $$

This bumping Latin café straddles a corner of the Bronx's Schuylerville section, and when the weather permits, grab a seat at its special palm tree-shaded sidewalk retreat. Inside, you'll find a friendly bar, ceiling fans and tropical fronds. The partners behind this operation have deep roots in the Bronx, and they've managed to hit on a great formula here—so much so, they've opened a second venture nearby called Cabo.

The classic Cuban-American black bean soup, *frijoles negro*, gets a bright, zesty kick from lime-spiked crème fraîche. *Palomilla*, a cut of tender beef, is topped with caramelized onions and paired with yucca fries; while a dessert of coconut rice pudding empanadas is filled with sweet dates and sided by vanilla dipping sauce.

Jake's Steakhouse

Steakhouse ✗✗

B1

6031 Broadway (bet. Manhattan College Pkwy. & 251st St.)

Subway: Van Cortlandt Park-242 St   Lunch & dinner daily
Phone: 718-581-0182
Web: www.jakessteakhouse.com
Price: $$$

This bustling and upscale restaurant is one of the borough's best steakhouses. Duck inside the limestone facade and you'll find a clubby, multi-level space with lots of private nooks, a lively, well-stocked bar with the latest games on, and an upstairs wall of windows overlooking Van Cortlandt Park.

A true American steakhouse ought to have a substantial shrimp cocktail, and at Jake's this classic starter arrives fresh and plump with the sweetness of the shrimp offset by a tangy cocktail sauce. Any steak on Jake's menu can be topped with Gorgonzola and a thatch of frizzled fried onions, though a succulent and well-marbled T-bone seared to rosy-pink perfection begs for little beyond a fork, knife and good conversation.

Joe's Place

 B3

1841 Westchester Ave. (at Thieriot Ave.)

Subway: Parkchester   Lunch & dinner daily
Phone: 718-918-2947
Web: www.joesplacebronx.com
Price: $$

From *abuelas* to *niños*, locals know to come to this "place" for solid Puerto Rican food. A glance at the wall of politicos and celebrities who have dined here proves how well-loved it truly is. The space is divided into two very different areas: a classic lunch counter also serving takeout, and a dark wood dining room.

A wonderful Nuyerican accent can be heard at gathering family tables and tasted in classic dishes like *mofongo al pilon de bistec* (savory shredded beef over mashed plantains) or *pernil con arroz y gandules* (roasted pork with pigeon peas and rice). Prices become even more reasonable when you realize that dishes are big enough to be split three ways. Daily *sopa* specials are a highlight, but end meals with hot and flaky cheese-filled *pastelito*.

La Morada

Mexican

A3

308 Willis Ave. (bet. 140th & 141st Sts.)

Subway: 3 Av - 138 St   Lunch & dinner Mon – Sat
Phone: 718-292-0235
Web: www.lamoradanyc.com
Price:

Tucked among the many little Willis Avenue bodegas, this sweet spot stands out for its authentic Oaxacan food. It's a homey, no frills sort of place that welcomes everyone, and the owner loves to chat about the traditions of Oaxacan cooking—or history or art as evidenced by the impromptu lending library that has emerged in the comfy back seating area.

This part of Mexico is known for its incredible moles, so sample a wonderfully complex red pumpkin seed version (*pipián rojo de pepitas*) with pork spare ribs. Another, the glossy *mole Oaxaqueño*, arrives fragrant with cloves, tomatillos, plantains, peanuts and chocolate, served over chicken. Don't miss the wildly fresh tamales, filled with silky chicken, spices and covered with a rich tomatillo sauce.

Leche y Miel

? D o m i n i c a n ?

5761 Broadway (bet. 236th & 237th Sts.)

Subway: 238 St   Lunch daily
Phone: 718-708-5787   Dinner Thu – Tue
Web: N/A
Price: ⊖⊗

Caught under the shadows of a big, neon McDonald's sign to its north, the entrance to this little Dominican-owned restaurant looks less than promising. But take a chance, drift inside, and you'll find big flavor awaits. The interior is simple and sparse, with a few tables in neat rows, a snatch of fresh flowers, an open kitchen and a stack of fine dining cookbooks. A lot of the menu at Leche Y Miel consists of Chef Rideiby Peña's cherished comfort foods from his beloved homeland. Classics like stewed tripe, cassava fritters and anything slathered in the powerful, delicious *sofrito*, are like a trip to the island without the airfare. Don't miss the wonderful daily specials or the wildly tender oxtail, a rich, smoky stew laced with—surprise—roasted eggplant.

Liebman's

D e l i

552 W. 235th St. (bet. Johnson & Oxford Aves.)

Subway: 231 St   Lunch & dinner daily
Phone: 718-548-4534
Web: www.liebmansdeli.com
Price: ⊖⊗

Some things never change (phew!) and thankfully this iconic kosher deli is still stuffing sandwiches and ladling matzoh ball soup (reputed for its healing powers), just as it has for over 50 years. Residents wax poetic about the place: a true-blue deli with a neon sign in the front window, the grill slowly roasting hot dogs, and meat-slicing machines churning out endless piles of pastrami.

Soulful classics include stuffed veal breast, potato latkes, and tongue sandwiches with tangy pickles. Some order to-go, but a hearty Reuben stacked with mounds of hot corned beef, sauerkraut, and Russian dressing is more enjoyable when freshly plated and served in a comfortable booth. End with a perfect little rugelach filled with chocolate and ground nuts.

Mexicosina

A3

503 Jackson Ave. (at 147th St.)

Subway: E 149 St   Lunch & dinner daily
Phone: 347-498-1339
Web: www.mexicosina.com
Price:

The light-filled interior of this Mexican powerhouse sitting on a quiet corner is a busy amalgam of rustic artifacts, wolf taxidermy, and the Virgin in all her glory with flowers and votives at her feet. And those huge jars of *jamaica*, *horchata*, and the *agua fresca del dia* are just as tasty and refreshing as they are decorative.

If they have the *tlayuda*, order it. Its crunchy paper-thin base is smothered in a veritable fiesta of refried black beans, *chicharrón*, lettuce, *queso Oaxaca*, *crema* and much, much more. Other equally terrific specials have included *chivo*, a rich goat stew in an intense habanero-spiked consommé, or tender and fatty lamb barbacoa tacos. Cold accompanying salsas are so divine one could skip the chips and just eat them—with a spoon.

Neerob

C2

2109 Starling Ave. (bet. Odell St. & Olmstead Ave.)

Subway: Castle Hill Av   Lunch & dinner daily
Phone: 718-904-7061
Web: N/A
Price:

Short on atmosphere but saturated in fiery flavor, this Bronx restaurant dishes out some of the best Bangladeshi fare this side of South Asia. Though harsh lighting, steam tables, and a cash register give the main room the feel of a fast food joint, none of that will matter after that first bite of sultry, explosively spicy cuisine.

Shingara, vegetable pakoras, and samosas are always available. This is in addition to a parade of daily specials: *chandal*, yellow lentils, is seasoned with garlic, ginger, and cumin; jumbo prawns or *golda chingri* are simmered in a thick sauce of spiced coconut milk; and gura mas, pan-fried small fish, swim in a tangy purée of greens and mustard oil. Order plenty of buttery, multi-layered *paratha* to scoop up the curries.

900 Park

 Italian ✗✗

900 Morris Park Ave. (at Bronxdale Ave.)

Subway: Bronx Park East
Phone: 718-892-3830
Web: www.900park.com
Price: $$

Lunch & dinner daily

Neither fancy nor innovative, there is a certain heartwarming quality that makes this an easy place to return to time and again. Couples often settle in the lounge near the fireplace while larger groups gather in the elevated dining room for platters of hot antipasti. White leather chairs, cotton panels, and rustic tables lend a breezy feel.

Italian and Italian-American classics span the wide menu, from grilled calamari with a mild tomato sauce topped with peppers and black olives, to ridged tubes of manicotti stuffed with ricotta and pecorino, cooked in a meaty Bolognese and finished with rich béchamel. Brick-oven pizzas are always worthy orders, especially the *Calabrese* decked with spicy *soppressata* and a few dollops of mozzarella.

Patricia's

 Italian ✗✗

1082 Morris Park Ave. (bet. Haight & Lurting Aves.)

Subway: Morris Park (& bus Bx8)
Phone: 718-409-9069
Web: www.patriciasnyc.com
Price: $$

Lunch & dinner daily

Much more than a neighborhood staple, Patricia's is an elegant restaurant committed to the convivial spirit of Southern Italy. Its seasonal fare is served in a gracious, brick-lined dining room among white tablecloths, chandeliers, and the warmth of a wood-burning oven.

That brick oven churns out pleasing pizzas with lightly charred crusts, like the Regina simply adorned in buffalo mozzarella, torn basil, and a drizzle of excellent olive oil. Spaghetti Frank Sinatra is a stain-making bowl of slippery pasta loaded with shrimp, clams, olives, and capers in chunky tomato sauce. A light touch is seen in the grilled vegetables, topped with paper-thin cremini mushrooms. Don't miss the flaky and gently poached *baccalà alla Livornese* in a sharp, tangy sauce.

Pine Bar & Grill

C2

1634 Eastchester Rd. (at Blondell Ave.)

Subway: Westchester Sq - Tremont Av
Phone: 718-319-0900
Web: www.pinebargrill.com
Price: $$

Lunch & dinner daily

Between this outpost and their popular sister restaurant, F & J Pine, the Bastone family has become a fixture on the Bronx restaurant scene, and their eateries thrive for good reason. Pine Bar & Grill, with its lovely muted yellow walls and black-and-white photos depicting the hometown borough, is, at heart, a red sauce joint of the old school variety—yet the menu reflects the neighborhood's sizable Latin-American population in dishes like pernil and coconut shrimp paella; or a tender trio of empanadas.

Don't miss the mouthwatering *pizzette* (especially good when Frankie's around); eggplant *rollatini*, stewed in a fragrant tomato sauce and drizzled with basil aïoli; or a juicy center-cut pork chop, finished with sweet and hot cherry peppers.

Roberto's

D3

603 Crescent Ave. (at Hughes Ave.)

Subway: Fordham Rd (Grand Concourse)
Phone: 718-733-9503
Web: www.roberto089.com
Price: $$

Lunch & dinner Mon – Sat

You can't miss this storied Italian-American favorite whose design falls somewhere between a cozy farmhouse and Mediterranean villa. In fact, Roberto's bright coral façade lets you know right away there's *allegria* to be had at this hopping respite.

This space is as ideal for big groups as it is for romantic evenings. Inside, you'll find a cozy, carved-wood bar and roomy farmhouse tables lit by candlelight. In addition to the regular menu (think wonderful, fun shapes of pasta *al cartoccio* as well as other classic entrées like grilled pork chop), it's always worth a look at the chef's delicious daily specials. Of course, save the best for last as evidenced by the *sbriciolata* crumb cake with amaretto, chunks of chocolate, ricotta and almonds.

Taqueria Tlaxcalli

B2

Mexican ✗

2103 Starling Ave. (bet. Odell St. & Olmstead Ave.)

Subway: Castle Hill Av   Lunch & dinner daily
Phone: 347-851-3085
Web: N/A
Price: 😊

What this sweet little Mexican spot lacks in looks it makes up for in personality—plus a warm, inviting atmosphere that draws a constant stream of locals. Behind the counter, a smiling staff prepares each order with machine gun speed, and professional servers are quick to help anyone not fluent in Spanish.

Daily specials could include anything from a complex *mole* to slow-braised goat with broth, though the menu is rife with options. Begin with a *torta*, stuffed with steak, layers of beans, avocado, onions, lettuce, and a bright chipotle mayo. In the *molcajetes*, grilled cactus strips, Mexican sausage, and tortillas are sautéed and then buried under a spicy green sauce and sprinkled with *queso*. A nice end is found in a cool disk of coconut flan.

Tra Di Noi 😊

D3

Italian ✗

622 E. 187th St. (bet. Belmont & Hughes Aves.)

Subway: Fordham Rd (Grand Concourse)   Lunch & dinner daily
Phone: 718-295-1784
Web: www.tradinoi.com
Price: $$

Decked out with crimson walls and red checkered tablecloths, this is the kind of place where diners feel like they're in on a delicious secret—and that's no coincidence, as Tra Di Noi is Italian for "between us." Responsible for the success behind this tiny spot is Chef/owner Marco Coletta, who directs the front and back of house with the precision of an air traffic controller and the passion of an Italian *nonno*.

This sincerity shines through in the cooking, from the ethereally light *gnocchi di patate* in a rich lamb ragù to the quickly pan-fried fillet of sole *Francese* nestled in a creamy lemon sauce with shrimp, parsley, and white wine. Only a few desserts are on offer, and all are made in house. For a classic finale, go with the ricotta cheesecake.

zero otto nove 🐧

Italian XX

The Bronx

D3

2357 Arthur Ave. (at 186th St.)

Subway:	Fordham Rd (Grand Concourse)	Lunch Tue – Sat
Phone:	718-220-1027	Dinner Tue – Sun
Web:	www.roberto089.com	
Price:	**$$**	

This Arthur Avenue favorite is easily recognized by the powder-blue FIAT parked outside, but is better appreciated for the wood-burning dome oven. Brick and cement archways, high ceilings, and a second-floor dining terrace strive to keep that oven—and its wares—within each table's line of vision.

The menu showcases Salerno-style cooking with pizzas, baked pastas, and wood-fired entrées. In fact any dish that is "al cartoccio" (in parchment) is sure to please. Open up this pouch to try the pitch-perfect al dente *radiatori* baked with porcini, cherry tomatoes, breadcrumbs, and loads of deliciously spicy sausage. The ragù Salernitano is a gut-busting triumph of stewed braciole, sausage, and tender meatballs. The Nutella calzone makes a sweet, rich finish.

Avoid the search for
parking. Look for 🛵.

Brooklyn

Downtown

BROOKLYN HEIGHTS · CARROLL GARDENS · COBBLE HILL

The Brooklyn Navy Yard may be a hub for commercial business and houses over 200 vendors, but the most impressive tenant remains the expansive **Brooklyn Grange Farm**. This leading green-roof consultant and urban farm is responsible for promoting healthy communities by providing them with fresh and locally sourced vegetables and herbs.

After admiring DUMBO's stellar views, stroll down cobblestoned Water Street. Then do like every proud local and walk straight into **Jacques Torres** for a taste of chocolate bliss. If savory is more your speed, then spend an afternoon

in Carroll Gardens, a historically Italian neighborhood that offers shoppers a spectrum of family-owned butchers and bakers along Court Street. Also set along this commercial paradise is **D'Amico**, an old-time gem dealing in specialty roasted coffees and teas. Step inside

for a rewarding whiff, before heading over to **Caputo's Fine Foods** for more substantial sustenance—think *salumi*-packed sandwiches, lard bread, and fresh mozz. Folks also favor **G. Esposito & Sons** for sausages, *sopressata*, arancini, and other Italian-American fun. Otherwise, rest your weary heels at **Ferdinando's Focacceria**, an age-old haunt famous for cooking up the classics, which taste as if they were transported straight from *nonna's* kitchen in Palermo and onto your palate. For the perfect finale, stop by **Court Pastry** for such sweets as cannoli, marzipan cookies, Italian ice, and the like. As Court Street blends into family-friendly Cobble Hill, find **Staubitz Market**—the most sociable butcher in town—blending the best of the old with the new by way of top-quality chops, cheeses, and charcuterie. But, those with tots in tow or groups looking for a change in mood (and food) may shift "hills" from Cobble to Boerum to feast on Middle Eastern hits at **Sahadi's** or **Damascus Bakery**, each lauded for outrageously good pitas, spreads and pastries.

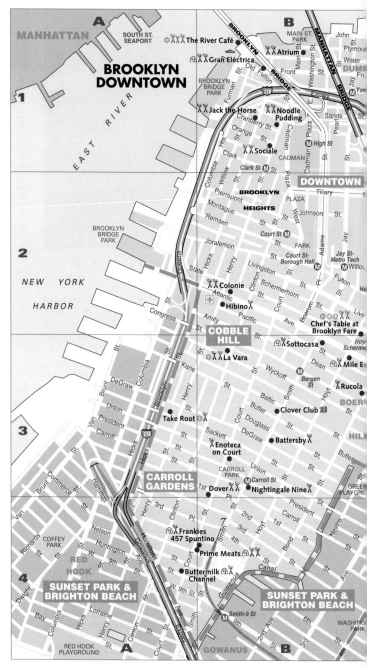

MANHATTAN

SOUTH ST. SEAPORT

✻✕✕✕ The River Café

ⓐ✕✕ Gran Eléctrica

BROOKLYN DOWNTOWN

BROOKLYN BRIDGE PARK

EAST RIVER

NEW YORK HARBOR

BROOKLYN BRIDGE PARK

✕✕ Jack the Horse

✕✕ Noodle Pudding

✕✕ Sociale

BROOKLYN HEIGHTS

✕✕ Colonie

● Hibino ✕

COBBLE HILL

✻✕✕ La Vara

Take Root ✻✕

✕ Enoteca on Court

CARROLL GARDENS

Dover ✕✕

Nightingale Nine ✕

ⓐ✕ Frankies 457 Spuntino

Prime Meats ⓐ✕✕

● Buttermilk Channel ⓐ✕

RED HOOK

SUNSET PARK & BRIGHTON BEACH

RED HOOK PLAYGROUND

MANHATTAN BRIDGE

BROOKLYN BRIDGE

✕✕ Atrium

DUMBO

Ⓜ High St

Ⓜ Clark St

DOWNTOWN

BROOKLYN PLAZA

Ⓜ Court St

Court St-Borough Hall

Jay St-Metro Tech Ⓜ

✻✻✻✕✕ Chef's Table at Brooklyn Fare

ⓐ✕ Sottocasa

ⓐ✕ Mile E

BOER

Ⓜ Bergen St

✕ Rucola

● Clover Club 🍴

● Battersby ✕

Ⓜ Carroll St

SUNSET PARK & BRIGHTON BEACH

Ⓜ Smith-9 St

GOWANUS

GREEN PLAYGR

HIL

WASHING PARK

438

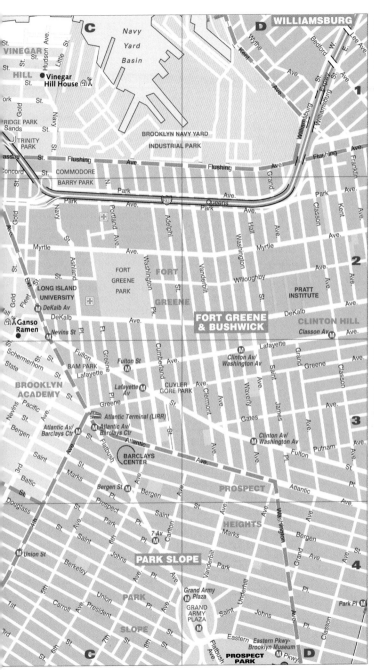

Atrium

B1

15 Main St. (bet. Plymouth & Water Sts.)

Subway: York St
Phone: 718-858-1095
Web: www.atriumdumbo.com
Price: $$$

Lunch & dinner daily

This industrial bi-level space has a rather iconic setting along the waterfront, between the Brooklyn and Manhattan bridges. Dark wood dominates the light-filled interior, amid metal accents and walls that sprout greenery to soften the room.

The food may have a farm-to-table focus, but a contemporary tilt is clear in everything that emerges from Atrium's bustling open kitchen. Elegant "baby greens" arrive as enticingly charred root vegetables over peppery arugula coulis; whereas crisply seared red snapper served over wild rice with dashi-simmered baby turnips, meaty mushrooms, and finished with a rich fumet makes the chef's (Laurent Kalkotour) French heritage abundantly clear. The chocolate-dipped crème fraîche and quark cheesecake is deservedly popular.

Battersby

B3

255 Smith St. (bet. Degraw & Douglas Sts.)

Subway: Bergen St (Smith St.)
Phone: 718-852-8321
Web: www.battersbybrooklyn.com
Price: $$

Dinner nightly

This intimate Smith Street stunner is the domain of Co-chefs Joseph Ogrodnek and Walker Stern, also of Dover. The tiny kitchen at the back of the minimally decorated room belies the abundance of brilliance delivered by the short and sweet menu.

Caserecci tossed with petite, al dente cauliflower florets, capers, currants, and a showering of crunchy breadcrumbs is a treat. Choosing the smaller portion size allows for more room to enjoy the lamb duo—rare seared loin and slow-braised belly—composed with a chickpea-and-piquillo pepper stew slicked with gorgeous lamb jus. For dessert, the chocolate mille-feuille with mint ganache and Fernet Branca whipped cream is like a Thin Mint made by very talented and very sophisticated Girl Scouts.

Buttermilk Channel

American 🍴

A4

524 Court St. (at Huntington St.)

Subway: Smith - 9 Sts.
Phone: 718-852-8490
Web: www.buttermilkchannelnyc.com
Price: $$

Lunch Sat – Sun
Dinner nightly

Doug Crowell and Chef Ryan Angulo run the sort of joint we'd all like to have at the end of our street. It's warm and relaxed, run with care and attention, offers an appealing menu for all occasions—and has prices that encourage regular attendance. The name may refer to the tidal strait but also evokes feelings of comfort and cheer in a place that's already cute and where the close-set tables and large bar both add to the animated atmosphere.

The kitchen seeks out worthy suppliers and with no little skill imbues each dish with that little extra something, be it the cod with Littleneck clams, the fresh linguini with beets or indeed the buttermilk-fried chicken. This care is even evident at weekend brunches on standouts like short rib hash.

Clover Club

American 🍴

B3

210 Smith St. (bet. Baltic & Butler Sts.)

Subway: Bergen St (Smith St.)
Phone: 718-855-7939
Web: www.cloverclubny.com
Price: $$

Lunch Sat – Sun
Dinner nightly

A former shoe store is now an atmospheric rest stop that fashions a spot-on vintage vibe with mosaic-tiled floors, glove-soft leather banquettes, and pressed-tin ceilings dangling etched-glass pendants that glow as warmly as single malt. The glossy mahogany bar (furnished with leather-upholstered bar stools) is overseen by natty bartenders artfully shaking and pouring a stellar selection of libations like the namesake Clover Club—a mixture of gin, dry vermouth, lemon, and raspberry syrup.

An excellent savory carte is a perfect counterpoint to such liquid indulgences. Highlights may include herb-marinated hanger steak over toasted baguette spread with horseradish cream; duck fat-fried potato crisps; oysters on the half-shell; and American caviar service.

Chef's Table at Brooklyn Fare ✿ ✿ ✿

200 Schermerhorn St. (bet. Bond & Hoyt Sts.)

Subway: Hoyt-Schermerhorn   Dinner Tue – Sat
Phone: 718-243-0050
Web: www.brooklynfare.com
Price: $$$$

Come dinnertime, this storefront attached to a gourmet grocer turns into something conceptual and remarkable. Here, Chef César Ramirez—the bespectacled authoritarian—stands center stage, surrounded by sous chefs and state-of-the-art everything. He personally welcomes every guest to his "table" which is actually a gleaming steel counter surrounding his kitchen, where each copper pot is watched-over and every porcelain vessel is cooled or warmed to match the temperature of the food it holds. The bar for painstaking detail seems to rise with each dish.

Expect a bang of flavor to open your meal, perhaps with a tart layering briny sea trout roe. Signatures like sea urchin piled over toasted brioche with a round of Périgord truffle never lose their impact. However, what was once an endless parade of seafood bites from faraway shores has grown and refined into equally lush mini-entrées. A square of Miyagi beef is *whoa*-inducing. Tiny wild strawberries, yogurt ice cream, and sake gelée balance each element with wondrous intensity.

The menu changes every night, but Chef Ramirez never veers from his brilliant melding of French and Japanese cuisines with modern style that keeps pleasure at the forefront.

Colonie

B2

Contemporary ✖✖

127 Atlantic Ave. (bet. Clinton & Henry Sts.)

Subway: Borough Hall
Phone: 718-855-7500
Web: www.colonienyc.com
Price: $$

Lunch Sat – Sun
Dinner nightly

Hip and lively (both the crowd and the green wall of lush plants that is), this is a buzzing retreat for taking in all that makes Brooklyn so enticing. There is the exposed brick dining room and the ceilings of distressed wood, of course, along with the requisite long bar and perhaps most important, a sharp crowd who give Colonie its measured dose of cool.

Start with crostini, perhaps laden with egg salad, a ribbon of lardo and drizzle of veal jus. A deeply nutty rye berry ragout brings together crispy mushrooms, cabbage, and a perfectly fried duck egg. Opt for the whole market fish, served deboned with tart and herbaceous salsa verde, crisp garlic, and roasted lemon. Be sure to save room for warm, yeasty sugar donuts stuffed with Chantilly cream.

Dover

B3

Contemporary ✖✖

412 Court St. (at 1st Pl.)

Subway: Carroll St
Phone: 347-987-3545
Web: www.doverbrooklyn.com
Price: $$$

Lunch Sat – Sun
Dinner nightly

Creative global accents are the guiding force behind the enticing lineup of plates at this tastefully spare candlelit bistro. Chefs Walker Stern and Joe Ogrodnek (the duo behind Battersby) prove the world is their oyster—raw or broiled and seasonally embellished—so settle in and expect to be impressed.

Sweet watermelon *aguachile* is boldly dressed with fresh lime juice, spicy green chiles, blistered shisito peppers and a hit of feta; while house-made links of merguez are nestled in a thick and creamy chickpea purée dotted with plumped golden raisins and accompanied by perfectly puffy wedges of hot pita.

Dessert is delicious and seasonal: picture a summery olive oil cake plated with white peach semifreddo and verjus gelée.

Enoteca on Court

Italian ✗

B3

347 Court St. (bet. President & Union Sts.)

Subway: Carroll St   Lunch & dinner daily
Phone: 718-243-1000
Web: www.enotecaoncourt.com
Price: 🍴

This Carroll Gardens wine bar is a fresh-faced take on *la Cucina Italiana*, almost in spite of its location next to the old-school stalwart Marco Polo. Slim, spare, and dishing out wood and brick details, the cozy spot accommodates neighborhood crowds at its L-shaped bar leading to the open kitchen and on to a handful of tables in the back.

A wood-burning oven brings a distinct personality to a range of specialties here like pizzas, baked pastas, and *spiedini* (skewered meat or seafood). The piping-hot panini are always a treat, made from a slab of fresh pizza dough that's crusty yet moist within, stuffed with sweet sausage, melted fresh mozzarella, a drizzle of olive oil, and tender broccoli rabe. The possibilities and tempting combinations are endless.

Frankies 457 Spuntino 😊

Italian ✗

B4

457 Court St. (bet. 4th Pl. & Luquer St.)

Subway: Smith - 9 Sts   Lunch & dinner daily
Phone: 718-403-0033
Web: www.frankiesspuntino.com
Price: $$

Frank Castronovo and Frank Falcinelli (collectively known as the Franks) have built a small empire for themselves based on delicious, seasonal Italian fare served in rustic little haunts. Frankies 457 Spuntino, a charming, brick-lined space with bare wood tables and a quiet, shady backyard strung with twinkling bistro lights, is a classic example of their easy Brooklyn style.

Seem familiar by now? Well, these guys wrote the book. Service is laid-back and unpretentious, perhaps because they know the food does the talking here: a wildly fresh fennel, celery root, and parsley salad arrives with aged pecorino and a delicate lemon vinaigrette; while a tender tangle of linguini is laced with a fresh tomato broth studded with fava beans and garlic.

Ganso Ramen

Japanese 🍴

C2

25 Bond St. (bet. Fulton & Livingston Sts.)

Subway: Nevins St
Phone: 718-403-0900
Web: www.gansonyc.com
Price: 🍴🍴

Lunch & dinner daily

A welcome sight amid the sneaker stores and pizza joints of commercial Fulton Mall, this friendly, comforting *ramen-ya* is a sure sign that things are changing in downtown Brooklyn. Inside, wood booths and tables sit atop stone floors while buzzing chefs are visible through encased glass. The same team has opened equally appealing spots, Ganso Yaki, and Sushi Ganso in Boerum Hill.

Cookbook author and owner Harris Salat ensures that these steaming bowls of springy noodles remain a notch above those slurp shops opening throughout the city. Nightly specials are deftly executed, including a Mongolian lamb ramen in chili-sansho broth topped with slices of lamb, fried onions, garlic chives, and *ajitama* egg. Try pillowy steamed buns stuffed with pork belly or tangy duck.

Gran Eléctrica

Mexican 🍴🍴

B1

5 Front St. (bet. Dock & Old Fulton Sts.)

Subway: High St
Phone: 718-852-2700
Web: www.granelectrica.com
Price: $$

Lunch Sat – Sun
Dinner nightly

Looking to market ingredients and a California-style approach to Mexican cuisine, this chic yet comfortable restaurant impresses with its lovely décor and lively vibe. Servers are engaged and enthusiastic about the menu's pleasures. An ideal visit starts with a margarita at the bar and moves to the garden as strings of lights flicker to life.

Mexico and Brooklyn are in balance on a menu that includes small plates such as *memelitas de frijoles*, a masa disc topped with mashed black beans, spicy salsa verde, *queso fresco*, and *crema*. Flavor is bright in the deliciously untraditional poblano *chile relleno* stuffed with Havarti, roasted tomato-jalapeño salsa, and tortillas. Try the *frijoles de la olla* (black beans topped with avocado) on the side.

Hibino

B2

333 Henry St. (at Pacific St.)

Subway: Borough Hall
Phone: 718-260-8052
Web: www.hibino-brooklyn.com
Price: 🍸

Lunch Mon – Fri
Dinner nightly

The team at this demure retreat isn't constrained by a menu. Instead, diners are greeted by servers bearing blackboards that list the day's offerings. The list of *obanzai* (Kyoto-style tapas) are enticing and include marinated, fried chicken thigh with tartar sauce, grilled pork sausage, or roasted oysters with spicy gazpacho. The kitchen's regional dedication is also evident in its offering of Osaka's traditional *hako* sushi. This box-pressed preparation might be served as a layering of quality rice, shiso, *kanpyo* (preserved gourd), and salmon. Meanwhile, lunch is a concise affair that reveals either a bento box or platter of nigiri accompanied by a neatly stuffed *futomaki*.

Of course, if lunch seems limited, come back for dinner when the kitchen truly shines.

Jack the Horse

B1

66 Hicks St. (at Cranberry St.)

Subway: High St
Phone: 718-852-5084
Web: www.jackthehorse.com
Price: $$

Lunch Sun
Dinner nightly

A Brooklyn Heights favorite, this sleepy American tavern is a consistent spot in a neighborhood that lacks a variety of serious eats. However, exposed brick walls covered with old-fashioned clocks set a cozy tone, and have regulars returning for the well-stocked bar, complete with myriad bitters.

Slurp a few bivalves at the Oyster Room next door before settling into a table, or if thirst beckons, sip an Old Fashioned with barrel strength Bourbon while perusing the menu. Some locals head straight for the burger—focaccia layered with Gruyère, caramelized Bourbon onions, and a juicy beef patty. Though ricotta and butternut squash ravioli, tossed in sweet brown butter and topped with crumbled smoky bacon, is a fine alternative.

La Vara ✿

Spanish XX

B3

268 Clinton St. (at Verandah Pl.)

Subway: Bergen St (Smith St.)
Phone: 718-422-0065
Web: www.lavarany.com
Price: $$

Lunch Sat – Sun
Dinner nightly

Chef Alexandra Raij knows her tapas. She helped kickstart the craze in Manhattan when she opened her beloved Tía Pol years ago. From there, she moved on to the equally popular El Quinto Pino. And in 2012, she brought her beloved style to Brooklyn via La Vara, which she co-owns with her husband, Eder Montero. It's been a hit since day one.

La Vara bills itself as "cocina casera" or home cooking, but this tapas den elevates the humble cuisine to such impressive levels that it's well worth the cab trip for non-Brooklynites. Product quality is excellent, and the playful spirit at work in the lineup of cold and hot small plates is the definition of creative cooking. Think crunchy fried sea anemone served in a chilled purée of almonds, bread, and garlic, drizzled with *huitlacoche* oil; or tender rabbit loin puddled in delicious sweet onion vinaigrette.

Tucked into a charming brownstone-lined enclave of Cobble Hill, this small, slender space is chic and cozy, with red brick walls and a little white marble counter lined with glossy, high-backed chairs. A curved tan leather booth and small white tables dot the room. It's an atmosphere meant to put you at ease, with a menu guaranteed to wow.

447

Mile End

Deli ✗

B3

97A Hoyt St. (bet. Atlantic Ave. & Pacific St.)

Subway: Hoyt-Schermerhorn
Phone: 718-852-7510
Web: www.mileendbrooklyn.com
Price:

Lunch & dinner daily

Boerum Hill's most bodacious deli serves up killer smoked meat and so much more. The tiny space gets lots of traffic, and those who can't find a seat along the counter or trio of communal tables can feast at home with takeout procured from the sidewalk window.

Now for the food: a cured and charred brisket sandwich, stacked onto soft rye bread and smacked with mustard, is the stuff that dreams are made of. The smoked mackerel sandwich heaped with fennel slaw, avocado, and chunky tartar sauce is an eclectic take on the deli theme, which also reveals poutine and a Middle East-inspired falafel platter. Don't overlook the hand-rolled, wood-fired Montreal-style bagels from owner and Montreal native Noah Bernamoff's SoHo offshoot, Black Seed Bagel shop.

Nightingale Nine

Vietnamese ✗

B3

329 Smith St. (bet. Carroll & President Sts.)

Subway: Carroll St
Phone: 347-689-4699
Web: www.nightingalenine.com
Price: **$$**

Lunch & dinner Tue – Sun

Housed in his old Seersucker restaurant space, Chef Robert Newton keeps the lines on his latest venture, Nightingale Nine, clean and stylish—with a long bar and row of tables hugging a blue wood banquette. Sleek black ceiling pendants light the tables, where the kitchen's delicious and creative Asian plates hit in happy abundance.

The Arkansas-reared chef has always loved Vietnamese cooking—and here, he ups the ante by implementing local and seasonal produce into his playful take on the same region's fare. The dinner menu features dishes like grilled pork chop with cucumber salad, fried egg, and jasmine rice; or a riff on jambalaya starring smoked pork sausage, Carolina shrimp, and crab paste.

Noodle Pudding

Italian ✗✗

B1

38 Henry St. (bet. Cranberry & Middagh Sts.)

Subway: High St
Phone: 718-625-3737
Web: N/A
Price: $$

Dinner Tue – Sun

With Dean Martin and Frank Sinatra rotating on the playlist and a dark wood bar full of regulars, Noodle Pudding embodies all the essential qualities of a winning neighborhood spot. It's the type of place to kick back and relax, dine on consistently good food, and even sit solo but never feel "alone."

The kitchen has mastered Italian-American classics, with honest ingredients and great preparation, like the balance of acidic and sweet components in the gently poached cod *Livornese*. The tantalizing egg-y, cheese-y and creamy carbonara that bathes mezze rigatoni, fava beans, and tiny pork sausage meatballs is "dyno-mite." Top off this smoky and sweet treat with an exemplary (and shareable) house-made cheesecake as well as a perfect shot of espresso.

Prime Meats

European ✗✗

B4

465 Court St. (at Luquer St.)

Subway: Smith - 9 Sts.
Phone: 718-254-0327
Web: www.frankspm.com
Price: $$

Lunch & dinner daily

Prime Meats stands tall and proud as a true original and local gem for German eats set to American beats. The booths in front are bright and snug, while bentwood chairs and net curtains tied into a knot add to that brasserie feel. A warm vibe and cheery servers complete the picture.

Hand-crafted sausages and burgers are all the rage here. Nibble away on homemade pretzels while perusing the lunch menu, which may be simple and sandwich-focused, but always showcases a gutsy edge. Bold flavors shine through in a creamy roasted squash soup; *jagerwurst*, a lightly charred, delicately smoky, and meaty sausage with red cabbage casserole; or Jen's German potato salad tossing waxy potato slices, chopped herbs, and thick bacon lardons in a pickled dressing.

The River Café

Contemporary

B1

1 Water St. (bet. Furman & Old Fulton Sts.)

Subway: High St
Phone: 718-522-5200
Web: www.therivercafe.com
Price: $$$$

Lunch Sat – Sun
Dinner nightly

Thanks to its enviable location and stunning skyline vistas, this waterside favorite more than lives up to its reputation as one of the dreamiest escapes in town. Delicate details like fresh, fragrant flowers, beautifully set tables, and cozy rattan chairs make for romantic environs—and though the tight space has a way of turning intimate whispers into public displays of affection, all will be forgiven after a bite or two of Chef Brad Steelman's solid-as-ever cuisine.

Launch into plump wild shrimp smothered in creamy Hollandaise and served with crunchy white asparagus for added texture; or the perfectly crisped crab cake arranged with creamy uni, avocado, and a light herb salad. Pearly white halibut with roasted maitakes is a testament to the kitchen's focus on simplicity and supreme freshness, while a glistening rack of mint- and mustard seed-glazed lamb—charred on the outside with an evenly pink interior—exemplifies its artistry.

Enjoy dessert, as the mouthwatering offerings (think milk chocolate soufflé with melted marshmallow, or dark chocolate marquise topped with a replica of the nearby Brooklyn Bridge) are a veritable education in soigné presentations and sumptuous flavors.

Rucola

 B3

190 Dean St. (at Bond St.)

Subway: Bergen St (Smith St.)
Phone: 718-576-3209
Web: www.rucolabrooklyn.com
Price: $$

Lunch & dinner daily

Nestled among the brownstone-lined streets of beautiful Boerum Hill, this inviting trattoria is open all day. Rucola's attractive interior rocks that prototypical rusticity of reclaimed wood and aged mirrors, while tables are set with sprigs of fresh wild flowers.

Yogurt and granola with local honey is part of the kitchen's repertoire, but the restaurant's Northern Italian influence fully comes into focus in the evenings. Vegetable antipasti, like spicy spears of pickled fennel, are offered alongside cured meats and imported cheeses. Arugula (that's *rucola in Italiano*) is tossed with shaved radish and a celery seed vinaigrette. Enjoyable entrées include a neat block of lasagna layering pasta sheets and hearty pork ragù with a creamy béchamel sauce.

Sociale

 B1

72 Henry St. (at Orange St.)

Subway: High St
Phone: 718-576-3588
Web: www.socialebk.com
Price: $$

Lunch & dinner daily

Sociale is every bit as swinging as its name implies, but true Italian hospitality is what makes the cozy Brooklyn Heights trattoria shine. Regulars at this warm and welcoming spot, housed in a former pharmacy dating back to the late 1800s, wedge up to the bar for glasses of mineral-rich Italian whites or crowd into the charming and lair-like dining room where the table inches away from yours may host your newest best friend.

The kitchen serves up rustic classics prepared with a dash of creativity, like grilled octopus with scallion vinaigrette or whole wheat pappardelle with rabbit ragout and black olives. Heartier items include roasted chicken with fried polenta, or mushroom- and ricotta-stuffed ravioli plated with zucchini carpaccio.

Sottocasa

B3

298 Atlantic Ave. (bet. Hoyt & Smith Sts.)

Subway: Hoyt-Schermerhorn
Phone: 718-852-8758
Web: www.sottocasanyc.com
Price: $$

Lunch Sat – Sun
Dinner nightly

Located just below street level on frenetic Atlantic Avenue, a nondescript façade holds a quiet den of serious Neapolitan pizza magic. Enter and you'll find a simple, narrow, wood-paneled room with whitewashed brick walls; a little bar showcasing a handful of wines; an enormous, two-ton clay oven (imported directly from Naples); and a little patio out back for alfresco dining.

The mood is decidedly relaxed, and while there are delicious salads, antipasti, and desserts to be tried at Sottocasa, the name of the game here is undoubtedly their wickedly good pizza, served folded, *bianche* or *rosse* (with—hurrah!—a gluten-free option as well). Regulars adore the *Diavola* pie, which comes laced with excellent mozzarella, fresh basil, black olives, and hot sopressata.

Vinegar Hill House 😊

C1

72 Hudson Ave. (near Water St.)

Subway: York St
Phone: 718-522-1018
Web: www.vinegarhillhouse.com
Price: $$

Lunch Sat – Sun
Dinner nightly

This local standout is situated in a waterfront neighborhood that feels not only charming but utterly untouched by time. The original carriage house was a butcher shop before becoming Vinegar Hill House—a lineage that seems apropos of such steady and perfectly delicious cooking. Chef/co-owner Jean Adamson's wood-fired fare is both rustic and enchanting.

Start with a wintry fennel salad dressed in lemony olive oil and arranged with fronds over a swipe of burnt onion crème (think of the best onion dip you've ever had). Then, dig into a roasted half chicken with copious jus and a splash of snappy sherry vinegar served in a cast iron skillet. Dark and impossibly moist chocolate Guinness cake is outrageously good, beneath a thick layer of cream cheese frosting.

Take Root

Contemporary ✗

A3

187 Sackett St. (bet. Henry & Hicks Sts.)

Subway: Carroll St
Phone: 347-227-7116
Web: www.take-root.com
Price: $$$$

Dinner Thu – Sat

The best way to describe the lovely Take Root is that it feels like an extraordinarily well-curated dinner party. The tiny restaurant is a two-woman operation: Chef Elise Kornack single-handedly runs the immaculate kitchen while her wife, Anna Hieronimus, amiably tends to the tranquil dining room.

If you're lucky enough to score one of the precious few seats here, make it your mission to arrive on time. The tasting menu's procession begins promptly, so stragglers may run the risk of missing out on those first luscious bites. And that would be wrong. Once seated, you're treated to a wonderfully relaxed and delicious experience. The décor is thankfully simple but soothing, with walnut tables and minimally dressed white walls. A wonderful playlist plays overhead.

Substitutions are not offered, but there's little chance you won't be happy with what's to come. Kornack weaves her culinary spell deftly, gracing blue point oysters with dots of "oyster pudding," aromatic chives and puffed buckwheat; or setting turnip, toasted almond, horseradish and celery over a disc of parmesan custard. Tortellini then arrives filled with luscious cranberry bean purée and bathed in a green tomato- chili- and pork jus.

453

Fort Greene & Bushwick

BEDFORD STUYVESANT · CLINTON HILL · CROWN HEIGHTS

Brooklyn is particularly big on international cuisine, and its every nook overflows with enticing eats. Set in the northwest corner and right across from Lower Manhattan lies Fort Greene, famous for West Indian and African communities (and cuisine). **Bati** is a traditional retreat for Ethiopean home food with a focus on vegetarian options. Since 1999, **Madiba** (named for the late-great Nelson Mandela) has amassed a cult-like following for faithfully conceived South African dishes. But, if good 'ole Caribbean food is what you're in the mood for, then get in line at **Gloria's Caribbean** for excellent roti, oxtail, jerk chicken, and more. Otherwise, simply imbibe the vibe and feel the love at

the annual West Indian Day parade—a veritable riot of color and flavor.

Then follow the culinary trail further east to Bedford-Stuyvesant. Here in Bed-Stuy

(as locals commonly refer to it), carb-junkies gather at **Clementine Bakery** for its nostalgic scene and addictive listing, while others who wish to plan a Southen-themed evening should stock up on wares from **Carolina Country Store**. Bringing crave-worthy signatures straight from the namesake states, this food truck sensation is every carnivores fantasy. Meanwhile, Mexico makes its presence known at old-timey **Tortilleria Mexicana Los Hermanos**,

a bona fide factory turning out some terrific tortillas in Bushwick. Similarly, **Caesar's Empanada Truck** is mobbed for its cheesy renditions of the eponymous treat. And, if all's well that ends well, then be sure to seal the deal over the 200-plus flavors found at **Dun-Well Doughnuts**. In the same vein, **Berg'n** in Crown Heights is a big and boisterous beer hall pouring myriad drafts or popping bottles of beer that pair perfectly with a litany of bites from **Ramen Burger**.

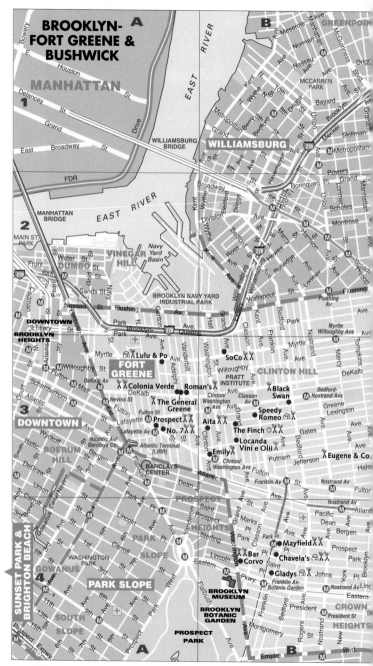

BROOKLYN-
FORT GREENE &
BUSHWICK

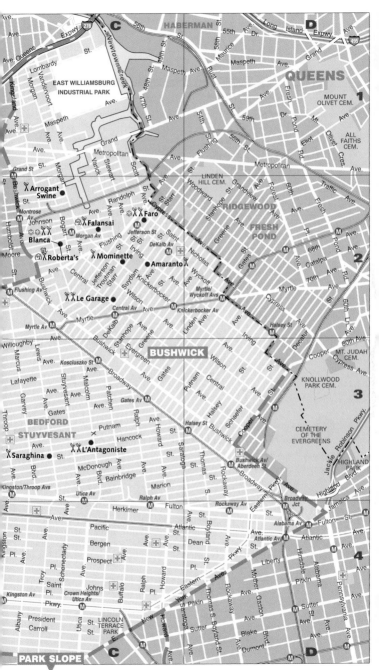

Ave. Queens
Lombardy
Vanderwoort
Morgan
Kingsland Ave.

EAST WILLIAMSBURG
INDUSTRIAL PARK

Maspeth Ave.
Grand St.
Metropolitan Ave.
Varick St.
Stewart
Scott

HABERMAN

56th St.
Maspeth Ave.
Rust
55th Dr.
Maurice
55th
Grand
Long Island Expwy

QUEENS

MOUNT
OLIVET CEM.

ALL
FAITHS
CEM.

Eliot
Olivet
Cres.

Fresh

Traffic

59th
Dr.
Mt.
Pond

Metropolitan
Ave.

LINDEN
HILL CEM.

Woodward
Grandview
Ave.
Starr
Stanhope
Greene

RIDGEWOOD

FRESH
POND

Forest

60th

68th
Catalpa

**Arrogant
Swine**

Montrose
Johnson
Ave.
Randolph
Ave.

Falansai

Blanca

Morgan Ave.
Flushing
Jefferson St

Roberta's

Central

Mominette

Jefferson
Trotman
Starr
Stuydm

Amaranto

DeKalb Av.
Nicholas
Wyckoff
Ave.
Gates
Ave.

Myrtle/
Wyckoff Avs

Le Garage

Wilson
Central Av
Ave.
Knickerbocker
Linden

Knickerbocker Av

Greene

Myrtle

Cypress
Myrtle

70th
St.
60th
Ln.

Halsey

Decatur
Cooper

Myrtle Av
DeKalb
Stanhope
Greene
Wilson
Irving

MT. JUDAH
CEM.

Willoughby
Lewis
Marcus
Lafayette
Garvey
Gates

Kosciuszko St
Stuyvesant
Malcolm
Patchen

BUSHWICK

Evergreen
Broadway
Gates
Putnam
Central

Ralph
Howard

Halsey
Schaefer

Cooper

Cypress Ave.

KNOLLWOOD
PARK CEM.

CEMETERY
OF THE
EVERGREENS

HIGHLAND
PARK

Jackie Robinson Pkwy.

BEDFORD
STUYVESANT

Saraghina

Throop
Gates
Putnam
Hancock
McDonough
Bainbridge

L'Antagoniste

Ralph
Saratoga
Thomas
Rockaway

Halsey St
Bushwick

Thomas
S.

Bushwick Av/
Aberdeen St

Broadway

Eastern Pkwy.

Highland Blvd.

Jamaica Ave.

Kingston/Throop Avs
Utica Av
Ralph Av
Herkimer

Fulton

Rockaway Av

Broadway
Jct.

Atlantic Av

Atlantic

Fulton

Pacific
Bergen
Prospect

Atlantic
St.
Dean
Boyland

Atlantic Av

Alabama Av

Hinsdale
Alabama

Troy
Saint
Johns
Schenectady
Buffalo
Crown Heights
Utica Av

Pl.
Ralph
Howard

Liberty
Pitkin

Mother Gaston

Pennsylvania Ave.

Kingston Av
Pkwy.

President
Carroll
Albany

Utica

LINCOLN
TERRACE
PARK

New
Stratford

Sutter
Blake
Dumont

Pitkin
York
Sutter

Thomas S. Boyland St

Rockaway

Blvd.

PARK SLOPE

457

Aita

Italian XX

B3

132 Greene Ave. (at Waverly Ave.)

Subway: Clinton - Washington Avs
Phone: 718-576-3584
Web: www.aitarestaurant.com
Price: $$

Lunch Tue – Sun
Dinner nightly

Tucked into a cozy corner, this quintessential trattoria echoes the beauty and charm of Clinton Hill. Set amidst a robust culinary scene, Aita finds a niche with its warm (never effusive) service and equally comforting décor of antique mirrors, wood paneling, and lacy curtains.

The kitchen certainly has a way with pasta, crafting thick, homemade noodles twirled with flavorful sauces, such as the *taglierini* with buttery clam broth that is slightly sweet with melted leeks and strewn with irresistibly briny littlenecks. Italian tradition echoes through beguilingly simple desserts, like a bowl of plump fresh berries with nothing more than a dollop of cream and end-of-meal biscotti.

The wines are as deliciously approachable as the cooking itself.

Amaranto

Mexican X

C2

887 Hart St. (bet. Knickerbocker & Irving Aves.)

Subway: DeKalb Av
Phone: 718-576-6001
Web: www.amarantobklyn.com
Price: $$

Lunch & dinner daily

Named for the staple grain of the Aztecs and emblazoned with a mural of Quetzalcoatl, this tidy but truly *caliente* restaurant makes its love of its homeland clear from first glance. Adding to the lure, the father-son duo delivers their own unique take on Mexican cuisine, which is irresistible at best.

Most dishes here, from enchiladas to tamales, are sure to incorporate their excellent masa. *Memelitas* may begin with griddled dough layered with crispy chorizo, vegetables, pinto beans, and more. Then, superb tortillas are folded with shredded chicken and draped with dark and luscious *mole poblano* enriched with cacao, almonds and spices. A range of other *moles* include *pipian verde* that dresses deliciously tender short ribs in a pool of nutty richness.

Arrogant Swine

Barbecue ✗

173 Morgan Ave. (bet. Meserole & Scholes Sts.)

Subway: Morgan Av
Phone: 347-328-5595
Web: www.arrogantswine.com
Price: ✿✿

Lunch & dinner Tue – Sun

A boon to this otherwise industrial warehouse neighborhood, Arrogant Swine's whitewashed brick walls and rows of picnic tables steadily fill with hungry patrons. Striking exterior wall murals and the aroma of sweet smoke both impress from the approach. Heat lamps extend the season for savoring slow-cooked pork outdoors, with rock music and a smoke-fueled barbecue buzz in the background.

Whole hog barbecue is the specialty here—smoked slow and whole over live embers, resulting in tender, glistening meat. The loin, shoulder, jowl, and more are then chopped or pulled and tossed with a Carolina-style vinegar sauce. Sides complete the downhome experience, especially their traditional cornpone (savory cornbread in an iron skillet with bacon drippings and slaw).

Bar Corvo

Italian ✗✗

791 Washington Ave. (bet. Lincoln & St John's Pls.)

Subway: Eastern Pkwy - Brooklyn Museum
Phone: 718-230-0940
Web: www.barcorvo.com
Price: $$

Lunch Sat – Sun
Dinner nightly

If it's not obvious from the crowds spilling onto the street, Chef Anna Klinger's Bar Corvo has the kind of charm people will wait for. Handmade furnishings, penny-tile flooring, and a cool retro décor blend seamlessly to lend the restaurant its eclectic, artsy vibe—and there's even a garden that's perfect for groups come summer.

The menu is cut from the same delicious cloth as Klinger's popular Al di Là Trattoria in Park Slope: picture concise, well-executed fare, featuring a plethora of seasonal produce. A short list of excellent pastas is rounded out by beautifully designed dishes like farro salad tossed with chicory, *ricotta salata*, sweet pea pods and mint. Juicy heritage pork chop comes with braised greens, creamy polenta and horseradish.

Black Swan

Gastropub ✗

B3

1048 Bedford Ave. (bet. Clifton Pl. & Lafayette Ave.)

Subway: Bedford - Nostrand Avs
Phone: 718-783-4744
Web: www.blackswannyc.com
Price: $$

Lunch & dinner daily

True to its gastropub spirit, Black Swan is a little rough around the edges, but that's just what makes it all the more endearing. A dark den where diners line the bar to down craft ales and catch a game on the TV, this former auto-body shop now boasts a moody back dining room with dark wood booths, long tables, and a skylight overhead.

The kitchen is slender, framed by windows, and items are routinely churned out from here. These include fish and chips, chicken curry pie, or the Camden—a John Lennon-inspired plate of French fries, smoky baked beans, fried egg, and bacon that pairs perfectly with a beer or cider. Some of the cooking is more ambitious, as in the hefty jerk pork chop, covered with a Jamaican blend of succulent spices and grilled to perfection.

Chavela's

Mexican ✗✗

B4

736 Franklin Ave. (at Sterling Pl.)

Subway: Franklin St
Phone: 718-622-3100
Web: www.chavelasnyc.com
Price: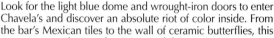

Lunch & dinner daily

Look for the light blue dome and wrought-iron doors to enter Chavela's and discover an absolute riot of color inside. From the bar's Mexican tiles to the wall of ceramic butterflies, this room is an explosion of artistic sensibilities.

Mexico City native, Chef Arturo Leonar is the man behind this menu and his guacamole—traditional or creative with smoked trout, *pico de gallo*, and *morita chile* salsa—is just as pleasing as the overall setting. Crisp *taquitos de cangrego* filled with the perfect balance of sweet crabmeat, salsa verde, and *crema Mexicana* are irresistible; while a thick, deliciously tender pork short rib stew named *costilla en salsa verde* is studded with nopales and served with a mountain of yellow rice and refried black beans for a wonderful finale.

Blanca ✿✿

C2

Contemporary ✗✗

261 Moore St. (bet. Bogart & White Sts.)

Subway: Morgan Av
Phone: 347-799-2807
Web: www.blancanyc.com
Price: $$$$

Dinner Wed– Sat

If you're lucky enough to score a seat at Blanca, you'll first pass through Roberta's corrugated metal façade, beyond the scent of a wood-burning pizza oven, and buzzing outdoor garden filled with masses of tattooed urbanites and millennials. Because deep within that compound—which first helped elevate seedy Bushwick into a haute foodie 'hood—lays this gleaming kitchen for serious eaters. Warm and fluid service keeps the mood friendly among the small group sitting side-by-side at the counter.

Blanca serves a carefully conceived 20-course tasting menu that promises immense creativity and an artist's ability to weave an unforgettable experience. This is dinner theater, with all eyes fixed on the open kitchen and its focused, muted chefs quietly tweezing each morsel of food into perfection.

Menus aren't presented until the end of the meal, but list dishes like creamy sunflower seed "milk" topped with crisp Pink Lady apple cubes and a mouth-coating grating of foie gras, tied together with chili and salt flakes. Fantastic pasta includes thick noodles "carbonara" with crisp and tender bits of lamb. Fragrant Makrut lime makes coconut ice and cashew ice cream refreshing and delicious.

461

Colonia Verde

Latin American

A3

219 DeKalb Ave. (bet. Adelphi St. & Clermont Ave.)

Subway: Clinton - Washington Avs
Phone: 347-689-4287
Web: www.coloniaverdenyc.com
Price: $$

Lunch Sat — Sun
Dinner Tue — Sun

The historic blocks with row homes on Fort Greene's DeKalb Ave. make for an equally appealing restaurant row. Thanks to a sunken front room that flanks the open kitchen's wood-fired oven, plus a glassed-in "greenhouse" that transitions to a pebbled outdoor garden, locals stroll into Colonia Verde no matter the time of year. And why not? The banter is lively and meals rewarding.

Its menu is a Brazilian-esque expression of the owners of Cómodo in SoHo. Curiously named dishes like poblano pepper fettuccine stars pasta tossed with a spicy, satisfying ragù made from roasted poblanos, pecans, and ground beef. For dessert, the Brooklyn Mess sweetens the deal: three scoops of coffee ice cream topped with mango, dulce de leche syrup, and toasted manioc flour.

Emily

Pizza

B3

919 Fulton St. (bet. Clinton & Waverly Aves.)

Subway: Clinton - Washington Avs
Phone: 347-844-9588
Web: www.pizzalovesemily.com
Price: $$

Lunch Sun
Dinner nightly

This charming Fort Greene trattoria arrives courtesy of Matt Hyland—a graduate of the Institute of Culinary Education and a former partner at Sottocasa. Named for his wife, this is a cozy, intimate reprieve from bustling Fulton Street, with a simple décor and small back bar where you can catch a glimpse of the kitchen's wood-fired pizza oven. The rustic tables bustle with young families from the neighborhood.

The menu is concise, creative, and often curious in the best possible way. Try Asian small plates like sticky-spicy Korean-style wings, tender Szechuan pork ribs, and comfort classics like excellent grass-fed, dry-aged burgers.

Lip-smacking pizzas are categorized as The Reds, Pinks (vodka sauce), Whites (sauce-free), and Greens (tomatillo sauce).

Eugene & Co.

B3

397 Tompkins Ave. (at Jefferson Ave.)

Subway: Kingston-Throop Avs   Lunch & dinner Tue – Sun
Phone: 718-443-2223
Web: www.eugeneandcompany.com
Price: $$

Straddling a corner of Brooklyn's increasingly trendy Bed-Stuy, you'll spot homey little Eugene & Co. by its sweet hanging planters and soft light emanating from large windows. It's the kind of rustic, farm-to-table restaurant you might find tucked away in a small town in California, featuring exposed brick walls lined with artwork and hand-tufted banquettes.

Cheerful waiters, clearly invested in the evening's menu, meander from table to table, discussing the food and dropping dishes like a ripe stone fruit and prosciutto salad with salted honey Cloumage cheese; or a tower of savory fried green tomatoes laced with buttermilk dressing. Moist meatloaf is then tucked into a soft roll and dressed with fresh cabbage, pickles, and barbecue sauce.

Falansai

C2

112 Harrison Pl. (at Porter Ave.)

Subway: Morgan Av   Lunch Tue – Fri
Phone: 347-599-1190   Dinner Tue – Sun
Web: www.falansai.com
Price: $$

Just say yes should someone invite you to sample the amazing food at Falansai. Bay Area food enthusiasts might recognize Chef/owner Henry Trieu from his days cooking at the popular Slanted Door; here at Falansai, a pretty little nook that feels miles from the gritty streets surrounding it, Trieu elevates the already complex Vietnamese cuisine to the next level. The results will knock your socks off—honestly, you might never look at a *bánh mì* the same way again.

Don't miss the tender shrimp fritters, enveloped in mashed cassava and chilies; fresh papaya salad laced with mint leaves, sweet poached shrimp, and crushed toasted peanuts; or a surprisingly complex and special coconut curry bobbing with sweet kabocha squash, Thai eggplant, and tender carrots.

Faro ✿

C2

436 Jefferson St. (bet. St Nicholas & Wyckoff Aves.)

Subway: Jefferson St
Phone: 718-381-8201
Web: www.farobk.com
Price: $$

Dinner nightly

There is an undeniable air of sophistication here, making Faro much more of a destination than neighborhood stop. The space looks like a cover shoot for an interior design magazine. Every wall, from the painted brick dining room to the back of the open kitchen, is covered in glossy white to complement the metal-framed seating and wood plank floor.

The smell of the kitchen's wood-burning fire perfumes everything here, acting as a savory prelude to the cuisine and reminding guests of their motto: "Earth, Wheat, Fire."

Chef Kevin Adey's worthy exploration of pasta begins with a traditional Southern Italian *frascatelli*, made with irregular bits of semolina dough mixed with tender peas and shoots dressed in bright mint oil. Offerings go on to include candy-shaped *caramelle* filled with ricotta, then tossed with bacon, charred ramps, and airy potato cream. From the carte, dry-aged duck breast is cooked to rosy red and fanned over green wheat and roasted kabocha squash, with orange squash purée and a drizzle of savory-sweet Thai caramel. Crushed *feuilletine* add a nice crunchy note to textbook-perfect golden sable crust filled with smooth chocolate custard and sliced bananas topped with butterscotch syrup.

The Finch

B3

212 Greene Ave. (bet. Cambridge Pl. & Grand Ave.)

Subway: Classon Av   Dinner Tue – Sat
Phone: 718-218-4444
Web: www.thefinchnyc.com
Price: $$

Brooklyn ▶ Fort Greene & Bushwick

If you've ever had Brooklyn envy, buckle your seatbelt. Tucked among rows of brownstones straight off the set of a movie, The Finch's charming location pulls at your heart strings long before Chef Gabe McMackin's outrageously good food warms your soul.

Duck behind the bright blue façade, and things get even better: a warm staff welcomes you to a charming, rustic décor, replete with wood beam ceilings and farmhouse chairs. At the heart of this expansive space, which sprawls out into a series of cozy nooks, is an open kitchen where the chef *extraordinaire* guides his team to excellence before an audience of diners seated at a Carrara marble counter.

Modern yet comforting, McMackin's dishes mix skill and personality. The food is well-executed, satisfying and carefully sourced from tender shishito peppers, blistered to perfection, with a squirt of lemon and crunchy sea salt, to shaved lamb tongue with fennel, green olives, orange and chili. Chewy *cavatelli* with yellow foot chanterelles, broccoli rabe, nettles and smoked yolk is yet another highlight, while six slices of spot-on Berkshire pork fanned over Calypso beans, littleneck clams, chicory and a sumptuously spicy broth is a fine way to end the affair.

The General Greene

American

 A3

229 DeKalb Ave. (at Clermont Ave.)

Subway: Lafayette Av
Phone: 718-222-1510
Web: www.thegeneralgreene.com
Price: $$

Lunch & dinner daily

Despite the fact that this sounds like Grandpa's pet-name for his antique tractor, The General Greene nicely straddles rusticity and hipness while serving three satisfying meals a day. Everything seems cool here, if perhaps a bit aloof, from the ambient lighting, comfy banquettes, and leather bar stools to their highly prized espresso machine and free WiFi for your iPad.

The menu has a playful Southern slant, as seen in the signature buttermilk-fried chicken served with gravy and mashed potatoes. While wood-fired pizzas (the Margherita?) taunt palates by perfuming the entire space, Arctic char caramelized until crisp and coupled with yuzu as well as dried red chilies, is a special for fitting reason. Cast-iron skillets of bread pudding seem to fly out the door.

Gladys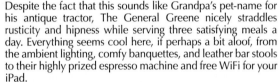

Caribbean

 B4

788 Franklin Ave. (at Lincoln Pl.)

Subway: Franklin Av
Phone: 718-622-0249
Web: www.gladysnyc.com
Price: $$

Lunch Sat – Sun
Dinner nightly

Ready to live the Caribbean dream? All it takes is a few sips of a rum cocktail at Chef/owner Michael Jacober's festive café. This turquoise destination is where locals come together for Happy Hour libations (the comprehensive list features bottles from Jamaica, Trinidad, and Barbados) as well as for luscious, flavor-packed dishes at budget prices.

The kitchen is liberal with Jamaica's signature jerk seasoning, a magical blend of allspice, Scotch bonnet pepper, and citrus that's applied to chicken, pork, seitan, and even whole lobsters. The latter are kept fresh in a tank and a thrown onto a pimento wood-fired grill. Save room for the succulent bowl of curry goat with chunks of potatoes and carrots, best enjoyed with a side of coconut-scented rice and peas.

L'Antagoniste

C3

238 Malcom X Blvd. (at Hancock St.)

Subway: Utica Av
Phone: 917-966-5300
Web: www.lantagoniste.com
Price: $$

Lunch Sat – Sun
Dinner nightly

From the razor-sharp service staff and its charming décor (think elegantly set wood tables and banquettes), to the killer but notably traditional French menu, everything about this buzzing hangout in burgeoning Bed-Stuy is bang-on. The fact that it is surrounded by bodegas and a fast food joint simply adds to the overall intrigue.

Owner Amadeus Broger is the master of operations here and appears to have just one, single formula in mind—and that is to churn out serious food in a fun and convivial setting. Don't miss the *soufflé au fromage*, rendered light and frothy with nutty Comté; the *tournedos Rossini*, tender filet mignon over a potato pancake, topped with foie gras medallions and finished with Madeira; or the perfectly executed duck *a l'orange*.

Le Garage

C2

157 Suydam St. (bet. Central & Wilson Aves.)

Subway: Central Av
Phone: 347-295-1700
Web: www.legaragebrooklyn.com
Price: $$

Lunch Sat – Sun
Dinner Tue – Sun

As the name implies, this chic Bushwick address once housed a garage. Nowadays, you'll find a bright and cheerful space boasting whitewashed brick walls, sleek blonde wood, and sunny yellow accents. The walls are hung with old black-and-white photographs of co-owner Catherine Allswang's previous restaurants in Paris. Now, with Le Garage, she partners with her daughter Rachel to bring a contemporary French menu to Brooklyn.

Classic dishes like leeks vinaigrette are cooked to silky perfection, and served chilled with finely diced hard-boiled egg. However, their heartier options are just as impressive: imagine the likes of slow-cooked pork cheek dressed with savory pan juices, pink grapefruit segments, braised radicchio, and peppery watercress.

Brooklyn ▶ Fort Greene & Bushwick

Locanda Vini e Olii

B3

129 Gates Ave. (at Cambridge Pl.)

Subway: Clinton - Washington Avs   Dinner nightly
Phone: 718-622-9202
Web: www.locandany.com
Price: $$

While regulars at this beloved Clinton Hill trattoria know just where to go, the uninitiated may be surprised to find it tucked underneath a sign that reads Lewis Drug Store. Old-school without feeling hyper-designed, the ambience at this re-purposed apothecary is truly special. Envision lace-covered windows, a penny-tile floor, and ladder-fronted shelves filled with vintage glassware and cookbooks.

Tuscany influences the cooking here, where the diverse list of antipasti includes *tripe alla Fiorentina*, and the pasta is expertly prepared, like a luscious tangle of *chitarra con le sarde*. Salads follow entrées on the menu, but no one will raise an eyebrow if you order the baby spinach with roasted beets and pecorino before the charred *poussin al mattone*.

Lulu & Po

A3

154 Carlton Ave. (at Myrtle Ave.)

Subway: DeKalb Av   Dinner Tue – Sun
Phone: 917-435-3745
Web: www.luluandpo.com
Price: $$

Nestled around the corner of an otherwise forgettable street lined with bodegas, somewhere between Fort Greene and Clinton Hill, the Lilliputian Lulu & Po carries a sweet name but packs a big foodie punch. For that reason alone, you'll battle neighborhood regulars for a table or spot at the bar, but you'll probably have a grand time doing it.

For the uninitiated, the setup is simple: you walk in, wait for a seat at one of the few tables that run the length of the room, and order from an ever-changing menu filled with delights. Try the creamy chicken liver pâté perked up with savory pancetta; tender grilled octopus with minty cilantro-jalapeño sauce; or a juicy half-chicken marinated with bright spices, then seared to perfection under the weight of a cast-iron pan.

Mayfield

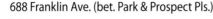

B4

American

688 Franklin Ave. (bet. Park & Prospect Pls.)

Subway: Park Pl
Phone: 347-318-3643
Web: www.mayfieldbk.com
Price: $$

Lunch Tue – Sun
Dinner nightly

Managing to be rustic yet hip, and dark yet welcoming, this Crown Heights hideaway has won the hearts of *nouveau* locals with its feel-good soundtrack and crave-worthy comfort food. A mix of distressed brick walls and sleek tiles fill the dining room, while brass mermaid door handles give the look a playful edge. Art deco-inspired fixtures hang over the inviting bar.

Tasso ham lends a smoky hint of the South to chewy mounds of hand-rolled linguini and tender coins of braised octopus tossed with a chunky *puttanesca* sauce of tomato, olives, capers, and garlic. Silky, organic chicken liver mousse is served alongside a stack of toasted baguette slices and fennel-apple salad. A *pot de crème* spiked with chilies is a welcome twist on the classic dessert.

Mominette

C2

French

221 Knickerbocker Ave. (bet. Starr & Troutman Sts.)

Subway: Jefferson St
Phone: 929-234-2941
Web: www.mominette.com
Price: $$

Lunch & dinner daily

Enter through the swinging wooden doors to discover that the less-than-glitzy surroundings seem a world away. Inside, Mominette's great vibe, classic bistro spirit, and highly romanticized glow are impossible to ignore—wallpaper crafted from sepia-toned newspapers keeps company with vintage chandeliers as well as risqué photos. Add to that a familial staff and fantastic food...et voilà...you have an instant fan favorite!

There is a reason why each diner becomes a regular here: the food is delicious and surprisingly authentic. And, the menu focuses on staples like escargots baked with tomatoes and garlic; a kerchief of puff pastry filled with roast duck infused with wine and tart cranberries; or braised pork tenderloin set atop a knoll of nutty lentils.

Brooklyn ▶ Fort Greene & Bushwick

469

No. 7

A3

American ✕✕

7 Greene Ave. (bet. Cumberland & Fulton Sts.)

Subway: Lafayette Av
Phone: 718-522-6370
Web: www.no7restaurant.com
Price: $$

Lunch Sat – Sun
Dinner nightly

With its worn-in good looks, it's no surprise that No. 7 is this neighborhood's favorite hangout—a place where a cool crowd sip at the lively bar and sink into the dining room's sumptuous, horseshoe-shaped banquette. Add to that a menu so intriguingly original, it started a movement (the brand now includes kiosks serving sandwiches and veggie burgers), and you've got a recipe for success.

A delicious alchemy is at work in the open kitchen creating the likes of braised pork shoulder-stuffed cabbage paired with grilled stone fruit panzanella. Starters and dessert here are every bit as fun as the main event. And the proof is in the perfectly ripe avocado topped with smoked trout, *tobiko*, and jalapeño oil; followed by the decadent brandy Alexander tiramisu.

Prospect

A3

American ✕✕

773 Fulton St. (bet. Oxford & Portland Aves.)

Subway: Lafayette Av
Phone: 718-596-6826
Web: www.prospectbk.com
Price: $$

Dinner Mon – Sat

This Fort Greene standout offers delicious cooking and just so happens to be pretty cool, too. The beverage menu features riffs on the Negroni cocktail—one for instance substitutes reposado tequila for gin. Walls are lined with reclaimed planks of the Coney Island boardwalk, and genuinely hospitable service tames the packed house.

Quality trumps quantity in the streamlined selection of product-driven creations. A neatly arranged row of silver dollar-sized kimchi pancakes, topped with tender strands of pulled pork make an enticing starter; while toothsome and tender house-made gnocchi is plated with snap peas, sautéed wild mushrooms, and sweet peas for a springtime treat. Finish with a contemporary take on banana cake enhanced with coconut cream foam.

Roberta's

Contemporary ✗

C2

261 Moore St. (bet. Bogart & White Sts.)

Subway: Morgan Av
Phone: 718-417-1118
Web: www.robertaspizza.com
Price: $$

Lunch & dinner daily

Entering through this (now) iconic red door is like a trip through the looking glass and into Bushwick's foodie wonderland. The city's love affair with Roberta's seems stronger each year, and for good reason. Everything from the industrial space to the underground Bohemian vibe epitomizes Brooklyn-chic. A new takeaway option has been added to the compound, so when the wait for a table is too long, snag a porchetta sandwich to-go.

Queens native Carlo Mirarchi leads a talented kitchen and its menu of beautifully prepared pasta, vegetables, and more. Many diners stick to the creatively named, less than purely Italian pizza, like the Speckenwolf, with freshly dried oregano, house-made mozzarella, thinly sliced speck, red onion, and roasted cremini mushrooms.

Roman's

Italian ✗

A3

243 DeKalb Ave. (bet. Clermont & Vanderbilt Aves.)

Subway: Lafayette Av
Phone: 718-622-5300
Web: www.romansnyc.com
Price: $$

Lunch Sat – Sun
Dinner nightly

Candlelight bounces off white-tiled walls and colorful mosaic throughout this cozy hideaway's small, tasteful dining room. Locals return for the two daily cocktails (one bitter, one sour) along with the short, none-too-complicated menu that is a study in the strength of focus. This is the type of inviting neighborhood joint that calls for a glass of wine and plate of soulful pasta at the bar.

Dishes are straightforward but satisfy in their careful execution. A squid salad with cannellini beans, tomato, herbs, and fantastic olive oil is elevated by seasoning and texture from toasted breadcrumbs. *Tortelli* stuffed with fluffy ricotta find a succulent home in pork ragù. A wonderfully rich and almost chocolate-hued braised beef rib tops buttery whipped potatoes.

Saraghina

C3

435 Halsey St. (at Lewis Ave.)

Subway: Utica Av
Phone: 718-574-0010
Web: www.saraghinabrooklyn.com
Price: $$

Lunch & dinner daily

If you build it, they will come: and sure enough, from the moment Saraghina opened its doors to a just-burgeoning Bed-Stuy, diners have flooded this cool, multi-room, restaurant decorated in garage-sale knickknacks, old butcher signs, and marmalade jars. It's downright adorable. But, it's the delicious food that fills the seats.

Still best known for their irresistible pizzas, blistered to puffy perfection, the menu offers all kinds of heavenly dishes not to miss, like the fried calamari and shrimp, served with tangy lemon and aïoli; or a wood fire-roasted side of cauliflower mixed with creamy mascarpone, tart *labneh* cheese, and Marcona almonds.

Just around the corner, at 433 Halsey, a sister bakery serves up fresh pastries and a mean espresso all day.

SoCo

B3

509 Myrtle Ave. (bet. Grand Ave. & Ryerson St.)

Subway: Classon Av
Phone: 718-783-1936
Web: www.socobk.com
Price: $$

Lunch & dinner Tue – Sun

Southern food meets bohemian city life at SoCo, an urbane, industrial-chic restaurant where guests are greeted at the door with a splash of wonderful jazz. The gracious, hospitable staff manages to meander through the young professionals and artsy Pratt students with ease, and if the cool charm of SoCo doesn't woo you, the outstanding Southern fare will certainly do the trick. Organic buttermilk-fried chicken arrives crispy and tender, and served over a delicious red velvet waffle; while fall-off-the-bone short ribs are braised in an irresistible coconut-molasses-ginger sauce, and served with creamy garlic mashed potatoes and tender okra. To finish, a soft peach cobbler is spiced to perfection.

Brunch is especially popular, so arrive early.

Speedy Romeo

B3

376 Classon Ave. (at Greene Ave.)

Subway: Classon Av

Phone: 718-230-0061

Web: www.speedyromeo.com

Price: $$

Lunch & dinner daily

Named for a racehorse and just as focused and quick, Speedy Romeo is in for a successful run. Part tavern, part roadside grill, its kitschy décor and modern touches transform this former automotive shop into a surprisingly attractive spot.

The owner benefited from years at Jean-Georges' empire, and that intelligence and experience is conveyed through the smart accents and whimsical menu that begins with Italian ingredients. Look to the wood-burning oven for smoky, meaty artichoke halves topped with lemon aïoli, sourdough crumbs, mint, and peppery arugula. Take a chance on the non-traditional but utterly fantastic pizza combinations, such as the St. Louis, layering a proper crust with meats, pickled chillies, and Midwestern Provel cheese.

Brooklyn ▶ Fort Greene & Bushwick

Your opinions are important to us. Please write to us directly at: michelin.guides@ us.michelin.com

Bordering Prospect Park, historic Park Slope brags of fancy trattorias and chic cafés perpetually crammed with stroller-rolling parents. Set in the heart of the 'hood, **The Park Slope Food Coop** is a veteran member- operated- and owned purveyor of locally farmed produce, grass-fed meat, and free-range poultry. Lauded as the largest of its kind in the country, membership is offered to anyone willing to pay a small fee and work a shift of less than three hours each month. The like-minded **Grand Army Plaza Greenmarket**, held every Saturday at Prospect Park, is a shopping haven among area residents craving organic, farm-fresh produce as well as cooking programs and demonstrations to boot.

Close at hand on Flatbush Avenue, **Bklyn Larder** is an artisanal provisions store that sells every imaginable type of cheese, meat, snack, beverage, and sweet. Devoted locals line up outside **The Ploughman**—a South Slope boutique—for an impressive bevy of beers, even more cheese, and over 20 varieties of cured meats. Favoring something sweet? Find it at **The Chocolate Room** where desserts are exclusively hand-crafted and composed of pure, all-natural ingredients. From myriad boxes and bars of chocolate, to cakes, cocoa, coffees, and teas, this is every sugar fiend's reverie. Over in Windsor Terrace, **Brancaccio's Food Shop** is a serious dine-in and take-out treat that keeps the crowds returning for more Italian-American eats (think caponota and meatballs) or even breakfast specials starring eggs, potatoes, cheese and meats. Ramen is another wildly popular

comfort food here, so on those cold, wintry days, head to **Chuko's** in Prospect Heights for an impressive selection with vegetarian options that are bound to stun. Further south, Ditmas Park residents make the pilgrimage to **Olympic Pita** for fresh, handmade bread or arguably the most perfect falafel in town. Finally, go big or go home—with a bold cup of tea (or coffee) at **Qathra Cafe**.

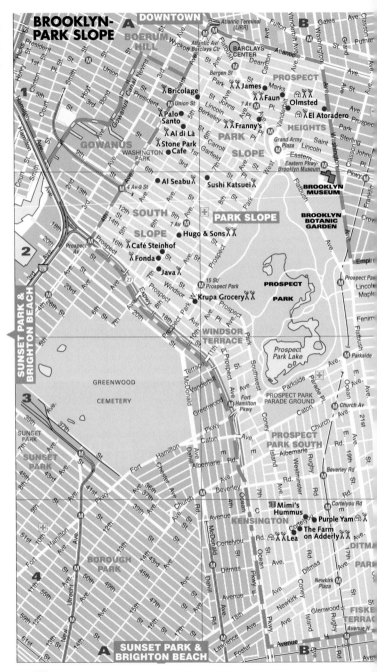

BROOKLYN-PARK SLOPE

A DOWNTOWN

BOERUM HILL

Atlantic Terminal (LIRR)

BARCLAYS CENTER

B

PROSPECT

Bricolage

James

Faun

Olmsted

Palo Santo

El Atoradero

Al di Là

Franny's

HEIGHTS

Stone Park Cafe

GOWANUS

WASHINGTON PARK

Grand Army Plaza

PARK SLOPE

Eastern Pkwy-Brooklyn Museum

BROOKLYN MUSEUM

Al Seabu

Sushi Katsuei

4 Av-9 St

SOUTH SLOPE

7 Av

PARK SLOPE

BROOKLYN BOTANIC GARDEN

Hugo & Sons

Café Steinhof

Fonda

Java

Empire

Prospect Park

Lincoln

Maple

Krupa Grocery

15 St/Prospect Park

PROSPECT PARK

Fenim

WINDSOR TERRACE

Parkside

GREENWOOD CEMETERY

Prospect Park Lake

PROSPECT PARK PARADE GROUND

Church Av

Fort Hamilton Pkwy

Parkside

Parade

Caton

PROSPECT PARK SOUTH

3

SUNSET PARK

SUNSET PARK

Beverley Rd

BOROUGH PARK

Cortelyou Rd

Mimi's Hummus

KENSINGTON

Purple Yam

The Farm on Adderly

Lea

DITMAS PARK

4

Newkirk Plaza

FISKE TERRACE

Avenue H

A SUNSET PARK & BRIGHTON BEACH **B**

SUNSET PARK & BRIGHTON BEACH

476

Al di Là

Italian 🍴

248 Fifth Ave. (at Carroll St.)

Subway: Union St

Phone: 718-783-4565

Web: www.aldilatrattoria.com

Price: $$

Lunch & dinner daily

When Al di Là opened nearly twenty years ago, it was a forward-thinking husband-and-wife operation serving rustic food to a gentrifying neighborhood. Today, it is every local's favorite spot for soul-satisfying pasta. This is a kitchen for that special kind of diner—one who is ruled by energy and ease. Lunches may bring a duo of *insalata di farro* tossed with roasted beets, red onion, spinach, goat cheese, and toasted pistachios paired with a daily *panino* such as pork belly with pickles, horseradish mayo, and salsa verde. Tables are laden with hearty and chewy ricotta *cavatelli* with smoky and enticingly charred cauliflower, anchovies, chili, and tomato sauce finished with grated pecorino.

The room may show wear, but consider that part of its charm.

Al Seabu

Malaysian 🍴

383 Fifth Ave. (bet. 6th & 7th Sts.)

Subway: 4 Av - 9 St

Phone: 718-369-0309

Web: N/A

Price:

Lunch Wed – Mon
Dinner nightly

The already impressive Park Slope dining scene gets another notch in its belt with Al Seabu, a little family-run restaurant with a seafood-centric menu and big personality. Decorated in cheerful sea-blue walls and industrial shelves lined with charming seashells, Al Seabu also boasts a friendly staff and fun, contemporary music. The overall effect is one of relaxed charm—and that's before the food knocks your socks off.

Don't miss the grilled *pulut panggang*, little cigars of sticky rice dabbed with coconut and shrimp paste; or fork-tender Nyonya beef *rendang* served with a pile of fluffy white rice and cool slices of cucumber and tomato to cut the heat. Fried *mantou*, hot sweet buns served with creamy condensed milk for dipping, makes for a dreamy finish.

Bricolage

A1

Vietnamese ✗

162 Fifth Ave. (bet. Degraw & Douglass Sts.)

Subway: Union St
Phone: 718-230-1835
Web: www.bricolage.nyc
Price: $$

Lunch & dinner daily

This delicious and fresh-faced Vietnamese gem is overseen by the team behind San Francisco's popular Slanted Door. Tucked into a simple, wood-and-exposed-brick space in family-friendly Park Slope, the restaurant's open kitchen bustles with energy as diners huddle in lively conversation. Bricolage bills itself as a gastropub (and the creative cocktails are certainly fantastic), but make no mistake—this is modern, next-level Vietnamese bar fare.

Crispy, golden imperial rolls arrive stuffed with shiny glass noodles, crunchy cabbage, earthy mushrooms, and minced pork; while a dish of "Unshaking Beef" is laced in a light, salty-sweet marinade and seared to tender, juicy perfection alongside a peppery watercress salad.

Café Steinhof

A2

Austrian ✗

422 Seventh Ave. (at 14th St.)

Subway: 7 Av (9th St.)
Phone: 718-369-7776
Web: www.cafesteinhof.com
Price: ⊜

Lunch Tue – Sun
Dinner nightly

Austrian flavors abound at this eccentric Park Slope café. The space is anchored by a large, wooden bar where a selection of beers on draught, generously measured libations, and fruit brandies are poured. Vintage posters hang on the walls and oldies play nostalgically in the background. Sturdy wood tables alongside large windows provide a cozy spot to feast on Austrian comfort food.

Old-world classics are executed with care; the expertly fried Wiener schnitzel is brightened with a few wedges of lemon and a side of thin, pickled cucumbers. Texture is also nailed in a side of pan-fried, golden-brown spaetzle that showcases chewy, butter-coated noodles. Linzer torte is the final Austrian flourish, satisfying with sour cherry jam and a flaky crust.

El Atoradero 🐵

B1

708 Washington Ave. (bet. Prospect Pl. & St. Marks Ave.)

Subway: Eastern Pkwy - Brooklyn Museaum
Phone: 718-399-8226
Web: www.elatoraderobrooklyn.com
Price: $$

Lunch Sat – Sun
Dinner nightly

Chef/owner Denisse Lina Chavez's beloved bodega-restaurant, El Atoradero, has sadly exited the Bronx to find a welcome reception in Brooklyn. The Mexican-born Chavez, a native of the Puebla region, has a serious indigenous ingredient pipeline to her home country going—an advantage that shows up in her delicious *mole poblano* and *pozole*. Tuck into tender tacos stuffed with fragrant, spicy *lengua* or plump *camarones*, or even nutty, pitch-perfect *mole poblano y pollo* dusted with sesame seeds. A daily special of lamb shoulder arrives perfectly juicy and flavorful, served with a side of rice and beans.

The new location offers a smattering of tables and a bar, housed in a homey interior with bright pineapple motifs that hark back to its original digs.

The Farm on Adderley

B4

1108 Cortelyou Rd. (bet. Stratford & Westminster Rds.)

Subway: Cortelyou Rd
Phone: 718-287-3101
Web: www.thefarmonadderley.com
Price: $$

Lunch & dinner daily

It's easy to fall in love with The Farm on Adderley with its cozy bar, enclosed back garden, and softly lit dining room, which oozes bonhomie. And then of course, there's the farm-to-table food: neighborhood regulars and borough-hopping gastronomes pack this charmer night and day for Chef Tom Kearney's irresistible dishes that may include fluffy cheddar omelets. Brunch is a standout, but really, any meal here is bound to sate.

Kick things off with a bright green salad, dotted with pickled red onion, thick slices of heirloom tomato and plump red raspberries. Then, try a tender nest of *spaghettini* laced with fresh tomato, capers, anchovies, and breadcrumbs; or opt for sizzling pork paired with sunchoke confit and crunchy pistachios.

Faun

Contemporary ✗✗

B1

606 Vanderbilt Ave. (bet. Prospect Pl. & St. Marks Ave.)

Subway: Bergen St (Flatbush Ave.)   Dinner Tue – Sun
Phone: 718-576-6120
Web: www. faun.nyc.
Price: $$$

Chef Brian Leth, who wooed many a culinary heart at Vinegar Hill House, takes the helm at this delicious Prospect Heights restaurant. Dressed in a pale palette with marble surfaces and an open kitchen, the space feels welcoming, intimate and tranquil, complete with a long bar for socializing and the kind of charming backyard diners clamor for on warm days.

Dig into crisp, homemade focaccia with good olive oil; or delicately fried fry pepper tucked beside delicate strands of fresh blue crab, cubes of cantaloupe, and crushed peanuts over a cool crème fraîche. Homemade *mezze maniche* is tossed with a ground pork ragù, laced with tomato, herbs and freshly grated pecorino. Wagyu coulotte is served over braised rainbow chard with a spicy horseradish cream.

Fonda

Mexican ✗

A2

434 Seventh Ave. (bet. 14th & 15th Sts.)

Subway: 7 Av (9th St.)   Lunch Sat – Sun
Phone: 718-369-3144   Dinner nightly
Web: www.fondarestaurant.com
Price: $$

A lively retreat set in a quiet neighborhood, Fonda is a local darling for creative Mexican food. Tiny tables are tightly packed into the dim room, where blood-red walls, a black ceiling, and paintings hanging over exposed brick create an intimate feel. Metal fans spin overhead and soft Mexican tunes are almost drowned out by animated conversations. Looking for tacos? Go elsewhere. This menu is more nuanced with such appetizing items as duck *zarape*, a mound of shredded duck between warm tortillas and blanketed in a roasted tomato-habanero sauce. *Pescado en chile atole* is equally layered with flavor, featuring ancho-rubbed red snapper over fingerling potatoes and tender poblanos.

The hibiscus margarita is tart yet moderately sweet and stunning in purple.

Franny's

Italian XX

B1

348 Flatbush Ave. (bet. Sterling & St. John's Pls.)

Subway: Grand Army Plaza
Phone: 718-230-0221
Web: www.frannysbrooklyn.com
Price: $$

Lunch Fri – Sun
Dinner nightly

This neighborhood staple keeps its crowds happy with two wood-burning ovens that churn out lovely thin-crust pizzas. The long bar will likely be your first stop with excellent cocktails that help pass the wait time. The warm space has colorful patterned floor tiles and neatly stacked cords of wood for those crackling ovens.

The open kitchen provides a bit of theater as pies are plucked from the oven—that delicate pizza topped with tomato, sausage, and mozzarella is simple and satisfying. True Italian spirit shines in the carefully executed bucatini with garlic, anchovies, chilies, and toasted breadcrumbs, even if portions are a bit shy. Thankfully there may be more room for dessert, so go for the crunchy *cannolo* filled with lemon ricotta.

Hugo & Sons

Italian XX

A2

367 Seventh Ave. (at 11th St.)

Subway: 7 Av (9th St.)
Phone: 718-499-0020
Web: www.hugoandsons.com
Price: $$

Lunch & dinner daily

Hugo & Sons may contain every requisite detail that conjures the look of rustic Italian hospitality straight from the heart of Park Slope, thanks to exposed brick, penny-tiled floors, and wood planters. Yet this is a special little family-focused place, where the skilled Chef/owner, Andrea Taormina, is attentive and hands-on.

The simple and uncomplicated cooking highlights the best of each ingredient. Crispy Brussels sprouts are true to their name, with loose and lightly charred outer layers, tender and moist within, finished with a zing of lemon zest, parsley, and aïoli. Heartier courses are thoroughly delicious, especially the pork braciole lined with breadcrumbs, pine nuts, raisins, and hard-cooked egg, then seared and served in a chunky tomato sauce.

James

B1

605 Carlton Ave. (at St. Marks Ave.)

Subway: 7 Av (Flatbush Ave.)
Phone: 718-942-4255
Web: www.jamesrestaurantny.com
Price: $$

Lunch Sat – Sun
Dinner nightly

This romantic restaurant holds a nostalgic sort of charm, as though it's been a fixture on the corner for a hundred years. It hasn't, of course, but its pressed-tin ceilings, silver bowls filled with bright citrus, white-washed exposed brick walls and tufted leather banquettes lend it an old-school sort of sophistication.

Chef/co-owner Bryan Calvert and his co-owner wife, Deborah Williamson, live just above the restaurant, pulling most of the herbs used in the kitchen's dishes straight from their rooftop garden. Items wander from sautéed Carolina shrimp over creamy "polenta" to crispy honey-glazed pork belly—all of it divine. The restaurant holds a popular burger night every Monday, with an expanded burger menu and happy hour prices all night.

Java

A2

455 Seventh Ave. (at 16th St.)

Subway: 7 Av (9th St.)
Phone: 718-832-4583
Web: N/A
Price: ☜

Dinner nightly

Java's corner in Park Slope has been an enduring first choice for the exotic eats of Indonesia since 1992. Tiny yet tidy, this dark wood-furnished space is brightened by tall windows covered in golden drapery, native artwork, and the smiles of a friendly staff wearing batik aprons.

A nibble from the bevy of fried appetizers is certainly recommended. Begin with *bakwan* or golden-fried corn fritters, but don't forget about the mouthwatering *sate*—charred skewers of chicken, beef, or seafood brushed with *kecap manis* and topped with diced tomato and crispy fried shallots. The array of saucy, simmered options includes *sambal goring udang*: excellent batter-fried shrimp doused in turmeric-tinted coconut milk infused with lemongrass, ginger, and basil.

Krupa Grocery

American XX

A2

231 Prospect Park West (bet. 16th St. & Windsor Pl.)

Subway: 15 St - Prospect Park   Lunch & dinner daily
Phone: 718-709-7098
Web: www.krupagrocery.com
Price: $$

A hit since it arrived on the scene in Windsor Terrace, Krupa Grocery makes you want to become a regular right out of the gate. Chef Jospeh Lee's food is so simple, fresh, and perfectly calibrated, it's hard to miss here. Get things started with a selection of country toast, served with delicious spreads like one of smashed pea and fava bean with pecorino, tarragon vinaigrette, and pea leaves; or whipped *lardo* with crisp radish, caper salad, and parsley. For dinner, try the buttermilk-fried skate, served over a bed of cracked hominy with basil seeds and salsa verde.

Designed with a long industrial bar that's perfect for solo eating or lingering couples, the interior is effortlessly cool, but the place to be come summer is undoubtedly the gorgeous backyard.

Lea

Italian XX

B4

1022 Cortelyou Rd. (at Stratford Rd.)

Subway: Cortelyou Rd   Lunch & dinner daily
Phone: 718-928-7100
Web: www.leabrooklyn.com
Price: $$

Italian is the name of the game at this stylish restaurant, where diners tuck into refined versions of the country's favorite dishes—try the tender eggplant, baked to silky perfection with fragrant basil, milky mozzarella and chunky tomato sauce. Don't miss a plate of chewy grilled squid, served over sheep's milk yogurt and cucumbers; or soft meatballs pocked with pine nuts and raisins in a mouthwatering sauce. A sublime, tart-like cheesecake is sure to seal the deal.

Settled on a prime corner location with sidewalk seating and a sexy, all-glass façade, Lea is a head-turner. The interior is fitted with unique accents (dismantled water tower "art," anyone?) while the overall vibe is breezy, stylish and welcoming.

Mimi's Hummus

Mediterranean

B4

1209 Cortelyou Rd. (bet. Argyle & Westminster Rds.)

Subway: Cortelyou Rd | Lunch & dinner daily
Phone: 718-284-4444
Web: www.mimishummus.com
Price: 🍜

Think meze and you have the right idea behind this heavenly destination for extra-delicious hummus. Though the space is teeny-tiny, a wise, thoughtful design and large windows ferrying swaths of natural light into the dining room make it very inviting. The open kitchen encourages a cheerful vibe and plenty of playful banter between the warm staff and upbeat patrons.

Oven-hot pitas arrive ready for scooping up the rich, creamy hummus (a mix of chickpeas, tahini, onion, and cumin). A variety of garnishes are also available, including meaty mushrooms, which are a worthy companion to the silky signature dish. Pickles are a necessary side with an Iraqi sandwich stuffed with hardboiled egg, fried eggplant slices, boiled potato...and yes...more hummus.

Olmsted

Contemporary 🍴🍴

B1

659 Vanderbilt Ave. (bet. Park & Prospect Pls.)

Subway: Grand Army Plaza | Dinner Tue – Sun
Phone: 718-552-2610
Web: www.olmstednyc.com
Price: $$

This exciting restaurant, dressed with bright whites, leafy plants and flaunting a vibe that can only be described as rustic-industrial-Euro chic, is where seasoned Chef Greg Baxtrom is laying his hat these days. A few advantageous counter stools offer a view of the kitchen and its myriad ingredients, many of which hail from the backyard.

The resulting food is so thoughtful and elegant that you can't help but wish this gem lived just around your corner. Kick things off with crunchy crawfish boil crackers or a Long Island fluke crudo paired with spring peas, a riot of herbs and lemon. Dave's Trout, a silky, skin-on fillet served in a delicate mushroom consommé with micro greens, sea salt and herb-infused oil, is an excellent next step.

Palo Santo

A1

652 Union St. (bet. Fourth & Fifth Aves.)

Subway: Union St
Phone: 718-636-6311
Web: www.palosantorestaurant.com
Price: $$

Lunch Sat – Sun
Dinner nightly

Jacques Gautier is the artiste behind this snug den cooking Latin and Caribbean cuisine. Nestled at the base of a townhouse, the dimly lit room makes for a lively (cue the salsa beats) yet intimate dining experience. Service can be slow, but nobody's in a hurry, so play along and make a night to remember. Closely set tables make privacy a challenge, but the arrival of crave-worthy pork tacos topped with avocado, radish, and cilantro will keep your eyes on the prize. Find equal appeal in a fillet of roasted fluke set atop pickled purple cabbage, paired with a pineapple-habanero sauce that will make you singe with abandon, and scattered with tomatillo salsa.

A slice of lime pie topped with lime custard and a dollop of cream makes for an addictive finale.

Purple Yam

B4

1314 Cortelyou Rd. (bet. Argyle & Rugby Rds.)

Subway: Cortelyou Rd
Phone: 718-940-8188
Web: www.purpleyamnyc.com
Price: $$

Lunch Sat – Sun
Dinner nightly

Owners Amy Besa and Romy Dorotan mix and match Southeast Asian dishes in such an appealing way at this neighborhood café, you'll have trouble figuring out what not to order. So follow the lead from the crowd—a smart, urbane mix of neighborhood types and savvy gourmands—and try a little bit of everything by sharing. Begin with *pa jun*, a delicious Korean scallion-and-shrimp pancake, and then move on to tender oxtail *kare-kare*, braised in peanut sauce and loaded with adobo, root vegetables and fermented fish paste. Other hits include the deliciously tangy and garlicky chicken adobo served with a refreshing green mango salad.

The décor is simple and comfortable—a long, narrow dining room lined with art leads to a pretty backyard garden.

Stone Park Cafe

A1

Contemporary

324 Fifth Ave. (at 3rd St.)

Subway: Union St
Phone: 718-369-0082
Web: www.stoneparkcafe.com
Price: $$

Lunch Tue – Sun
Dinner nightly

A true neighborhood place that feels fuss-free, laid-back, and just right for lingering, this little corner eatery makes the most of its large windows peering onto Park Slope's vibrant thoroughfare and small nearby park. The airy interior has exposed brick walls, a long bar near the entrance for pre-dinner cocktails, and a candlelit, sunken dining room scattered with linen-topped tables.

Satisfying light fare includes charred baby octopus with chorizo and fingerling potatoes, or grilled lacinato kale served over a frisée salad with tangy buttermilk dressing. Mains like pork loin over Brussels sprouts and rainbow carrots are hearty, and may be tailed by such inventive treats as a mini ravioli-shaped puff pastry baked atop a nutty and crumbly apple cookie.

Sushi Katsuei

B2

Japanese

210 Seventh Ave. (at Third St.)

Subway: 7 Av (9th St.)
Phone: 718-788-5338
Web: www.sushikatsuei.com
Price: $$

Lunch Sat – Sun
Dinner nightly

Park Slope's serious sushi den is the kind of place where the *itamae* will adamantly decline requests for soy sauce. But rest assured it comes from a place of love, because that beautiful piece of nigiri has already been brushed with soy sauce, sprinkled with yuzu and sea salt, or dabbed with *yuzu kosho*. In other words, it's fantastic as is.

A handful of straightforward cooked items like free-range chicken teriyaki or tempura udon are great if the kids are in tow, but the real focus is sushi best enjoyed in an omakase that won't break the bank. Be sure to choose the option that includes sashimi and begin this repast with velvety slices of medium fatty tuna and sparkling sea bass, followed by a maki of mackerel, slivered cucumber and pickled ginger.

Red Hook rests on Brooklyn's waterfront, where diligent locals and responsible residents have transformed the area's aged piers and deserted warehouses into cool breweries, bakeries, and bistros. Following suit, the **Red Hook Lobster Pound** is a popular haunt for seafood fans, but if sugar is what you favor, then **Baked** is best, followed by **Steve's Authentic Key Lime Pie**. Close the deal at **Cacao Prieto**, widely cherished for family farm-sourced chocolates and spirits. Just as **Red Hook Village Farmers' Market** (open on Saturdays) brings pristine produce from its Community Farm to the locality, trucks and tents in Red Hook Ball Fields cater to natives in the know with *delicioso* Central American and Caribbean cuisine. Dining destinations in their own right, these diners-on-wheels may only be parked on weekends from May through October, but leave an impression that lasts through the year. Meanwhile, carnivores on a mission venture west to Gowanus where **Fletcher's Brooklyn Barbecue** proffers tons of variety and quality; while Bensonhurst best-seller **Bari Pork Store** sticks to perfecting the pig. Foodies can also be found scouring the shelves of **G & S Salumeria and Pork Store** for cold cuts to be stuffed into delicious sandwiches. But, even flesh

fiends need a break—perhaps at **Four & Twenty Blackbirds**—a bakeshop with *the* best black bottom oatmeal pie in town. Or, look for **Raaka Chocolate** showcasing beans in all their glory, while ensuring a healthy relationship with the environment. Pair these sweets with cherries from **Dell's Maraschino** and know you're in for a serious treat. An afternoon in Sunset Park is a must, especially for mouthwatering Mexican flavors. Then cool off with an original ice pop (*paleta*) at **Sley Deli**— an authentic grocer booming with business in Borough Park. Flea market cult-favorite **Bon Chovie** has also settled into the neighborhood and serves its signature fried anchovy snacks among other piscine treats to go with addictive Old Bay fries and cases of icy, chilled beer. Of course, die-hard butter cookie fans can't imagine going a day without a whiff from **St. Anthony's Bakery**. Across from

Maimonides Medical Center, **Fei Long Market** is a giant emporium flooded with Asian foodies in search of dried squid, eel, and all things exotic. Slightly south, where Mexico meets China, sidewalks teem with vendors steaming tofu, and fishmongers purveying wonderfully offbeat eats—bullfrog anyone? More mainstream but equally tasty is **Ba Xuyên**, a modest storefront revered for its deliciously crusty *bánh mì*. Moving from the Far East to a flock of kosher restaurants, **Di Fara** is a popular pizzeria with a mini offshoot (**MD Kitchen**) in Midwood. **Totonno's Pizza** is another sought-after haunt for Neapolitan-style pies; and **Joe's of Avenue U** is divine for crispy chickpea panelle.

At the southernmost end of Brooklyn is Brighton Beach, best known for its borscht and blintzes. This dominantly Russian quarter is also home to Ukranian hot spot **Café Glechik**, churning out staples for its patrons packed within. But for a true alfresco snack to tote, **Gold Label International Food** remains unrivaled. Bakery buffs take a time out at **Toné Café**, where an ancient tandoor-like oven turns out impeccable Georgian bread (*shoti*). Couple these killer carbs with juicy kielbasa from **Jubilat Provisions** for a real deal feast.

Customs, traditions, and cuisine come alive in culinary bastion **Moldova**, while over at **Octopus Garden** the nostalgic scene is never-ending with Italian regulars stocking up on goods for the Christmas Feast of the Seven Fishes. Also set within this Eastern European enclave is **Mansoura**, a Syrian institution proudly preparing savories and pastries. **Le Sajj** dishes up Lebanese food with live tunes (on Saturdays); and across the way, local sensation, **Lindenwood Diner** is loved for liberally spiced Cajun food. And while there is no confusing the Chesapeake with Sheepshead Bay, **Randazzo's Clam Bar** promises to provide you with a superior seafood experience. However, never forget that beef is always king here, and there are big, bold flavors to be had at **Brennan & Carr**—where the menu doesn't change, but NY'ers love it all the same.

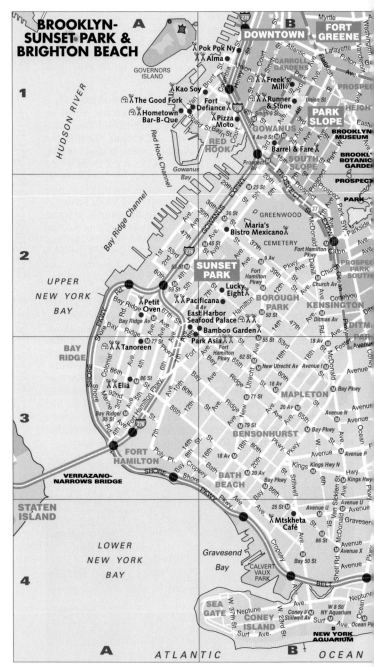

BROOKLYN-
SUNSET PARK &
BRIGHTON BEACH

A

B

GOVERNORS
ISLAND

Pok Pok Ny
Alma

DOWNTOWN

**FORT
GREENE**

Myrtle

Washington

Lafayette

Vanderbilt

Fulton

PROSPECT

CARROLL
GARDENS

Atlantic

Court

Smith

Henry

Union

Freek's
Mill

Runner
& Stone

Union Pl

**PARK
SLOPE**

HEIGH

Kao Soy

The Good Fork

Hometown
Bar-B-Que

Fort
Defiance

Pizza
Moto

Brunt
Board St
Bay St

Columbia

9th Smith-9 St

3rd

GOWANUS

4 Av-9 St

15th

Prospect

**BROOKLYN
MUSEUM**

**BROOKL
BOTANIC
GARDEN**

**RED
HOOK**

Barrel & Fare

**SOUTH
SLOPE**

Gowanus
Bay

29th St

25 St

20th

Prospect

Prospect Park SW

PROSPECT

PARK

PROSPECT

1

HUDSON RIVER

Red Hook

Bay Ridge Channel

Gowanus Channel

36th
Ave.

47th
Ave.

53rd
Ave.

60th

25 St

9 Av

GOWANUS EXPWY

36 St

GREENWOOD

Maria's
Bistro Mexicano

CEMETERY

Fort Hamilton
Pkwy.

9th

37th

Caton

Church

Church Av

Parkside

Coney

**PROSPECT
PARK
SOUTH**

KENSINGTON

**DITM.
PAR**

2

UPPER
NEW YORK
BAY

1st
2nd

4th

Bay Ridge

59 St

67th

Petit
Oven

Pacificana

East Harbor
Seafood Palace

Bamboo Garden

Park Asia

**SUNSET
PARK**

Lucky
Eight

7th

8 Av

Hamilton

50 St

55 St

14th

47th

Fort
Hamilton
Pkwy.

53rd

**BOROUGH
PARK**

Ditmas Av

18 Av

McDonald

Foster

**DITM.
PAR**

Tanoreen

Eliá

77 St

86 St

Fort
Hamilton
Pkwy.

62 St

65th

New Utrecht Av

Avenue I

18 Av

71 St

79 St

Ridge

New Utrecht

20th

18th

80th

MAPLETON

Bay Pkwy

20 Av

65th

Avenue N

**BAY
RIDGE**

Shore Pkwy

Colonial

86th

92nd

95 St

4th

5th

6th

7th

BENSONHURST

Kings Hwy N

Bay Pkwy

Avenue O

Avenue P

Ocean

3

**FORT
HAMILTON**

**VERRAZANO-
NARROWS BRIDGE**

7th

14th

8th

16th

Poly Pl.

Bay

Cropsey

SHORE

18 Av

20 Av

**BATH
BEACH**

Bath

Bay Pkwy

86th

Stillwell

Kings Hwy

Van Sicklen St

Avenue P

Kings Hwy

Avenue U

Gravesen

**STATEN
ISLAND**

25 St

Mtskheta
Café

Avenue U

86 St

McDonald

Avenue

Avenue U

Graveser

4

LOWER
NEW YORK
BAY

Gravesend
Bay

CALVERT
VAUX
PARK

Bay 50 St

Shell Rd.

Avenue X

Avenue

BELT

**SEA
GATE**

W. 37th St

Neptune

Stillwell Av

**CONEY
ISLAND**

Coney I/
Stillwell Av

Surf

Coney I/
NY Aquarium

Surf Ave.

W 8 St/
NY Aquarium

Ocean Pky.

Neptune

Ocean Pky

**NEW YORK
AQUARIUM**

A

ATLANTIC

B

OCEAN

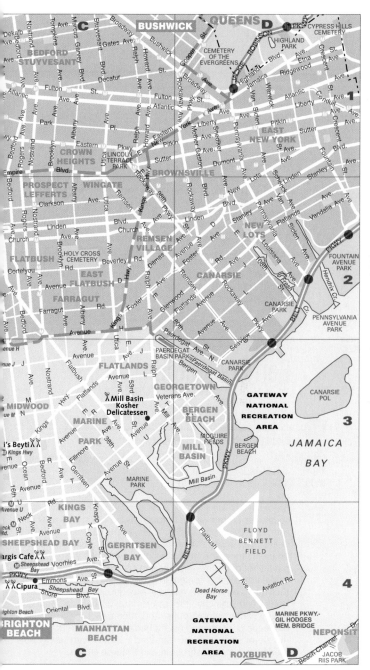

Alma

B1

Mexican ✗✗

187 Columbia St. (at Degraw St.)

Subway: Carroll St
Phone: 718-643-5400
Web: www.almarestaurant.com
Price: $$

Lunch Sat – Sun
Dinner nightly

This festive stalwart with a renowned rooftop has come a long way since its early days along this rather unromantic waterfront. Mexican artifacts and mirrors line the brick walls of this multi-story spot with a margarita-fueled vibe and food that puts a smile on every face.

Alma's pleasing Mexican cooking focuses on good, clean ingredient combinations in a nuanced menu of simple, flavorful dishes. Go for a delicious standard like plump, tender short rib enchiladas in soft, flour tortillas with roasted *ranchero*, Gouda cheese, and pumpkin seed sauce. Be sure to add on baked *arroz con queso*, a decadent side of rice with tomato, poblano, and sharp cheddar. The classic palate-cooling flan is topped with an enticingly sticky mantel of caramel.

Bamboo Garden

B2

Chinese ✗

6409 Eighth Ave. (at 64th St.)

Subway: 8 Av
Phone: 718-238-1122
Web: N/A
Price: 🍴

Lunch & dinner daily

Brooklyn's Dyker Heights, a residential neighborhood in the southwest corner of the borough, is awash in delicious dim sum, but Bamboo Garden holds a special place in locals' hearts. An impressive display of roasted meats is the key differentiator of this bright and bustling gem that also proffers piping hot dim sum—and the servers are more than happy to explain their cart's content to newbies.

Kick things off with the *har gow*, a tender quartet of dumplings stuffed with crunchy little rock shrimp; or the flaky, perfectly savory barbecue pork puffs. And, then move on to succulent barbecue pork, fanned over a bed of fluffy white rice with a drizzle of soy; or crispy pan-fried noodles with tender stir-fried beef, straw mushrooms, and Chinese greens.

Barrel & Fare

B1

American ✗

494 Fourth Ave. (at 12th St.)

Subway: 4 Av - 9 St
Phone: 917-909-1088
Web: www.barrelandfare.com
Price: $$

Lunch Sat – Sun
Dinner nightly

This small, inviting (and probably underappreciated) neighborhood spot surprises with unexpectedly good American fare. Begin with fun snacks like mini lobster rolls, glazed pork belly, or one-dollar Blue Point oysters freshly shucked for happy hour. Plump, golden-fried croquettes are filled with supremely cheesy macaroni and topped with garlicky aïoli. Brunch is popular, but dinner is when this kitchen does its most ambitious cooking. Try more substantial entrées like roasted chicken or house-made ravioli. Duck breast is prepared here with rare skill leaving it tender, flavorful, and rendered crisp over a mound of buttery barley and mushrooms.

The location seems petite and somewhat spare, but warm and friendly service makes up for it.

Cipura

C4

Mediterranean ✗✗

1901 Emmons Ave. (entrance on E. 19th St.)

Subway: Sheepshead Bay
Phone: 718-758-5353
Web: www.cipurany.com
Price: $$$

Lunch & dinner daily

This stylized Turkish-leaning but Mediterranean-at-heart spot is already getting buzz, helping it stand above the crowd of surrounding lounges and catering halls. The elegant interior feels a world away, thanks to shimmering mosaic columns and spacious tables.

The menu is extensive and focuses on a range of specialties, so be sure to start with a combo of cold appetizers such as *levrek marine*, branzino fillet marinated in lemon, olive oil, and capers, or a fava bean purée folded with caramelized onion and garlic. The thick and spicy feta cheese spread with jalapeños and roasted red pepper is yet another treat. These arrive with hot *pida* for ripping apart and scooping up spreads. Finish with an ultra-juicy grilled Cornish hen coupled with grilled vegetables.

East Harbor Seafood Palace

Chinese **XX**

A2

714-726 65th St. (bet. Seventh & Eighth Aves.)

Subway: 8 Av   Lunch & dinner daily
Phone: 718-765-0098
Web: N/A
Price: $$

Dim sum is a well-orchestrated dance at this boisterous hall, where small crowds wait for a spot at one of the large round tables for an indulgent weekend brunch. Steaming carts roll by and waiters ferry trays briskly into the red dining room with shiny gold accents. Service is quick but helpful; the constant clatter of chopsticks and rollicking groups are part of the fun. Eyes can guide the ordering when it comes to the dim sum carts, stocked with authentically prepared bites. Try the plump shrimp *siu mai* followed by rice noodles wrapped around crunchy whole shrimp and doused in a salty-sweet soy sauce. Snappy, stir-fried green beans are addictively crunchy. Don't miss the Singapore *mei fun*, a mound of vermicelli noodles with shrimp, pork, and scallions.

Eliá

Greek **XX**

A3

8611 Third Ave. (bet. 86th & 87th Sts.)

Subway: 86 St   Dinner Tue – Sun
Phone: 718-748-9891
Web: www.eliarestaurant.com
Price: $$

This sliver of Mykonos in Bay Ridge evokes the Greek island spirit with its white walls, baby-blue accents, and rustic wood-beamed ceilings. Choose between the charming backyard patio, the small bar, or a table surrounded by woven chairs.

Then, tuck into a menu of Greek classics, beginning with the deliciously familiar flavors of spanakopita, elegantly presented as small triangles of buttery filo filled with earthy spinach, tender leeks, and a whisper of salty feta. Slightly charred and nicely crunchy grilled shrimp arrive on a bed of plump Israeli couscous tinted pink with pomegranate syrup. Crowd-pleasing options include house-made ravioli filled with shredded braised lamb. *Rizogalo* (rice pudding) is topped with preserved cherries and crunchy granola.

Brooklyn ▶ Sunset Park & Brighton Beach

Fort Defiance

American ✗

A1

365 Van Brunt St. (at Dikeman St.)

Subway: Smith - 9 Sts (& bus B61)
Phone: 347-453-6672
Web: www.fortdefiancebrooklyn.com
Price: $$

Lunch daily
Dinner Wed – Mon

Surprisingly mellow for a restaurant named after a Revolutionary War fort, this Southern tavern (of sorts) is a warm and inviting space where one meal can easily bleed into the next. With a reputation for cocktails, a classic wood bar, and tables covered in colorful oilcloths depicting flora and fauna, this is a lively but not-too-crowded watering hole with solid cooking and heaps of character. A meal could start with crostini topped with local ricotta, shiitake mushrooms, kale, and parmesan. On a blustery day in windswept Red Hook, perhaps the smoky lentil soup will do.

Locals return time and again for classics like faultless deviled eggs dusted with paprika. A lean towards the South is seen in the hearty muffuletta of New Orleans fame.

Freek's Mill

American ✗✗

B1

285 Nevins St. (at Sackett St.)

Subway: Union St
Phone: 718-852-3000
Web: www.freeksmill.com
Price: $$

Lunch Sat – Sun
Dinner nightly

This contemporary American small plates restaurant calls an industrial stretch of Gowanus home. Inside, you'll find a cozy, intimate space with exposed brick walls, filament light bulbs as well as a wood burning oven in the back of the dining room—it's that Brooklyn feel we've come to know and love, and Freek's Mill does it just so.

The cuisine is seasonal, light, and fresh, with each plate delivering something unique and unexpected. Try the fried soft-shell crab—its streak of cashew butter balanced by a sweet and spicy *sambal* and chopped baby bok choy; or the deliciously caramelized barbecue kohlrabi with buttery grits and wilted mustard greens. Close out with a beautifully aged duck breast coupled with refried cranberry beans and a rosemary-honey glaze.

Brooklyn ▶ Sunset Park & Brighton Beach

The Good Fork

Contemporary 🍴

A1

391 Van Brunt St. (bet. Coffey & Van Dyke Sts.)

Subway: Smith - 9 Sts (& bus B61)
Phone: 718-643-6636
Web: www.goodfork.com
Price: $$

Lunch Sat – Sun
Dinner Tue – Sun

The Good Fork is a perfect neighborhood restaurant with a serious local following. Located on the food-centric Van Brunt Street near the Red Hook Waterfront, this inviting spot swaps New York pretense for pure passion—it's the dream of a married couple who built the restaurant from scratch, literally. Co-owner Ben Schneider crafted the space, while his classically trained wife, Chef Sohui Kim, helms the kitchen.

Her cuisine emphasizes Korean and other global flavors as well as a commitment to locality. Homemade dumplings are filled with nicely seasoned pork, crisped, and served with black vinegar dipping sauce. Market-fresh bluefish is not only superbly cooked but creatively served with buttery taro root mash, citrus sauce, and pickled radish.

Hometown Bar-B-Que

Barbecue 🍴

A1

454 Van Brunt St. (entrance on Reed St.)

Subway: Smith - 9 Sts (& bus B61)
Phone: 347-294-4644
Web: www.hometownbarbque.com
Price: $$

Lunch & dinner Tue – Sun

Texas-style barbecue has come to Brooklyn, even if this 'cue begins in an 18-foot smoke pit located a few blocks away, thereby keeping its on-site kitchen free from wood smoke. Instead, it remains focused on creamy mac n' cheese, whiskey sour pickles, and mayo-mustardy potato salad. Meats arrive sweet and tender enough to have a caramel crunch, while smoky sausages snap and explode with juice and chili-spiced bite—each is sold by the plump quarter-pound link. Ribs are cooked until the moment before they fall off the bone; and desserts feature Steve's Key lime pie locally made in Red Hook.

The warehouse-like space is clad in repurposed wood with communal picnic tables lending an intimate and friendly vibe. Water Taxi is the easiest way here from Manhattan.

Kao Soy

B1

Thai 🍴

283 Van Brunt St. (bet. Pioneer St. & Visitation Pl.)

Subway: Smith - 9 Sts (& bus B61)
Phone: 718-875-1155
Web: N/A
Price: ⌘⌘

Lunch & dinner daily

The flavors of Northern Thailand are sparkling and alive at this Red Hook hangout, featuring a bright, basic, and brick-walled dining room. Inside, tables loaded with vibrant dishes flaunting heightened levels of fire are bound to tingle palates and tempt passersby.

Kao soy, the famous curry from Chiang Mai, is a signature for a fitting reason. Topped with crispy egg noodles, this combo unites dark meat chicken, egg noodles, crushed peanut, and lime. A tart green mango salad mingled with crispy anchovies and sweet cashew nuts is a delight on its own; while banana blossom fritters should be dunked in thick peanut-chili sauce for more flavor. Bitter melon soup served with a whole deep-fried red snapper is yet another intriguing offering.

Lucky Eight

B2

Chinese 🍴

5204 Eighth Ave. (bet. 52nd & 53rd Sts.)

Subway: 8 Av
Phone: 718-851-8862
Web: N/A
Price: ⌘⌘

Lunch & dinner daily

For an intimate alternative to the nearby Eighth Avenue banquet halls, this cozy restaurant is a reliable spot for Cantonese specialties from quick stir-fries to roasted meats. Beyond the bustling takeaway counter, turquoise fish tanks, and butchers at work, the mellow dining room houses small tables. English-speaking waiters can help maneuver through the menu against a soundtrack of clinking plates and bowls from the nearby kitchen.

The expertly cooked noodle soups are a must—springy egg noodles swim in piping-hot chicken broth, studded with generous chunks of tender roasted duck. The roast barbecue pork platter contains juicy, thin layers of pork with just the right whisper of fat. Greens like *choy sum* are steamed to a vibrant emerald-green.

Maria's Bistro Mexicano

Mexican 🍴

B2

886 Fifth Ave. (bet. 38th & 39th Sts.)

Subway: 36 St   Lunch & dinner daily
Phone: 718-438-1608
Web: N/A
Price: $$

In a vibrant pocket of Brooklyn, locals flock to this timeworn façade for generous portions of fresh, well-priced, and tasty Mexican cuisine. Complete with a backyard, the décor of this quirky neighborhood staple is distinctly Mexican, from its bright woven textiles and vibrant pink walls, to lava rock *molcajetes* that top each table.

Start your meal with a delicious and filling chorizo taco topped with onion, tomato, and cilantro. *Crepas de elote* are stuffed with bits of tender onion, juicy corn, and poblano peppers. The chile poblano is a house specialty that satisfies with its one-two punch: the first is plumped with a savory combination of cheeses, while the other is stuffed with a beguiling mixture of chicken, almonds, diced plantain, and crunchy apple.

Mill Basin Kosher Delicatessen

Deli 🍴

C3

5823 Avenue T (bet. 58th & 59th Sts.)

Subway: N/A   Lunch & dinner daily
Phone: 718-241-4910
Web: www.millbasindeli.com
Price: $$

This middle-aged Brooklyn treasure is as old-school as it gets, and though it's a bit of a trek to Mill Basin, anyone looking for a real Jewish deli won't think twice. Part deli counter, part artsy dining room, and part party hall, Mark Schachner's beloved spot serves up all the classics—from beef tongue sandwiches to gefilte fish.

The wildly overstuffed sandwiches (all served with homemade pickles and coleslaw) are a home run, as in soft rye bread with pastrami, which is steamed not once but twice, leaving the meat juicy yet hardly fatty. Then dive into a heap of thin latke chips that are fried until golden-brown, crunchy on the outside, tender and chewy on the inside. Garnished with a mound of shiny caramelized onions, this is a sweet treat indeed.

Mtskheta Café

Central Asian

 B4

2568 86th St. (bet. Bay 41st St. & Stillwell Ave.)

Subway: 25 Av
Phone: 718-676-1868
Web: N/A
Price: 🍷

Lunch & dinner Thu – Tue

Deep in the heart of Brooklyn bordering Bath Beach, Mtskheta Café pumps out Georgian classics in a green-hued, faux-brick dining room complete with paper napkins, a campy jungle mural, and television looping foreign music videos. While the décor may lack, the service and food excel, setting this impossible-to-pronounce restaurant apart from the nearby bodegas and elevated subway tracks.

Whether or not you can deduce what's on the Cyrillic menu, friendly servers stand by, directing guests to native dishes like *badrijani,* an almost overwhelming helping of eggplant stuffed with fluffy walnut purée. It's light compared to the mutton *bozbashi,* though—a heady soup of tarragon, cilantro and lamb fat that adds a layer to any blustery day.

Nargis Cafe

Central Asian

 C4

2818 Coney Island Ave. (bet. Kathleen Pl. & Avenue Z)

Subway: Sheepshead Bay
Phone: 718-872-7888
Web: www.nargiscafe.com
Price: $$

Lunch & dinner daily

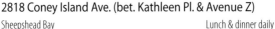

This industrial strip is ground zero for Central Asian hot spots, where Nargis Cafe endures as a real treat. Composed of a front bar area and larger, brighter dining room, the entire space is brought together with marvelous Persian rugs and exotic pierced-metal sconces.

Nargis hits a strong stride among the locals for its convivial vibe and unique repertoire of dishes that may include a *bojon* salad of smoky eggplant tossed with garlic, peppers, carrots, and cucumber. Kebabs are taken seriously here, so try the succulent lamb with chopped onion and dill. Uzbek *plov* studded with chickpeas, lamb, and raisins is simple but imperative. For dessert, the honey-sweet *chak-chak* is fried but surprisingly light and exquisitely indulgent.

Pacificana

Chinese XX

B2

813 55th St. (at Eighth Ave.)

Subway: 8 Av
Phone: 718-871-2880
Web: N/A
Price: $$

Lunch & dinner daily

Among the best of the superior Chinese options in this far-flung pocket of Brooklyn, Pacificana is a bustling, airy second-floor jewel. After getting a number (which will be called out in Mandarin, Cantonese, and finally English) and waiting in the inevitable line, settle into a large, circular table along with other diners and prepare for a feast. The fun begins when silver dim sum carts start to roll by, hauling delicacies from the open kitchen.

Service is curt as signature temptations such as plump pork dumplings and shrimp rice noodle rolls are plopped onto the table. Chicken with crunchy mustard greens, paired with preserved black beans and a steaming bowl of fluffy white rice is nothing short of heavenly so plan to linger here a while.

Park Asia

Chinese XX

A2

6521 Eighth Ave. (bet. 65th & 66th Sts.)

Subway: 8 Av
Phone: 718-833-1688
Web: N/A
Price: ⊜

Lunch & dinner daily

Park Asia's lavish design overhaul is giving Dyker Heights' popular Dim Sum Row a jolt of style these days, wowing new and old customers with its floor-to-ceiling windows, soaring ceilings, a sparkling chandelier, and light-flooding sky lights. If it all seems a bit showy for your average weekend dim sum rush, not to worry: Park Asia takes its food just as seriously.

Servers are well-mannered and friendly, delivering delicious, well-executed Chinese dishes like plump shrimp paired with crispy bacon, as well as succulent minced beef wrapped in glutinous rice noodles and drizzled with a sweet-savory sauce. A pile of snappy *choy sum* is dusted with fried garlic chips; and warm fried crullers wrapped in rice noodles are topped with sweet soy for a saucy finish.

Petit Oven

French

A2

276 Bay Ridge Ave. (bet. Ridge Blvd. & Third Ave.)

Subway: Bay Ridge Av
Phone: 718-833-3443
Web: www.petit-oven.com
Price: $$

Dinner Wed – Sun

Unassuming but worth your attention, this little Bay Ridge site offers a petite, tidy room that is simply done and fills quickly. The ambience here brings a gracious welcome, and the air wears a palpable note of authenticity.

Chef/owner Katarzyna Ploszaj styles her agreeable and refreshingly relaxed cuisine through a classic French lens. Appetizers may include a novel riff on Greek salad composed of thinly shaved Brussels sprouts mingled with diced feta, a handful of black olives, sliced red onion, and a sprig of fragrant oregano all licked with olive oil and a bright hit of lemon juice. Expect equally impressive entreés like a cooked duck breast, crisped and rosy, with red onion-ginger marmalade, and duck fat-roasted potatoes scented with thyme.

Pizza Moto

Pizza

B1

338 Hamilton Ave. (bet. Centre & Mill Sts.)

Subway: Smith – 9 Sts
Phone: 718-834-6686
Web: www.pizzamoto.com
Price: $$

Dinner Tue – Sun

 Welcome to the first brick and mortar location of this longtime Smorgasburg favorite, now a simple neighborhood pizzeria with a warm and welcoming atmosphere. The space started out as a bakery long ago, but the heart of today's operation is actually a century-old oven that was only recently discovered and restored.

The menu is full of surprises that go well beyond pizza joint standards, including surprisingly good pasta dishes. For instance, pillowy gnocchi should be a contender for top billing as it is tossed with chunky beef shank ragù, enriched with marrow, red wine, and then elegantly garnished with cress. Still, that pepperoni pizza is really good, with a puffed and charred crust topped with coins of smoky chorizo, pecorino, and tart tomato sauce.

Pok Pok Ny

Thai ✗

B1

117 Columbia St. (bet. Degraw & Kane Sts.)

Subway: Carroll St
Phone: 718-923-9322
Web: www.pokpokny.com
Price: $$

Lunch Sat – Sun
Dinner nightly

It takes a special talent to bridge the gap between Brooklyn and Northeast Thailand, but Chef Andy Ricker does so deftly, having dedicated his life to the study of Northern Thai cuisine. Pok Pok Ny is the delicious manifestation of that education, along with his ongoing travels.

Tucked into the Columbia Street waterfront district, this casual spot offers seating along a long bar, as well as at little tables covered in checkered colorful plastic. Service is equally laid-back—the young, trendy servers mill about in chambray shirts, while crooning Thai pop music wafts overhead. Don't leave without trying the *khao soi kai*, a rich coconut curry with springy egg noodles and tender chicken; or *laap*, a warm hand-minced pork salad.

Runner & Stone 🐾

Contemporary ✗✗

B1

285 Third Ave. (bet. Carroll & President Sts.)

Subway: Union St
Phone: 718-576-3360
Web: www.runnerandstone.com
Price: $$

Lunch & dinner daily

This ambitious Gowanus operation has a clear sense of purpose. Its name refers to the two stones used to grind grain; the location is just blocks from where the city's first tide-water grist mill once stood; and a Per Se alum heads the fantastic bakery. Inside, the theme continues with walls constructed of concrete blocks shaped like flour sacks.

Lunchtime sandwiches showcase their beloved array of house-baked breads, like whole wheat *pain au lait* grilled with cheddar and pickled peppers, or falafel-inspired broccoli fritters swaddled in a warm pita with shots of harissa and walnut-yogurt sauce. Come dinnertime, try impressive house-made pastas or the crowd-pleasing fish of the day, like monkfish fillet that is seared golden and buttery inside.

Taci's Beyti

 Turkish

C3

1953-55 Coney Island Ave. (bet. Avenue P & Quentin Rd.)

Subway: Kings Hwy (16th St.)   Lunch & dinner daily
Phone: 718-627-5750
Web: www.tacisbeyti.com
Price: $$

Find safety from the evil eye at Taci's Beyti, a bright Turkish spot tucked into a busy thoroughfare in Midwood, where smiling strangers chat at communal tables amid dozens of *nazar boncugu* amulets. Homey and cozy, families dig into rustic dishes as servers spring to and fro with platters of golden, fresh, fragrant food and pile tables high with *pide*, *tabuli*, grape leaves, and almond-stuffed apricots.

Turkish options are few and far between in this predominately Orthodox neighborhood, and dishes here reflect this mergence of ethnicities, as in the unexpected but appealing combination of hummus topped with pastrami. Indulge in dishes that focus on vivid Aegean flavors, like the artichoke heart salad with potatoes and sweet peas (a meal unto itself).

Tanoreen

 Middle Eastern

A3

7523 Third Ave. (at 76th St.)

Subway: 77 St   Lunch & dinner Tue – Sun
Phone: 718-748-5600
Web: www.tanoreen.com
Price: $$

One of the city's finest Middle Eastern experiences is tucked into an unassuming Bay Ridge corner and run by Chef/owner Rawia Bishara and her daughter.

Meals graciously commence with pickled vegetables and *za'atar*-dusted flatbread and are followed by a tableful of unique plates brimming with flavors and colors. Turkish salad is actually a bright red tomato spread shot with *harissa* and dressed with bits of diced cucumber and a drizzle of excellent olive oil. Appetizers are numerous, but try to fit in the chicken *fetti*: an entrée of basmati rice pilaf studded with toasted, broken vermicelli and topped with spicy bits of chicken, slivered toasted almonds, a generous drizzle of yogurt-tahini sauce, and chopped parsley for a fresh, final note.

 Brooklyn ▲ Sunset Park & Brighton Beach

 503

Williamsburg

GREENPOINT

Williamsburg—traditionally an Italian, Hispanic, and Hasidic hub—is now a mecca for hipsters and artists. Here in Billyburg, creative culinary endeavors abound and include several, small-scale stores preparing terrific eats—imagine the artisan chocolate line crafted at **Mast Brothers Chocolate** and you'll start to get the picture. Bring an appetite or posse of friends to **Smorgasburg**, where sharing is crucial for a true gustatory thrill. This open-air market is held on the waterfront from spring through fall and headlines everything from beef sliders and brisket, to *bulgogi* and

chana masala. Less interested in eating and more so in cooking? Sign up for a class at *Brooklyn Kitchen*, where home cooks can keep up with haute chefs by learning how to pickle, bake, and ferment...even kombucha!

Over on Metropolitan Avenue, cute takeout shop **Saltie** serves a tempting list of sammies and sweets; while **Pies 'n' Thighs** soothes the soul with down-home goodness. And, there's no going wrong with a cup of joe from **Toby's Estate** or **Blue Bottle Coffee Co.** on Berry Street. In need of a different type of pick-me-up? **Maison Premiere** is perfect. The vague signage may be of little help, but the line out the door is enough of a clue that this boîte is *the* spot for stellar sips. Within its distressed walls, freshly shucked oysters are washed down with absinthe, icy juleps, and other skillfully made libations. Inspired by the art of butchery, **Marlow & Daughters** is adored for regionally sourced meat, house-made sausages, and dry goods. Locals who live and breathe by meat and cheese make routine trips to **Best Pizza**, a destination that delivers on what its name proclaims. In keeping with the vibe of the 'hood, the interior is disheveled by design, but that doesn't keep peeps from coming in for a slice of "white." Tried and true **Fette Sau** brings rudimentary comfort with roadhouse-style barbecue to residents; and **BrisketTown** on Bedford has been winning over hearts for a while now.

Greenpoint bakeries offer stacks of traditional Polish pastries, but for a change of pace head to **Ovenly**, just steps away from WNYC Transmitter Park, for a slice of pitch-dark Brooklyn blackout cake.

BROOKLYN-
WILLIAMSBURG

A

B

MANHATTAN

1

2

3

4

EAST RIVER

EAST RIVER

FDR

FDR

Third Ave.

Second Ave.

First Ave.

23rd St.

20th St.

14th St.

13th St.

E. 10th St.

Avenue C

Avenue D

Avenue 6th

Avenue

Houston St.

Columbia St.

Grand St.

WILLIAMSBURG
BRIDGE

Grand St.

54th Ave.

Ash St.

Box St.

Paige St.

McGuinness

Commercial St.

Dupont St.

Franklin St.

Freeman St.

Green St.

Huron St.

India St.

Java St.

West St.

Greenpoint Ave.

Greenpoint Ave.

Manhattan Ave.

Leonard St.

Eckford St.

Noble St.

Oak St.

Calyer St.

Meserole Ave.

Lorimer St.

Manhattan Ave.

N. 15th St.

12th Ave.

Kent Ave.

N. Wythe Ave.

N. 7th Berry St.

Bedford Ave.

Driggs Ave.

Union Ave.

N. 9th 10th St.

MCCARRE
PARK

Bedford Av

5th St.

Grand Ave.

1st St.

Metropolitan Ave.

Salt +
Charcoal

Roebling St.

Metropolitan Ave.

N. 2nd

N. 3rd

Havemeyer St.

Borinquen Pl.

Metropolit
Grand St.

Broadway

Division Ave.

Marcy Av

Roebling St.

Lee Ave.

Bedford Ave.

Clymer St.

Taylor St.

Wilson St.

Ross St.

Rutledge St.

Heyward St.

Wallabout St.

Keap St.

Hewes St.

Marcy Ave.

Broadway

Hooper St.

5th St.

2nd St.

Hewes St.

Harrison Ave.

Broadway

Lorimer St.

Nostrand Ave.

Park Ave.

Navy
Yard
Basin

DOWNTOWN

VINEGAR
HILL

John St.

Water St.

Front St.

York St.

Sands St.

Gold St.

Nassau St.

Hudson Ave.

Navy St.

Tillary St.

Flushing Ave.

COMMODORE
BARRY PARK

Park

Brooklyn-

Carlton Ave.

BROOKLYN NAVY YARD
INDUSTRIAL PARK

Hall St.

Classon Ave.

Clinton Ave.

Park Ave.

Ave.

278

Williamsburg

Queens

Grand Ave.

WILLIAMSBURG

FORT GREENE &
BUSHWICK

Glasserie

Achilles Heel

Anella

Karczma

Paulie Gee's

Le
For

Krolewskie
Jadlo

Cherry Point

El Born

Sauvage

Luksu
at Tør

Allswell

Baya

Zenkichi

Rider

Lilia

Fro

Ramen Yebisu

Llama Inn

Egg

Delaware
and Hudson

Kings Cour
Imperial

Aurora

Extra
Fancy

St.
Anselm

Maison Premiere

Samurai
Mama

Manila Social Club

Aska

Bozu

Zizi Limona

Rye

Semilla

Marlow
& Sons

Diner

Xixa

Bárano

Meadowsweet

Peter Luger

Shalom
Japan

506

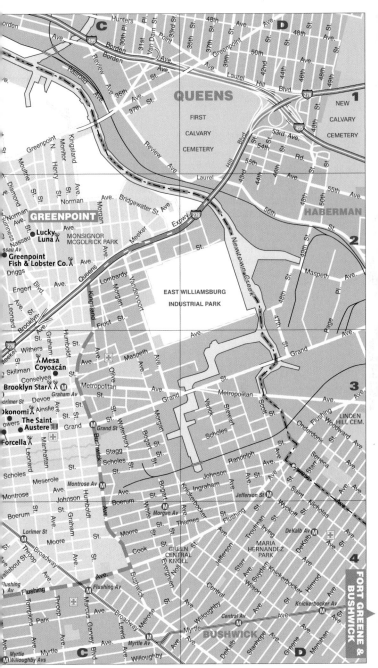

QUEENS

FIRST
CALVARY
CEMETERY

NEW
CALVARY
CEMETERY

HABERMAN

GREENPOINT

MONSIGNOR
MCGOLRICK PARK

Lucky
Luna

Greenpoint
Fish & Lobster Co.

EAST WILLIAMSBURG
INDUSTRIAL PARK

LINDEN
HILL CEM.

Mesa
Coyoacán

Brooklyn Star

Okonomi

The Saint
Austere

Forcella

GREEN
CENTRAL
KNOLL

MARIA
HERNANDEZ
PARK

BUSHWICK

FORT GREENE &
BUSHWICK

507

Achilles Heel 😊

B1

180 West St. (at Green St.)

Subway: Greenpoint Av   Dinner nightly
Phone: 347-987-3666
Web: www.achillesheelnyc.com
Price: $$

Ace restaurateur Andrew Tarlow (of Diner, Marlow & Sons, The Reynard and more) brings next-level bar food to a tavern in Greenpoint—and the result is predictably spectacular. Located near the East River, Achilles Heel is beautifully worn, with big windows and an authentic dockside tavern warmth. Chef Lee Desrosiers heads the tiny kitchen, where the menu is succinct but surprise dishes are common.

A crisp three-bean salad is paired with thick aïoli and soft-crumb sourdough; while lobster mushrooms are pooled in a perfect tomato dashi. Don't miss the Hell Chicken (served on Sundays only)—an otherworldly chicken extravaganza that's smoked, grilled, braised, then grilled again, and served with chicken jus, chicken schmaltz and garlicky miso.

Allswell

B2

124 Bedford Ave. (at N. 10th St.)

Subway: Bedford Av   Lunch & dinner daily
Phone: 347-799-2743
Web: www.allswellnyc.com
Price: $$

For remarkably good food and drinks, head to this rustic, farm-to-table favorite with the soul of a time past. The simple interior reflects the straightforward pleasure of this gastropub fare.

Burgers are popular, but the cooking here is thoroughly delicious. Start with potato-ricotta gnocchi tossed with walnuts, wild mushrooms, and finished with rosemary oil for a smart and pleasing interplay of flavors. The veal *piccata* is also excellent, pounded thin and served in a marvelous lemon-caper sauce splashed with white wine, alongside artichoke hearts and bright green fava beans. An intensely chocolaty tart with buckwheat crust is brought to an entirely new level with taste bud-tingly anise ice cream. Their always-changing frittatas are a brunchtime highlight.

Anella

American ✗

222 Franklin St. (bet. Green & Huron Sts.)

Subway: Greenpoint Av
Phone: 718-389-8100
Web: www.anellabrooklyn.com
Price: $$

Lunch & dinner daily

Tucked into the renovated landscape of upper Franklin Street, Anella charms locals and visitors alike with their beautifully composed fare. The owners, also involved in nearby Jimmy's Diner, know their audience well—the space is all weathered wood planks, sepia-toned mirrors and creaky floors; and while a darling bar springs to life come happy hour, teetotalers are bound to delight in their list of loose teas. The food is light and well-executed, with a lunch menu featuring a BLT on ciabatta with beefsteak tomatoes, crispy bacon and spicy remoulade. Then savor a vibrant tomato soup with thyme and white cheddar before moving on to seared striped bass with lentils and cauliflower.

Close with an apple crémeux accompanied by almond cake and rum ice cream.

Aurora

Italian ✗✗

70 Grand St. (at Wythe Ave.)

Subway: Bedford Av
Phone: 718-388-5100
Web: www.aurorabk.com
Price: $$

Lunch & dinner daily

A waning sun over the twinkling East River; a chilled glass of Italian white in an ivy-covered garden: these are the details that set your heart in motion at this beloved little neighborhood trattoria. And, that's long before you sink your teeth into their homemade dishes laced with pristine seasonal ingredients. *La vita é bella*, indeed.

Aurora takes Italian cooking back to its rustic roots with simply dressed market greens; impeccably executed pastas; and beautifully seasoned meats and whole fish. A lovely plate of *fave e pecorino* arrives bursting with fresh fava beans, sharp pecorino, and springy additions like fennel, pea shoots and mint; while a thick tangle of al dente spaghetti is paired with plump shrimp, chili and a touch of mullet roe.

Aska ✿ ✿

Scandinavian 🍴🍴🍴

47 S. 5th St. (bet. Kent & Wythe Aves.)

Subway: Marcy Av   Dinner Tue – Sat
Phone: 929-337-6792
Web: www.askanyc.com
Price: $$$$

Finally, Chef Fredrik Berselius has opened this second incarnation of Aska, and it is already a must on any serious diner's list. The cuisine is his own Nordic fusion of the Northeast's bounty, importing as little as possible and showcasing produce from the Catskills, as well as the restaurant's own plot at the nearby Farm on Kent.

The interior has a theatrical quality; the dining room is purposefully dark as if to heighten its contrast with the overly bright open kitchen. Chefs often come forward to present certain courses, as if breaking the fourth wall.

The heart of Aska's innovation is in its use of myriad cooking techniques, like fermentation, smoking, and preserving. Elements of dining here are more about discovery than comfort, and may focus on an introduction to new tastes. Lamb's heart slowly cooked with hay down to ash served with pickled sunchoke purée is unforgettable, but whether it is pleasurable may be a source of debate. The carefully composed Finnish Carelian caviar with grilled onion bulbs, cultured cream, and ramp seeds in a complex lemon verbena-onion broth is extraordinary in presentation and flavor. Courses may ebb and flow, but the overall experience is fantastic.

Barano

Italian

B3

26 Broadway (bet. Kent & Wythe Aves.)

Subway: Marcy Av   Dinner nightly
Phone: 347-987-4500
Web: www.baranobk.com
Price: $$$

Hot off the success of his time at Rubirosa in SoHo, Chef Al Di Meglio brings his distinctive take on the cooking of Ischia to Barano. The stylish newcomer sits at the base of a new residential development, just a stone's throw from the East River. Inside, you'll find a stylish décor featuring sepia mirrors, polished tables, and columns lined in pearly mosaic tiles. The vibrant bar, fully open kitchen, and wood-burning oven add to its appeal.

Everything here is executed with great care, but the pasta and pizza are particularly noteworthy. Sensational nettle tortellini are tucked with mushrooms and bathed in a purée of mild spring garlic ramps and sweet peas; while tender bucatini are twirled with an irresistible rabbit ragù.

Bozu

Japanese

B3

296 Grand St. (bet. Havemeyer & Roebling Sts.)

Subway: Bedford Av   Dinner nightly
Phone: 718-384-7770
Web: www.oibozu.com
Price: $$

It's almost impossible to believe, but little Bozu preceded the Williamsburg dining boom and has been flourishing for over a decade now. That's practically a dinosaur in these parts, but this hep cat shows no signs of slowing down. It's still jumping every night of the week with an energetic crowd. And why not? Eating here is a blast, and their sushi is the bomb—quite literally.

The unique sushi bombs (flat coin-like rice cakes topped with fish, spicy sauces and such) are one of the kitchen's signature dishes and for good reason. But do try the tender pork Betty and delicious fried *tako* balls too. The menu here has been described as "authentically inauthentic." But however named, the important thing is that the food is executed with care and attention.

Brooklyn Star

C3

593 Lorimer St. (at Conselyea St.)

Subway: Lorimer St - Metropolitan Av
Phone: 718-599-9899
Web: www.thebrooklynstar.com
Price: $$

Lunch Sat – Sun
Dinner nightly

Chef Joaquin Baca's handiwork at Brooklyn Star displays a fun and creative streak that yields admirable results. Pork chops are brined with molasses, striped bass is poached in duck fat, and roasted chicken is glazed with sweet tea and plated with dirty rice. Gluttony will convince you to bolster a meal here with bacon-jalapeño cornbread or buttermilk biscuits. But, let restraint chime in with a tasty raw kale salad; starring golden raisins, toasted peanuts, lemon vinaigrette, and a lacy cheddar crisp on top, it's pleasure on a plate.

Though the focus is on the eats, the room is comfortably outfitted with brick red terrazzo floors and grey-trimmed walls. Blonde wood tables are set with bottles of hot sauce, pepper vinegar, and wild flowers.

Cherry Point

B2

664 Manhattan Ave. (bet. Bedford & Norman Aves.)

Subway: Nassau Av
Phone: 718-389-3828
Web: www.cherrypointnyc.com
Price: $$$

Lunch Sat – Sun
Dinner nightly

This charming Greenpoint restaurant used to be a butcher shop, as evidenced by the glass-enclosed meat case built into the end of its stylish bar. The rustic space now houses a lively open kitchen, great music, and jumbo windows that look out over the neighborhood, offering prime people-watching. Most importantly, though, Cherry Point is home to food and drink compliments of Chef Julian Calcott and wine and cocktail aficionado, Garret Smith.

Tender grilled oysters are laced in an excellent, smoky Hollandaise with roasted, blackened lime. Then crispy and supremely fresh local baby greens are elevated to noteworthy salad status with pristine anchovies. A nightly special featuring a juicy, bone-in pork chop is rubbed with *koji* and laced with *chimichurri*.

Delaware and Hudson ✿

American 🍴🍴

B3

135 N. 5th St. (bet. Bedford Ave. & Berry St.)

Subway: Bedford Av

Lunch & dinner Tue – Sun

Phone: 718-218-8191
Web: www.delawareandhudson.com
Price: $$$

Just removed from the busy thoroughfare, find this understated gem adorned with little more than photographs of field-fresh produce, votives, and a tulip for each table. Service is as laid back and attentive as the ambience.

That easygoing feel extends to the menu, which capitalizes on the best ingredients of the moment. Thanks to an impressive resume, Chef Patti Jackson's foundation in Italian cooking adds delicious dimension to this regional American food. Start off with an array of openers, ranging from the cool and bracing flavors of mustard-pickled sardines over arugula, to a paper-thin crostini topped with a quenelle of chicken liver pâté and julienned radish. The golden-brown chickweed pie is a signature for good reason. By the grace of the chef's upbringing in Pennsylvania Dutch country, her warm, yeasty pretzel rolls may be among the best on this side of the Delaware. Follow this with twice-cooked nuggets of buttery spaetzle composed with a springtime mélange of chopped morels and slivered green onion.

End your meal on a strong, sweet note with a duo of desserts like almond cake topped with rhubarb compote, and a pitch-perfect panna cotta over a smear of lemon curd.

Diner

B3

85 Broadway (at Berry St.)

Subway: Marcy Av   Lunch & dinner daily
Phone: 718-486-3077
Web: www.dinernyc.com
Price: $$

Williamsburg's restored 1920s-era diner is a modern day catalyst that lures locals and visitors into its dingy quarters. Settle atop swivel stools lining a counter or wood-slat booths for a feast of unfussy American food. In lieu of a menu, friendly servers notate the kitchen's carte and daily specials onto paper-topped tables, all the while explaining each item in detail.

The signature grass-fed burger is thoroughly suitable for the setting, but it's the less expected items that really wow. Take for example the chicken soup special floating with tender lima beans and garnished with parsley for restorative flavor and perfect texture. Desserts are equally impressive as evidenced in coconut panna cotta with fragrant fennel seed and blood orange coulis.

Egg

B3

109 N. Third St. (bet. Berry St. & Wythe Ave.)

Subway: Bedford Av   Lunch daily
Phone: 718-302-5151
Web: www.eggrestaurant.com
Price: ᴄᴏ

It was only a matter of time before owner George Weld would have to find larger digs for his home of the city's best biscuits. Egg's ravenous following is now accommodated in a much larger location that's light and bright with seating at a number of counters and ample table space; yet it's still common to be faced with a queue.

Breakfast is served all day, every day, and stars those fantastic buttermilk biscuits. The fresh-baked beauties are split open and smothered with pork sausage-studded sawmill gravy, stacked with country ham, house-made fig jam, and Vermont cheddar cheese; or simply accompanied by molasses, honey, or jelly. Lunchtime brings savory fare like Carolina kale wilted in a spicy tomato broth poured over a wedge of crumbly cornbread.

El Born

Spanish XX

B2

651 Manhattan Ave. (bet. Nassau & Norman Aves.)

Subway: Nassau Av
Phone: 347-844-9295
Web: www.elbornnyc.com
Price: $$

Lunch Sat – Sun
Dinner nightly

Named for a trendy neighborhood in Barcelona, this Greenpoint tapas den has a decidedly urban feel. A glossy interior features a neon squiggle suspended from the ceiling; red Shaker-style chairs; and a long bar with twelve contemporary (but comfy!) stools for perching.

Chef Alberto Astudillo's menu slides effortlessly between Andalusia, Catalonia, and Castilla-La Mancha, giving each of his dishes a dusting of European flair. *Croquetas*, warm and oozing with goat cheese, are served with apple compote; while shaved summer squash straddles sweet-and-salty perfection with *jamon Ibérico*, blueberries, and padrón pepper vinaigrette. For a finale packed with serious flavors, go for a plate of stone-grilled octopus seasoned with olive oil, thyme, and paprika.

Extra Fancy

Seafood X

B3

302 Metropolitan Ave. (at Roebling St.)

Subway: Bedford Av
Phone: 347-422-0939
Web: www.extrafancybklyn.com
Price: $$

Dinner nightly

Williamsburg's restaurant scene is awash in excellence these days, yet this guy still manages to find its own niche. Their particular bag is fresh seafood, rendered in an inventive American fashion, and served in a charming, rustic dining room awash in warm woods and nautical lighting fixtures. Out front, you'll find a lively, packed bar; toward the back, cozy seating and a truly welcoming service staff.

Pristine dorade ceviche arrives bursting with crisp onion and bright cilantro; while a lovingly constructed lobster roll teems with sweet, fresh lobster. Wild-caught King salmon confit is paired with smoked crème fraîche, dill and toasted bagel crumbs. Don't miss the superb Jonah crab bucatini with tender Littleneck clams, lemon and parsley.

Forcella

Pizza

C3

485 Lorimer St. (bet. Grand & Power Sts.)

Subway: Lorimer St - Metropolitan Av

Phone: 718-388-8820

Web: www.forcellaeatery.com

Price: ☜

Lunch Sat – Sun

Dinner nightly

The Big Apple's love affair with authentic Neapolitan pizza shows no signs of slowing, and Forcella deserves a spot on everyone's must-hit list. Opened in 2012, Forcella crafts each pizza with style, grace, and top ingredients. It all begins with Caputo 00 flour and ends in a big, domed, wood-burning oven to pump out perfectly blistered, pillowy crusts like clockwork.

The warm, rustic dining space is simple but comfortable, with a welcoming bar that offers a great view of the *pizzaiolo* performing his magic. You can create your own pizza with any number of fresh ingredients, or try one of their signature pies, like the Montanara, a unique house specialty that's fried, then decked with creamy *fior di latte* and slid into the oven for finishing.

Glasserie

Middle Eastern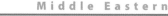

B1

95 Commercial St. (bet. Box St. & Manhattan Ave.)

Subway: Greenpoint Av

Phone: 718-389-0640

Web: www.glasserienyc.com

Price: $$

Lunch Sat – Sun

Dinner nightly

Housed in an old glass factory, the beautiful Glasserie is colorful, rustic and industrial, with lots of original details, a welcoming bar, and a small door that peeks into the bustling kitchen. Add to this lovely setting a straight-up delicious Middle Eastern menu from a wildly talented kitchen, and you begin to understand why the crowds are flocking to this hot spot.

Manning the kitchen is Eldad Shem Tov, a talented chef who favors organic and locally sourced ingredients. Highlights may include the table-shared mezze feast—served with ten or so incredible small dishes—or the rabbit taco, spiked with harissa and folded into a thin kohlrabi "taco" with herbs and radish. The silky chicken liver mousse, served with *arak*, is a crowd-pleaser and fittingly so.

Greenpoint Fish & Lobster Co.

Seafood ✗

C2

114 Nassau Ave. (at Eckford St.)

Subway: Nassau Av
Phone: 718-349-0400
Web: www.greenpointfish.com
Price: $$

Lunch & dinner daily

Fronted by green awnings, and flooded with light, this corner gem is equal parts sustainably sourced fish market and fantastic eat-in spot. Walk past iced specimens to claim a seat at the white marble counter; then dig into the day's catch dressed-up with global influences.

New England clam chowder is given the classic treatment, while grilled sea bass skewers are accompanied by a Thai coconut-and-peanut dipping sauce. Local fluke touched by extra virgin olive oil, a squeeze of Meyer lemon, and Maldon sea salt is an example of the first-rate crudo of the day; while Baja-style fish tacos feature tortillas stuffed with fried pollack, shredded cabbage, and chipotle-lime mayonnaise. For the fish-free, a raw vegan kelp noodle-pad Thai is remarkably satisfying.

Karczma

Polish ✗

B1

136 Greenpoint Ave. (bet. Franklin St. & Manhattan Ave.)

Subway: Greenpoint Av
Phone: 718-349-1744
Web: www.karczmabrooklyn.com
Price: ⊘

Lunch & dinner daily

Located in a slice of Greenpoint that still boasts a sizeable Polish population, Karczma offers a lovely old-world ambience that may belie its age (opened for five-plus years) but perfectly matches its very traditional, budget-friendly menu. Hearty offerings may include peasant-style lard mixed with bacon and spices, or a plate of Polish specialties piled high with pierogies (three varieties, steamed or fried, topped with sliced onions and butter), kielbasa, potato pancakes, hunter's stew, and stuffed cabbage. Grilled plates can be prepared for two or three, while others, like the roasted hocks in beer, could easily feed an army.

The quaint, farmhouse-inspired interior is efficiently staffed with smiling servers in floral skirts and embroidered vests.

Kings County Imperial

Chinese ✗

B3

20 Skillman Ave. (at Meeker Ave.)

Subway: Lorimer St - Metropolitan Av
Phone: 718-610-2000
Web: www.kingscountyimperial.com
Price: $$

Dinner nightly

While this 'hood has enjoyed a rush of good restaurants in recent years, Kings County Imperial creates a stir within the stir. The décor is nothing to write home about—though it's cute and disheveled in all the right ways and boasts a mean "backyard." But, their pan-Chinese dishes have certainly set tongues a wagging.

Think juicy white broiler chicken dumplings laced with cinnamon-red oil and Kings County Soy Works (carried on tap, fresh from the Pearl River Delta in Southern China); or creamy *kung pao* sweet potatoes paired with silky king trumpet mushrooms. A salt-and-pepper pork chop dish features outstanding quality meat; while tender tea-smoked *moo shu* duck, marinated for 48 hours, is paired with soft homemade wheat pancakes.

Krolewskie Jadlo

Polish ✗

B2

694 Manhattan Ave. (bet. Nassau & Norman Aves.)

Subway: Nassau Av
Phone: 718-383-8993
Web: www.krolewskiejadlo.com
Price:

Lunch & dinner daily

Krolewskie Jadlo ("king's feast" in Polish) sits in a Greenpoint enclave that was once home to a large number of Polish immigrants. Although the size of the community has decreased through the years, the area still thrives with a distinct Eastern European soul.

The room is pleasant and routinely packed with crowds basking in the enjoyable authenticity. The Polish plate brings all one could hope for in a hearty old-world platter: cabbage rolls stuffed with ground beef and braised in tart tomato sauce; pan-fried potato pierogis; and a link of smoky kielbasa. Other items are just as tasty, like the pounded pork shoulder steak, grilled and brushed with honey, and served with pickled cabbage and beets.

Known for their dessert make sure to end on a sweet note.

Le Fond

French

 B2

105 Norman Ave. (at Leonard St.)

Subway: Nassau Av
Phone: 718-389-6859
Web: www.lefondbk.com
Price: $$

Lunch Sun
Dinner Tue – Sun

Chef-owner Jake Eberle's cute corner restaurant shows us that not every dish needs reimagining and not every recipe requires reinterpretation. He's a French-trained chef whose cooking is crisp, clean, and comfortingly classic—and his well-balanced menu includes words like "roulade" and "blancmange" that here seem curiously reassuring. That's not to say his food doesn't pack a punch: the rich, meaty cassoulet could keep an army on the march for days.

Globe lights hang from the ceiling to illuminate a sea-blue room with bespoke wooden furniture. The acoustics can be bouncy and those lacking the necessary padding will find the seating a little numbing. But, there is honest toil and earnest endeavor happening here and it deserves support.

Lilia

Italian

B3

567 Union Ave. (at N. 10th St.)

Subway: Lorimer St - Metropolitan Av
Phone: 718-576-3095
Web: www.lilianewyork.com
Price: $$$

Dinner nightly

Who's not happy to see Missy Robbins back on the culinary scene, whipping up pastas that could bring the savviest diner to their knees? Tucked amongst the mish-mash of shiny new condos and the roar of the BQE that make up this part of Williamsburg, sleek Lilia occupies an old corner auto shop. The transformation is dramatic, replete with iron casement windows, unique tiling, and contemplative artwork.

Most of the dishes at Lilia ooze authenticity, made all the better by a warm, knowledgeable service staff who are happy to elaborate on details. Dinner might begin with cured sardines laid over a thick slice of sourdough, dotted with dill and capers; or chewy rigatoni *diavola* in a chunky tomato-based salsa humming with chili pepper and salty pecorino.

519

Llama Inn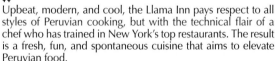

B3

Peruvian ✗✗

50 Withers St. (bet. Lorimer & Union Sts.)

Subway: Lorimer St - Metropolitan Av   Dinner nightly
Phone: 718-387-3434
Web: www.llamainnnyc.com
Price: $$

Upbeat, modern, and cool, the Llama Inn pays respect to all styles of Peruvian cooking, but with the technical flair of a chef who has trained in New York's top restaurants. The result is a fresh, fun, and spontaneous cuisine that aims to elevate Peruvian food.

Fish courses are notable, and nowhere is that more clear than in the fresh and expertly cut raw sea bream *tiradito* with persimmon, ginger, yuzu, and nutty poppy seeds. Fluke ceviche is just as memorable, served in a bit of dashi with lime, onion, cilantro, aji, and wonderfully spicy *leche de tigre*. Then move on to devour decadent little skewers of pork belly brushed with Chinese five-spice, soy, garlic, and barbecue sauce. Excellent desserts include airy coffee mousse with chocolate and *lucuma*.

Lucky Luna

C2

Fusion ✗

167 Nassau Ave. (at Diamond St.)

Subway: Nassau Av   Lunch Wed – Sun
Phone: 718-383-6038   Dinner Tue – Sun
Web: www.luckyluna-ny.com
Price: $$

There's no other restaurant around like Lucky Luna. Seriously. Their delicious menu is a hybrid of Taiwanese and Mexican cuisine. The pizzazz on the plate is served in a simple yet tidy assemblage of glossy black tables, and an ambitious beverage program makes the small bar a total draw.

Mom's sweet-and-sour cucumber salad, flavored with ginger and garlic, is a bracing start for Peking duck confit *bao* spread with hoisin mayonnaise, garnished with crispy duck *chicharrònes* and duck fat popcorn dusted with Chinese five spice. Another hit: the taco of "reverse" carnitas is a pile of succulent pork shoulder that's been seared then braised in a broth of beer, oranges, and tomatoes, and finally topped with crunchy bits of radish and spicy pickles.

Luksus at Tørst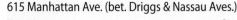

C o n t e m p o r a r y

 B2

615 Manhattan Ave. (bet. Driggs & Nassau Aves.)

Subway: Nassau Av | Dinner Tue – Sun
Phone: 718-389-6034
Web: www.luksusnyc.com
Price: $$$$

Tucked behind a little beer bar in Greenpoint, it doesn't get a lot more hip than Luksus at Tørst. The man to thank for this den of Scandinavian deliciousness is Daniel Burns, who took a chance on a highly unique concept and never looked back. It's a lovely and snug space with a lot of heart, but what keeps people loyal are the culinary surprises that the passionate Burns brings to the table again and again—along with a downright magical bread he bakes on premises.

Inside the small room, the open kitchen teems with activity. A handful of tables and stools lining a counter offer great views of the action—the effect is something like having an amazingly talented chef cook privately in your home. Burns and his sous chef hand-deliver each dish, always with an explanation and sometimes, if you're lucky, with a second helping of that fabulous bread.

Dinner might include creative dishes like one of cabbage chips dusted with smoky paprika; or a pristine, deep-fried oyster surrounded by cauliflower custard. Silky pork neck might get paired with roasted parsley root and crabapple purée.

Save room for inventive desserts like parsnip ice cream, featuring crispy, wafer-like studs of chanterelle.

Maison Premiere

Seafood

B3

298 Bedford Ave. (bet. S. 2nd & Grand Sts.)

Subway: Bedford Av
Phone: 347-335-0446
Web: www.maisonpremiere.com
Price: $$$

Lunch Sat – Sun
Dinner nightly

This ultra-retro tavern may feel dark and old-timey, like a watering hole where the Founding Fathers would have stopped for fortification before fending off the British. But, the massive, U-shaped bar is particularly coveted, so arrive early or prepare to wait for your absinthe drip.

To accompany the stellar sips, a vast selection of oysters, clams, and group-friendly seafood plateaux seem to pop up on every table. The kitchen's talent is equally clear in such preparations as luscious sea urchin served in a chilled shellfish consommé with fragrant lemongrass and thin slices of sweet grapes. Heartier appetites will delight in a thick, juicy pork Porterhouse, glazed with jus, served alongside braised kale, roasted beets, and finished with zippy horseradish cream.

Manila Social Club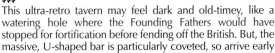

Asian

B3

2 Hope St. (At Roebling St.)

Subway: Lorimer St - Metropolitan Av
Phone: 718-384-4396
Web: www.manilasocialclub.com
Price: $$

Lunch Sat – Sun
Dinner Wed – Sat

Everything's buzzing at the Manila Social Club, a sibling-run Filipino restaurant with a ton of heart and some formidable culinary talent. Straddling a bustling corner of Roebling Street, it's a small but lovely space, with a sweet little bar that doubles as a welcome refuge for waiting customers.

Chef Björn DelaCruz may be self-trained but delivers one surprise after another. Filipino guilty pleasures like Spam fries are served with banana ketchup and pickled mango sauce; while perfectly fried whole snapper gets a delicious lift from jasmine rice tucked with cubed sweet chayote and hints of absinthe. Big spenders can impress their friends by calling ahead to order the $100 Golden Cristal donut for a dessert made with ube (sweet purple yam).

Marlow & Sons

American

B3

81 Broadway (bet. Berry St. & Wythe Ave.)

Subway: Marcy Av
Phone: 718-384-1441
Web: www.marlowandsons.com
Price: $$

Lunch & dinner daily

Nestled behind a little specialty goods store offering excellent bread, coffee and to-go items, the popular Marlow & Sons sports a rustic hideaway vibe—replete with thick wood communal tables and flickering votives. The place is charming enough to warrant a visit even if the food wasn't ace, but as it happens, the rotating breakfast, lunch and dinner menus are divine.

Kick things off with a smoky bowl of tomato soup sporting a delicate flutter of basil leaves; and then move on to the scrumptious brick chicken, a menu mainstay of moist chicken legs that get their crisp skin from being cooked under a brick. Paired with seasonal sides like a soft pile of corn, caramelized onions and slow-roasted cherry tomatoes, the result is homespun bliss.

Mesa Coyoacán

Mexican

C3

372 Graham Ave. (bet. Conselyea St. & Skillman Ave.)

Subway: Graham Av
Phone: 718-782-8171
Web: www.mesacoyoacan.com
Price: $$

Lunch Wed – Sun
Dinner nightly

Mexico City native, Chef Ivan Garcia has settled into this Brooklyn hot spot, where wolfish appetites are sated with richly flavored fare. Fronted by windows that open up to bustling Graham Avenue, the long space is outfitted with patterned wallpaper, snug banquettes, and communal tables. The kitchen's spirited cooking is simply a joy. Partake in tacos featuring hand-crafted tortillas, like the *suadero* stuffed with beef brisket and avocado salsa; or *torta tinga de pollo*, packed with shredded chipotle-braised chicken, mashed black beans, pickled jalapeños, and a toasted roll to sop up that delish sauce. Reposado and diced mango enhances the *pastel tres leches*—and to keep the tequila flowing, hit up nearby Zona Rosa.

Meadowsweet

B3

Mediterranean 🍴🍴

149 Broadway (bet. Bedford & Driggs Aves.)

Subway: Marcy Av

Phone: 718-384-0673

Web: www.meadowsweetnyc.com

Price: $$

Lunch Sat – Sun
Dinner Wed – Mon

Tucked next to the steely skeleton of the Williamsburg Bridge, Meadowsweet cuts a stylish industrial figure with its glass-fronted façade, whitewashed brick walls, and original mosaic-tiled floors. Leather banquettes line the wall, and pendant bulbs illuminate one of several beautiful oil paintings of a meadow. Inside, the restaurant jumps with Williamsburg's finest —along with more than a few bridge-hoppers from Manhattan and beyond. And that's on a slow night.

The fuss is quite merited. Despite ample competition in this section of town, Chef/owner Polo Dobkin and wife, Stephanie Lempert, manage to elevate the kitchen's dishes into next level territory, and they do so in a lovely, urbane setting with loads of charm and friendly service.

The inventive American menu gets a lift from Mediterranean accents: a bowl of deliciously chewy squid ink "fettuccine" arrives with Spanish octopus, chorizo, hot chili and breadcrumbs; while tender duck finds its match in braised red cabbage, poached Seckel pear, and roasted pear-and-black currant coulis. There's an impressive list of cocktails and wine; not to mention a globetrotting beer selection ranging from Austrian lagers to Japanese ales.

Okonomi

J a p a n e s e 🍴

C3

150 Ainslie St. (bet. Leonard & Lorimer Sts.)

Subway: Lorimer St - Metropolitan Av
Phone: 718-302-0598
Web: www.okonomibk.com
Price: 😒

Lunch daily
Dinner Mon – Fri

A small counter and a handful of tables is the extent of this tiny café headed by Chef Yuji Haraguchi, famous for his ramen pop-ups. Regardless of the time of day, Okonomi's delightfully unconstrained Japanese cuisine is a compelling reason to visit.

Locally grown produce and domestic fish are the foundation of the high-quality *ichiju sansai*, a set lunch of *shioyaki* (salt-grilled) or miso-marinated broiled fish, rice, miso soup, and *shira-ae* (wilted greens with a tofu dressing). Come evening, the focus shifts to ramen, with each steaming bowl bearing the distinctive hand of the skilled chef. A surf-and-turf broth stocked with thin, straight noodles and roasted fish is just one example; while broth-less *mazemen* is dressed for the season.

Paulie Gee's

P i z z a 🍴

B2

60 Greenpoint Ave. (bet. Franklin & West Sts.)

Subway: Greenpoint Av
Phone: 347-987-3747
Web: www.pauliegee.com
Price: 😒

Dinner nightly

Owner Paul Giannone, aka Paulie Gee, channeled a lifelong love of pizza into this charmingly delicious spot that feels as if it has been around forever. Rustic in appearance, the room's cool concrete and brick are warmed by the glow of the wood-burning oven imported from Naples. From here, Giannone and his son work their magic.

The addictive crust is beguilingly moist and chewy, perfumed with smoke, and adroitly salted. Killer wood-fired pies dominate the menu with tempting combinations, excellent ingredients, and whimsical names. Offerings may include the Harry Belafontina—fontina, tomatoes, beefy meatballs, cremini mushrooms, and golden raisins. Vegans get equal respect here, with an added menu of vegan cheese and house-made vegan sausage.

Peter Luger ✿✿

Steakhouse ✗

B3

178 Broadway (at Driggs Ave.)

Subway: Marcy Av   Lunch & dinner daily
Phone: 718-387-7400
Web: www.peterluger.com
Price: $$$$

More than just an icon of the New York dining scene—Peter Luger is an idolized classic. Run on wheels by a team of gloriously forthright waiters, this munificent paean to beef doesn't just serve legendary steaks, it provides a side helping of history too. The wood paneling and beer-hall tables tell of family gatherings, friends united, deal making, success celebrated and stories swapped. It's evocative and unforgettable. It's also unapologetically old-school—computerization and credit cards remain fanciful futuristic concepts, so you'll need to come with a few Benjamins tucked into your wallet.

Start with a thick slice of bacon to get your taste buds up to speed before the steak arrives. These slabs of finely marbled Porterhouse are dry-aged in-house for around 28 days, which means there's tenderloin on one side of the bone and strip steak on the other. They are then broiled to perfection, sliced before being brought to the table, and served with their own sauce as well as a host of sides, which range from their version of German fried potatoes to creamed spinach.

If you can still feel a pulse after that, there's always cheesecake served with their equally famous "schlag" to finish you off.

Ramen Yebisu

B3

126 N. 6th St. (bet. Bedford Ave. & Berry St.)

Subway: Bedford Av
Phone: 718-782-1444
Web: www.ramenyebisu.com
Price: 🍣

Lunch & dinner daily

At this popular Williamsburg *ramen-ya*, Chef and Hokkaido native Akira Hiratsuka ladles signature bowlfuls of Sapporo-style ramen, characterized by its seafood-infused broth and wavy noodles aged for 48-hours. The results are distinct and delicious. Among the host of options to be tried are *shoyu* (soy-based), *shio* (salt-based), or the special house ramen brimming with a bounty of shellfish. A recent unique offering featured a fiery broth infused with a blend of 12 spices and fish sauce and filled with bone-in pork rib, cabbage, and red chilies.

Slurp your soup at one of two seating options in the moody, dark-walled space: perched atop tall tables or at a counter looking into the kitchen, where a refrigerator unit is stocked with custom-made noodles.

Rider

XX

B2

80 N. 6th St. (at Whythe Ave.)

Subway: Bedford Av
Phone: 718-210-3152
Web: www.riderbklyn.com
Price: $$

Lunch Sat – Sun
Dinner nightly

Some may think this hip, new bi-level eatery is an offshoot of the Brooklyn performance space National Sawdust, but in fact Rider vies for top billing. Downstairs, you'll find an industrial vibe outfitted with concrete flooring, exposed brick walls, and comfy banquettes; upstairs is polished, low-lit and moodier.

Patrick Connolly has put together an exciting menu designed for sharing, with a refreshing focus on vegetables. The execution and flavors transcend the trendiness of the space, offering unfussy, timeless dishes that may be considered small plates, but are generously portioned. Try gemelli bathed in mushroom ragù with crisp breadcrumbs, or grilled mortadella on sourdough with ricotta, toasted sunflower seeds and a nasturtium "pesto."

Rye

American 🍴

B3

247 S. 1st St. (bet. Havemeyer & Roebling Sts.)

Subway: Marcy Av
Phone: 718-218-8047
Web: www.ryerestaurant.com
Price: $$

Lunch Sat – Sun
Dinner nightly

Rye's Classic Old Fashioned—a carefully crafted swirl of liquid amber—is the perfect personification of Chef Cal Elliott's beloved gastropub: strong, satisfying, and comforting. Anchored by a reclaimed mahogany bar, the Brooklyn speakeasy is accented accordingly with creaky plank flooring, a pressed-tin ceiling, and exposed filament bulbs overhead. For even more reasons to imbibe, climb down to the basement offshoot, The Bar Below Rye.

Bar snacks such as oysters, cheeses, and duck rillettes with pickled watermelon lead to a succinct lineup of cooking that includes crispy skin seared Scottish salmon dressed with seasonal vegetables and preserved lemon. For dessert, the warm and fudgy molten chocolate cake is another classic Rye gets just right.

The Saint Austere

Contemporary 🍽

C3

613 Grand St. (bet. Leonard & Lorimer Sts.)

Subway: Lorimer St - Metropolitan Av
Phone: 718-388-0012
Web: www.thesaintaustere.com
Price: 🍺

Dinner nightly

Sometimes all one needs is a fine glass of wine and a little snack (or three). For this, The Saint Austere fits the bill nicely. Platings bring on far-flung influences—as in the *bánh Mi(lano)*, pork terrine, thinly shaved mortadella, and house-pickled vegetables sandwiched into a toasted baguette moistened by a chili-flecked dressing. However, the menu's truest muse is a general coupling of Italian and Spanish flavors, such as pork belly *croquetas* accompanied by a dipping sauce of crushed chicken livers; or slow-cooked polenta topped with sweet onions caramelized in sausage drippings.

The spartanly adorned room offers a hospitable bar in addition to three communal tables. And the wine list proffers a gently priced selection of mostly European labels.

Salt + Charcoal

Japanese ✗

B3

171 Grand St. (at Bedford Ave.)

Subway: Bedford Av
Phone: 718-782-2087
Web: www.saltandcharcoal.com
Price: $$

Lunch & dinner daily

The attention-grabbing, mouthwatering name says it all: this place is all about *robata* items, cooked over Japanese charcoal and dressed with a selection of salts. Inside the tiny corner space, minimal seating is amplified by a counter accented with black-glazed brick and mid-century modern chairs. And, highly-coveted sidewalk tables serve as a front row for Bedford Avenue's hipster parade.

Skewers and small plates of charred nibbles include sweet miso-glazed *goma fu*, fish collar of the day, or strips of boneless Kurobuta pork short rib. Even the flame-free items are enticing, including soba, *hako* sushi, house-made chilled tofu accompanied by a trio of salts, as well as a refreshing salad comprised of four different varieties of seaweed.

Samurai Mama

Japanese ✗

B3

205 Grand St. (bet. Bedford & Driggs Aves.)

Subway: Bedford Av
Phone: 718-599-6161
Web: www.samuraimama.com
Price: ⊜⊜

Lunch & dinner daily

For an authentic taste of Japan in Williamsburg, Chef Makoto Suzuki's cozy den is the place to be. Save for a handful of seats and high-backed wooden booths, a communal table touched by seasonal flora hosts the majority of its occupants. Raw offerings include taco-style sushi, the fish cradled by a sheet of toasted nori, but the menu's crux is on cooked bites—think handmade pork gyoza, kabocha squash simmered in dashi, and nicely done tempura. A truly special treat here is the udon, a tangle of plump, chewy house-made noodles crafted from California-milled flour and filtered water bobbing in luscious broths. Try the seafood curry variation—a rich, bonito and curry powder-spiked broth stocked with sweet shrimp, mussels, and scallops.

Sauvage

B2

905 Lorimer St. (at Nassau Ave.)

Subway: Nassau Av
Phone: 718-486-6816
Web: www.sauvageny.com
Price: $$$

Lunch Sat – Sun
Dinner nightly

Sauvage means "wild and natural" in French, and that's a perfectly apt description for this handsome restaurant with its small and thoughtful list of naturalist wines. Select one of the organic, biodynamic offerings; then sit back and relax while you take in the leather booths, that beautiful walnut bar, hand-blown glass chandeliers and tropical plants.

But enough about drinks and décor, because the kitchen happens to be whipping up some dishes that absolutely thrill. Highlights include the creamy Santa Barbara sea urchin served with nage, tart rhubarb and ponzu; or even those feather-light ricotta dumplings. Pooled in a lovely barley consommé kissed with chives, they're also paired with braised radishes, fingerling potatoes, sweet cipollini and herbs.

Shalom Japan 😊

B3

301 S. 4th St. (at Rodney St.)

Subway: Marcy Av
Phone: 718-388-4012
Web: www.shalomjapannyc.com
Price: $$

Lunch Sat – Sun
Dinner nightly

The curious moniker of this sweet spot refers to the backgrounds of its husband-and-wife team, Chefs Aaron Israel and Sawako Okochi. Each has an impressive resume, and together the result is a unique labor of love. Nightly specials are displayed via a wall-mounted blackboard with small plates progressing to a handful of entrées.

Monkfish hot pot features *ankimo*-enriched miso broth, ground shrimp balls, glass noodles, and a heap of fragrant fresh herbs. The house-baked sake *kasu* challah with raisin butter is a highly recommended start. But, it may also turn up as toro toast smeared with scallion and wasabi cream cheese and topped with finely chopped, smoked lean tuna belly. Still craving more? Experience it once again in the warm chocolate bread pudding.

Semilla

Contemporary ✗

B3

160 Havemeyer St., No. 5 (bet. S. 2nd & S. 3rd Sts.)

Subway: Marcy Av   Dinner Tue – Sat
Phone: 718-782-3474
Web: www.semillabk.com
Price: $$$

Brooklyn ▶ Williamsburg

Vegetables bask in the spotlight at this stellar South Williamsburg counter, where the formidable team of Chefs José Ramírez-Ruiz and Pamela Yung apply their fine dining aptitude to produce an improvisational feast out of the season's bounty.

Turning the notion of service on its head, members of the kitchen step away from their stations to deliver their intricate compositions—each of them plated on hand thrown pottery. The briefest of descriptions is offered upon presentation, which means that a mouthful of "grilled squash," for example, might also deliver raw slivers of *pattypan*, creamy peanut sauce, and a dusting of dried mint. Embellishments like foie gras and trout roe are used sparingly and to splendid effect, never outshining the true flavor of the produce. Semilla's bread is house-made, excellent, and used to accentuate the menu; as seen in a wedge of flax seed-barley sourdough with cultured butter to accompany a roasted carrot "mille-feuille," alongside smoked potato purée and fava greens sauce.

Although the duo of sweets to finish may include options that disappoint, dessert can also be an electrifying success as in the egg yolk-saffron sorbet, cloud of smoked cream, and passion fruit.

St. Anselm

B3

355 Metropolitan Ave. (bet. Havemeyer & Roebling Sts.)

Subway: Bedford Av

Phone: 718-384-5054

Web: N/A

Price: $$

Lunch Sat – Sun
Dinner nightly

Step through the heavy wood-framed glass door and let the smell of charred meat and grassy notes from *chimichurri* greet you. The low ceiling is shingled with distressed wood to lend a rustic note to the room. Its open floor plan accentuates the bright flames from the sizzling grill, visible through the kitchen.

Settle down at the bar to sample offbeat wines and cocktails. A genuine sense of contentedness fills the packed room, as guests enjoy small plates of monster prawns, grilled quickly in their steaming shells, finished with garlic, parsley, and a hint of spice. Sweet tea-brined young Bobo chicken served with head and feet intact may seem like it isn't for everyone, but it should be. Perfectly moist and whole-roasted, it is pure, hands-on pleasure.

Xixa

B3

241 S. 4th St. (bet. Havemeyer & Roebling Sts.)

Subway: Marcy Av

Phone: 718-388-8860

Web: www.xixany.com

Price: $$

Dinner Wed – Sun

Flaunting the trademark style of Chef Jason Marcus, this Mexican romp packs Williamsburg denizens into a slender space set aglow by etched brass ceiling pendants.

A delicious alchemy is at work here, as evidenced in the crabmeat-topped tamale flan sauced with fava bean-poblano purée; baked lamb meatballs in chipotle cream accompanied by grilled garlic and cheese sprinkled Texas toast; or strawberry *tres leches* with fragrant cilantro ice cream.

Like the menu, the beverage listing is loads of fun. Wines are whimsically arranged under headings of iconic women (Rieslings listed in the Helen Mirren section are described as concentrated and transcendent), and deconstructed margaritas feature a shot of tequila poured over frozen cubes of fruit juices.

Zenkichi

B2

Japanese

77 N. 6th St. (at Wythe Ave.)

Subway: Bedford Av
Phone: 718-388-8985
Web: www.zenkichi.com
Price: $$

Dinner nightly

Though this Japanese standby might have seemed more novel a few years ago, Zenkichi still retains plenty of magic. The atmosphere is relaxed but focused, and the omakase is surprisingly well-priced for this neighborhood. Secluded booths offer a sexy vibe for date night, where couples can ring a bell for service. And Akariba, a cool little cash-only bar connected to the restaurant next door, serves up such treats as oysters and sake.

In addition to the à la carte and dessert menus, this kitchen also offers three variations on omakase: traditional, vegetarian, and wheat-free. But unlike the typical omakase, there's something here for everyone, and the pre-determined dishes may unveil Saikyo miso cod or a heap of summer vegetables in Tosazu gelée.

Zizi Limona

B3

Middle Eastern

129 Havemeyer St. (at S. 1st St.)

Subway: Lorimer St - Metropolitan Av
Phone: 347-763-1463
Web: www.zizilimona.com
Price: $$

Lunch Fri – Sun
Dinner nightly

This hip Middle Eastern gem brings such bright complexity and care to its exotic menu that it's hard to put Zizi Limona's food in a box.

Nestled inside a charming café with cute brasserie details and colorful Mediterranean tiles, the mood is delightfully relaxed, with neighborhood regulars sipping cold, refreshing cocktails and catching up with friends and family. A small opening even offers a view into the tiny, lively kitchen. Though it's virtually impossible to make a bad choice here, don't skip on the delicious chicken shawarma served over thick, luscious hummus and finished with a few tender chickpeas and tahini. Other delights include golden cauliflower florets, served in a pan over a thick bed of tahini, dotted with toasted black cumin, sweet onions and parsley.

Queens

Nearly as large as Manhattan, the Bronx, and Staten Island combined, Queens covers 120 square miles on the western end of Long Island. Reputedly the most ethnically varied district in the world, its diversified nature is reflected in the numerous immigrants who arrive here each year for its affordable housing, strong sense of community, and cultural explosion. Such a unique convergence of cultures results in this stately borough's predominantly global and very distinctive flavor. Though Superstorm Sandy was especially damaging to the Rockaways, these streets continue to prosper with amazing and affordable international eats even today.

GLOBE-TROTTING

Begin your around-the-world feast in Astoria, a charming quarter of old-world brick row houses and Mediterranean groceries. Discover grilled octopus bookended by baklava at one of the many terrific Greek joints. Then, prolong your culinary spree over juicy kebabs at **Little Egypt** on Steinway Street; or chow on equally hearty Czech *tlačenka* at the popular **Bohemian Hall & Beer Garden**. On lazy days, brew buffs can be found at Astoria's hottest beer havens—**Sweet Afton**—for an intimate setting with a serious selection, or equally sublime **Studio Square** for the ultimate alfresco experience. Showcasing equally exquisite beverages alongside beautiful baked goods, **Leli's Bakery** may be a relatively young member of Astoria's dining scene, but hooks its troops with age-old roots—their commercial kitchen in the Bronx has been supplying fine dining establishments with a wealth of sweetness since

time immemorial. Founded in 1937, **La Guli** is an Italian *pasticceria* whose expert talent has been feeding families with rich and creamy cakes and cookies. Staying true to tradition, **The Lemon Ice King of Corona**, brought to you by the Benfaremo family, is a nostalgic ode to Italian ice complete with sugar-free selections for health-embattled hordes. But, for an unapologetically potent treat, **To Laiko** is the area's favorite for a delicious frappe.

Sojourning south and then to the east, **La Boulangerie** brings a slice of France to Forest Hills by way of fresh-baked loaves of white bread and crusty baguettes. Of course, cheese couples best with bread, and the choices are abundant at **Leo's Latticini** in Corona. Surprisingly, eating in **Terminal C** at La Guardia Airport is now considered a gastronomic delight with wonderful food and beverage outposts churned out by star chefs like Andrew Carmellini and Michael Lomonaco. Hopping airports, JFK's **Delta Terminal 4** is also becoming known as a culinary emporium replete with such acclaimed offerings as **Shake Shack** courtesy of restaurateur Danny Meyer, and **Uptown Brasserie** from the much raved-about chef, Marcus Samuelsson. Frequent flyers with refined palates will appreciate Dave Cook's *Eating in Translation*, a daily newsletter citing fantastic food finds at unusual locations—including airports! Speaking of outposts, **Sylvia's**—once a Harlem landmark—has also set up shop here (in Jamaica) and cooks up generous portions of its Southern comfort food. And, **M. Wells Dinette** housed inside MoMA PS 1 delivers insanely inventive items to curious visitors and the lucky locals of Long Island City. Offering an imaginative blend of diner signatures, Quebecois favorites, and "are you serious!?" combos, this sequel to the original, outstanding diner continues to charm crowds by simply doing their thing. While in this 'hood, feel the sass and spirit at PS 1's "Warm Up"—one of Gotham's greatest summer soirées featuring a DJ, turntables, and all that jazz. And housed in the historic Falchi Building, **Doughnut Plant** boasts an outré selection, crafted from the best ingredients in town—tres leches doughnuts anyone? And, what

goes best with dessert? Coffee of course, with a crowning range of roasted beans available at **Vassilaros and Sons**. Enhancing this quarter's global repute is **Güllüoglu**, a Turkish bakery and café whose elegant space and tasty bites bring Istanbul to life. But, if Pakistani flavors are a particular fave, then **Bundu Khan** is worth a trip for every type of grilled delight. Close out these global eats at cozy **Café Norma**—a hot spot for homey, comfort fare.

ASIA MEETS THE AMERICAS

Flushing still reigns as Queens' most vibrant Asian haven and NYers are always dropping in for dim sum, Henan specialties, or a savory bowl of *pho* like you'd find streetside in Saigon. Food vendors at Flushing's mini-malls offer feasts from far flung corners of China that are light on the pockets but big on flavor. Of both local note and city-wide acclaim, **New World Mall Food Court** is a clean, airy space serving excellent Asian food. You'll find everything at these inviting stalls from hand-pulled noodles (at **Lanzhou**) and fiery Sichuan dishes at **Chengdu**

Snacks, to Taiwanese shaved ice for the end of the night. And the offerings don't stop here. Over on Main Street, vegans feel the love and care at **New Bodai Vegetarian** where such kosher-friendly dishes as vegetarian duck and seaweed sesame rolls keep the crowds returning time and again. These same health food fans as well as epicureans from all walks may then trek east to arrive at **Queens County Farm Museum**, considered one of the largest working farms in the city that supports sustainable farming, farm-to-table meals, and is rife with livestock, a greenhouse, and educational programs. Speaking of livestock, **Chand Halal Meat** is a specialty market where the butchers know your name and game: beef, goat, or lamb. From Flushing to Floral Park, **Real Usha Sweets & Snacks** cooks India's favorite street eats, which also make for excellent dinner party treats. Think *chana chor*, *papadi*, and banana chips—a Kerala specialty. Also reminiscent of flavors from the sub-continent, **Singh's Roti Shop and Bar** prepares Caribbean delicacies like curry chicken, saltfish, and *aloo pie* to gratify its contiguous community. Shifting gears from south to Central Asia, as many as 40,000 immigrants traveled to New York after the fall of the Soviet Union. They staked their claim in Forest Hills, and **King David Kosher Restaurant** remains a paragon among these elder statesmen and their large families for Bukharian specialties.

Energy and variety personify Elmhurst, the thriving hearth of settlers primarily from Latin America, China, and Southeast Asia. **The Royal Kathin**,

a celebration that occurs at the end of Thailand's rainy season, pays homage to the spirit of Buddhist monks. While Elmhurst's adaptation of this festival may lack the floods, it certainly proffers a bounty of authentic Thai bites. Whitney Avenue is home to a booming restaurant row with an array of small Southeast Asian storefronts. Indulge your *gado gado* yearning at **Upi Jaya** before getting your *laksa* on at **Taste Good**. Elmhurst spans the globe, so if the pungent flavors of Southeast Asia don't fit the bill, relocate from Asia to the Americas by way of thick, creamy Greek yogurt at **Kesso Foods**. This mini shop is a gem among locals, while **Cannelle Patisserie**'s carb-o-licious goodies keep the entire borough abuzz.

Jackson Heights is home to a large South Asian community. Take in the bhangra beats blaring from cars rolling along 74th Street. This dynamic commercial stretch is dotted with numerous Indian markets, Bengali sweet shops, and Himalayan-style eateries serving all types of *tandoori* specialties and steaming Tibetan *momos*. In keeping with the fact that Latin Americans also make up a large part of the demographic here, Roosevelt Avenue swarms with authentic taquerias, aromatic Colombian coffee shops, and sweet Argentinean spots to sate their vast range of assorted tastes.

WANDERING THROUGH WOODSIDE

Take this thriving thoroughfare west to Woodside, where Irish bars mingle with Thai spots. Once home to an enormous Irish population, Woodside now shares its streets with Thai and Filipino communities—even if the kelly green awnings of decade-old pubs scatter these blocks and clover-covered doors advertise in Gaelic. Set alongside **Donovan's**, an age-old Irish respite grilling up one of the best burgers in town, is **Little Manila**—an eight-block stretch of Roosevelt Avenue where you can stock up on Filipino groceries galore. Also find folks join the line outside **Jollibee**, a fast-food chain serving up flavors from home. If Filipino sounds too funky, rest assured as **Piemonte Ravioli** carries every choice of fresh pasta for an Italian *cena con la famiglia*. Down south in Sunnyside, you may also eat your way through Korea, Romania, China, Turkey, Mexico, and more.

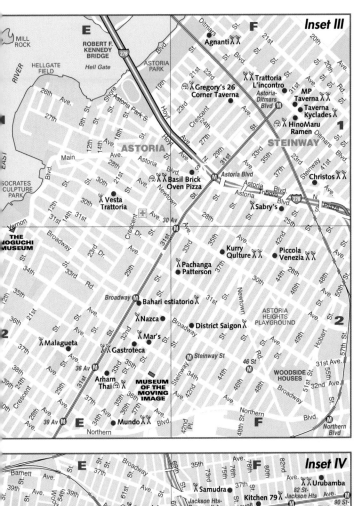

Inset III

MILL ROCK

ROBERT F. KENNEDY BRIDGE

HELLGATE FIELD

Hell Gate

ASTORIA PARK

EAST RIVER

SOCRATES SCULPTURE PARK

ASTORIA

STEINWAY

Agnanti ✗✗

Trattoria L'incontro ✗✗

Gregory's 26 Corner Taverna ✗

MP Taverna ✗✗

Taverna Kyclades ✗✗

HinoMaru Ramen ✗

Christos ✗✗

Basil Brick Oven Pizza ✗✗

Vesta Trattoria ✗

Sabry's ✗

THE NOGUCHI MUSEUM

Kurry Qulture ✗✗

Piccola Venezia ✗✗

Pachanga Patterson ✗

Bahari estiatorio ✗

ASTORIA HEIGHTS PLAYGROUND

Nazca ✗

District Saigon ✗

Mar's ✗

Malagueta ✗

Gastroteca ✗✗

Steinway St

WOODSIDE HOUSES

Arharn Thai ✗

MUSEUM OF THE MOVING IMAGE

Mundo ✗✗

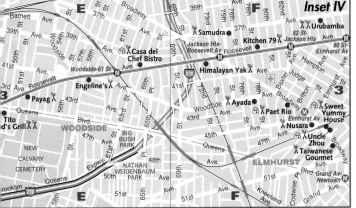

Inset IV

Barnett Ave.

Samudra ✗

Urubamba ✗✗

Casa del Chef Bistro ✗

Kitchen 79 ✗

Jackson Hts-Roosevelt Av

Himalayan Yak ✗

Engeline's ✗

Payag ✗

Ayada ✗

Paet Rio ✗

Sweet Yummy House ✗

Tito Rod's Grill ✗✗

Nusara ✗

WOODSIDE

BIG BUSH PARK

Uncle Zhou ✗

Taiwanese Gourmet ✗

ELMHURST

NEW CALVARY CEMETERY

NATHAN WEIDENBAUM PARK

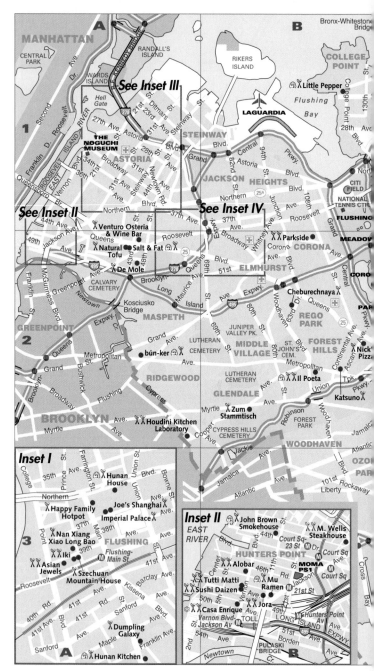

MANHATTAN

CENTRAL PARK

Franklin D. Roosevelt Dr.

Second Ave.

A

RANDALL'S ISLAND

WARDS ISLAND

Hell Gate

See Inset III

27th Ave.

21st St. 23rd St. Ditmars

31st St. Astoria

THE NOGUCHI MUSEUM

ASTORIA

26th St. 30th St. 31st St. 34th St. 36th St. Broadway

Vernon Blvd.

ROOSEVELT ISLAND

Queensboro Br.

EAST RIVER

Steinway St. Grand

Newtown Rd.

31st Ave. Broadway

34th Ave. 35th Ave. Steinway St.

Northern Blvd.

B

Bronx-Whitestone Bridge

RIKERS ISLAND

LAGUARDIA

STEINWAY

Blvd. Central Pkwy.

82nd St. Astoria Blvd.

94th St.

JACKSON HEIGHTS

Northern Blvd. (25A)

108th St.

Flushing Bay

College Point Blvd.

28th Ave.

North

CITI FIELD

NATIONAL TENNIS CTR.

FLUSHING

See Inset II

44th St. Jackson Ave.

49th Ave.

Queens Blvd.

✕ Venturo Osteria & Wine Bar

✕ Natural Tofu ● Salt & Fat ✕✕ 48th St.

43rd Ave.

✕ De Mole

See Inset IV

37th Ave. Roosevelt Ave.

Northern Blvd. Broadway

51st Ave. Queens Blvd.

Junction Blvd.

Corona

ELMHURST

✕✕ Parkside

CORONA

MEADOW

CORO

PAR

Roosevelt Ave.

Grand Ave.

(25)

69th St.

80th St.

CALVARY CEMETERY

Franklin St.

McGuinness Blvd.

GREENPOINT

Greenpoint Newtown Cr.

Brooklyn Queens Expwy.

Kosciusko Bridge

MASPETH

Brooklyn Long Island Expwy.

Maurice Ave.

Woodhaven

Cheburechnaya ✕

Queens

REGO PARK

PAP

(25)

Queens

Metropolitan Ave.

Grand Ave.

Bushwick Ave.

Flushing Ave.

Cypress Ave.

Grand Ave.

JUNIPER VALLEY PK.

LUTHERAN CEMETERY

MIDDLE VILLAGE

ST. JOHN'S CEM.

FOREST HILLS

Continental Ave.

Ascan Ave.

✕ Nick's Pizza

bún-ker ✕

RIDGEWOOD

BROOKLYN

Myrtle Ave.

LUTHERAN CEMETERY

GLENDALE

Myrtle Ave.

Cypress Hills St.

✕✕ Houdini Kitchen Laboratory

Cooper

CYPRESS HILLS CEMETERY

Metropolitan Ave.

(A) ✕ Il Poeta

Union Tpk.

Woodhaven Blvd.

Tpk.

Pkwy.

Katsuno ✕

✕ Zum Stammtisch

Robinson

FOREST PARK

WOODHAVEN

Jackie Ave.

Jamai

Atlantic

OZO

PAR

Inset I

College Point

35th Ave.

Prince St.

Farrington St.

Union St.

Bowne St.

Northern Blvd.

Ave.

(A) ✕ Hunan House

✕ Happy Family Hotpot

37th Ave.

Joe's Shanghai ✕

Imperial Palace ✕

✕ Nan Xiang Xiao Long Bao

38th Ave.

FLUSHING

✕✕ Iki

39th Ave.

✕✕ Asian Jewels

Flushing-Main St Ⓜ

41st Ave.

Roosevelt Ave.

✕ Szechuan Mountain House

Barclay Ave.

Kissena

40th Rd.

41st Rd.

Sanford Ave.

41st Ave. Ave.

Blvd.

✕ Dumpling Galaxy

Maple Ave.

Franklin Ave.

Sanford

A

(A) ✕ Hunan Kitchen ●

Inset II

EAST RIVER

✕ John Brown Smokehouse

44th Dr.

Court Sq-23 St Ⓜ

HUNTERS POINT

46th Ave.

11th St.

Center Blvd.

✕✕ Alobar

✕✕ Tutti Matti

✕ Sushi Daizen

50th Ave.

Vernon Blvd.

Jackson Ave.

(A) ✕ Mu Ramen

✕ Jora

(A) ✕ Casa Enrique

Vernon Blvd-Jackson Av Ⓜ

49th Ave.

TOLL

2nd St.

Newtown Cr.

54th Ave.

✕✕ M. Wells Steakhouse

Court Sq Ⓜ

D

MOMA PS1

21st St.

Court Sq

Ⓜ Hunters Point Av

LONG ISLAND EXPWY.

51st Ave.

Borden Ave.

PULASKI BRIDGE

B

Cross

Bay

542

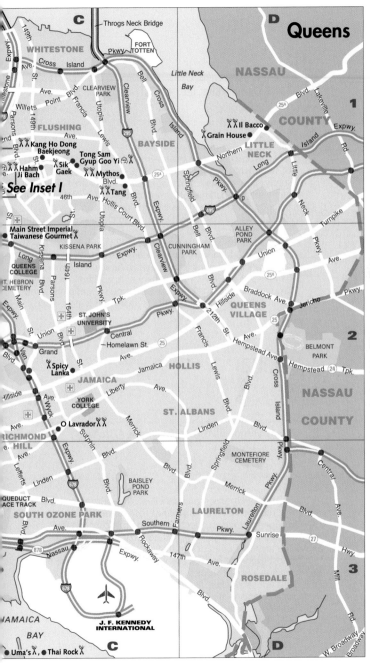

Queens

Throgs Neck Bridge

WHITESTONE

FORT TOTTEN

NASSAU

Little Neck Bay

CLEARVIEW PARK

COUNTY

149th Ave.

Cross Island

Willets Point Blvd.

Francis Lewis Blvd.

FLUSHING

149th St.

Parsons Blvd.

✕✕ Kang Ho Dong Baekjeong

✕✕ Hahm Ji Bach

✕ Sik Gaek

Tong Sam Gyup Goo Yi ✕

46th Ave.

✕✕ Mythos

✕✕ Tang

Hollis Court Blvd.

BAYSIDE

Utopia Pkwy.

Clearview Expwy.

✕✕ Il Bacco

● Grain House

LITTLE NECK

Northern Blvd.

Long Island Expwy.

Lakeville Rd.

Springfield Blvd.

Bell Blvd.

Little Neck Pkwy.

Union Turnpike

Main Street Imperial Taiwanese Gourmet ✕

KISSENA PARK

Long Island

Kissena Blvd.

164th St.

QUEENS COLLEGE

MT. HEBRON CEMETERY

Parsons Blvd.

ST. JOHN'S UNIVERSITY

CUNNINGHAM PARK

Clearview Expwy.

212th St.

Hillside Ave.

ALLEY POND PARK

Braddock Ave.

QUEENS VILLAGE

Union Tpk.

Jericho Tpk.

BELMONT PARK

NASSAU COUNTY

Main St.

Van Wyck Expwy.

Union Grand

Central —Homelawn St.

Francis Lewis Blvd.

HOLLIS

Hempstead Ave.

Hempstead Tpk.

✕ Spicy Lanka

JAMAICA

YORK COLLEGE

Liberty Ave.

Jamaica Ave.

ST. ALBANS

Linden Blvd.

Cross Island Pkwy.

Hillside Ave.

RICHMOND HILL

O Lavrador ✕ ✕

Merrick Blvd.

MONTEFIORE CEMETERY

Central Ave.

AQUEDUCT RACE TRACK

SOUTH OZONE PARK

Lefferts Blvd.

Linden Blvd.

BAISLEY POND PARK

Farmers Blvd.

Springfield Blvd.

LAURELTON

Laurelton Pkwy.

Sunrise Hwy.

Nassau Expwy.

Southern Pkwy.

Rockaway Blvd.

147th Ave.

ROSEDALE

W. Broadway

JAMAICA BAY

✈ J. F. KENNEDY INTERNATIONAL

● Uma's ✕, ● Thai Rock ✕

See Inset I

Agnanti

F1

Greek ✗✗

19-06 Ditmars Blvd. (at 19th St.)

Subway: Astoria - Ditmars Blvd
Phone: 718-545-4554
Web: N/A
Price: $$

Lunch & dinner daily

Situated on a corner lot, this taverna offers stunning panoramas of midtown, the Queensboro Bridge, and Astoria Park; on sunny days, outdoor tables speckle the front area. The view alone sets this darling apart from the host of Greek restaurants that popularized Astoria as a dining destination.

Yet the food offers its own view of Greek cuisine. Here, East meets West in a menu section reserved for Turkish classics with a unique spin, such as *midia dolma* or mussels with pine-nut studded rice. Other usual suspects also make an appearance including tzatziki with cucumber, lemon, and garlic—a marvelous accompaniment to zucchini-and-cheese croquettes. But don't fill up until you've sampled smoky swordfish kabobs basted with rosemary and lemon sauce.

Alobar

B3

American ✗✗

46-42 Vernon Blvd. (bet. 46th Rd. & 47th Ave.)

Subway: Vernon Blvd - Jackson Av
Phone: 718-752-6000
Web: www.alobarnyc.com
Price: $$

Lunch Sat – Sun
Dinner Tue – Sun

This leisurely gastropub radiates old-world appeal through the red brick exterior and dining room adorned with antiques, copper-rimmed architect lamps, and rustic wood tables. From the softly lit, stocked bar to the cozy banquettes, this space has an attention to design that enhances each meal.

Most everyone here begins with a selection from the pickled menu—curried apples, mushrooms—perhaps to pair with the house chicken liver or country pâté (sadly, most of the charcuterie is no longer made in-house). From there, the inventive pleasures range from half chicken with roasted sweet yellow corn and chipotle honey to the bacon-chocolate bread pudding oozing with chunks of chocolate, served with salted caramel, crème anglaise, and a satisfying crust.

Arharn Thai

Thai 🍴

E2

32-05 36th Ave. (bet. 32nd & 33rd Sts.)

Subway: 36 Av
Phone: 718-728-5563
Web: www.thaiastoria.com
Price:

Lunch & dinner daily

The look here may be demure with its pale pink walls and gilded artwork, but this gem serves up a bounty of bold, northern-leaning specialties. And though tables are draped in embroidered linen, glass tops encourage diners to partake in the flavor-packed cooking as lustily as they please.

A shelf of snacks is the extent of the restaurant's retail component, but these will be the last thing on your mind after consuming their excellent *gai yang* sided by sweet chili sauce; or *nua nam tok*, a warm salad of grilled steak tossed with roasted rice powder, red onion slivers, and fragrant herbs. The *yum woon sen* combines glass noodles with stir-fried ground pork, fresh chilies, and a liberal amount of bright dressing redolent of lime and fish sauce.

Asian Jewels

Seafood 🍴🍴

A3

133-30 39th Ave. (bet. College Point Blvd. & Prince St.)

Subway: Flushing - Main St
Phone: 718-359-8600
Web: www.tunseng.com
Price: $$

Lunch & dinner daily

Arguably the best dim sum in Flushing, this spectacular gem is an absolute must for anyone seeking serious seafood and very authentic Cantonese cooking. A longtime resident of 39th Avenue, the expansive dining room is outfitted with round, banquet-style tables, bamboo plants, and ornate chandeliers.

Let the feasting begin with memorable crab-and-pork soup dumplings, before moving on to the thrill-inducing dim sum carts. Taste the likes of steamed rice rolls with honey-roast pork; pork spareribs with rice starch and black beans; chicken and ham wrapped in yuba; and poached jellyfish with scallions and sesame. The signature Dungeness crab—steamed and stir-fried with ginger and green onions, served with Japanese eggplant and garlic—is simply outstanding.

Ayada

Thai

77-08 Woodside Ave. (bet. 77th & 78th Sts.)

Subway: Woodside - 61 St

Phone: 718-424-0844

Web: N/A

Price: $$

Lunch Mon – Fri
Dinner nightly

A bright green sign leads the way to little Ayada, where the décor's a bit plain but the food is anything but. Inside the popular Thai restaurant, guests are greeted with a smattering of tables; a simple, but homey setting; and a warm, family-focused staff to walk them through the menu.

And what a menu it is, with dishes like the crispy catfish salad, paired with green mango and laced with a perfectly balanced lime dressing; a whole, deep-fried snapper, served with shredded green mango and tamarind sauce; a bowl of chewy drunken noodles sporting crisp green beans and tender chicken in a fragrant chili-garlic sauce; or fresh ripe mango and sticky rice, steamed to pearly, translucent perfection and carrying flavors of of sweetened coconut milk.

Bahari estiatorio

Greek X

31-14 Broadway (at 31st St.)

Subway: Broadway

Phone: 718-204-8968

Web: www.bahariestiatorio.com

Price: $$

Lunch & dinner daily

Astoria is awash in good Greek food, but Bahari estiatorio still sets itself apart. Hiding behind an unassuming façade, the dining room is clean, generously sized and simple—think exposed red brick, white walls, and tables draped with paper placemats featuring the Greek Isles. Service is friendly and knowledgeable.

Everything on the menu here is a temptation, but a collection of traditional casserole dishes under the *mageirefta* portion of the menu offers the coziest of baked Greek dishes. One example, *saganaki methysmeno*, arrives bubbling with caramelized *kefalograviera* cheese, and a tomato and red wine sauce. *Papatsouki*, or tender roasted eggplant stuffed with ground beef and a layer of fluffy caramelized béchamel, is deliciously decadent.

Basil Brick Oven Pizza

Italian ✕✕

F1

28-17 Astoria Blvd. (bet. 28th & 29th Sts.)

Subway: Astoria Blvd   Lunch & dinner daily
Phone: 718-204-1205
Web: www.basilbrickoven.com
Price: $$

In an area crying out for a reliable neighborhood Italian joint, Basil's was an instant hit upon opening. The tiny front room is dominated by a dome wood-burning pizza oven, but down a long and narrow hallway there's a larger dining room with dark wood floors, exposed brick walls, and lantern-like light fixtures that is a cozy spot for devouring pizza or daily specials.

Meals here must include thin-crust pizza crafted from well-salted dough. If you can look beyond the classic *Margherita*, the *Napoletana* with black olives or the *salsiccia* with caramelized onions both delight. Specials might reveal oven-roasted swordfish, tender and served with oven-roasted root vegetables. Thick, fluffy squares of tiramisu have earned their own loyal following.

bún-ker

Vietnamese ✕

A2

46-63 Metropolitan Ave. (at Woodward Ave.)

Subway: Grand St (& bus Q54)   Lunch Sat – Sun
Phone: 718-386-4282   Dinner Tue – Sun
Web: www.bunkervietnamese.com
Price:

Located along an industrial stretch of Ridgewood, this charismatic Vietnamese restaurant doesn't offer much in the way of location—which is even more reason to suspect the throngs of people clamoring for it to open on a Saturday are here for something special. It's the food, of course, though the funky hipster surf shack interior and warm staff certainly add to the appeal.

You really can't miss on bún-ker's menu, a whirlwind of Vietnamese dishes sporting a California-like freshness. But, highlights include the bang-on *bánh xèo*, a crispy crêpe featuring tender shrimp, bacon, bean sprouts, and fresh herbs; the excellent *pho ga* bobbing with tender poached chicken, chewy rice noodles, sprouts, lime, and jalapeño; or any of the mouthwatering daily specials.

Casa del Chef Bistro

E3

Contemporary   ✗

39-06 64th St. (bet. 39th & Roosevelt Aves.)

Subway: 69 St   Dinner Tue – Sun
Phone: 718-457-9000
Web: www.casadelchefny.com
Price: $$

Heart, passion, and skill—this inviting bistro embodies the spirit of its dedicated owners. Chef Alfonso Zhicay earned his stripes at some of New York's finest, including Blue Hill at Stone Barns; his daughter is the one-woman show behind the personal, warm service. In a cozy room with large glass windows, elegant (and often vegetable-driven) dishes comfort and surprise.

The four-course prix-fixe is a remarkable value, perhaps beginning with a mushroom confit tart showcasing meaty strips of portobellos, mushroom purée, and truffle oil. Move on to savory pasta courses like orzo folded with seasonal vegetable ragout, topped with parmesan foam. Chocolate-hued braised short ribs sit among braised savoy cabbage, buttery potatoes, and a hit of citrus-horseradish.

Cheburechnaya

B2

Central Asian   ✗

92-09 63rd Dr. (at Austin St.)

Subway: 63 Dr - Rego Park   Lunch & dinner daily
Phone: 718-897-9080
Web: N/A
Price:

This may be a kosher spot with no bagel in sight, but one look at its counter loaded with layers of bowl-shaped *noni toki* bread and you quickly realize that a meal here is a dining adventure. Specializing in Bukharian (Central Asian) cuisine, longstanding Cheburechnaya has been a neighborhood pioneer.

The focused menu is more engrossing than the décor, and it's easy to want every cumin- and paprika-laced item on it. Bring your own vodka and start with the house specialty, *chebureki*, an empanada-like deep-fried wrap stuffed with either hand-cut lamb seasoned with cumin, chili, cilantro, and paprika; or fennel-sparked cabbage. It may serve as the perfect complement to smoky lamb fat, tender quail, veal heart, and seared beef sweetbread kebabs.

Casa Enríque

Mexican XX

B3

5-48 49th Ave. (bet. 5th St. & Vernon Blvd.)

Subway: Vernon Blvd - Jackson Av
Phone: 347-448-6040
Web: www.henrinyc.com
Price: $$

Lunch Sat – Sun
Dinner nightly

Chiapas. Puebla. San Luis Potosí. One can literally taste the regions and cities that Chef Cosme Aguilar's amazingly complex menu explores—including his own childhood recipes to honor his mother's memory. A steady stream of hungry diners seeks out this rather small, tasteful dining room for friendly yet professional service and soul-warming fare. Aim for the large, fantastic communal table.

Start your meal with hearty *rajas con crema*, combining none-too-spicy poblanos with sweet, fresh corn, Mexican sour cream, and cheese served alongside a stack of fresh and slightly toasty tortillas. This kitchen's tender chicken enchiladas with *mole de Piaxtla* may induce swooning, thanks to a sauce that is unexpectedly sweet yet heady with bitter chocolate, raisins, almonds, cloves, cinnamon, chilies, garlic, sesame, and so much more, with incomparable results. It's the kind of food that thrills palates (and tempts wanton thoughts). Expect the *chamorros de borrego al huaxamole* to arrive falling off the bone and redolent of epazote, allspice, and *pulla* chilies. Its fruity-spicy broth is drinkable.

Every bit of every spongy and buttery layer of the cow and goat's milk *pastel tres leches* is absolutely worth the indulgence.

Christos

F1

41-08 23rd Ave. (at 41st St.)

Subway: Astoria - Ditmars Blvd   Dinner nightly
Phone: 718-777-8400
Web: www.christossteakhouse.com
Price: $$$

This beloved Astoria steakhouse has a lot going for it, but its cause for celebration is that authentic Greek accent that imbues everything here. Excellent quality beef, as in the signature prime "wedge" for two, is dry-aged in-house, charbroiled to exact specification, and finished with sea salt and dried oregano. Vibrant starters and sides underscore the Aegean spirit at play with pan-fried *vlahotyri* cheese, charred octopus with roasted peppers and red wine dressing, and smoked feta mashed potatoes.

Christos has a commanding presence on a quiet tree-shaded corner just off bustling Ditmars Blvd. Mixing shades of brown, the cozy and elegant dining room has a separate bar area and is lined with fish tanks stocked with live lobsters.

De Mole

A2

45-02 48th Ave. (at 45th St.)

Subway: 46 St - Bliss St   Lunch & dinner daily
Phone: 718-392-2161
Web: www.demolenyc.com
Price:

If the words sweet, competent, clean, and authentic come to mind, you're most likely thinking of this heart-warming haunt for delightful Mexican. Albeit a tad small, with a second dining room in the back, rest assured that De Mole's flavors are mighty, both in their staples (burritos and tacos) and unique specials—seitan fajitas anyone?

This delightful pearl rests on a corner of low-rise buildings where Woodside meets Sunnyside, yet far from the disharmony of Queens Boulevard. Fans gather here for hearty *enchiladas verdes con pollo*, corn tortillas smeared with tomatillo sauce and *queso blanco*. Crispy chicken *taquitos* are topped with rich sour cream; steamed corn tamales are surprisingly light but filled with flavor; and the namesake *mole* is a must.

District Saigon

F2

37-15 Broadway (bet. 37th & 38th Sts.)

Subway: Steinway St

Lunch & dinner daily

Phone: 718-956-0007

Web: www.district-saigon.com

Price: $$

This delicious Vietnamese café brings a welcome hit of Southeast Asian flavor to Astoria's bustling Broadway. The dining room is sleek, modern and rustic, with a smattering of small tables lining its glass façade; a slender banquette-lined corridor; and communal live-edge wood tables.

The talented kitchen at District Saigon serves up an array of irresistible street snacks (think: *satay*, rolls, or pork and chicken liver pâté with baguette), alongside heartier fare like *pho*, noodle bowls, and grilled pork chops. Dig into plump summer rolls filled with cool rice vermicelli, crunchy bean sprouts, fresh mint, and poached shrimp. Or order the excellent crispy catfish, served over the same vermicelli, tossed with slivered green onion, carrot, and dill.

Dumpling Galaxy

A3

42-35 Main St. (in Arcadia Mall)

Subway: Flushing - Main St

Lunch & dinner daily

Phone: 718-461-0808

Web: www.dumplinggalaxy.com

Price: ⊜

Neon bounces off all the new, shiny surfaces at Dumpling Galaxy, inside the Arcadia Mall. Navigate beyond the phone retailers and stalls to find this huge, modern space full of red booths and hanging red lights. Spiffy and inviting, this establishment is lauded for crafting scores of dumpling variations, plus comforting entrées that shouldn't be ignored. Fill your table with a dumpling feast, stuffed chock-full of duck and mushroom, spicy-sour squash, or lamb and celery redolent of lemongrass and spices. Larger dishes are equally memorable; those cold, thick, slurp-inducing green bean noodles soaked in heady, tart black vinegar with raw white sesame seeds, cilantro, cucumbers, and wood-ear mushrooms will have you coming back for more...and then some more.

Queens

Engeline's

E3

58-28 Roosevelt Ave. (at 59th St.)

Subway: Woodside - 61 St   Lunch & dinner Tue – Sun
Phone: 718-898-7878
Web: N/A
Price: ⚭

This may be *the* place for your local Filipino gossip. An all-day hangout, the bakery-restaurant is all ease and conviviality. A display case stocked with traditional sweets—maybe a soft cassava cake—is alone worth the visit. So, come as you are and settle into the well-maintained dining room for a more thorough introduction to this island nation's cuisine.

Discerning just what's in each dish can prove challenging, but find straightforward pleasure in all-day breakfast treats like eggs with *longganisa* or *sarsiadong bangus*—fried milkfish steaks simmered in a subtle yet flavorful fish sauce and topped with scrambled eggs. *Chicharon bulaklak* and accompanying house-made *suka* (coconut-sugarcane vinegar steeped with bird chilies) lends quite the kick to fried chicken skin.

Gastroteca

Italian ✗✗

E2

33-02 34th Ave. (at 33rd St.)

Subway: 36 Av   Lunch & dinner daily
Phone: 718-729-9080
Web: www.gastrotecaastoria.com
Price: $$

Astoria gets a much-needed jolt of rustic Italian cooking with Gastroteca, a charming new restaurant courtesy of Chef/owner John Parlatore. Tucked into a lovely corner location with enormous framed windows, exposed brick, and movies being projected onto the wall behind the bar, this is a fun spot but with a serious menu—the latter brought to life by a technically talented culinary team.

The ingredient-driven menu offers a wonderful selection of crostini to start. Don't miss the one with Sicilian pineapple, mascarpone, chili flakes, or the avocado—before diving into the likes of *linguini al limone* with a poached egg and grated lemon zest; or fragrant, oven-roasted rosemary chicken, paired with creamy mashed potatoes and chicken gravy.

Grain House

Chinese

D1

249-11 Northern Blvd. (bet. 249th St. & Marathon Pkwy.)

Subway: N/A　　　　　　　　　　　　　　　　　Lunch & dinner daily
Phone: 718-229-8788
Web: N/A
Price: $$

It may be situated at the eastern edge of Queens, but a meal at Grain House is worth the trek to Little Neck. The room is amiably attended to and minimally adorned, with blue and white ceramic pieces lending a distinct Chinese tone to the otherwise staid but comfortable room.

Grain House brings joy to enthusiasts of Chinese cookery with a menu representing the many regions of the country's culinary map. "Home-style" specialties include the salted, tea-smoked duck—which is, in a word, perfection— and Sichuan dishes factor prominently, as in a platter of impossibly crispy, fried tofu smacked with ground cumin and dried chilies. Succulent, soothing, and braised in a clay pot, the cabbage casserole proves this kitchen knows how to wow with subtlety, too.

Gregory's 26 Corner Taverna

Greek

F1

26-02 23rd Ave. (at 26th St.)

Subway: Astoria - Ditmars Blvd　　　　　　　　　Lunch & dinner daily
Phone: 718-777-5511
Web: N/A
Price: $$

Judge a book by its cover and miss the rustic pleasures found within this old-fashioned Greek taverna. Disheveled charm fills the tiny two-room interior, festooned with Greek flags, bunches of artificial grapes, and framed countryside scenes. The bare tables are topped with butcher paper and the service is slow as molasses, but the cooking is honest and intensely flavorful.

Begin with *tirokafteri*, a spicy, satisfying spread of thick feta blended with pickled red chili peppers and served with hot pita points. A stuffed green horn pepper might be next, over a bed of fried squash slices and a well of garlicky *scordalia*. The seafood combo offers the simple pleasures of stuffed clams, mussels, lobster, and shrimp with lots of butter, lemon, and parsley...Greek style!

Hahm Ji Bach

Korean ✗✗

41-11 149th Pl. (bet. Barclay & 41st Aves.)

Subway: Flushing - Main St   Lunch & dinner daily
Phone: 718-460-9289
Web: www.hahmjibach.com
Price: $$

This beloved Queens institution enjoys fine digs where they serve popular and praise-worthy Korean food. The contemporary dining room is spacious and airy, with the warm, always informative, staff buzzing from table to table. It's not uncommon for the manager to roll up her own sleeves when the pace elevates—and elevate it does, for this is not your average Korean barbecue.

It's hard to go wrong on Hahm Ji Bach's delightful menu, but don't miss the *samgyeopsal*, tender slabs of well-marinated pork belly sizzled to crispy perfection tableside for you to swaddle in crisp lettuce with paper-thin daikon radish, spicy kimchi, and bright scallions; or the *mit bachan*, a hot clay pot with soft steamed eggs, kimchi, tofu, pickled cucumbers, and spicy mackerel.

Happy Family Hotpot

Chinese ✗

36-35 Main St. (bet. 37th Ave. & Northern Blvd.)

Subway: Flushing - Main St   Lunch & dinner daily
Phone: 718-358-6667
Web: www.happyfamilyhotpot.com
Price:

You'll think you've died and gone to Hong Kong. Every table at this popular Flushing hot pot spot is fitted with iPads and a square cooker, and the interior is ultra sleek. Think tufted white leather walls and flat-screen televisions dangling over the tables.

It's a stylish place to cool your heels but the real star of the show exists within the kitchen's authentic hot pot selection—pork brain, anyone? You can build your own, choosing from 70+ dunkables like tender pork belly that cooks in a flash; paper-thin taro root; tender baby greens; flavorful head-on shrimp; or chewy udon noodles. From there, choose either the mild white broth or an irresistibly spicy red one bobbing with peppercorns. Better yet, get both, also known as a half and half.

Himalayan Yak

F3

Tibetan

72-20 Roosevelt Ave. (bet. 72nd & 73rd Sts.)

Subway: 74 St - Broadway   Lunch & dinner daily
Phone: 718-779-1119
Web: N/A
Price: $$

Broadly appealing yet truly unique, Himalayan Yak transports diners from Jackson Heights to Central Asia for a hybrid of Nepalese, Tibetan, and Indian cuisines. The room is a bit worn—a testament to its long-standing popularity—but orange walls invoke mountain sunsets; carved dark wood and colorful fabrics create a far-flung ambience.

Start with an order of *momo* or steamed minced meat-filled dumplings seasoned with scallions, cilantro, and ginger. Then sample yak in the form of sausage, stew, or cheese. *Labsha* is a beef and daikon curry served with *tingmo*, a multi-layered steamed bun for sopping up the mildly spiced sauce, which simply must not be missed. And finally the lassi, a traditional yogurt-based drink, is the perfect complement to every meal.

HinoMaru Ramen

F1

Japanese

33-18 Ditmars Blvd. (bet. 33rd & 34th Sts.)

Subway: Astoria - Ditmars Blvd   Lunch & dinner daily
Phone: 718-777-0228
Web: www.hinomaruramen.com
Price: $$

What this simple spot lacks in décor, it makes up for in charming details (think friendly service, an energetic open kitchen, and a chalkboard menu). Order a Sapporo on tap and a small plate like shrimp *nikuman*, shrimp tempura wrapped in a steamed bun, and prepare for the main event: truly remarkable ramen. The menu lists several slurp-worthy varieties, including a to-die-for Hakata-style *tonkatsu*. This pork bone distillation is vigorously simmered to produce a creamy broth infused with bone marrow and stocked with straight noodles, *char siu*, nori, and fishcake. Equally delicious is the vegetarian variety, a soy milk base teeming with carrots, ginger, and broccoli.

For Manhattan residents, Lucky Cat, an offshoot, sits on busy East 53rd Street.

Houdini Kitchen Laboratory

Pizza

A2

15-63 Decatur St. (at Wyckoff Ave.)

Subway: Halsey St   Lunch & dinner daily
Phone: 718-456-3770
Web: N/A
Price:

Located in an industrial stretch of Ridgewood, this inventive pizzeria more than lives up to its creative name. Taking residence in a repurposed brewery built in the late 1800s, the red brick structure sits near the borough's massive cemeteries where this establishment's namesake has been laid to rest. While the "lab" isn't especially large, it feels cavernous nonetheless thanks to immensely high ceilings, a sparse arrangement of tables with views of the cement dome oven, and an ample covered terrace.

This kitchen whips up a small but selective menu of salads and wood-fired pies that includes the Houdini Green—a chewy crust spread with quality sauce and topped with fresh mozzarella, creamy knobs of goat cheese and flame-kissed veggies.

Hunan House 😊

Chinese 𝗬

A3

137-40 Northern Blvd. (bet. Main & Union Sts.)

Subway: Flushing - Main St   Lunch & dinner daily
Phone: 718-353-1808
Web: www.hunanhouseflushing.com
Price:

Located along quiet Northern Boulevard in Flushing, Hunan House offers a delicious reprieve from the street. The interior is crisp and sophisticated, with dark, ornately carved wood and thick linen tablecloths. But, the real draw here is the wonderfully authentic Hunanese fare, with its myriad fresh river fish; flavorful preserved meats; complex profiles; and mouth-puckering spice.

Hunan House's menu is filled with exotic delights, but don't miss the wonderful starter of sautéed sour string beans featuring minced pork, chilies, ginger, and garlic; smoky dried bean curd with the same preserved meat; or spicy sliced fish-Hunan style, perfectly cooked and served in a delicious pool of fiery red sauce and plated with tender bulbs of bok choy.

Hunan Kitchen

Chinese

 A3

42-47 Main St. (bet. Blossom & Franklin Aves.)

Subway: Flushing - Main St   Lunch & dinner daily
Phone: 718-888-0553
Web: N/A
Price:

As New York's Sichuan renaissance continues apace, this pleasant and unpretentious Hunanese spot has popped up on Flushing's Main Street. The look here is tasteful and uncomplicated; the cooking is fiery and excellent.

The extensive menu of Hunan specialties includes the likes of the classic regional dish, pork "Mao's Style" simmered in soy sauce, Shaoxing wine, oil, and stock, then braised to tender perfection. Boasting heat and meat in equal amounts, the spicy-sour string beans with pork expertly combines rich and savory aromatics, vinegary beans, and fragrant pork with tongue-numbing peppercorns. The barbecue fish Hunan-style is a brilliant menu standout.

Smaller dishes, like winter melon with seafood soup, round out an expertly prepared meal.

Iki

Japanese

 A3

133-42 39th Ave. (bet. College Point Blvd. & Prince St.)

Subway: Flushing - Main St   Lunch & dinner daily
Phone: 718-939-3388
Web: www.ikicuisine.com
Price: $$$

While One Fulton Square hasn't quite caught on, this upscale gem tucked into the Hyatt Place Hotel is a worthy anchor and addition to the local scene. Duck inside the modern glass façade and you're greeted with curving leather booths and beautiful blonde flooring. You've seen this before, you think to yourself, but this is a curious outlier— think Queens in high heels.

Diners can opt for omakase or à la carte. While the former might begin with a chilled bowl of soft tofu topped with creamy uni; the latter showcases cool kanpachi, *shima aji, tai* and *kinmedai* nigiri. Then, tender-cooked rice, cooked in an earthenware pot, is tinted with the addition of dashi, topped with maitakes, and folded with flakes of salmon for a bright assortment.

Il Bacco

Italian

253-24 Northern Blvd. (bet. Little Neck Pkwy & Westmoreland St.)

Subway: N/A   Lunch & dinner daily
Phone: 718-224-7657
Web: www.ilbaccoristorante.com
Price: $$

With its striking Mediterranean façade, crimson awnings, and rooftop garden, Il Bacco is hard to miss. This local favorite offers a stylish Little Neck-by-way-of-Tuscany setting for enjoying their thoughtfully crafted classics with top-notch ingredients. A seasoned staff guides patrons through the many menu temptations.

The kitchen dutifully honors Italian-American staples with skill. The pizza oven is a beauty, churning out perfect pies, while tables pile up with salads of fennel, red radicchio, pitted olives, and orange, as well as pastas like house-made spinach fettuccine with peas, cream, mushrooms, and parmesan. Portions are generous but do not sacrifice quality, which is clear in the hefty rack of lamb with brandy sauce and simple roasted potatoes.

Il Poeta 😊

B2

Italian

98-04 Metropolitan Ave. (at 69th Rd.)

Subway: Forest Hills - 71 Av   Lunch Mon – Fri
Phone: 718-544-4223   Dinner nightly
Web: www.ilpoetarestaurant.com
Price: $$

Queens is teeming with family-owned Italian restaurants dishing up the red sauce, and yet Il Poeta manages to carve out a unique place among its competitors by cooking real classics that locals can't help but enjoy. Perched on a quaint corner of Forest Hills, the refreshed décor is simple but elegant, with a suited staff and vibrant pieces of art lining the walls.

Chef Mario di Chiara knows a thing—or ten—about Italian fare: you can't miss with items like *cannelloni gratinati al profumo di tartufo*, a homemade pasta plump with veal and carrot, baked in buttery béchamel, and kissed with truffle oil; or *pollo spezzatino alla pizzaiola con salsiccia*, a rustic chicken stewed in a light-as-air tomato sauce pocked with sweet porky sausage and roasted peppers.

Imperial Palace

A3

Chinese

136-13 37th Ave. (bet. Main & Union Sts.)

Subway: Flushing - Main St
Phone: 718-939-3501
Web: N/A
Price: $$

Lunch & dinner daily

You might mistake Imperial Palace for one of those red awning-covered restaurants on this strip of Chinese eateries—but don't. While it may share the same lettered signage, wide windows, and nondescript facade, inside find some of the best sticky rice and Dungeness crab Flushing has to offer.

Seafood is front and center, with servers promptly presenting everything from deep-fried jumbo shrimp tossed with candied sesame walnuts to shrimp-stuffed tofu with slices of conch. It's easy to plow through all the fresh shellfish dishes with a chilled beer and sweet rice, but try to leave room for the clam casserole: a spicy broth full of Cantonese flavors, loads of onions, and small, briny clams, finished with a sprinkling of crisp coriander stems.

Joe's Shanghai

A3

Chinese

136-21 37th Ave. (bet. Main & Union Sts.)

Subway: Flushing - Main St
Phone: 718-539-3838
Web: www.joeshanghairestaurants.com
Price: $$

Lunch & dinner daily

Diners at this venerable Flushing institution are greeted with menus and a dish of black vinegar dipping sauce, as it's practically a given that you'll be ordering their famous *xiao long bao* here. Despite stiff competition, these soup dumplings—soft and delicate with perfectly spiraled shoulders and a mouthful of lip-smacking golden broth wrapped inside—still stand a head above the rest. In fact, these chefs have made it their mission to ensure biting into them is a sensual experience.

But there are other pleasures to be had here, too, such as steamed cabbage in light broth scattered with dried shrimp, or the popular Shanghainese lion's head meatballs. Made from ground pork, the latter are incredibly light and lacquered with a dark, savory glaze.

John Brown Smokehouse

B3

Barbecue

10-43 44th Dr. (bet. 10th & 11th Sts.)

Subway: Court Sq - 23 St
Phone: 347-617-1120
Web: www.johnbrownseriousbbq.com
Price: $$

Lunch & dinner daily

Regional barbecue has arrived in the city, but John Brown continues his reign as the true "bawss" for Kansas-style bites. The décor is minimal with a front area plating infinite orders, but find a seat in the back and settle in for a serious shindig. Amid sepia-toned photos and a flat-screen showing football (a religion here), find famished city folk ordering perfectly done proteins served with a thick and rich barbecue sauce.

Rib tips and burnt ends are juicy, tender, and sumptuous when paired with baked beans studded with bits of smoked meat or killer mac-and-cheese that is appropriately bright orange, creamy, and sparked by black pepper. An order of the corn pudding is a must, and nicely caps off a meal here. Finger-licking is an inevitable end.

Jora

B3

Peruvian

47-46 11th St. (at 48th Ave.)

Subway: Vernon Blvd - Jackson Av
Phone: 718-392-2033
Web: www.jorany.com
Price: $$

Lunch Fri – Sun
Dinner nightly

Peruvian pottery and tapestries set a casually elegant scene at this newcomer, which is quickly earning a loyal following for frothy pisco sours and spicy dishes full of fresh flavor. Beyond the pale limestone façade, the deep, narrow dining room is filled with light from arched windows and boasts a wall covered in river stones as well as a relaxed bar with striking artwork.

The diversity of Peruvian cuisine is on tasty display here, from classic dishes like *ceviche mixto* with slices of crunchy red onion, oversized kernels of corn and sweet potato, to *chupe de camarones*—a thick, restorative soup of rice, seafood, and gently poached eggs. A juicy skirt steak with sautéed onions, peppers, cilantro, and sweet plantains on the side will satisfy carnivores.

Kang Ho Dong Baekjeong

Korean

 C1

152-12 Northern Blvd. (bet. 153rd & Murray Sts.)

Subway: Flushing - Main St (& bus Q13)   Lunch & dinner daily
Phone: 718-886-8645
Web: n/a
Price: $$

The Korean barbecue of the moment is a short LIRR trip away, and well worth the ride. This was the first East Coast branch of (Korean wrestler and TV personality) Kang Ho Dong's growing empire—and it is already among the best in the city. A younger sib now resides in midtown.

The menu is focused, the space is enormous, the air is clean, and the service is friendly. Start your grill off with steamed egg, corn, cheese, and more to cook along the sides while marbled pork belly or deeply flavorful marinated skirt steak strips sizzle at the center. *Bibimbap* is a classic rendition, mixing beef seasoned with *gochujang*, vegetables, sesame, nori, and crisp sprouts in a hot stone bowl—so hot that it sears the bottom rice to golden while cooking the raw egg on top.

Katsuno

Japanese

 B2

103-01 Metropolitan Ave. (at 71st Rd.)

Subway: Forest Hills - 71 Av   Dinner Tue – Sun
Phone: 718-575-4033
Web: www.katsunorestaurant.com
Price: $$

To find Katsuno, look for the white lantern and those traditional *noren* curtains. Featuring less than ten tables, what this Japanese jewel lacks in size it makes up for in flavor and attitude. The owner's wife greets each guest at the door, while Chef Katsuyuki Seo dances around the miniscule kitchen crafting precise Japanese dishes from top-quality ingredients. His elegant plating of sashimi may reveal the likes of amberjack topped with a chiffonade of shiso, luxurious sea urchin, translucent squid crested with needle-thin yuzu zest, as well as supremely fresh fluke, tuna, and mackerel. Meanwhile, carb fans will enjoy a warm bowl of soba in duck broth with tender duck breast; or the fantastically brothy *inaniwa udon*, served only on special nights.

Kitchen 79

F3

Thai

37-70 79th St. (bet. Roosevelt & 37th Aves.)

Subway: 82 St - Jackson Hts
Phone: 718-803-6227
Web: www.kitchen79nyc.com
Price: 💰

Lunch & dinner daily

Shiny black subway tiles and glowing fixtures set a date-worthy tone at this new Thai standout. Patient, helpful servers assist in exploring the menu, focused mainly on dishes of southern Thailand. Patrons can choose to be as adventurous as the sometimes familiar yet authentic and funky menu allows.

Thick green curry (*gaeng kiew warn*) is packed with tender shrimp, bamboo shoots, eggplant, Chinese long beans, and holy basil simmered in coconut milk with pleasantly restrained spicing. A whole flounder (*pla neung ma nao*) is brilliant, distinct, and steamed to perfection with sour and spicy notes from garlic, minced ginger, and a Thai hot sauce. Flat noodles (*ka nom jeen gang tai pla*) with pumpkin, mackerel, and curry paste is a powerful, spicy dish.

Kurry Qulture

F2

Indian XX

36-05 30th Ave. (bet. 36th & 37th Sts.)

Subway: 30 Av
Phone: 718-674-1212
Web: www.kurryqulture.com
Price: $$

Lunch Sat – Sun
Dinner nightly

Noted Chef Hemant Mathur and owner Sonny Solomon bring their considerable talents to this contemporary collaboration set on a busy stretch of Astoria. Inside, the vibe is friendly and casual, in an attractive room that extends from a front bar to brick-lined dining room and open back patio.

The regional (and sub-regional) Indian cooking is both tasty and high achieving, beginning with *mirchri ka salan* featuring a complex peanut- coconut and sesame seed-base spiced with fresh-ground tamarind, curry leaf, and fenugreek. More notable is the fact that this may be a mere accompaniment to a very interesting South Indian riff on vegetarian biryani, made wonderfully fragrant with fluffy rice and jackfruit. The slow-cooked *bhuna gosht* is silky, gamey excellence.

Little Pepper

B1

18-24 College Point Blvd. (bet. 18th & 20th Aves.)

Subway: Flushing - Main St (& bus Q20A)   Lunch & dinner Fri – Wed
Phone: 718-939-7788
Web: N/A
Price: 😊

Set on an ordinary block of residences and businesses is Little Pepper, a tiny yet extraordinary rendition of Sichuan cooking. The room wears a delicate vibe with hand-painted murals, marble-tiled floors, and a cozy service bar. But, the real focus remains on the food, which is honest, bold, and always on-point.

Sample soft and yielding *mapo* tofu, sweet with minced pork, fiery with chilies, and smoky with ground peppercorns sinking into a thick, oily gravy; or shredded pork tossed with potato strands and pickled cabbage to truly appreciate their excellent (if occasionally) underrated food. Pine nuts sautéed with corn and snow pea leaves are marvelous for mellow palates, while chicken stir-fried with dried red chilies is a hit among those on a spice trip.

Main Street Imperial Taiwanese Gourmet

C2

59-14A Main St. (bet. 59th & 60th Aves.)

Subway: Flushing - Main St (& bus Q44)   Lunch & dinner daily
Phone: 718-886-8788
Web: N/A
Price: 😊

It's a real journey to this Taiwanese treasure—not only in its trek from the closest subway stop, but more importantly, in the experience. Here, the staff speaks their mother tongue for the most part, incense wafts from an altar, and the food is otherworldly.

Dishes present dazzling, authentic flavors, easily savored in the peaceful atmosphere. Sweet, head-on shrimp arrive steamed and still in the shell, housing juice that accentuates the concentrated flavor when dipped in soy sauce. Likewise, the stinky tofu (a traditional delicacy) gets its flavor from a light sauté and a finish of kimchi-style pickles. And if you're any sort of fan of the famed oyster pancake, this outstanding version will remain in your memory long after the lengthy ride home.

Malagueta

E2

25-35 36th Ave. (at 28th St.)

Subway: 36 Av
Phone: 718-937-4821
Web: www.malaguetany.com
Price: $$

Lunch & dinner daily

Complete with a wine-red awning, this culturally rich corner is a beloved spot for authentic Northeastern Brazilian fare. From its personable and dedicated staff to the comfortable and unassuming setting to the zesty and colorful cooking, Malagueta is an Astoria standout.

The kitchen deftly mixes smoky, sour, hot, and salty flavors, all stewed to a mellowness, in perfectly balanced specialties like *corvina com vatapa*, a pan-roasted fillet of pollack served with a lush and deliciously complex mélange of salt cod, dried shrimp, yucca, and coconut milk. And while Brazil's national dish, *feijoada completa*, is prepared solely for Saturday evening dining, dessert lovers will appreciate that the excellent coconut flan is offered as a daily indulgence.

Mar's

E2

34-21 34th Ave. (at 35th St.)

Subway: Steinway St
Phone: 718-685-2480
Web: www.lifeatmars.com
Price: $$

Lunch Sat – Sun
Dinner nightly

Oh, Astoria, fine—you're finally the coolest kid on the culinary block. Mar's, a charming oyster bar plucked out of another century, is a good example of why: with its weathered seaside tavern décor, whitewashed walls, and curving bar, you'll feel dropped into a sun-bleached, turn-of-the-century photo.

Most of the menu is given over to raw seafood and New England classics; part, to Mediterranean tavern small plates like sweetbreads and steak tartare. Kick things off with the excellent Mar's chowder, bobbing with briny clams, tender potatoes, bacon, and thyme. Then move on to sautéed sweetbreads with buttery fingerlings, pickled onion, and a swirl of balsamic reduction; or the house lobster roll kicked up with salty batons of Granny Smith apple.

MP Taverna

Greek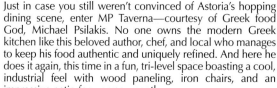

31-29 Ditmars Blvd. (at 33rd St.)

Subway: Astoria - Ditmars Blvd
Phone: 718-777-2187
Web: www.michaelpsilakis.com
Price: $$

Lunch & dinner daily

Just in case you still weren't convinced of Astoria's hopping dining scene, enter MP Taverna—courtesy of Greek food God, Michael Psilakis. No one owns the modern Greek kitchen like this beloved author, chef, and local who manages to keep his food authentic and uniquely refined. And here he does it again, this time in a fun, tri-level space boasting a cool, industrial feel with wood paneling, iron chairs, and an impressive patio for warmer months.

For a more intimate feel, head to the second floor decked with leather chairs and chandeliers, or better yet, the rooftop terrace. Any place you land, be prepared for delicious fare: a perfectly cooked fillet of sole arrives stuffed with spinach, feta, and dill, and is finished in a wine-caper sauce.

Mundo

International

37-06 36th St. (at 37th Ave.)

Subway: 36 St
Phone: 718-706-8636
Web: www.mundonewyork.com
Price: $$

Dinner nightly

The Mediterranean hot spot that turned the city on to "Red Sonja"—a popular Turkish dish of red lentil and bulgur wheat—has relocated to larger digs. Mundo's new space is tucked into Queens' trendy Paper Factory Hotel, and both are a stunning addition to this industrial stretch of Long Island City. The interior is now a sexy, bi-level affair, complete with a spiral staircase and lounge.

Kick things off with the *cuatro sabores*, a medley of dips (think caramelized carrot or fava and dill) served with warm naan. Then move on to the Argentinian baked empanadas, with braised short ribs or Swiss chard and feta; feather-light Turkish meatballs, paired with spicy cilantro tzatziki; or the Egyptian artichoke "Nile's Flower" with a verdant dill-fava mousse.

Mu Ramen

Japanese ✗

12-09 Jackson Ave. (bet. 47th Rd. & 48th Ave.)

Subway: Vernon Blvd - Jackson Av
Phone: 917-868-8903
Web: N/A
Price: **$$**

Lunch Thu – Fri
Dinner nightly

What began as a pop-up found an insanely popular home behind an unmarked door in this industrial yet residential nook of Long Island City. Lines never cease; arrive early if possible. A thick wood block serves as a communal table in the dining room, where slurpers can witness the focus and dedication of chefs working within an open kitchen in the back.

The kitchen's methodical devotion results in a superior bowl of ramen. In the spicy miso ramen, springy noodles (from Sun Noodle) are nested in a red miso- and pork-based soup of rich bone broth that slowly simmers for over 24 hours. Topped with scallion, ground pork, sesame, and chili oil, it is one of many rewarding bowls. *Okonomiyaki* are ethereally light, with smoked trout and shaved bonito.

M. Wells Steakhouse

Gastropub ✗✗

B3

43-15 Crescent St. (bet. 43rd Ave. & 44th Rd.)

Subway: Court Sq - 23 St
Phone: 718-786-9060
Web: www.magasinwells.com
Price: **$$$$**

Lunch Thu – Fri
Dinner Thu – Sat

First impressions can be deceiving at this hip Queens gastropub. From the outside, M. Wells Steakhouse looks like the old auto body garage it's housed in, but step inside and the interior is all gloss and swagger. The dining room is a dark, sultry space—from its gold-and-black wallpapered ceiling and crystal chandeliers, to its sexy red walls, stunning bar area, and open, wood-burning kitchen. Of course, the service is just as polished as the design.

Though the kitchen bills itself as a steakhouse, you can't go wrong with the excellent raw bar, fish entrées, and unique appetizers. And while it's true that the quality of cooking has been less impressive as of late, sinfully gooey *pommes aligot*, dusted with cracked black pepper, are as outstanding as ever.

Mythos

Greek **XX**

C1

196-29 Northern Blvd. (bet. 196th St. & Francis Lewis Blvd.)

Subway: N/A

Phone: 718-357-6596

Web: www.mythosnyc.com

Price: **$$**

Lunch & dinner daily

A gathering place for Greeks and non-Greeks alike, this family-run and friendly restaurant tempts with impeccably fresh fish, cooked over charcoal and basted simply with olive oil, lemon juice, and herbs. Beyond the whitewashed exterior and dark blue awning is a large dining room with rows of neat tables for indulging in Hellenic pleasures, from zesty appetizers to boisterous conversations.

Settle into an array of *pikilia*; cold appetizers such as *melitzansalata*, eggplant whipped with herbs and olive oil. Chargrilled fish, priced by the pound, has a delightfully smoky essence and moist flesh. Whole smelts are a rare and traditional treat, simply pan-fried with a lemony herb dressing. Finish with a choice of authentic, nutty, and syrup-soaked pastries.

Nan Xiang Xiao Long Bao

Chinese **X**

A3

38-12 Prince St. (bet. 38th & 39th Aves.)

Subway: Flushing - Main St

Phone: 718-321-3838

Web: N/A

Price: ⊛⊛

Lunch & dinner daily

Also known as Nan Xiang Dumpling House, it is easily found among a strip of restaurants reflecting the diversity of Flushing's dominant Asian population. Simply decorated, the comfortable dining room features rows of closely set tables and a mirrored wall that successfully gives the illusion of space.

The enjoyable and interesting menu focuses on noodle-filled soups, toothsome stir-fried rice cakes, and the house specialty, juicy dumplings. These are made in-house and have a delicate, silky wrapper encasing a flavorful meatball of ground pork or crab with rich tasting broth. Eating the specialties may take some practice, but take your cue from the slurping crowd: puncture the casing on your spoon to cool the dumplings and avoid scalding your mouth.

Natural Tofu

Korean

40-06 Queens Blvd. (bet. 40th & 41st Sts.)

Subway: 40 St   Lunch & dinner daily
Phone: 718-706-0899
Web: N/A
Price: $$

This is the sort of place you've walked by a hundred times and never noticed, but look up, because the house-made tofu here is unrivaled. The space may be more functional than cozy, but this staff knows how to treat their customers—from welcoming each table with a succulent assortment of *banchan* to happily adjusting a dish's spice level.

They also clearly know the many secrets of tofu: the kitchen makes its own, on view at the front of the restaurant, then deploys it in a series of silken *soondubu* (soft bean curd stews). Served scalding hot in a *ddukbaegi* or glazed earthenware cauldron, this bubbling piquant broth contains your choice of pork, seafood, or even beef intestine—but kimchi, the funky favorite, is the hands-down winner.

Nazca

Peruvian

34-20 Broadway (at 35th St.)

Subway: Broadway   Lunch Fri – Sun
Phone: 929-522-0297   Dinner nightly
Web: N/A
Price: $$

When the façade is open and music fills the air, you know the party is on at Nazca—a delicious restaurant that hits all the usual Peruvian standbys, but does so with style. Inside, you'll find exposed red brick walls, wood plank flooring, a handful of tables, and a row of booths that can be made private with floor-to-ceiling drapes.

The menu offers up traditional Peruvian cooking, like beef heart anticuchos, *papa rellenas*, *tiradito*, *lomo saltado*, and rotisserie chicken. A perfect little cocktail glass of fresh jumbo shrimp ceviche is filled with tart and spicy l*eche de tigre* and set in a ring of crunchy corn kernels. The slow-cooked goat stew, *seco de cabrito*, is simmered with corn-based beer called *chicha de jora* with warm and hearty results.

Nick's Pizza

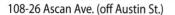

Pizza ✗

108-26 Ascan Ave. (off Austin St.)

Subway: 75 Av
Phone: 718-263-1126
Web: N/A
Price:

Lunch & dinner daily

This family-friendly pizzeria opened among the quaint Tudor-style architecture of Forest Hills in 1993, and hasn't looked back. What's not to love here? The staff is casual and gracious; the dark green vinyl booths and Formica tables give it a homey, throwback appeal; and the pizza is downright superb. Strictly speaking, Nick's isn't on the Neapolitan bandwagon—nor is it doing your typical New York slice thing. Rather, Nick's is just Nick's: honest, delicious pizza, offered in two pie sizes (small or large), and laced with a thick crush of tomatoes, mozzarella, and toppings like bright green broccoli and peppers. Save room for their world-class cannoli.

For heartier appetites, a location in the Upper East Side along Second Avenue offers an extended menu.

Nusara

Thai ✗

82-80 Broadway (at Whitney Ave.)

Subway: Elmhurst Av
Phone: 718-898-7996
Web: www.nusarathaikitchen.com
Price: $$

Lunch & dinner daily

Despite its less-than-impressive strip mall surroundings, this Thai kitchen—a haven of soft pink walls and cordial servers—is nothing short of wonderful. Bypass the small selection of snacks available for purchase, and instead settle in to a table to peruse the menu and prepare for the aromatic and savory feast ahead.

Begin with the *som tum* Lao-style, a traditional green papaya salad made less so with the stimulating addition of salty anchovies. Then crispy pork may top the pick-your-protein options for noodles and entrées. Additionally, those deep-fried bits of pork belly are a treat when thrown into creamy red chili- and coconut-based *chu chee* curry. And as an ideal accompaniment to any of the curries, look no further than the salted fish fried rice.

O Lavrador

Portuguese

138-40 101st Ave. (bet. Cresskill & Sanders Pls.)

Subway: Sutphin Blvd - Archer Av - JFK Airport
Phone: 718-526-1526
Web: www.olavradorrestaurant.com
Price: $$

Lunch & dinner daily

This throwback pleases with rib-sticking Portuguese fare and an attention to hospitality. Choose between two experiences: the long, well-worn bar (which may be rowdy with soccer fans) or the spacious dining room, reached through lovely arches. Seasoned servers know how to charm and keep customers patient, as dishes are made to order and can take time.

Zoom in on anything with *bacalhau* here, a superior air-dried fish (not salt-cured) with excellent flavor and texture. The *bacalhau à pescador* sates with a stew of clams, mussels, shrimp, calamari, and potatoes. Another appealing soup is *caldo verde* full of meaty collards and smoky chorizo. Round out this elaborate feast with *feijoada de mariscos*, a slurry of white beans, seafood, and of course, more chorizo.

Pachanga Patterson

Mexican

33-17 31st Ave. (at 34th St.)

Subway: 30 Av
Phone: 718-554-0525
Web: www.pachangapatterson.com
Price: $$

Lunch Sat – Sun
Dinner nightly

This unassuming spot for tasty Mexican food with a twist has been a smash from the start, offering much more than guacamole with chips and a margarita (though these happen to be excellent here).

Floor-to-ceiling windows, fairy lights, and quirky artifacts adorn the space while enhancing the feel-good, neighborhood vibe.

The fuchsia-painted kitchen brims with bold flavors, skill, and creativity that incorporate worldly influences. Try tacos that fold crisp and faintly honeyed pig's ear with pickled onion and none-too-spicy habanero mayo into soft, warm tortillas. Earthenware-baked enchiladas are a particular treat, perhaps rolled with shredded bits of braised lamb in rich and luscious *mole coloradito*, topped with a delicately set fried egg.

Paet Rio

F3

Thai ✗

81-10 Broadway (bet. 81st & 82nd Sts.)

Subway: Elmhurst Av
Phone: 917-832-6672
Web: N/A
Price:

Lunch & dinner daily

With so many Thai places around, it's easy to get lost in this exceptional concentration; just be sure to find yourself at Paet Rio. The design of this long and inviting room may elevate the experience, but it is their spicy and unusual cooking that makes everything shine.

The menu here is a dance of sensations—tart, spicy, sour, fresh—as seen in Chinese broccoli leaves (*miang kha-na*) with pork, chilies, peanuts, garlic, and lime. Grilled squid (*pla muek yang*) has an addictive fiery sauce, while fermented pork and sticky rice sausage (*sai krok Isan*) is pleasurably sour with cabbage, chili, and peanuts. End this steamy affair over noodles sautéed with pork, squid, and soy sauce (*kua gai*); or *khao phat pla kem* featuring a tasty twist on the tired fried rice.

Parkside

B2

Italian ✗✗

107-01 Corona Ave. (at 51st Ave.)

Subway: 103 St - Corona Plaza
Phone: 718-271-9871
Web: www.parksiderestaurantny.com
Price: $$$

Lunch & dinner daily

A veteran on the Corona dining scene, Parkside carries that old-fashioned kind of New York energy—back when waiters donned tuxedos, hosts boomed hello, and walls boasted classic photos of the city's elite. And though the neighborhood has changed much since Parkside first opened its doors, the fantastic Italian-American food they dole out stands the test of time. Join in the celebratory mood and make some new friends (no one really dines alone here) while tucking into tender ribbons of savory fettuccini Alfredo; succulent veal *pizzaiola* laced with a delectable marinara; or top it all off with a cannoli freshly piped with ricotta and studded with candied fruit.

The irresistible desserts are wheeled around to guests on a rolling tray, of course.

Payag

Filipino ✗

E3

51-34 Roosevelt Ave. (at 52nd St.)

Subway: 52 St
Phone: 347-935-3192
Web: www.payagrestaurant.com
Price: $$

Lunch & dinner Wed – Mon

Thoughtfully crafted with ingenuity and spirit, Payag is intended to feel like a home. From the open and light design that evokes a *bahay kubo* (Tagalog for "house") to the chatty and knowledgeable servers, this restaurant brings a welcoming air to this quiet corner. With bamboo touches and live Filipino music on the weekends, Payag strives to preserve a cultural identity both on and off the menu.

The dishes showcase a regional approach to the multi-island nation's cuisine. National favorite *kinilaw na isda*, a sour ceviche of delicate white fish, ginger, and cucumber, is a refreshing start to the meal. Then move on to the beautiful *bulalo*, a tender beef shank specialty from Batangas, gently simmered in a broth with yellow corn, cabbage, and baby bok choy.

Piccola Venezia

Italian ✗✗

F2

42-01 28th Ave. (at 42nd St.)

Subway: 30 Av
Phone: 718-721-8470
Web: www.piccola-venezia.com
Price: $$$

Lunch Mon – Fri
Dinner nightly

This old-time idol deserves its landmark status as it has been going strong since opening in 1973. With Italian-American cooking so rampant in the city, it's wholly refreshing to happen upon a classic of such welcoming comfort. The décor is outdated, but white tablecloths are clean and crisp, and glasses gleam at the prospect of great wine varietals.

With a trio of pasta, you needn't choose between *fusi* swirled in a grappa- mushroom- and Grana-sauce; squid ink *taglierini*; or *maltagliati* in a roasted tomato and basil sauce with a touch of cream. *Spiedini alla Romana* sees thick slabs of focaccia and mozzarella dredged and fried, served with an anchovy and caper sauce, and pork osso buco is of the falling-apart-tender variety—perfect with the velvety polenta.

Sabry's

Seafood

24-25 Steinway St. (bet. Astoria Blvd. & 25th Ave.)

Subway: Astoria Blvd   Lunch & dinner daily
Phone: 718-721-9010
Web: N/A
Price: $$

There are no distractions at this authentic Egyptian café. The look is simple and alcohol isn't offered since this is a strictly Muslim establishment, but friendly service provides the small space with just enough ambience.

Seafood is without a doubt the star attraction here. Whole fish are pulled from their icy display and thrown onto a sizzling flattop to be barbecued Egyptian-style (blackened and sprinkled with spices and chopped herbs); and the fried shrimp are also a very popular option. But, no matter what main you decide on, a platter of cool and creamy spreads is the only accompaniment you'll need—especially since it's served with pillows of wonderfully chewy pita that arrives so hot you might burn your fingers ripping into it.

Salt & Fat

Contemporary ✗

41-16 Queens Blvd. (bet. 41st & 42nd Sts.)

Subway: 40 St   Dinner Tue – Sun
Phone: 718-433-3702
Web: www.saltandfatny.com
Price: $$

An ode to the pleasures of the pig, this is the pleasantly casual home to Sunnyside-rasied Chef/owner Daniel Yi. Dark woods, playful pig motifs, and soft lights decorate the simple space, known for its friendly, personal service.

There's probably no better way to welcome diners to this aptly named bistro than with a bag of salty bacon-fat popcorn. Yet, also renowned are the *bao* and beer pairings that change frequently. Other options include wide strands of golden-yellow pappardelle dressed with grilled ramps, sweet peas and smoky bacon lardons. Deep-fried chicken wings coated with a garlic-infused caramel sauce and sprinkled liberally with crispy garlic chips boasts its own decadent prowess. Finish with the Rice Krispies treats and heave a sigh of relief.

Samudra

F3

75-18 37th Ave. (bet. 75th & 76th Sts.)

Subway: 74 St - Broadway   Lunch & dinner daily
Phone: 718-255-1757
Web: N/A
Price: ⊜⊜

Excellent and affordable Southern Indian food arrives via this humble little gem in Jackson Heights. Guests are greeted by a long and simply decorated room laced with a few hand-woven textiles from India; and Samudra's owner (a personable presence when he's in-house) certainly adds to the cozy ambience by smiling and greeting guests upon entry.

Of course, the real star of the show here is the vegetarian menu, which features 16 different kinds of dosas, including a perfectly crispy Mysore masala version stuffed with turmeric-tinged mashed potato. South Indian fermented dough specialties, like an *idli-vada* combo, arrive on a silver tray with sides of tangy tomato- and coconut-chutney—and is just another sample of the delicacies on offer here.

Sik Gaek

C1

161-29 Crocheron Ave. (bet. 161st & 162nd Sts.)

Subway: Flushing - Main St (& bus Q12)   Dinner Tue – Sun
Phone: 718-321-7770
Web: N/A
Price: $$

There may be glitzier Korean spots in town, but insanely delicious, exceedingly simple Sik Gaek assures a good time, every time. Dressed in silly costumes, the staff is always having a blast in this seasonally decorated shack-like dining room featuring corrugated metal roofs, street lights, buckets for shells, and walls papered in dollar bills. Booths along the edge are filled with noisy regulars.

The kitchen serves the ocean's bounty, starting with a deliciously crisp and gargantuan pancake, *pajeon*, studded with seafood and kimchi begging to be dipped in enticingly salty soy-sesame sauce. A cloudy soup bobbing with tofu arrives piping hot, boasting that sharp, nutty, telltale flavor of fermented bean curd, and seems to have its own restorative powers.

Spicy Lanka

Sri Lankan ✗

159-23 Hillside Ave. (bet. 160th St. & Parsons Blvd.)

Subway: Parsons Blvd   Lunch & dinner daily
Phone: 718-487-4499
Web: N/A
Price:

It's worth the trek to this far-out Jamaica restaurant for its veritable explosion of hip-hop beats, brightly colored murals of palm trees, and an unbridled enthusiasm for heat and colliding Sri Lankan flavors.

The heady aroma of spices that fills the dining room can be attributed to any number of specialties. Find a blast of flavor on the plate by way of the biryani, which is steamed for hours in a blend of cardamom, nutmeg, bay leaves, and star anise, then tossed with garlic- and ginger-marinated chicken and okra. String hoppers are another fragrant specialty, featuring rounds of steamed rice flour noodles meant to be drenched in a host of spicy embellishments, like dried chili-speckled *dhal*, coconut *sambal*, or fish curry infused with Ceylon cinnamon.

Sushi Daizen

Japanese ✗✗

47-38 Vernon Blvd. (bet. 47th Rd. & 48th Ave.)

Subway: Vernon Blvd - Jackson Av   Dinner Tue – Sun
Phone: 718-729-1297
Web: www.sushidaizen.com
Price: $$$$

The staff is upbeat, and the room is attractively minimal in design, but what really stands out here is the adoration of this little *sushi-ya's* devoted clientele. The mood is light and engaging as everyone digs into their omakase, with options to add sashimi or a small list of à la carte pieces.

Start your meal with a cool appetizer of enoki mushrooms in soy and dashi broth, or crisp green beans over creamy tofu. A knob of pickled ginger freshly sliced before your eyes signals the beginning of your sushi course, a progression of neatly trimmed, hand-formed morsels of fish. Highlights include excellent poached tiger shrimp, Santa Barbara sea urchin, and *kawa kawa* from Japan. A fatty tuna hand roll at the end of your meal serves a perfect finale.

575

Sweet Yummy House

F3

83-13 Broadway (bet. Cornish & Dongan Aves.)

Subway: Elmhurst Av   Lunch & dinner daily
Phone: 718-699-2888
Web: N/A
Price: $$

This tiny, impeccably clean dining room is drawing diners left and right to Elmhurst these days. But wait, you argue—isn't this just another Chinese joint along a stretch of Broadway filled with such Chinese joints? Not quite. In fact, Sweet Yummy House is a diamond in the rough for those hunting down authentic spice levels and Taiwanese specialties they've never heard of.

A meal might kick off with a duo of sautéed cabbages, one cooked in a delicate Taiwanese style, the other in the Shanghai tradition, sporting fiery oil. Then move on to tender, crispy chicken and pickled turnips in a nose-twitching spicy sauce; before lingering over deep and dark cold jelly, rendered Chengdu-style, with slippery mung bean noodles and lip-numbing Sichuan peppercorns.

Szechuan Mountain House

A3

3916 Prince St., Ste. G03 (at 39th Ave.)

Subway: Flushing - Main St   Lunch & dinner daily
Phone: 718-888-7893
Web: N/A
Price: $$

The moniker of this cozy spot connotes shelter against the elements, and its comforting menu follows suit with a range of stir-fries, soups, casseroles, and stews hailing from China's Sichuan province. Adding to the earthy vibe is a rustic interior complete with a koi pond at the entrance, brick-faced walls and a slate-tile floor, as well as large tables crowded with diners and heaped with platters.

Evidenced by its oft-ordered presence throughout the room, pork belly is clearly a crowd-pleaser—its long, thinly sliced strips of fatty meat presented hanging on an A-frame rack above a bowl of chili-garlic sauce for dipping. This is also the case for their myriad preparations of frog; fish simmered in a tart and spicy bath of pickled greens; and braised chicken with dried chilies.

Taiwanese Gourmet

Chinese ✗

84-02 Broadway (at St. James Ave.)

Subway: Elmhurst Av
Phone: 718-429-4818
Web: N/A
Price: 🍷🍷

Lunch & dinner daily

A truly local spot, Taiwanese Gourmet puts diners in the mood with its semi-open kitchen (a rarity for Chinese restaurants) and tasty food. Natural light floods the walls, which showcase an impressive collection of ancient warrior gear, all beautifully framed as if museum-ready. Menu descriptions are minimal but the staff is happy to elaborate.

Excellent technique shines through the Taiwanese specialties, notably in strips of "shredded beef" sautéed in a dark, meaty paste, and tossed with dried tofu that balances complex flavors with fresh Chinese celery—a hands down winner on the menu. Likewise, the stir-fry of wonderfully briny clams and basil offers a perfect balance of sweet and salty flavors with oyster sauce, soy, rice wine, and red chilies.

Tang

Korean ✗✗

196-50 Northern Blvd. (at Francis Lewis Blvd.)

Subway: N/A
Phone: 718-279-7080
Web: N/A
Price: $$

Lunch & dinner daily

When craving authentic Korean specialties, Tang is an absolute must-visit. The restaurant's impeccably cool style extends from its angled exterior ablaze in beams of yellow light to its sleek interior with exposed brick walls and bare wood tables. The attractive art gallery next door is attached and doubles as a private dining space.

Meals begin with an unending supply of wonderfully crisp and mild house kimchi. Also try the hearty *bibimbap* of marinated beef strips, root vegetables, and mushrooms alongside a bowl of ox-bone broth. The main attraction is the sensational *jeon*, traditional Korean pancakes grilled to order (weekend dinners only). Round out the meal with steamed pigs feet accompanied by Tang's special fiery, salty, shrimp-based dipping sauce.

Taverna Kyclades

✗

F1

33-07 Ditmars Blvd. (bet. 33rd & 35th Sts.)

Subway: Astoria - Ditmars Blvd   Lunch & dinner daily
Phone: 718-545-8666
Web: www.tavernakyclades.com
Price: ⊜⊜

Forget the no-frills surroundings and focus instead on the fantastically fresh fish. This beloved Greek spot (with a second location in the East Village) has folks happily dining elbow to elbow in a tiny yet lively space where the bustling kitchen is in view and seafaring scenes paint the walls. Quick, straightforward servers may address you in Greek if you look the part—that's just how local it gets here.

Grab a seat on the enclosed patio for some serenity and get things going with garlicky and bubbling hot crab-stuffed clams; or the cold, classic trio of powerful *skordalia*, cooling tzatziki, and briny *taramosalata* served with toasted pita triangles. Order a side of *horta* (steamed escarole and dandelion) to accompany a plate of sweet and delicate mullets, served with a side of lemon potatoes.

Thai Rock

✗

C3

375 Beach 92nd St. (at Beach Channel Dr.)

Subway: Beach 90 St   Lunch & dinner daily
Phone: 718-945-5111
Web: www.thairock.us
Price: $$

The "rock" in Thai Rock is not just a reference to the restaurant's location in the beachside Rockaways, but a nod to the live music that takes over after the sun dips down. Inside, you'll find tightly packed wooden tables and comfortable high-backed chairs, but the large uncovered patio overlooking the bay is certainly the place to be come summer.

The menu covers the usual Thai standards—think pad Thai, curries, and various stir fries—as well as a few Northern Thai specialties, with aplomb. Don't miss the plump and tender dumplings stuffed with crunchy turnips, peanuts, and fragrant garlic; refreshing chicken *larb gai*, laced with a bright and zesty lime sauce featuring mint and scallion; or the delicious and very savory Issan sausage.

Tito Rad's Grill

Filipino

E3

49-10 Queens Blvd. (bet. 49th & 50th Sts.)

Subway: 46 St - Bliss St   Lunch & dinner daily
Phone: 718-205-7299
Web: www.titorads.com
Price: ⊜⊜

This eclectic grill seduces with its perfectly encapsulated fusion of the Malay, Spanish, Chinese, and Japanese flavors that typify the wholly unique cuisine of the Philippines. Cozy touches accent the décor and a mix of light stone with dark wood strikes just the right balance between contemporary and familiar.

Bold and generously portioned, the authentic specialties here have amassed a devout following. Highlights from the extensive pork- and seafood-dominated menu might include *binagoongang baboy*, tender chunks of pork cooked in a shrimp paste-sparked sauce made rich with melted fat; and *adobo* fried rice studded with crunchy and delicious bits of pork belly skin. If it's on offer, be sure to opt for the *inihaw na panga* or grilled tuna jaw.

Tong Sam Gyup Goo Yi

Korean ᛉ

C1

162-23 Depot Rd. (bet. Northern Blvd. & 164th St.)

Subway: Flushing - Main St (& bus Q13)   Lunch & dinner daily
Phone: 718-359-4583
Web: N/A
Price: $$

Murray Hill is no stranger to Korean food, but this prized, pig-loving barbecue destination is always packed. Inside, the bright room's décor forgoes all frills to focus on regional specialties. Smiling servers are earnest and hospitable.

Begin with the usual but very exquisite *banchan*-like pickled turnips, fermented bean paste soup, and specially aged house kimchi—funky, garlicky, and a total pleasure. Bowls of glassy *naengmyun* noodles dancing in a chilled broth with kimchi are just as popular. Yet what makes this place unique is that barbecue grill on each table, used for sizzling slices of flavorful duck with miso, garlic cloves, and bean sprouts; spicy, tender bits of octopus; and sweet, fatty pork with soy sauce, red chili paste, and scallions.

Trattoria L'incontro

Italian ✖✖

F1

21-76 31st St. (at Ditmars Blvd.)

Subway: Astoria - Ditmars Blvd   Lunch & dinner Tue – Sun
Phone: 718-721-3532
Web: www.trattorialincontro.com
Price: $$

A litany of delights sets the stage for an entertaining evening at this beloved institution of Italian-American pleasure. Frescoes of tranquil Italian scenes adorn coral walls in the unfussy dining room, complete with white-clothed tables spread at an ample distance. Service is relaxed, professional, and even theatrical in their performance of reciting special upon special.

Flavors are classic and robust, from eggplant rollatini stuffed with ricotta and herbs to the ravioli *golosi*, filled with both ground filet and veal, then topped with a sauce of mushrooms and sausage. Tender veal scaloppini is gently dredged and pan-fried, then bathed in a silky sauce of wine, butter, garlic, and lemon. Crunching through crisp cannoli is a divine finale.

Tutti Matti

Italian ✖✖

B3

47-30 Vernon Blvd. (bet. 47th Rd. & 48th Ave.)

Subway: Vernon Blvd - Jackson Av   Lunch & dinner daily
Phone: 718-937-2900
Web: www.tuttimattilic.com
Price: $$

This fine trattoria is the perfect addition to the teeming Long Island City scene. The décor is attractive and the vibe friendly. Envision a slender space opening to a rear dining room, with mezzanine seating, whitewashed brick, rustic wood slats, and a wall of wine storage.

Part of the space is devoted to the pizza station, where a dedicated *pizzaiolo* churns out delicious-smelling (and tasting) pies from a wood-burning oven. The pies are offered as *"tradizionali"* or as *"speciali da provare,"* referring to the Amalfi coast-style pizza. Pastas, like the house-made *maccheroncini scoglio*, tossed with a pristine assortment of seafood in a bright tomato sauce, are equally tasty; as are heartier entrées like veal scallopini with Sicilian lemon and orange sauce.

Uma's

Central Asian

C3

92-07 Rockaway Beach Blvd. (bet. Beach 92nd & 94th Sts.)

Subway: Beach 90 St   Lunch & dinner daily
Phone: 718-318-9100
Web: N/A
Price: $$

Thanks to a warm, unpretentious vibe, ukulele tunes, and the talented husband-and-wife team at its helm, this Far Rockaway haven of central Asian cuisine is as easy and breezy as its unique surf town environs.

Uma's unique interplay of flavors guarantees a delightful meal that's as hearty and fragrant as it is unpretentious: shredded Korean-style carrot salad is dressed with chili flakes and aromatic herbs, and the signature butternut squash manti—here topped with caramelized onions—are an utterly satisfying vegetarian take on the typically meat-stuffed dumplings. Daily specials are always a treat, and may reveal succulent braised lamb seasoned with cumin and rosemary, plated with sundried apricots as well as a fluffy mound of kasha.

Uncle Zhou

Chinese

F3

83-29 Broadway (at Dongan Ave.)

Subway: Elmhurst Av   Lunch & dinner Wed – Mon
Phone: 718-393-0888
Web: N/A
Price: ෩

Gifted cooks have been setting up in Elmhurst to show off their skills, but the chef/visionary of this modestly decked, massively popular Henanese gem has been a fixture from the start. Seat yourself inside the butterscotch-hued room, surrender to the affable staff, and await a memorable feast.

Opening this culinary show are pickled cucumbers and briny bamboo shoots with mushrooms, followed by pan-seared lamb dumplings or hugely fortifying "Dial oil" noodles sautéed with dried red chilies. For the consummate finale, pre-order "Taosibao," an impressive showpiece of rice-stuffed quail inside a squab, inside a chicken, inside a duck. Not only is this trumped-up version of *turducken* technically superb, but every element is flavored by an aromatic broth.

Urubamba

✗✗

F3

86-20 37th Ave. (at 86th St.)

Subway: 82 St - Jackson Hts
Phone: 718-672-2224
Web: N/A
Price: $$

Lunch & dinner daily

Named for Peru's intensely beautiful river, the Rio Urubamba, this hacienda-inspired space features indigenous paintings and artifacts that echo the rustic fare pouring out of the kitchen.

On weekends, the eatery serves traditional *desayuno*, a gut-busting feast of *chanfainita* beef stew and other hearty favorites. Here, tamales are a broad and flat banana leaf wrapped and stuffed with chicken and olives—a tasty contrast to the familiar Meso-American counterpart. For ultimate comfort, go for the *seco de cabrito*, a fantastically tender lamb and *aji panca* stew served with chunks of cassava and extra sauce in a tiny clay kettle. The dense *alfajor* cookie sandwich filled with dulce de leche and *crema volteada* flan is a perfectly decadent ending.

Venturo Osteria & Wine Bar

✗

A2

44-07 Queens Blvd. (bet. 44th & 45th Sts.)

Subway: 46 St - Bliss St
Phone: 718-406-9363
Web: www.venturovino.com
Price: $$

Lunch Sat – Sun
Dinner nightly

Chef Michelle Vido helms a dedicated kitchen that surprises with excellence and generosity at this delicious Sunnyside *osteria*. Having amassed a loyal following for her cooking at Vesta, this offshoot deserves its own high praise.

Distressed wood accents and calming pale-blue walls reinforce the chill Mediterranean vibe here, even at peak times. And of course house-made elements define every single dish on the menu, from slices of freshly baked focaccia to creamy mozzarella drizzled with herbed oil. Clever touches also abound, as seen in a refreshing lemon vinaigrette-dressed escarole salad that is given a hint of sweetness from diced, dried figs, as well as in pasta like the pumpkin-shaped *zucca* served with beef ragù and shaved young pecorino.

Vesta Trattoria

 Italian

E1

21-02 30th Ave. (at 21st St.)

Subway: 30 Av
Phone: 718-545-5550
Web: www.vestavino.com
Price: $$

Lunch Sat – Sun
Dinner nightly

Ever-changing daily specials and a respectable wine list—celebrated with a weekday happy hour—have fostered the favorable reputation of Astoria's favorite trattoria. Local foodies fill the wee room, a moderately dressed space with sage-green banquettes and a wall-mounted blackboard displaying the names of farms and producers sourced for the menu's array of contemporary Italian food.

To that end, tender meatballs are braised in a serrano chili-sparked tomato sauce; and free-range chicken Milanese is plated with a swipe of roasted lemon purée. For dessert, *la torta del piccolo bambino Gesu Cristo* reveals a block of excellent sticky toffee pudding cake that arrives warm, caramel-soaked, and capped with a refreshing scoop of crème fraîche sorbet.

Zum Stammtisch

German

B2

69-46 Myrtle Ave. (bet. 69th Pl. & 70th St.)

Subway: N/A
Phone: 718-386-3014
Web: www.zumstammtisch.com
Price: $$

Lunch & dinner daily

Family owned and operated since 1972, this unrelenting success story has expanded over the years and welcomed Stammtisch Pork Store & Imports next door.

Zum Stammtisch hosts a crowded house in a Bavarian country inn setting where old-world flavor is relished with whole-hearted enthusiasm. The goulash is thick and hearty, stocked with potatoes and beans, but that's just for starters. Save room for *sauerbraten, jägerschnitzel,* or a platter of succulent grilled sausages that includes *bratwurst, knockwurst,* and hickory-smoked *krainerwurst* served with sauerkraut and potato salad. The *Schwarzwälder Kirschtorte* (classic Black Forest cake) layers dense chocolate sponge with Kirsch-soaked cherries and cream, and is absolutely worth the indulgence.

Staten Island

Staten Island

Staten Island may be the least populated borough of NYC, but the building of the Verrazano-Narrows Bridge ended its once bucolic existence. This fact is especially apt because one of the strongest, most accurate simplifications is that this "island" is home to a large Italian-American population, and no self-respecting foodie visits here without picking up a *scungilli* pizza from **Joe & Pat's**, or a slice from **Nunzio** and **Denino's**. These shores, marinas, and waterfronts, once in shambles thanks to Superstorm Sandy, are slowly but surely recovering. In fact, **Skippy's**, originally a famous food truck, is back in (big) business with its hot dogs prepared in various regional styles for the residents of Mariner's Harbor right on Richmond Terrace. In fact, anyone with preconceived notions about this "forgotten borough" can leave them at the ferry door. Though deemed at one time the largest landfill in the world, Staten Island is currently being transformed into a verdant and very vast public park.

CULINARY CORNUCOPIA

While it is revered as an Italian-American hub, Staten Island continues to surprise visitors with its ethnically diverse enclaves. Take a culinary tour of the Mediterranean and Balkans at **Dinora**, proffering an abundance of olives, cheeses, and halal-butchered meat. Or, stop by those popular old-time Polish delis, which seem to comfortably thrive on their takeout business and homemade jams alone. Of course, **Giuliano's Prodotti Italiani** continues to keep patrons happy with such Old Country classics as handmade pizzas, pastas, calzones, and more.

Spice heads will rejoice at the fantastic Sri Lankan food finds in the area surrounding Victory Boulevard. A spectrum of restaurants (think storefronts) reside here, including **New Asha** serving this country's fiery cuisine. Of course, **Lanka Grocery** is an epicurean's dream featuring a riot of colorful, authentic ingredients Staying within South Asia—its cuisine and culture—this borough is also home to Jacques Marchais Museum of Tibetan Art, an institution aimed at advancing Tibetan and Himalayan art. Steps from these subcontinent gems, discover authentic taquerias and a large Liberian outdoor market in the vicinity of Grasmere, where a small but special selection of purveyors supply West African staples and other regional eats.

Staten Island

STREETS

Clarke Ave.	1 B3
Clove Rd.	2 B2
Lily Pond Ave.	3 B2
Ocean Terrace	4 B2
Page Ave.	5 A4
Richmond Hill Rd.	6 A3
Richmond Rd.	7 B3
School Rd.	8 B2
Vanderbilt Ave.	9 B2
Outerbridge Crossing	10 A3

Take these to enjoy at home; or cook up a globally inspired feast with locally farmed produce from **Gerardi's** farmer's market in New Brighton or **St. George Greenmarket**, open on Saturdays. Historic Richmond Town pays homage to the sustainable food movement here by organizing the family-focused festival **Uncorked!**, which features the best in homemade cuisine and wine. They even offer recipes for traditional American classics. For rare and more mature varietals, **Mission Fine Wines** is top-notch, but if yearning for more calorie-heavy (read heavenly) eats, **The Cookie Jar** is way above par. Opened in 2007, this youngest sibling of **Cake Chef**, a beloved bakeshop up the road and **Piece-A-Cake** further south on New Dorp Lane, not only incites its audience with a range of sweets but savory focaccias and soups galore.

FOOD, FUN & FROLIC

Given its booming culinary scene and cultural merging, it should come as no surprise that the Staten Island of the future includes plans for a floating farmer's market, aquarium, and revamped waterfronts, giving residents and tourists another reason to sit back and savor a drink at one of the bars along Bay Street. Couple these sips with abundant small plates at **Adobe Blues**, a cantina preparing sumptuous Southwestern food and prettified with a fireplace, clay walls, and collectibles depicting the island's rodeo days…yee-haw! Residents adore this neighborhood hangout for its modest demeanor coupled with gratifying grub, and will probably continue to flood it till the end of time. After dawdling on Lafayette Avenue, drive through some of the city's wealthiest zip codes starring mansions with magnificent views of Manhattan and beyond. Whether here to glimpse the world's only complete collection of rattlesnakes at the zoo, or seek out the birthplaces of such divas as Christina Aguilera and Joan Baez, a visit to Staten Island is nothing if not interesting.

Angelina's

Italian ✗✗

A4

399 Ellis St. (at Main St.)

Bus: N/A

Lunch & dinner Tue – Sun

Phone: 718-227-2900

Web: www.angelinasristorante.com

Price: $$$

It's no secret that Angelina's is Staten Island's place to celebrate Italian-American culture. Packed by 7:00 P.M. and boasting stunning river sunset views, it also offers live music and a massive atrium attracting revelers from near and far.

The multi-level Victorian may conjure New Orleans, but Angelina's keeps the focus clearly on Italian-American cooking with excellent pastas and plush red wines. The classic baked clams oreganata has that idyllic blend of butter and garlic. *Spaghettini al pomodoro* is as lovely as it sounds, with long-simmered tomato ragù, basil, and a sprinkling of Parmigiano. The popular *trenette nere con frutti di mare* piles a mountain of shrimp, clams, mussels, and scallops on thick squid ink pasta bathed in chunky tomato sauce.

Bayou

Cajun ✗✗

B2

1072 Bay St. (bet. Chestnut & St. Marys Aves.)

Bus: 51, 81

Lunch & dinner daily

Phone: 718-273-4383

Web: www.bayounyc.com

Price: $$

Southern food isn't novel to the city, but Cajun cuisine on Staten Island is a whole new realm. Bayou delivers with its veritable setting and spread. The space is a bit bawdy with gold and green accents, but linen-covered tables, luminous mirrors, and chandeliers lend refinement. Live music on occasion also adds to the lure.

Kitchen offerings begin with wonderfully decadent nachos featuring crawfish tails and crispy tortilla chips smothered in red beans, cheese, *pico de gallo,* and pickled jalapeños. Follow this up with a soul-satisfying and deliciously fragrant chicken-andouille sausage gumbo kicked up a notch with celery and peppers. Banana-chocolate bread pudding with vanilla ice cream turns heavenly when kissed with a boozy Bourbon cream sauce.

Beso

Spanish ✗

B2

11 Schuyler St. (bet. Richmond Tr. & Stuyvesant Pl.)

Bus: N/A   Lunch & dinner daily
Phone: 718-816-8162
Web: www.besonyc.com
Price: $$

Well-located? Yes, just by the Richmond County Courthouse. Good food and helpful staff? Of course. Great for groups or solo diners? You know it. Beso seems to have it all, including an interior that spotlights quaint accents like beautiful antique sideboards.

Grazing menus are all the rage, so it's worth exploring their vibrant tapas, which includes *empanada de res* stuffed with sautéed beef and served with a yucca-tomato sauce. *Pan y cerdo* or garlic-infused shredded roast pork slathered over a crostini and topped with melted Mahon along with avocado-*pico de gallo* is a savory treat, while *bistek Cubano* reveals a sherry wine- and garlic-marinated skirt steak grilled until tender and garnished with mojito sauce. Finish with a classic, ultra-smooth coconut flan.

Bin 5

Contemporary ✗✗

B2

1233 Bay St. (bet. Maryland & Scarboro Aves.)

Bus: 51, 81   Dinner Tue – Sun
Phone: 718-448-7275
Web: www.bin5nyc.com
Price: $$

At this intimate bistro in Rosebank, dinner comes with a view of the Manhattan skyline. Complete with teardrop chandeliers and exposed brick, Bin 5's romantic setting has for long drawn locals seeking good food and quiet conversation (plus that fantastic panorama!).

The playful menu—complete with solid daily specials—may reveal a perfect pan-seared and golden-brown pork loin, set atop slices of pickled red and green peppers and surrounded by a generous amount of pan sauce made from prosecco and vinegar. Then, cauliflower florets are pulsed to form couscous-like beads and cooked in the style of fried rice, studded with veggies and seasoned by soy. A tall wedge of pistachio-walnut cake dusted with powdered sugar is a light, fluffy and fitting finale.

Bocelli

Italian XX

B2

1250 Hylan Blvd. (bet. Parkinson Ave. & Quintard St.)

Bus: 78
Phone: 718-420-6150
Web: www.bocellirest.com
Price: $$$

Lunch & dinner daily

Tucked into a workaday shopping mall, Bocelli doesn't make much of an impression at first glance. But, make your way past the simple façade, and wow, behold a gorgeous sloping staircase as well as a vast, theatrical dining room with polished dark wood, stunning light fixtures, and well-spaced tables that are luxuriously set. Could the delicious looking Italian menu be just as special?

The answer is most delightedly yes. An appetizer of *spiedini alla Romana* arrives topped with a delicious lemon, anchovy, and caper sauce; while a generous bowl of *rigatoni ripieni alla Sangiovese* is stuffed with savory beef tenderloin tips that have been braised in Sangiovese. At the end, a decadent chocolate three-layer cake gets a luscious hit from salty peanut butter.

Cafe Luna

Italian XX

A3

31 Page Ave. (bet. Boscombe Ave. & Richmond Valley Rd.)

BusBus: 74
Phone: 718-227-8582
Web: www.cafelunanyc.com
Price: $$

Lunch Mon – Fri
Dinner nightly

This well-run local institution proves that one should never judge a restaurant by its strip mall cover. With its Italian-American cooking, romantic fireplace, enclosed wine room, and covered veranda, Cafe Luna has a friendly, warm, and familial air thanks to the Sicilian owners who hail from Palermo.

Their perfectly prepared pastas mean the standards are taken care of, and it's easy to leave here satisfied. Start with short little corkscrews of fresh fusilli *puttanesca* in a strong, plum tomato sauce enhanced by anchovies, red chili flakes, garlic, basil, and black olives. Deliciously fresh red snapper *marechiaro* combines briny clams and sweet mussels with a fresh fish fillet and light tomato sauce with hints of chili flakes and lots of fresh parsley.

Carol's Cafe

American   ✗

B2

1571 Richmond Rd. (at Four Corners Rd. & Seaview Ave.)

Bus: 74, 76, 84, 86
Phone: 718-979-5600
Web: www.carolscafe.com
Price: $$

Dinner Wed – Sat

♿

Dining here is like dining in Chef/owner Carol Frazzetta's kitchen—almost literally, because she lives on the premises. Her delightful personality fills the space, from the fresh flowers and pink linens, to shareable dishes and that homemade chocolate stout triple layer cake.

Not only has Frazzetta owned the building since the 1970s, but she clearly knows her neighbors, many of whom flock to the café for a roster of daily specials (top hits include "wild game of the day" like grilled buffalo ribeye and a marvelous prosciutto- and tomato-stuffed bread). The chef's slow-cooked *spaghetti al pomodoro* is another fan fave, topped with a chiffonade of basil and peppered with parmesan, before serving. Like everything else, it's simple, well-made, and *delizioso*.

Dosa Garden

Indian   ✗

B2

323 Victory Blvd. (bet. Cebra Ave. & Jersey St.)

Bus: 46, 48, 61, 66
Phone: 718-420-0919
Web: N/A
Price: ♿

Lunch Tue – Sun
Dinner nightly

The spicy, complex, and fragrant *dosas* of Dosa Garden make this casual stop a thoroughly impressive hidden gem. The ambience feels more storefront eatery than sit-down restaurant, with just a few hints of South Asian décor, but the warm, made-to-order dishes and aromas from the kitchen are transporting.

The kitchen boasts a tandoor oven but also churns out an array of elaborate *dosas,* like the tantalizingly crisp Mysore masala served with a sour yogurt sauce, spread with spicy chutney, and folded with potatoes, peppercorns, curry leaves, chili, and cumin. Don't miss the unique *rasa vada*, crunchy lentil doughnuts soaked in a deliciously spicy *rasam*. Curries are amazingly delish, like the shockingly deep brown Chettinadu fish, accented with mustard seeds.

Enoteca Maria

B2

27 Hyatt St. (bet. Central Ave. & St. Marks Pl.)

Bus: N/A
Phone: 718-447-2777
Web: www.enotecamaria.com
Price: $$

Lunch Wed – Fri
Dinner Wed – Sun

No need to venture far on Staten Island for excellent Italian. Enoteca Maria is just blocks from the St.George Terminal and brought to you by Jody Scaravella, whose cookbook *Nonna's House* has been earning him (and this tiny gem) much applause. With its Carrara marble and lively vibe, most foodies flock here for a certain authenticity that is rarely sacrificed.

Each night, the menu changes depending on which *nonna* is presiding over the kitchen, as in Nina from Belarus, who might serve a *salat Odessa* mingling grilled eggplant, red onion, tomato and parsley. *Lasagna de Adelina* arrives as an inspired layering of zucchini, basil pesto and cream cheese, all topped with parmesan. And for a bit of sweet, try the *torta di vaniglia di Melissa* served with whipped cream.

Fushimi

B3

2110 Richmond Rd. (bet. Colfax & Lincoln Aves.)

Bus: 51, 81
Phone: 718-980-5300
Web: www.fushimigroup.com
Price: $$$

Lunch & dinner daily

Fushimi is the ultimate spot for hungry locals in search of a dependable club scene sans commute. On any given night, its cozy booths are packed with islanders slinging back colorful cocktails and digging into architecturally designed sushi and sashimi from the Asian-fusion menu. Presentations are a knockout here, and the creativity and precision extends to the quality and combination of ingredients as well. Case in point: the aptly named Staten Island, a shrimp tempura roll topped with thin slices of seared filet mignon and dollops of mint-honey mustard and spicy aïoli.

Sink your teeth into the long-braised short ribs, which are fall-off-the-bone tender and served with Korean *galbi* sauce and "pee wee" potato chips made from those adorably tiny tubers.

Giuliana's

 Italian ✗✗

4105 Hylan Blvd. (at Osborn Ave.)

Bus:	54, 78, 79
Phone:	718-317-8507
Web:	www.giulianassi.com
Price:	$$

Lunch & dinner Tue – Sun

Staten Island may swarm with Italian-American eateries, but this festive classic does a masterful job in keeping its kitchen distinct and the patrons loyal. Giuliana's is the queen bee amid shops, catering halls, and ample competition. The interior is modest and charming, with framed pictures of smiling patrons and a fully stocked bar.

Hearty *stracciatella* is loaded with spinach and a comforting sauce of eggy parmesan, finished with a generous shower of black pepper. Seek out the *perciatelle con sarde*, a Sicilian-style pasta tossed in a powerful blend of fennel, saffron, raisins, sardines, anchovy paste, and crunch of toasted breadcrumbs. A trio of gelatos—pistachio, chocolate, and bitter almond, served with biscotti—is a divine ending.

Lakruwana

Sri Lankan ✗

668 Bay St. (at Broad St.)

Bus:	51, 76
Phone:	347-857-6619
Web:	www.lakruwana.com
Price:	

Lunch & dinner Tue – Sun

Prepare for a sensory overload the moment you set foot into Lakruwana—the Sri Lankan hot spot is covered from floor-to-ceiling in murals, sculptures, flags, and more. The bright kaleidoscope of textures and colors is a welcome sight in an otherwise downtrodden part of the borough, as is the energetic owner who drifts from table to table.

Those familiar with Indian food will love Lakruwana's abundance of curries, green chili-spiked *kuttu roti*, as well as refreshingly salty-and-sour *lassi*. But their flavorful fare is considerably spicier, packing heat into everything from fiery red chili *lunu miris* chutney to devilled chicken. Loaded with ginger and garlic, this stellar tomato-based chicken specialty comes with cooling *raita* and tangy vegetable curry.

595

Maizal

B2

990 Bay St. (bet. Lynhurst & Willow Sts.)

Bus:	51, 76	Lunch Sun
Phone:	347-825-3776	Dinner nightly
Web:	www.maizalrestaurant.com	
Price:	$$	

This lovely, festive, and downright delicious Mexican restaurant is the perfect reprieve should you need a night off from Staten Island's endless stream of Italian fare. Featuring bright artwork, rustic wood tables, a well-stocked bar and semi-open kitchen, the mood at Maizal is fun and informal, with live music offered on weekends.

Kick things off with the house-made guacamole, mashed to order in a *molcajete* and spiced to request. Then tuck into tender chicken enchiladas rolled in warm handmade corn tortillas and laced with a smoky chile-ancho sauce; or one of the authentic house specials like *tikin xic* grouper, a subtle Mayan dish where citrus- and annatto-marinated fish is steamed to delicate and mouthwatering perfection in a banana leaf.

Mario's

B3

1657 Richmond Rd. (bet. Buel & Liberty Aves.)

Bus:	n/a	Lunch & dinner daily
Phone:	718-979-1075	
Web:	www.mariossiny.com	
Price:	$$	

Does Staten Island really need another Italian-American restaurant? A fair question, but Chef/owner Mario Gentile confirms the answer is a yes. And, after a bite or two of his delicious red sauce food, you might be inclined to agree. Sprawled on a stretch of Richmond Road dotted with florists and bridal shops, Mario's offers big windows for people watching, leather banquettes, and oversized artwork.

It's practically law in this borough to start your meal with calamari, and this respite doesn't disappoint—it's refreshingly light and served with a scrumptious, herby lemon sauce. Move on to a tender poached pear salad with crushed walnuts, creamy Gorgonzola, and crispy prosciutto; or fall-off-the-bone osso buco plated with a soft pile of saffron risotto.

Phil Am Kusina

B2

Filipino ✗

556 Tompkins Ave. (bet. Clifton Ave. & Hylan Blvd.)

Bus: 53
Phone: 718-727-3672
Web: www.philamkusina.com
Price: ⊜

Lunch & dinner daily

This charming dining room is located amidst a mostly residential neighborhood blocks away from busy Bay Street. The peaked-roof interior is brightened by skylights and pale peach walls, and the jovial vibe is amplified by genuinely gracious service.

The menu offers a wide range of Filipino specialties including fried delights, noodle preparations, and simmered specialties like *humba*—a lusciously tender and fatty pork shank slow-simmered with soy sauce and pineapple. A side of crispy garlic-flecked rice is the perfect accompaniment to this sweet-and-salty treat. Inspired to whip something up in the comfort of your own kitchen? Just head across the street, where a long-standing Filipino grocery store shares the same name and family ownership.

San Rasa

B2

Sri Lankan ✗

19 Corson Ave. (bet. Daniel Low Ter. & Monroe Ave.)

Bus: 51
Phone: 718-420-0027
Web: www.sanrasa.com
Price: ⊜

Lunch & dinner Wed – Mon

A little excursion to Staten Island is a must for knock-your-socks-off Sri Lankan food. Life is short, and honestly—so is that charming ferry ride, which deposits you on this local island destination for the best Sri Lankan food. Inside the bright, large dining space, you'll find wood accents and vessels lined up for their popular Sunday lunch buffet.

San Rasa's food is prepared fresh to order, offering the perfect excuse to nurse a cold, salty lassi while you wait. Dinner may begin with a starter of string hoppers or crispy little pancakes laced in a rich fish curry carrying hints of clove, fennel, and cardamom; and then move on to the *lampri*, a succulent little bundle of beef curry wrapped in banana leaf with nutty yellow rice, eggplant, and cashews.

Trattoria Romana da Vittorio

Italian ✗✗

1476 Hylan Blvd. (at Benton Ave.)

Bus: 54, 78, 79   Lunch & dinner Mon – Sat
Phone: 718-980-3113
Web: www.trattoriaromanasi.com
Price: $$

This delicious Staten Island via Lazio trattoria serves up heaping platters of al dente pasta and irresistible nightly specials, alongside bubbling pizzas that roll out of its brick oven in the back. Owned and guided by local personality and beloved chef, Vittorio Asoli (his cooking classes are televised on a local community channel), Trattoria Romana da Vittorio offers a cozy reprieve from the busy avenue outside, with diners huddling over snug tables or gathering at a communal table to chat up their neighbors.

Don't miss the juicy chicken *scarpariello*, caramelized to perfection and simmered in a delicate white wine sauce with rosemary and garlic; or tender *trippa alla Romana*, served in a fresh tomato sauce with a hunk of crusty bread for dipping.

Vida

American ✗

381 Van Duzer St. (bet. Beach & Wright Sts.)

Bus: 78   Dinner Tue – Sat
Phone: 718-720-1501
Web: www.vidany.com
Price: $$

All the locals love Vida, where popular Chef/owner Silva Popaz has created a cozy little restaurant with a firm commitment to simple, but well-executed, dishes. Inside the café-like atmosphere, you'll find unique artwork lining brightly painted walls, and a smattering of tables surrounding a long communal wood table in the center.

The charming Popaz travels quite often, and the flavors she picks up along her journeys tend to make their way back into her menu at Vida. The "Mexican Duo"—her most popular dish—features pulled pork- and chicken-stuffed tortillas, topped with a vibrant Chimayo chile and tangy cheese sauce, and paired with tender stewed beans sporting bright green onion; while a delicate bread pudding arrives puddled in creamy vanilla ice cream.

MICHELIN
IS CONTINUALLY INNOVATING FOR SAFER, CLEANER, MORE ECONOMICAL, MORE CONNECTED AND BETTER ALL AROUND MOBILITY.

Tires wear more quickly on short urban journeys.

TRUE!

You tend to accelerate and brake more often when driving around town so your tires work harder!
If you are stuck in traffic, keep calm and drive slowly.

Tire pressure only affects your car's safety.

FALSE!

Driving with underinflated tires (0.5 below recommended pressure) doesn't just impact handling and fuel consumption, it will take 8,000 km off tire lifespan.
Make sure you check tire pressure about once a month and before you go on vacation or a long journey.

If you only encounter **winter weather from time to time** - sudden showers, snowfall or black ice - **one type of tire** will do the job.

?

TRUE!

The revolutionary **MICHELIN CrossClimate** - the very first summer tire with winter certification - is a practical solution to keep you on the road whatever the weather.

Fitting **2 winter tires** on my car guarantees maximum safety.

FALSE!

In the winter, especially when temperatures drop below 44.5°F, to ensure better road grip, all four tires should be identical and fitted at the same time.

2 WINTER TIRES ONLY =
risk of compromised road grip.

4 WINTER TIRES =
safer handling when cornering, driving downhill and braking.

If you regularly encounter rain, snow or black ice, choose a **MICHELIN Alpin tire**. This range offers you sharp handling plus a comfortable ride to safely face the challenge of winter driving.

MICHELIN

MICHELIN IS COMMITTED

▶ MICHELIN IS THE **GLOBAL LEADER IN FUEL-EFFICIENT TIRES** FOR LIGHT VEHICLES.

▶ **EDUCATING YOUNGSTERS ON ROAD SAFETY FOR BIKES,** NOT FORGETTING TWO-WHEELERS. LOCAL ROAD SAFETY CAMPAIGNS WERE RUN IN **16 COUNTRIES** IN 2015.

QUIZ

1   TIRES ARE BLACK SO WHY IS THE MICHELIN MAN WHITE?

Back in 1898 when the Michelin Man was first created from a stack of tires, they were made of natural rubber, cotton and sulphur and were therefore light-colored. The composition of tires did not change until after the First World War when carbon black was introduced. But the Michelin Man kept his color!

2   HOW LONG HAS MICHELIN BEEN GUIDING TRAVELERS?

Since 1900. When the MICHELIN guide was published at the turn of the century, it was claimed that it would last for a hundred years. It's still around today and remains a reference with new editions and online restaurant listings in a number of countries.

3   WHEN WAS THE "BIB GOURMAND" INTRODUCED IN THE MICHELIN GUIDE?

The symbol was created in 1997 but as early as 1954 the MICHELIN guide was recommending "exceptional good food at moderate prices." Today, it features on the MICHELIN Restaurants website and app.

If you want to enjoy a fun day out and find out more about Michelin, why not visit the l'Aventure Michelin museum and shop in Clermont-Ferrand, France:

www.laventuremichelin.com

Where to **Eat**

Alphabetical List
of Restaurants_____608

Restaurants
by Cuisine_____620

Cuisines
by Neighborhood_____632

Starred Restaurants_____648

Bib Gourmand_____651

Under $25_____653

Indexes

Alphabetical List of Restaurants

A

ABC Cocina		XX	108
ABC Kitchen		XX	108
Aburiya Kinnosuke		XX	242
ABV		X	198
Abyssinia		X	198
A Casa Fox		XX	220
Achilles Heel	🛱	X	508
Acme		XX	146
Africa Kine		X	199
Agern	❀	XX	243
Agnanti		XX	544
Ai Fiori	❀	XxX	278
Aita		XX	458
al Bustan	🛱	XX	242
Alcala		XX	244
Aldea	❀	XX	109
Al di Là		X	478
Aldo Sohm Wine Bar		🍸	279
Allswell		X	508
Alma		XX	492
Almayass		XX	110
Alobar		XX	544
Al Seabu		X	478
Amaranto		X	458
Amma		XX	244
Anassa Taverna		XX	245
Andanada	❀	XX	398
Andaz		X	368
Añejo		X	279
Anella		X	509
Angelina's		XX	590
Angkor	🛱	XX	368
Anjappar		X	110
annisa		XX	146
Antique Garage		X	328
Aquavit	❀❀	XxX	246
Ardesia		🍸	280
Arharn Thai	🛱	X	545
Armani Ristorante		XX	245
Arrogant Swine		X	459
Asian Jewels		XX	545
Aska	❀❀	XxX	510
atera	❀❀	XX	352
Atlantic Grill		XX	369
Atoboy	🛱	X	111
Atrium		XX	440
Aunt Jake's		X	38
Aureole	❀	XxX	281
Aurora		XX	509
Autre Kyo Ya		XX	54
Au Za'atar		X	54
Avant Garden		X	55
A Voce Madison		XX	111
Awadh		XX	399
Ayada		X	546

B

Babbalucci		X	199
Babbo	❀	XX	147
Babu Ji		X	55
Bacaro		X	220
Bahari estiatorio		X	546
Baker & Co.	🛱	XX	148
Balaboosta		XX	328
Balade		XX	56
Balthazar		XX	329

Balvanera	X	221	Bistro Vendôme		XX	247
Bamboo Garden	X	492	Black Ant (The)		XX	58
Bao (The)	X	56	Black Swan		X	460
Barano	XX	511	Blanca	✿✿	XX	461
Barawine	XX	200	Blaue Gans		XX	354
Barbetta	XxX	282	Blenheim		XX	150
Bar Boulud	XX	399	Blossom		XX	18
Barbounia	XX	112	BLT Prime		XX	113
Barbuto	XX	148	BLT Steak		XxX	247
Bar Corvo	XX	459	Blue Hill	✿	XX	151
Bar Masa	XX	280	Blue Ribbon		XX	329
Barney Greengrass	X	400	Blue Ribbon Sushi		XX	330
Bar Primi	⊛	XX	57	Blue Water Grill		XX	113
Barraca	XX	149	BLVD Bistro		X	201
Barrel & Fare	X	493	Boathouse Central Park		XX	370
Basil Brick Oven Pizza	⊛	XX	547	Bobby Van's		XX	248
Bâtard	✿	XX	353	Bocca		XX	114
Battersby	X	440	Bocelli		XX	592
Bayou	XX	590	Bo Ky		X	38
Becco	XX	282	BONDST		XX	152
Beccofino	X	420	Boqueria		XX	114
Bell Book & Candle	XX	149	Boulud Sud		XxX	401
Benares	XX	283	Bowery Meat Company		XX	58
Beso	X	591	Bozu		X	511
Betony	✿	XxX	284	Braai		X	285
Bettolona	X	200	Brasserie 8 1/2		XxX	285
Beyoglu	⊛	X	369	Brasserie Ruhlmann		XX	286
BG	X	283	Bread & Tulips		XX	115
Bhatti	X	112	Breslin (The)	✿	X	116
biáng!	⊛	XX	57	Bricolage		X	479
Bin 5	XX	591	Brinkley's		X	39
Bin 71	▤	400	Brisas del Caribe		X	421
Birds & Bubbles	XX	221	Brooklyn Star		XX	512
Bistro SK	X	420	Bruno		X	59

Bukhara Grill	XX	248
bún-ker	⊛ X	547
Burger & Barrel	XX	330
Bustan	XX	401
Buttermilk Channel	⊛ X	441
Buvette	X	152

C

Cacio e Pepe	X	59
Café Altro Paradiso	XX	331
Café Boulud	✿ XXX	371
Café China	✿ XX	249
Cafe Clover	XX	153
Cafe Cluny	XX	153
Café Frida	XX	402
Cafe Katja	X	222
Cafe Luna	XX	592
Café Mingala	X	370
Café Mogador	X	60
Cafe Sabarsky	X	372
Café Steinhof	X	479
Cagen	✿ XX	61
Caravaggio	XXX	372
Carbone	✿ XX	154
Carol's Cafe	X	593
Casa del Chef Bistro	⊛ X	548
Casa Enríque	✿ XX	549
Casa Lever	XXX	250
Casa Mono	✿ XX	117
Casellula	🍲	286
Cata	XX	222
Caviar Russe	✿ XXX	251
Cecil (The)	XX	201
Ceetay	X	421
Chaiwali	XX	202
Charlie Bird	XX	331
Chavela's	⊛ XX	460
Cheburechnaya	X	548
Chefs Club	XXX	332

Chef's Table at Brooklyn Fare	✿✿✿	XX	442
Cherche Midi		XX	332
Cherry Point		XX	512
Chez Napoléon		X	287
ChikaLicious		🍲	60
China Blue		XX	354
Cho Dang Gol	⊛	X	287
Chomp Chomp	⊛	X	155
Chop-Shop		X	18
Christos		XX	550
Ciccio	⊛	X	333
Cipura		XX	493
Clam (The)		XX	155
Clement		XXX	288
Clinton St. Baking Company		X	223
Clocktower (The)		XXX	115
Clover Club		🍲	441
Co.		X	19
cocoron		X	223
Colonia Verde		XX	462
Colonie		XX	443
Community Food & Juice		XX	202
Cómodo		XX	333
Còm tam Ninh Kieu		X	422
Congee Village	⊛	X	224
Contra	✿	XX	225
Cookshop		XX	19
Coppelia	⊛	X	20
Corner Social		XX	203
Cosme		XX	118
Cotenna	⊛	X	156
Covina		XX	118
Craft		XX	119
Craftbar		XX	119
Crispo		XX	156
Cull & Pistol		XX	20
Curry-Ya		X	62

D

Da Franco & Tony Ristorante		XX	422
Daniel	✿✿	XxXxX	373
Danji		X	288
da Umberto		XX	21
db Bistro Moderne		XX	289
DBGB Kitchen & Bar		XX	62
Degustation		XX	63
Delaware and Hudson	✿	XX	513
Del Frisco's		XxX	289
Delhi Masala		X	203
Del Posto	✿	XxX	22
De Mole		X	550
Dieci		X	63
Dim Sum Go Go	✸	X	39
Diner		X	514
dinnertable		X	64
Dinosaur Bar-B-Que		X	204
Dirt Candy		XX	224
Dirty French		XX	226
District Saigon		X	551
Dojo Izakaya		🍴	64
DOMODOMO	✸	X	157
Don Antonio by Starita	✸	XX	290
Donguri		X	374
Donostia	✸	X	65
Don's Bogam		XX	250
Dosa Garden		X	593
Dover		XX	443
Dovetail	✿	XxX	403
Dumpling Galaxy		X	551
Dutch (The)		XX	334

E

East 12th Osteria		XX	65
East Harbor Seafood Palace	✸	XX	494
East Pole		XX	374
Eddy (The)		XX	66
Edi & The Wolf		X	66
Ed's Lobster Bar		X	334

Egg	✸	X	514
El Atoradero	✸	X	480
El Born		XX	515
Eleven Madison Park	✿✿✿	XxxX	120
Eliá		XX	494
Eli's Table		XX	375
El Nuevo Bohío		X	423
El Parador	✸	XX	252
El Paso		X	204
El Porrón		X	375
El Quinto Pino		XX	21
Emilio's Ballato		XX	335
Emily		X	462
Empellón Taqueria		XX	157
Emporio		XX	335
Engeline's		X	552
EN Japanese Brasserie		XxX	158
Enoteca Maria	✸	X	594
Enoteca on Court		X	444
Enzo's of Arthur Ave		X	423
Estela		XX	336
Estiatorio Milos		XxX	290
Estrellita Poblana III		X	424
Eugene & Co.		X	463
Extra Fancy		X	515
Extra Virgin		XX	158

F

Falansai	✸	X	463
Farm on Adderley (The)		XX	480
Faro	✿	XX	464
Fat Radish (The)		XX	226
Fatty Fish		X	376
Faun		XX	481
Feast		X	67
Fedora		XX	159
Felidia		XxX	252
15 East		XX	121
Fig & Olive		XX	376
Finch (The)	✿	XX	465

Fishtag		XX	402
F & J Pine Restaurant		XX	424
Flat Top		X	205
Flex Mussels		XX	377
Flinders Lane		X	67
Fonda		X	481
Foragers City Table		XX	23
Forcella		X	516
Fort Defiance		X	495
44 & X Hell's Kitchen		XX	291
Frankie & Johnnie's		XX	291
Frankies 457 Spuntino	⊕	X	444
Franny's		XX	482
Freek's Mill	⊕	XX	495
Freud		XX	159
Fumo		XX	205
Fung Tu		XX	227
Fushimi		XX	594

G

Gabriel Kreuther	⊛	XxX	292
Gallagher's		XX	293
Gander (The)		XX	121
Ganso Ramen	⊕	X	445
Gastronomia Culinaria	⊕	X	404
Gastroteca		XX	552
Gato		XX	160
Gelso & Grand		X	40
General Greene (The)		X	466
Gennaro		XX	404
Gigino at Wagner Park		XX	98
Giorgione		XX	336
Giuliana's		XX	595
Gladys	⊕	X	466
Glasserie	⊕	XX	516
Gnocco		X	68
Goemon Curry		X	337
Golden Unicorn		X	40
Good		XX	160
Good Enough to Eat		X	405
Good Fork (The)	⊕	X	496
Gotham Bar and Grill	⊛	XxX	161
Gradisca		XX	163
Graffiti		🍴	68
Grain House		X	553
Gramercy Tavern	⊛	XxX	122
Gran Eléctrica	⊕	XX	445
Great N.Y. Noodletown		X	41
Greek (The)		XX	355
Greenpoint Fish & Lobster Co.		X	517
Gregory's 26 Corner Taverna	⊕	X	553
Grünauer Bistro		XX	377
Günter Seeger NY	⊛	XxX	162

H

Hahm Ji Bach	⊕	XX	554
Hakata Tonton		X	163
Hakkasan		XxX	293
Haldi		X	123
HanGawi	⊕	XX	253
Hanjan		XX	123
Happy Family Hotpot		X	554
Harry's Cafe & Steak		XX	98
Hasaki		X	69
Hatsuhana		XX	253
Havana Café	⊕	XX	425
Hearth		XX	69
Hecho en Dumbo	⊕	X	164
Hibino		X	446
Hide-Chan Ramen	⊕	X	254
High Street on Hudson	⊕	XX	164
Hill Country		X	124
Hill Country Chicken	⊕	X	124
Himalayan Yak		X	555
HinoMaru Ramen	⊕	X	555
Hirohisa	⊛	XX	338
Hometown Bar-B-Que	⊕	X	496
Hot Kitchen		X	70
Houdini Kitchen Laboratory		XX	556
Houseman		XX	337

Huertas		XX	70
Hugo & Sons		XX	482
Hunan Bistro	☺	X	71
Hunan House	☺	X	556
Hunan Kitchen	☺	X	557

I

Iki		XX	557
Il Bacco		XX	558
Il Buco		X	165
Il Buco Alimentari e Vineria	☺	XX	165
Il Cortile		XX	41
Il Gattopardo		XX	294
Il Poeta	☺	XX	558
Il Riccio		XX	378
Il Salumaio		X	378
Imperial Palace		X	559
Impero Caffè		XX	23
Inatteso Pizzabar Casano		XX	99
Indian Accent		XxX	294
I Sodi		XX	166
I Trulli		XX	125
Ivan Ramen		X	227

J

Jack the Horse		XX	446
Jake's Steakhouse		XX	425
James		XX	483
Java		X	483
Jean-Georges	☺☺☺	XxxX	406
Jewel Bako	☺	X	72
J.G. Melon	☺	X	379
Jin Ramen	☺	X	206
Joe's Place		X	426
Joe's Shanghai		X	559
John Brown Smokehouse	☺	X	560
John Dory Oyster Bar (The)		X	125
JoJo		XX	379
Jones Wood Foundry		X	380
Jora		XX	560

Joseph Leonard		X	166
J. Restaurant Chez Asta	☺	X	206
Jubilee		XX	254
Jukai		XX	255
Jungsik	☺☺	XxX	356
Jun-Men Ramen Bar		XX	24
Junoon	☺	XxX	126

K

Kafana		X	71
Kaia		X	380
Kajitsu	☺	XX	256
Kang Ho Dong Baekjeong		XX	561
Kang Suh		XX	295
Kanoyama	☺	X	73
Kao Soy		X	497
Karczma		X	517
Katsuno		X	561
Kat & Theo		XX	127
Katz's	☺	X	228
Keens		XX	295
Kesté Pizza & Vino		X	167
Khe-Yo	☺	XX	355
Kiin Thai	☺	XX	167
Kiki's	☺	X	228
Kings County Imperial	☺	X	518
Kingsley		XX	74
Kitchen 79		X	562
Ko	☺☺	XX	75
Kokum		X	127
Kosaka		XX	168
Kristalbelli		XX	296
Krolewskie Jadlo		X	518
Krupa Grocery		XX	484
Kung Fu Little Steamed Buns Ramen	☺	X	296
Kunjip		X	297
Kura		X	74
Kurry Qulture		XX	562
Kurumazushi		XX	255
Kyo Ya	☺	XX	76

L

La Esquina		X	42
Lafayette		XX	168
La Grenouille		XxX	257
Lakruwana		X	595
La Masseria		XX	297
Lambs Club (The)		XX	298
L'Amico		XxX	24
La Morada	🍃	X	426
Landmarc		XX	357
Land of Plenty	🍃	XX	257
Lan Sheng		X	298
L'Antagoniste		XX	467
La Pecora Bianca		XX	128
L'Apicio		XX	77
L'Appart	✿	XX	100
Larb Ubol	🍃	X	299
L'Artusi		XX	169
La Sirena	✿	XxX	25
Las Ramblas		🍴	169
Laut	🍃	X	128
Lavagna		X	77
La Vara	✿	XX	447
Lea	🍃	XX	484
Le Bernardin	✿✿✿	XxxX	300
Leche y Miel		X	427
Le Cirque		XxxX	258
Le Coq Rico		XX	129
Le Coucou		XxX	339
Le Fond		X	519
Left Bank		XX	170
Le Garage		XX	467
Legend Bar & Restaurant		XX	26
Le Gigot		XX	170
Le Relais de Venise (L'Entrecôte)		XX	258
Le Turtle		X	229
Liebman's		X	427
Lil' Frankie's	🍃	X	78
Lilia		XX	519
Limani		XxX	299

Lincoln		XxX	405
Little Beet Table (The)		XX	129
Little Owl (The)		X	171
Little Park		XX	357
Little Pepper	🍃	X	563
Llama Inn	🍃	XX	520
Locanda Verde		XX	358
Locanda Vini e Olii		X	468
Loi Estiatorio		XX	301
Louie and Chan		X	229
Lucky Bee (The)		X	230
Lucky Eight		X	497
Lucky Luna		X	520
Lugo		XX	301
Luksus at Tørst	✿	XX	521
Lulu & Po	🍃	X	468
Lupa	🍃	XX	171
Lupulo		XX	26
Lusardi's		XX	381
Luzzo's		X	78

M

Macao Trading Co.		XX	358
Macchina		XX	407
Macondo		XX	230
Madangsui		XX	302
Maialino		XX	130
Main Street Imperial Taiwanese Gourmet		X	563
Maison Harlem		X	207
Maison Premiere		X	522
Maizal		X	596
Malagueta		X	564
Malai Marke		XX	79
Malaparte		X	172
MáLà Project	🍃	X	79
Mandoo Bar		X	302
Manila Social Club	🍃	X	522
Má Pêche		XX	303
Mapo Tofu	🍃	X	259

Marc Forgione	XX	359
Marcha Cocina	X	207
Marea	❀❀ XxX	304
Margaux	XX	172
Maria's Bistro Mexicano	X	498
Mario's	XX	596
Mari Vanna	XX	130
Market Table	XX	173
MarkJoseph	XX	99
Marlow & Sons	X	523
Mar's	X	564
Marta	XX	131
Mary's Fish Camp	X	173
Masa	❀❀❀ XX	305
Maya	XX	381
Mayfield	XX	469
Maysville	XX	131
Maz Mezcal	X	382
Meadowsweet	❀ XX	524
Meijin Ramen	X	382
Melba's	X	208
Mercato	X	303
Mercer Kitchen	XX	339
Mermaid Inn (The)	X	80
Mesa Coyoacán	X	523
Metrograph Commissary (The)	XX	231
Mexicosina	⊛ X	428
Mezzaluna	X	383
Mezzogiorno	XX	407
Mighty Quinn's	X	80
Mile End	⊛ X	448
Mill Basin Kosher Delicatessen	X	498
Mimi	X	174
Mimi's Hummus	🍴	485
Minetta Tavern	❀ X	175
Miss Korea	XX	306
Miss Lily's	X	174
Miss Mamie's Spoonbread Too	⊛ X	408
Modern (The)	❀❀ XxX	307
Molyvos	XX	306
Mominette	X	469
Momofuku Noodle Bar	⊛ X	81
Momofuku Ssäm Bar	⊛ X	81
Momokawa	⊛ X	132
Momoya	XX	408
Moti Mahal Delux	XX	383
Motorino	X	82
Mozzarella & Vino	XX	308
MP Taverna	XX	565
Mr Chow	XX	259
Mr. Taka	X	231
Mtskheta Café	X	499
Mundo	XX	565
Mu Ramen	⊛ X	566
Musket Room (The)	❀ XX	340
M. Wells Steakhouse	XX	566
Mythos	XX	567

N

Nakajima at Jado Sushi	XX	208
Nan Xiang Xiao Long Bao	X	567
Narcissa	XX	82
Nargis Cafe	XX	499
Natural Tofu	X	568
Navy	X	341
Nazca	X	568
Nebraska Steakhouse	XX	101
Neerob	X	428
Nerai	XX	260
New Leaf	XX	209
New Malaysia	⊛ X	42
New Wonjo	XX	308
Nick's Pizza	X	569
Nightingale Nine	X	448
900 Park	XX	429
Nishi	XX	27
Nix	❀ XX	176
No. 7	XX	470
Nocciola	XX	209
Noche Mexicana II	X	409
NoMad	❀ XX	133

Nom Wah Tea Parlor		X	43
Noodle Pudding		XX	449
Noreetuh		X	83
Norma's		XX	309
North End Grill		XxX	101
Nougatine		XX	409
Novitá		XX	132
Nuaa (The)		XX	384
Nusara		X	569
Nyonya	🕲	X	43

O

Oda House		X	83
Odeon (The)		XX	359
Oiji		XX	84
Okonomi		X	525
O Lavrador		XX	570
Olmsted	🕲	XX	485
Ootoya		XX	134
Oriental Garden		X	44
Orsay		XX	384
Oso	🕲	X	210
Osteria al Doge		XX	309
Osteria del Circo		XX	310
Osteria Laguna		XX	260
O Ya		XX	134

P

Pachanga Patterson		X	570
Pacificana		XX	500
Paet Rio	🕲	X	571
Pagani		XX	177
Palo Santo		X	486
Pampano		XX	261
Panca		X	177
Papatzul		X	341
Paradou		X	178
Park Asia		XX	500
Park Avenue		XX	135
Parkside		XX	571

Parlor Steak & Fish		XX	385
Pastai		XX	27
Patricia's		XX	429
Patroon		XxX	261
Paulie Gee's	🕲	X	525
Payag		X	572
Pearl & Ash	🕲	XX	342
Pearl Oyster Bar		X	178
Peasant		XX	342
Peking Duck House		XX	44
Pera		XX	262
Periyali		XX	135
Per Se	✿✿✿	XxXxX	311
Persepolis		XX	385
Peter Luger	✿	X	526
Petit Oven		X	501
Petrossian		XxX	310
Phil Am Kusina		X	597
Phoenix Garden	🕲	X	262
Piccola Venezia		XX	572
Pier A		XX	102
Pine Bar & Grill		XX	430
Piora	✿	XX	179
Pippali	🕲	XX	136
Pizza Moto		X	501
pizzArte		XX	312
P.J. Clarke's		X	263
Pó		XX	180
Pok Pok Ny		X	502
Porsena	🕲	XX	84
Porter House		XxX	312
Prime Meats	🕲	XX	449
Print		XX	313
Prospect		XX	470
Prune	🕲	X	85
Public	✿	XX	343
Purple Yam	🕲	X	486
Pylos		XX	85

Q

Quality Eats	XX	180
Quatorze Bis	XX	386

R

Racines NY		XX	360
Radiance Tea House		X	313
Rai Rai Ken		X	86
Ramen Misoya		X	86
Ramen Yebisu		X	527
Raoul's		XX	345
Rebelle	✿	XX	344
Red Cat (The)		XX	28
RedFarm		X	181
Red Rooster		XX	210
Regency Bar & Grill (The)		XX	386
Remi		XxX	314
Ribalta	⊕	XX	181
Ribbon (The)		XX	410
Ricardo Steakhouse		XX	211
Rider	⊕	XX	527
Risotteria Melotti		XX	87
Ristorante Morini		XxX	387
River Café (The)	✿	XxX	450
Robataya		XX	87
Roberta's	⊕	X	471
Roberto's		XX	430
Rocking Horse Cafe		XX	28
Rockmeisha		🍶	182
Roman's		X	471
Root & Bone		X	88
Royal Seafood		X	45
Rubirosa	⊕	XX	345
Rucola		X	451
Runner & Stone	⊕	XX	502
Russ & Daughters Cafe	⊕	XX	232
Russian Samovar		XX	314
Rye	⊕	X	528

S

Sabry's		X	573
Saint Austere (The)		🍶	528
Sakagura		XX	263
SakaMai		XX	232
Salinas		XX	29
Salt + Charcoal		X	529
Salt & Fat	⊕	X	573
Samudra		X	574
Samurai Mama		X	529
San Matteo	⊕	X	387
San Rasa	⊕	X	597
Santina		XX	182
Saraghina		X	472
Saravanaas		X	136
Sauce		X	233
Sauvage		XX	530
Saxon + Parole		XX	183
Scarlatto		XX	315
Schilling		X	102
Sea Grill (The)		XxX	315
Seamore's		XX	45
Seamstress		XX	388
2nd Avenue Deli		X	264
Semilla	✿	X	531
Sessanta		XX	347
Settepani		XX	211
Sevilla		X	183
Shalom Japan	⊕	X	530
Shanghai Café	⊕	X	46
Shanghai Heping		XX	46
Shanghai Pavilion		XX	388
Shuko		XX	184
Sigiri		X	88
Sik Gaek		X	574
Simone (The)		XX	389
Sip Sak	⊕	XX	264
Smith & Wollensky		XX	265
Snack EOS		X	316
Sobakoh		X	89

Indexes ▲ Alphabetical List of Restaurants

Soba Totto		XX	265
Soba-Ya	🕸	X	89
Socarrat		XX	29
Sociale		XX	451
SoCo		XX	472
Somtum Der	🕸	X	90
Soto	🌸🌸	XX	185
Sottocasa	🕸	X	452
Speedy Romeo	🕸	X	473
Spicy Lanka		X	575
Spiga		XX	410
Spitzer's Corner		X	233
Spotted Pig	🕸	X	184
Standard Grill		XX	186
St. Anselm		X	532
Stanton Social (The)		XX	234
Stella 34		XX	316
Stone Park Cafe		X	487
Streetbird Rotisserie	🕸	X	212
Supper	🕸	XX	90
SushiAnn		XX	266
Sushi Daizen		XX	575
Sushi Dojo		X	91
Sushi Ginza Onodera	🌸	XX	267
Sushi Inoue	🌸	XX	213
Sushi Katsuei		X	487
Sushi Nakazawa		XX	186
Sushi of Gari	🌸	X	390
Sushi Seki		X	389
Sushi Yasaka		X	411
Sushi Yasuda	🌸	XX	268
Sushi Zo	🌸	XX	187
Sutton Inn		XX	266
Sweet Yummy House	🕸	X	576
Szechuan Gourmet	🕸	X	317
Szechuan Mountain House		X	576

T

Taboon		XX	317
Taci's Beyti		XX	503
Taiwanese Gourmet		X	577

Takashi		🎋	188
Take Root	🌸	X	453
Tamarind		XxX	360
Tamba		X	137
Tang		XX	577
Tang Pavilion		XX	318
Tanoreen	🕸	XX	503
Tanoshi		X	391
Taqueria Tlaxcalli		X	431
Tastings Social Presents Mountain Bird		XX	212
Taverna Kyclades		X	578
Tavola		X	318
Tempura Matsui	🌸	XX	269
Tertulia	🕸	XX	188
Thai Rock		X	578
Thái Soh		X	47
Thelma on Clinton	🕸	XX	234
Tía Pol		X	30
Tiella		XX	391
Timna		X	91
Tiny's		X	361
Tipsy Parson		XX	30
Tito Rad's Grill		XX	579
Tocqueville		XX	137
Toloache		XX	319
Tong Sam Gyup Goo Yi	🕸	X	579
Tori Shin	🌸	XX	320
Toro		XX	31
Trading Post		XX	103
Tra Di Noi	🕸	X	431
Trattoria L'incontro		XX	580
Trattoria Romana da Vittorio		XX	598
Tre Otto		XX	214
Trestle on Tenth		XX	31
Tribeca Grill		XX	361
Tsushima		XX	270
Tulsi	🌸	XX	271
Tuome		X	92
Turkish Kitchen	🕸	XX	138
Tutti Matti		XX	580

21 Club		XX	319
Txikito		XX	33

U

Uma's		X	581
Uncle Boons	✿	XX	346
Uncle Zhou	☺	X	581
Untitled		XX	189
Upland		XX	138
Urubamba		XX	582
Ushiwakamaru	✿	XX	32
Utsav		XX	321
Uva	☺	X	392

V

Vai		XX	411
Vaucluse		XxX	392
Venturo Osteria & Wine Bar		X	582
Vesta Trattoria		X	583
Via Carota		XX	189
Vic's		XX	190
Vida	☺	X	598
Vinatería		XX	214
Vinegar Hill House	☺	X	452
Virginia's		XX	92

W

Wa Jeal		XX	393
Wallflower		XX	190
Wallsé	✿	XX	191
Wasan		X	93
Wassail		XX	235
Waverly Inn (The)		XX	192
Wolfgang's		XX	270

X

Xe Lua		X	47
Xixa	☺	X	532

Y

Yakiniku Futago		X	139
Yakitori Totto		X	321
Yefsi		XX	393
Yerba Buena Perry		XX	192
Yopparai		X	235
Yuzu		X	215

Z

Zenkichi		XX	533
zero otto nove	☺	XX	432
00+Co	☺	X	93
Zizi Limona		X	533
Zoma	☺	X	215
Zum Stammtisch		X	583
Zutto		X	362
ZZ's Clam Bar	✿	X	193

Indexes ▶ Alphabetical List of Restaurants

Restaurants by Cuisine

American

Alobar		XX	544
Anella		X	509
Barrel & Fare		X	493
Bell Book & Candle		XX	149
BG		X	283
Birds & Bubbles		XX	221
Blenheim		XX	150
Blue Hill	✿	XX	151
Boathouse Central Park		XX	370
Bobby Van's		XX	248
Brooklyn Star		XX	512
Buttermilk Channel	☺	X	441
Carol's Cafe		X	593
Casellula		🍲	286
Cherry Point		XX	512
Clinton St. Baking Company		X	223
Clover Club		🍲	441
Community Food & Juice		XX	202
Cookshop		XX	19
Corner Social		XX	203
Craft		XX	119
Delaware and Hudson	✿	XX	513
Diner		X	514
Dovetail	✿	XxX	403
Dutch (The)		XX	334
Egg	☺	X	514
Eli's Table		XX	375
Eugene & Co.		X	463
Farm on Adderley (The)		XX	480
Faro	✿	XX	464
Finch (The)	✿	XX	465
Fort Defiance		X	495
44 & X Hell's Kitchen		XX	291
Freek's Mill	☺	XX	495
General Greene (The)		X	466
Good		XX	160
Good Enough to Eat		X	405
Gotham Bar and Grill	✿	XxX	161
Harry's Cafe & Steak		XX	98
High Street on Hudson	☺	XX	164
Hill Country Chicken	☺	X	124
Houseman		XX	337
Jack the Horse		XX	446
James		XX	483
J.G. Melon	☺	X	379
Krupa Grocery		XX	484
Lambs Club (The)		XX	298
Little Beet Table (The)		XX	129
Little Owl (The)		X	171
Little Park		XX	357
Lulu & Po	☺	X	468
Market Table		XX	173
Marlow & Sons		X	523
Mayfield		XX	469
Maysville		XX	131
Metrograph Commissary (The)		XX	231
New Leaf		XX	209
No. 7		XX	470
Norma's		XX	309
North End Grill		XxX	101
Odeon (The)		XX	359
Patroon		XxX	261
Pier A		XX	102
Print		XX	313
Prospect		XX	470
Quality Eats		XX	180
Red Cat (The)		XX	28
Red Rooster		XX	210
Ribbon (The)		XX	410
Root & Bone		X	88
Rye	☺	X	528
Speedy Romeo	☺	X	473
St. Anselm		X	532
Sutton Inn		XX	266

Thelma on Clinton	⊛	XX	234
Tiny's		X	361
Tipsy Parson		XX	30
Trading Post		XX	103
21 Club		XX	319
Untitled		XX	189
Vida	⊛	X	598
Vinegar Hill House	⊛	X	452
Waverly Inn (The)		XX	192

Argentinian

Balvanera		X	221

Asian

Ceetay		X	421
Chop-Shop		X	18
Fung Tu		XX	227
Laut	⊛	X	128
Lucky Bee (The)		X	230
Manila Social Club	⊛	X	522
Momofuku Noodle Bar	⊛	X	81
Momoya		XX	408
Nightingale Nine		X	448
Purple Yam	⊛	X	486
Radiance Tea House		X	313
RedFarm		X	181
Zutto		X	362

Austrian

Blaue Gans		XX	354
Cafe Katja		X	222
Cafe Sabarsky		X	372
Café Steinhof		X	479
Edi & The Wolf		X	66
Freud		XX	159
Grünauer Bistro		XX	377
Schilling		X	102

Wallsé	❁	XX	191

Bangladeshi

Neerob		X	428

Barbecue

Arrogant Swine		X	459
Dinosaur Bar-B-Que		X	204
Hill Country		X	124
Hometown Bar-B-Que	⊛	X	496
John Brown Smokehouse	⊛	X	560
Mighty Quinn's		X	80

Brazilian

Malagueta		X	564

Burmese

Café Mingala		X	370

Cajun

Bayou		XX	590

Cambodian

Angkor	⊛	XX	368

Caribbean

Gladys	⊛	X	466

Central Asian

Cheburechnaya		X	548
Mtskheta Café		X	499
Nargis Cafe		XX	499
Oda House		X	83
Uma's		X	581

Chinese

Bamboo Garden		⅄	492
Bao (The)		⅄	56
biáng!	⊛	⅄⅄	57
Bo Ky		⅄	38
Café China	✿	⅄⅄	249
China Blue		⅄⅄	354
Congee Village	⊛	⅄	224
Dim Sum Go Go	⊛	⅄	39
Dumpling Galaxy		⅄	551
East Harbor Seafood Palace	⊛	⅄⅄	494
Golden Unicorn		⅄	40
Grain House		⅄	553
Great N.Y. Noodletown		⅄	41
Hakkasan		⅄⅄⅄	293
Happy Family Hotpot		⅄	554
Hot Kitchen		⅄	70
Hunan Bistro	⊛	⅄	71
Hunan House	⊛	⅄	556
Hunan Kitchen	⊛	⅄	557
Imperial Palace		⅄	559
Joe's Shanghai		⅄	559
Kings County Imperial	⊛	⅄	518
Kung Fu Little Steamed Buns Ramen	⊛	⅄	296
Land of Plenty	⊛	⅄⅄	257
Lan Sheng		⅄	298
Legend Bar & Restaurant		⅄⅄	26
Little Pepper	⊛	⅄	563
Lucky Eight		⅄	497
Main Street Imperial Taiwanese Gourmet		⅄	563
MáLà Project	⊛	⅄	79
Mapo Tofu	⊛	⅄	259
Mr Chow		⅄⅄	259
Nan Xiang Xiao Long Bao		⅄	567
Nom Wah Tea Parlor		⅄	43
Oriental Garden		⅄	44
Pacificana		⅄⅄	500
Park Asia		⅄⅄	500
Peking Duck House		⅄⅄	44
Phoenix Garden	⊛	⅄	262
Royal Seafood		⅄	45
Shanghai Café	⊛	⅄	46
Shanghai Heping		⅄⅄	46
Shanghai Pavilion		⅄⅄	388
Sweet Yummy House	⊛	⅄	576
Szechuan Gourmet	⊛	⅄	317
Szechuan Mountain House		⅄	576
Taiwanese Gourmet		⅄	577
Tang Pavilion		⅄⅄	318
Uncle Zhou	⊛	⅄	581
Wa Jeal		⅄⅄	393

Contemporary

ABC Kitchen		⅄⅄	108
Acme		⅄⅄	146
Aldo Sohm Wine Bar		〼	279
Ardesia		〼	280
atera	✿✿	⅄⅄	352
Atrium		⅄⅄	440
Aureole	✿	⅄⅄⅄	281
Barawine		⅄⅄	200
Bâtard	✿	⅄⅄	353
Battersby		⅄	440
Betony	✿	⅄⅄⅄	284
Bin 5		⅄⅄	591
Blanca	✿✿	⅄⅄	461
Blue Ribbon		⅄⅄	329
Brasserie 8 1/2		⅄⅄⅄	285
Bruno		⅄	59
Cafe Clover		⅄⅄	153
Cafe Cluny		⅄⅄	153
Casa del Chef Bistro	⊛	⅄	548
Caviar Russe	✿	⅄⅄⅄	251
Chefs Club		⅄⅄⅄	332
Chef's Table at Brooklyn Fare	✿✿✿	⅄⅄	442
ChikaLicious		〼	60
Clement		⅄⅄⅄	288
Clocktower (The)		⅄⅄⅄	115
Colonie		⅄⅄	443
Contra	✿	⅄⅄	225
Craftbar		⅄⅄	119
db Bistro Moderne		⅄⅄	289
dinnertable		⅄	64
Dover		⅄⅄	443

East Pole	XX	374
Eddy (The)	XX	66
Eleven Madison Park ✿✿✿	XxxX	120
Estela	XX	336
Fat Radish (The)	XX	226
Faun	XX	481
Feast	X	67
Fedora	XX	159
Flat Top	X	205
Foragers City Table	XX	23
Gabriel Kreuther ✿	XxX	292
Gander (The)	XX	121
Good Fork (The) 🐕	X	496
Graffiti	▤	68
Gramercy Tavern ✿	XxX	122
Günter Seeger NY ✿	XxX	162
Jean-Georges ✿✿✿	XxxX	406
JoJo	XX	379
Joseph Leonard	X	166
Kingsley	XX	74
Ko ✿✿	XX	75
Left Bank	XX	170
Le Turtle	X	229
Luksus at Tørst ✿	XX	521
Marc Forgione	XX	359
Mercer Kitchen	XX	339
Modern (The) ✿✿	XxX	307
Momofuku Ssäm Bar 🐕	X	81
Musket Room (The) ✿	XX	340
Narcissa	XX	82
Nishi	XX	27
NoMad ✿	XX	133
Nougatine	XX	409
Olmsted 🐕	XX	485
Park Avenue	XX	135
Parlor Steak & Fish	XX	385
Pearl & Ash 🐕	XX	342
Per Se ✿✿✿	XxxXxX	311
Piora ✿	XX	179
Prune 🐕	X	85
Regency Bar & Grill (The)	XX	386
Rider 🐕	XX	527
River Café (The) ✿	XxX	450
Roberta's 🐕	X	471
Runner & Stone 🐕	XX	502
Saint Austere (The)	▤	528
Salt & Fat 🐕	X	573
Sauvage	XX	530
Saxon + Parole	XX	183
Seamstress	XX	388
Semilla ✿	X	531
Simone (The)	XX	389
Standard Grill	XX	186
Stone Park Cafe	X	487
Take Root ✿	X	453
Tastings Social Presents Mountain Bird	XX	212
Tocqueville	XX	137
Trestle on Tenth	XX	31
Tribeca Grill	XX	361
Virginia's	XX	92

Deli

Barney Greengrass	X	400
Katz's 🐕	X	228
Liebman's	X	427
Mile End 🐕	X	448
Mill Basin Kosher Delicatessen	X	498
Russ & Daughters Cafe 🐕	XX	232
2nd Avenue Deli	X	264

Dominican

Leche y Miel	X	427

Eastern European

Kafana	X	71

Ethiopian

Abyssinia	X	198
Zoma 🐕	X	215

European

Le Cirque	XxxX	258
Prime Meats 🐕	XX	449

Filipino

Engeline's	X	552
Payag	X	572
Phil Am Kusina	X	597
Tito Rad's Grill	XX	579

French

Balthazar		XX	329
Bar Boulud		XX	399
Bistro SK		X	420
Bistro Vendôme		XX	247
Brasserie Ruhlmann		XX	286
Buvette		X	152
Café Boulud	✿	XxX	371
Cherche Midi		XX	332
Chez Napoléon		X	287
Daniel	✿✿	XxXxX	373
DBGB Kitchen & Bar		XX	62
Dirty French		XX	226
Jubilee		XX	254
Lafayette		XX	168
La Grenouille		XxX	257
L'Antagoniste		XX	467
L'Appart	✿	XX	100
Le Coq Rico		XX	129
Le Coucou		XxX	339
Le Fond		X	519
Le Garage		XX	467
Le Gigot		XX	170
Maison Harlem		X	207
Mimi		X	174
Mominette		X	469
Orsay		XX	384
Paradou		X	178
Petit Oven		X	501
Petrossian		XxX	310
Quatorze Bis		XX	386
Racines NY		XX	360
Raoul's		XX	345
Rebelle	✿	XX	344
Vaucluse		XxX	392
Wallflower		XX	190

Fusion

annisa		XX	146
Autre Kyo Ya		XX	54
Dieci		X	63
Fushimi		XX	594
Lucky Luna		X	520
Má Pêche		XX	303
Noreetuh		X	83
Public	✿	XX	343
Shalom Japan	☺	X	530
Stanton Social (The)		XX	234
Streetbird Rotisserie	☺	X	212
Tuome		X	92

Gastropub

ABV		X	198
Achilles Heel	☺	X	508
Allswell		X	508
Black Swan		X	460
Breslin (The)	✿	X	116
Brinkley's		X	39
Burger & Barrel		XX	330
Jones Wood Foundry		X	380
Minetta Tavern	✿	X	175
M. Wells Steakhouse		XX	566
P.J. Clarke's		X	263
Spitzer's Corner		X	233
Spotted Pig	☺	X	184

German

Zum Stammtisch	X	583

Greek

Agnanti		XX	544
Anassa Taverna		XX	245
Bahari estiatorio		X	546
Eliá		XX	494
Estiatorio Milos		XxX	290
Greek (The)		XX	355
Gregory's 26 Corner Taverna	☺	X	553
Kiki's	☺	X	228
Limani		XxX	299
Loi Estiatorio		XX	301

Molyvos	XX	306
MP Taverna	XX	565
Mythos	XX	567
Nerai	XX	260
Periyali	XX	135
Pylos	XX	85
Snack EOS	X	316
Taverna Kyclades	X	578
Yefsi	XX	393

Indian

Amma		XX	244
Andaz		X	368
Anjappar		X	110
Awadh		XX	399
Babu Ji		X	55
Benares		XX	283
Bhatti		X	112
Bukhara Grill		XX	248
Chaiwali		XX	202
Delhi Masala		X	203
Dosa Garden		X	593
Haldi		X	123
Indian Accent		XxX	294
Junoon	✿	XxX	126
Kokum		X	127
Kurry Qulture		XX	562
Malai Marke		XX	79
Moti Mahal Delux		XX	383
Pippali	⊛	XX	136
Samudra		X	574
Saravanaas		X	136
Tamarind		XxX	360
Tamba		X	137
Tulsi	✿	XX	271
Utsav		XX	321

Indonesian

Java	X	483

International

ABC Cocina	XX	108
Cecil (The)	XX	201

Fatty Fish	X	376
Flinders Lane	X	67
Mundo	XX	565

Italian

Ai Fiori	✿	XxX	278
Aita		XX	458
Al di Là		X	478
Angelina's		XX	590
Armani Ristorante		XX	245
Aunt Jake's		X	38
Aurora		XX	509
A Voce Madison		XX	111
Babbalucci		X	199
Babbo	✿	XX	147
Bacaro		X	220
Baker & Co.	⊛	XX	148
Barano		XX	511
Barbetta		XxX	282
Barbuto		XX	148
Bar Corvo		XX	459
Bar Primi	⊛	XX	57
Basil Brick Oven Pizza	⊛	XX	547
Becco		XX	282
Beccofino		X	420
Bettolona		X	200
Bin 71		🍷	400
Bocca		XX	114
Bocelli		XX	592
Bread & Tulips		XX	115
Cacio e Pepe		X	59
Café Altro Paradiso		XX	331
Cafe Luna		XX	592
Caravaggio		XxX	372
Carbone	✿	XX	154
Casa Lever		XxX	250
Charlie Bird		XX	331
Ciccio	⊛	X	333
Cotenna	⊛	X	156
Crispo		XX	156
Da Franco & Tony Ristorante		XX	422
da Umberto		XX	21
Del Posto	✿	XxxX	22
East 12th Osteria		XX	65

Indexes ▶ Restaurants by Cuisine

Emilio's Ballato		XX	335	Locanda Verde	XX	358
Emporio		XX	335	Locanda Vini e Olii	X	468
Enoteca Maria	⊛	X	594	Louie and Chan	X	229
Enoteca on Court		X	444	Lugo	XX	301
Enzo's of Arthur Ave		X	423	Lupa	⊛ XX	171
Felidia		XxX	252	Lusardi's	XX	381
F & J Pine Restaurant		XX	424	Macchina	XX	407
Frankies 457 Spuntino	⊛	X	444	Maialino	XX	130
Franny's		XX	482	Malaparte	X	172
Fumo		XX	205	Mario's	XX	596
Gastronomia Culinaria	⊛	X	404	Marta	XX	131
Gastroteca		XX	552	Mercato	X	303
Gelso & Grand		X	40	Mezzaluna	X	383
Gennaro		XX	404	Mezzogiorno	XX	407
Gigino at Wagner Park		XX	98	Mozzarella & Vino	XX	308
Giorgione		XX	336	900 Park	XX	429
Giuliana's		XX	595	Nocciola	XX	209
Gnocco		X	68	Noodle Pudding	XX	449
Gradisca		XX	163	Novitá	XX	132
Hearth		XX	69	Osteria al Doge	XX	309
Hugo & Sons		XX	482	Osteria del Circo	XX	310
Il Bacco		XX	558	Osteria Laguna	XX	260
Il Buco		X	165	Pagani	XX	177
Il Buco Alimentari e Vineria	⊛	XX	165	Parkside	XX	571
Il Cortile		XX	41	Pastai	XX	27
Il Gattopardo		XX	294	Patricia's	XX	429
Il Poeta	⊛	XX	558	Peasant	XX	342
Il Riccio		XX	378	Piccola Venezia	XX	572
Il Salumaio		X	378	Pine Bar & Grill	XX	430
Impero Caffè		XX	23	pizzArte	XX	312
Inatteso Pizzabar Casano		XX	99	Pó	XX	180
I Sodi		XX	166	Porsena	⊛ XX	84
I Trulli		XX	125	Remi	XxX	314
La Masseria		XX	297	Ribalta	⊛ XX	181
L'Amico		XxX	24	Risotteria Melotti	XX	87
La Pecora Bianca		XX	128	Ristorante Morini	XxX	387
L'Apicio		XX	77	Roberto's	XX	430
L'Artusi		XX	169	Roman's	X	471
La Sirena	✿	XxX	25	Rubirosa	⊛ XX	345
Lavagna		X	77	Saraghina	X	472
Lea	⊛	XX	484	Sauce	X	233
Lil' Frankie's	⊛	X	78	Scarlatto	XX	315
Lilia		XX	519	Sessanta	XX	347
Lincoln		XxX	405	Settepani	XX	211

Sociale		XX	451
Spiga		XX	410
Stella 34		XX	316
Supper	🐸	XX	90
Tavola		X	318
Tiella		XX	391
Tra Di Noi	🐸	X	431
Trattoria L'incontro		XX	580
Trattoria Romana da Vittorio		XX	598
Tre Otto		XX	214
Tutti Matti		XX	580
Uva	🐸	X	392
Venturo Osteria & Wine Bar		X	582
Vesta Trattoria		X	583
Via Carota		XX	189
Vic's		XX	190
Vinatería		XX	214
zero otto nove	🐸	XX	432

Jamaican

Miss Lily's		X	174

Japanese

Aburiya Kinnosuke		XX	242
Bar Masa		XX	280
Blue Ribbon Sushi		XX	330
BONDST		XX	152
Bozu		X	511
Cagen	🌼	XX	61
cocoron		X	223
Curry-Ya		X	62
Dojo Izakaya		🍱	64
DOMODOMO	🐸	X	157
Donguri		X	374
EN Japanese Brasserie		XxX	158
15 East		XX	121
Ganso Ramen	🐸	X	445
Goemon Curry		X	337
Hakata Tonton		X	163
Hasaki		X	69
Hatsuhana		XX	253
Hibino		X	446
Hide-Chan Ramen	🐸	X	254
HinoMaru Ramen	🐸	X	555

Hirohisa	🌼	XX	338
Iki		XX	557
Ivan Ramen		X	227
Jewel Bako	🌼	X	72
Jin Ramen	🐸	X	206
Jukai		XX	255
Jun-Men Ramen Bar		XX	24
Kajitsu	🌼	XX	256
Kanoyama	🌼	X	73
Katsuno		X	561
Kosaka		XX	168
Kura		X	74
Kurumazushi		XX	255
Kyo Ya	🌼	XX	76
Masa	🌼🌼🌼	XX	305
Meijin Ramen		X	382
Momokawa	🐸	X	132
Mr. Taka		X	231
Mu Ramen	🐸	X	566
Nakajima at Jado Sushi		XX	208
Okonomi		X	525
Ootoya		XX	134
Rai Rai Ken		X	86
Ramen Misoya		X	86
Ramen Yebisu		X	527
Robataya		XX	87
Rockmeisha		🍱	182
Sakagura		XX	263
SakaMai		XX	232
Salt + Charcoal		X	529
Samurai Mama		X	529
Shuko		XX	184
Sobakoh		X	89
Soba Totto		XX	265
Soba-Ya	🐸	X	89
Soto	🌼🌼	XX	185
SushiAnn		XX	266
Sushi Daizen		XX	575
Sushi Dojo		X	91
Sushi Ginza Onodera	🌼	XX	267
Sushi Inoue	🌼	XX	213
Sushi Katsuei		X	487
Sushi Nakazawa		XX	186
Sushi of Gari	🌼	X	390

Indexes ▶ Restaurants by Cuisine

Sushi Seki		𝗫	389
Sushi Yasaka		𝗫	411
Sushi Yasuda	⁂	𝗫𝗫	268
Sushi Zo	⁂	𝗫𝗫	187
Takashi		🍴	188
Tanoshi		𝗫	391
Tempura Matsui	⁂	𝗫𝗫	269
Tori Shin	⁂	𝗫𝗫	320
Tsushima		𝗫𝗫	270
Ushiwakamaru	⁂	𝗫𝗫	32
Wasan		𝗫	93
Yakiniku Futago		𝗫	139
Yakitori Totto		𝗫	321
Yopparai		𝗫	235
Yuzu		𝗫	215
Zenkichi		𝗫𝗫	533

Korean

Atoboy	🍃	𝗫	111
Cho Dang Gol	🍃	𝗫	287
Danji		𝗫	288
Don's Bogam		𝗫𝗫	250
Hahm Ji Bach	🍃	𝗫𝗫	554
HanGawi	🍃	𝗫𝗫	253
Hanjan		𝗫𝗫	123
Jungsik	⁂⁂	𝗫𝗫𝗫	356
Kang Ho Dong Baekjeong		𝗫𝗫	561
Kang Suh		𝗫𝗫	295
Kristalbelli		𝗫𝗫	296
Kunjip		𝗫	297
Madangsui		𝗫𝗫	302
Mandoo Bar		𝗫	302
Miss Korea		𝗫𝗫	306
Natural Tofu		𝗫	568
New Wonjo		𝗫𝗫	308
Oiji		𝗫𝗫	84
Sik Gaek		𝗫	574
Tang		𝗫𝗫	577
Tong Sam Gyup Goo Yi	🍃	𝗫	579

Lao

| Khe-Yo | 🍃 | 𝗫𝗫 | 355 |

Latin American

A Casa Fox		𝗫𝗫	220
Colonia Verde		𝗫𝗫	462
Cómodo		𝗫𝗫	333
Coppelia	🍃	𝗫	20
Havana Café	🍃	𝗫𝗫	425
Macondo		𝗫𝗫	230
Marcha Cocina		𝗫	207
Palo Santo		𝗫	486
Yerba Buena Perry		𝗫𝗫	192

Lebanese

al Bustan	🍃	𝗫𝗫	242
Almayass		𝗫𝗫	110
Balade		𝗫𝗫	56

Macanese

| Macao Trading Co. | | 𝗫𝗫 | 358 |

Malaysian

Al Seabu		𝗫	478
New Malaysia	🍃	𝗫	42
Nyonya	🍃	𝗫	43

Mediterranean

Aldea	⁂	𝗫𝗫	109
Barbounia		𝗫𝗫	112
Boulud Sud		𝗫𝗫𝗫	401
Cipura		𝗫𝗫	493
Covina		𝗫𝗫	118
Degustation		𝗫𝗫	63
Extra Virgin		𝗫𝗫	158
Fig & Olive		𝗫𝗫	376
Gato		𝗫𝗫	160
Kat & Theo		𝗫𝗫	127
Landmarc		𝗫𝗫	357
Margaux		𝗫𝗫	172
Meadowsweet	⁂	𝗫𝗫	524
Mimi's Hummus		🍴	485
Rucola		𝗫	451
Upland		𝗫𝗫	138
Vai		𝗫𝗫	411

628

Mexican

Alma	XX	492
Amaranto	X	458
Añejo	X	279
Black Ant (The)	XX	58
Café Frida	XX	402
Casa Enríque	⌂ XX	549
Chavela's	⌂ XX	460
Cosme	XX	118
De Mole	X	550
El Atoradero	⌂ X	480
El Parador	⌂ XX	252
El Paso	X	204
Empellón Taqueria	XX	157
Estrellita Poblana III	X	424
Fonda	X	481
Gran Eléctrica	⌂ XX	445
Hecho en Dumbo	⌂ X	164
La Esquina	X	42
La Morada	⌂ X	426
Maizal	X	596
Maria's Bistro Mexicano	X	498
Maya	XX	381
Maz Mezcal	X	382
Mesa Coyoacán	X	523
Mexicosina	⌂ X	428
Noche Mexicana II	X	409
Oso	⌂ X	210
Pachanga Patterson	X	570
Pampano	XX	261
Papatzul	X	341
Rocking Horse Cafe	XX	28
Taqueria Tlaxcalli	X	431
Toloache	XX	319
Xixa	⌂ X	532

Middle Eastern

Au Za'atar	X	54
Balaboosta	XX	328
Bustan	XX	401
Glasserie	⌂ XX	516
Taboon	XX	317
Tanoreen	⌂ XX	503

Timna	X	91
Zizi Limona	X	533

Moroccan

Café Mogador	X	60

Persian

Persepolis	XX	385

Peruvian

Jora	XX	560
Llama Inn	⌂ XX	520
Nazca	X	568
Panca	X	177
Urubamba	XX	582

Pizza

Co.	X	19
Don Antonio by Starita	⌂ XX	290
Emily	X	462
Forcella	X	516
Houdini Kitchen Laboratory	XX	556
Kesté Pizza & Vino	X	167
Luzzo's	X	78
Motorino	X	82
Nick's Pizza	X	569
Paulie Gee's	⌂ X	525
Pizza Moto	X	501
San Matteo	⌂ X	387
Sottocasa	⌂ X	452

Polish

Karczma	X	517
Krolewskie Jadlo	X	518

Portuguese

Lupulo	XX	26
O Lavrador	XX	570

Puerto Rican

Brisas del Caribe	X	421
El Nuevo Bohío	X	423

Joe's Place   X   426

Russian

Mari Vanna	XX	130
Russian Samovar	XX	314

Scandinavian

Agern	❀ XX	243
Aquavit	❀❀ XxX	246
Aska	❀❀ XxX	510

Seafood

Asian Jewels	XX	545
Atlantic Grill	XX	369
Blue Water Grill	XX	113
Clam (The)	XX	155
Cull & Pistol	XX	20
Ed's Lobster Bar	X	334
Extra Fancy	X	515
Fishtag	XX	402
Flex Mussels	XX	377
Greenpoint Fish & Lobster Co.	X	517
John Dory Oyster Bar (The)	X	125
Le Bernardin	❀❀❀ XxxX	300
Maison Premiere	X	522
Marea	❀❀ XxX	304
Mar's	X	564
Mary's Fish Camp	X	173
Mermaid Inn (The)	X	80
Navy	X	341
O Ya	XX	134
Pearl Oyster Bar	X	178
Sabry's	X	573
Santina	XX	182
Sea Grill (The)	XxX	315
Seamore's	XX	45
ZZ's Clam Bar	❀ X	193

Senegalese

Africa Kine	X	199
J. Restaurant Chez Asta	⊛ X	206

Singaporean

Chomp Chomp	⊛ X	155

South African

Braai	X	285
Kaia	X	380

Southern

BLVD Bistro	X	201
Melba's	X	208
Miss Mamie's Spoonbread Too	⊛ X	408
SoCo	XX	472

Spanish

Alcala		XX	244
Andanada	❀	XX	398
Barraca		XX	149
Beso		X	591
Boqueria		XX	114
Casa Mono	❀	XX	117
Cata		XX	222
Donostia	⊛	X	65
El Born		XX	515
El Porrón		X	375
El Quinto Pino		XX	21
Huertas		XX	70
Las Ramblas		🍽	169
La Vara	❀	XX	447
Salinas		XX	29
Sevilla		X	183
Socarrat		XX	29
Tertulia	⊛	XX	188
Tía Pol		X	30
Toro		XX	31
Txikito		XX	33

Sri Lankan

Lakruwana		X	595
San Rasa	⊛	X	597
Sigiri		X	88
Spicy Lanka		X	575

Steakhouse

BLT Prime	𝕏𝕏	113
BLT Steak	𝕏x𝕏	247
Bowery Meat Company	𝕏𝕏	58
Christos	𝕏𝕏	550
Del Frisco's	𝕏x𝕏	289
Frankie & Johnnie's	𝕏𝕏	291
Gallagher's	𝕏𝕏	293
Jake's Steakhouse	𝕏𝕏	425
Keens	𝕏𝕏	295
Le Relais de Venise (L'Entrecôte)	𝕏𝕏	258
MarkJoseph	𝕏𝕏	99
Nebraska Steakhouse	𝕏𝕏	101
Peter Luger	✿ 𝕏	526
Porter House	𝕏x𝕏	312
Ricardo Steakhouse	𝕏𝕏	211
Smith & Wollensky	𝕏𝕏	265
Wolfgang's	𝕏𝕏	270

Thai

Arharn Thai	🕸	𝕏	545
Ayada		𝕏	546
Kao Soy		𝕏	497
Kiin Thai	🕸	𝕏𝕏	167
Kitchen 79		𝕏	562
Larb Ubol	🕸	𝕏	299
Nuaa (The)		𝕏𝕏	384
Nusara		𝕏	569
Paet Rio	🕸	𝕏	571
Pok Pok Ny		𝕏	502
Somtum Der	🕸	𝕏	90
Thai Rock		𝕏	578

Uncle Boons	✿	𝕏𝕏	346

Tibetan

Himalayan Yak	𝕏	555

Turkish

Antique Garage		𝕏	328
Beyoglu	🕸	𝕏	369
Pera		𝕏𝕏	262
Sip Sak	🕸	𝕏𝕏	264
Taci's Beyti		𝕏𝕏	503
Turkish Kitchen	🕸	𝕏𝕏	138

Vegan

Avant Garden		𝕏	55
Blossom		𝕏𝕏	18
00+Co	🕸	𝕏	93

Vegetarian

Dirt Candy	𝕏𝕏	224
Nix	✿ 𝕏𝕏	176
Wassail	𝕏𝕏	235

Vietnamese

Bricolage		𝕏	479
bún-ker	🕸	𝕏	547
Còm tam Ninh Kieu		𝕏	422
District Saigon		𝕏	551
Falansai	🕸	𝕏	463
Thái Sơn		𝕏	47
Xe Lua		𝕏	47

Indexes ▶ Restaurants by Cuisine

Cuisines by Neighborhood

MANHATTAN

Chelsea

American
Cookshop	XX	19
Red Cat (The)	XX	28
Tipsy Parson	XX	30

Asian
Chop-Shop	X	18

Chinese
Legend Bar & Restaurant	XX	26

Contemporary
Foragers City Table	XX	23
Nishi	XX	27
Trestle on Tenth	XX	31

Italian
da Umberto		XX	21
Del Posto	❀	XXxX	22
Impero Caffè		XX	23
L'Amico		XxX	24
La Sirena	❀	XxX	25
Pastai		XX	27

Japanese
Jun-Men Ramen Bar		XX	24
Ushiwakamaru	❀	XX	32

Latin American
Coppelia	⊛	X	20

Mexican
Rocking Horse Cafe	XX	28

Pizza
Co.	X	19

Portuguese
Lupulo	XX	26

Seafood
Cull & Pistol	XX	20

Spanish
El Quinto Pino	XX	21
Salinas	XX	29
Socarrat	XX	29
Tía Pol	X	30
Toro	XX	31
Txikito	XX	33

Vegan
Blossom	XX	18

Chinatown & Little Italy

Chinese
Bo Ky		X	38
Dim Sum Go Go	⊛	X	39
Golden Unicorn		X	40
Great N.Y. Noodletown		X	41
Nom Wah Tea Parlor		X	43
Oriental Garden		X	44
Peking Duck House		XX	44
Royal Seafood		X	45
Shanghai Café	⊛	X	46
Shanghai Heping		XX	46

Gastropub
Brinkley's	X	39

Italian
Aunt Jake's	X	38
Gelso & Grand	X	40
Il Cortile	XX	41

Malaysian
New Malaysia	⊛	X	42
Nyonya	⊛	X	43

Mexican
La Esquina   X   42

Seafood
Seamore's   XX   45

Vietnamese
Thái Sơn   X   47
Xe Lua   X   47

East Village

American
Root & Bone   X   88

Asian
Momofuku Noodle Bar   ⊛ X   81

Austrian
Edi & The Wolf   X   66

Barbecue
Mighty Quinn's   X   80

Central Asian
Oda House   X   83

Chinese
Bao (The)   X   56
biáng!   ⊛ XX   57
Hot Kitchen   X   70
Hunan Bistro   ⊛ X   71
MáLà Project   ⊛ X   79

Contemporary
Bruno   X   59
ChikaLicious   ▤   60
dinnertable   X   64
Eddy (The)   XX   66
Feast   X   67
Graffiti   ▤   68
Kingsley   XX   74
Ko   ⊛⊛ XX   75
Momofuku Ssäm Bar   ⊛ X   81

Narcissa   XX   82
Prune   ⊛ X   85
Virginia's   XX   92

Eastern European
Kafana   X   71

French
DBGB Kitchen & Bar   XX   62

Fusion
Autre Kyo Ya   XX   54
Dieci   X   63
Noreetuh   X   83
Tuome   X   92

Greek
Pylos   XX   85

Indian
Babu Ji   X   55
Malai Marke   XX   79

International
Flinders Lane   X   67

Italian
Bar Primi   ⊛ XX   57
Cacio e Pepe   X   59
East 12th Osteria   XX   65
Gnocco   X   68
Hearth   XX   69
L'Apicio   XX   77
Lavagna   X   77
Lil' Frankie's   ⊛ X   78
Porsena   ⊛ XX   84
Risotteria Melotti   XX   87
Supper   ⊛ XX   90

Japanese
Cagen   ⊛ XX   61
Curry-Ya   X   62
Dojo Izakaya   ▤   64
Hasaki   X   69

Jewel Bako	✿	𝕏	72
Kanoyama	✿	𝕏	73
Kura		𝕏	74
Kyo Ya	✿	𝕏𝕏	76
Rai Rai Ken		𝕏	86
Ramen Misoya		𝕏	86
Robataya		𝕏𝕏	87
Sobakoh		𝕏	89
Soba-Ya	⊕	𝕏	89
Sushi Dojo		𝕏	91
Wasan		𝕏	93

Korean
Oiji		𝕏𝕏	84

Lebanese
Balade		𝕏𝕏	56

Mediterranean
Degustation		𝕏𝕏	63

Mexican
Black Ant (The)		𝕏𝕏	58

Middle Eastern
Au Za'atar		𝕏	54
Timna		𝕏	91

Moroccan
Café Mogador		𝕏	60

Pizza
Luzzo's		𝕏	78
Motorino		𝕏	82

Seafood
Mermaid Inn (The)		𝕏	80

Spanish
Donostia	⊕	𝕏	65
Huertas		𝕏𝕏	70

Sri Lankan
Sigiri		𝕏	88

Steakhouse
Bowery Meat Company		𝕏𝕏	58

Thai
Somtum Der	⊕	𝕏	90

Vegan
Avant Garden		𝕏	55
OO+Co	⊕	𝕏	93

Financial District

American
Harry's Cafe & Steak		𝕏𝕏	98
North End Grill		𝕏x𝕏	101
Pier A		𝕏𝕏	102
Trading Post		𝕏𝕏	103

Austrian
Schilling		𝕏	102

French
L'Appart	✿	𝕏𝕏	100

Italian
Gigino at Wagner Park		𝕏𝕏	98
Inatteso Pizzabar Casano		𝕏𝕏	99

Steakhouse
MarkJoseph		𝕏𝕏	99
Nebraska Steakhouse		𝕏𝕏	101

Gramercy, Flatiron & Union Square

American
Craft		𝕏𝕏	119
Hill Country Chicken	⊕	𝕏	124
Little Beet Table (The)		𝕏𝕏	129
Maysville		𝕏𝕏	131

Asian
Laut	⊕	𝕏	128

Barbecue
Hill Country		𝕏	124

Contemporary
ABC Kitchen		𝕏𝕏	108
Clocktower (The)		𝕏x𝕏	115
Craftbar		𝕏𝕏	119
Eleven Madison Park	✿✿✿	𝕏x𝕏x𝕏	120
Gander (The)		𝕏𝕏	121
Gramercy Tavern	✿	𝕏x𝕏	122
NoMad	✿	𝕏𝕏	133
Park Avenue		𝕏𝕏	135
Tocqueville		𝕏𝕏	137

French
Le Coq Rico		𝕏𝕏	129

Gastropub
Breslin (The)	⌘	X	116

Greek
Periyali		XX	135

Indian
Anjappar		X	110
Bhatti		X	112
Haldi		X	123
Junoon	⌘	XxX	126
Kokum		X	127
Pippali	☺	XX	136
Saravanaas		X	136
Tamba		X	137

International
ABC Cocina		XX	108

Italian
A Voce Madison		XX	111
Bocca		XX	114
Bread & Tulips		XX	115
I Trulli		XX	125
La Pecora Bianca		XX	128
Maialino		XX	130
Marta		XX	131
Novitá		XX	132

Japanese
15 East		XX	121
Momokawa	☺	X	132
Ootoya		XX	134
Yakiniku Futago		X	139

Korean
Atoboy	☺	X	111
Hanjan		XX	123

Lebanese
Almayass		XX	110

Mediterranean
Aldea	⌘	XX	109
Barbounia		XX	112
Covina		XX	118
Kat & Theo		XX	127
Upland		XX	138

Mexican
Cosme		XX	118

Russian
Mari Vanna		XX	130

Seafood
Blue Water Grill		XX	113
John Dory Oyster Bar (The)		X	125
O Ya		XX	134

Spanish
Boqueria		XX	114
Casa Mono	⌘	XX	117

Steakhouse
BLT Prime		XX	113

Turkish
Turkish Kitchen	☺	XX	138

Greenwich, West Village & Meatpacking District

American
Bell Book & Candle		XX	149
Blenheim		XX	150
Blue Hill	⌘	XX	151
Good		XX	160
Gotham Bar and Grill	⌘	XxX	161
High Street on Hudson	☺	XX	164
Little Owl (The)		X	171
Market Table		XX	173
Quality Eats		XX	180
Untitled		XX	189
Waverly Inn (The)		XX	192

Asian
RedFarm		X	181

Austrian
Freud		XX	159
Wallsé	⌘	XX	191

Contemporary
Acme		XX	146
Cafe Clover		XX	153
Cafe Cluny		XX	153
Fedora		XX	159
Günter Seeger NY	⌘	XxX	162
Joseph Leonard		X	166
Left Bank		XX	170

French
Piora	❀	XX	179
Saxon + Parole		XX	183
Standard Grill		XX	186

French
Buvette		X	152
Lafayette		XX	168
Le Gigot		XX	170
Mimi		X	174
Paradou		X	178
Wallflower		XX	190

Fusion
annisa		XX	146

Gastropub
Minetta Tavern	❀	X	175
Spotted Pig	✿	X	184

Italian
Babbo	❀	XX	147
Baker & Co.	✿	XX	148
Barbuto		XX	148
Carbone	❀	XX	154
Cotenna	✿	X	156
Crispo		XX	156
Gradisca		XX	163
Il Buco		X	165
Il Buco Alimentari e Vineria	✿	XX	165
I Sodi		XX	166
L'Artusi		XX	169
Lupa	✿	XX	171
Malaparte		X	172
Pagani		XX	177
Pó		XX	180
Ribalta	✿	XX	181
Via Carota		XX	189
Vic's		XX	190

Jamaican
Miss Lily's		X	174

Japanese
BONDST		XX	152
DOMODOMO	✿	X	157
EN Japanese Brasserie		XxX	158
Hakata Tonton		X	163
Kosaka		XX	168
Rockmeisha		🍴	182
Shuko		XX	184
Soto	❀❀	XX	185
Sushi Nakazawa		XX	186
Sushi Zo	❀	XX	187
Takashi		🍴	188

Latin American
Yerba Buena Perry		XX	192

Mediterranean
Acme		XX	146
Extra Virgin		XX	158
Gato		XX	160
Margaux		XX	172

Mexican
Empellón Taqueria		XX	157
Hecho en Dumbo	✿	X	164

Peruvian
Panca		X	177

Pizza
Kesté Pizza & Vino		X	167

Seafood
Clam (The)		XX	155
Mary's Fish Camp		X	173
Pearl Oyster Bar		X	178
Santina		XX	182
ZZ's Clam Bar	❀	X	193

Singaporean
Chomp Chomp	✿	X	155

Spanish
Barraca		XX	149
Las Ramblas		🍴	169
Sevilla		X	183
Tertulia	✿	XX	188

Thai
Kiin Thai	✿	XX	167

Vegetarian
Nix	❀	XX	176

Harlem, Morningside & Washington Heights

American
Community Food & Juice		XX	202
Corner Social		XX	203

Indexes ▲ Cuisines by Neighborhood

636

New Leaf		XX	209
Red Rooster		XX	210

Barbecue
Dinosaur Bar-B-Que		X	204

Contemporary
Barawine		XX	200
Flat Top		X	205
Tastings Social Presents Mountain Bird		XX	212

Ethiopian
Abyssinia		X	198
Zoma	🙂	X	215

French
Maison Harlem		X	207

Fusion
Streetbird Rotisserie	🙂	X	212

Gastropub
ABV		X	198

Indian
Chaiwali		XX	202
Delhi Masala		X	203

International
Cecil (The)		XX	201

Italian
Babbalucci		X	199
Bettolona		X	200
Fumo		XX	205
Nocciola		XX	209
Settepani		XX	211
Tre Otto		XX	214
Vinatería		XX	214

Japanese
Jin Ramen	🙂	X	206
Nakajima at Jado Sushi		XX	208
Sushi Inoue	✿	XX	213
Yuzu		X	215

Latin American
Marcha Cocina		X	207

Mexican
El Paso		X	204
Oso	🙂	X	210

Senegalese
Africa Kine		X	199
J. Restaurant Chez Asta	🙂	X	206

Southern
BLVD Bistro		X	201
Melba's		X	208

Steakhouse
Ricardo Steakhouse		XX	211

Lower East Side

American
Birds & Bubbles		XX	221
Clinton St. Baking Company		X	223
Metrograph Commissary (The)		XX	231
Thelma on Clinton	🙂	XX	234

Argentinian
Balvanera		X	221

Asian
Fung Tu		XX	227
Lucky Bee (The)		X	230

Austrian
Cafe Katja		X	222

Chinese
Congee Village	🙂	X	224

Contemporary
Contra	✿	XX	225
Fat Radish (The)		XX	226
Le Turtle		X	229

Deli
Katz's	🙂	X	228
Russ & Daughters Cafe	🙂	XX	232

French
Dirty French		XX	226

Fusion
Stanton Social (The)		XX	234

Gastropub
Spitzer's Corner		X	233

Greek
Kiki's	🙂	X	228

Italian

Bacaro		X	220
Louie and Chan		X	229
Sauce		X	233

Japanese
cocoron		X	223
Ivan Ramen		X	227
Mr. Taka		X	231
SakaMai		XX	232
Yopparai		X	235

Latin American
| A Casa Fox | | XX | 220 |
| Macondo | | XX | 230 |

Spanish
| Cata | | XX | 222 |

Vegetarian
| Dirt Candy | | XX | 224 |
| Wassail | | XX | 235 |

Midtown East & Murray Hill

American
Bobby Van's		XX	248
Patroon		XxX	261
Sutton Inn		XX	266

Chinese
Café China	✿	XX	249
Land of Plenty	🕸	XX	257
Mapo Tofu	🕸	X	259
Mr Chow		XX	259
Phoenix Garden	🕸	X	262

Contemporary
| Caviar Russe | ✿ | XxX | 251 |

Deli
| 2nd Avenue Deli | | X | 264 |

European
| Le Cirque | | XxxX | 258 |

French
Bistro Vendôme		XX	247
Jubilee		XX	254
La Grenouille		XxX	257

Gastropub
| P.J. Clarke's | | X | 263 |

Greek
| Anassa Taverna | | XX | 245 |
| Nerai | | XX | 260 |

Indian
Amma		XX	244
Bukhara Grill		XX	248
Tulsi	✿	XX	271

Italian
Armani Ristorante		XX	245
Casa Lever		XxX	250
Felidia		XxX	252
Osteria Laguna		XX	260

Japanese
Aburiya Kinnosuke		XX	242
Hatsuhana		XX	253
Hide-Chan Ramen	🕸	X	254
Jukai		XX	255
Kajitsu	✿	XX	256
Kurumazushi		XX	255
Sakagura		XX	263
Soba Totto		XX	265
SushiAnn		XX	266
Sushi Ginza Onodera	✿	XX	267
Sushi Yasuda	✿	XX	268
Tempura Matsui	✿	XX	269
Tsushima		XX	270

Korean
| Don's Bogam | | XX | 250 |
| HanGawi | 🕸 | XX | 253 |

Lebanese
| al Bustan | 🕸 | XX | 242 |

Mexican
| El Parador | 🕸 | XX | 252 |
| Pampano | | XX | 261 |

Scandinavian
| Agern | ✿ | XX | 243 |
| Aquavit | ✿✿ | XxX | 246 |

Spanish
| Alcala | | XX | 244 |

Steakhouse

BLT Steak	XxX	247
Le Relais de Venise (L'Entrecôte)	XX	258
Smith & Wollensky	XX	265
Wolfgang's	XX	270

Turkish

Pera		XX	262
Sip Sak	⊛	XX	264

Midtown West

American

BG	X	283
Casellula	🍸	286
44 & X Hell's Kitchen	XX	291
Lambs Club (The)	XX	298
Norma's	XX	309
Print	XX	313
21 Club	XX	319

Asian

Radiance Tea House	X	313

Chinese

Hakkasan		XxX	293
Kung Fu Little Steamed Buns Ramen	⊛	X	296
Lan Sheng		X	298
Szechuan Gourmet	⊛	X	317
Tang Pavilion		XX	318

Contemporary

Aldo Sohm Wine Bar		🍸	279
Ardesia		🍸	280
Aureole	❀	XxX	281
Betony	❀	XxX	284
Brasserie 8 1/2		XxX	285
Clement		XxX	288
db Bistro Moderne		XX	289
Gabriel Kreuther	❀	XxX	292
Modern (The)	❀❀	XxX	307
Per Se	❀❀❀	XxXxX	311

French

Brasserie Ruhlmann	XX	286
Chez Napoléon	X	287
Petrossian	XxX	310

Fusion

Má Pêche	XX	303

Greek

Estiatorio Milos	XxX	290
Limani	XxX	299
Loi Estiatorio	XX	301
Molyvos	XX	306
Snack EOS	X	316

Indian

Benares	XX	283
Indian Accent	XxX	294
Utsav	XX	321

Italian

Ai Fiori	❀	XxX	278
Barbetta		XxX	282
Becco		XX	282
Il Gattopardo		XX	294
La Masseria		XX	297
Lugo		XX	301
Mercato		X	303
Mozzarella & Vino		XX	308
Osteria al Doge		XX	309
Osteria del Circo		XX	310
pizzArte		XX	312
Remi		XxX	314
Scarlatto		XX	315
Stella 34		XX	316
Tavola		X	318

Japanese

Bar Masa		XX	280
Masa	❀❀❀	XX	305
Tori Shin	❀	XX	320
Yakitori Totto		X	321

Korean

Cho Dang Gol	⊛	X	287
Danji		X	288
Kang Suh		XX	295
Kristalbelli		XX	296
Kunjip		X	297
Madangsui		XX	302
Mandoo Bar		X	302
Miss Korea		XX	306
New Wonjo		XX	308

Mexican
Añejo — X — 279
Toloache — XX — 319

Middle Eastern
Taboon — XX — 317

Pizza
Don Antonio by Starita — ⊕ XX — 290

Russian
Russian Samovar — XX — 314

Seafood
Le Bernardin — ❀❀❀ XxxX — 300
Marea — ❀❀ XxX — 304
Sea Grill (The) — XxX — 315

South African
Braai — X — 285

Steakhouse
Del Frisco's — XxX — 289
Frankie & Johnnie's — XX — 291
Gallagher's — XX — 293
Keens — XX — 295
Porter House — XxX — 312

Thai
Larb Ubol — ⊕ X — 299

SoHo & Nolita

American
Dutch (The) — XX — 334
Houseman — XX — 337

Contemporary
Blue Ribbon — XX — 329
Chefs Club — XxX — 332
Estela — XX — 336
Mercer Kitchen — XX — 339
Musket Room (The) — ❀ XX — 340
Pearl & Ash — ⊕ XX — 342

French
Balthazar — XX — 329
Cherche Midi — XX — 332
Le Coucou — XxX — 339
Raoul's — XX — 345
Rebelle — ❀ XX — 344

Fusion
Public — ❀ XX — 343

Gastropub
Burger & Barrel — XX — 330

Italian
Café Altro Paradiso — XX — 331
Charlie Bird — XX — 331
Ciccio — ⊕ X — 333
Emilio's Ballato — XX — 335
Emporio — XX — 335
Giorgione — XX — 336
Peasant — XX — 342
Rubirosa — ⊕ XX — 345
Sessanta — XX — 347

Japanese
Blue Ribbon Sushi — XX — 330
Goemon Curry — X — 337
Hirohisa — ❀ XX — 338

Latin American
Cómodo — XX — 333

Mexican
Papatzul — X — 341

Middle Eastern
Balaboosta — XX — 328

Seafood
Ed's Lobster Bar — X — 334
Navy — X — 341

Thai
Uncle Boons — ❀ XX — 346

Turkish
Antique Garage — X — 328

TriBeCa

American
Little Park — XX — 357
Odeon (The) — XX — 359
Tiny's — X — 361

Asian
Zutto — X — 362

Austrian
Blaue Gans — XX — 354

Chinese

China Blue		XX	354

Contemporary

atera	✿✿	XX	352
Bâtard	✿	XX	353
Marc Forgione		XX	359
Tribeca Grill		XX	361

French

Racines NY		XX	360

Greek

Greek (The)		XX	355

Indian

Tamarind		XxX	360

Italian

Locanda Verde		XX	358

Korean

Jungsik	✿✿	XxX	356

Lao

Khe-Yo	⊛	XX	355

Macanese

Macao Trading Co.		XX	358

Mediterranean

Landmarc		XX	357

Upper East Side

American

Boathouse Central Park		XX	370
Eli's Table		XX	375
J.G. Melon	⊛	X	379

Austrian

Cafe Sabarsky		X	372
Grünauer Bistro		XX	377

Burmese

Café Mingala		X	370

Cambodian

Angkor	⊛	XX	368

Chinese

Shanghai Pavilion		XX	388
Wa Jeal		XX	393

Contemporary

East Pole		XX	374
JoJo		XX	379
Parlor Steak & Fish		XX	385
Regency Bar & Grill (The)		XX	386
Seamstress		XX	388
Simone (The)		XX	389

French

Café Boulud	✿	XxX	371
Daniel	✿✿	XxXxX	373
Orsay		XX	384
Quatorze Bis		XX	386
Vaucluse		XxX	392

Gastropub

Jones Wood Foundry		X	380

Greek

Yefsi		XX	393

Indian

Andaz		X	368
Moti Mahal Delux		XX	383

International

Fatty Fish		X	376

Italian

Caravaggio		XxX	372
Il Riccio		XX	378
Il Salumaio		X	378
Lusardi's		XX	381
Mezzaluna		X	383
Ristorante Morini		XxX	387
Tiella		XX	391
Uva	⊛	X	392

Japanese

Donguri		X	374
Meijin Ramen		X	382
Sushi of Gari	✿	X	390
Sushi Seki		X	389
Tanoshi		X	391

Mediterranean

Fig & Olive		XX	376

Mexican

Maya		XX	381
Maz Mezcal		X	382

Persian
Persepolis XX 385

Pizza
San Matteo ⊕ X 387

Seafood
Atlantic Grill XX 369
Flex Mussels XX 377

South African
Kaia X 380

Spanish
El Porrón X 375

Thai
Nuaa (The) XX 384

Turkish
Beyoglu ⊕ X 369

Upper West Side

American
Dovetail ⊛ XxX 403
Good Enough to Eat X 405
Ribbon (The) XX 410

Asian
Momoya XX 408

Contemporary
Jean-Georges ⊛⊛⊛ XxxX 406
Nougatine XX 409

Deli
Barney Greengrass X 400

French
Bar Boulud XX 399

Indian
Awadh XX 399

Italian
Bin 71 ⊞ 400
Gastronomia Culinaria ⊕ X 404
Gennaro XX 404
Lincoln XxX 405
Macchina XX 407
Mezzogiorno XX 407
Spiga XX 410

Japanese
Sushi Yasaka X 411

Mediterranean
Boulud Sud XxX 401
Vai XX 411

Mexican
Café Frida XX 402
Noche Mexicana II X 409

Middle Eastern
Bustan XX 401

Seafood
Fishtag XX 402

Southern
Miss Mamie's Spoonbread Too ⊕ X 408

Spanish
Andanada ⊛ XX 398

THE BRONX

Asian
Ceetay X 421

Bangladeshi
Neerob X 428

Deli
Liebman's X 427

Dominican
Leche y Miel X 427

French
Bistro SK X 420

Italian
Beccofino X 420
Da Franco & Tony Ristorante XX 422
Enzo's of Arthur Ave X 423
F & J Pine Restaurant XX 424
900 Park XX 429
Patricia's XX 429
Pine Bar & Grill XX 430
Roberto's XX 430
Tra Di Noi ⊕ X 431
zero otto nove ⊕ XX 432

Latin American

Havana Café	🍴	✗✗	425

Mexican
Estrellita Poblana III		✗	424
La Morada	🍴	✗	426
Mexicosina	🍴	✗	428
Taqueria Tlaxcalli		✗	431

Puerto Rican
Brisas del Caribe		✗	421
El Nuevo Bohío		✗	423
Joe's Place		✗	426

Steakhouse
Jake's Steakhouse		✗✗	425

Vietnamese
Còm tam Ninh Kieu		✗	422

BROOKLYN

Downtown

American
Buttermilk Channel	🍴	✗	441
Clover Club		🍸	441
Jack the Horse		✗✗	446
Vinegar Hill House	🍴	✗	452

Asian
Nightingale Nine		✗	448

Contemporary
Atrium		✗✗	440
Battersby		✗	440
Chef's Table at			
Brooklyn Fare	❀❀❀	✗✗	442
Colonie		✗✗	443
Dover		✗✗	443
River Café (The)	❀	✗✗✗	450
Take Root	❀	✗	453

Deli
Mile End	🍴	✗	448

European
Prime Meats	🍴	✗✗	449

Italian
Enoteca on Court		✗	444
Frankies 457 Spuntino	🍴	✗	444

Noodle Pudding		✗✗	449
Sociale		✗✗	451

Japanese
Ganso Ramen	🍴	✗	445
Hibino		✗	446

Mediterranean
Rucola		✗	451

Mexican
Gran Eléctrica	🍴	✗✗	445

Pizza
Sottocasa	🍴	✗	452

Spanish
La Vara	❀	✗✗	447

Fort Greene & Bushwick

American
Eugene & Co.		✗	463
Faro	❀	✗✗	464
Finch (The)	❀	✗✗	465
General Greene (The)		✗	466
Lulu & Po	🍴	✗	468
Mayfield		✗✗	469
No. 7		✗✗	470
Prospect		✗✗	470
Speedy Romeo	🍴	✗	473

Barbecue
Arrogant Swine		✗	459

Caribbean
Gladys	🍴	✗	466

Contemporary
Blanca	❀❀	✗✗	461
Roberta's	🍴	✗	471

French
L'Antagoniste		✗✗	467
Le Garage		✗✗	467
Mominette		✗	469

Gastropub
Black Swan		✗	460

Italian

Aita		XX	458
Bar Corvo		XX	459
Locanda Vini e Olii		X	468
Roman's		X	471
Saraghina		X	472

Latin American
| Colonia Verde | | XX | 462 |

Mexican
| Amaranto | | X | 458 |
| Chavela's | ✿ | XX | 460 |

Pizza
| Emily | | X | 462 |

Southern
| SoCo | | XX | 472 |

Vietnamese
| Falansai | ✿ | X | 463 |

Park Slope

American
Farm on Adderley (The)		XX	480
James		XX	483
Krupa Grocery		XX	484

Asian
| Purple Yam | ✿ | X | 486 |

Austrian
| Café Steinhof | | X | 479 |

Contemporary
Faun		XX	481
Olmsted	✿	XX	485
Stone Park Cafe		X	487

Indonesian
| Java | | X | 483 |

Italian
Al di Là		X	478
Franny's		XX	482
Hugo & Sons		XX	482
Lea	✿	XX	484

Japanese
| Sushi Katsuei | | X | 487 |

Latin American
| Palo Santo | | X | 486 |

Malaysian
| Al Seabu | | X | 478 |

Mediterranean
| Mimi's Hummus | | ▤ | 485 |

Mexican
| El Atoradero | ✿ | X | 480 |
| Fonda | | X | 481 |

Vietnamese
| Bricolage | | X | 479 |

Sunset Park & Brighton Beach

American
Barrel & Fare		X	493
Fort Defiance		X	495
Freek's Mill	✿	XX	495

Barbecue
| Hometown Bar-B-Que | ✿ | X | 496 |

Central Asian
| Mtskheta Café | | X | 499 |
| Nargis Cafe | | XX | 499 |

Chinese
Bamboo Garden		X	492
East Harbor Seafood Palace	✿	XX	494
Lucky Eight		X	497
Pacificana		XX	500
Park Asia		XX	500

Contemporary
| Good Fork (The) | ✿ | X | 496 |
| Runner & Stone | ✿ | XX | 502 |

Deli
| Mill Basin Kosher Delicatessen | | X | 498 |

French
| Petit Oven | | X | 501 |

Greek
| Eliá | | XX | 494 |

Mediterranean
| Cipura | | XX | 493 |

Mexican
| Alma | | XX | 492 |

Maria's Bistro Mexicano	X	498

Middle Eastern
Tanoreen	㋬ XX	503

Pizza
Pizza Moto	X	501

Thai
Kao Soy	X	497
Pok Pok Ny	X	502

Turkish
Taci's Beyti	XX	503

Brooklyn

Williamsburg

American
Anella	X	509
Brooklyn Star	XX	512
Cherry Point	XX	512
Delaware and Hudson	✿ XX	513
Diner	X	514
Egg	㋬ X	514
Marlow & Sons	X	523
Rye	㋬ X	528
St. Anselm	X	532

Asian
Manila Social Club	㋬ X	522

Chinese
Kings County Imperial	㋬ X	518

Contemporary
Luksus at Tørst	✿ XX	521
Rider	㋬ XX	527
Saint Austere (The)	🍴	528
Sauvage	XX	530
Semilla	✿ X	531

French
Le Fond	X	519

Fusion
Lucky Luna	X	520
Shalom Japan	㋬ X	530

Gastropub
Achilles Heel	㋬ X	508
Allswell	X	508

Italian
Aurora	XX	509
Barano	XX	511
Lilia	XX	519

Japanese
Bozu	X	511
Okonomi	X	525
Ramen Yebisu	X	527
Salt + Charcoal	X	529
Samurai Mama	X	529
Zenkichi	XX	533

Mediterranean
Meadowsweet	✿ XX	524

Mexican
Mesa Coyoacán	X	523
Xixa	㋬ X	532

Middle Eastern
Glasserie	㋬ XX	516
Zizi Limona	X	533

Peruvian
Llama Inn	㋬ XX	520

Pizza
Forcella	X	516
Paulie Gee's	㋬ X	525

Polish
Karczma	X	517
Krolewskie Jadlo	X	518

Scandinavian
Aska	✿✿ XxX	510

Seafood
Extra Fancy	X	515
Greenpoint Fish & Lobster Co.	X	517
Maison Premiere	X	522

Spanish
El Born	XX	515

Steakhouse
Peter Luger	✿ X	526

QUEENS

American
Alobar	XX	544

Barbecue
John Brown Smokehouse ⊛ X   560

Brazilian
Malagueta   X   564

Central Asian
Cheburechnaya   X   548
Uma's   X   581

Chinese
Dumpling Galaxy   X   551
Grain House   X   553
Happy Family Hotpot   X   554
Hunan House   ⊛ X   556
Hunan Kitchen   ⊛ X   557
Imperial Palace   X   559
Joe's Shanghai   X   559
Little Pepper   ⊛ X   563
Main Street Imperial
   Taiwanese Gourmet   X   563
Nan Xiang Xiao Long Bao   X   567
Sweet Yummy House   ⊛ X   576
Szechuan Mountain House   X   576
Taiwanese Gourmet   X   577
Uncle Zhou   ⊛ X   581

Contemporary
Casa del Chef Bistro   ⊛ X   548
Salt & Fat   ⊛ X   573

Filipino
Engeline's   X   552
Payag   X   572
Tito Rad's Grill   XX   579

Gastropub
M. Wells Steakhouse   XX   566

German
Zum Stammtisch   X   583

Greek
Agnanti   XX   544
Bahari estiatorio   X   546
Gregory's 26 Corner Taverna ⊛ X   553
MP Taverna   XX   565
Mythos   XX   567
Taverna Kyclades   X   578

Indian

Kurry Qulture
   XX   562
Samudra   X   574

International
Mundo   XX   565

Italian
Basil Brick Oven Pizza   ⊛ XX   547
Gastroteca   XX   552
Il Bacco   XX   558
Il Poeta   ⊛ XX   558
Parkside   XX   571
Piccola Venezia   XX   572
Trattoria L'incontro   XX   580
Tutti Matti   XX   580
Venturo Osteria & Wine Bar   X   582
Vesta Trattoria   X   583

Japanese
HinoMaru Ramen   ⊛ X   555
Iki   XX   557
Katsuno   X   561
Mu Ramen   ⊛ X   566
Sushi Daizen   XX   575

Korean
Hahm Ji Bach   ⊛ XX   554
Kang Ho Dong Baekjeong   XX   561
Natural Tofu   X   568
Sik Gaek   X   574
Tang   XX   577
Tong Sam Gyup Goo Yi   ⊛ X   579

Mexican
Casa Enríque   ❀ XX   549
De Mole   X   550
Pachanga Patterson   X   570

Peruvian
Jora   XX   560
Nazca   X   568
Urubamba   XX   582

Pizza
Houdini Kitchen Laboratory   XX   556
Nick's Pizza   X   569

Portuguese
O Lavrador   XX   570

Seafood

Asian Jewels		XX	545
Mar's		X	564
Sabry's		X	573

Sri Lankan
| Spicy Lanka | | X | 575 |

Steakhouse
| Christos | | XX | 550 |

Thai
Arharn Thai	😊	X	545
Ayada		X	546
Kitchen 79		X	562
Nusara		X	569
Paet Rio	😊	X	571
Thai Rock		X	578

Tibetan
| Himalayan Yak | | X | 555 |

Vietnamese
| bún-ker | 😊 | X | 547 |
| District Saigon | | X | 551 |

STATEN ISLAND

American
| Carol's Cafe | | X | 593 |
| Vida | 😊 | X | 598 |

Cajun
| Bayou | | XX | 590 |

Contemporary
| Bin 5 | | XX | 591 |

Filipino
| Phil Am Kusina | | X | 597 |

Fusion
| Fushimi | | XX | 594 |

Indian
| Dosa Garden | | X | 593 |

Italian
Angelina's		XX	590
Bocelli		XX	592
Cafe Luna		XX	592
Enoteca Maria	😊	X	594
Giuliana's		XX	595
Mario's		XX	596
Trattoria Romana da Vittorio		XX	598

Mexican
| Maizal | | X | 596 |

Spanish
| Beso | | X | 591 |

Sri Lankan
| Lakruwana | | X | 595 |
| San Rasa | 😊 | X | 597 |

Starred Restaurants

*W*ithin the selection we offer you, some restaurants deserve to be highlighted for their particularly good cuisine. When giving one, two, or three Michelin stars, there are a number of elements that we consider including the quality of the ingredients, the technical skill and flair that goes into their preparation, the blend and clarity of flavours, and the balance of the menu. Just as important is the ability to produce excellent cooking time and again. We make as many visits as we need, so that our readers may be assured of quality and consistency.

A two or three-star restaurant has to offer something very special in its cuisine; a real element of creativity, originality, or "personality" that sets it apart from the rest. Three stars – our highest award – are given to the choicest restaurants, where the whole dining experience is superb.

Cuisine in any style, modern or traditional, may be eligible for a star. Due to the fact we apply the same independent standards everywhere, the awards have become benchmarks of reliability and excellence in over 20 countries in Europe and Asia, particularly in France, where we have awarded stars for 100 years, and where the phrase "Now that's real three-star quality!" has entered into the language.

The awarding of a star is based solely on the quality of the cuisine.

✿✿✿

Exceptional cuisine, worth a special journey

One always eats here extremely well, sometimes superbly. Distinctive dishes are precisely executed, using superlative ingredients.

Chef's Table at Brooklyn Fare	XX	442
Eleven Madison Park	XxxX	120
Jean-Georges	XxxX	406
Le Bernardin	XxxX	300
Masa	XX	305
Per Se	XxXxX	311

✿✿

Excellent cuisine, worth a detour

Skillfully and carefully crafted dishes of outstanding quality.

Aquavit	XxX	246	Jungsik	XxX	356
Aska	XxX	510	Ko	XX	75
atera	XX	352	Marea	XxX	304
Blanca	XX	461	Modern (The)	XxX	307
Daniel	XxXxX	373	Soto	XX	185

✿

A very good restaurant in its category

A place offering cuisine prepared to a consistently high standard.

Agern	XX	243	Casa Enríque	XX	549
Ai Fiori	XxX	278	Casa Mono	XX	117
Aldea	XX	109	Caviar Russe	XxX	251
Andanada	XX	398	Contra	XX	225
Aureole	XxX	281	Delaware and Hudson	XX	513
Babbo	XX	147	Del Posto	XxxX	22
Bâtard	XX	353	Dovetail	XxX	403
Betony	XxX	284	Faro	XX	464
Blue Hill	XX	151	Finch (The)	XX	465
Breslin (The)	X	116	Gabriel Kreuther	XxX	292
Café Boulud	XxX	371	Gotham Bar and Grill	XxX	161
Café China	XX	249	Gramercy Tavern	XxX	122
Cagen	XX	61	Günter Seeger NY	XxX	162
Carbone	XX	154	Hirohisa	XX	338

Jewel Bako	X	72	Rebelle	XX	344
Junoon	XxX	126	River Café (The)	XxX	450
Kajitsu	XX	256	Semilla	X	531
Kanoyama	X	73	Sushi Ginza Onodera	XX	267
Kyo Ya	XX	76	Sushi Inoue	XX	213
L'Appart	XX	100	Sushi of Gari	X	390
La Sirena	XxX	25	Sushi Yasuda	XX	268
La Vara	XX	447	Sushi Zo	XX	187
Luksus at Tørst	XX	521	Take Root	X	453
Meadowsweet	XX	524	Tempura Matsui	XX	269
Minetta Tavern	X	175	Tori Shin	XX	320
Musket Room (The)	XX	340	Tulsi	XX	271
Nix	XX	176	Uncle Boons	XX	346
NoMad	XX	133	Ushiwakamaru	XX	32
Peter Luger	X	526	Wallsé	XX	191
Piora	XX	179	ZZ's Clam Bar	X	193
Public	XX	343			

Bib Gourmand

This symbol indicates our inspectors' favorites for good value.
For $40 or less, you can enjoy two courses and a glass of wine or a dessert
(not including tax or gratuity).

Achilles Heel	X	508	Freek's Mill	XX	495
al Bustan	XX	242	Ganso Ramen	X	445
Angkor	XX	368	Gastronomia Culinaria	X	404
Arharn Thai	X	545	Gladys	X	466
Atoboy	X	111	Glasserie	XX	516
Baker & Co.	XX	148	Good Fork (The)	X	496
Bar Primi	XX	57	Gran Eléctrica	XX	445
Basil Brick Oven Pizza	XX	547	Gregory's 26 Corner Taverna	X	553
Beyoglu	X	369	Hahm Ji Bach	XX	554
biáng!	XX	57	HanGawi	XX	253
bún-ker	X	547	Havana Café	XX	425
Buttermilk Channel	X	441	Hecho en Dumbo	X	164
Casa del Chef Bistro	X	548	Hide-Chan Ramen	X	254
Chavela's	XX	460	High Street on Hudson	XX	164
Cho Dang Gol	X	287	Hill Country Chicken	X	124
Chomp Chomp	X	155	HinoMaru Ramen	X	555
Ciccio	X	333	Hometown Bar-B-Que	X	496
Congee Village	X	224	Hunan Bistro	X	71
Coppelia	X	20	Hunan House	X	556
Cotenna	X	156	Hunan Kitchen	X	557
Dim Sum Go Go	X	39	Il Buco Alimentari e Vineria	XX	165
DOMODOMO	X	157	Il Poeta	XX	558
Don Antonio by Starita	XX	290	J.G. Melon	X	379
Donostia	X	65	Jin Ramen	X	206
East Harbor Seafood Palace	XX	494	John Brown Smokehouse	X	560
Egg	X	514	J. Restaurant Chez Asta	X	206
El Atoradero	X	480	Katz's	X	228
El Parador	XX	252	Khe-Yo	XX	355
Enoteca Maria	X	594	Kiin Thai	XX	167
Falansai	X	463	Kiki's	X	228
Frankies 457 Spuntino	X	444	Kings County Imperial	X	518

Kung Fu Little Steamed Buns Ramen	✗	296
La Morada	✗	426
Land of Plenty	✗✗	257
Larb Ubol	✗	299
Laut	✗	128
Lea	✗✗	484
Lil' Frankie's	✗	78
Little Pepper	✗	563
Llama Inn	✗✗	520
Lulu & Po	✗	468
Lupa	✗✗	171
MáLà Project	✗	79
Manila Social Club	✗	522
Mapo Tofu	✗	259
Mexicosina	✗	428
Mile End	✗	448
Miss Mamie's Spoonbread Too	✗	408
Momofuku Noodle Bar	✗	81
Momofuku Ssäm Bar	✗	81
Momokawa	✗	132
Mu Ramen	✗	566
New Malaysia	✗	42
Nyonya	✗	43
Olmsted	✗✗	485
Oso	✗	210
Paet Rio	✗	571
Paulie Gee's	✗	525
Pearl & Ash	✗✗	342
Phoenix Garden	✗	262
Pippali	✗✗	136
Porsena	✗✗	84
Prime Meats	✗✗	449
Prune	✗	85
Purple Yam	✗	486
Ribalta	✗✗	181
Rider	✗✗	527
Roberta's	✗	471
Rubirosa	✗✗	345
Runner & Stone	✗✗	502
Russ & Daughters Cafe	✗✗	232
Rye	✗	528
Salt & Fat	✗	573
San Matteo	✗	387
San Rasa	✗	597
Shalom Japan	✗	530
Shanghai Café	✗	46
Sip Sak	✗✗	264
Soba-Ya	✗	89
Somtum Der	✗	90
Sottocasa	✗	452
Speedy Romeo	✗	473
Spotted Pig	✗	184
Streetbird Rotisserie	✗	212
Supper	✗✗	90
Sweet Yummy House	✗	576
Szechuan Gourmet	✗	317
Tanoreen	✗✗	503
Tertulia	✗✗	188
Thelma on Clinton	✗✗	234
Tong Sam Gyup Goo Yi	✗	579
Tra Di Noi	✗	431
Turkish Kitchen	✗✗	138
Uncle Zhou	✗	581
Uva	✗	392
Vida	✗	598
Vinegar Hill House	✗	452
Xixa	✗	532
zero otto nove	✗✗	432
00+Co	✗	93
Zoma	✗	215

Under $25

Abyssinia	✗	198
Africa Kine	✗	199
Al Seabu	✗	478
Arharn Thai	⊛ ✗	545
Arrogant Swine	✗	459
Bamboo Garden	✗	492
Barney Greengrass	✗	400
Bhatti	✗	112
Bo Ky	✗	38
Brisas del Caribe	✗	421
bún-ker	⊛ ✗	547
Café Mingala	✗	370
Café Mogador	✗	60
Café Steinhof	✗	479
Chavela's	⊛ ✗✗	460
Cheburechnaya	✗	548
ChikaLicious	🍧	60
Cho Dang Gol	⊛ ✗	287
Clinton St. Baking Company	✗	223
cocoron	✗	223
Congee Village	⊛ ✗	224
Curry-Ya	✗	62
Còm tam Ninh Kieu	✗	422
De Mole	✗	550
Dojo Izakaya	🍧	64
Donostia	⊛ ✗	65
Dosa Garden	✗	593
Dumpling Galaxy	✗	551
Egg	⊛ ✗	514
El Nuevo Bohío	✗	423
Engeline's	✗	552
Enoteca on Court	✗	444
Estrellita Poblana III	✗	424
Forcella	✗	516
Ganso Ramen	⊛ ✗	445
Goemon Curry	✗	337
Great N.Y. Noodletown	✗	41
Happy Family Hotpot	✗	554
Hibino	✗	446
Hide-Chan Ramen	⊛ ✗	254
Hill Country Chicken	⊛ ✗	124
Houdini Kitchen Laboratory	✗✗	556
Hunan House	⊛ ✗	556
Hunan Kitchen	⊛ ✗	557
Il Salumaio	✗	378
J. Restaurant Chez Asta	⊛ ✗	206
J.G. Melon	⊛ ✗	379
Java	✗	483
Jin Ramen	⊛ ✗	206
Jun-Men Ramen Bar	✗✗	24
Kao Soy	✗	497
Karczma	✗	517
Katz's	⊛ ✗	228
Kesté Pizza & Vino	✗	167
Kitchen 79	✗	562
Krolewskie Jadlo	✗	518
Kung Fu Little		
Steamed Buns Ramen	⊛ ✗	296
Kunjip	✗	297
La Morada	⊛ ✗	426
Lakruwana	✗	595
Larb Ubol	⊛ ✗	299
Las Ramblas	🍧	169
Leche y Miel	✗	427
Legend Bar & Restaurant	✗✗	26
Liebman's	✗	427
Lil' Frankie's	⊛ ✗	78
Little Pepper	⊛ ✗	563
Lucky Eight	✗	497
Main Street Imperial		
Taiwanese Gourmet	✗	563
Mandoo Bar	✗	302
Mapo Tofu	⊛ ✗	259
Meijin Ramen	✗	382

Mexicosina	⊛ X	428	Royal Seafood	X	45
Mighty Quinn's	X	80	Saint Austere (The)	👘	528
Mile End	⊛ X	448	Samudra	X	574
Mimi's Hummus	👘	485	Samurai Mama	X	529
Miss Mamie's Spoonbread Too	⊛ X	408	San Matteo	⊛ X	387
Motorino	X	82	San Rasa	⊛ X	597
Mtskheta Café	X	499	Saravanaas	X	136
Nan Xiang Xiao Long Bao	X	567	2nd Avenue Deli	X	264
Neerob	X	428	Shanghai Café	⊛ X	46
New Malaysia	⊛ X	42	Sigiri	X	88
Nick's Pizza	X	569	Sobakoh	X	89
Noche Mexicana II	X	409	Soba-Ya	⊛ X	89
Nom Wah Tea Parlor	X	43	Spicy Lanka	X	575
Nyonya	⊛ X	43	Taiwanese Gourmet	X	577
Okonomi	X	525	Taqueria Tlaxcalli	X	431
Paet Rio	⊛ X	571	Taverna Kyclades	X	578
Park Asia	XX	500	Thái Sơn	X	47
Paulie Gee's	⊛ X	525	Tito Rad's Grill	XX	579
Phil Am Kusina	X	597	Tía Pol	X	30
Rai Rai Ken	X	86	Uncle Zhou	⊛ X	581
Ramen Misoya	X	86	Xe Lua	X	47
Ramen Yebisu	X	527	Zoma	⊛ X	215
Rockmeisha	👘	182			

Credits

Page 9: H. Soto - Pages 12-13: Peter L. Wrenn - Page 14: HP - Page 16: HP
Page 17: Peter L.Wrenn - Page 22: AS - Page 25: AS - Page 32: MR - Page 34: AS
Page 36: AS - Page 37: Peter L.Wrenn - Page 48: AS - Page 49: AS;HP
Page 50: HP; Jeanine Hart - Page 51: AS - Page 61: AS - Page 72: Maralayna
Page 73: AS - Page 75: MR - Page 76: AS - Page 94: Jeanine Hart
Page 96: Jeanine Hart - Page 97: Jeanine Hart;AS - Page 100: Maralayna
Page 104: HP - Page 105: AS - Page 109: Daniel Krieger - Page 116: Nicole
Franzen Page 117: Kelly Campbell - Page 120: Francesco Tonelli - Page 122:
Daniel Krieger Page 126: Ronnie Bhardwaj - Page 133: Francesco Tonelli
Pages 140-142: AS - Page 143: HP - Page 147: Kelly Campbell - Page 151: Andre
Baronowski - Page 154: Daisy Zeijlon - Page 162: Maralayna - Page 175: Ngoc
Ngo Page 176: Maralayna - Page 179: Luca Pioltelli - Page 185: Tokio Kuniyoshi
Page 187: Maralayna - Page 191: Wallsé - Page 193: Daisy Zeijlon
Pages 194-195: AS - Page 213: MR - Page 216: Maralayna - Page 218: HP
Page 219: Maralayna - Page 225: AS - Page 236: AS - Page 237: HP
Page 238: HP; Jeanine Hart - Page 239: AS - Page 243: AS - Page 246: Patricia
Chang - Page 249: Isabel Parra - Page 251: Caviar Russe - Page 256: Chihiro
Kimura - Page 267: H. Soto - Page 268: MR - Page 269: Tempura Matsui
Page 271: Chef Eric McCarthy - Page 272: AS - Pages 273-275 HP
Page 278: Noah Fecks - Page 281: MR - Page 284: Signe Birck - Page 292: AS
Page 300: Daniel Krieger Page 304: Noah Fecks - Page 305: Patrick Crawford/
Blackletter - Page 307: AS - Page 311: AS - Page 320: Michka Mochizuki
Page 324: HP - Page 325: Maralayna Page 326: HP - Page 327: Jeanine Hart
Page 338: Naoko Takagi - Page 340: Signe Birck - Page 343: Garrett Rowland
Page 344: Patricia Chang - Page 346: Patricia Chang - Page 348: Jeanine Hart;
Maralayna - Pages 350-351: Jeanine Hart - Page 352: MR - Page 353: Daniel
Krieger - Page 356: A. Banchan - Page 363: Jeanine Hart - Page 364: HP
Page 366: HP - Page 367: AS - Page 371: Noah Fecks - Page 373: Eric Laignel
Page 390: MR Page 394: Jeanine Hart - Page 396: Jeanine Hart - Page 397: AS
Page 398: Maralayna - Page 403: Nathan Rawlinson - Page 406: Francesco
Tonelli - Pages 412-413: Ivo M. Vermeulen/The New York Botanical Garden
Page 414: Robert Benson/The New York Botanical Garden
Pages 415-417: Maralayna - Page 433: Zhe Fan - Pages 434-435: Peter L.Wrenn
Page 436: AS;HP - Page 437: AS - Page 442: Annie Gonzalez - Page 447:
Lauren Volo - Page 450: VivaVioletaPhotography - Page 453: Melissa Horn
Page 454: Maralayna - Page 455: Jeanine Hart - Page 461: Patricia Chang
Page 464: MR - Page 465: Jessica Harvill - Pages 474-475: MR
Pages 488-489: MR - Page 504: HP; MR - Page 505: AS; HP
Page 510: Maralayna - Page 513: John Taggart - Page 521: Signe Birck
Page 524: Evan Sung - Page 526: Michael Berman - Page 531: AS
Pages 534-535: Jeanine Hart - Page 536: Maralayna - Page 537: HP
Page 538: HP - Pages 539-540: Jeanine Hart - Page 549: Patricia Chang
Pages 584-585: Jeanine Hart - Page 586: Maralayna - Page 588: Maralayna; AS
Page 589: Maralayna - Page 599: Peter L. Wrenn

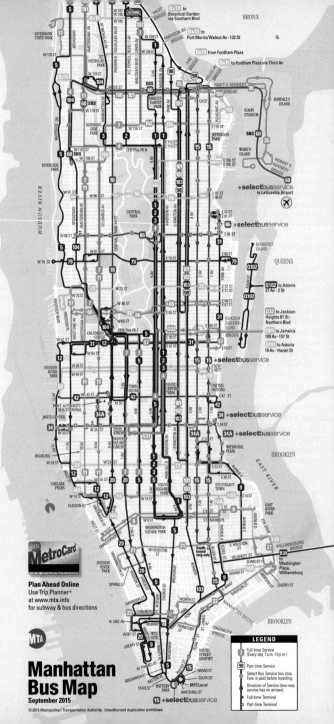

Manhattan Bus Map

September 2015

©2015 Metropolitan Transportation Authority. Unauthorized duplication prohibited.